# Series II

# Lectionary Preaching Workbook

## Cycle B

**for use with Common, Lutheran, and Roman Catholic Lectionaries**

# PERRY H. BIDDLE, Jr.

**C.S.S. Publishing Co., Inc.**

Lima, Ohio

Copyright © 1987 by
The C.S.S. Publishing Company, Inc.
Lima, Ohio



**Library of Congress Cataloging-in-Publication Data**

Biddle, Jr., Perry H., 1932-
Lectionary preaching workbook, series II.

Bibliography: [v. 2], p.:
Contents: — [v. 2] Cycle B.
1. Preaching.  2. Lectionaries.  3. Common lectionary.  4. Bible — Homiletical use.  I. Title.
BV4211.2.B53 1987 251                                          87-6411
ISBN 0-89536-879-X (v. 2)

7865 / ISBN 0-89536-879-X                    PRINTED IN U.S.A.

*To my father, P. H. Biddle, Sr.*
*ordained to the Presbyterian ministry in 1926*
*and a continuing inspiration to me and many others*

# Table of Contents

# Preface

When C.S.S. Publishing Company invited me to write a three volume *Lectionary Preaching Workbook* over the three year cycle of the Common Lectionary, beginning with cycle B, I was challenged almost to the point of turning down the invitation! However, the positive response to my earlier books for the working pastor encouraged me to undertake the enormous project of writing commentary and homiletical moves for each lectionary reading and variations from the Common Lectionary in the Lutheran and Roman Catholic lectionaries for some 156 Sundays. That works out to be five months of Sundays!

My friend and colleague in ministry, Dr. Robert H. Crumby, Jr., and my wife, Sue, gave me needed encouragement to undertake the project. I discussed the direction the project should go with my friend from seminary days, Dr. Don Wardlaw, Professor of Worship and Preaching, McCormick Theological Seminary, and with Dr. John Killinger, Jr. and Dr. David Buttrick. Dr. Buttrick introduced me to the concept of "homiletical moves" in his D. Min. course at Vanderbilt Divinity School on "The Phenomenology of Preaching." I am grateful to Dr. Buttrick for giving valuable guidance and comments on the project at various stages. Dr. Killinger was my major professor at Vanderbilt Divinity School for a Doctor of Ministry degree in preaching, literature and worship in 1972-73. He kindly recommended me to the publisher for this project. I continue to be inspired by his writing and friendship. I also wish to thank Rev. Michael Sherer, my editor, for many valuable suggestions and helpful criticisms.

The assistance of a word processor has been invaluable in writing these lectionary commentaries and moves. The flexibility in composing and editing as the manuscript was being written was beyond my imagining before purchasing the word processor. From my first hand experience in writing sermons, I can recommend to the preacher the use of a word processor in sermon preparation.

I wish to thank the congregation of First Presbyterian Church, Old Hickory, Tennessee, where I have served as pastor since 1974, for their patience and encouragement in our common venture of preaching and hearing sermons. Many of the Sunday lectionary selections were developed into sermons and preached to this congregation during 1986. I have benefited from the valuable comments from members of the congregation, including the comments of my wife, Sue, my best sermon critic.

Finally, I would like to thank Sue for enduring many hours of being a "computer user's widow" while I was studying for and writing the Workbook. She continues to share her life with me and has given me daily inspiration for carrying through the project.

I offer these Workbook chapters to you, the working pastor, with the prayer that God will enable you to use them as you prepare for your weekly preaching task. I assume responsibility for any shortcomings and mistakes in the Workbook. May God richly bless you in your high and holy mission of proclaiming God's word to a troubled world!

Perry H. Biddle, Jr.
Old Hickory, Tennessee

Advent 1986

# Introduction

## A. Use of the Workbook

1. The *Workbook* is designed to help the working pastor plan and develop sermons each week. It is printed with wide margins in which you may write your notes and ideas as you use the workbook during the week. The *Workbook* will work for you as you make use of its resources and guidance in planning for preaching. Just as the success of laboratory discoveries depends to a great extent on the "labor" and less on the "oratory" of the laboratory, so the success you will find in using this workbook will depend on your "work" and less on the "book." This writer developed many of the lectionary readings into sermons which were preached in a congregation within Metro Nashville, Tennessee, during 1986. The research in commentaries and reflection on Scripture in preparing this *Workbook* involved many hours of work which are offered in the hope that it will make the preparation of sermons more stimulating and will in turn enable the preacher to "move" the congregation to deeper commitment to Christ and the Kingdom.

One way in which the *Workbook* may be used is to read over the Scripture passages and the *Workbook* material for the coming Sunday on the preceding Monday morning. This initial work will give the preacher an introduction to the three lessons and how they relate to one another, if they do. Notes may be written in the margins as ideas come to the preacher. In addition to reading the commentary material in this *Workbook,* the preacher is strongly encouraged to read one or more commentaries on the passage which appears to be the basis for the coming week's sermon. If the preacher is preparing for a Sunday morning and evening sermon and mid-week service, then all three lessons may be studied in preparation for the services. But if only one sermon is to be prepared, the preacher is encouraged to select the Scripture passage to be developed as early in the week as possible.

*Planning ahead* in using this lectionary will greatly increase the preacher's effectiveness in the use of time and in preparation. Planning ahead for thirteen weeks or a quarter is a minimum optimum period. The preacher should read ahead thirteen weeks, select the passage(s) to be preached and the central theme to be developed in each sermon, and then develop a file folder for each sermon, labeled to be used for collecting ideas, illustrations, clippings, and the like, for each particular sermon. The minister's general reading of novels, plays, biography, history, etc., will feed these files so that when the time for preparing a specific sermon comes, the minister will have useful material already in hand.

My friend, Don Wardlaw, likes to point out to preachers that they need to give "the little elves inside them" time to process and rework the materials the preacher sends down to them through reading and thinking. If the preacher waits to the last day or so to send down the material into his or her subconscious the preacher will find the little elves will send it right back up unprocessed, says Wardlaw. By working thirteen weeks ahead, the minister may gain insights from the subconscious that otherwise would never appear. God's Spirit is a source of miracles but the preacher shouldn't put the Spirit to the test by not allowing sufficient time for the Spirit to work creatively is developing the sermon.

In addition to the general planning thirteen weeks ahead, the preacher will find more intensive two-week planning helpful. This demands self-discipline but pays off in more effective work in preparing to preach. By reading the commentary materials for the sermon *two weeks* in advance (on the Monday or Tuesday two weeks earlier) the preacher can take even greater advantage of the "little elves" inside who process the ideas and begin looking for ways to apply the sermon to life! Then the week in which the sermon is to be preached can be used to bring together illustrations and more insights for developing the sermon before actually writing the manuscript or outline from which the sermon is delivered.

Through advance planning for the sermon the minister can gather more appropriate and interesting illustrative material for the sermon and can avoid the "canned" and shop-worn illustrations that tend to bore the hearer and seem unreal to contemporary life.

Then work on the passage proceeds during the week, using commentaries, word studies, concordance, and other tools of the preacher. The preacher will find that even short periods of work time, scattered throughout the week, will be much more productive than one longer period on Friday or Saturday, since she or he will have time to reflect on the passage while doing pastoral work, reading, doing community service, carrying out administrative duties, and the like. The work of the subconscious mind in creating the message cannot be overestimated. Artists make use of the "incubating time" for ideas which later enables the creative juices to flow. The preacher, no less than the painter, poet, novelist or other artist would do well to put the subconscious mind to work, allowing the Holy Spirit to work over a longer period of time and in greater depth in forming the sermon.

2. While the format of the *Workbook* is the Lectionary, this does not rule out the preacher using it for sermon preparation when not following the lectionary. More and more preachers from non-liturgical churches are discovering the advantages of following the Lectionary in preaching, advantages both for themselves and their congregations. Many preachers generally follow the Lectionary, but break away from it for special events in the congregation, or in response to world events which call for the preacher to address them. One need not be a slave to the Lectionary to make use of it. After all, the Lectionary was made by human beings for human beings, and not vice versa!

There are many different lectionaries. One used in this *Workbook* is the Common Lectionary prepared by the Consultation on Common Texts of the Church Hymnal Corporation. The *Workbook* also lists Lutheran and Roman Catholic variations from the Common Lectionary when they appear and deals with them as well. (On one Sunday in Cycle B this resulted in eight different pericopes!)

The function of a Sunday lectionary is to relate the time of the church between Christ's resurrection and Second Coming to the time of salvation spelled out in Scripture. The Lectionary has two Christological annual cycles: Advent/Christmas/Epiphany, and Lent/Easter/Pentecost. Perhaps the most important contribution the Lectionary can make to worship is in integrating the church's liturgical, educational and ecumenical life.

While it may appear that the Church Year runs through a cycle that repeats itself each year, a spiral or screw is a better image than a circle for the Lectionary cycle. For the purpose of the Church Year is to move us upward toward Christ and not to merely repeat the same themes of Advent, Christmas, Easter, Pentecost. There should be movement toward a Christ-like life for the preacher and hearer.

The Lectionary used here follows a three year cycle: Years A, B, and C, respectively. One may begin with any cycle, at any time in the cycle in preaching from the Lectionary and using it in worship and study of Scripture within the congregation. Thus the preacher need not wait until Advent of year A to begin using the Lectionary but may begin at whatever time she or he decides to begin following it.

3. It should be noted that the so-called Christian "Year" is really only half a year, with Advent being the beginning, and December the first calendar month. While the end of the festival six months of the year is regulated by the movable date of Easter it ends with Pentecost. The Sundays that follow Pentecost are not really a season and have no theme like Advent, Christmas and Easter have. These summer and fall Sundays and Sundays after Epiphany before Lent are "ordinary Sundays."

Christmas and Easter are the *two centers* of the Christian Year, and they developed rather independently at different times and places. It is not within the scope of this introduction to give the background of the development of these two foci of the Christian Year, but the preacher may want to study the development of the Lectionary and Christian Year in books listed in the bibliography.

4. One benefit of following the Lectionary is that the preacher may join a "Lectionary Study Group" which meets weekly, usually early in the week to discuss the lectionary readings for the coming Sunday. Usually one member of the group is designated to present the exegetical work on the passages. The members of the group reflect on ways in which the passage may be applied to contemporary life, share illustrations, insights, etc. Such groups may consist of three to seven persons or even just two. A group larger than seven can be too large for the kind of participation by members which is desirable. A spin-off of such a group is that it is also a peer support group and may be a source of ecumenical fellowship among clergy. In one small town in Kentucky, several of the clergy of the area met at a local radio station on Fridays at noon to discuss the Lectionary readings with each other for the radio audience. This stimulated the listeners, many of whom would be in church the following Sunday where the sermon was based on the passages discussed. Listeners read the Scripture and reflected on its meaning for their lives. A variation of this is one in which the minister invites a group from the congregation to meet to discuss the lectionary readings for the coming Sunday.

Following the Lectionary enables the congregation to hear and meditate on most of the major Scripture passages over a three year cycle. There is a renewed emphasis in the Church on *hearing Scripture* as well as hearing the sermon based on Scripture. There is a widespread biblical illiteracy in churches of North America and the use of the Lectionary is helping overcome this.

By using the Lectionary the minister may print in the weekly bulletin and/or newsletter the Scripture passages for the coming week, asking that the congregation read and reflect on them for the coming Sunday. Pew Bibles can enable those who come early for worship to read over and meditate on the readings for that particular Sunday. More church school classes of all ages are following the Church Year in their weekly studies, thereby enabling them to focus on a theme common both to their church school class and to the readings and sermon of worship on any given Sunday.

### B. Design of the Workbook

1. The *Workbook* begins with the designation of the Sunday in the year, and cycle of the Lectionary, (B), for example, for Sundays of this volume. This is followed by a very brief "Comments on the Lessons," which gives an overview of variations from the (C) Common (Consensus) Lectionary by the (L) Lutheran and (RC) Roman Catholic versions, and in some cases a statement of the theme of a lesson.

This is followed by the "Commentary," which seeks to give the preacher insights into the particular passage, its central thrust, the movement of the action of the passage, relationship to other passages, hints for application to contemporary life (for some passages), and meaning of key words. This is not intended to be an exhaustive commentary but rather a condensed, straightforward commentary on the passage. One or more additional commentaries should be studied in connection with this summary.

Next comes the "Theological Reflections," an attempt to locate any common themes in the passages and relate them, and to restate the central thrust of each passage. The purpose is to enable the preacher to take an overview of the passages just dealt with in the Commentary section.

The "Homiletical Moves" are just that: "moves" to " move" the preacher to "move" the congregation to faith in Christ or more faithful obedience to Christ. The "moves" should not be mistaken for the usual three point outline. In fact, an effort has been made to avoid only three "moves" for a given passage, so this will not be done. The use of these "moves" will be discussed further in the section on preaching which follows. Each sermon is given a suggested title, but this is only a hint for the preacher as she or he chooses a title for the sermon she or he develops. The title may serve as a foil, as a title that serves as a contrast to the one the preacher chooses for the sermon. Often, in developing a sermon, the preacher needs a catalyst, a foil, a starter idea in order to get the creative juices flowing and come up with what is appropriate for the unique sermon being developed. The preacher may choose not to title the sermon, but usually it is helpful to "name the baby," either before or after you have conceived and developed the manuscript, to help your hearers grasp the central movement of the passage.

There is one passage each week singled out as "This Preacher's Preference" to be developed as the sermon. This is usually the Gospel passage, but may be another one. If the preacher is developing more than one sermon for the week, then other passages will, of course, need to be developed also.

A hymn for the particular Sunday is suggested which seeks to embody the theme or move of one or more of the pericopes for that Sunday. This is only a suggested hymn and the preacher will want to select *the hymn* which seems most appropriate for the congregation that Sunday. Most hymnals contain a listing of Scripture passages which form the basis for particular hymns, plus a listing of hymns by topics such as thanksgiving, love, Christ the King, etc. This hymn may be used as a concluding hymn of the service through which the congregation sings its faith and rededicates its life to God. Or all hymns used in the service may be selected because of their relation to the sermon and worship theme.

Finally, a prayer is included which seeks to incorporate the themes of the various pericopes for the particular Sunday. This prayer, like the homiletical moves and sermon title, should serve to enable the preacher to develop a prayer or prayers which relate to the Scripture passages. The preacher may want to use the prayer as her or his own prayer in developing the sermon. It is not intended to be a polished, final form of the prayer which the preacher uses in leading the congregation in praying, but a foil or catalyst for developing prayer(s).

An introduction to each season of the Church Year is also included to enable the preacher to interpret the movement of the Liturgical Year and lectionary readings to the congregation. The seasons and themes of the Church Year are repeated each year, but rather than thinking of this as a circle which simply repeats itself, it is more appropriate to think of it as a *spiral moving upward* toward Christ in ever widening circles as the years come and go in which the preacher and congregation grow in their knowledge and love of God and of God's creation, including all persons.

### C. Preaching With Homiletical Moves

The homiletic of this *Workbook* is a radical break from the stock homiletic design of the eighteenth and nineteenth centuries which has continued until recent years. This stock homiletic consisted of an introduction, followed by a text (often a brief one, or even a single verse or phrase of Scripture). The text was reduced to a propositional topic, which in turn was developed in a series of "points" (usually three) and the sermon ended in a conclusion. The points were often categorical and alliteration was frequently used to make them easier to remember. An outline was often forced on the text with a "cookie cutter" method of stamping out sermons. Such sermons were sometimes nicknamed "Three points and a poem," since a poem or stanza of a hymn was often used to wrap up the message on a note of inspiration.

It is no accident that such a rationalistic, objective homiletic came about at the same time as the scientific method for the "stock homiletic" isolated a topic for study, and a general deduction is followed by a descriptive statement, sprinkled with illustrations that may not illustrate the topic. Mixed with this is what David Buttrick calls "pop-Schleiermacher" in which the rational homiletic is altered by the preacher's own "consecrated imagination." Using this approach, the preacher often seizes an idea which interests her or him and then seeks a text to validate the idea, and then proceeds to make "points" for the sermon. This results in a romantic notion of inspiration joined to a rational method, which is found in most homiletic texts now available.

Harry Emerson Fosdick developed what has come to be known as "the project method," which begins with people and their problems. Another form of preaching, used commonly by fundamentalists, is to claim to be doing biblical preaching while merely walking through a text offering truths culled from the verses. Listeners have trouble seeing any unity or sequence to such sermons.

The method of developing the "Homiletical Moves" of the *Workbook* is based on a different approach to biblical preaching. This new approach takes account of recent biblical studies which ask of the Scripture passage: (1) What is the form? (2) What is the plot, structure or shape of the passage? (3) What is the "field of concern" or hidden perspective? (4) What is the "logic" of movement in the passage? (The text is seen as a moving picture, versus the "still-life" approach of the rationalistic method.) (5) What is the addressed "world" of the passage? (6) What is the passage trying to do? David Buttrick has called this a "patchwork phenomenological" approach in an article in *Interpretation* (p. 54, January 1981; Vol. XXXV, No. 1, Published by Union Theological Seminary, 3401 Brook Road, Richmond, Virginia 23227). He has developed it further in a recent landmark book entitled *Homiletic* (Fortress Press, 1987). The user of this *Workbook* is urged to become familiar with this book and its approach to homiletics and the article from *Interpretation*. In his book Buttrick sets forth a dynamic approach to structure and preaching:

*Preaching should favor mobile structures, foregoing fixed topics and categorical development. What we encounter in Scripture is* movement *(emphasis added) of thought or event or image by some "logic." How can a movement of language designed to assemble in hermeneutic faith be reduced to a propositional statement? . . . However, in our age, the "sacred canopy" is tattered, and we sense emerging a preference for mobile forms (e.g. process theologies and the recent froufou about "story"). If there is* analogia *nowadays it is not static or vertical (between an isolated self and the fixity of God", but relational — the relating of an on-the-move purposeful God with his lag-behind pilgrim people. So sermon structures ought to travel through congregational consciousness as a series of immediate thoughts, sequentially designed and imaged with technical skill so as to assemble in forming faith . . . What is more important than form is "logic of movement." While a sermon on a biblical narrative need not be full-scale story, it can move with narrative logic as the hearing and understanding of a story in consciousness. Likewise, a sermon on a vision need not be a vision but can move as an eye moves while envisioning and interpreting a scene. Obviously one of the tasks of a new homiletic theory that dares abandon deductive logic is to explore the different "logics" of language in consciousness. Homiletics may well discover that different biblical rhetorics will demand different homiletic strategies including variable logic of movement.*

The interpretation of a passage should be whole in the mind of a preacher before it is broken into a designated homiletic strategy. Although sermons should be a plotted sequence of language units, says Buttrick, they need *not* follow the sequence found in a particular passage in a legalistic fashion. Nor should a sermon be bound by biblical form. This is to say that in order to preach a biblical narrative one need not adopt a story form. For example, in order to interpret a poem one need not write a poem about it! Buttrick says that what is more important than form is what he terms "logic of movement" (hence the "Homiletical Moves" of this *Workbook*). A preacher must be a poet, exegete and theologian, asserts Buttrick, simply because sermon structures must be shaped so that the language of preaching "plays" in a theological field of concern and so the preacher must use "Theologic" in moving from text to sermon.

A popular TV ad for a fast food chain featured an older woman asking, "Where's the beef?" The preacher should ask "Where is the gospel?" in developing the sermon and in preaching it. The gospel is good news of God's initiative, God's action, God's movement: "for God so loved . . . he gave his only Son . . ." (John 3:16) In this and other texts the preacher should begin by asking, "What is the passage trying to do?" Sermons should be built as moving modules of language.

In using this *Workbook* the preacher should search for "images" which will form in the hearer's mind and in turn move the hearer to action. The dynamic nature of the human psyche is described by Ira Progoff:

*From Whence do the goals of persons come? From the psyche, which is the organ of direction and meaning in life for human beings. But the psyche, as an active organ of life is ever in flow. It is a movement of images of many kinds, visual and non-visual, that supplies the contents of consciousness. The goals of personal desire are drawn from this flow. They come forth from the movement of imagery and in their symbolic forms they project themselves, literally throw themselves forward, and establish themselves concretely as goals for future activity. (p. 91,* The Dynamic of Hope *by Ira Progoff, New York: Dialogue House Library, 1985).*

The preacher would benefit from studying how language forms in the mind and the critical role images play in shaping thought and action. Buttrick has conducted extensive research in the phenomenology of preaching with particular attention to how language forms images in the mind. One of the reasons people like *stories in sermons is because they form images.* Care should be taken to make such images clear and avoid their cancelling out one another.

The point of view of the sermon is critical, just as it is in a novel or short story. The preacher controls the point of view and should get it set quickly in the sermon. People can't shift back and forth in points of view quickly. For this reason "I" should usually be avoided in the sermon, because it causes a point of view shift.

The "Homiletical Moves" of the *Workbook* are offered as suggestions for the preacher to consider in developing her or his own sermon. They may be seen as foils against which the preacher poses another "move", or as catalysts to help the preacher develop "moves" for the particular sermon she or he is preparing. By no means should they be seen as set in concrete or as the only way to develop a particular passage, for to do this would deny the approach the *Workbook* takes to preaching, namely that sermons are dynamic messages for a particular congregation at a particular time and place by a particular preacher. This rules out "canned sermons" from books, or "canned outlines" or "canned illustrations." The "moves" of the Workbook are offered to stimulate the preacher to develop the form of the sermon appropriate for her or his congregation.

### D. Becoming More Creative in Preaching

The most serious criticism of much preaching today is not that it is heretical but that it is *boring!* Most congregations are over-stimulated during the week by TV, movies, sporting events, festivals, and when they go to church they are too often bored by dull sermons. One writer about contemporary preaching tells of going to a church service which was so dull that the preacher himself actually yawned in the pulpit!

In order for the sermon to become more "moving," the preacher must be "moved" by the Scripture and its relevance for the congregation. The new homiletic described in the section above canhelp eliminate dullness in the pulpit. David Buttrick concludes an article on "Interpretation and Preaching" by saying:

*When a new homiletic, tuned to hermeneutic sensitivity and a tough phenomenological analysis of language, emerges and filters down to the pastor's study, we may see a generation of preachers who find Scripture exciting and who find speaking in grace an act of radical obedience. (p. 58,* Interpretation, *January, 1981)*

The real key to becoming more creative lies in what you do with the knowledge you have. Creative preaching calls for an attitude or outlook which allows you to search for ideas and manipulate your knowledge and experience. It calls for an openness to God, and an openness to what God is doing in the world, and where God is calling his people to join with him in work. Preachers who enjoy their work will come up with more ideas, will be more creative in the pulpit, than those who find it a weekly dreaded chore.

Earlier in this essay, it was suggested that the preacher begin working on the sermon on Monday in order to allow time for the sermon to simmer in the subconscious during the week. Another reason for beginning early is to allow for the text and ideas for developing the sermon to be played with during the week in the preacher's mental playground. One of the leading authorities on creative thinking has this to say about the relationship between play and creativity:

> *. . . Necessity may be the mother of invention, but play is certainly the* father *. . . A playful attitude is fundamental to creative thinking. Indeed, I'll bet that you generate most of your new ideas when you are playing in your mental playground. That's because your defenses are down, your mental locks are loosened, and there is little concern with the rules, practicality, or being wrong. (p. 97,* A Whack on the Side of the Head *by Roger Von Oech, New York: Warner Brooks, 1983).*

Two keys to creative sermon development and delivery are *playfulness* and *intensity*. Those who have this approach to preaching are enthusiastic and creative. They come up with fresh approaches to familiar texts, doctrines, issues. Someone has said that it is not so important to be serious as it is to be serious about the important things. While a monkey may look serious and in the depths of concentration, it may be it is serious because it itches somewhere! Plato has written that life must be lived as play. The person who is playing is still learning and living.

All too often we find that the deadline of eleven o'clock Sunday morning is our source of inspiration. Reinhold Niebuhr once commented that the prophets of old spoke only when inspired by the Spirit, but parish preachers must speak every week, inspired or not. While every working pastor is under the gun to deliver a message each Sunday, this necessity may not be the best source of inspiration.

Indeed, a survey of thousands of people indicates that, while necessity is a source of inspiration for one group, the other group of folks find their best inspiration in just playing around with ideas, doing unrelated activities, toying with a problem, not taking themselves too seriously and just relaxing. The preacher who starts on the sermon *early in the week* will find there are moments of reflection and playing around with the sermon all during the week while driving to the hospital, mowing the grass, making pastoral calls and listening to the hurts and joys of folks, wrestling with the family budget, cooking, cleaning house and in social time with family and friends. This is not to say the preacher must be so absorbed with the sermon that she or he cannot relax and think of something else during the week. Rather, it is to say that the preacher may find that the mind with enough time and a playful attitude can work during the week like a fishing net or a vacuum cleaner.

Our thinking about what we collect during the week grows through metaphorical thinking: we understand the unfamiliar by means of the similarities it has with the familiar. The Bible makes the unfamiliar spiritual world familiar to us through the familiar physical world by means of the use of metaphors. Jesus' parables and teachings are prime examples of the use of metaphors.

The preacher who seeks to preach creative, stimulating, biblical sermons would do well to read widely, attend plays, movies, and to listen critically to what is being said and done in the world. This critical faith-stance will enable the preacher to declare God's word to the congregation so that they, too, may see the world from a faith-critical stance. The images and "moves" of the sermon can help this happen. The congregation then lives out the sermon during the week, reflecting on the good news from God as it impacts the world in which they live.

In order to make sermons more effective as instruments of God's word to the world, great care should be given to the introduction to the sermon. Professional platform speakers put great emphasis on "The Introduction" to their talks. Other parts of their routine speeches may change, but the introduction, once shaped to do its job of introducing the topic, remains the same. One novelist has a hobby of browsing through book stores and reading the first line of novels to discover the "hook" the writer uses to catch the reader's attention.

Studies of audiences reveal that the first sentence of a sermon, like a conversation, is a "tuning in" and therefore a lot of content should not be put in it. In fact, "tuning in" occurs in the first two or three sentences and for this reason they must be kept simple. Imagine you are focusing a camera with the introduction. You are trying to get your hearers to "see" an image. An introduction should be no longer than seven sentences, and the last one should stop the action. "It should be a simple sentence, a kind of conclusion that gives closure," says Buttrick. "Then follows a long pause as speaker and hearer take a deep breath and get ready to move into the sermon proper. The introduction is to set you up so you can begin the sermon," according to Buttrick. (p. 45, "A Phenomenological Approach to Preaching" by Perry H. Biddle, Jr., an article based on class notes by David Buttrick,

Vanderbilt Divinity School, in *Sharing the Practice,* published by The Academy of Parish Clergy, October/November/December 1984)

The preacher using this *Workbook* is urged to read recent books on homiletics and to take advantage of workshops on preaching which will help hone the preacher's skills in developing and delivering the sermon. The present introduction to the *Workbook* can only sketch some of the insights and new approaches in homiletics, therefore further reading in David Buttricks's new book *Homiletic* (Fortress Press, 1987) and other new books in the field are highly recommended.

### E. Key to code for texts

(C) = Common (Consensus). Where the Lutheran and Roman Catholic lectionaries agree with (C), then no other notation appears.

When the Lutheran lectionary carries a different reading or selection of verses, then this pericope is noted by (L).

And a similar variation in the Roman Catholic lectionary is noted by (RC).

### F. Reading and use of Lectionary Scripture

1. For greater teaching effect, the congregation should be furnished the lectionary readings for each Sunday in the previous Sunday's bulletin with a request that the congregation read them during the week. A note in each Sunday's bulletin suggesting that the worshipers read the Scripture *before* the service begins from their personal Bibles or pew Bibles will also encourage familiarity with the texts.

2. When the Scripture is read in the worship service, the minister should encourage *listening* to and *seeing* the reader of Scripture, rather than suggesting that the congregation follow in their pew Bible. The oral/visual impact of watching and hearing the reader is much more effective than reading and listening at the same time.

3. It is helpful to give the congregation some introduction to each passage of Scripture, and, when beginning a new book of the Bible, to give a brief introduction to the nature of the book, setting, audience, etc.

4. The reader of Scripture should practice reading it aloud and should seek to read thoughts in a sentence rather than following punctuation pauses.

5. Lay readers can be very effective in reading Scriptures in worship, if given some training and if encouraged to prepare for the role of reading aloud to a congregation.

6. It may be helpful to let the congregation know that the sermon will be based on a particular Scripture of the Lectionary and that other pericopes are being read for their teaching value and are not related to the sermon. When two or all three Lectionary readings have a common theme and are the basis for the sermon this information should be shared with the congregation.

### G. Overview of the Lectionaries

1. The lectionary provides three readings for every Sunday over a three-year cycle, with readings drawn from the Old Testament, the Epistles (and Revelation), and the Gospels respectively. The purpose of this choice is to provide a witness to the unity of the Old and New Testaments and thus to the continuity of the plan of salvation. God's work of salvation is announced and initiated in the Old Testament and reaches its full realization in the passion of Christ. Through the apostolic preaching it reaches all the generations which follow them. One of the main reasons for a three year cycle is that this cycle allows for giving attention to each of the Synoptic Gospels in due course: Matthew is read in Year A; Mark in Year B, and Luke in Year C. However, this plan is not rigid. John's Gospel is used in the seasons of Christmas, Lent and Easter and John 6 is used on six Sundays in Year B, which helps fill in since Mark is a shorter Gospel.

2. The lectionary may be viewed as two halves: (1) the festival half (Advent — Pentecost Day),

and (2) the non-festival half (Trinity Sunday — Christ the King which concludes the church year). During the festival half, the convergences of the Common, Lutheran and Roman Catholic lectionaries are striking. But during the non-festival half there are differences between the Common and Lutheran lectionaries which are of two types: (1)In the Old Testament texts, the readings follow their own cycle in the Common Lectionary and often continue a series of stories from Sunday to Sunday (the story of David, for example in year B). By contrast, in the Lutheran lectionary each Old Testament lesson tends to relate to the Gospel reading for the day. This results in the Old Testament readings differing widely during this period, while the Gospels tend to agree. The Common lectionary planners thought it highly important that the biblical books be heard in their literary integrity week by week, rather than their having a thematic unity with the Gospel readings during the non-festival period. But during the seasons of Advent, Christmas, Lent and Easter they do tend to have a common theme each Sunday. Thus the Common Lectionary combines the two historic principles used in developing lectionaries: a. ''Continua'' or continuous readings which take place after Epiphany and following Pentecost, and b. ''selecta'' or selected passages for their particular theme used during Advent, Christmas, Lent and Easter to Pentecost Day.

2. In the Common and Lutheran lectionaries there are two opposite ways of determining which texts belong to which Sunday. Only rarely are all the twenty-eight Pentecost texts needed and, in most years, the extra texts are simply discarded. In the Common and Roman Catholic lectionaries, texts are assigned to Sundays by *counting backwards* from Christ the King Sunday, and those remaining texts are discarded from *the beginning* of the church season's list. But, in the Lutheran lectionary, texts are assigned beginning at Trinity Sunday and moving toward Christ the King Sunday, with the left-over texts discarded at the *end* of the church year.

Those using this *Workbook* should *note carefully* that identical Gospel themes appear in both Common/RC and Lutheran lectionary series, but for any given church year they may fall on *different* Sundays. In this *Workbook* a combination of titles are used for the Sundays: Proper, Pentecost, Ordinary Time and calendar dates in order to assist in identifying the Sunday for using the particular texts. In the second (''non-festival'') half of the church year, the Common Lectionary uses ''Proper 4, 5, 6, etc.'' while the Lutheran version follows ''Sundays after Pentecost'' to mark the Sunday. In the Roman Catholic lectionary the reference is to ''Sundays in Ordinary Time.''

A principle used in the Lutheran lectionary is that of choosing the Old Testament lesson to coordinate with the Gospel. While this ''typological'' arrangement has its weakness, it does provide the preacher with a clear clue as to sermon preparation. Note: the preacher should always *start* with the Gospel and proceed to the Old Testament passage. Depending upon the season of the year the Epistle reading may or may not be related in theme to the other readings.

Some of the Roman Catholic readings are from extra-canonical books and in the Common lectionary these are replaced with canonical readings. Also, in the Common lectionary some of the Roman Catholic readings were lengthened and others ''filled in,'' where the Roman planners skipped verses or portions of verses.

In the chart below of texts in the non-festival half of the church year the Gospel readings only are listed. Where there are differences, the Common/RC reading is first, followed by the Lutheran. Once the Gospel lesson is located the preacher may find the other lessons on the pages indicated:

| Common/RC | Lutheran Lectionary | Gospel Text(s) | Pages |
|---|---|---|---|
| May 29 — June 4 | Pentecost 2 | Mark 2:23—3:6<br>Mark 2:23-28 | 170 |
| June 5-11 | Pentecost 3 | Mark 3:20-35 | 178 |
| June 12-18 | Pentecost 4 | Mark 4:26-34 | 183 |
| June 19-25 | Pentecost 5 | Mark 4:35-41 | 187 |
| June 26 — July 2 | Pentecost 6 | Mark 5:21-43<br>Mark 5:21-24a, 35-43 | 192 |
| July 3-9 | Pentecost 7 | Mark 6:1-6 | 196 |
| July 10-16 | Pentecost 8 | Mark 6:7-13 | 201 |
| July 17-23 | Pentecost 9 | Mark 6:30-34 | 206 |
| July 24-30 | Pentecost 10 | John 6:1-15 | 210 |
| July 31 — August 6 | Pentecost 11 | John 6:24-35 | 215 |

In this *Workbook,* Common texts are listed and interpreted first.

# Preaching Resources for Cycle B

*(Highly recommended)*

## Commentaries on Gospel of Mark

*Kelber, Werner H., *Mark's Story of Jesus,* Fortress Press (Excellent brief introduction of Mark's gospel).

Achtemeier, *Mark Proclamation Commentaries,* Fortress Press.

Cranfield, C.E.B., *The Gospel According to Saint Mark,* Cambridge University Press.

Moule, *Mark, Cambridge New English Bible.*

*Nineham, *Saint Mark, Pelican New Testament Commentaries,* Penguin Books.

Schweizer, Eduard, *The Good News According to Mark,* John Knox Press.

*Williamson, Lamar, Jr., *Mark (Interpretation series: A Bible Commentary for Teaching and Preaching),* John Knox Press.

Kee, and others, *The Gospels, Interpreter's Concise Commentary,* Abingdon Press.

*Interpreter's Bible,* Volume 7, Abingdon Press.

Martin, Ralph P., *Mark, (Knox Preaching Guides),* John Knox Press.

*Hamilton, Neill Q., *Recovery of the Protestant Adventure,* The Seabury Press (While not a commentary in usual sense, this book shows the relevance of Mark's gospel for Americans today. Excellent resource for preaching from Mark).

## Commentary on John's Gospel

*Brown, Raymond E., *The Gospel of John* (2 volumes), Doubleday and Company (A classic by a leading Roman Catholic scholar, useful for dealing with texts from John in Year B)

## Commentaries for Lessons

*Interpreter's Concise Commentary Series,* Edited by Charles M. Laymon, Abingdon Press.

*Interpreter's Bible,* pertinent volumes, Abingdon Press.

Fuller, *Preaching the Lectionary,* Revised Edition, The Liturgical Press, Collegeville, Minnesota, 1984. (Includes Cycles A,B,C).

*Proclamation 3,* Series B. Fortress Press.

*Preaching the New Common Lectionary,* Year B, Abingdon Press.

Sloyan, *A Commentary on the New Lectionary,* A,B,C, Paulist Press, Paramus, New Jersey.

*1 Corinthians* by Barrett, Black/Harper Publishers.

*2 Corinthians* by Barrett, Black/Harper, Publishers.

*Epistles of John* by Brown, Anchor Bible.

*Epistles of John* by Westcott (1966).

*Ephesians* by Barth, Anchor Bible.

*Ephesians* by Johnston, New Century Bible.

*(The readings in cycles B ''jump around'' from book to book during the year so all the individual commentaries on each book of the Bible used will not be cited.)*

**Old Testament**

Achtemeier, Elizabeth, *The Old Testament and the Proclamation of the Gospel,* Westminster Press.

McCurley, *Proclaiming the Promise,* Fortress Press.

*The Old Testament Library,* Westminster Press (see pertinent commentaries).

*Interpreter's Concise Commentary,* Abingdon Press (see pertinent commentaries).

*Story and Faith: A Guide to the Old Testament,* by James L. Crenshaw, Macmillan Company, 1986.

**One Volume Commentaries**

*Peake's Commentary,* (1962), Thomas Nelson Publishing Company, edited by M. Black and H. H. Rowley.

*Jerome Bible Commentary,* edited R. Brown, et al.

**Commentaries on Several Books of the Bible**

*New Testament Theology* by J. Jeremias, Charles Scribner's Sons.

*Biblical Preaching* (An Expositor's Treasury), edited by James W. Cox, The Wesminster Press.

*The Torah: A Modern Commentary,* Edited by W.G. Plaut, Union of American Hebrew Congregations, New York City (An exciting Jewish commentary on first five books of the Bible with fresh insights and illustrations).

**Church Year**

*Handbook of the Christian Year,* by Hickman, Saliers, Stookey, White, Abingdon Press (Highly recommended as companion to this Workbook in designing worship).

*Worship* by H. O. Old, John Knox Press (Deals with historical and theological rationale for Reformed worship by a leading scholar in field).

*The Origins of the Liturgical Year* by T.J. Talley, Pueblo Publishing Company.

*The Liturgical Year* by Adolf Adam, Pueblo Publishing Company.

*Common Lectionary* (The Lectionary Proposed by the consultation on Common Texts), The Church Hymnal Corp., 800 Second Ave., New York, New York 10017.

*A Handbook for the Lectionary* by Horace T. Allen, Jr., The Geneva Press, Philadelphia.

*Doxology* by Geoggrey Wainwright, Oxford University Press (A systematic theology of worship).

**Enriching Preaching from the Lectionary Resources**

*"In Season," Edited by Rev. Dean Lueking, Cathedral Publishing Company *(Sermons on the Lectionary Readings by Working Pastors,* published weekly by Cathedral Publishing, 324 E. Fourth Street, Royal Oak, Michigan, 48068).

*C.S.S. *Sermon Books* (Books of sermons for Church Seasons).

*Augsburg Sermons,* Augsburg Publishing House (A year of sermons).

*Homily Service, Liturgical Conference* (Roman Catholic), Washington, DC (Monthly magazine with exegesis and sermons).

*Emphasis,* C.S.S. Publishing Company (Monthly publication of illustrations for each lesson).

*The Westminster Concise Handbook for the Bible,* D. V. Wilson, Westminster Press, 1979 (Gives overview of each book of Bible).

**Worship/Lectionary Aids**

*Let us Pray,* W. S. Carter, Series B, C.S.S. Publishing Company.

Carl, H. H., *Lectionary Worship Aids,* Series B., C.S.S. Publishing Company.

Joyce, Jon, *Scripture Notes — Series B,* C.S.S. Publishing Company.

*Word and Witness,* Published by Sunday Publications, Inc., 1937 10th Avenue, N., P. O. Box 9501, Lake Worth, Florida 33466.

*Reformed Liturgy and Music,* Published quarterly by Joint Office of Worship, Presbyterian Church (USA), hymns, anthems and other liturgical resources for each Sunday.

*An Inclusive Language Lectionary,* Philadelphia: Westerminster Press, 1983-85. One volume for each of Years A, B, C. Paraphrases the lessons in inclusive language. Sponsored by National Council of Churches.

*Preaching Through the Year,* David Steel, John Knox Press (suggestions for preaching from the lectionary with balance between freedom and order).

**Liturgical Preaching**

**Homiletic* by David Buttrick, Fortress Press. 1987 (A fresh approach to preaching by one of America's leading homileticians based on extensive research in preaching and communication of the spoken word).

**Preaching* by Fred Craddock, Abingdon Press.

*What is Liturgical Preaching?* Fuller.

Bosch, *The Sermon as Part of the Liturgy,* Concordia.

Best, *From Text to Sermon,* John Knox Press.

Keck, *The Bible in the Pulpit,* Abingdon Press.

Smith, Moody D., *Interpreting the Gospels for Preaching,* Fortress Press.

*Williams, Michael E., *Preaching Peers,* (Nashville: Discipleship Resources, 1987) A very useful guide to the formation of peer study groups of pastors to develop more effective preaching skills.

Craddock, Fred, *As One Without Authority,* (Nashville: Abingdon Press, 1979) Calls into question the deductive sermon with points, subheads, introduction, and formal conclusion. Argues for the inductive method of preaching in which Scripture and experience are so narrated that the form of the sermon becomes invisible.

Efrid, James M., *How to Interpret the Bible,* (Atlanta: John Knox Press, 1984) Examines various methods of biblical interpretation with a focus on ''the original meaning of Scripture.'' Helpful for the preacher in getting an overview of various books of the Bible and how to interpret them for congregations today.

# The Gospel Of Mark

Space does not permit a full introduction of the Gospel of Mark, therefore the user of the workbook should read one or more introductions to recent commentaries on Mark, such as *The Gospel of Mark* by D. E. Nineham *(The Pelican New Testament Commentaries),* and *The Gospel According to Saint Mark* by C. E. B. Cranfield *(The Cambridge Greek Testament Commentary).* The following brief introduction to Mark is intended to aid the preacher in gaining an overview of the Gospel.

*Author*

While scholars are not fully agreed on the identity of the author of Mark, a number of leading scholars such as Cranfield say that it is virtually certain that the Mark who is the associate of Peter and the author of the Gospel is also the Mark of Acts and the Pauline epistles. He was a Gentile author, deeply Christian, with good intellectual ability but without formal education to express himself in better Greek. Other scholars such as Kelber say that Mark is an anonymous Jewish Christian author.

*Date*

The date of writing the Gospel seems to be sometime in the latter part of A.D. 65-75.

*Place of Writing*

Rome is the traditional place for the writing of Mark, but the arguments for this are not conclusive. Antioch has the next best claim. More recently a scholarly consensus is beginning to emerge which points to Galilee or southern Syria as a likely place for the Markan Gospel. The internal logic, rather than external evidence, points to this area as the site of the writing of Mark.

*Priority of Mark*

It is now widely agreed that Mark was the first Gospel to be written. Part of the evidence for this is the fact that over ninety percent of Mark's verses are found in Matthew, and over fifty percent in Luke. Where either Matthew or Luke differs from Mark, the other Synoptic Gospel usually agrees with Mark. Mark is the shortest Gospel.

*Nature of the Gospel*

Mark is neither history nor biography. Mark, like the other Gospels, is intended to convey a religious message and demand a religious decision. To understand the Gospel we must use all the historical and critical resources available, in order to grasp the meaning of the Gospel considered as a spiritual message addressed to the church for which it was originally written. Only then can we begin to gain the message of the book for the Church of today. The Gospel is not a photographic panorama of the whole of Christ's life, as if someone with a video or audio recorder took it all down as it happened. Rather the Gospel is a series of essentially independent stories which have been preserved and to some extent modified in the context of the church's life and worship before it was included in the Gospel. Mark does directly attest to the beliefs about and understanding of Christ's ministry in the Christian Church around A.D. 75.

When Mark is read straight through (and the preacher is urged to do this early on), we see that Jesus is presented as the Son of God in a prominent way. Mark presents Jesus, not primarily as a teacher, but as the mysterious Son of God. Mark pictures Jesus as One whose work is to bring home to his generation the conviction that the End time was near, and as one who sought by his ministry and death to hasten the coming of the Kingdom of God. The Gospel ends at 16:8 in the best manuscripts.

*Audience to Which Mark Is Written*

Mark was written to people who already were Christians in order to give them a brief account of the facts about Jesus of Nazareth. The audience was Greek speaking Christians living in various parts of the Mediterranean world. Mark presents an understanding of Jesus and his work of salvation which is closely related to that in the letters of Paul. Therefore, the letters of Paul help us understand the religious message of Mark. Mark helps the reader to understand why the view of Jesus held in the conservative Jewish Christian communities was so unsatisfactory to the Gentile Christian church. In order to understand Mark, we must refrain from injecting Matthean or Lukan or Fourth Gospel elements into Mark's Gospel.

### Structure of Mark

*I. Ministry in Galilee (1:1—8:26)*

1. Baptism of Jesus
2. Beginning of Jesus' ministry in Galilee
3. Developing opposition
4. Parables of Jesus
5. Sending out of the Twelve
6. Jesus' visit to Tyre and Sidon

*II. Ministry in Judea (8:27—13:37)*

1. Announcement of Jesus' approaching death
2. Journey from Galilee to Judea
3. Palm Sunday and the cleansing of the Temple
4. Other teaching in Judea

*III. The Last week: death and resurrection (chapters 14-16)*

Note that the Gospel falls into two rather sharply divided parts, each containing its own characteristics. From 1:1 to 8:26 the emphasis falls on the miraculous deeds of Jesus and such teaching as is recorded. Teaching is directed to the crowd, is couched in parables, and is concerned with the coming of God's kingdom. Jesus seeks to prevent the recognition of his Messiahship (the Messianic secret), and there is almost no teaching about it.

But after 8:31 we notice a marked change in all these respects. Here miraculous healings are very rare, and the emphasis is now on Jesus' teaching which for the most part is directed to the disciples. Now the teaching assumes the knowledge of Jesus' Messiahship. Messiah's work involves grievous suffering both for the Messiah himself and his followers. But the final outcome of this suffering is the glorious triumph of God's cause which Messiah was expected to bring in.

But between these two parts is the story (8:27-30) of the Great Confession when Jesus and the twelve are alone near Caesarea Philippi. Peter speaks for all the disciples to say that Jesus is the Messiah (8:29) and this is recognized as the first recognition of Jesus' Messiahship by human beings. Jesus changed his tactics after being recognized for what he was. But Jesus continued to hide his Messiahship from outsiders who might misunderstand it.

Note that 16:9-20 are generally considered to be a later addition by the early church.

### Preaching Themes and Emphasis of Mark

*1. Mark presents Jesus as both human and divine,* a theological point of the Nicene Creed, and the church through the ages. Mark begins his Gospel with "The beginnings of the Gospel of Jesus Christ, the Son of God." Mark portrays Jesus as both human and divine with anger, pity, sorrow, etc. He was tempted. He prayed like any human being, and he experienced despair on the cross. But he was also the Son of God who forgave sin, cast out demons, calmed storms, healed, and raised the dead.

*2. Action thrust of Jesus' ministry.* Mark shows us Jesus as always on the move, and "straightway" is a common word in Mark. Jesus tried to do as much as possible in the little time left before the End. He had divine power to do wonderful things for people. But his greatest power was revealed in his death for the sins of the world. Mark portrays Jesus as teaching not only by words but by his life and works. Jesus is often addressed as "Teacher" in Mark and he taught, not only in parables, but by his miracles and life itself. Notice that Mark gives more place to miracles than any other Gospel does. Miracles express Jesus' authority and power.

*3. The centrality of the cross in Mark.* As early as 1:14 where the arrest of John the Baptizer occurs we can see a foreshadowing of the arrest of Jesus also, since John was his forerunner. Opposition to Jesus builds as indicated in 2:1—3:6, which culminates in a plot to put him to death. Jesus is rejected by his home town in 6:1-6a, which foreshadows his rejection by the people in general. And from the time of Peter's confession, the references to Jesus' approaching Passion and Resurrection become more and more plain. The story of the Passion and Resurrection forms the climax of Mark, and it dominates from 8:27—16:8. Jesus came to suffer and die for human beings so that they might be reconciled to God, and so that the Kingdom of God might come. The conflict between Jesus' opponents and Jesus reaches a climax on Good Friday at the cross.

The great emphasis which Mark put on the cross and resurrection is revealed by the amount of space and material devoted to this theme. As the preacher works through the Gospel of Mark, the preacher should take into account this focus on the cross and resurrection of Mark as he or she prepares and preaches from Mark. This is the heart of the Gospel and should be proclaimed in some form *every preaching occasion.*

# The Christian Year

As a result of the modern Liturgical Movement, many Protestant as well as Roman Catholic churches are following the seasons of the Christian Year. The colors used on specific days and seasons were formally defined in 1570 in the reformed missal under Pius V which has been changed little in recent time. The colors are as follows:

| | |
|---|---|
| Advent to Christmas Eve | Violet/Blue/Black |
| Christmas to Epiphany | White/Gold |
| Sundays after Epiphany | Green |
| Septuagesima to Ash Wednesday | Violet/Blue/Black |
| Throughout Lent | Veiling of colours |
| Passion Sunday to Easter Eve | Red/Rose |
| Easter | White/Gold |
| Pentecost | Red |
| Trinity | White/Gold |
| Sundays after Trinity | Green |
| Ordinary weekdays | Green |
| Blessed Virgin Mary | White/Red |
| Apostles, evangelists, martyrs | Red |
| Saints other than martyrs | White/yellow |
| Baptisms/confirmation | White/Red |
| Ordination/marriage | White |
| Funeral | Violet/Blue/Black |
| Dedication of a church | White |

(Page 40, *The Westminister Dictionary of Worship,* Edited by J.G. Davies, Wesminster Press, 1972).

In the Roman Catholic Church the post-Vatican II, *Ordo Missae* (1969) generally reaffirmed the current practice:

*White* for Easter, Christmas, feasts of Christ (other than Passion), All Saints, feast of Mary, etc.

*Red* for Passion and Palm Sundays, Good Friday, Pentecost, feasts of the Passion of Christ and of martyrs,

*Violet* for Advent and Lent, and possibly for funeral masses in place of black

*Rose* for Gaudet Sunday (Advent III) and Laetare Sunday (Lent IV)

*Green* at other times.

For further suggestions on use of liturgical colors see page 36, *Handbook of the Christian Year* by Hickman and others. Purples, grays and blues have been used for seasons of a preparatory and penitential character. White and gold are used on joyous seasons and events with a special christological flavor. Texture as well as color may be varied with the church year. These visual symbols are more than decorations as they serve as visual proclamations of the Gospel. Often a visual image will remain in people's minds after words are forgotten.

# The Advent and Christmas/Epiphany Seasons

The theology of this season is powerful because it unites the celebration of the expectation and birth of Jesus with his life, suffering, death and resurrection. The Appalachian folk carol catches up the unity of this season with the Lent/Easter/Pentecost season in its haunting words: "I Wonder as I Wander . . . how Jesus the Savior did come for to die." A vivid reminder of this same connection between the Incarnation and the Atonement is found in the huge star that is lighted during the Christmas season on a hill overlooking Bethlehem, Pennsylvania, which can be seen for miles around. It shines forth as a reminder of the star which guided the Wise Men and then stood over the stable where Jesus was born. Now at Easter the same huge steel framework is used to light an enormous cross that recalls Jesus' death for our sins. If you look closely at the lighted star at Christmas, you can see the outline of the same lights that help to form the cross at Easter! This is quite unintentional, but it expresses good theology: the star announcing the Incarnation foreshadows the cross and atonement: "Jesus the Savior did come for to die."

The great message of this season is summed up in "the Word became flesh and dwelt among us" (John 1:14). Historically, the orginal special day of this whole cycle of Advent/Christmas/Epiphany was Epiphany. This day of celebrating the manifestation of God's light and power in Christ was, after Easter and Pentecost, the third chief event in the Christian calendar of the early church. In the earliest lectionaries and sermons for Epiphany, stress was placed on John 1:1—2:11. The earliest themes associated with it were light, Jesus' advent into the world, his baptism, and the first miracle at Cana of turning water into wine. The common theme in all of these events is the affirmation that God was in Christ being made manifest to human beings even to the ends of the earth.

## Advent

The color is purple. Advent is the season beginning with the fourth Sunday before Christmas continuing to Christmas Eve. The theme is both threat and promise. It is a time of great tension with its primary concern of eschatology. Advent looks back at the first coming of Christ and forward to his coming again. We begin the Christian Year by thinking about the End of history. The Advent hymns often have a note of threat and promise, in contrast to Christmas hymns and carols. Thus the readings and sermons for Advent deal not so much with preparation for Christmas but with the expectation of Christ's coming to rule, to judge and to save. The prayer of Advent is summed up in the words: "Thy kingdom come, thy will be done, on earth . . ." The prophetic note is strong in this season but it is judgment on evil with a strong note of hope and expectation of Christ's coming reign.

Some liturgical leaders suggest that Advent hymns may be sung *before* Advent begins during November when sermons deal with eschatology and the coming rule of Christ as King (Christ the King Sunday and others). Then appropriate Christmas carols may be interspersed with Advent hymns during Advent season. Otherwise congregations would be confined to singing only a few of the lovely Christmas carols and hymns only on Christmas Eve (counted as an integral part of the following day as in the Jewish Sabbath) and on Christmas Day. Advent hymns might be sung on the first Sunday of Advent, with carols and hymns on the next three Sundays of Advent. This may offend liturgical "purists," but after all the Christian Year was made by and for human beings and not vice versa!

## Christmas

The color is white for Christmas Eve and Christmas Day to signify joy. The Christmas celebration begins on Christmas Eve, as noted above. Many churches celebrate with a candlelight communion service on Christmas Eve and may also celebrate with a worship and communion service on Christmas Day. When Advent is properly observed, then Christmas becomes far more than a sentimental remembrance of the birth and childhood of Jesus. Christmas should focus on the Incarnation and its meaning for human beings. The Incarnation and the Atonement, however, cannot be separated since they are all one piece of God's saving action in Jesus Christ. The Child that was born was born to die as our Redeemer. Preaching on Christmas Eve and Day should focus on the joy which Christ brings into our lives by forgiving our sins and giving us eternal life. This joy is a gift of the Holy Spirit and is independent of circumstances of life. The fulfillment of Old Testament prophecy in the birth of Jesus points us to God's continuing work of salvation.

The prayer of Christmas is summed up in the words of "O Little Town of Bethlehem": "cast out our sin and enter in, be born in us today.'' The goal of preaching at Christmas is to enable people to so hear God's Word that they may invite the Living Christ to be ''born in us today.''

The period between Christmas and Epiphany became for some elements of the early church a time of baptisms, second only to the Easter Vigil and Great Fifty Days. In Roman Catholic tradition there is an observance of feasts of martyrs and saints during this period, reminding us of the connection between Christmas/Epiphany and our dying and rising again with Christ.

## Epiphany

Epiphany gets its name from a Greek word which means ''manifestation'' and the thrust of this Day and Season is on the revelation of God in Jesus Christ, the Light of the World. White is the color, along with gold and yellow for Epiphany Day, the Baptism of our Lord, and Transfiguration. White is a symbol of joy and celebration, hence its use on these days. Green is used on the other Sundays of Epiphany season. Green symbolizes growth, growth in our knowledge of the God manifested in Jesus Christ. Epiphany Day itself is a celebration of Jesus' manifestation of God to the world. It is a day of splendor and light. The Wise Men representing the human race bearing precious gifts are integral parts of the Epiphany celebration. Two other events associated with it are Jesus' baptism in the Jordan and the wedding at Cana.

January was selected as Epiphany Day because it was the winter solstice on which day the birth of the sun god was celebrated. Although the solstice was moved to December 25th in 331 B.C., January 6th continued to be celebrated. Christians later substituted Epiphany for the solstice. Jesus is referred to as the Sun of Righteousness, and light and its rebirth is a theme of Epiphany.

Epiphany is a time to witness to the light manifested in Jesus Christ through a new thrust in evangelism. Christ, the Sun of Righteousness, breaks through the darkness of evil in the world and casts it out. There is a focus on worship as we reflect on the disciples' experience at the Transfiguration.

The Epiphany star and Epiphany candle may be used to symbolize the meaning of this season. The star which guided the Wise Men to the stable can guide us to the Child born there. The candle sheds its light in a darkened world. The candle gives its light by burning itself up. We see a symbol in the candle of Christ who burned himself out on the cross as the Light of the World.

The number of weeks in Epiphany depends upon the date of Easter, hence the season may be longer or shorter. It may be six to nine Sundays in length, since the former pre-Lenten season of three Sundays was made part of Epiphany in the new lectionary.

# Advent 1

| **Common** | **Lutheran** | **Roman Catholic** |
| --- | --- | --- |
| Isaiah 63:16—64:8 | Isaiah 63:16b-17; 64:1-8 | Isaiah 63:16-17, 19; 64:2-7 |
| 1 Corinthians 1:3-9 | 1 Corinthians 1:3-9 | 1 Corinthians 1:3-9 |
| Mark 13:32-37 | Mark 13:33-37 | Mark 13:33-37 |

## Comments on the Lessons

The Isaiah reading is virtual consensus and contains a plea for the coming of God the Redeemer. The 1 Corinthians pericope is virtual consensus also, but is not a continuous reading of the epistle. For this reason the introduction (vv. 1-2) is omitted. With the third reading there is virtual consensus. The pericope is in the context of the whole eschatological discourse. Because of the length of the preceding readings it seems appropriate to begin at verse 32 (or 33 L, RC). In each instance, where there are differences among the three lectionaries, the longer reading will be dealt with, leaving it to the preacher to make the necessary adjustment if a shorter reading is used.

## Commentary

*Isaiah 63:16—64:8 (C)*
*Isaiah 63:16b—17; 64:1-8 (L)*
*Isaiah 63:16-17, 19; 64:2-7 (RC)*

The people pray to God asking why their hearts have been hardened. Why have they turned away from God's leading to act as if they were not God's chosen people. "Come down," they cry in so many words, "help us! Overthrow our enemies and bring us back to you! For you, God, are the Father and Redeemer of Israel." This pericope is a selection from the psalm of lament found in Isaiah 63:7—64:11. The Jerome Bible calls it "one of the jewels of the Bible." The historical context of the lament is the post-exilic period when the Israelites, having returned from exile with high hopes fueled by Deutero-Isaiah's prophecies, find there is no real basis for their hopes. The temple still lay in ruins.

In this pericope the psalmist confesses both his own sins and those of the nation Israel which he sees as the cause of the delay in the restoration of Jerusalem. Notice that the prophet identifies himself with his recently conquered people. On the basis of God's redemptive work in the past he pleads for a renewal of such divine action. "O that thou wouldst rend the heavens and come down, that the mountains might quake at thy presence —" (64:1) These words remind us of God's advent to Moses on Sinai: "And the Lord came down upon Mount Sinai, to the top of the mountain; and the Lord called Moses to the top of the mountain . . ." (Exodus 19:20) This cry of the prophet for God to rend the heavens and come down undoubtedly influenced Mark's description of Jesus' baptism when the heavens were "rent" (a more accurate translation than "were opened" 1:10). A free translation of the Greek would be: "he saw the heavens in the process of being ripped apart." The passive verb used here is the same one used of the temple curtain being torn in two from top to bottom when Jesus died on the cross. The Hebrew prayer for divine intervention was answered in the ministry of Jesus and in his death. The cry for divine intervention has long been associated with Advent.

This psalm of Isaiah has been called probably the most powerful psalm of communal lamentation in the Bible. The structure is not readily apparent. A broad outline is: (1) the prayer that God should turn towards Israel (63:5), (2) related to this is the prayer that God should intervene (63:19b), and (3) at the end (64:11) an anxious prayer which had been joined earlier to the introductory prayer (v. 15b) is offered to God.

To properly understand the introductory prayer "look down from heaven and see" (63:15, 16) we must take into account a characteristic which marks supplication in the Old Testament, namely the fact that the prayer for God's help is invariably preceded by a prayer asking that he should turn toward the suppliant.

It is significant that the community of Israel as it prays to God asserts it cannot put its trust in Abraham or Jacob for they do not know it. The way God is the father of Israel is different from that of earthly fathers. God is a living and present father who sees, knows and acts. The unique thing which makes God Israel's father is the fact that his people may call upon him, and he in turn can be gracious to his people.

After the introductory prayer comes the lament itself. It is made up of: (1) the complaint regarding enemies (v. 18), and (2) the lament in the first person plural (v. 19). God is reproached by being asked why he made Israel turn aside from obeying him. Israel is forced into this question by her belief that all things come from God. It was to avoid a dualism which posits an evil force outside God, contesting with God, that allowed the Israelite to believe that God could harden his heart. Another profound question of faith is expressed in the question of how God can allow his foes, the foreign armies, to desecrate his sanctuary. Notice that the question is not put about God but to God himself!

In verse 19a we have a statement as the third part of the lament which goes beyond the questions. This expresses something of "darkness" regarding God. Here is one of the most profound confrontations of man with God in all Scripture. When the Israelites pray to God they come to an abyss. "We have become like those over whom thou hast never ruled, like those who are not called by thy name (19)." This lament as very relevant for our present day because it anticipates the arguments of atheism. The essential difference is that the laments are offered by God's people to God himself.

The central part of the psalm is the wish that God might appear with power and in sovereign majesty to give help to Israel. (63:19b—64:4a) Note that this corresponds to the plea that God should turn towards Israel in 63:15. God reveals himself to deliver his people when things are at their worst.

The nations tremble when God draws near, such is his awesome power. The terrible acts of God include the overthrow of Israel's adversaries and the establishment of Israel's power. Verse 4b is a final piece of praise: "no eye has seen a God besides thee, who works for those who wait for him." The psalmist prays that God will meet "him that joyfully works righteousness, those that remember thee in thy ways"(5).

An overview of the development of laments from the exile onwards reveals that there is less and less charge brought against God and finally it disappears. In its stead, greater importance is given to the confession of sin. God's wrath was brought about by Israel's unfaithfulness and transgression.

God is called "our Father" in 63:16 and 64:8, phrases which are found only in this one psalm! The reason for avoiding this term for God lies in the cultural backgroud in which pagans believed in the physical fatherhood of the gods as a basic aspect of religious myth. The Hebrew saw himself, not as a child of God, but a creature of God. Notice that the Fatherhood of God is never asserted until after the Exile, at which time the danger of its being misunderstood may have diminished. Israel turns to her Father God in confidence in her time of need. Notice that in 63:16 the stress falls on God's being a Father, in 64:8 the emphasis is on the fact the speakers are God's children. The psalmist describes himself as a creature, or like clay with God as the potter. The prayer in verse 9 takes for granted that God cannot overlook his people's sin. The psalmist prays that God will look again toward sinful Israel for, after all, "we are all thy people." There is a sharp break off in the psalm here. It has been suggested that 63:17b belongs here, since it is out of context where it now stands. This would have the psalm end: "Return for the sake of thy servants, the tribes of thy heritage."

### *1 Corinthians 1:3-9*

This pericope contains the greeting and opening of Paul's epistle. This was not the first letter Paul wrote to the church at Corinth, for he tells us in 1 Corinthians 5:9 that he had written a previous letter to them. Note the fact that Paul associates Jesus Christ with God our Father as the source and giver of grace and peace. The word "grace" is a word play on the normal greeting, and the word "peace" expresses the Hebrew greeting "shalom." Thus Paul combines references to both God's prior acts (through Iarael) and now through Jesus Christ.

Paul thanks God for their variety of charismatic gifts (v. 4) — their speech and knowledge. Later he will criticize them for the way they are using these gifts. He doesn't doubt they are authentic gifts. But he goes on to remind them that, in spite of all their present knowledge, they are waiting for the "revealing of our Lord Jesus Christ." (v. 7) By this Paul sets the charismatic gifts in an eschatological context.

Notice the main thrust throughout these opening verses is on the *action of God*. They need to be sustained by God and preserved by him until the day of Christ's return. The second coming of Christ is a major emphasis throughout the Advent season. Paul clearly sets forth the tension between Christ's coming and his coming again at the Day of the Lord. Because God is a faithful God who has called them into the fellowship of Jesus Christ, the Church, the members of the church may face the judgment unafraid.

Paul makes it clear that God's work in all this is through Christ, the agent of redemption. Here are three "not yets" which the Corinthian charismatics were in danger of forgetting in their enthusiasm with the gifts they already have: (1) they are still waiting for the revealing of the Lord Jesus Christ, (2) they will be sustained by him until the end, and (3) they will be preserved by him guiltless until the Day of Jesus Christ. It is these reminders that make this pericope especially appropriate for Advent. Later in the letter, Paul criticizes the Corinthians for their use or misuse of their charismatic gifts. Chapters 12, 14 especially reflect this criticism of Corinthian life and thought. This can be regarded as a spelling out of the implications of the eschatological pointers in this opening thanksgiving.

Notice that Paul gives thanks to God on behalf of the Corinthians precisely for the gifts (vv. 5) which are creating trouble within the church. The problem is not a lack of such gifts but their abuse. But, in spite of their abuse, the gifts still are a sign of God's continuing favor and grace. God remains faithful even when his gifts are misued!

*Mark 13:32-37 (C)*
*Mark 13:33-37 (L) (RC)*

In year B, as in other years of the lectionary cycle, we begin Advent with gospel readings not from the beginning of the gospel but with the future-eschatological passage in the synoptic apocalypse. This apocalypse concludes in Mark as in Matthew and Luke with a series of eschatological parables. Today's pericope is one of these: the parable of the doorkeeper.

The central thrust of this passage is that, since no one knows the exact schedule for the end of this age and the coming of the kingdom, everyone should be ready for that Day, *watching continuously*. Variations of these watchfulness sayings are found also in Luke and Matthew. Mark has arranged them editorially here for his purposes. "To be on the alert" is the unifying theme of the whole chapter 13 of Mark. The kind of alertness differs (vv. 5, 9, 23, 29, 33, 35, 37), but the theme of all of these verses is summed up in the final word of the chapter: *watch*.

Scholars tend to agree that verse 32 must be a genuine saying since no one in the early church would have invented it. The absolute use of the title son is significant. The parable of the doorkeeper has also been called the Parable of the Absent Householder. It recalls the Waiting Servants of Luke 12:35-40. In the context of Mark it refers to the Second Advent, which is a major emphasis of the Advent Season. But, when spoken by our Lord on the eve of his passion, the parable may well have referred to the brief time before his return from the grave and vindication by God.

It should be noted that the parable shades into direct advice to the disciples. The point of the parable, as noted earlier, is found in the words of command to the porter to *watch*. The figures in the parable are only thinly disguised representations of those for whom the teaching is intended.

In its long and complicated history, this parable has acquired secondary features, in contrast to the Lucan form. (Luke 12:35-38) They are: (1) "A man going on a journey" which is a phrase from the parable of the talents, (2) "puts his servants in charge, each with his work", from the parable of the faithful and unfaithful servants. (Matthew 24:45 and Luke 12:42) The reference to a man going on a journey clearly applies to Jesus' ascension and identifies his return with the parousia. The "servants" clearly applies the parable to the post-Easter church waiting for the parousia which is delayed. The church had to adapt this parable to this situation since there was not one final crisis, but a phased out process. This process was: the ascension of Jesus, his waiting in heaven and his final return. This parable was not spoken to prepare the disciples for a long period of waiting for the second coming, but rather to enforce on the disciples the necessity for alertness in a crisis imminently upon them. This final eschatological crisis would overtake the disciples as a result of his ministry. One final note is that the fourfold division of the day (evening, midnight, cockcrow, and morning) which replaces the Palestinian division of the first, second and third watches is an accommodation to Roman usage.

## Theological Reflections

The second and third pericopes put the Church today firmly in place "between the times," the time of Jesus earthly ministry and his coming again at the end of the age. This strident theme, alongside the Isaiah passage which is a calling for God's intervention to save Israel then, sets the tone for the Advent season: *watching*. While the Old Testament hopes for Messiah who is still to come, the

New Testament hopes for the Christ who has come and is coming again. For this reason the Christian hope is based on historical knowledge of its object. The past events recorded in Scripture witnessing to Jesus Christ nourish our hope for the future. This hope is not an unknown, but is based on our experience of the faithfulness of Him who is the same yesterday, today and forever. (Hebrews 13:8) The future has lost its power to terrify. Hope for the Christian is always a good hope. In Jesus Christ hope is always eschatological. This means that its object is always future, and yet already present. The Christian's future is not a fixed, fatalistic one, always out of reach, but rather the future comes to us! As we move toward it, it moves toward us! Christ is the one who comes! The message of Advent is that in Christ what is hoped for is on the way to meet us, already breaking into the present moment!

## Homiletical Moves

*Isaiah 63:16—64:8*
### Our Cry to God in Time of Urgent Need

1. A prayer for God to turn towards us (63:15)
2. Confession of sin (and complaints against God) (63:19b—64:5a)
3. An anxious prayer to our Father for help (63:16; 64:8), which is answered in Jesus Christ, already come and coming again

*1 Corinthians 1:3-9*
### Waiting for the Day of Our Lord Jesus Christ

1. We eagerly expect Christ's coming again
2. God will sustain us to the end
3. God will preserve us guiltless through Christ, for God is faithful

*Mark 13:32-37*
### Keep on Watching for Jesus!

1. We don't know when Jesus is coming again (v. 32)
2. Don't be caught napping when Jesus returns (v. 36)
3. Continue actively watching by faithful discipleship (v. 37)

### *This Preacher's Choice*

*Mark 13:32-37*

The central thrust of this pericope is watchfulness in light of the coming again of the Ascended Christ. The preacher may want to "block out" the movements of the passage: (1) a man goes on a journey; (2) leaves his servants in charge, each with his work to do; (3) and commands the doorkeeper to be on the watch, for the master is certainly coming again! In developing this there is a definite allusion to Jesus' ascension in the reference to a man going on a journey. The Jesus who came once left for a time. The church has its work to do, with each member carrying out his or her task. They are warned not to sleep, since they never know when the master will return. The Jesus whose first coming we prepare to celebrate at Christmas is the One who is coming again at the end of the age. The preacher may want to point out the aspects of culture which tend to put the Christian to sleep, particularly the security of affluence, the secularism of the age which denies the transcendent, and the commercialism of the season which dwells on sentimentality about the birth of a baby, but forgets that the coming Jesus is coming to judge and reign as King of Kings. Ways in which Christians can be "watching" for the coming Lord can help Christians deal constructively with this season of the year. Watching through increased reflection on Scripture, renewed prayer, and deeds of mercy in the name of Christ may be suggested. The mood of *expectation* should permeate the message.

**Hymn for Advent 1:**  *Watchman, Tell us of the Night*

**Prayer**
*O God, who ripped open the heavens and sent Jesus Christ into this world, help us to watch with eagerness for his return. Keep us faithful in service to you and the world. Keep us from dozing off into indifference, apathy, or despair over his return. May we be sustained by you, guiltless, until the Day of the Lord. Amen*

# Advent 2

| **Common** | **Lutheran** | **Roman Catholic** |
|---|---|---|
| Isaiah 40:1-11 | Isaiah 40:1-11 | Isaiah 40:1-5, 9-11 |
| 2 Peter 3:8-15a | 2 Peter 3:8-14 | 2 Peter 3:8-14 |
| Mark 1:1-8 | Mark 1:1-8 | Mark 1:1-8 |

## Comments on the Lessons

While there is virtual consensus on the first reading, the RC lectionary omits verses 6-8 which are an important part of the passage in which the prophet comforts Jerusalem with the promise of the coming God. There is virtual consensus on the second reading with verse 15a offering a good conclusion. Third reading has consensus. In the Isaiah passage Yahweh orders a highway built in the wilderness, so that his exiled people can return in a second Exodus across the wilderness desert to Zion. With the proclamation of comfort there is action to deliver the people from servitude in Babylon. The turning point in Israel's fortunes come at the point of the announcement that Israel's "time of service is ended her iniquity as pardoned." The Peter pericope contrasts God's view of time with the human view and defends the delay in the coming of the Day of the Lord, as God's gracious provision for our repentance and salvation here and now. The Markan passage contains John the Baptizer's radical call for repentance in light of the coming One who will baptize with Holy Spirit. We stand on this side of the cross and find in Christ the One who is God's highway of salvation. His death and resurrection give comfort to sinners through the forgiveness of sins. Repentance, a traditional theme of Advent, is reflected in the Markan pericope. God's grace in Christ provides the forgiveness the repentant sinner seeks. John could only call for repentance, Christ offers salvation to all.

## Commentary

*Isaiah 40:1-11 (C)*
*Isaiah 40:1-11 (L)*
*Isaiah 40:1-5, 9-11 (RC)*

The pericope for today forms the prologue to Deutero-Isaiah (chapters 40-55) and the form in which we have these chapters goes back basically to Deutero-Isaiah himself. This prophet carried out his mission during the exile just as Cyrus the Persian ruler began his conquest of the Babylonian Empire. Jerusalem had fallen to the Babylonian onslaught and Jerusalem was captured in 597 BC. King Jehoichin and his family were carried off into captivity in the first deportation of exiles. Some ten years later Judah was again trying to defend herself against the Babylonian army. But in 587 BC Jerusalem was destroyed. Its walls were pulled down, the temple was burned and the Davidic family was removed from the throne. Additional Judeans were deported. The book of Lamentations describes the horrors which took place in Jerusalem's fall. For this reason Lamentations should be read side by side with Deutero-Isaiah. The good news Isaiah announces is the coming to an end of the exile and the salvation which is at hand.

While several of the prophetic books begin with an account of the prophet's call, the placing of the message "Comfort, comfort . . ." tells us that the really important thing is the introduction of the message. The message, not the messenger, is the thrust of the pericope. The introduction of the messenger is peripheral which forms a just a part of the larger whole. And it is presented in veiled terms: verses 6-8 are the equivalent of the messenger's call.

The main thrust of Deutero-Isaiah and of this introductory pericope is the good news of the coming of Yahweh. In the later poems of the prophet, it becomes clear that God comes to liberate and restore Israel. The poem uses the form of dialogue which is the usual literary form in Deutero-Isaiah. While the book has been called the "Book of Consolation" because of its opening words, the book is much more than this, although this is a dominant theme. This pericope is like an overture to a great symphony. Watch for its recurring themes in future passages. In Deutero-Isaiah it is sometimes difficult to distinguish the speakers. Some have suggested that the two unidentified speakers, in addition to Yahweh and the prophet, are voices of the heavenly council. Whether members of the heavenly council or not, the voices are Yahweh's messengers who give the prophet his commission.

The content of Isaiah's preaching was two-fold: (1) he had to convince the despondent exiles that God was again moving in history and was responsible for the meteoric rise of Cyrus and other events in the international scene, and (2) Isaiah had to convince his own people that Cyrus' conquest would bring a new day for the exiles and the Judeans. This included the good news that God had forgiven the people and was about to inaugerate an act of salvation to free them from the oppressive servitude of the exile.

As noted above, verses 6-8 contain the prophet's call. The two passages which precede and follow it (vv. 3ff and 9ff) are two cries which form, as it were, a framework for the prophet's call. The first (vv. 3ff) is an order given to unspecified listeners to prepare a way in the wilderness. The other (v. 9ff) is a summons to Zion to get up into a high mountain and announce to the cities of Judah, "Behold your God." These three sections are introduced by the cry, "Comfort my people." These three sections make up one cry. They set the pattern for all that follows.

The opening words "Comfort, comfort . . ." sound forth like a general's marching orders to an army at ease. They are passed throughout the army until every man has heard them and has obeyed. Comfort is not just soothing words but action! A great highway through the desert to home in Jerusalem is to be constructed. Notice that the one who comforts is God, and Israel is the receiver of God's comfort. Comforting signifies God's direct intervention in human history to help and restore. Notice that the comforting is spoken of in the past tense. The force of this in past tense is noteworthy. To the question, "Who helps Israel in her distress?" comes the reply: "Yahweh has comforted his people. (Isaiah 49:13)

The turning point in Israel's fortunes is announced in the verse: "her time of service is ended . . . her iniquity is pardoned." (v. 2) The change in Israel's life is based on the gift of divine forgiveness. For Second Isaiah there is no divorce of religion from politics. God and history are vitally linked. Isaiah's words of comfort put him in the company of the pre-exilic prophets of doom who took as their chief task the emphasis to Israel of her accumulated iniquity. God's forgiveness of his people has far greater impact than his relationship to them. It has an impact on world history. It should be noted that concerns which would appear at first glance to belong only to the personal, such as failure and forgiveness, are made by Isaiah the basis of changes in world history.

The key to the entire passage is in verse 8: "But the word of our God will stand for ever." While grass may wither, flowers fade, and man himself pass on like grass, God's word endures forever. Man cannot annul it. But note carefully that it is not only the spoken word of Yahweh, but the *deed it accomplishes* which has enduring reality.

The call for a highway in the desert is a call for the preparation for a second Exodus through the desert back to Jerusalem. In Babylonian religion, special processional ways were built, along which the images of the gods were carried so all could see them. Nature is to be transformed and a clear way for God is to be prepared. Jerusalem is called upon to be a herald of God's coming (v. 9) and to declare to the cities of Judah: "Behold your God!" (v. 9) The image of the king as a shepherd was a familiar one in the ancient world. This deliverer God is a gentle shepherd who gathers the lambs in his arms and gently leads those that are with young. (v. 11) The announcement of God's presence is a prominent Advent theme. Immanuel, *God with us,* is the good news of Advent, indeed, of the whole Christian Year!

*2 Peter 3:8 15a (C)*
*2 Peter 3:8-14 (L)*
*2 Peter 3:8-14 (RC)*

Second Peter is by an unknown author who wrote between A.D. 100 and 125 and is concerned mainly with the Gnostic heresy. Gnosticism taught that a secret, superior "knowledge" was necessary in order to be a Christian. It taught that all things physical were inferior to things spiritual, and for this reason Jesus' earthly life was of little or no importance in contrast to his spiritual self. It has no place for the belief in the second coming of Christ. Throughout the first three centuries the churches refused to accept 2 Peter as a genuine epistle of Peter.

The pericope begins with the declaration that God's time scheme is different from ours. With the Lord a day is as a thousand years, and a thousand years as one day. The author says the Lord is not tardy, but rather is patient, giving time to all so that they may repent and turn to him. The delay of the return of Christ is only apparent due to the relativity of time, and this gives people additional opportunity to be saved.

But the Lord will come as a thief in the night. This reference to Jesus' parable (Matthew 24:43) is cited to stress that Christians must expect the Day of the Lord at any moment. This gives motivation for holiness and godliness in living. The coming catastrophic judgment on the universe should motivate people to do serious reflection and also to live a godly life.

*Watchfulness* is an essential part of Christian living. Christians should live as if it were the last hour. (1 John 2:18) When understood correctly, the expectation of Christ's imminent return is cause, not for despair, but for renewed zeal in holy living. No matter how much we attempt to demythologize the New Testament, we cannot escape the hope of a new heaven and earth it offers as the final goal of history. Christ spoke of his return, and the church through the ages has affirmed its faith in the One who will come to "judge the quick and the dead."

### Mark 1:1-8 (C)

Although the first eight verses of Mark's Gospel seem to be given over entirely to John the Baptizer, they have much to say about the credentials of Jesus. They treat John almost entirely as the forerunner of Messiah, although he was an outstanding religious leader in his own right. What is important about John for Mark is the fact that the story of Jesus begins with him. John is primarily a figure of hope since his appearance marks "the beginning of the gospel."

Putting John the Baptizer center stage on the second and third Sundays of Advent is the established pattern of the Lectionary. John prepares the way for Jesus' ministry. John's call to repentance prepares the church today for the appropriate celebration of the Incarnation at Christmas. According to Mark, the preaching of John had a two pronged thrust: (1) the preaching of repentance and baptism and the forgiveness of sins, and (2) the announcment of the coming of the mightier One who will baptize with the Holy Spirit.

Notice that John the Baptizer picks up the Deutero-Isaiah pericope for today of Isaiah 40:1-11 and prefaces it with a verse from Malachi (3:1), altering "my face" to "thy face." This makes it an address to Christ. We have learned from the Dead Sea Scrolls that both these techniques of combining two widely separated texts and altering them for the author's purpose were common practices.

These two references from the Old Testament say that the Messiah would be preceded by a forerunner. The rest of the account of John emphasizes that John was this prophesied forerunner. The fact that John lived and worked in the wilderness is made in order to show he fulfilled this prophecy. However, the better exegesis of Isaiah 40:1 ff indicates that it is not a "voice in the wilderness" as Mark says (1:3), but rather "A voice cries: 'In the wilderness prepare the way of the Lord . . .' " But Mark's interest in the matter is theological, not historical or geographical.

The whole population comes out to be baptized by John. John was seen as the fulfillment of the prophecy that Elijah would return to earth as the forerunner of Messiah. (Malachi 4:1-6) Thus John is a link with what has gone before. He stands as a bridge between the Old and New Testaments. He is the last of the prophets. He calls the people to repent and return to God in light of the expected final reconcilation and transformation.

John calls the people to repent of their arrogant assumption that they are alone favored by God, to repent of their failure to meet God's moral demands, and their self-righteousness that led them to feel themeselves better than those around them. John's message was good news in that it was a call to repent, confess and to be forgiven. But he announced the One "mightier than I" who would baptize with the Holy Spirit. Thus John's baptism is an anticipation of Jesus' baptism. Although John's followers held him in high regard, Mark and the early church make it clear that John is only the forerunner. Jesus is Messiah! Jesus is the real "beginning."

## Theological Reflections

The Advent themes of repentance in preparation for the coming of Messiah and the expectation of Christ's return at the End of the Age are prominent in the readings for today. Deutero-Isaiah announces good news, and so does John the Baptizer. God is acting in history to deliver his people from their bondage. For Isaiah it was servitude in a foreign land. For John it was bondage to sin. The expectation of the Second Coming of Christ at the End gives the Advent season an anticipation far more profound that the yearly "getting ready for Christmas rush." It calls every Christian to repentance and to an expectation of God's radical action at the Day of the Lord. It puts an edge on the Advent season, a keen sense of joyful anticipation of Christ's return as King of Kings and

Lord of Lords.

## Homiletical Moves

*This Preacher's Choice*

*Isaiah 40:1 11*
## You Can Go Home Again!

Isaiah has a vision of the heavenly council in which heavenly beings are commanded to comfort Israel in exile, in deed as well as word, by preparing the great highway on which God will return to Jerusalem. The word "comfort" is a plural imperative which suggests that comfort will be proclaimed by the three voices that follow. The tension in this pericope is Israel's exile in Babylon and how to get home again to Palestine. God announces a second Exodus of Israel out of servitude, this time out of Babylon instead of Egypt.

One possible set of "moves" would follow this pattern:

1. Israel's time of service (like military service in warfare) is ended and her iniquity is pardoned. Earlier in Israel's life God had declared war against his people's sin, bringing battle and destruction upon them. But now God announces an end to the war, and calls for comfort for Israel. God acts in gracious mercy toward his people. We who stand on this side of the Cross can rejoice that God has in Christ broken the power of sin and evil and pardoned our sins.

2. Life is like the flowers and grass, fleeting, fading and temporary, but God's word stands forever. The buying and selling, giving and receiving of the holiday season may demand our full attention for a few weeks, but it is soon over. Indeed, human life itself is very limited in comparison to God's time in which a thousand years are but as a day, and a day a thousand Years. (2 Peter 3:8-14) That God's word endured is attested by the fact Israel was released from servitude in Babylon and returned to Palestine. God has kept his word to us in Jesus Christ, the same yesterday, today and forever.

3. Jerusalem is called as a herald to announce, "Behold your God!" (v. 9) This is the good news of the Advent season: God has appeared in Jesus Christ. This is the Immanuel — God with us — Israel longed for. He is the royal way out of servitude into the Promised Land. God comes with power and might to rule, but he comes gently like a shepherd who cares for the lambs, taking them up in his arms, and carefully watching over the unborn. The God to whom we are pointed this Advent season is the crucified and ascended Good Shepherd who gave his life for the sheep!

*2 Peter 3:8-15a*
## Living Now in Light of Eternity

1. Secular humanity, like the Gnostics, denies the Second Coming of Christ. (vv. 3, 4) The transcendental dimension of life is denied in a world in which science and technology seem to offer all the answers.

2. The day of judgment will come with fire to destroy the ungodly. (vv. 7, 12) The real possibility of a nuclear holocaust gives new meaning to this ancient prophecy. Movies picturing a world after such a man-made disaster point up the precariousness of life on planet Earth.

3. God is patient with us now in order to give us time to repent and turn to him for forgiveness. (v. 9)

4. In light of God's forbearance and the coming judgment, we are to live now lives of faithful obedience "without spot or blemish and at peace." (v. 14)

*Mark 1:1-8*
## Preparing the Way for Jesus

1. John the Baptizer preaches a message of repentance for the forgiveness of sins. We prepare

for Christ to be born anew in our hearts by repenting and accepting God's forgiveness.

2. John was the forerunner, who ends the prophetic tradition and points to the Mightier One. Gruenwald's Isenheim Altarpiece of the crucifixion in Colmar, France, puts John the Baptizer at the foot of the cross pointing with a bony finger to Christ, while holding the Old Testament Scriptures foretelling the Servant who would suffer.

3. John points to Jesus who will baptize with the Holy Spirit. We who live on this side of the cross have received the fulfillment of this prophecy. Pentecost inaugurated this baptism with the Holy Spirit which continues as God transforms repentant sinners.

**Hymn for the Sunday:**   *Heralds of Christ*

**Prayer**

*Lord God who delivered your people from bondage in Egypt and from servitude in Babylon, deliver us in our time from bondage to self, greed, and security. Comfort us by preparing a way back to you, the way of repentance and forgiveness. May we know the joy of beholding you, face-to-face, in Christ Jesus this Advent season. Keep us watchful for Christ's coming again at the end of this age. Amen*

# Advent 3

| Common | Lutheran | Roman Catholic |
| --- | --- | --- |
| Isaiah 61:1-4, 8-11 | Isaiah 61:1-3, 10-11 | Isaiah 61:1-2, 10-11 |
| 1 Thessalonians 5:16-24 | 1 Thessalonians 5:16-24 | 1 Thessalonians 5:16-24 |
| John 1:6-8, 19-28 | John 1:6-8, 19-28 | John 1:6-8, 19-28 |

## Comments on the Lessons

There is near consensus on the first reading. Isaiah 61:4, 8 introduces restoration themes which blend well with the John the Baptizer material and provide appropriate Advent themes. There is consensus on the second and third pericopes. John the Baptizer figures prominently in the readings for the second and third Sundays of Advent as the one who points to the coming Messiah.

## Commentary

*Isaiah 61:1-4, 8-11*

The pericope is from the third section of the Book of Isaiah (chapters 56-66), which has come to be known as Trito-Isaiah. This section comes mostly from a time when the city of Jerusalem has been rebuilt. So has the temple. This section seems to assume that the new exodus Deutero-Isaiah announced has already occurred. The author(s) of the material are in Jerusalem. While some scholars see this material deriving from the school of Deutero-Isaiah, there is agreement among many scholars that chapters 60-62 form the nucleus of the message of this third section of the Book. The prophet lived after the exile. The section forms a literary unit. It is significant that chapters 60-62 contain a message which is exculsively one of salvation.

The opening verses (1-3) are a proclamation by a man who is aware that God has sent and equipped him to proclaim the message of salvation. He describes his mission in terms of servanthood. This passage had a profound effect on Jesus' understanding of his own mission. Jesus alluded to it in answer to John (Matthew 11:2-6; Luke 7:18-23) and quoted from it in his sermon at Nazareth. (Luke 4:16 22)

Notice that the series of infinitives which set forth the purpose for which the messenger was sent are dependent on the verb (to send). In a somewhat strange way they combine the prophet's task with its results: "to proclaim . . . to declare . . . to bind up . . . to comfort . . . to give." The prophet speaks and it happens! To proclaim salvation is almost the same as bringing it about!

Identifying speaker and audience is important in understanding a passage of Scripture. This pericope opens with a confessional statement about God (vv. 1-4), then it appears God speaks (vv. 5-9), and finally it seems the community speaks (vv. 10 11). While nothing in the speeches gives a clue to who the audience is, we can assume it is the community of the prophet's day. There are echoes of the Servant Songs here which indicate that the prophet thought of himself as fulfilling the mission of the Servant. The mission is to Israel to declare to her the arrival of the promised salvation. But the "poor," "brokenhearted," etc. are not Israel as a whole, but the devout core of the faithful. The prophet is to bring about a reversal of the fate of the deprived and destitute. In previous texts for Advent from the Old Testament we have seen the yearning for release from servitude and oppression. The new element that has entered the scene is the figure appointed to take action. By the speaker's proclamation he will not only announce good tidings but bring them to pass. In Hebrew thought, word/deed are a unity. To say the word is to do the word!

The speaker's words have a "bite" in the real world of people, food, prisons, etc., in that the proclamation is depicted in political rather than spiritual terms. It can be compared to Moses' liberation of Israel from bondage in Egypt.

Isaiah was aware of being sent to "comfort all who mourn" (v. 2), and what gives comfort is the action of God indicated by the "insteads" that follow. Then verses 4-11 go on to say how and in what this change in Zion's fortunes is brought about. Briefly, it is brought about in: (1) the rebuilding of the city, and (2) the restoration of her honor. The saving action of God brings forth the response of a song of praise by those saved: "I will greatly rejoice in the Lord, my soul shall exult in my God . . ." (v. 10)

In verse 11 salvation is compared to the bursting forth of plants in a garden: "For as the earth brings forth its shoots, and as a garden causes what is sown in it to spring up." This picks up and continues the image in verse 3, "the planting of the Lord that he may be glorified."

In verse 10 we have a model of worship: a hymn of praise by the community to God, in response to its acceptance of the message of salvation. While Deutero-Isaiah has such hymns sung by the whole community, Trito-Isaiah puts it in the mouth of an individual. But the significant thing is that Trito-Isaiah continues to connect the proclaiming of salvation and the community's answer to it, as does Deutero-Isaiah.

The central thrust of this pericope is that God is acting to bring about righteousness and justice in the world. God will set things right that humans have made wrong. To ensure this continuing, God will make an everlasting covenant with his people and their descendants, so that the whole world will know that they are a people blessed by God.

### 1 Thessalonians 5:16-24

"Rejoice always," urges Paul. Joy in the light of God's coming salvation is a theme of Advent. In the Roman Missal this Sunday was known as Gaudete from the opening word of the introit. The theme of joy and rejoicing is found in the Magnificat, the "psalm" reading from Luke 1:46b ff for today. The Magnificat is especially associated with Advent. In this concluding exhortation, Paul emphasizes the kind of life a Christian should live in light of the coming of our Lord Jesus Christ. (v. 23) While the second coming is the major thrust of Advent I, and other Advent lectionary readings put the stress on the first coming of Christ, the mention of the second coming here is like an echo of a major Advent theme. Christians should rejoice in contemplating both the first and second comings of our Lord, saving events which cannot be separated.

"Rejoice" is a favorite admonition of Paul's and is found more than two dozen times in his letters. Here it marks a turning point in Paul's exhortation, moving the thought from an ethical to religious theme. Believers are to pray continually and give thanks in all circumstances. The reason for this rejoicing, praying and giving thanks is that it is the will of God. If the Thessalonians who were in a young church wondered about the second coming and how they should live here and now, Paul gives clear directions for living "between the times". These same themes are found in other letters of Paul and so are pointed to again and again as belonging to the essence of the Christian life.

Paul calls on his hearers not to quench the Spirit or despise prophesying. Rather, they are to test everything and hold to what is good. While the Spirit and the prophetic energy given by the Spirit can be unsettling, nevertheless it is essential for renewal. The word quench is associated with the Spirit as it is compared to fire which may be quenched by water. This testing an order to discover the good and reject the evil is found in the epistle of John: "Beloved, do not believe every spirit, but test the spirits to see whether they are of God; for many false prophets have gone out into the world." (4:1) Paul contrasts the one "good" with the many forms of evil. The good has integrity, unity, wholeness, while evil is divided, schismatic, diffuse. Note that prophesying is not only prediction but includes also the inspired word of preaching.

Next Paul prays for his audience, asking that the God of peace sanctify them wholly. This is the goal of Christian living "between the times" — to become more Christ-like by the power of God. Paul mentions "spirit and soul and body" and this is the only place where he makes such a division in the New Testament. We should not take this as a division of the human being into three parts, but rathar as a way of viewing the unity of human life from three points of view. Paul's prayer is that they be kept sound and blameless at "the coming of our Lord Jesus Christ." He assures them that God is faithful and will do just what he has prayed for. The faithfulness of God is the central theme of the Bible. God is faithful in spite of the faithlessness of his people. This is good news for us who live "between the times" waiting for the coming again of our Lord Jesus Christ.

### John 1:6-8, 19-28

The role of John the Baptizer as the forerunner of Jesus is a major Advent theme and is the central thrust of this pericope. John climaxes the Old Testament prophets and is commissioned by God (Malachi 3:1) to point to Jesus. (v. 23) While some see John's role in verse 7 contradicting that in verse 31, where the author says John the Baptizer came that Jesus might be revealed to Israel, the idea is that ultimately John's message will, like that of Jesus, touch all people. It should be noted that the Fourth Gospel stresses more the role of John as a witness than as a baptizer.

The well-known Isenheim altarpiece by Gruenwald dramatically portrays the role of John as witness to Jesus. Taking poetic license the artist has placed John the Baptizer at the foot of the cross, although John was executed at the outset of Jesus' ministry. John stands with a book in his left hand, presumably the Old Testament and points with a bony, gnarled finger of his right hand to the crucified Messiah. A lamb at his feet has a cross beside it, symbol of Jesus as the lamb of God who dies.

The Fourth Gospel takes pains to emphasize that John was not the light, but was a witness to the light, and that John himself admitted he was only a voice crying in the wilderness to prepare for the Lord. There was a rivalry between the followers of John and those of Jesus when this Gospel was written, and the author underlines John's claim to a lesser role than that of Jesus.

Some scholars have suggested that verses 6-7 were the original opening of the Gospel. But they were displaced when the Prologue was added. One clue to this is the fact that "There was a man sent from God . . ." would be a normal opening for a historical narrative.

We must read verse 7 in light of verse 19 since light can ordinarily be seen and there is no need for someone to witness to it. But in verse 19 we see John gives witness to Jesus, the light, before the hostile Jews who have not yet seen Jesus. Some think that John's followers even claimed that John was the light, but verse 8 makes it very clear that John came only to bear witness to the light and was not the light himself. Evidence for the fact that there were loyal followers of John is found in Acts 19:1-7, which relates Paul's mission among a group of disciples who had received John's baptism but not that of the Holy Spirit. A small sect called Mandeans found in Iraq claim to go back in history to John the Baptizer as their founder.

John fulfills the prophetic role announcing the Messiah's coming (Isaiah 40:3), a role foretold in the Old Testament. While John is unconscious of this role, Jesus later ascribed it to him. (Matthew 11:14) John prepares for Jesus through calling the people to repentance. John's message has a greater urgency than that of any prophet before him. God's kingdom is at hand. Hence the urgency to repent and be ready! Repentance stands at the point where the rule of God and the nations of the world confront one another.

Repentance has two facets: one negative, one positive. Repentance means literally "to change one's mind," but in the New Testament it is closely related to the Old Testament word which implies a coming to one's senses, a deliberate turning away from one's sinful past in order to do an about face toward God. In the New Testament it means more than just a change of mind and has the thrust of a whole reorientation of the personality, a conversion. It includes the idea of regretting, thinking again, and being converted. It should be noted that one does not live in a state of repentance. Rather it is the transition from one state to another. The negative aspect of repentance presupposes a state of sin. In the other gospels we note that John preached repentance, not only to notorious sinners, but to the Pharisees and Sadducees. John's preparation of the way for Jesus, his witness to the light, his call to repentance is directed to good religious folk as well as to sinners.

The positive aspect of repentance is a door to the future. Too much preaching has dwelt on sin in all its fascinating details rather than opening a door to the future. Repentance opens to the sinner a new way of living in communion with God, rejoicing, praying constantly and giving thanks. This new way of life is a result of a radical reorientation of one's life. Repentance is a gift of God that leads to salvation. While John's message in the Fourth Gospel is not spelled out as one of repentance the Synoptic Gospels make John's message of repentance primary.

## Theological Reflections

Isaiah's message of good news to the destitute and oppressed was fulfilled in the Light to whom John pointed. God continues to work to bring about righteousness and justice in the world. John the Baptizer not only pointed to Jesus as the Lord but, by his call for repentance, prepared the hearts of all who heard to receive him. Paul's message is one from this side of the cross, in which he urges his hearers to rejoice in their new life in Christ and to live in constant communion with God through prayer in an attitude of thanksgiving. The overall theological movement of the pericopes is that of God's faithfulness in spite of man's unfaithfulness. "He who calls you is faithful, and he will do it." (1 Thessalonians 5:24) This is the good news for us during Advent, as we wait with keen expectation for the coming of our Lord Jesus Christ. God is not absent or sleeping. He is at work in spite of our sin and "every form of evil." (1 Thessalonians 5:22) We need not simply recall the facts of Jesus' first coming, or the promise of his Second Coming, but we can live here and now in daily communion with the God of peace who is sanctifying our lives by his Spirit. This is indeed good news!

## Homiletical Moves

*Isaiah 61:1-4; 8-11*
### Good News to the Afflicted

1. God has acted in Christ, the anointed Servant
2. The action of God in Christ is good news in very concrete ways:
   a. good tidings to the afflicted (poor) means physical help
   b. binding up the brokenhearted
   c. proclaiming liberty to the captives and the opening of the prison to those who are bound
   d. comfort to the mourners
3. God's greatest act of deliverance is in the new covenant, an everlasting one made in Jesus Christ
4. Therefore, let us greatly rejoice in the Lord for he has clothed us with the garments of salvation and the robe of righteousness.

*1 Thessalonians 5:16-24*
### Rejoice Always, Pray Constantly Giving Thanks Always

1. Test everything, holding fast to the good, abstaining from evil
2. God will be sanctifying you wholly by his Spirit as we await the coming of our Lord Jesus Christ
3. God is faithful in spite of our unfaithfulness
4. Rejoice in the daily presence of the Living Christ in your life as you live in expectation of Christ's Second Coming

*This Preacher's Choice*

*John 1:6-8, 19-28*
### The Witness to the Light

1. John the Baptizer is a model for witness
   a. He disclaimed being the Light
   b. He pointed to the Light
   c. In humility he acknowledged his unworthiness to untie Jesus' sandal
2. We are called by God to point to the crucified Christ as the Light of the World
3. We are to prepare for Christ's coming by repentance and turning to God in faithful trust
4. Those who know the Risen Christ point to Christ by their lives as well as their words, and are the ultimate irrefutable argument for the Christian faith.

**Hymn for Advent 3:** *Come, Thou Long-expected Jesus*

**Prayer**

*O Lord, we wait on tiptoe, straining forward to see the Coming of Christ, yet living here and now in joy, prayer and gratitude for your saving work. Give us the wisdom to test the temptations that confront us and to hold fast to the good, while abstaining from all evil. We pray that by your Spirit you will continually be sanctifying our lives so that we may be kept sound and blameless for the coming again of our Lord Jesus Christ. We affirm once again our trust in your faithfulness to do this, as you have worked in our lives in the past. In this we rejoice and give thanks. Amen*

# Advent 4

| Common | Lutheran | Roman Catholic |
|---|---|---|
| 2 Samuel 7:8-16 | 2 Samuel 7:(1-7) 8-11, 16 | 2 Samuel 7:1-5, 8-11, 16 |
| Romans 16:25-27 | Romans 16:25-27 | Romans 16:25-27 |
| Luke 1:26-38 | Luke 1:26-38 | Luke 1:26-38 |

## Comments on the Lessons

There is virtual consensus on the first reading, with consensus on the second and third readings. In the first reading verses 8-16 give the essential themes while avoiding the difficulties of a very edited and longer pericope. In this passage God promises David an eternal dynasty. David had proposed building a house for God, but God promises that he will make a house for King David. This is a very fitting text for Advent 4 since the fulfillment of God's promise comes when the Word, the Son of David, who is the Son of God comes and dwells with us. He makes his tabernacle among us. (John 1:14) The Romans pericope is a doxology which states that the divine plan of salvation, though attested by the prophets was in its fullness, a secret until the coming of Christ.

## Commentary

*2 Samuel 7:8-16 (C)*
*2 Samuel 7:(1-7) 8-11, 16 (L)*
*2 Samuel 7:1-5, 8-11, 16 (RC)*

This is a theological commentary inserted into the book later as an explanation of why David was not chosen to build the temple. Note its relationship to Psalm 89 on which it appears to be based to some extent. The key to understanding this passage and the entire chapter 7 is the wordplay on the various meanings of the word "house." In verses 1-2 it means a palace, while in verses 5-7, 13 it means "temple." These meanings are contrasted with the meaning "dynasty" in verses 11, 16, 19, 25, 27, 29 and in verse 18 where it means "family status." It should be remembered that the dynasty of David was not everlasting but fell in 587 (586) B.C. This was sometime before the author of this passage penned it. He may have had in mind a literal restoration of the kingdom of David while also anticipating the coming Kingdom of God.

This passage is the classical location of the expectation of the eternal rulership of David's house and the ultimate source of all messianic hopes about the revival of David's house after the fall of Jerusalem in 587 B.C.

David's motive for proposing to build a house for God is based on his conscience. He has built a palace for himself in Jerusalem but the ark was still in a tent. The significance of the tent in the wilderness was that it symbolized that God was always with his people, wherever they might go. Notice that a tent was the dwelling of the socially inferior nomads, in contrast to a house of cedar which symbolized permanence and grandeur. While the temple, which was later built by David's son, Solomon, may have helped unify and purify the national worship of Israel, it stood at the same time in the way of a higher and more universal faith in the God who dwells with the humble and contrite. Jeremiah seems to be the first to have seen this universal aspect. It appears that the tent in the earlier period of Israel's history was believed to be, not the dwelling of God, but simply the place where he chose to meet his people through their representative Moses. It is clear that the writer is making a strong point that the temple is *not* the earthly dwelling place of God.

Whether or not the prophecy in verse 11 was intended to be read as prophecy is open to debate. But it can be so interpreted, especially in light of the fact that Jesus said he was the living temple who could be destroyed and raised again in three days. (Mark 14:58; 15:29; John 2:19)

God chose, not David, a man of war, but his son, Solomon, the man of peace, to build the temple. The name Solomon and the Hebrew word "shalom" meaning peace are closely related. Notice that an eternal kingdom is promised, not to the family of David, but to Solomon personally. (vv. 12, 13)

*Romans 16:25-27*

This doxology appears in various manuscripts at three different places: after 14:23, after 15:33 and in its canonical position here. Similarities can be seen in this doxology and Colossians 1:26-27 and Ephesians 3:9-10. It is probably the work of an editor of Romans. It was probably added as a conclusion to the three different versions of Romans that were circulated in early times that ended with chapters 14, 15 or 16.

The theme of the doxology is that the prophesied divine plan of salvation in its fullest form was a secret until the coming of Christ. It was then revealed and became known to the Gentiles who believed and obeyed. The idea of a secret purpose revealed in Christ is quite prominent in the later epistles and not unknown in the earlier ones. But it is not a prominent theme in this epistle and so we should not expect it to be the central thrust of the final doxology. Scholars suspect that it was not an original part of the epistle at all.

Nevertheless, the doxology is a summary of the gospel Paul preached and loved. It is a gospel which strengthens a believer. The verb strengthen seems to refer to the need for help in defeating the heretics referred to in verses 17-21. Preaching is another word for gospel. In other epistles of Paul he refers to the secret of the gospel. (1 Corinthians 2:6-7; Colossians 1:24-29; 2:2-3; and also in Romans 11:25) Since it is known that Romans was put last in some collections of Paul's letters this doxology would have brought the whole collection of Paul's letters to a close. It reminds one of the doxology in Ephesians 3:20-21 and may have been based on that model.

Scholars have suggested that this doxology was adapted from an original Jewish doxology. It came from a particular form of Judaism which pictures God speaking out of silence.

*Luke 1:26-38*

Artists have portrayed in paintings the angel Gabriel announcing to Mary that she would conceive and bear a son which show the words going into Mary's ear. This is an attempt to dramatize the fact that Jesus was conceived, not by a human father in normal sexual intercourse, but by the Holy Spirit through her hearing the Word. The angel comes to a virgin betrothed to a man named Joseph. Betrothal lasted for a year and was as binding as marriage. It was an official relationship and could only be dissolved by divorce. If a man to whom a woman was betrothed should die she was considered a widow. This accounts for the strange phrase "a virgin who is a widow." Betrothal often involved cohabitation which culminated in the legal recognition of marriage. A man and woman betrothed were bound by a bond that only death could break. Girls were often betrothed at a young age and so it is likely that Mary was quite young.

Since the child is to inherit the throne of his father, David (verse 32), Luke makes a point of saying that Joseph is of the house of David. (verse 27) This may strike the modern mind as peculiar to trace Jesus' lineage through his father when Luke makes it clear Mary has no husband (literally has not had sexual intercourse with a man). But for the Hebrew mind this was no problem. In fact, until verse 34, the Lukan account seems to assumed that Joseph will be the father.

Notice the pattern of the annunciation, a pattern found in annunciation of the angel to Zechariah of John's birth and in Old Testament stories of annunciation: (1) the greeting (v. 28), (2) the person's startled reaction (v. 29), (33) the person is reassured (v. 30), (4) the birth is announced (vv. 31 33), (5) an objection is raised (v. 34), (6) a final reassurance or sign is given (v. 36), and (7) the word is accepted (v. 38).

Another significant feature of this passage is that it is filled with the language of the Jewish scriptures. Phrases such as "Hail, the Lord is with you," "the Holy Spirit will come upon you," and so forth. The passage is filled with songs. We best sing our faith! Even a cursory reading of the passage reveals its liturgical character.

The Holy Spirit comes upon Mary in the same way Luke understood the Holy Spirit came upon the disciples at Pentecost. The "overshadowing" reminds us of the presence of God in the Old Testament sanctuary. Note that the same verb used here is also used at the Transfiguration. (Luke 9:34) Here at the annunciation is the fulfillment of God's promise to dwell with his people.

Mary's response is a model for human response to God's initiative in any age. She puts herself at the disposal of God's purpose. The angel's assurance that "with God nothing will be impossible" (v. 37), is the ultimate creed. Here is a model for the church's affirmation at the manger, cross and any other occasions when "man's extremity is God's opportunity." It points the church beyond this earth-bound view of life to the Transcendent who continues to break in and startle.

## Theological Reflections

God acts to fulfill his plan of salvation by assuring David that his son would have a dynasty, a "house" which would last forever. In the annunciation to Mary that she would bear a son who will be given the throne of his father, David, and will reign forever, we see this prophecy fulfilled. In these two stories we see the mighty warrior David seeking to build a "house" for God, but God rejects his offer with the counterplan of building a house for him. Contrast Mary the young maiden betrothed but yet innocent with David the man of the world. She is the passive one to whom God speaks to assure her she will conceive a son, thus building a "house" or temple in which God will dwell among his people. She responds with words of obedience and her life put at God's disposal. The doxology from Romans sings of the secret of the ages now revealed in Jesus Christ. Both this doxology and the annunciation account are liturgical in character and express the essence of the Gospel: Emmanuel, God with us in Jesus Christ.

## Homiletical Moves

*2 Samuel 7:8-16*
*2 Samuel 7:(1-7) 8-11, 16*
*2 Samuel 7:1-5, 8-11, 16*
### The House That God Builds

1. God responds to David's proposal to build a house for God to dwell in by promising an everlasting "house" to David
2. God fulfilled his promise through Jesus Christ whose body is the temple which was destroyed but raised up in three days
3. Christ's Body on earth is the Church in which God dwells by the Holy Spirit
4. Therefore, instead of trying to build a house for God, accept Christ's gracious offer of eternal life
5. Come and dwell in Christ in whom we live, and move and have our being now and in the Age to come.

### The Secret is Out!

1. The mystery of God's revelation was kept secret for long ages
2. In Jesus Christ, life, death and resurrection, the secret is revealed
3. Through this revealed secret God is able to strengthen you and bring about the obedience of faith he desires

*This Preacher's Choice*

*Luke 1:26-38*
### Mary's Obedience, A Model of Faith

1. God takes the initiative in coming to us
2. Our response initially is often one of fear, questioning, disbelief
3. But with God nothing is impossible, therefore obedience is our appropriate response to God

The preacher will want to get in touch with the flow of this passage in order to proclaim the good news of God's initiative in coming to us. The wonder, fear, questioning, and finally, humble obedience are very human reactions to the miraculous. But the passage shouts out to us that "with God nothing will be impossible." Here at the last Sunday of Advent, as we look forward to the celebration of the Incarnation at Christmas, we would do well to lift up the awesome miracle of Emmanuel: God with us.

**Hymn for Advent 40:**  *O Come, O Come, Emmanuel*

**Prayer**
*Almighty God who establishes kings and kingdoms and who is Lord of history, we thank you for the everlasting kingdom you established in the coming of Jesus Christ. We stand in awe of the Incarnation for our minds are too small and feeble to grasp its full meaning. Like Mary, we react in fear, awe, and questioning of how can this be. But grant that when you speak to us we may have the strength, faith, and humility to respond to you in humble obedience knowing that with you nothing is impossible. Amen*

# Christmas 1

| Common | Lutheran | Roman Catholic |
|---|---|---|
| Isaiah 61:10—62:3 | Isaiah 45:22-25 | Sirach 3:2-6, 12-14 |
| Galatians 4:4-7 | Colossians 3:12-17 | Colossians 3:12-21 |
| Luke 2:22-40 | Luke 2:25-40 | Luke 2:22-40 |

## Comments on the Lessons

In speaking of the restoration and the new name, the first lesson can be seen as foreshadowing the presentation in the temple. The first Isaiah pericope tells of God's salvation which begins in Zion but is intended for all nations. The second Isaiah passage stresses that all people are invited to partake in the divine salvation, and that membership in the people of God is based on the free assent of the individual to his claims. The Galatians passage refers to Jesus' birth under the Law which complements the presentation theme of the Lukan passage. Colossians describes Christian virtues as though they were garments one puts on, directing that everything be done in the name of the Lord Jesus, another reference to Jesus' name. Finally, the Lukan pericope has virtual consensus and is the account of Jesus' presentation in the temple.

## Commentary

### Isaiah 61:10—62:3 (C)

This passage by Trito-Isaiah, as the author(s) are known, proclaims salvation and is directly connected with the message of 61:1ff. Some commentators place verse 11 before verse 10 since the latter is a unit in itself which corresponds to the hymns of praise which form end pieces in 2 Isaiah's larger passages. Verse 10 is the community's acceptance of the message of salvation. One major difference between 2 Isaiah and 3 or Trito-Isaiah is that the former offers hymns sung by the community, while Isaiah 61 is a psalm sung by an individual. In verse 11 the prophet likens salvation's springing up to the growth of plants in a garden, it is cultivated and grows as a process.

The passage can be divided into two parts: (1) 61:10-11 is a joyful celebration of the salvation which God has brought about or at least promised; (2) followed by 62:1-3 really goes with the rest of chapter 62, rather than 61 and refers to the nations and the kings seeing the glory of Zion. This connects it with the Epiphany season which is fast approaching. We should also note that 61:10, 11 is appropriate as a post-Christmas reading, since it points to Zion and stresses the experience of salvation and shows an interest in the nations.

According to Hebrew belief, the name contains within it the interior character and being of the people. Thus a new name means a new people. God's glory is revealed in action, in the vindication and salvation of Zion which all nations will see.

The crown of beauty and royal diadem (v. 3) describe the royal headdress which are a symbol of God's kingship. It is not yet on his head but is in his hand. God is winning his sovereignty by the redemption of his people. The crown is a visual representation of Israel's glory and expresses the close relationship between God and Zion. In the New Testament we see that Jesus' cross is his crown by which his glory is revealed to all the world and by which he draws all people to himself.

### Isaiah 45:22-25 (L)

These verses are part of one of the trial speeches in which God confronts the nations or gods of the nations. In verse 22 we see that the victor does not glory in his feat. God's victory in the lawsuit against the gods of the nations means that there is no longer overthrowing and destroying but convincing. God's goal in his mission of salvation is free confession, a confession motivated by the realization that the only true God is the God of Israel. "To me every knee shall bow, every tongue shall swear" (v. 23) is a novel idea resulting from the free assent of the individual to God's claims. The author, 2 Isaiah, believed that in his day a final break had been made between the people of God and any form of its former existence as a political entity. Now all people are invited to participate in divine salvation. Membership in the people of God is based on a free confession of those who have discovered that he alone is God. Notice that these two crucial items in the Christian church are already present in 2 Isaiah.

### Sirach 3:2-6, 12-14 (RC)

This book in its original form was composed in BC 180 or so. The pericope is concerned with filial piety. The author expands the thrust of the fifth commandment calling for honoring of one's parents, with the promise of long days for obedience. The Old Testament carries the stiffest penalties for breaking this commandment. The person who curses father or mother is to be put to death. (Leviticus 20:9) The honoring of father and mother goes beyond, but includes, showing respect and kindness to parents. In Jesus' day, to avoid giving material help to parents, sons might tell them that all their goods were Korban, that is, formally dedicated to God. Then, when an aged parent asked for help, they would reply, "We cannot help you since all our goods are dedicated to God." This was a clever trick to avoid doing one's duty to parents. Jesus quoted the fifth commandment to the rich young ruler as one of the basic commandments which everyone who seeks goodness ought to obey. The author says that respect for a father atones for sins. This appears to be more a works righteousness approach than a salvation by grace alone one. But the point is stressed that care for parents, especially in old age (vv. 12-14) is commendable. Even if his mind fails one is to make allowances for the failing parent.

This passage is particularly relevant for a society such as America's, with its rapidly increasing class of older citizens and the youth culture which puts down the aged. Verse 14 definitely seems to point to an eternal treasury of good works in which support for one's father will be added to balance against one's sins. From a New Testament point of view this is works righteousness rather than living an ethical response to salvation in Jesus Christ through caring for parents in an honorable fashion.

### Galatians 4:4-7 (C)

Here we have one of Paul's rare accounts of an event in the life of the historical Jesus. Note that verses 4-7 contain the note of joy, but only as Christmas leads to Good Friday and Easter. They remind us that "Jesus our savior was born for to die," as the folksong puts it. The baby born of woman redeems those under the law by his death and resurrection. This is dramatically illustrated in a huge cross made of steel overlooking Bethlehem, Pennsylvania, which is lighted at Christmas. The same frame is used during Holy Week to light a huge cross. If you look carefully at the lights in the star at Christmas you can see the outline of the cross. The cross in the star tells us that the incarnation and atonement cannot be separated. The good news is that not only has a baby been born but his work of redemption has freed those bound by sin under the law.

Notice that verse 4 points out that the pre-existent Christ became incarnate at a time set by God to ransom those who were in bondage. God is the prime figure who determines the appropriate time for Jesus' birth. Jesus was wholly human in flesh and bone as we are. He lived his life in full solidarity with those "under the law." He was vulnerable to all the conditions of human life which threaten us today: fear, loneliness, temptation, doubt, suffering and finally, on the cross, being forsaken by God.

The critical issue in this passage is the liberation of those who are bound under the law. Calvin has said that by putting the chains on himself Jesus takes them off the other. We are adopted as sons of God by faith in Jesus Christ. We are thereby given full rights as heirs and full access to the Father. Symbolic of this relationship are the words "Abba! Father!" in Aramaic and English by which our adopted relationship is expressed. This suggests that what we have here is a fixed liturgical form which may have been used in a prayer offered by new converts to express their new access to God through Christ. Note that God sends the Son and gives the Spirit. This passage is the strongest statement of the incarnation in Paul's letters. Redemption of those under the law and their adoption as sons of God are the two purposes of Jesus' coming into the world.

### Colossians 3:12-17 (L)
### Colossians 3:12-21 (RC)

This pericope must be read in both verse 1 and verse 10, in which Paul indicates that the Colossians have been raised with Christ and have put on the new nature which is being renewed in knowledge after the image of its creator. The five characteristics of the new life in Christ contrast with the five fold list of vices in verses 5 and 8. These are not cardinal virtues but are set forth aa typical of the attitudes and characteristics the Christian faith teaches. They are referred to as if they were pieces of clothing or parts of a soldier's uniform. While most of the charateristics praised by Paul are mentioned by non-Christian writers, the virtue of "lowliness" outside of Jewish and Christian thought was listed among the vices! It was a sign of weakness, not strength, for it referred to abject humiliation. Jesus, by his life of service to others, and especially in the act of washing the disciples' feet dramatized the meaning of humiliation. But the cross itself shows lowliness raised to its ultimate level — the humiliation of crucifixion. No wonder the cross was a source of ridicule for non-Christians, for it indicates weakness and submission raised to the nth degree!

The passage is addressed to those who have already been raised to a new life in Christ. Since they have already put on a new nature in Christ they are to put on these virtues also. In verse 15 Paul says let the peace of Christ rule (umpire) in your hearts. Let his peace call the plays, make the decisions.

The phrases "God's chosen ones," "holy and beloved" are drawn from the Old Testament where they are used of Israel. For Paul, love is the supreme mark of the new life in Christ. Like a belt holding the clothing in place, love binds all the other virtues in place in the Christian's life. "Perfect harmony" includes the ideas of wholeness, completeness and integrity.

It should be noted that the "peace of Christ" is not peace of mind, not just psychological adjustment. It has cosmic significance and is given to the whole community of faith. The peace of God dwells in the one body, the community of believers. "In your hearts" indicates the depth and sincerity of commitment to Christ's rule.

Thankfulness is closely related to the attitude of faith. Everything the Christian does should exhibit thankfulness as one lives the new life. This is a spirit of gratitude which marks one's daily life as well as public worship. The church has always been a singing church and here Paul mentions psalms, hymns and spiritual songs with which to praise God. Whether this refers to three types of music is not clear.

In verses 18-21 Paul lists some of the household duties of a Christian. Similar tables are found in other New Testament books which emphasize a need to respect one another and to let love rule in one's daily living. Verse 18 must be understood in the context of the culture to which it was addressed. It is balanced by the command to husbands to love their wives. This gives mutuality in marriage. Children are to obey their parents, and fathers (and mothers by implication) are to avoid provoking their children. This is expanded further in Ephesians 6:1-4. This table of household duties has vital significance for marriage and family life today when set in the context of Christian love and mutuality.

*Luke 2:22-40 (C)*
*Luke 2:25-40(L)*
*Luke 2:22-40(RC)*

The author of this passage has four main purposes: (1) to show that from infancy Jesus' life was marked by obedience to the law of Moses, (2) to declare the greatness of the child Jesus, through two pious Jews, Simeon and Anna, (3) to shift the family and action of the Gospel to Nazareth, and (4) to introduce another Christian hymn known as "Nunc Dimittis" from the first words of the Latin translation. The latter consists of phrases and lines from the Old Testament, mostly Isaiah 49 and 52.

An imposing image this passage gives is that of an old man with hope and faith holding a baby. This is a very fitting image for the last Sunday of the year, as we often think of the old year as an old man and the new year as a baby!

We do not know anything else about Simeon and Anna except what is found here. They express faith in Jesus as Savior, Christ and universal Lord. Compare this with announcement of the angel of a "Savior, who is Christ the Lord." (2:11) The consolation of Israel was the salvation Messiah was to bring.

Luke wants his readers to understand that the Mosaic law is strictly observed in Jesus' life. Like John, he was circumcised on the eighth day and his pre-natally revealed name is given: Jesus = he saves. Note that verses 22, 23, 24, 27, 39 all point to obedience of Mosaic law. Christianity is the fulfillment of Judaism. Jesus' parents offer the sacrifice of "a pair of turtle-doves, etc.," which was the sacrifice of the poor on this occasion.

The center of interest in this passage is Jesus who is seen as the fulfillment of the prophecy of Messiah. Messiah brings a light of revelation for the Gentiles, and he brings a glory to the people

Israel. Messiah is a challenge to his times. (v. 34)

Anna, who is eighty-four, or, if this number refers to the years she has been a widow, it would make her over a hundred years old, is a pious woman. She was continually in the temple praying and fasting. Since she and Mary are both present, this event must have occurred in one of the court-yards where women were allowed. Anna gives thanks to God and expresses her hope that the redemption of Jerusalem would be found in Jesus.

The life of Jesus is decisive. History is dated from his birth forward and backward. Professor Alfred North Whitehead has written: "The life of Christ has the decisiveness of a supreme ideal, and that is why the history of the world divides at this point of time." (p. 47 *Religion in the Making*) This decisiveness of Jesus provides a theme for a sermon on Jesus and the new year soon to begin.

## Theological Reflections

The naming and restoration themes in the Isaiah 61, 62 passages foreshadow the naming of Jesus in the temple. The Galatian passage points to the Incarnation at the decisive time determined by God. Jesus' life and death for the redemption of those under the law and to enable them to become adopted sons and daughters of God is lifted up here. The implications of the new life of one raised with Christ are spelled out further in the Colossian passage. Luke wants to focus on the main events of Jesus' circumcision and dedication in the temple, including obedience to Mosaic law and fulfillment of the prophecy of Messiah. God's mighty acts in sending Jesus into the world at the right time to redeem and save and the implications of this are the themes running through these pericopes like a common thread.

## Homiletical Moves

*Isaiah 61:10—62:3*
### A Joyful Celebration of Salvation

1. God is working to cause righteousness and praise to spring forth
2. God will give a new name, foreshadowing the naming of Jesus in the temple (Lukan passage)
3. Therefore, let us greatly rejoice for he has clothed us with the garments of salvation in Jesus Christ

*Isaiah 45:22-25*
### Turn to God in Christ and Be Saved

1. There is no other God like the God revealed in Jesus Christ
2. God calls for the free assent of individuals to his claims: "every knee shall bow, and every tongue shall swear"
3. God's call is universal: "all the ends of the earth!"

*Sirach 3:12-21*
### Honoring Parents Is God's Will

1. God commands honoring of one's parents (v. 2, and 5th commandment: Exodus 20:12)
2. Respect for parents will influence one's children to show respect
3. Make allowances for parents in failing health
4. Honor is shown in providing for material and emotional support of one's parents in old age (Mark 7:10-13)
5. Caring for parents should be done out of Christian love in gratitude for their care in the past and not done grudgingly

*Galatians 4:4-7*
### Jesus Was Sent in the Fullness of Time!

1. God sent forth his Son in the fullness of time, born of woman, born under the law to redeem those under the law
2. God sent his Son that we might be adopted as sons
3. Jesus was born to die to free sinners from sin and death
4. We can cry "Abba! Father!" as sons and heirs of God by the spirit

*This Preacher's Choice*

*Colossians 3:12-21*
## Above All Put on Love

1. Since you have been raised with Christ put to death what is earthly in you. (3:5, 8)
2. Put on as God's chosen ones:
    a. compassion
    b. kindness
    c. lowliness
    d. meekness
    e. patience
    f. love
3. Let the peace of God umpire in your hearts as you live in the Body of Christ, the Church
4. Do everything in the name of the Lord Jesus with thankfulness to God

*Luke 2:22-40*
## Our Eyes Have Seen God's Salvation in Jesus

1. Jesus' life from infancy was lived in obedience to the law of Moses:
    a. circumcised on eighth day
    b. named Jesus as commanded by angel to Mary
    c. presented at the temple
2. Jesus is the Lord's Christ (Messiah), who is God's salvation to all peoples, as Savior, Christ and Lord.
3. Let us give thanks to God for salvation through Jesus Christ in worship and by lives of obedience to God

**Hymn for Christmas 1:**   *Lord, Now Lettest Thy Servant Depart*

**Prayer**

*O God of salvation who has revealed Messiah by the new name "Jesus" born of woman under the law to set us free from the bondage of sin, grant us your peace. Give us peace in the depths of our hearts that we may live lives of wholeness in the Body of Christ, the Church. Help us who have been raised to a new life with Christ die to earthly things. Enable us to put on the garments of salvation and to live in love with one another, giving thanks to you through Christ. Let us see our salvation in Jesus that we may live lives of grateful obedience. Amen*

# Christmas 2

| Common | Lutheran | Roman Catholic |
|---|---|---|
| Jeremiah 31:7-14 | Isaiah 61:10—62:3 | Sirach 24:1-4, 8-12 |
| Ephesians 1:3-6, 15-18 | Ephesians 1:3-6, 15-18 | Ephesians 1:3-6, 15-18 |
| John 1:1-18 | John 1:1-18 | John 1:1-18 |

## Comments on the Lessons

The pericope from Jeremiah is the festal restoration lesson associated with Christmas. The Sirach (or Ecclesiasticus) reading parallels the wisdom theme of the John passage. The Isaiah passage (L) was dealt with in Christmas 1 and is concerned with the growth of righteousness and the new name.

## Commentary

*Jeremiah 31:7-14 (C)*

Homecoming is the thrust of this passage. God will bring home the dispersed Jews and assemble them in their homeland. This prediction is of the immediate return of the people from the many lands to which they have been sent in exile. Compare this passage with the ideas and phrases of Second Isaiah who was concerned with the return from the whole Diaspora. Scholars see these as ideas foreign to Jeremiah and later than Jeremiah. Some see only verse 9c as likely to be from Jeremiah. Verse 14 seems particularly foreign to Jeremiah's thought.

In verse 7 we should probably adopt the reading of the LXX and other MSS for "for the chief of the nations" and read "on the top of the mountains." "The chief (first) of the nations" was apparently a popular and prideful term for Israel. Note in verse 10 that "the coastlands" is a favorite word of Second Isaiah. So is the address to the nations of the world, and phrase "as a shepherd his flock." And the image of the well-watered garden is also found in Isaiah 58:11. The restored nation is described in idyllic terms. This is particularly appropriate as an image in a land such as Palestine where rainfall is limited and often uncertain.

But in verse 14 note that the reference to priests is unlikely to have come from Jeremiah who so often was in conflict with the priests of his day. The meaning of the verse is that sacrifices will be so abundant that priests will have plenty to eat. The land will flourish with an abundance of good things to comfort the exiles and make them happy. Their days of pain and suffering are over. Now there is only singing and joy.

*Isaiah 61:10 62:3 (L) (See Christmas 1)*

*Sirach 24:1-4, 8-12 (RC)*

Wisdom is personified as a woman who praises herself on earth and in heaven. "Her people" must refer to Israel. "The assembly of the Most High" and "his host" apparently refer to the heavenly council of ministers who surround God's throne. This is the second of two principal poems praising wisdom and may be compared to 1:1-10. Each introduces a major section of the book. In fact, chapter 24 is a pivotal chapter in the whole book which sums up the entire doctrine of wisdom.

Wisdom is pictured as being in union with God and yet distinct from him. These same characteristics were applied to the person of the Word, as also to the person of the Spirit. In verse 4b wisdom has enthroned herself alongside God himself. In RC theology the liturgy applies this passage by "accommodation" to the Blessed Virgin.

Wisdom is said to be the first of created things. (v. 9) This idea is taught in Proverbs 8:22-31. In addition, there seems to be a reference to the creation account in Genesis. There God creates by speaking (Word). Note that, as a mist covered the earth before other things are created, so wisdom speaks of herself as being like mist.

In verses 8-12 wisdom speaks of Israel as her particular dwelling place. In verses 10-12 we see that wisdom obeys the divine command to dwell in Israel. God entrusts the revelation of himself to Israel which can be compared to Romans 9:4. In verse 10 we have a reference to wisdom's part in Israel's worship in the allusion to the "pillar of cloud" in which wisdom was present. This presence of God as a pillar of cloud came down to mark his presence first in the tabernacle and later in the temple. The reference to "ministered" indicates that Mosaic worship was the gift of God's revelation (wisdom) to Israel.

Note that in verse 11b there is a reference not only to the laws of worship but to the moral and civil laws contained in the revelation for which "wisdom" stands. The priesthood in Jerusalem (with the king's cooperation) had the authority to interpret and apply these laws.

In verses 13-14 we find wisdom's beneficent operation in and through Israel described under the figure of flourishing and graceful trees. The Cedars of Lebanon were known for their majestic growth and the beauty and durability of its wood. The cypress was like cedar in its qualities, and the Hermon range parallels the Lebanon range. The roses referred to are oleanders which were especially abundant about Jericho. These, and the trees mentioned, stand for the moral excellence which indwelling wisdom gives to Israel among the nations.

### Ephesians 1:3-6, 15-18

The authorship of Ephesians is still debated. Either Paul or a follower of Paul wrote it. We will refer to the author as Paul. It lacks a formal structure.

In verse 3 the "heavenly places" is an expression found only in this letter. It refers to the unseen spiritual world behind and above the material universe. It is used five times here to describe the cosmic sphere in which Christ rules and to which Christians have been raised to new life in him. But note also that it is the realm where the powers of darkness and evil are still active. The "spiritual blessings" refers to God's eternal purpose by which God has willed that all people should be holy and blameless before him. Note that holiness and blamelessness are associated primarily with the believer's election to sonship, while also including the idea of moral purity.

In verse 5 "to be his sons" refers to adoption as sons and occurs several places in Paul's letters. Adoption as sons emphasizes both God's initiative in establishing this relationship with men and women and their responsibility to God to obey him. Throughout this hymn there is an emphasis on God's freedom, the eternal nature of his redemption and Christ's role in revealing and mediating God's grace. Christ is the pre-existent Beloved through whom God had bestowed his grace. "The Beloved" has Messianic connotations.

In verses 15-18 we have the thanksgiving proper. The loyalty of the readers of the letter is acknowledged, a loyalty expressed in their faith in the Lord Jesus and by their relationships within the church. It is characteristic of Paul's letters that the opening words of thanksgiving become at once a prayer of petition for his readers' continuing and increasing faith. It becomes a diplomatic, indirect exhortation to the readers! He prays that God may give them a spirit of wisdom and of revelation in the knowledge of God.

The author uses the term "eyes of your hearts" to refer to the way in which God is known. This recalls the term "eyes of the soul," a term frequently found in Greek and Hellenistic religious thought. Paul is referring to the actual transformation of the whole person which happens as one is opened to receive the grace of God given in Christ Jesus. It must be remembered that for Hebrew thought the heart is not the seat of emotions but of the will, the moral understanding and the essential being.

In verse 18 "enlightened" is a perfect participle which conveys the idea of a state of enlightenment, rather than a process of enlightenment. The enlightenment of the heart is not an intellectual act only, but is a flooding of the whole inward being with the light of God's truth. It is the gift of spiritual sight to the spiritually blind.

### John 1:1-18

It is commonly accepted that the Prologue (verses 1-18) of John is an earlier hymn of the Johannine community which was attached to the Fourth Gospel at some later stage of its composition. Either John or the final redactor made this addition.

This is John's "nativity story," since John doesn't include stories like those of Matthew and Luke to describe Jesus', the Word's, entry into human history. The lectionary places it on Christmas 2 Sunday, assuming that Luke 2:1-20 telling the story of Jesus' birth has already been read. The preacher would do well to read that Lukan passage in conjunction with this Prologue since the Prologue is a comment upon that story. The Prologue puts the birth of Jesus into perspective and prevents us from reading the Lukan nativity story as just a fairy tale with all the romantic feelings that surround the birth of a baby, or the rags to success (?) story the ordinary mind loves to believe in. The Prologue brings out the pre-existence of Jesus and the full, utter seriousness of the incarnation. And it reminds us, as the mountain folk song puts it, that "Jesus our Savior was born for to die." The Prologue puts the birth in connection with Jesus' whole life, culminating on the cross. The very name Christmas (Christ-Mass) points to the celebration of the Lord's Supper and Jesus' death and resurrection.

The "Word" (Greek "logos") is more than speech. He is nothing less than God in action, creating (Genesis 1:3), revealing (Amos 3:7-8), redeeming (Psalm 107:19-20). The Prologue is the reflection of Genesis 1, the Old Testament creation hymn. Both begin "In the beginning . . ." It may be related to Mark 1:1 "beginning of the gospel" and apparently is imitated in 1 John 1:1-4. The Word spoken by God is basic in all these passages. They reflect the Hebrew connection of word/deed: God spoke and it was done! This is true of creation, of the gift of the law, and the message of the prophets.

The word is also the wisdom of God. Note the earlier Sirach pericope which describes Wisdom as a woman. Some find in feminine Wisdom the feminine aspect of God. We should not press the masculine/feminine metaphors here since God transcends human nature, for, if we do, we get a mixed metaphor with the Word (Jesus, masculine), related also to Wisdom (feminine).

The Prologue is divided into four units by verses:

1. 1-5
2. 6-8
3. 9-13
4. 14-18.

The units move from eternity (vv. 1-5) into time (6-8) and alternate between accounts of Jesus (1-5, 9-14, 16-18) and John the Baptizer (6-8, 15). The Prologue is structured as narrative (1-13, 15, 17-18), and confession (14, 16). It should be noted that the prologue summarizes the themes developed in the Gospel: Jesus as the agent of creation, as the life of the world, as the light of the world, who is rejected by his own people, but is acknowledged by all who believe in him. While the Greek Logos has its roots in Greek philosophy, and Stoics and Platonists made much of the Logos as the "mind of God," John's use has a very definite Hebraic flavor. Augustine wrote that none of the philosophers caught the originality of the Gospel in an affirmation that the Word became flesh.

## Theological Reflections

God's initiative in saving his people is the central thrust of the pericopes. God acts to bring his people home again. God acts in Wisdom personified as a woman. And God sent forth the Word to be made flesh end dwell among human beings, who died and was raised the third day. Through faith in Christ we have been adopted as sons and daughters of God. For this reason we can be thankful and continue to grow in faith, receiving from God a spirit of wisdom and knowledge. The Prologue of John puts the birth of Jesus in the nativity stories in eternal perspective: in the beginning was the Word, and the Word was with God and the Word was God (v. 1). The revelation of God through the only son, Jesus Christ the Word made flesh who dwelt among us, is the good news.

## Homiletical Moves

*Jeremiah 31:7-14 (C) (L)*
### God's Homecoming and Ours

1. God will bring home his people from Exile
2. God will care for his flock Israel like a shepherd
3. God has come in Jesus Christ, the Good Shepherd, to bring us home to him by his atoning death
4. Therefore, hear God's gracious invitation in Christ to come to him, all you who labor and are heavy-laden and he will give you rest
5. God will comfort you and give you gladness for sorrow

*Sirach 24:1-4, 8-12 (RC)*
### In Praise of Wisdom

1. Wisdom was in the beginning and was spoken by God

2. Wisdom took root among God's chosen people
3. Therefore, forsake folly and choose wisdom
4. God has chosen us in Christ as his special possession and given us the gospel, which is a stumbling block and foolishness to some, but the power of God for those being saved

*Ephesians 1:3-6, 15-18*
## Destined to Be God's Sons and Daughters

1. God has blessed us in Christ with every spiritual blessing
2. God chose us before the foundation of the world to be holy and blameless before him
3. He destined us to be his sons and daughters according to the purpose of his will
4. May you have the eyes of your hearts enlightened so that you may know the hope to which you have been called and the riches of the glorious inheritance in the saints

*This Preacher's Choice*

*John 1:1-18*
## The Word Became Flesh and Dwelt Among Us

1. In the beginning was the Word (the Son) and all things were made through him
2. The Word became flesh and dwelt among us giving us grace upon grace
3. Jesus in whom was life and light has made known the mystery of God
4. Therefore, receive Christ and become children of God through faith in Christ, living in obedience to God

**Hymn for Christmas 2:**   *O For a Thousand Tongues to Sing*

**Prayer**
   *Eternal God who sent forth your Son as the Word made flesh who dwelt among us, full of grace and truth, we thank you with our voices and lives for bringing us home to you. You made us for yourself and outside of fellowship with you we can find no rest or peace for our souls. You have given your Wisdom to your people and we pray that you will enable us to follow the paths of Wisdom in all our living. Thank you for revealing yourself to us in your only Son. May we live graceful lives each day. Amen*

# The Epiphany of Our Lord

(January 6)

| Common | Lutheran | Roman Catholic |
|---|---|---|
| Isaiah 60:1-6 | Isaiah 60:1-6 | Isaiah 60:1-6 |
| Ephesian 3:1-12 | Ephesians 3:2-12 | Ephesians 3:2-3, 5-6 |
| Matthew 2:1-12 | Matthew 2:1-12 | Matthew 2:1-12 |

## Comments on the Lessons

There is consensus on the first reading which ends at verse 6 with an appropriate mention of gold and frankincense. Notice that it speaks of light and glory in the sight of all nations. There is virtual consensus on the second reading which is an old Epiphany epistle. The gospel reading has consensus also. It should be noted that the Epiphany readings are the same each year.

## Commentary

### Isaiah 60:1-6

It appears that in its original context the first part of this reading points to the fulfillment of Isaiah 40ff which describes the return of the exiles to Jerusalem. The present passage portrays the light that has now come and the glory of the Lord that has been revealed. The second part (vv. 3-6) foretells the eschatological pilgrimage of the Gentiles to Jerusalem that will follow the rebuilding of the city. The reading for today is particularly suited for Epiphany when given a Christian interpretation. The Incarnation can be given the place of the return from Babylon as God's great saving act. By doing this we see that Christ is the light that has indeed shone in the darkness. In Christ the glory of the Lord has risen upon the world. Then as the Gentiles respond to this revelation, symbolized in the journey of the Magi with gold and frankincense to the infant Jesus, the eschatological pilgrimage of the Gentiles is fulfilled.

These initial verses (1-6) are just the beginning of the longer oracle that continues through verse 22. Notice in the pericope for today that Jerusalem after the exile is pictured as a woman mourning in the dust, grieving over her lost children. The prophet bids her to rise and be radiant with joy because all her exiled children, along with the wealth of the nations, will be brought back to her.

But the "woman" Jerusalem is to shine primarily by reflecting the the light of the glory of God. God now dwells in her midst, a foreshadowing of the Incarnation by which God dwells with his people in the person of Jesus Christ. The command "arise" is originally a cultic direction. Darkness and thick darkness are frequently used in describing revelation. (Exodus 20:21, Pslam 97:2) The thrust of the ingathering is of the dispersion generally.

The nations not only come to Zion in camel caravans, but they contribute their wealth and pay homage. This bringing of gifts can be compared to the gifts which the queen of Sheba gave to Solomon. (1 Kings 10:2) Foreigners proclaim the praise of the Lord. (v. 6) They recite God's mighty acts which are worthy of praise. The pilgrims themselves will be an acceptable offering and will assist in beautifying the temple.

Risen Zion welcomes her children home and their gifts replace her poverty with wealth.

### Ephesians 3:1-12 (C)
### Ephesians 3:2-12 (L)
### Ephesians 3:2-3, 5-6 (RC)

This pericope combines the same two themes as the Isaiah reading: (1) the revelation or epiphany of God (v. 3) and the inclusion of the Gentiles in the salvation offered in Christ (Messiah). The passage is part of a prayer for wisdom (vv. 1-20) which begins with verse 1, is interrupted from verses 2-13, and continues with verse 14. Paul was a prisoner in Rome because he had aroused the hostility of the Jews by declaring the equality of the Gentiles in the church. The mystery which Paul alludes to refers to God's eternal purpose now revealed to his chosen to call Gentiles as well as Jews to share in Christ's redemptive work.

The inclusion of the Gentiles in the plan of salvation was an event of truly cosmic significance "made known to the principalities and powers in the heavenly places." (v. 10) But what does it mean for the church to be truly ecumenical in the sense of our text? When denominations each claim to be the one and only true church, when the church sets itself over against Jews and in other ways denies the true universality of its message it denies the thrust of Epiphany.

Epiphany can be one moment in the church's life when the church takes a wide and broad view of its message and mission. Often hymns catch the heart of the Gospel in ways prose alone fails. The hymn sings "There's a wideness in God's mercy, like the wideness of the sea" and reminds us of our own narrow vision of God and his mercy.

We are living in a truly ecumenical time when Christians are being drawn closer to one another as they draw closer to Christ, even as spokes of a wheel come nearer to each other as they come nearer to the center of the wheel. Now that the church is essentially Gentile, it is the task of the church to make room for Jews. The contemporary Jewish/Christian dialogue seeks to clarify the ground we have in common and to enable us to overcome those prejudices and dogmas which divide us. This is happening in local groups meeting to reflect on Jewish and Christian beliefs and practices. Epiphany is a time to deal with the universal revelation of God in Christ and its implications for Christians and Jews today.

### Matthew 2:1-12

There are many different traditions from primitive Christianity that go into the makeup of the Magi story. Notice that this is not a birth story, although it is commonly read as a nativity story at Christmas. Matthew gives the birth story in 1:18-25. The visit of the Magi symbolizes the divine preparation for the advent of Jesus, and the gifts, fit for a king, point to the kingly rights of the child and the worldwide acclaim he is to receive later. As we read this story we should remember that Matthew is not trying to present a complete chronological account of Jesus' birth and infancy. Since Herod ordered all male children in Bethlehem and that region who were two-years-old and under to be killed this implies that Jesus himself was already about two when the Magi arrived from the East.

The Magi were a combination of astrologer and magicians. They were the closest to astronomers that the ancient world knew, and they used their knowledge of the movement of the stars to tie it in with the destiny of human beings. They were wise and learned men among the Gentiles. Since they are Gentiles they receive their proclamation through created nature. They recognized the saving import of the star. But notice that they could not gain a full understanding of the revelation of the Messiah from nature alone. This is a secret found in Scripture of special revelation God gave to the Jews alone.

But notice the paradox. The Jews who have the Scriptures with the prophecies of the coming of Messiah cannot recognize him when he appears. But the Magi, guided by star and Scripture accept Jesus as Messiah and worship him. But in sharp contrast stand the chief priests and scribes of the people who do not believe. They conspire to put him to death.

Notice that the Magi from the East came to Jerusalem saying, "Where is he who has been born king of the Jews? (v. 2) This is the same title given to Jesus at the crucifixion. "The King of the Jews" was the charge put over Jesus' head as he hung on the cross. This title was given him by the Magi, but rejected by Herod, and those who advised him.

See the parallel between the infancy narrative and the crucifixion. Jesus is taken away by his parents to another land (Egypt) and then returns. At his crucifixion Jesus dies but is brought back to life by God in the resurrection.

The gold and frankincense are suggested by the first reading (Isaiah). Matthew does quote from Micah's prophecy that the Davidic Messiah would be born in Bethelehem. In Jewish eyes this qualifies him to be Messiah. Raymond Brown sees in this infancy narrative "a gospel in miniature." He points out that the Gospel is good news but that it must have a passion and rejection as well as success. This account and the remainder of chapter 2 has these factors. (p. 183, *The Birth of the Messiah,* Garden City: Image Books, 1979)

This pericope points us to the fact that Christ appeared not only for Israel but for the whole world, symbolized by the Magi. But Jesus is also the true king of Israel. The tie to Bethelehem makes this plain. But right here at his birth and infancy the cross casts its shadow. The political and religious establishment reveal their hostility to Jesus. The little nation, indeed, the whole world is too small for two kings — Herod and Jesus. The world still struggles with loyalties torn between the kings of this world and the King Jesus who claims his kingdom by dying and being raised from the dead. Love still arouses the hostility and hatred of the evil powers of this world. Witness those in any nation who work for peace and justice, who seek to practice the teachings of Jesus in daily living, who love their enemies rather than seeking to kill them.

## Theological Reflections

The twin themes of the lessons for today are God's revelation in Christ and the fact this is a revelation to the Gentiles as well as Jews, a worldwide revelation. God has taken the initiative. Mankind responds with either humble worship after the fashion of the Magi, or in hostility like Herod. The reader is confronted with the choice: worship the King of the Jews, or seek to kill him. There is no middle ground. Wherever Jesus appears he calls for a decision.

## Homiletical Moves

*Isaiah 60:1-6*
### Arise, Shine, for Your Light Has Come!

1. Into the darkness of sin and evil Jesus Christ has come as the Light of the World
2. The light and love of Christ from the cross draws all peoples to him
3. The Wise Men who brought gold, frankincense, and myrrh to the Christ child and worshiped him are models for all humanity
4. Come out of the darkness of your sin into the Light of Christ and worship him with all you have and are, for he is your Light that has come!

*Ephesians 3:1-12*
### The Mystery Made Known by Revelation

1. The mystery is how Gentiles are fellow heirs in Christ Jesus through the Gospel
2. By the preaching of the unsearchable riches of Christ the wisdom of God is being made known to principalities and powers
3. God is working out his eternal purpose in Christ Jesus our Lord
4. Therefore, accept Christ as the Lord of your life and come boldly through faith in Christ to partake of the Gospel

*This Preacher's Choice*

*Matthew 2:1-12*
### What Will You Do With the King of the Jews?

1. The Magi followed the star and the Scriptures to the King of the Jews in Bethlehem
2. When they found Jesus they rejoiced with great joy, fell down and worshiped him and gave him gifts fit for a king
3. The Magi departed to their own country by another way for they were changed persons
4. Herod sought out the young Jesus to have him put to death for he could brook no rival. (v.17)
5. The King of the Jews was crucified: what will you do with him?

**Hymn for Epiphany:**  *We Three Kings*

**Prayer**

*O God who has revealed yourself in Jesus Christ to Jew and Gentile alike, we humbly bow before you, rejoicing in your great gift of love. We have too often missed the star and the direction of Scripture as they pointed us to the King of the Jews. Guide us to the King that we may worship him in spirit and in truth. We worship the King on the Cross who has broken the powers of evil of this world. Because he was raised from the dead, we are new men and women who cannot return home the same way but must take another route. Amen*

# The Baptism of Our Lord

Epiphany 1

| **Common** | **Lutheran** | **Roman Catholic** |
|---|---|---|
| Genesis 1:1-5 | Isaiah 42:1-7 | Isaiah 42:1-4, 6-7 |
| Acts 19:1-7 | Acts 10:34-38 | Acts 10:34-38 |
| Mark 1:4-11 | Mark 1:4-11 | Mark 1:7-11 |

## Comments on the Lessons

The Genesis passage depicts God's creative Word being spoken over the chaos of darkness and deep waters. Although this Genesis passage is part of the readings at the Easter vigil, here it is given prominence in a Sunday reading. This helps link creation and redemption. The reading from Mark says that Jesus will baptize with the Holy Spirit. It also gives an account of Jesus' baptism by John in the Jordan, including the descending of the Spirit upon Jesus. The Acts (C) reading vividly portrays baptism in the early church by the Holy Spirit with the laying on of hands. Note that Mark 1:4-6, which all three lectionaries have in common, makes even clearer the contrast between John the Baptizer and Jesus and distinguishes John's messianic preaching from the general thrust of his preaching. Isaiah 42:1-7 describes the calling of the Servant who is given God's Spirit to bring forth justice to the nations. This is part of the first of the four so-called Servant Songs. The language of the songs is clearly messianic. Notice the link of the prophecy of Messiah with the beginning of Jesus' ministry at his baptism.

## Commentary

### Genesis 1:1-5 (C)

These first five verses of the Bible are among the best known and certainly the most important in all of Scripture. In spite of this they are also often the most misunderstood. This is due to a misunderstanding of the style and character of the literature. To rightly understand them we must be clear about the kind of material found here and its relationship to the rest of Scripture. Right off it should be evident that we are not dealing with science and history as we conceive of them. Rather, we are dealing with a poetic kind of language which conveys the deepest truths of the universe in a way which no other kind of language can do. The ultimate question of creation of "Where did it all come from?" is not answered in the test tube or found with an electron microscope. Rather, the writer of Genesis posits God as the creator of the heavens and the earth. One of the young child's earliest questions is "Who made the stars?" Genesis gives the answer. When the scientist has pushed to the limits of discovery, or the philosopher the limits of knowledge, there is the annoying question that won't go away but which Genesis answers in a few words: God created the heavens and earth. These first verses of Genesis which lead on to the first eleven chapters embody a peculiar and perceptive intellectual tradition. It has found that all other questions of life such as issues of meaning and power are subordinated to this fundamental one of the relation of the creator and creation. Upon reflection we see that upon this issue everything else hinges. This includes human authority, power and the fact of order and freedom in human life.

While these verses describing creation have parallels in other ancient creation stories of the Near East, the writer has handled the stories in a distinctly theological fashion. Notice that there is a radical break with the "mythological" view of reality which puts all the real action with the gods while giving no significant value to creation in and of itself. The writer wants us to understand that the ultimate meaning of creation is to be found in the purpose of the creator who is God. And he asserts that the world has been created good and valued as such by its creator. From this it follows that creation must be valued by the creators to whom it is entrusted.

Note that God creates by the Word: "And God said, 'Let there be . . .' " In verse 2 we read that the Spirit of God was moving over the face of the waters. This working of the Spirit in creation should be recalled when reflecting on the baptism of Jesus and the giving of the Spirit to those who are baptized in obedience to Jesus.

Recent scholarship has pointed out the contrast between verses 1 and 2. Verse 1 has more than one possible interpretation. The usual translation makes an absolute claim for creation as a decisive act of the Creator God. But the verse may be translated. "When God began to create . . ." which would make it related closely to the material which follows. To do this gives the meaning that creation is God's work which he not only began but continues. This has impact on the other pericopes in which God's Spirit is at work.

Another issue in verses 1 and 2 involves whether or not God created out of nothing, or out of chaos. Verse 1 suggests that God created out of nothing, which is the traditional understanding. But verse 2 makes it clear that there was an existing chaos. It appears that verse 2 is a more primitive notion. Verse 1 is more reflective about its theological claim.

*Isaiah 42:1-7 (L)*
*Isaiah 42:1-4, 6-7 (RC)*

Following the Babylonian conquest and destruction of Jerusalem in 587 BC the military and intellectual elite of the city were deported to Babylon. The author of Isaiah 40-55 was among the exiles. Known as Deutero-Isaiah, he spoke to a people who had lost both home and political identity. The writer adapts the theology of Isaiah to the new conditions found in Babylon on the Euphrates. He writes of the servant to whom scholars have given various identies: the prophet Deutero-Isaiah himself, the king, or the people collectively, or some unknown person. Many scholars today prefer the collective identity. There is no mistaking that the language of the Servant Songs is messianic. The term "Servant" was commonly used of the king in ancient Near Eastern cultures. Much of what is said about the Servant could also be said about the king. The song of the pericope for today falls into two parts: verses 1-4, which portrays the Servant's official commission, and part two, verses 5-7, plus 8 and 9. This latter part was formerly not part of this song, but now is included. It outlines the Servant's universal mission. Throughout the song the speaker is none other than Yahweh, the God who is the Creator. Filled and guided by the Spirit, the Servant will mete out justice to the nations. This work of justice is the most conspicuous assignment given him.

In its broadest sense justice indicates the divinely willed order of life which will prevail over disorder and chaos. The specific meaning of justice is given in verses 3 and 7. Verse 3, while not speaking of the suffering of the Servant himself, outlines the compassion of the Servant for the suffering people: ". . . a bruised reed he will not break . . . he will faithfully bring forth justice." Justice involves essentially an active concern for the oppressed. Through the work of the Servant the poor of the earth will know that their day has come. In a quiet and unobtrusive fashion which does not call attention to itself the Servant will carry out his mission. (v. 2) This will produce a covenant with the people of Israel and the outcome will be salvation for the nations. After Israel's kingship collapses Deutero-Isaiah reformulates salvation along the line of royal ideology. The Hebrew thought form does not always make a clear distinction between the individual and the collective "person", much as "Uncle Sam" represents the people of a nation. If one accepts the collective identity of the Servant, then it is the people of Israel themselves who will receive and implement the messianic promises.

*Acts 19:1-7 (C)*

Paul, as customary, preaches in the synagogue, this time at Ephesus. He encounters some disciples who have not received the Holy Spirit, although they had made a profession of faith in Jesus as the Christ. Luke assumes that these twelve are Christians. However, it is strange that they have never heard of the Holy Spirit. It is more likely that they are members of a sect of John the Baptizer. Paul describes John's baptism as one of repentance. (Luke 3:3) He portrays John's message as proclaiming the coming One. Notice that the disciples are rebaptized in the "name of . . . Jesus" and that following the laying on of hands they receive the Spirit. Luke sees them as similar to the converts of Samaria. Luke wants us to understand that Paul has the apostolic power to convey the Spirit. He offers as proof of the Spirit's presence the speaking in tongues and prophesying.

*Acts 10:34-38 (L, RC)*

Luke uses the Semitic style in presenting Peter's sermon. Romans 2:11 also asserts the belief that God shows no partiality. The statement that the righteous in every nation are acceptable to God does not imply that there is salvation apart from Christianity. Rather, this opens the way for the Gentile mission. These verses are the opening words of Peter's Proclamation to the household of Cornelius at Caesarea. It is evident that while Peter is the dominant figure in the first half of Acts (chapters 1-12), it is Paul who is the unquestioned main figure of the second half (chapters 13-28). Both men preached sermons often, and their famous speeches in Acts have attracted the attention and study of scholars. While C. H. Dodd and others argued a generation ago that these speeches contain the pattern of the earliest Christian kerygma, more recent scholars identify them as Luke's own compositions. The speeches of both Peter and Paul can be understood as summaries of Lukan theology.

Peter's sermon follows the conversion of Cornelius (chapter 10) which is a milestone event in that it marks the breakthrough toward the Gentiles. Note that Cornelius is the first Gentile to become a Christian. The forceful sermon of Peter carries the argument in favor of the Gentiles. This is followed by the giving of the spirit and the Gentiles' baptism. (vv. 44-45, 47-48)

Peter begins his appeal to the Gentiles with the affirmation that God is impartial. Fear of God and ethical behavior are marks of those who claim Jesus as the Christ. Cornelius was one of many Gentiles known as "Godfearers," who were attracted to the Jewish faith but had not become converts. Notice that the doing of good works is one mark of Luke's ethical system. Peter traces the origin of the Gospel and shows its destiny. While the good news was at first intended only for Israel, this was soon expanded to include all nations. Luke refers to the "good news of peace by Jesus Christ." (v. 36) This is a theme in Luke. While Jesus was born into a society marked by violence (Zealots, Romans), he is the prince of peace. Peter traces the gospel's movement beginning with John's baptismal message and continuing on through Galilee and Judea. Then the gospel moves on out to the whole Roman Empire, reaching Rome itself.

The main thrust of Peter's messages are: (1) Jesus was anointed at baptism, (2) lived a life in the Spirit with power, (3) he went about doing good and healing all that were oppressed by the devil. The healings and miracles were evidence of God's power with him. The remaining verses of Peter's sermon (39-43) bear witness to the death and resurrection of Jesus. It includes the command of Jesus to preach to the people and to witness to his role as the one ordained by God to judge the living and the dead. Peter sums up his message by saying that all the prophets point to Jesus as the one who gives forgiveness to all who believe in him. The pericope for today must be seen in the context of the occasion on which it was preached, to whom, and the results. The cross and resurrection are an integral part of Peter's sermon and must be included in our consideration of the pericope.

*Mark 1:4-11 (C)*
*Mark 1:4-11 (L)*
*Mark 1:1-11 (RC)*

The first three verses give the title and introduction to the gospel and will be included as part of the commentary, although omitted by (C) and (L).

This pericope is part of the prologue to Mark (1:1-13) and includes John the Baptizer who prepares the way (1-3), announces and baptizes Jesus (4-11). Immediately, Jesus is driven by the Spirit into confrontation with Satan. (12-13) And from this empowering and confrontation Jesus emerges to begin his public ministry which begins with the preaching of the kingdom of God. (14-15)

The ministry of John is the earliest account of John and his work. The Jewish historian Josephus, writing in the last part of the first century, said of John that he was "a good man, and commanded the Jews to exercise virtue . . . and piety towards God, and so to come to baptism." But John's baptism was to repentance for the forgiveness of sins only. It foreshadowed the gospel of Jesus Christ which followed.

We are not told the manner of baptism John used. It was a form probably not unique to John but was already being used. It appears to have been a communal washing of sins, not one individual baptizing another as we think of it. Undoubtedly it involved immersing oneself in the Jordan in John's practice.

The description of John the Baptizer is that of an ascetic. "Camel's hair" may refer either to a skin from a camel or to cloth made from camel's hair worn as a garment. Since the latter was cheap and in common use, this is probably what John wore. The leather girdle John wore around his waist recalls the girdle Elijah wore: "He wore a garment of haircloth with a girdle of leather about his loins." (1 Kings 1:8) Mark wants us to know that John stands in the prophetic tradition of Elijah. He even wears the uniform of a prophet! But his role as prophet went beyond his clothing. He ate locusts and wild honey, common food among the poor Bedouin of the Near East.

John's message is given in only meager outline: One is coming after me who is mightier than I.

John is the messianic forerunner. Note that the word "mightier" is usually associated with supernatural beings!

While some argue that the words "I have baptized you" indicate individuals being baptized by John, this is not conclusive, especially in light of the crowds (Matthew 3:5) that went out to John. "With water" is more apt to describe immersion than the "in water" of the Greek text. Both are equally correct, although "with water" is more explicit.

Jesus came to be baptized by John in the Jordan and, in doing so, he identified himself with sinners, although sinless. When he came up out of the water, immediately Jesus saw the heavens opened and the Spirit descending upon him "like a dove." A voice from heaven came: "Thou art my beloved Son, with thee I am well pleased." (v. 11) Jesus' baptism marks the real beginning of the Gospel story. Mark is not interested in telling us what Jesus was doing before this event. It is one of the most historically sound events of Jesus' life. However, Jesus' baptism was a source of embarrassment for the early Christians for two reasons: (1) Since John baptized for the forgiveness of sin, it was inferred that Jesus was a sinner who had repented like others being baptized, and (2) it put Jesus in an inferior position to John. John's religious movement and Jesus' existed side by side and were even rival groups. But John's Gospel has John expressly deny all claims to superiority, and even leaves out the account of the baptism.

The fact that Mark says Jesus "saw" the heavens opened indicates that, in Mark's view, only Jesus shared this experience. The historical evidence points to this as a personal religious experience. John was not aware of Jesus' messiahship according to the views of all the Synoptic writers. (Matthew 11:2-6; Luke 7:18-23) "The heavens opened" is too mild. The violent Greek word used here means "split apart." Jews of that period commonly believed that direct communication from heaven was very rare and involved a splitting of the barrier between heaven and earth. The description of the descending of the spirit "like a dove" points to a personal experience. The identification of the spirit and the dove came about only at a secondary stage. Note that both Matthew and Luke describe Jesus' baptism as an objective event, however.

The voice is addressed to Jesus, not to the bystanders. Paul's experience on the road to Damascus is another striking example of this kind of experience. It included both hearing and seeing and was described as a "heavenly vision."

What the voice from heaven said has commonly been thought to refer to both Psalm 2:7 and Isaiah 42:1 (see alternate pericope for today). Psalm 2:7 had to do with the enthronement of a king, or adoption rites (kings were thought to be adopted as sons by gods when enthroned). Isaiah 42:1 is the consecration of God's Servant. But more recent scholarship is challenging this. It is known that in the Judaism of this period, when large parts of Scripture were said off by heart, it was the regular custom to quote only the beginning of a passage, with the continuation of the passage kept in mind. Now the really decisive clause from Isaiah 42:1 "I have put my spirit upon him" does not appear in the Markan quotation. In all probability, the Mark 1:11 proclamation means that what Isaiah 42:1 promised, i.e. that God would lay his spirit on his servant, has just been fulfilled.

If the proclamation interprets the descent of the Spirit as fulfillment of Isaaah 42:1, this has far-reaching consequences for an understanding of the baptism of Jesus: First, the thrust of the event of Jesus' baptism is on the gift of the Spirit. Second, the proclamation originally had nothing to do with the enthronement of the king or adoption rites. It does not take us into the realm of ideas about the Messiah as king. Rather, it confronts us with scriptural statements about the servant of God. In the Judaism of Jesus' day the imparting of the Spirit almost always meant prophetic inspiration. A man is grasped by God who authorizes him to be his messenger through whom he speaks. Thus, when Mark says that the Spirit descends on Jesus, the meaning is that Jesus is called in this way to be God's messenger of the inbreaking of the Kingdom.

### Theological Reflections

Both the Genesis and the baptism of Jesus pericopes for today share a trinitarian formula rarely found in the Scripture. Genesis places God (the Father), the Spirit of God, and God's Word (God said . . .) all at the beginning of creation. The trinitarian God who was in the beginning continues the work of creation. After the Fall of Adam God began the work of re-creating, which culminated in the life and work of Jesus, the New Adam. The baptism pericope gives the call of Jesus by the Father to be God's messenger, and the descent of the Spirit upon him, anointing him for the task. From that time Jesus knew he was in the grasp of the Spirit. God was setting him apart for his service, equipping him with the Spirit and authorizing him to preach the breaking in of the Kingdom.

58

The event reflects the Isaiah 42:1 pericope foretelling the giving of the Spirit to the Servant by God to carry out his mission. Reflecting on this promise of God from the time of Jesus' baptism onward, Jesus was conscious of being God's servant promised by Isaiah. When later in his ministry Jesus is asked about the evidence of his authority (Mark 1:27-33), he responds with a counter-question whether the baptism of John was or was not from God. This was hardly an evasion of the question. Rather, it means that Jesus is saying in his defense, "My authority rests on John's baptism." In concrete terms this means that Jesus is saying: "My authority is based on what happened when John baptized me in the Jordan and the Spirit came upon me." Here is the starting point for the message of Jesus: the call which Jesus experienced when baptized by John the Baptizer.

The creator God is also the redeemer God who appears as Father, Son (word), and Spirit. The God who manifested his power in the work of creation is the same God who manifests his power in the call of Jesus to the task of re-creating, and inaugurating the Kingdom of God. Jesus reveals the presence of God through his life, death and resurrection. He refers to his death as a "baptism": "I have a baptism to be baptized with; and how I am constrained until it is accomplished!" (Luke 12:50) In this "second baptism" Jesus dies in order to redeem all creation from the power of evil. Jesus, the Word, through whom all things were created in the beginning (John 1:3) is the One through whom God inaugurates the New Creation.

## Homiletical Moves

*Genesis 1:1-5*
### The God Who Created and Is Creating Still

1. God is the uncreated Creator (v. 1)
2. God moves to bring order out of chaos
3. God the Father is working still, and Jesus, the Word, is working. (John 5:17) Jesus, the New Adam, is bringing in the New Creation
4. Therefore, invite Christ to become Lord of your life and make you a new creation

*Isaiah 42:1-7*
### The Servant's Mission to a Broken World

1. In Jesus we see the Servant who is chosen by God
2. God has empowered the Servant Jesus with the Spirit
3. The Servant himself is a covenant to the people to bring in the New Order marked by justice, light and freedom
4. Therefore, accept the Servant Christ as your Savior and Lord and join in his mission to a broken world

*Acts 19:1-7*
### Baptism in the Name of Jesus

1. The disciples, like us, had a need for power
2. Paul baptizes in the name (nature) of the Lord Jesus
3. The Holy Spirit came upon them through the laying on of hands and gave them power for mission
4. You have been baptized in the name of Jesus, therefore claim the power of the Holy Spirit for your mission in the world
5. If you have not been baptized, repent of your sins, and accept Christ as your Savior and Lord and go out in mission

*Acts 10:34-38*
### God Shows No Partiality

1. The Word of good news of peace by Jesus Christ was sent to Israel and Judea
2. This word is now available to you who fear God and do what is right
3. This word is the good news of Jesus' life, death, and resurrection which gives forgiveness to all who believe
4. Therefore, turn from sin to God and believe the good news!

*Mark 1:4-11*
## Jesus' Call to Mission

1. John came preaching a baptism of repentance for the forgiveness of sins
2. John foretells the coming One who will baptize with the Holy Spirit
3. Jesus is baptized and the Spirit comes upon him
4. Jesus experiences God's call as the call to be God's servant in fulfillment of Isaiah's prophecy (42:1 ff)
5. Therefore, repent and turn to God, calling upon him for forgiveness and the power of the Spirit for service

### *This Preacher's Choice*

A preacher following the lectionary would be led to the Markan pericope for the sermon. Listening to the passage the preacher will discover the flow of the passage from John's preaching of repentance for the forgiveness of sins, to John's foretelling of the One who will baptize with the Holy spirit. This sets the stage for the epiphany of Jesus at his baptism when God calls him to be his messenger. The preacher will need to decide whether to deal with this as a public event seen and heard by all, or a personal religious experience of Jesus. If the latter choice is made, the preacher will develop the meaning of Isaiah 42:1 ff for Jesus' ministry as the Servant anointed by the spirit for mission. The preacher may want to develop implications of Jesus' baptism for our sins, our baptism as our call to mission, whether lay or clergy, and the gift of the Spirit to empower us for our mission. This mission of justice, light and freedom has specific implications for the mission of the church as God's Servant People which may be developed in the sermon.

**Hymn Choice for the day:**   *Guide Me, O Thou Great Jehovah*

**Prayer**

We praise you, O God Creator and Redeemer, for the revelation of your loving kindness in Jesus Christ. We thank you for his baptism for our sins in the Jordan and on the cross. We pray that we may be empowered by the spirit to be faithful to our call to mission in the world. Forgive us when we fail, and call us back to faithfulness. Amen

## Epiphany 2          Epiphany 2          Ordinary Time 2

| Common | Lutheran | Roman Catholic |
|---|---|---|
| 1 Samuel 3:1-10 (11-20) | 1 Samuel 3:1-10 | 1 Samuel 3:3-10, 19 |
| 1 Corinthians 6:12-20 | 1 Corinthians 6:12-20 | 1 Corinthians 6:13-15, 17-20 |
| John 1:35-42 | John 1:43-51 | John 1:35-42 |

### Comments on the Lessons

There is virtual consensus on the first reading. In (C) verses 11-20 are an option when the purpose of Samuel's call is considered important to the reading and therefore needs to be included. On the second reading there is virtual consensus. The gospel is especially fitting for one of the Sundays after Epiphany which, in the approach of the Consultation on Common Texts, is to be a series of epiphanies of Jesus as the Messiah. These culminate in the Transfiguration on the last Sunday after Epiphany.

### Commentary

*1 Samuel 3:1-10 (11-20) (C)*
*1 Samuel 3:1-10 (L)*
*1 Samuel 3:3-10, 19 (RC)*

Samuel was twelve-years-old when he heard God's call to him in the night, says Jewish tradition. This is the same age at which Jesus discoursed in the temple in Jerusalem. The stories of the birth and childhood of Samuel must have been in the mind of Luke as he began the writing of his gospel. The main part of chapter 3 contains an outstanding narrative with a double purpose: (1) to announce the punishment of the house of Eli, and (2) to relate the call of Samuel. Samuel's call emerges from a theophany (a visible manifestation of a deity), and we learn that Samuel was from his boyhood up the kind of person who is capable of receiving God's word. This is not a natural trait but is a divinely given qualification.

Samuel spends the night in the sanctuary in expectation of a divine revelation. While the person would normally remain awake, sleep would not necessarily invalidate the experience. In verse 1 we read that the word of God was rare or precious at that time. While it would be true to say that in any age the word of God was rare and precious for Israel, the mention of it here increases the significance of it for young Samuel.

The writer feels it is important to mention that young Samuel has grown used to his service in the sanctuary. But in the very sanctuary where one would expect visions of God to occur and words from God to be heard there was silence except on rare occasions. The basic reason for this, of course, is the conduct of the house of Eli. Eli has limited vision, among other infirmities. This may account for his not sleeping in the sanctuary himself. We don't know why this was the priestly duty, but it may have been someone was needed there during the night to keep the lamp burning, or to simply keep watch by the ark to receive divine instructions. But this watch for a long time had been unsuccessful.

With this background description, toward morning, while the lamp of God had not yet gone out, the drama now becomes active. (v. 4) The Lord calls to Samuel twice and the lad answers "Here I am!" He ran to Eli thinking the aging priest had called him, only to be told he had not and that he should lie down again. This happens three times without Samuel or Eli knowing what is happening. But on the fourth call Samuel gives the answer prompted to him by Eli, "Speak, Lord, for thy servant hears." In Hebrew the word "hears" means "is ready to hear."

The lamp was near the ark of God, the portable shrine or chest symbolizing the presence and power of God. While simple in its earliest form, it later became quite ornate. It is when Samuel replies to God's call with the obedient words, "Speak, for thy servant hears" that the Lord spoke his message to Samuel. Something now is about to take place for which the earlier call was just a preparation. Samuel is about to hear a real threat in which guilt and punishment are closely bound together as cause and effect.

In verse 19 we learn that Samuel grew and the Lord was with him and let none of his words fall to the ground. God must chasten as well as offer salvation. It was necessary that the first revelation God makes to Samuel should be a tragic one since the house of Eli had fallen into iniquity. The purpose of Samuel's call is to raise up a new, faithful priest to replace the worthless sons of·Eli.

*1 Corinthians 6:12-20 (C, L)*
*1 Corinthians 6:13-15, 17-20 (RC)*

Corinth was notorious in the ancient world for its lax morality. There was a saying, "To make a visit to Corinth demands much money." Temple prostitution in which a man paid a sum to have sexual intercourse with a temple prostitute as a way of gaining union with a god was one of Corinth's best known religious rites. The libertines there argued that satisfying sexual desire was like taking food into the body to satisfy hunger. It was only a natural thing. But Paul rejected this analogy.

While Paul had preached and taught that Christians were free from the Jewish law, this did not mean they were free to be licentious. The phrase "All things are lawful for me" seems to reflect this misunderstanding of Christian freedom. Paul points out that not everything is expedient. Not all things are helpful. He emphasizes that the body was not made for immorality, but for the Lord, and the Lord for the body. The gnostic Christians at Corinth claimed that anything goes since they believed that their Christian experience enabled them to transcend the realities of the material world. But Paul will not tolerate this perversion of Christian freedom.

Paul refutes the gnostic claim that the Christian experience delivers the soul from the body. Rather, the whole person, body and soul alike are brought under the lordship of Christ, says Paul. "The body is not meant for immorality, but for the Lord, and the Lord for the body." (v. 13) The body is not something evil and should not be dedicated to evil such as fornication, but to the Lord. For the Lord has given himself to the body (in the Eucharist). While the early gnostics tended to disparage the body as material and thus evil, the Christian doctrines of Incarnation and Resurrection opposed such teaching. Christ was raised with a resurrection body.

Paul says that because their bodies are already members of Christ, the Corinthian Christians are not to take the members of Christ and make them members of a prostitute. Prostitution is not just a casual act, like eating and drinking, but involves a union of the person's very being with another person. He reminds them that in marriage as God created it "the two shall become one flesh." Since sexual immorality involves the whole person, it deprives Christ of his own property.

The gnostics tended to go to one of two extremes. Either they encouraged people to sow their wild oats, engaging in temple prostitution, etc., in the belief that the soul would not be endangered by this, or a very rigorous asceticism was followed with the spiritual element being used to crush the material. Paul says that the immoral man sins against his own body. He points out another reason for abstaining from immorality: the body is a temple of the Holy Spirit within you, which you have from God. (v. 19)

But the most telling argument of all for shunning evil is that the Christian was bought with a price: Christ's death on the cross. The Christian did not belong to herself or himself but to God for this reason. "So glorify God in your body," exhorts Paul. With his "body" a convert is a member of Christ. He belongs to the one who bought him with a price. The body is an instrument of the Spirit.

The Christian religion has been called the most materialistic of all the religions of the world. This passage is one evidence of this fact. Paul refuses to allow the gnostics to so spiritualize the Christian religion that what one does with the body has no connection with what one does with the spiritual person. Rather, the human being is a *unity*. And the Christian is a body whose ruler is the Lord himself. And the body is a temple of the Holy Spirit.

*John 1:35-42 (C, RC)*

Here is John's version of the call of the first disciples. In the Fourth Gospel witnessing to Christ begins with John the Baptizer. It is important to see the distinction between the Synoptic account of the relation between John the Baptizer and Jesus and that of the Fourth Gospel. And we should not let one bleed over into the other. The Fourth Gospel says that both John the Baptizer and Jesus ministered in Judea at the same time. (1:29—4:3) But the Synoptics portray the beginning of Jesus' ministry after John is imprisoned and place its beginning in Galilee.

The Fourth Gospel introduces the story of the Master and the disciples with the profound witness that Jesus is *the Lamb of God*. In the Isenheim altarpiece by Grunewald of the crucifixion in Colmar,

France, the artist has taken poetic license to place John the Baptizer at the crucifixion. He stands to the right of the picture holding the Old Testament scriptures in his left hand and pointing to Jesus with his index finger of the right hand as if to say "There is the fulfillment of the prophecies of scripture." At his feet stands a lamb with a small cross by its head. The artist is telling us in symbols what John the Baptizer said in words: "Behold, the Lamb of God!" Once you have gazed on this dramatic scene of the crucifixion you will never again see the cross of Jesus in the same way. The artist has linked symbols which leave indelible images in the mind.

Before the Messiah performs any Messianic act he gathers around himself the people of the Messiah. Or as John puts it, before Jesus is manifested in his glory he is revealed to some of the brethren by his Father. John makes it plain that when Peter is called as a disciple he already senses something of his Messianic powers since Andrew invites Peter to come to Jesus with the words: "We have found the Messiah."

John the Baptizer fulfills a unique role in salvation history. He was a man sent from God who was given direct illumination from God so that he might bear witness to the true light of the world. John the Baptizer is unique in this role. Other disciples are dependent upon a human witness for the divine illumination about the real nature of Jesus as Messiah. But notice that John the Baptizer does not share in the evangelistic mission of the church. As Matthew and Luke say of John, among those born of women there is no greater than John the Baptizer. But even so he who is least in the kingdom of heaven is greater than he.

On the day after John's first confession of Jesus as the Lamb of God, it was repeated by him in the presence of two of his disciples. They are turned to follow Jesus from following John. Andrew was one, and we are not told the name of the other disciple. They ask where Jesus is staying. They go and spend the rest of the day with him. Thus John's witness to Jesus evokes the two essentials for discipleship: following and abiding.

Notice that when Jesus and Peter meet, Peter is given a new name. In the Old Testament a decisive encounter with God such as that of Jacob, or Abram brought forth a new name indicating the change of character effected by the encounter. Now Simon (heard) becomes Peter (the rock man). The name Rock may also suggest that Peter will be the foundation of the church. We can surmise both of these implications of Peter's new name although John does not bring out either interpretation.

### John 1:43-51 (L)

This is a continuation of the calling of the disciples which began in the preceding passage. But now Jesus has gone to Galilee where he finds Philip, who finds Nathanael (the name means "God gives" or "God has given"), who says to him: "We have found him of whom Moses in the law and also the prophets wrote, Jesus of Nazareth, the son of Joseph." (v. 46) But Nathanael objects with a scornful question: "Can any good thing come out of Nazareth?" So to prove his statement Philip invites him, "Come and see." As Nathanael approaches him, Jesus comments, "Behold, an Israelite indeed, in whom is no guile!" Nathanael asks how he knows him, to which Jesus replies that before Philip called him he saw him under the fig tree. This image of sitting under a fig tree recalls the prophecy of Micah, "But they shall sit every man under his vine and under his fig tree, and none shall make them afraid." (4:4)

Nathanael recognizes the Messianic reference and replies, "Rabbi, you are the Son of God! You are the King of Israel!" Because there was no guile, no deceitful cunning, in Nathanael in contrast to guileful Israel, he could recognize Jesus as Messiah. He could see Jesus as the King of Israel. He could see that Jesus was the one to bring to new birth the life of God's people, Israel, in the role of king and leader.

Jesus tells him he will see greater things than he has already seen. He tells Nathanael that he will see heaven opened and the angels of God ascending and descending upon the Son of man. (v. 51) This will fulfill the vision Jacob saw long before. Nathanael will see in Jesus not only the reality of the new life of Israel but will see in him the reality and new life of the whole of humanity. This was what Jacob's vision was about, not just the destiny of Israel as God's chosen people. Both Jesus and Nathanael were using terms from current Messianism of their age. However, the Son of man, applied to Jesus, is the only name that derives from Jesus' own application of such a title to himself.

## Theological Reflections

The major concern of the passages for today is with correct hearing and interpretation of the Word of God. Samuel, the lad in the house of God, hears God call him three times but misunderstands the call. Then Eli gives him the response to make the fourth time and Samuel hears and obeys. The libertines in Corinth have misunderstood God's call to freedom and take it to mean licentiousness. They have not heard God's call to join their bodies exclusively to Christ and not to prostitutes. They have not heard God's call to belong to Christ alone who bought them with the price of his death. They have not caught the meaning of morality, which as G. K. Chesterton once said, "Art, like morality, consists in drawing the line somewhere." But Paul insists that a line be drawn in Christian conduct. The gospel readings are concerned with the disciples hearing and responding to Jesus' call to follow him. Two hear Jesus' call and leave John the Baptizer to follow him. The number grows. Jesus calls Philip who tells Nathanael he has found the Messiah. Thus right hearing of God's word is a common theme in the pericopes. And hearing, in the Hebrew understanding of the word, implies obeying what is heard!

## Homiletical Moves

*1 Samuel 3:1-10 (11-20)*
### Speak, For Thy Servant Hears!

1. God calls but the lad Samuel does not understand
2. Eli, the priest, understands and coaches Samuel
3. Samuel hears correctly
4. God gives Samuel a task
5. Hear and obey God's call to service

*1 Corinthians 6:12-20*
### Liberty Is Not License!

1. The body is meant, not for immorality, but for the Lord
2. Your bodies are members of Christ the Lord
3. Your body is a temple of the Holy Spirit
4. You are not your own but were bought with a price: Christ's death
5. So glorify God in your body

*John 1:35-42 (C, RC)*
### Behold, The Lamb of God!

1. John the Baptizer witnesses to Jesus as the Lamb of God
2. Two of John's disciples turn and follow Jesus the Messiah
3. When Simon meets Jesus he is given a new name: Peter, Rock
4. Jesus, the Lamb of God, calls us to follow him

*This Preacher's Choice*

*John 1:43-51 (L)*
### The Son of God, the King of Israel!

1. Jesus calls Philip to follow him
2. Nathanael questions who Jesus is, coming from Nazareth
3. Nathanael recognizes Jesus as the Son of God and King of Israel
4. Jesus tells him that his mission is not just to Israel but to all humanity
5. Jesus calls us to go into all the world with the Gospel

**Hymn for Ordinary Time 2:** *Jesus Calls Us*

**Prayer**

*O God who called Samuel of old, and who called the disciples to follow Jesus, open our ears to your call in our time. May we respond in joyful obedience at once. Keep us from confusing your call to freedom with the human love for license to follow the way of the flesh. Remind us that we were bought with the price of Christ's death on the cross and therefore belong to him. Remind us that our bodies are the temple of the Holy Spirit. Help us to live as members of the body of Christ in faithful obedience to his call to service in the world. Amen*

# Epiphany 3     Epiphany 3     Ordinary Time 3

| Common | Lutheran | Roman Catholic |
| --- | --- | --- |
| Jonah 3:1-5, 10 | Jonah 3:1-5 | Jonah 3:1-5 |
| 1 Corinthians 7:29-31 (32-35) | 1 Corinthians 7:29-31 | 1 Corinthians 7:29-31 |
| Mark 1:14-20 | Mark 1:14-20 | Mark 1:14-20 |

## Comments on the Lessons

There is near consensus on the Jonah passage which is important since it is the only Jonah pericope in the Sunday lectionary. It describes Jonah's call to repentance and Nineveh's response. There is near consensus on the epistle reading. It is especially fitting for Epiphany. There is virtual consensus on the gospel reading. We will note a parallel between Jonah's call for repentance and Jesus' message that in the light of the kingdom of God being at hand people should repent and believe in the gospel.

## Commentary

*Jonah 3:1-5, 10*

While the book of Jonah is one of the most familiar of all Bible stories, and its dramatic events make a lasting impression on children and adults alike, the book has been misused and misunderstood. Because of its fantastic account of a man being swallowed by a great fish (commonly called a whale in popular usage) the story is surrealist in nature. The point of the story is not whether or not a person can be swallowed by a great fish and live for three days, but rather the universal mission of Israel to preach to all the nations the wideness of God's mercy and his forgiveness. All too often the central thrust of the book has been swallowed up by the great fish and lost, never to be cast up on shore alive but lost in the debate over sizes of great fish, man's need for air, water, etc., and on and on.

The fundamentalist/liberal debate of the past took this book and its story as a test of faith. Fundamentalists, holding that every word of the Bible was inspired in the original monographs (which don't exist now) and claiming that all stories are literally true, refused to accept the possibility that Jonah may be a parable rather than a historical account. Liberals tended to take the story as an example of unbelievable biblical material which put the whole biblical story in question and often ignored the call for active mission work in which people are called to repent of sin.

Jonah is unique among all the prophetic books. For one thing, it doesn't contain any oracles in verse against Israel and foreign nations. Rather, it is a didactic narrative about the prophet himself. This is another surrealist aspect of the book. Instead of being a straightforward prophecy by an obedient servant of the Lord as other prophetic books are, it features a recalcitrant prophet who flees from his mission and sulks when his hearers repent! The book has taken older material from popular legend, the great fish story, for example, and used it for its own purpose. The story of the rapidly growing plant which provides shelter for a day and then withers seems to be drawn from oral tradition. They give a colorful background to the author's story.

The central thrust of the book of Jonah is its call to Israel to repent and to remember her mission to preach the wideness of God's mercy, including his forgiveness, to all nations. The author seems to have lived in the post exilic-period sometime between the Exile and 200 B.C., since he shows the influence of Jeremiah and Second Isaiah. He opposes the kind of narrow Jewish nationalism revealed in Ezra and Nehemiah. The book may be described as a written sermon based on the prophecy of Jeremiah: "If that nation, concerning which I have spoken, turns from its evil, I will repent of the evil that I intended to do to it." (Jeremiah 18:8) Jonah clearly alludes to this passage when he says, "When God saw what they did, how they turned from their evil way, God repented of the evil which he had said he would do to them; and he did not do it." (3:10)

While there are many ways to approach the book of Jonah, including taking it as literal history, or allegory, legend or folklore, the best solution is to see Jonah as a *parable*. It is a kind of tract which can be compared to a historical novel with a propagandist thrust. The argument for treating

Jonah as a parable is overwhelming. As someone has said, if something looks like a duck, waddles like a duck and quacks like a duck, it must be a duck! If a story, like Jonah, reads like a parable, makes its point like a parable, and exhibits all the characteristics of a parable, it must be a parable. In modern times Jonah is not interpreted as history, since it lacks the kind of details and names we would expect in literal history. There would be attempts to explain things like the great fish swallowing Jonah (size and exact kind of fish, how Jonah survived, etc.), and the remarkable coincidences in the book. The sudden and complete conversion of Nineveh reads like a parable, not an event in real life, since there was no opposition. And the only motivation was Jonah's threat. There is no other mention of the conversion of this huge city in either other parts of the Bible or history.

The pericope for today picks up immediately after the great fish deposits Jonah on the shore. The word of God comes to him a second time, telling him to go to Nineveh and proclaim the message he will be given. This time Jonah obeys the command of God and goes to Nineveh. It was called a great city, three day's journey in breadth. The size of the city creates problems, if we take the story as actual history, unless we do some interpreting. One explanation is to take Nineveh as referring not just to a city alone, but to the so-called ''Assyrian triangle'' which includes the territory from Khorsabad in the north to Nimrud in the south, about twenty-six miles. But to get side-tracked on the size of Nineveh is as distracting as the debate about the great fish's species and size . . .

Jonah had gone only one day's journey into the city crying, ''Yet forty days (the LXX says ''three days'') and Nineveh shall be overthrown!'' (v. 4) The reaction of the Ninevites is amazing: they repent at once. What preacher is not envious of Jonah's track record here? To express their repentance the people proclaimed a fast and everyone put on sackcloth.

Their repentance and conversion moves God to change his mind. So God decides not to destroy Nineveh as planned, and as Jonah preached he would do. Thus Jonah, in spite of his lack of courage and disobedience earlier in the story, appears to be the most successful missionary of all time, outranking even Paul himself!

The story of Jonah is referred to in the New Testament on several occasions. As Jonah was a sign to the people of Nineveh, so Jesus would be to those of his generation. Matthew speaks of the three days in the fish as a symbol of the resurrection after three days in the tomb, but Matthew's use of Jonah seems out of keeping with the context. For Jesus the thing that mattered most about Jonah was that he preached to Nineveh.

But notice the contrast between Jesus' rejoicing over those who are converted during his ministry, while Jonah sulks in anger over those who repent under his preaching. What Jonah feared might happen did happen: the people of Nineveh believed God. Jonah believed that God was the God of the Jews only and like many of his fellow-Jews, he was very jealous of this privilege.

A final note, this little book is one of the most important in the Old Testament, for it deals with the mystery of the mercy of God. The teller of the parable caricatures the narrow-minded Israelite mentality in order to preserve the sovereign freedom of God. Paul, in writing to the Romans, dealt with the same issue when he wrote: ''Is he not the God of Gentiles also?'' (3:29)

## *1 Corinthians 7:29-31 (32-35) (C)*
## *1 Corinthians 7:29-31 (L, RC)*

Paul and the young church expected the imminent return of Christ and so writes to advise the Corinthians how to live in the brief time remaining. In verse 26 Paul speaks of the ''present distress'' which refers to the Messianic woes before the End. Jesus tells the disciples, ''Truly, I say to you, this generation will not pass away before all these things take place.'' (v. 30) Paul makes the point that an unmarried person can concentrate on the Lord's service in contrast to the married person who has to think of and give pleasure to the partner.

Paul was undoubtedly idealizing the effectiveness of a celibate Christian's witness. It may be that Paul was trying to justify his own personal inclination, when he wished that all Christians might follow his example in foregoing marriage in light of the imminent End. The fateful hour of the divine deliverance was expected at any moment. In this brief interval believers are not to be concerned with outward affairs. He wants his hearers to keep a single-minded concentration on the things of the Lord. However, this stance is not consistent with earlier admonitions of Paul. Earlier in verse 4 Paul urges husbands to show wives consideration and vice versa.

In verses 32-35 Paul assumes that marriage is a primary distraction from the affairs of the Lord. Paul qualifies his advice by saying that he does not mean to lay any restraint on them, but writes this for their benefit, to promote good order and to secure their undivided devotion to the Lord. (v. 35)

Basic to understanding this passage is Paul's affirmation that "each has his own special gift from God, one of one kind and one of another." (v. 7) Most Christians do not have the gift of celibacy. They find that the witness of the Christian marriage and the Christian family is a positive aspect of serving Christ. We are told that on the world mission field the witness of Christian family life to unbelievers is one of the most effective witnesses to the gospel and its power to transform human relationships. So rather than the church taking this section from Paul's letter as normative for Christians today, we must interpret it in light of the young church's expectation of the immiment return of Christ and the End of the Age. Rather than being a negative, marriage for many Christians is a good gift of God. (For a further development of the goodness of marriage see the author's devotional book for newlyweds: *The Goodness of Marriage,* (Nashville: Upper Room Press, 1984.)

### *Mark 1:14-20*

In these verses we have two events in the beginning of Jesus' activity in Galilee: the announcement of Jesus' preaching of the Kingdom of God, and the calling of some of the disciples to follow him. As the Messiah and herald of the rule of God, Jesus begins the first stage of his final battle with the evil powers. John the Baptizer, the forerunner, has completed his task. The right moment has come for the principal's work to begin. Mark wants us to understand this announcement of the beginning of Jesus' work to be a kind of manifesto which sums up the essential meaning of the whole public ministry which follows.

The meaning of "the gospel of God" could be either "the good news about God," but more likely means "the good news *from* God. This is the news of God's intention to bring in his kingdom at once. The Aramaic word here means more accurately "the kingship" or sovereign rule of God. It did not refer to a place or realm or even a group of people. Rather the thrust of the phrase is on the autonomous sovereign action by which God would assert his authority and bring everything into conformity with his will forever. Note here and elsewhere in the New Testament that the kingdom is something whose coming and existence will depend entirely on *divine* power.

"The time is fulfilled" refers to the notion that from the beginning God had determined the length of time that must elapse before the coming of the kingdom and that time is now at hand. "At hand" seems to refer to the kingdom's coming in the immediate future, although C. H. Dodd and others have translated it "has arrived." In the Old Testament the kingship of God was thought of in two ways: God is thought of as being even now the King of Isral and of the whole world, but other passages refer to the divine kingship in terms of expectation and hope, as something yet to be realized. Mark is recording Jesus' annoucement that the Old Testament's object of hope which was in the future is now present. Yet, paradoxically, Jesus can still speak about it as future. He teaches his disciples to pray "Thy kingdom come."

Jesus calls his hearers to repent in light of the coming of the kingdom. The word "repent" in the Greek "metanoein" means literally "to change one's mind." As it is used in the New Testament it resembles the Old Testament word "shubh" meaning "to turn back," which implies coming to one's senses. The thrust is that of turning away from one's sins and turning towards God. This implies a change of conduct. In the New Testament repent means much more than changing one's mind. It implies a 180 degree turn about in one's life, a whole reorientation of the personality, a conversion. Too often we have thought of it as something only negative, being sorry enough to turn from sinful ways, rather than seeing the even more important aspect of repentance which is turning *to God*. "Repent and believe the gospel" sums up what preachers in the young church thought one must do to be saved (Acts, etc.).

Before Mark gives us a sample day in the life of Jesus, beginning at verse 21 he records the calling of four disciples. It does not note a time or place, and it appears that Mark himself added "by the sea of Galilee." Commentators conclude this addition from the awkward way the words fit into the context in the original Greek. We can't be clear about why Mark did this.

In this section we have the first of a series of stories which illustrate the authority of Jesus. His word claims the total allegiance of his followers. He asserts his right to their complete renunciation of other duties to follow him. Jesus' call will not allow for any delay. The call of God comes with such divine power that it can create the response it demands. The call is to go after Jesus.

The term "fishers of men" refers to helping Jesus in his task of catching human beings, drawing them out of the waters of this world into the net of the eschatological life of the age to come. In the Old Testament this metaphor was used in a bad sense only, and so also in Rabbinic literatue. But it was suggested by what Simon and Andrew were already doing. It means they are to share in the task of winning further converts to his movement.

In verse 20 we see that following Jesus may involve the severing of personal and family ties as well as economic ties as noted earlier. The Greek word for ''hired servants'' is often used in a bad sense. It could be that the contrast here is between the apostles who respond to Jesus' call and the ''hirelings'' who remain behind to work for pay.

The original point of this story was that of the nature of Christ's call and the Christian's response. This is still the point of the account for the reader today.

## Theological Reflections

In both Jonah and Mark we have the accounts of God's calling individuals and their response. This two-fold movement is at the core of the Biblical story. God acts. Human beings respond. In Jonah's case, the initial response was disobedience. Only later does Jonah obey God's call to preach to Nineveh. Jonah's actions express repentance, the theme of his preaching, in a very concrete fashion. He not only changes his mind, but this change results in changed actions, in a 180 degree turn from cowardly, sinful actions, to faithful obedience. The disciples respond to Jesus' call to follow him with an immediate act of obedience. Jesus has just begun to preach the Gospel of God and to call people to repent and believe. Now four persons who hear the Gospel and Jesus' personal call to follow him do so at once. They illustrate the kind of obedience to Christ's call that the kingdom demands. In the epistle Paul advises his readers how they are to live in light of the expected immediate return of Jesus at the End. In a a sense, this is a call to renounce personal concerns in light of the expected consummation of the Kingdom. They are to devote their full attention to the affairs of the Lord.

## Homiletical Moves

*This Preacher's Choice*

*Jonah 3:1-5, 10*
## The People of Nineveh Believed God

1. Jonah preaches in Nineveh God's warning that the city is about to be destroyed
2. The people believed God, repented, and put on sackcloth and sat in ashes as evidence of their repentance
3. When God saw how they turned from evil he repented of the plan to destroy the city
4. Believe God's offer of forgiveness in Christ, repent, and turn to him and he will forgive

*1 Corinthians 7:29-31 (32-35)*
## Living in the Interim

1. The form of this world is passing away
2. Give your undivided devotion to the Lord
3. Live free from anxieties in the interim
4. Seek ways to please the Lord

*Mark 1:14-20*
## Jesus Came Preaching

1. Jesus announced that the kingdom of God was at hand
2. Jesus calls for repentance in light of the kingdom
3. Jesus calls people to believe in the gospel
4. Jesus finds four men and calls them to immediately leave their work, family, and personal interests and follow him
5. Hear and obey Christ's call to follow him

**Hymn for Ordinary 3:**  *Once to Every Man and Nation*

**Prayer**

O God who called Jonah to a task of service, help us to hear your call to us so that we may obey at once. May we not be like Jonah who fled in the opposite direction. but like the four disciples who immediately left their nets and followed Jesus. We repent of our sinful ways, claiming the good news of the gospel for our pardon. In light of the coming of your kingdom we turn from self and sin to live in the freedom and joy of forgiveness. We trust your promises to forgive us, and to receive us gladly. Amen

# Epiphany 4     Epiphany 4     Ordinary Time 4

| Common | Lutheran | Roman Catholic |
|---|---|---|
| Deuteronomy 18:15-20 | Deuteronomy 18:15-20 | Deuteronomy 15-20 |
| 1 Corinthians 8:1-13 | 1 Corinthians 8:1-13 | 1 Corinthians 7:32-35 |
| Mark 1:21-28 | Mark 1:21-28 | Mark 1:21-28 |

## Comments on the Lessons

There is consensus on the first reading. In it God promises prophets like Moses for the people to speak God's word to them. Since 1 Corinthians 7:32-35 was an option on the previous Sunday it will not be dealt with again here. There is near consensus on this second reading. There is consensus on the third reading.

## Commentary

*Deuteronomy 18:15-20*

The central thrust of this passage is that the Israelites are not to resort to pagan divination, because God will raise up a prophet or prophets (the word "prophet" is singular collective and thus means many prophets) to reveal his will to them. This "prophet" will be like Moses who is regarded as the prototype of the true prophet. The true prophet is identified by the fact that his prophecy is brought to fulfillment according to God's purpose. However, this delay in testing whether the prophecy is fulfilled or not means that one cannot instantly ferret out true from false prophets.

In order to understand this passage we must look at the verses which precede it in the chapter. In verses 1-3 we have pre-Deuteronomic elements and verse 3 itself contains some of the earliest material which is very matter-of-fact regulations. But beginning with verse 4 we have the hortatory style of "you shall give him" which is specifically Deuteronomic.

Note that in verses 9-22 the comprehensive law about the prophets is very clearly arranged. It may be outlined: (1) verses 9-14 deals with mantic (divination) practices which are not allowed, (2) then positively with the office of a prophet itself which was founded at Sinai (vv. 15-18), and (3) finally with disobedience to the word of the prophet and with the possibility of the corruption of the prophet's office. These statements appear to come from the earliest period of the monarchy.

In verse 16 we learn that the prophet is to mediate God to Israel, to mediate his presence, his words and his authority: "I will raise up for them a prophet like you (Moses) from among their brethren; and I will put my words in his mouth, and he shall speak to them all that I command him."

These prophets are understood by the writer of Deuteronomy to stand in a charismatiac succession from Moses. Much later this text was interpreted eschatologically in pre-Christian circles as a prediction that God would send one final prophet — the "eschatological prophet" as scholars today call him. Jesus' own understanding was in line with this. He understood his mission as one of announcing the dawning of God's kingdom, with himself as the last messenger immediately before its consummation. While this title of prophet after the example of Moses served well in Hebrew circles, when the Christian faith moved into the Greek world the title was replaced by Lord, Son of God and Word.

Deuteronomy outlines the function of this prophet yet to come by saying that he will be for Israel the mouth of God. But we must not think of him in terms of the great prophets who were primarily concerned with judgment. But rather we should conceive of the prophet in terms of the way Moses carried out his office of prophet: interceding, suffering as the representative, actually dying, and therefore this picture of the prophet is in line with that of the suffering servant of Second Isaiah.

There was an old tradition regarding Moses at Sinai in which Israel had begged to spare the necessity of hearing the divine voice directly. Moses was to listen to it and then give Israel God's word. God granted this request. Thus the role of prophet as mediator came into being. From this side of the cross we see that Jesus fulfilled this role of the prophet who was yet to come.

*1 Corinthians 8:1-13 (C, L)*

The question which this passage seeks to answer is "May a Christian eat food consecrated to a pagan god?" The problem arises from the fact that much of the meat sold in market places had come from animals sacrificed to pagan gods in temples. Often slaughterhouses were located next to temples. Parts of the slain animals were burned on the altar fire, but the leftovers were given to priests, or to other worshipers, or were sold in the market place. Some of the worshipers used portions of the food consecrated to a god to give a banquet at home or in the temple in honor of the god. It was believed that in eating the food offered to the god one communed with the god. People were invited to feast in the name of the god.

It is not difficult to see that many Christians had scruples about eating such meat. Paul mentions this in Romans 14:20, "Everything is indeed clean, but it is wrong for any one to make others fall by what he eats; it is right not to eat meat or drink wine or do anything that makes your brother stumble."

On the other hand, many Christians felt superior to such scruples and were contemptuous toward those whose consciences were troubled by eating meat offered to idols. These were the superior people Paul mentions with their "knowledge," but Paul rebukes them for lacking love. " 'Knowledge' puffs up, but love builds up." (v. 1) But these Corinthians held that all the questions associated with eating or not eating meat was of no consequence. Paul apparently is agreeing with people when he quotes their argument in verse 1a and verse 4. But this knowledge was being used by the libertines in Corinth to feel superior to those who were troubled in consience. But Paul's advice on this matter is not consistent with his words in Acts 15:29: ". . . That you abstain from what has been sacrificed to idols and from blood and from what is strangled and from unchastity. If you keep yourselves from these, you will do well. Farewell."

In verses 2, 3 Paul points out that the true blessedness of the Christian life consists not in superior knowledge but in our being known by God. And Paul says that it is in loving God that one is known by God. The test of whether or not one's knowledge is true is that of loving. (13:1) It may well be that verse 3 should read "But if one loves others one is known by God." This meaning is found in the earliest papyrus manuscript and is supported by the context.

A more difficult problem in interpretation is found in verses 4-6 where Paul seems to both deny and to concede the existence of many gods. Apparently the influence of contemporary theology on Paul explains this seeming paradox. The Hebrew was a radical monotheist, at least in the time of Paul, and saw the gods of the pagans as mere idols. Yet Paul was realistic enough not to deny the existence of invisible powers and principalities and authorities. In 2 Corinthians 4:4 Paul even refers to the "god of this world." With this in the culture of Paul's day it is not hard to understand the apparent equivocal teaching concerning those who eat meat offered to idols.

Social clubs and guilds held banquets in pagan temples. (v. 10) Many Christians felt that, since there was no worship of the pagan god involved, there was no valid reason for them not to attend. But Paul warns of the influence this could have on a weaker Christian brother for whom eating meat offered to an idol would be a violation of conscience and destructive. The "weak" to whom Paul refers is the Christian who has an uneasy conscience about anything associated with idol worship.

While for some Christians the purchasing of meat in markets which dealt in meat offered to idols would be of no consequence, for others it was a great obstacle. Some people who ate meat offered to an idol might even relapse into pagan worship. So in order to prevent such temptation, Paul urges that the stronger people refrain from eating meat offered to idols in order to protect the weaker brother and keep him from falling.

One may ignore the pagan gods and assert that they do not exist. But, says Paul, one cannot ignore the Christian brother or sister who has a tender conscience about meat offered to idols.


*Mark 1:21-28*

The city of Capernaum was on the northwest shore of the Sea of Galilee. It apparently was the headquarters of Jesus' mission. The spirit or demon in the man was called unclean because the person with an unclean spirit was separated from the worship of God. Unclean spirit is a common term in the New Testament for a demon. Regarding evil spirits Richardson says, "The general pattern of thought is that the whole world lies in the power of the Evil One (2 John 5:19) and Christians must wage war against supernatural forces of wickedness (Ephesians 6:12) . . . Men and women are unhealthy as sinners or as vexed by evil spirits; hence Jesus frequently exorcised the demons . . ."

(p. 2324, *A Theological Wordbook of the Bible,* New York: The Macmillan Company, 1950).

The man with the unclean spirit cried out, "What have you to do with us, Jesus of Nazareth? Have you come to destroy us? I know who you are, the Holy One of God." (v. 24) Jesus of Nazareth would seem to imply that Jesus was born in Nazareth, since it was the custom of that day to use the birthplace, not the present residence, to identify a person: cf. Paul of Tarsus, Joseph of Arimathea. Mark and John do not know of the Bethlehem tradition apparently. Another possibility is that "of Nazareth" is not a place reference but a party name like Simon the Zealot, since "of Nazareth" literally means "the Nazarene."

The demon asked if Jesus had come to destroy him. It is significant that demons readily recognized Jesus and his power over them. Mark's answer is quite clear that "Yes, he has." This may not have been so much a question as an exclamation, a cry "You have come to destroy us!!!"

The title for Jesus of "the Holy One of God" is an appropriate one, since it indicates Jesus was a superhuman person. Only the demons recognize Jesus as he really is. Mark keeps the reader informed by means of the dialogue with demons.

Jesus rebuked the demon, not for giving him the title "Holy One of God," but in order to suppress the use of the title. Again and again, Jesus speaks to the demons who recognize him and commands them "Be silent." This is the way Mark answers the urgent question of his day of why wasn't Jesus recognized as the Son of God during his earthly ministry. Indeed, he was recognized, says Mark, but only by the demons. And when he was, he silenced them. Mark says that Jesus' fame spread everywhere throughout all the surrounding region of Galilee (v. 28), which is typical of Mark's vagueness about his geographical descriptions.

## Theological Reflections

The Deuteronomy passage foretells the coming of the prophet like Moses, which we see fulfilled in the life and work of Jesus. In Mark's gospel we find that Jesus not only speaks God's word as prophet, but he commands demons and they obey! His words have immediate effect on evil. The demons, in contrast to Jesus' opponents in the flesh, recognize him and obey his command.

Paul deals with the sensitive matter of whether a Christian can, in good conscience, eat meat offered to idols and at the same time show love for a weaker brother who may not be as strong in the faith. To love one's neighbor through refraining from eating meat is commendable, says Paul.

## Homiletical Moves

*Deuteronomy 18:15-20*
### A Prophet Like Moses

1. God has, in Christ, raised up a prophet like Moses
2. Christ has spoken the words the Father has commanded
3. In Christ we have seen God and live!
4. Trust'and follow Christ in whom we live, move and have our being

*I Corinthians 8:1-13 (C, L)*
### Love Builds Up

1. We know that an idol has no real existence
2. But not all possess this knowledge and so their consciences are defiled by eating meat offered to idols
3. Take care lest your liberty become a stumbling block to others
4. If one loves his brother/sister that person is known to God
5. Therefore, love your neighbor as yourself

*This Preacher's Choice*

*Mark 1:21-28*
### The Holy One Commands Unclean Spirits!

1. Jesus taught as one who had authority in the synagogues
2. The unclean spirit recognized that Jesus was the Holy One of God

3. Jesus rebukes the unclean spirit and commands him to come out
4. The unclean spirit comes out
5. Jesus' fame spreads throughout the region of Galilee.
6. Let Christ free you from unclean spirits of sin

**Hymn for Ordinary Time 4:**   *All Hail the Power of Jesus' Name*

**Prayer**

*O God who has sent Jesus, the Holy One, into the world as prophet to mediate your Word to us, make us sensitive to hear that Word. May we not only hear the Word but gladly obey the Word. Help us to express love for our neighbor by not doing things which will cause our neighbor to stumble and fall. May we express love for our neighbor and so be known by you. May we never trust knowledge, but rather follow the way of love which builds up. Amen*

# Epiphany 5    Epiphany 5    Ordinary Time 5

| Common | Lutheran | Roman Catholic |
|---|---|---|
| Job 7:1-7 | Job 7:1-7 | Job 7:1-4, 6-7 |
| 1 Corinthians 9:16-23 | 1 Corinthians 9:16-23 | 1 Corinthians 9:16-19, 22-23 |
| Mark 1:29-39 | Mark 1:29-39 | Mark 1:29-39 |

## Comments on the Lessons

There is consensus on the first reading from Job which laments the inevitability of human suffering. There is virtual consensus on the second reading. Note that verses 20-21 are an integral part of the passage. There is consensus on the third reading.

## Commentary

The book of Job is a unique book written in the late sixth or early fifth century B.C. It is composite in nature and is composed of prose and poetry by multiple authors. In its external form it is like other literary compositions in the ancient world. If we take the prose and poetry of Job together, the book is best characterized as a disputation. In this case, a prose narrative introduces a problem, which is then dealt with in debate form, and the deity ultimately gives a resolution. But if we consider the poem in isolation, the term ''lament'' best describes the initial dialogue. There are parallels to Job from the ancient Near East which function as a model of an answered lament. Such composition offers examples for others who are engulfed in suffering for which there is no suitable explanation. The therapeutic effect of such texts comes from the individual sufferer discovering appropriate responses to his or her own suffering and thus profiting from the experience of others.

The author(s) of Job addresses two aspects of a single problem: one theoretical and the other practical. The first problem concerns the question of divine justice or theodicy. The second deals with the way in which a person responds to suffering. Upon reflection, we see that these are the fundamental questions of reality with which we continue to wrestle today (note recent books seeking to explain why bad things happen to ''good'' people, etc.). Such questions as can faith survive in a world where assurances of rational order have vanished, and what is the appropriate behavior with which to respond in such a harsh environment?

Job was written to deal with the assumption of the ancient world that said a virtuous deed was rewarded and a wicked act was punished. This was an axiom of the principle of a harmonious universe. Job and his friends are of a common mind in taking for granted the dogma of reward and punishment. Although Job calls this dogma into question his argument against the deity loses all its force once the dogma is discarded. This loss results from the breaking of the causal connection between sin and suffering.

The dominant theme in the speeches of Job's friends is the inscrutable divine act. In this lies a direct link with the character of the Deity's conduct found in the prose section. The sovereign of the universe *is not subject to human ideas about what constitutes justice,* and this is the message which the writer declares with great force.

Notice in reading the book of Job that Job does not receive a single answer to his relentless questioning regarding divine justice. The power of faith transformed mystery into a relationship with God that acknowledged divine sovereignty and human mortality. The problem of God's justice is not resolved, but humans are assured that they may bring their doubts and even their accusations before the sovereign God, fully assured that their doubts and accusations will not bring down God's wrath on them.

The other problem with which the Book of Job deals is one for which a practical answer may not be found. This is the problem of undeserved suffering. What should one's response be to suffering which one doesn't deserve? The book presents several possible answers from Job and his friends. Job's final submission is exactly what his friends have encouraged him to do: confess your sins and submit to God's will. But Job gives an additional response to the question which the poet seems to recommend to readers: pour out your soul to God. Job does this in anger and desperation, but he directs his passion to God. He is able to do this because he is convinced that a relationship with God permits honest expression of feelings and thoughts, negative as well as positive. But note carefully that the poet avoids his hint that Job could always depend upon God to answer when summoned. To do so would have resulted in a dogma that enslaves God, similar to the presumption about the operation of the principle of reward and punishment.

In the particular verses of the pericope of Job we find that Job explores the universal human condition as one in which the general human lot, shared by Job, is one of misery. While Job's friend Eliphaz attributes human misery to sinfulness, Job attributes it to other causes. He sees human life as lived out in the conditions of hard service. The word "saba," which is translated "hard service" in 7:1, usually refers in the Bible to military service. It appears 480 times, and only in Job 7:1 and a few other pieces does the word refer to slave service. Job and Second Isaiah (Isaiah 40:2) share this extremely rare usage. This suggests that it would be appropriate to exegete the passage as one in which the plight of Job in his sufferings is compared to Israel in exile. The interpreter would do well to explore the themes of each book in the light of the other.

The miserable conditions of human life as a slave in 7:1-6 is followed in 7:7-21 by an accusation against God for this harsh treatment. This tends to confirm the suspicion that in 3:17-19 the terms "wicked, taskmaster, and master" refer, in a veiled fashion, to God. Job raises and deals with some of the most basic problems of the human condition. While Job's answers may not be the answers we want, they are the answers which the pre-Christ Hebrew found. The Christian interpreter must deal with undeserved suffering in light of the cross and Christ's death for us, the sinless for the sinful. The cross points to God as a God of suffering love who suffers with his creatures, who loves the sinner and redeems the sinner at the cost of his only Son, Christ the Savior. The Christian preacher is led to the foot of the cross for the ultimate answer to the problem of the innocent suffering and the justice of God.

### 1 Corinthians 9:16-23 (C, L)
### 1 Corinthians 9:16-19, 22-23 (RC)

Paul says he deserves no credit for preaching the Gospel. He cannot help but preach the Gospel! Paul does take pride, however, in preaching without compensation and the ground of this pride he will not give up. Paul evidently had been criticized by some for not letting his converts pay him for his preaching. They see this as reflecting a lack of confidence in his authority as an apostle. He is entrusted with a commission he says. Paul agrees that he has a right to ask for payment. We know that he actually did accept money from churches in Macedonia. But there were particular unique reasons for his not accepting payment for preaching at Corinth. This is another example of his becoming all things to all people in order that he might save some.

To answer the question of why receiving support would hinder Paul's goal we must look at what was happening in Corinth. False teachers turned up at Corinth who sponged on the congregation and nearly got a following from them. Paul very definitely does not want to give any hint of being a wandering preacher like his opponents. If they associated him with the wandering free-loaders then the Corinthians would misunderstand his Gospel. They might confuse his preaching with the work of a miracle worker or "another Christ," but not see him as preaching Christ crucified.

In verses 19-23 Paul picks up again the theme from chapter 8: the Christian is free except from the duty to love. We must read this section within its context to properly understand it. Paul went so far in his efforts to win people to the Gospel that he was charged with hypocrisy, as when he went to Jerusalem for the last time and appeared in the temple as a Jewish-Christian. Paul is here focusing on consideration and tact and this should not be misunderstood as cowardice or compromise. Paul at every point identifies himself with others so that the Gospel may be preached more effectively. As a wise missionary Paul takes his place beside those he would win for Christ.

In verse 23 we have a transition from Paul's renunciation for the sake of others to self-discipline for his own sake. (vv. 24-27) In next Sunday's Epistle reading we will deal with the latter passage in C and L lectionaries.

### Mark 1:29-39

In last week's Gospel reading we saw that Jesus began his ministry in Capernaum, according to Mark, with a day of healing, beginning with the healing of the man with an unclean spirit. This apparently was on a sabbath. Now we have additional healings on the same day: of Simon's mother-in-law, and all who were sick or possessed with demons. The next morning, a great while before day, Jesus rose and went out to a lonely place to pray. He went on to other towns to preach in synagogues and to cast out demons throughout Galilee.

Jesus' healing of Simon's mother-in-law is a second example of Jesus' power to make whole. Note that Jesus does not use some magical formula in order to call down some supernatural power but rather he himself is the power to heal. Because of this healing we know that Peter was married, for he had a mother-in-law. Since Simon Peter lived in Capernaum, this may have been the reason Jesus made his headquarters there. Being a disciple of Jesus did not mean repudiating normal human relationships. It seems that Peter's wife accompanied him on his preaching journeys, as did the wives of the other apostles.

Notice how Mark describes two specific healings and then goes on to say that Jesus healed all who were brought to him who were sick or possessed by demons. The whole city gathered about the door of the house to witness the healings. But Jesus did not permit the demons to speak because they knew him. He did not want the Messianic secret revealed too soon, which would have aborted his ministry. While the demons recognized Jesus, only the centurion at the foot of the cross can truly confess him as the Son of God, because the Jesus he sees is not the wonder-worker but the crucified Savior.

The miracles play an important role in Mark's Gospel. Miracles may be divided into four classes: (1) exorcisms, (2) healing miracles, (3) raisings of the dead, (4) nature miracles. How important miracles are for Mark is indicated by the fact that forty-seven percent of the verses of the first ten chapters deal directly or indirectly with miracles. According to Jesus, his miracles are the activity of God, wrought by God's Spirit which are manifestations of his kingdom. The miracles signify that Satan has been bound and that those whom Satan has bound have been loosed. The miracles are also an expression of God's pity for his people. But the miracles are not compelling proofs of Jesus' divinity for we read of the cities which do not repent, and even the disciples can misunderstand them. The true significance of the miracles is recognized only by faith.

Jesus' withdrawal to pray very early in the morning, a great while before day, reveals something of Jesus' own prayer life and the strength he drew from communion with the Heavenly Father. Peter and those with him did not appreciate his need for prayer and were activists who sought out Jesus to tell him the crowds were looking for him. Jesus was renewed by prayer in order to set out preaching and healing throughout the area of Galilee. Notice that Jesus preached in the synagogues as he did in his home village of Nazareth. And he went about working the miracles of casting out demons.

## Theological Reflections

It appears that the reading from Job was chosen for this Sunday in order to have a background of human misery for the healing work of Jesus described in the Gospel. It is from the miseries that Job describes that Jesus has come to save human beings, then and now.

In the epistle Paul deals with his call to preach the Gospel and to adapt himself to all kinds of people in order to become more effective in winning people to the Gospel. He does it all for the sake of the Gospel, the Gospel of Jesus who came to save us from sin and its misery. In Jesus crucified we see the justice of God revealed in the mercy of God, and the mercy of God revealed in the justice of God. In the Christ on the cross we see the divine answer to the mystery of why the innocent suffer as Christ the sinless One suffers for sinners. God himself is a God of suffering love and those who suffer do not suffer alone. God is with them in the depths of suffering. To suffer is to participate with Christ in his suffering and in doing so to find meaning in innocent suffering.

## Homiletical Moves

*Job 7:1-7*
## Our Hard Service on Earth

1. Human beings have a life of hard service on earth
2. Our life is as a breath and may come to an end without hope
3. But in Christ we find strength and courage when we suffer
4. God in Christ suffered and is with us in our suffering
5. Come to Christ all you who labor and are heavy-laden and he will give you rest

*1 Corinthians 9:16-23*
## Woe Is Me If I Do Not Preach the Gospel

1. Paul is entrusted with a commission to preach
2. Though free in Christ, Paul makes himself all things to all people in order to win some
3. Paul does all his identifying with people for the sake of the Gospel that he might share its blessings
4. Let us become more faithful witnesses to the Gospel

### This Preacher's Choice

*Mark 1:29-39*
## Jesus Came to Preach and Heal!

1. Jesus went to a lonely place before dawn to pray
2. Jesus healed the sick and those with demons
3. Jesus went throughout Galilee preaching and casting out demons
4. Invite Christ to cast evil powers out of your life and heal your brokenness

**Hymn for Ordinary Time 5:**  *We Sing the Mighty Power of God*

**Prayer**

*O God who has revealed yourself in Jesus Christ as a God of suffering love who is with us in our suffering. We praise and adore you. We thank you for those like Paul who preached the Gospel. May we have the grace to identify with those to whom we witness the good news of Jesus Christ. May we be willing to walk in their shoes. Grant us the courage to come boldly before the throne of grace in prayer as Jesus did in order to commune with you and gain strength for our work in your kingdom. In the name of Christ. Amen*

| Epiphany 6 | Epiphany 6 | Ordinary Time 6 |

| Common | Lutheran | Roman Catholic |
| --- | --- | --- |
| 2 Kings 5:1-14 | 2 Kings 5:1-14 | Leviticus 13:1-2, 44-46 |
| 1 Corinthians 9:24-27 | 1 Corinthians 9:24-27 | 1 Corinthians 10:31—11:1 |
| Mark 1:40-45 | Mark 1:40-45 | Mark 1:40-45 |

### Comments on the Lessons

The (C) (L) reading from 2 Kings is chosen rather than the Leviticus of the (RC) lectionary, because of its prophetic quality in contrast to the legal concerns of Leviticus 13. The 2 Kings passage is the account of the healing and cleansing of Naaman the leper who was a Syrian. The Leviticus reading deals with legal requirements for cleansing lepers. The 1 Corinthians 9:24-27 reading is chosen because of its good content and unity, which compares the Christian life to a race and the discipline involved. The thrust of the (RC) reading is glorifying God in all one does. There is consensus on the Markan reading which is an account of Jesus healing a leper. This reading may account for the selection of the Leviticus reading on leprosy. Leprosy was a catch-all term for any number of skin diseases and included molds, etc. Therefore, our understanding of the biblical term must not be confined to Hansen's disease only.

### Commentary

*2 Kings 5:1-14 (C, L)*

In the first movement of the story Naaman, a commander of the army of the king of Syria, who was held in high favor, is informed by a Hebrew slave girl that there was a prophet in Israel (Elisha) who could heal him. She waited on Naaman's wife and told her Elisha in Israel could cure him. Naaman is given a letter of introduction to the king of Israel. But Israel had suffered greatly from Syrian raiders and so the king of Israel takes offense at the letter. He suspected the king of Syria was making a quarrel with him.

The next movement is Elisha's intervention to say he would see Naaman: "Let him come now to me, that he may know that there is a prophet in Israel." When Naaman arrives at Elisha's house with his horses and chariots, Elisha refuses to see him in person, but sends a messenger with instructions for Naaman to wash in the Jordan river seven times as the way to be cured of his leprosy. This aloofness of Elisha incenses Naaman, the honored army commander. Naaman expresses national pride in the rivers of Syria which he thinks are better than all the waters of Israel. He wonders aloud why he could not wash in Syrian water and be cleansed. He turned away from Elisha's house in a rage. But his advisers calm his anger and hurt pride and counsel him to follow the instructions. Naaman expected Elisha to send him off to do some great thing to get cured, or expected Elisha to come out and call on the name of the Lord God, wave his hand over the leprous spot and cure it. Instead, Naaman is given a simple act: to wash seven times in the Jordan. Seven was the complete number. Washing seven times indicates completeness, wholeness, perfection.

If Elisha's instructions proved ineffective, it would be Elisha, not Naaman, who would lose face. Naaman accepted the advice, went to the Jordan and dipped himself seven times and was cured. His flesh was "restored like the flesh of a little child, and he was clean." (v. 14)

Notice that neither the name of the king of Syria or king of Israel is mentioned. From the story it is assumed that the Syrians held the upper hand. The value of the gift sent with Naaman could be as high as $80,000. There are a number of New Testament accounts of the healing of leprosy, including the one in the Markan reading for today.

*Leviticus 13:1-2, 44-46 (RC)*

As noted in "Comments on the Lessons" earlier, leprosy in the Bible is a generic term which includes various skin diseases, including what is known as leprosy today, Hansen's disease, and blemishes and molds in houses and clothing. God gives Moses instructions on diagnosing leprosy and taking the leper to Aaron the priest or one of his sons, the priests. (vv. 1-2) Such a man is unclean and the priest must so pronounce him. The leper must then wear torn clothes, appearing thus like a mourner, and must go into isolation. He must let his hair hang loose and shall cover his upper lip and cry, "Unclean, unclean." Letting the hair hang loose would make the leper appear as though dead. The judgment that a person with leprosy is unclean is based on the belief that, since the person was ritually impure, the defilement could be transmitted to others in the community. Notice that, even after being cured, the leper was not officially "clean" until ritually purified. The disease described in verse 3 is leprosy, which involved white hair and infiltrated lesions. Such an infection involved the deeper layers of the epidermis.

In the Markan lesson for today we will see how Jesus healed a leper, a sign of the Messiah who could perform miracles and heal diseases.

### *1 Corinthians 9:24-27 (C, L)*

Paul is fond on drawing on sports events for illustrating the Christian life. He would be familiar with the Isthmian games held at Corinth. Thinking about these various athletic contests led Paul to mix metaphors of foot race and boxing as he urges his readers to discipline their lives. This writer visited both Corinth and the home of the Olympian Games, Olympus, Greece, where the great athletic contests of the ancient world were held. Starting blocks for runners have been unearthed and can be seen by visitors. Paul's use of illustrations from sporting events suggests to the preacher today that apt illustrations can be drawn from current sports which have captured the attention of his or her congregation. One outstanding published minister always included an illustration from golf in his sermons. People of all ages can appreciate such illustrations of discipline and heroics. This little paragraph is just packed with figures from athletic contests which make his message come alive.

He begins with the foot race where, obviously, only one person can win. Paul wants his hearers to run with the same determination, to be goal-oriented! He urges them to be intentional about their Christian living and to discipline themselves daily in order to reach their goal.

While Paul urged his hearers to run the race and win the prize, he must also have realized that in the church all can win the prize. Writing to the church at Philippi, Paul says, "Not that I have already obtained this or am already perfect; but I press on to make it my own, because Christ Jesus has made me his own. I press on toward the goal for the prize of the upward call of God in Christ Jesus. (3:12, 14) Paul cites the vigorous discipline of the runner who seeks to win the prize. Like runners in the Boston Marathon or other races, the Christian must exercise self-control and keep his or her eyes set on the goal. But athletic contests award prizes which perish, an ivy or pine wreath, but the Christian faith awards the imperishable life in the resurreation to those who persevere in the faith.

Paul says that the runner must not run aimlessly but with the goal always in mind. Here, Paul shifts from the second person to the first and from the metaphor of running to boxing. He says he does not shadow box, merely beating the air. But he pummels his body and subdues it in order to win the prize. Our real opponent, says Paul, is not flesh and blood, however. "For we are not contending against flesh and blood, but against the principalities, against the powers, against the world rulers of this present darkness, against the spiritual hosts of wickedness in the heavenly places." (6:12) We should not blame others for our failures, but recognize that we are often our own worst enemy and that supernatural forces tempt and lead us into evil. Paul uses a technical term from boxing for a knockout blow. But it is a blow delivered to himself.

Then Paul shifts the figure of speech to the herald announcing the results of games, or calling the contestants to their places. He identifies himself with the herald, and this term is one of the regular ones used for preaching the Gospel. It is the most fitting comparison of all, as Paul compares himself with one of the officials of a sports contest who could be ruled out of the contest. Paul illustrated that "the medium is the message" as he lived out a disciplined life, pressing on toward the goal of the prize of the imperishabie resurrection life. He disciplined his body and life so that he might win rather than be disqualified.

### *1 Corinthians 10:31—11:1 (RC)*

Earlier Paul had dealt with eating meat offered to idols and the question of Christian liberty and conscience. Here Paul returns to the topic of chapter 8. Now he draws his final conclusions. He says that correct eating and drinking are not enough. Rather, the whole life of the believer should be one that glorifies God. ''Do all to the glory of God,'' (v. 31) says Paul. The aim of Christian liberty is not to give offense to those who are weak. Paul divides human beings into three groups: Jews, Greeks and the church of God. The first two had been isolated and the church of God had preached Christ crucified to them. The purpose is that many may be saved. His last appeal is to his own example as a person who seeks to imitate Christ. The community of faith is asked to imitate the Christ who dwells in Paul.

Paul says ''Be imitators of me'' and does this without arrogance, because he himself imitates Christ. This is much more than following the ethical example of Christ. Note in Paul's writings and life that he shows little knowledge of or interest in the earthly life of Jesus or Jesus' tradition. Rather, he seeks to imitate the life of Christ who came down from heaven, humbled himself and suffered and died for others. Notice how the life of Paul reproduces the same kind of self-emptying, humiliation and suffering. See Philippians 2:6-11 for the classic description of Christ's self-emptying.

### Mark 1:40-45

In this brief miracle story we find the basic three step pattern common to such stories: (1) the diagnosis, indicated by the fact the man was a leper and asked for healing, (2) the cure by word and touch, and (3) the demonstration by going to the high priest as prescribed by Levitical law (see reading from Leviticus for today). Notice that the man is told to say nothing to anyone about his cure. This is clearly a Markan redaction in which the Messianic secret is emphasized. But the leper, as we might expect of a healed person, disobeys the command and his cure becomes the talk of the village. As a result, Jesus could no longer enter any town but was out in the country. And people from everywhere came to him. Mark uses commands to silence here and with the demon, etc., in order to forestall any misunderstanding of Jesus as Messiah and to point to the greatest miracle of all — the cross. But the command to keep the healing secret is disobeyed and this puzzles us. It appears we are dealing with a characteristic part of Mark's theory of the messianic secret — it is penetrated again and again. Mark seems to want to show that while the messiahship of Jesus is indeed a mystery it must not be revealed too soon, but can only be understood in the light of the cross. But at the same time it cannot be fully suppressed but must come out. And it does come out in the preaching of the church after the resurrection, which the compulsive telling of his cure by the leper foreshadows. Note carefully that we, at this point, are not dealing with history as we know it but with an artificial construction with a theological purpose created by Mark.

Notice that the leper kneels before Jesus, as an act of homage and as a posture of supplication before a man of God. Here it expresses the earnest seeking for healing of the leper. The leper is sure Jesus can heal him, if he is willing to do so. Jesus was moved with pity and stretched out his hand, touched him and said, ''I will; be clean.'' Mark's emphasis is on Jesus' power to heal. Mark's main intent is on who Jesus was rather than on what he taught. The phrase ''moved with pity'' may not be as simple as it seems. It is probably a substitution for ''being angry'' which appears in some ancient MSS. It is omitted in later accounts in Matthew and Luke. It seems to have been difficult for ancient interpreters to deal with the notion of Jesus being angry, just as it is difficult for us. While there are a number of reasons why Jesus was angry, it is most likely he was angry with Satan for disfiguring the leper with his illness. All disease was thought to be the devil's work, and in his healings Jesus is waging war against Satan's power.

## Theological Reflections

The power of God to heal Naaman the leper through Elisha the prophet is a theme also in the Markan account of Jesus healing the leper. Leviticus is chiefly concerned with the legal aspects of leprosy and being declared cured. The two passages from the letter to the Corinthians have a common focus: the goal of the Christian life. Paul urges his readers to discipline themselves as a runner or boxer undergoes training and discipline in order to win. In the second passage Paul urges his readers to imitate him as he imitates Christ. Paul imitates Christ in his self-emptying, his humiliation, and suffering. In the passage from Mark, Jesus heals a leper, commands him to tell no one but he immediately tells everyone! So Jesus could not openly enter a town but was out in the country. Even so the people came to him from every quarter. The thrust here is on Jesus' power to heal. It appears that Jesus was angry toward Satan for disfiguring the leper, rather than being moved with pity, since some ancient MSS read ''anger.'' God's power at work in healing human illness and the goal of Christ-like living are two central themes of the passages for today.

## Homiletical Moves

*2 Kings 5:1-14 (C, L)*
### God Heals Naaman the Leper

1. Naaman, a Syrian army commander, who has leprosy is referred to Elisha the prophet in Israel
2. Naaman expects a dramatic healing by Elisha
3. Elisha commands Naaman by a messenger to dip himself seven times in the Jordan
4. Naaman is incensed at first, but his advisors counsel him to obey
5. Naaman dips himself seven times and his flesh is made clean by God's healing power
6. God has made us clean (forgiven) by baptism, so let us live as new men and women!

*Leviticus 13:1-2, 44-46 (RC)*
### Leprosy, Living Death in the Ancient World

1. The person with a skin disease is examined by a priest
2. If the person has leprosy the person is excluded from the human community, and wears his hair loose like one who is dead, and torn clothes like one in mourning
3. God in Christ came to heal the outcasts of society, lepers, disfigured, broken persons, so that they might be restored to community and have life again.
4. Trust in Christ and he will heal your brokenness and restore you to life in community

*1 Corinthians 9:24-27 (C, L)*
### So Run That You May Obtain the Prize!

1. Runners discipline themselves and go for the prize in a race
2. Christians are to exercise self-control as they seek, not a perishable prize, but the imperishable prize of the resurrection life
3. Knock yourself out to subdue your body and thus run the race of the Christian life and not be disqualified in the end
4. So run the race of life that you may receive the prize!

*1 Corinthians 10:31—11:1 (RC)*
### Do All to the Glory of God!

1. Give no offense to anyone so that many may be saved
2. Do all to the glory of God
3. Be imitators of Paul as he is of Christ in self-emptying, humiliation and suffering

*This Preacher's Choice*

*Mark 1:40-45*
### The Leper Made Clean

1. A leper came to Jesus seeking healing
2. Jesus moved with pity (or anger at Satan) heals him
3. Jesus commands the leper to tell no one but he tells everyone
4. Jesus could no longer openly enter a town
5. Jesus was out in the country and the people came to him from every quarter
6. Come to Christ and you will find healing for your life, then follow him

**Hymn for Epiphany 6:**  *O For a Thousand Tongues to Sing*

**Prayer**

*O God who healed Naaman the leper and who healed the leper who came to Jesus, heal us of our brokenness and sin. When we are alienated from others, restore us to community. when we have lost sight of the prize of the Christian race of life, grant us a fresh vision of our goal. May we not run aimlessly through life, or box the air, but rather discipline our total lives so that we may win the prize of the imperishable life through the resurrection of Christ. Help us to do all to your glory and to be imitators of Christ. Amen*

# Epiphany 7     Epiphany 7     Ordinary Time 7

| Common | Lutheran | Roman Catholic |
|---|---|---|
| Isaiah 43:18-25 | Isaiah 43:18-23 | Isaiah 43:18-19, 21-22, 24-25 |
| 2 Corinthians 1:18-22 | 2 Corinthians 1:18-22 | 2 Corinthians 18-22 |
| Mark 2:1-12 | Mark 2:1-12 | Mark 2:1-12 |

## Comments on the Lessons

There is virtual consensus on the first reading. Verse 20 is omitted by (RC) but provides important descriptive imagery. Verse 23 is also needed for cumulative effect of the poetry. Isaiah identifies the ''new thing'' that God is doing as forgiveness. (vv. 19, 25) There is consensus on both second and third readings.

## Commentary

*Isaiah 43:18-25 (C, L)*
*Isaiah 43:18-19, 11-22, 24-25 (RC)*

Second Isaiah spoke this prophecy while many Israelites were in exile in Babylon, where God had sent them in punishment for Israel's sins. But now the exile was about to end and God was going to bring them home in a second Exodus. The former things (v. 18) refer to the Exodus from Egypt. God is going to send to Babylon and break open the prison and lead Israel home. In verses 18, 19 there is a concentration on the new thing God is about to do. The stress on not remembering the former thing is another way of saying, ''Stop looking mournfully backward and clinging to what has gone before and turn to open your minds to the fact that a new, miraculous act of God is breaking in from the future! The future should be your goal, not a dwelling on the past.'' This new thing God is about to do is something Israel had given up hope for or belief in. She thought that God's saving acts were over. This new thing is about to happen and Israel herself will experience it.

Israel's return to Palestine, this ''new thing'' promised by God will be through the wilderness. The description in 40:3 is part of this new Exodus story: ''A voice cries: 'In the wilderness prepare the way of the Lord, make straight in the desert a highway for our God'.'' The future remembrance will not be of exodus from Egypt but of the new redemption. Water in the desert (v. 20) was one of the great gifts God gave Israel as she wandered in the wilderness. God's provisions will be bountiful in this new Exodus. Note the change from the second to the third person in verse 20b to verse 21.

Notice the contrast between Israel's actions in sacrifice in Isaiah 1:10-15 and 43:22-28. In the first passage Israel is described as giving great attention to the details of sacrifice and worship: ''I have had enough of burnt offerings of rams and the fat of fed beasts . . . Bring no more vain offerings; incense is an abomination to me . . .'' (vv. 11, 13) But because Israel was sinful, all her sacrifices were not acceptable. But in the latter passage no sacrifice is offered. It could not be in exile. But Israel remains sinful. So from this we see that sacrifice neither could atone for sin nor avert judgment. Nor does sacrifice merit redemption. Sin is sin and remains the same. The only way of dealing with it is by God's free grace and forgiveness, ''I, I am He who blots out your transgressions for my own sake, and I will not remember your sins.'' (v. 25) God forgives sins for his own sake, which indicates not self-concern but God's unmerited grace, the ''agape'' of the New Testament. This is a necessity of God's character, the nature of his divine love.

We find here (43:22-28 and in 50:1-3) trial speeches which resemble disputations. In them God opposes his people Israel. The central thrust of these trial speeches is a claim. Israel charges God with not being faithful to the covenant, and God answers, ''Therefore I profaned the princes of the sanctuary, I delivered Jacob to utter destruction and Israel to reviling.'' (v. 28) The argument of Israel which lies behind verses 22-24a goes like this as Israel protests to God: ''How could you do this to us, when we have been so faithful in bringing our sacrifaces to you?'' God replies by saying in so many words, ''In all your pious sacrifices you did not really serve me. Instead, I was obliged to serve you . . . You have burdened me with your sin, you have wearied me with your iniquities.'' (v. 24) The trial speech proper begins with verse 26.

While God challenges Israel to summon him to court, this is not done. Second Isaiah sees himself as in the succession of the pre-exilic prophets of doom. He underlines what other prophets before had said about Israel's worship having lost touch with reality. And with this goes a dismissal of the plea made by Israel in her accusation against God. While Israel claims to have truly served God with sacrifices, God says Israel did not really serve him. Rather, Israel made God her servant! She turns the relationship upside down. Instead of being God's servant Israel burdens God with her sins and makes him her servant! There is a play on words in the Hebrew which is lost in translation, a play on the word ''abad'' meaning to serve or to work. God says to Israel, ''I did not make you work (serve), instead you made me work (serve). (vv. 23b, 24b) God charges Israel with making him into a servant with her sins, But this reversal of roles is really impossible according to the Old Testament understanding of God. For God is Lord. The very nature of the divinity is lordship. But when Israel makes God into a servant, if he is made to serve Israel by burdening God with her sins and iniquities, then his divinity is taken from him. In verse 24 we see this reversal for just a quick glance, but in verse 25 this immediately changes as God asserts his lordship as the master who can blot out Israel's sin. Israel cannot force God to carry her sins or forgive them. Rather, God acts according to his divine nature to forgive them.

In verse 25 we see the thrust of this verse to be the vanity of Israel's worship and her mistaken history. But at the same time there is the central proclamation of God's forgiveness! This is the good news in contrast to what precedes and follows. God forgives for his own sake. He forgives, not because as the French philosopher, Voltaire, said ''That is God's business,'' but because God's nature is grace, grace revealed later in the Christ on the cross dying for the sins of the world. This is not cheap grace, as Bonhoeffer warned, but costly grace, which cost God the death of his Son. And it must not be taken lightly or cheaply.

### 2 Corinthians 1:18-22

Some Corinthians apparently had accused Paul of vacillating in decisions and saying both Yes and No at the same time. They thought him guilty of ''manic indecisiveness'' as someone has described contemporary problems of personality. This passage was written to Corinth when the crisis there was over and the relationship with the church and Paul restored. But during the crisis Paul had twice changed his travel plans. First, he had paid a quick visit to Corinth, but this visit sadly failed to effect the changes Paul sought at Corinth. Then he postponed visiting them again in order for Titus to have an opportunity to straighten things out. It was this frequent change of plans that was the basis for the charge that Paul was not dependable but rather fickle. In verses 15-22 Paul denies that he has been fickle and says that, because of his very position as a minister of the faithful God he could not be fickle. Then in the following passage he gives his reason for his change of plans. (1:23—2:4) At every stage of his plans Paul says that his decisions were made in the full confidence that he and the Corinthians were bound together then and in the future: ''as you have understood in part, that you can be proud of us as we can be of you, on the day of the Lord Jesus.'' (v. 14) The change of plans had led to two charges against Paul: (1) that he was vacillating and not serious and responsible in his words and deeds, and (2) that he was like a worldly man who is selfish, acting without commitment to God.

This accusation hurt Paul so much that he put himself under oath (v. 25) to defend his actions. ''As surely as God is faithful'' (v. 18) is the basic defense Paul uses in answering the charges against him. He writes of the fulfillment of God's promises to his people in the past. While this may seem digression from his major defense, Paul wants to undergird his actions with theological motives. Paul says that his faithfulness is based in his grateful response to God, who has called him to be an apostle and who has graciously acted in the gospel of Jesus Christ. This has been sealed by the Spirit in their hearts as a guarantee. The ''seal'' may refer to baptism by which believers were set apart and marked by God as his own, and given God's protection, as well as his call to be an apostle. Paul uses a legal figure of a guarantee in referring to the Spirit. (v. 22) It was the first installment of a payment which bound the purchaser to complete the payment of the full price. Paul is saying that God, in giving his Spirit at the beginning of the Christian life, at baptism, has bound himself to give all the other blessings that belong to complete salvation. The thrust of Paul's argument is that since he is thus sealed by God's Spirit he is established and supported by God and therefore cannot be justly accused of being fickle and of vacillating. Also, the gift of the Spirit after Christ's resurrection was a promise and pledge from God of the New Age that is breaking in from the future.

Paul declares that the Son of God, Jesus Christ, whom he preached, was not Yes and No, but in him it is always Yes. (v. 19) And he goes on to say that all of God's promises find their Yes in Christ. And for this reason, says Paul, we affirm "Amen" through him to the glory of God. Amen means "so be it" and may well have been the response given by worshipers upon hearing God's promises read in scripture as well as in preaching. The Amen is the expression of grateful response on the part of God's people to his saving work. Amen, a Hebrew word meaning "so be it," was taken over into Greek as a term of affirmation.

Notice that the Trinity is referred to in verse 21 where Paul writes, "But it is God who establishes us with you in Christ, and has commissioned us . . . and given us his Spirit." God, Christ and the Spirit are united in the divine work of redemption. While this is not a formal statement of the doctrine of the Trinity, it expresses the faith and experience of the early church out of which it molded the doctrine of the Trinity.

*Mark 2:1-12*

While some scholars think this is a composite unit (vv. 1-5a, 10b-12), giving the account of a miracle story with verses 5b-10a, being inserted and combined with it, this belief may be due to a failure to recognize the very close connection between the healing of sickenss and the forgiveness of sins. When this connection is recognized, then there is no need to posit the combining of two passages. Rather, the whole hangs together nicely, except for 10a which may be viewed as Mark's own comment in parentheses. This may have its source in Peter.

The setting is a house in which Jesus is preaching the word to those assembled. The word refers to everything Jesus had to say to people about God's purposes. The house was so crowded that the paralytic carried by four friends on a pallet could not get into the house. So they removed the roof and let him down to the place where Jesus was preaching in the house. The roof was most likely formed by beams and rafters across which matting, branches and twigs, covered by earth were laid and packed hard by foot. It was probably a one-story house and access to the roof would be by an outside staircase.

"Their faith" refers not only to the faith of Jesus' hearers but also to the faith of the paralytic. Jesus usually looked for faith in the person who was sick and sought healing. Jesus' declaration, "My son, your sins are forgiven" (v. 5) is an authoritative word. This is what arouses the anger of the scribes sitting there. They called it blasphemy since Jesus claimed the power to forgive sins, a power reserved for God alone. It seems at first sight easier to declare forgiveness of sins which cannot be verified than to restore a sick man to health, but Jesus voluntarily undergoes the test. Notice that verse 12 refers to the miracle of healing only and not to the forgiveness of sins. Son of man (v. 10) is a title Jesus used of himself and for his hearers this may have had one of two meanings: (1) that Jesus was calling himself a typical human being which was the common meaning of "son of", or (2) that Jesus linked himself to the figure in Daniel 7:13-14 who was thought of in popular thought as the coming Messiah. Jesus does not fully make known his own understanding of this term. Each meaning alone or even together could have appealed to him. This may be another one of the ways in which Jesus so typically spoke so that his hearers had to determine their own personal attitude toward him. This would be a process of their coming to understand his words. The most striking thing about Jesus' use of this title is that after Caesarea Philippi, he reinterprets it in terms of the suffering servant of Isaiah. This means that the "son of man" of apocalytic thought becomes king only through suffering!

## Theological Reflections

God's promise of a new Exodus back to the holy land from exile in Babylon, a new thing, includes also forgiveness of sins. God accuses Israel of not calling on him or bringing him sacrifices, but rather has burdened him with their sins. But he promises to blot out their transgressions for his own sake, for this is his nature. Paul defends himself from accusations of those who say he is fickle by pointing out that God is a faithful God who has spoken a divine Yes in Jesus Christ and has sealed Paul for service by the Spirit. Jesus heals the paralytic let down into the house. But first he forgives his sins. Jesus recognizes an organic connection between disease and sin, and makes war on both. The healing is a sign of the forgiveness of sins.

## Homiletical Moves

*Isaiah 43:18-25 (C, L)*
*Isaiah 43:18-19, 21-22, 24-25 (RC)*
### God's Promise to Do a New Thing

1. God tells Israel to remember not former things
2. God is doing a new thing, is bringing Israel home through the wilderness to Palestine
3. The new thing will include blotting out Israel's transgressions and forgetting her former sins
4. This promise of a new thing is fulfilled in Christ's death on the cross for the forgiveness of sins
5. Trust in Christ to forgive your sins and do a new thing in your life

*2 Corinthians 1:18-22*
### God's Yes in Christ

1. God is faithful
2. All the promises of God find their Yes in Christ
3. God has put his seal on us and given us his Spirit
4. Say "yes" to God's *Yes* in Jesus Christ and obey him

*This Preacher's Choice*

*Mark 2:1-12*
### Jesus Heals the Paralytic Let Down Through the Roof

1. Four friends brought a paralytic man on his pallet to Jesus for healing
2. They tear a hole in the roof and let him down to Jesus
3. Jesus declares his sins are forgiven
4. The paralytic rose up and took up his pallet
5. They were all amazed and glorified God and said, "We never saw anything like this!"
6. Believe in Christ's power to forgive you and make you whole

**Hymn for Epiphany 7:** *Praise, My Soul, the King of Heaven*

**Prayer**

O God who has promised a new thing and has fulfilled it in Jesus' death on the cross for the forgiveness of sins, make us to remember no longer the former things but to know your redeeming love here and now. Forgive us when we have been vacillating, fickle in the decisions of life, and living a life of manic indecisiveness. Heal us, as Jesus healed the paralytic and set us on our feet. Send us forth to witness to the forgiveness of Christ and the love which never will let us go. Amen

Year B
# Epiphany 8     Epiphany 8     Ordinary Time 8

| Common | Lutheran | Roman Catholic |
|---|---|---|
| Hosea 2:14-20 | Hosea 2:14-16 (17-18) 19-20 | Hosea 2:16-17, 21-22 |
| 2 Corinthians 3:1-16 | 2 Corinthians 3:1b-6 | 2 Corinthians 3:1-6 |
| Mark 2:18-22 | Mark 2:18-22 | 2:18-22 |

## Comments on the Lessons

There is virtual consensus on the first and second readings and consensus on the third reading. The Hosea reading compares God's relationship to Israel with that of a husband to an unfaithful wife. In this analogy God at times is the husband and at others the judge in the court to which the unfaithful wife has been brought. The children of the couple are individuals within Israel. In the Corinthians letter Paul asserts his credentials as an apostle by saying that the Corinthians themselves are a letter from Christ delivered by him, written on tablets of human hearts. The Markan reading is a pronouncement story and two parables, the new patch and the wineskins.

## Commentary

*Hosea 2:14-20 (C)*
*Hosea 2:14-16 (17-18) 19-20 (L)*
*Hosea 2:16-17, 21-22 (RC)*

The thrust of Hosea's prophecy is that the northern kingdom, Israel, has been faithless to God and has yielded to Baal worship. This may be dated about 750-721 B.C. Hosea describes God as a wronged husband who seeks to recover his wife who has gone after lovers in harlotry. Hosea had been commanded by God to use his own marriage to Gomer as a prophetic symbol of God's dilemma in the face of Israel's faithlessness and succumbing to Baal worship. The setting for this allegory/drama is the cult of Israel which has been corrupted by the fertility religion of the Baals in Canaan. It was probably delivered in the earliest part of Hosea's ministry when there was abundant prosperity, a confident cult and untroubled times. The basic motivation for Israel's adopting the Baal fertility worship is her anxiety to gain from the land what is needed for basic needs of life and to make life pleasant. Israel's guilt is due, not to her being materialistic, but in thinking that the Baals were the source of what she needed.

Putting the pericope in context of what has gone before, the "therefore" of verse 14 is the third "therefore" and introduces the announcement of what God will do in response to Israel's unfaithfulness. God promises to assume by himself the responsibility for the reconcilation of his faithless wife, Israel. This third announcement fulfills and completes the previous two and brings to consummation the pleading with which it began. (v. 2) Notice the daring language.

The Baal cult has emphasized the sacred marriage between the deity and the worshipers. God had married Israel in the wilderness, not just a place, but more a time and situation in which the pristine relation between God and his people was pure and untarnished. Israel relied totally on God. God will make love to Israel in the wilderness, which literally means "speak to her heart." The term "allure" in the RSV is not strong enough, but "entice" which means to persuade irresistably, to overwhelm the loved one, is a better translation. God woos back the unfaithful wife, Israel, who has gone whoring after Baal worship. When entering the promised land Israel sinned at the valley of Achor. (Joshua 7:20-26) The literal meaning of Baal is "mater," or "lord."

God promises to remove the Baals from the mouth of Israel, and instead to make for Israel a covenant with the beasts, birds and creeping things, and to make Israel lie down in safety. The creation of peace will affect two spheres: (1) the living things, and (2) will eliminate all threat and harm of war. The land referred to is the place where Israel resides. Note that the peace envisioned is a local affair concerned only with Israel and is not a world-wide peace. The peace is the blessing of the re-established covenant. The wonder of all this is that Israel does not receive the blessing as a reward for the obedience required, but rather *as a gift of grace and as a sign* that God himself has brought them again into covenant!

God tells Israel, "And I will betroth you to me in righteousness and in justice, in steadfast love, and in mercy. I will betroth you to me in faithfulness; and you shall know the Lord." (vv. 19, 20) Note the five concepts of (1) righteousness, (2) justice, (3) devotion, (4) compassion, and (5) faithfulness. These are the bride-price with which God will establish the marriage and represent attitudes and actions of God. Of course, the analogy cannot be pushed to completion, since there is no father to receive the bride-price. But these express the attitudes and actions of God which satisfy all the requirements of the marriage as a covenant and lead to its consummation. They describe the normative quality of living in the various kinds of relations society provides. Righteousness means the saving help of God for Israel. It is not a state of being but an act whose quality of rightness lies in the vindication of a relationship, God's election of Israel. Justice is the rights and claims which belong to a given relation. Devotion is conduct which favors another within a relationship, especially a covenant. Compassion is active sympathy toward one who stands :n a relationship of dependence or need. Faithfulness is the divine reliability and consistency of purpose and character with which God deals with his people Israel. These concepts describe what God could expect from Israel as his covenant people, but also they sum up what Israel could expect from its covenant God. God commits himself to give these "gifts" as the price of wedding Israel, even though the old covenant is broken and finished. These describe the promise of a great and unanticipated grace! This description of a new covenant is a forerunner of the new covenant Jeremiah will describe later (Jeremiah 31:31ff), and the first description of the Church as the eschatological bride of Christ. (Ephesians 5:23ff)

### 2 Corinthians 3:1-6 (C) (RC)
### 2 Corinthians 3:1b-6 (L)

Paul had been accused of commending himself to the Corinthians it appears and now he answers this charge. The accusers seem to think he was an egotistical braggart. One of the charges against Paul made by the false apostles in Corinth was that he had not brought letters of recommendation from other churches. It was customary for wandering preachers to get and take with them letters from the congregations where they visited and to carry them to their next place to preach. It was usual for these letters to list the miracles they had performed, their ability to speak in tongues, and the ecstasies and visions they had displayed. But Paul admits he doesn't have any such letters. The "again" indicates that the previous statements of Paul's had brought forth the same accusation.

Paul says he doesn't need written letters as submitted by other apostles, but that the Corinthians themselves are his letter of recommendation, a letter written on *our* (preferred to the "your" of the RSV) hearts. Such a letter can be known and read by all, and they are a letter from Christ delivered by Paul. Christ is the author and Paul is the scribe. The letter is written, not with ink, but with the Spirit on the tablets of human hearts. Although the Corinthian church was far from perfect, yet through their thriving community they commended the gospel to all the world. It is not written on tablets of stone, like the law God gave Moses for Israel, but is written on human hearts.

In verses 4-6 the theme is the sufficiency from God. Paul admits that he and and his associates are not competent of themselves but their competence is from God. God has made him competent as the minister of a new covenant in the Spirit. (cf. Jeremiah 31:31) This new covenant stands in sharp contrast with the old legal code of Moses. While Paul's opponents boasted of their miracles and other mighty works as personal achievements, Paul has no such sufficiency. God has made Paul a minister of the new covenant, the covenant made in the blood of Christ on the cross. This new covenant is in the Spirit, not the written code, for the written code kills, says Paul, but the Spirit gives life. The covenant in the Bible was not between equals, but between God and his people, a superior and inferior party. God's making of such a covenant was an expression of his gracious character. In this new covenant the Christian lives, not as an isolated individual who comes to the Garden alone and walks and talks with Jesus alone, but as a member of the people of God. To become a Christian is to enter into a community of believers through the initiation rite of baptism. For Paul, to become a Christian and to become a member of the church are identical. There are no "Lone Ranger" Christians.

### Mark 2:18-22

The nature of this pericope is a pronouncement story to which are coupled two parables, that of the new patch and the wineskins. Because John the Baptizer's disciples and the Pharisees were fasting people, the Pharisees came to Jesus and asked him why his disciples did not fast. Jesus responds with a question: "Can the wedding guests fast while the bridegroom is with them? (v.19) This pronouncement story follows the usual form of such stories with three divisions: (1) the setting which in this case is the fasting of John's disciples and the Pharisees, (2) the action, the people come and ask Jesus a question about fasting, and (3) the pronouncement which is that one doesn't fast at weddings. This has all the marks of an authentic incident in the life of Jesus. Jesus expresses in his reply an indication of the joy of the kingdom which is already breaking into the present from the future.

The two brief parables coupled to this incident may have been told separately before being joined to it, but in any case they fit perfectly. Both parables describe the new which bursts through the old. Note that one part of this does not fit with the rest, and that is the comment of Jesus that the bridegroom will be taken away and then they will fast. Some think this must be a later addition. It may have been added by the church to justify fasting by the Christian community.

The idea of the bridegroom had, due to Old Testament influence, gained Messianic significance. Jesus is saying that the time while he is present is a time for joy, not for mourning or fasting, although that time will come. The point of these two parables is that the new movement, the Kingdom of God, cannot be confined within the limits of the old religion.

The saying that the bridegroom is taken away and then they will fast points to Jesus' death on the cross. Mark wants the cross to overshadow the gospel story almost from the beginning of Jesus' ministry. In order to accomplish this Mark turns the Jesus tradition from a collection of miracle stories into the proclamation of the cross.

## Theological Reflections

Hosea is an account of the gracious God who is faithful to the covenant and to the covenant people, Israel, even when Israel is unfaithful. The allegory of a marriage between a husband and unfaithful wife who goes into harlotry dramatizes this relationship. For the husband is faithful and woos the unfaithful wife back. This is due, not to Israel's obedience or good works, but to God's sheer grace. Paul makes the point that God has made him competent to be a minister of the new covenant written in the spirit. Here again the grace of God expressed in covenant relationship with his people is the theme. Mark records an incident in which Jesus points out that the New Age is breaking in, like new wine in old wineskins that burst as the fermenting new wine expands. And like an unshrunk patch put on an old garment which makes a tear, so the Kingdom cannot be confined in the old religion of the law. The joy of the Kingdom and bridegroom who is now present is another thrust of this passage. In saying that the bridegroom must later go away, Jesus is pointing to the cross, even this early in his ministry. Then will be the appropriate time for fasting, says Jesus.

## Homiletical Moves

*This Preacher's Choice*

*Hosea 2:14-20 (C)*
*Hosea 2:14-16 (17-18) 19-20 (L)*
*Hosea 2:16-17, 21-22 (RC)*
**You Shall Know the Lord!**

1. God woos Israel and speaks to her heart tenderly to win her back from harlotry with Baals
2. God makes for Israel a covenant and makes peace
3. God betroths Israel in steadfast love and mercy
4. Because Israel is betrothed to God she shall know the Lord
5. The Church is Christ's Bride, therefore live as faithful members of the Bride of Christ in community

*2 Corinthians 3:1-6 (C) (RC)*
*2 Corinthians 3:1b-6 (L)*
**You Are a Letter from Christ**

1. The Corinthians are a letter from Christ delivered by Paul
2. The "letter" is written not on tablets of stone like the Law, but on tablets of human hearts, not with ink but with the Spirit
3. God gave Paul competence to be a minister of the new covenant, not in a written code which kills but in the Spirit which give life

4. Let us live as "letters of God" in the world bearing faithful witness to the Gospel

*Mark 2:18-22*
## Joy, Not Fasting, While the Bridegroom Is Present

1. People ask Jesus why his disciples do not fast like John's and the Pharisees
2. Jesus replies that one does not fast while the bridegroom is with them
3. Jesus says the bridegroom will be taken away and then they will fast, pointing to his coming death on the cross
4. A new patch is not put on old cloth, or new wine into old wineskins, and neither can the old religion contain the Kingdom which is breaking in now
5. Rejoice for the Living Christ is with you by the Spirit

**Hymn for Epiphany 8:** *Fairest Lord Jesus*

**Prayer**

*We turn to you, the covenant-keeping God, to confess that we have been unfaithful while you have remained faithful. Forgive us and receive us back into the family of faith. Thank you for writing on our hearts a letter from Christ for all to see. May we so live that others may read this letter written with the Spirit of the Living God. Reaffirm us in the covenant you have made with us through Jesus' death on the cross. May we live now rejoicing that the bridegroom, even Jesus the Risen Lord, is with us by the power of the Spirit. Enable us to live as members of the new covenant in the Kingdom which is continually breaking in from the future. Amen*

# The Transfiguration of Our Lord

| **Common** | **Lutheran** |
|---|---|
| 2 Kings 2:1-12a | 2 Kings 2:1-12a |
| 2 Corinthians 4:3-6 | 2 Corinthians 3:12—4:2 |
| Mark 1:40-45 | Mark 1:40-45 |

## Comments on the Lessons

Notice that the passage from 2 Kings relates to the Transfiguration account of the gospel. It tells of Elijah's assumption into heaven and his passing on to Elisha his double measure of power. The first epistle passage describes those whose eyes are blinded to the gospel and are perishing, and the preaching by Paul of the gospel of Jesus Christ who gives light. The 2 Corinthians 3:12—4:2 passage tells of Moses, who put a veil over his face so the Israelites could not see the fading splendor, and the coming of Christ who reveals the glory of the Lord which changes us. Mark gives his account of the Transfiguration in which Jesus took Peter, James and John up a high mountain where they saw Moses, representing the Law, and Elijah representing the prophets and Jesus himself was transfigured.

## Commentary

*2 Kings 2:1-12a*

The Old Testament records that only Elijah and Enoch were considered worthy to be taken up into heaven without passing through death. This account of Elijah's being taken into heaven in a chariot of fire was chosen for this place in the lectionary because of Elijah's appearance in the Transfiguration story of Mark in today's reading. This is one of a collection of readings about Elisha. While it may appear from the stories about the two prophets that Elijah was the greater and that Elisha lived only in his reflected glory, this is not the case since Elisha touched lives at much deeper levels than did Elijah.

Elijah and Elisha were on their way from Gilgal, some seven miles north of Jerusalem, when they came to Bethel which, along with Gilgal, Bethel and Jericho were centers of prophetic communities. Gilgal was a significant shrine in Israel's early history as a cult-centre. The two prophets then miraculously crossed the waters of the Jordan, as Israel had crossed the Red Sea and later had crossed the Jordan coming into the promised land.

Notice that the term "sons of the prophets" refers not to physical relationship, but means "members of the prophetic order" or guild of prophets. Elisha asks a blessing from the departing Elijah: "I pray you, let me inherit a double share of your spirit." (v. 9) In Hebrew families the eldest son received a double inheritance. So Elisha is asking for the portion of the first-born so that he might follow him in his prophetic office. So Elisha is not seeking to excel his master but to be recognized and equipped as the true successor of Elijah.

Elijah says the wish will be granted on the condition that Elisha has a vision of Elijah's translation into heaven. This implies that only to those who are fit to receive spiritual gifts can such gifts be given. Elisha had the vision, received the gift and picked up Elijah's cloak that fell from him. (v. 13) This passing of Elijah's mantle has come to symbolize the passing of leadership in the church from one leader to another.

In verse 11 "the" whirlwind with the definite article after the chariot and horses of fire may suggest a connection between the two. The whirlwind was a natural phenomena. It suggests a dust devil, which might accompany the sirocco east of the Jordan. Fire suggests the sirocco. A dust storm as it appears in the distance might be compared to horses and chariot which created clouds of dust. But we need not seek a rationalistic interpretation. Rather, it may be that in verse 12 Elisha means that Elijah was more important and powerful than chariots and horsemen. It could mean that the title "the chariotry of Israel and the horsemen thereof," originally the title of Elisha, is now transferred to Elijah. An explanation may be found in the cult legend in which the horse was well known as the cult-animal of the sun. The story of Elijah may be combined here with an older solar cult legend. The element of fire is a common motif in theophanies. God revealed himself to Moses in the burning bush and led the children of Israel in the wilderness with a pillar of fire by night and a cloud by day.

## 2 Corinthians 4:3-6 (C)

Paul is writing at a time when the End was believed imminent; this explains the blindness of the unbelievers and the hope of the apostles. Evidently Paul had been accused of not making the Gospel clear. He says the Gospel is veiled only to those who are perishing. The god of this world (v. 4) is Satan who has blinded the minds of the unbelievers.

Paul is seeking to explain why some believe and live, and others do not believe and are perishing. Could it be that some have suggested that Paul himself is at fault for not making the Gospel clear? But no one should blame his or her unbelief on another. God holds each person responsible for a positive or negative response to the Gospel. In the previous chapter (3:15) Paul has spoken of the "veil" over the hearts of Jews. Now in this chapter he is thinking of people in general whose minds are veiled to the Gospel. Some do not clearly face the Gospel, and so are perishing. The present participle for "perishing" indicates they are on their way to full and final destruction.

In this passage Paul sees this world as a battleground between Satan and God. In this battle God is in final control for Christ has won the victory over sin and death. Jesus' death on the cross was like the "D-Day Invasion" of Europe in World War II. While the war was not yet over, the invasion by the Allies spelled the beginning of the end for the Nazi government.

The "glory of Christ" (v. 4) means both the exalted nature and visible expression of Christ's divine splendor and nature. "Light" is another visible expression of this divine splendor. Paul says he and those with him preach not themselves, but Jesus Christ as Lord. The earliest creed of the church was simply "Jesus is Lord." Paul and his associates were the servants of the Corinthians for Christ's sake. Note that Paul does not say "Christ's servants" but "your servants." He serves them in preaching, teaching, and pastoral care. He offers this service for Jesus' sake, a service to others in obedience to Christ.

In verse 6 there is a reference to God's creating light out of darkness (Genesis 1:3), and Paul says it is this same God who has shone in our hearts to give us the light of salvation in Christ. Paul saw the external light of God in the face of Christ on the road to Damascus when he was converted. But this was more than external light; it involved his whole life and brought about a life-changing conversion. Paul saw every spiritual blessing as a gift from God for use in his ministry.

We should note that Paul's words in this passage echo themes found in the account of the Transfiguration in the Gospel reading. Note especially the theme of "light" which is central to the Transfiguration story. We should also note that what follows in verses 7-12 resemblea in many ways the nature of Jesus' instructions to the disciples after the Transfiguration. It could be said that the Epiphany of Christ takes its truest form within our lives as we reenact the suffering and death of Christ. The life of Paul is a prime example of this reenactment. Note the word "manifested" (v. 11) which expresses the meaning of Epiphany.

## 2 Corinthians 3:12-4:2 (L)

Paul describes how Moses put a veil over his face to hide from the people how temporary the old covenant was to be. In verse 14 the old covenant refers to the books of the law. When one sees Christ, one sees how transient the old covenant really is and knows the freedom and glory of the new covenant. (vv. 15-17) Note how close Paul comes here to identifying the Spirit known within the church with the risen Lord Jesus: "Now the Lord is the Spirit, and where the Spirit of the Lord is, there is freedom." (v. 17)

While the knowledge that Christ has outdated the law is veiled from the Jews, they have only to turn to Christ for the veil to be removed, says Paul. The Christian can boldly unveil his or her face and reflect and behold as in a mirror the Lord's glory. (v. 16)

In the first verses of chapter 4 Paul picks up the themes of 2:16 and 3:12. Because Paul had been given such a glorious ministry he could never be a traitor to it, like the false apostles who accused him in Corinth. He could never indulge in disgraceful, underhanded ways, and refused to practice cunning or to tamper with God's Word. Instead, Paul openly states the truth of the Gospel and in so doing commends himself to every person's conscience.

*Mark 9:2-9*

While the mountain of the story has traditionally been identified with Mount Tabor, modern commentators prefer Mount Hermon (9,200 feet). An entirely different approach is to view this narrative not as involving a mountain geographically, but rather to see it as a vision of Jesus in heavenly glory as the Messiah. Luke 9:28-36 gives a parallel account and says the event began as prayer and grew from that into an intense religious experience. The aura of unnatural brilliance is often associated with mystical experiences and with revelations of God. (Exodus 34:29 ff; Acts 9:3) A number of scholars see this as a piece of theological symbolical writing, a legendary development of a Resurrection-story which was read back into the earthly life of Jesus. Bultmann is one who sees it as originally a Resurrection story. But in objection to this, several differences must be noted: (1) All the aocounts of the Resurrection appearances begin with Jesus being absent, but here he is present at the beginning, (2) In the Resurrection stories something said by Jesus has an important place, but here Jesus is silent, (3) the story lacks the features to be expected in a appearance to Peter, (4) it is surprising to find Moses and Elijah in a Resurrection story, since in the Easter stories only angels appear, and never at the same time as Jesus, and (5) this theory leaves unexplained Peter's curious suggestion: "Master, it is well that we are here; let us make three booths, one for you and one for Moses and one for Elijah." (v. 5) But there is evidence for its historical basis, such as the reference to the six days, after which came the sabbath, Peter's use of "Rabbi", which is not used in the New Testament outside the Gospels and thus was not likely to have been used in a symbolic narrative written by the early church. Finally, Mark gives no hint that all that he relates is something other than historical event.

The central thrust of the Transfiguration is the glory of Christ. The Transfiguration reminds us of the baptism of Jesus when he heard a voice from heaven saying, "Thou art my beloved Son; with thee I am well pleased." (1:11) The voice at the Transfiguration speaks to the disciples, not to Jesus, and says, "This is my beloved Son; listen to him." (9:7) This event anticipates the Resurrection. However, Mark does not have an actual resurrection appearance.

Notice the parallels with Moses with God on Mount Sinai. (Exodus, chapters 24, 34) There are the six days of waiting, the cloud, the glory, the voice, the descent from the mountain. Moses' face shone because he had been in the presence of God. Notice also that the Transfiguration comes in the central part of Mark 8:22—10:52. We are given clues to understanding stories in the Bible by *how* it is told or *when* it is told. Its location within the context here is in a section which begins and ends with healings of blind men. And, between these healings, the disciples themselves remain blind to the real nature of Jesus' Messiahship and mission. They are unable to accept the cross and death, for they understand Messiah in terms of a political king.

One of Mark's goals in writing the Gospel is to help the reader transpose the events about an apparently past Jesus into the contemporary situation of the witnessing community. Jesus admonishes the disciples after his Transfiguration, "And as they were coming down the mountain, he charged them to tell no one what they had seen, until the Son of man should have risen from the dead." (v.9) The vision of the transformation of Jesus modeled the kind of shift in perception which takes place when the reader of Mark sees that the book is dealing with the resurrected Jesus. He is making the point that the risen, living, contemporary Son of man is none other than the Jesus of the Gospel stories, but now transformed in the enlightened perception of the believer hearing the story.

In the verse preceding the Transfiguration, Jesus tells the disciples, "Truly, I say to you, there are some standing here who will not taste death before they see that the kingdom of God has come with power." (9:1) Since Peter, James and John are the witnesses of the Transfiguration they are the "some" referred to. The kingdom of God come with power means the recognition of the transformed Jesus as a heavenly being with dynamic access to the reader's life. Mark uses the account of the Transfiguration as a parable of the way in which the historical Jesus becomes the risen Christ in the here and now.

Both Elijah and Moses had come to be associated with the coming of Messiah in Judaism and Christianity. Their appearance here signals the anticipated Messiah and the End time fulfilled in Jesus. The fact that they disappear and leave only Jesus with the disciples says that the old is ended and the new has begun. Note that, as at Jesus' baptism, he does not speak or act. Rather, God the Father speaks and acts. And the message is for Jesus' followers.

Peter would like to preserve this high point by building booths for Jesus, Moses and Elijah. He spoke, not knowing what to say, and all three disciples were very afraid. They are told to be silent about this until after the resurrection. (v. 9) Neither the three disciples nor those who might hear their story are ready to be witnesses to Jesus' messianic role. Until the cross, the full story cannot be told or understood. Here in the Transfiguration the disciples are given a glimpse of who Jesus really is. But they miss the meaning of it. But there is one more mountain for the disciples and those after them yet to climb: Golgotha, where the glory of God will be revealed for all the world to see in the death of God's son.

## Theological Reflections

The account of Elijah and Elisha in 2 Kings relates to the Transfiguration in the Gospel, not only because Elijah appears there with Moses, but because Elijah's departure into heaven foreshadows the discussion with the disciples and the uncertainty about Jesus' departure in Mark's account of the Transfiguration. God is acting in a miraculous way in both instances. Paul writes to explain why some are blind to the Gospel, while others believe in 2 Corinthians 4:3-6. He sees the world as a battleground between God and Satan. The glory of Christ (v. 4) and the mentioning of light both parallel the glory of Jesus at the Transfiguration. In the second passage from Corinthians, Paul compares the old covenant which was only temporary with the new covenant in Christ. He comes close to identifying the Spirit with the risen Lord. Mark points us to the glory of the Transfigured Jesus on the mountain. The disciples do not understand the meaning of it, but will later after the cross and resurrection. All these passages show the necessity of faith in order to see and understand the glory of God revealed in Jesus Christ. Some are blinded to it, but need to have their blindness healed, and the veil removed. But to those who believe is given the "light of the knowledge of the glory of God in the face of Christ." (2 Corinthians 4:6)

## Homiletical Moves

*2 Kings 2:1-12a*
### Elijah's Departure Into Heaven

1. Elijah and Elisha meet with the sons of the prophets who predict Elijah will be taken from Elisha
2. Elijah and Elisha cross over the Jordan on dry ground
3. Elisha asks for a double share of Elijah's spirit, which is promised to him if he sees Elijah taken from him
4. Elijah is taken up into heaven by a whirlwind in a chariot of fire seen by Elisha
5. Elisha saw him no more, but takes up Elijah's mantle and prophetic role
6. Let us be faithful servants of God in our time of service

*2 Corinthians 4:3-6 (C)*

### The Glory of God in the Face of Christ
1. The Gospel is veiled to those who are perishing for the god of this world has blinded their minds
2. What Paul preaches is Jesus Christ as Lord
3. Paul and associates are servants of the Corinthians for Jesus' sake
4. The God who said "Let light shine . . ." has shone in our hearts to give us the light of the knowledge of the glory of God in the face of Christ
5. Because we have seen God in Christ let us live in faithful obedience

*2 Corinthians 3:12—4:2 (L)*
### Freedom Where the Spirit of the Lord Is

1. We are bold, not like Moses who put a veil over his face
2. The minds of Jews have a veil over them when the old covenant is read
3. But when a person turns to the Lord the veil is removed
4. The Spirit of the Lord gives freedom
5. We are beholding the glory of the Lord and are being changed into his likeness
6. Live in freedom by the Spirit of the Lord

*This Preacher's Choice*

*Mark 9:2-9*
### See the Beloved Son, Jesus, and Listen to Him!

1. Jesus takes Peter, James and John up a high mountain by themselves

2. Jesus is transfigured before them, and his garments became white
3. Moses and Elijah, representing the Law and the Prophets appear
4. A voice from heaven declares Jesus is the beloved Son to whom they should listen
5. Jesus charges the disciples not to tell what they had seen until after the resurrection
6. Because we have seen God in Christ let us live as faithful witnesses to that vision

**Hymn for the Transfiguration of Our Lord:** *O Wonderous Sight, O Vision Fair* or *Christ Upon the Mountain Peak*

**Prayer**

*Holy God who has called the prophets and disciples of old, lift the veil from our minds that we may behold anew your glory in the face of Christ. Let us see the light of the Gospel of the glory of Christ. Give us faithful hearts raised on high by this great vision's mystery. May we know the freedom given by the Spirit of the Lord. And may we continually be changed into the likeness of Christ. Grant that we may be faithful in witnessing to what we have seen and heard. Amen*

# The Lent and Easter/Pentecost Seasons

This is the season which celebrates the heart of the Christian faith: the life, suffering, death, resurrection and ascension of Jesus Christ. During the previous cycle of Advent and Christmas/Epiphany we celebrated the Incarnation in which "the Word became flesh and dwelt among us." (John 1:14) Now we are focusing on the Atonement by which God in Christ has made us at-one with him by grace through faith. God sent forth the Son in the fullness of time to suffer and die for our sins and to be raised for our salvation. The risen Christ ascended into heaven, from which we expect his return in power and glory. By the gift of God's Holy Spirit the power of Christ's death and resurrection are made available for our lives.

Since the beginning of Christian worship the events of Christ's passion, death and resurrection have shaped life and worship for Christians for each week, the Christian Year, and for daily worship in community and as individuals. We can properly observe Lent, Easter and Pentecost only as we do so understanding their relationship to each other and to the mystery of salvation in Christ. These occasions are formed in the pattern of his death and resurrection and Spirit which gives eternal life.

## The Season of Lent

Purple is the color of Lent, and during this season the joyous Gloria and alleluia are omitted from worship. The word "lent" is related to the words "long" and "lengthen." The word came into use in reference to the lengthening of the hours of sunlight in the springtime. The season has been called "the Easter penitential period" to keep the focus on Easter rather than Lent itself. The Sundays during the Lenten season are not considered a part of Lent, therefore we speak of Sunday *in* Lent not *of* Lent. The beginning of Lent depends on the date of Easter. Lent begins forty-six days before Easter, and the season of Lent proper is a season of forty days.

The intention of Lent was to imitate Jesus who, after his baptism in the Jordan, fasted for forty days. The Church saw in the observance of Lent an echo of the forty days Moses fasted on Sinai (Exdous 34, 28), and the forty days Elijah fasted on his journey to Mount Horeb (1 Kings 19:8), as well as Israel's wandering in the wilderness, etc. Christians in the second century were already observing a two-day grief-inspired fast in preparation for the feast of Easter. The first Ecumenical Council of Nicaea speaks of the forty-day period of preparation for Easter as something that was familiar to all.

The fast of Lent meant that people took only a single daily meal which was eaten in the evening. Abstaining from meat and wine was added later on, as was abstinence from dairy products and eggs which continued until the Middle Ages and later. Fasting for medical reasons was not uncommon among the Greeks and Romans. Christians of the early church saw fasting as a source of fervor in prayer, comparing the prayer of one fasting to the soaring of a young eagle, in contrast to the prayer of an immoderate eater.

The purpose of observing Lent was to prepare for receiving the spirit, which was a powerful instrument in the fight against evil spirits. Fasting during Lent was also preparation for baptism and the eucharist, and was also a way of being able to help the poor with money, which otherwise would have been spent for food. The church was very much aware of the danger that fasting might become an external formality, and it remembered the warnings of Jesus in the Sermon on the Mount.

Vatican II wrote directions for observing Lent which put even greater emphasis on the recalling of baptism or preparation for it, and penance. The purpose remained to prepare the faithful for Easter. Penance is stressed as a detestation of sin because it is an offense against God. Penance should be not only internal and individual but also external and social. The practice of this should be adapted to local regions and individual circumstances.

Ash Wednesday which is the beginning of Lent was so named, because penitents put on penitential garments and had ashes sprinkled on them. Wearing of sackcloth and the use of ashes was familiar to the Old Testament and in pagan societies. Jesus speaks of this in upbraiding Chorazin and Bethsaida for not doing penance: "If the mighty works done in you had been done in Tyre and and Sidon, they would have repented long ago in sackcloth and ashes." (Matthew 11:21) Sometime in the twelfth century, the rule developed that the ashes used to either sprinkle on the heads of men or mark with a sign of the cross on the foreheads of women should come from the burning of palm branches left from the previous year. Ash Wednesday in the Roman Catholic and other traditions is still observed as a day of universal fasting on which ashes are to be distributed.

Vatican II relaxed some of the strictness of Lent and allows meat to be eaten on Fridays and breakfast before Communion.

Many churches, Protestant and Catholic, observe Lent with special weekday services, such as weekday noon services for business people who come to church for lunch and a Lenten service, or special evening services focusing on the themes of Lent. Lent can take on greater meaning as people come to better understand its purpose in a positive way. Lent can be a means of self-discipline and self-denial in preparation for the celebration of Eastertide and Pentecost. Lent is a time when many church members give more of their time and energy to church programs, thus making this a period of growth in service to God and others. Some churches suggest one or more books for reading during Lent which assist in spiritual formation.

Planning services during Lent and throughout the year should involve lay persons as well as the pastor. This can be part of the congregation's Lenten journey and ''work of the people'' as the word ''liturgy'' means literally.

## Holy Week

While some Protestant churches single out only Palm/Passion Sunday and Thursday before Easter for special observance, others are holding special midday or evening services each day of Holy Week. The services often follow the movements of Jesus as tradition outlines them:

| Monday | Cleansing of the Temple |
| Tuesday | Verbal conflict with Jesus' enemies |
| Wednesday | Day of silence and retreat in Bethany |
| Thursday | Final conversations with the disciples |
| Friday | The crucifixion |
| Saturday | Jesus' body in the tomb |

Maundy Thursday is often observed with a celebration of the Lord's Supper and candles are lighted by those in the congregation. ''Maundy'' is derived from the new ''mandate'' or ''commandment'' Jesus gave to the disciples to ''love one another,'' and from his command to celebrate the Lord's Supper in remembrance of him until he returns.

Other special observances are held on Good Friday. Three hour services, usually noon — 3:00 p.m, began in the Roman Catholic tradition in the seventeenth century and are now common in Protestant churches. Often churches join together for community Good Friday services in which a different speaker presents a brief meditation on each of Jesus' seven last words from the cross.

In strict liturgical observance the altar is stripped, candles are left unlit and the cross is veiled in black for Good Friday to remind all of Jesus' death.

Lent ends officially at noon on Saturday before Easter. From sunset on Holy or Maundy Thursday until sunset on Easter Day has come to be known as the Triduum. In the early church after a long rigorous fast of Lent the church celebrated the whole Paschal mystery (the saving work of Christ and the church's participation in it) on Easter Eve and on into Easter Day in *one unified liturgy*.

Black American churches have found special meaning in the powerful themes of exodus, *deliverance* from death, and liberation from slavery, themes which have enriched worship particularly during the Passover-Easter period. Other ethnic groups and cultures have traditions to enrich the Church's worship as they are shared with one another.

## Easter

The celebration of Easter in worship is both the source and summit of the whole Christian Year. We declare that Christ who was crucified, dead and buried is risen and exalted to the Godhead. We celebrate his presence in our midst by the Holy Spirit. While it has been said that every Sunday is a ''little Easter'' it could more accurately be said that Easter is a ''big Sunday'' in that Sunday, the Lord's Day, is the celebration of Christ's resurrection on the first day of the week.

The color for Easter is white. The alternate color is gold which expresses the prominence of this peak of the Christian Year. The mood is joy. The cross-resurrection are at the center of the celebration of Easter.

Although Easter is the climax of the church's worship on one day, the celebration continues throughout Eastertide. There is a dramatic contrast between Lent and Easter/Pentecost in that Lent is penitential with a mood that is sober, reflective and watchful. There was an ancient practice of omitting

"Alleluias" and "Glorias" during Lent. But Easter/Pentecost is exuberant. This joy in the Living Christ should be expressed not only in the sermon but in the entire worship service through music and visual images.

Worship and preaching should keep in tension the connection between Christ's death, resurrection and the gift of the Holy Spirit. Easter has been called the "Eighth Day" which ushers in the end time and promises the light of eternal life. Christ risen from the dead is the New Adam whose resurrection is the beginning of a New Humanity and New Creation.

## Pentecost

Pentecost is a reliving of the meaning of Eastertide, the period from Easter until Pentecost. In celebrating the outpouring of the Holy Spirit at Pentecost, the Church was no longer desolate for the Living Christ had returned by the Spirit to the disciples. It celebrates the "birthday" of the Church. Pentecost is one of the major church festivals and ranked second only to Easter until more emphasis began to be placed on Christmas. Pentecost gathers three festivals of the church: Ascension, Pentecost and Trinity.

The color for Pentecost is white. The Passover-Pentecost period has been called one great extended Lord's Day feast in that it lifts up all the redeeming work of God in Christ. White is a symbol of joy, and Pentecost is a rejoicing in the Presence of God by the Spirit.

Ascension Day, the fortieth day after Easter, is not a completely separate historical commemoration from that of Pentecost. Until the end of the fourth century the ascension of Christ and the descent of the Spirit were celebrated on the same Lord's Day. The exaltation of the risen Christ is vitally linked to his giving of the Holy Spirit. The color is white for Ascension Day also.

Trinity Sunday is celebrated the Sunday following Pentecost. The color is white for this day also. It celebrates the mystery of the nature of the Godhead, Father, Son and Holy Spirit, one God in three persons. The use of the Nicene Creed is particularly appropriate on Trinity Sunday and is preferred over the Apostles' Creed or a modern creed, since it states the church's belief regarding the persons of the Trinity, with special emphasis on the nature of Jesus Christ. Preaching on the Trinity on this Sunday each year can be an exciting and challenging venture as the preacher seeks to set forth the Scriptural understanding of God's revelation of himself. Notice that the first and last Sundays in the season after Pentecost are days with special emphases: Trinity, and Christ the King, respectively. White is used on both of these Sundays, although green is the color for Sundays after Pentecost generally. The time between these two special Sundays is called "ordinary time."

# Lent 1

| **Common** | **Lutheran** | **Roman Catholic** |
|---|---|---|
| Genesis 9:8-17 | Genesis 22:1-18 | Genesis 9:8-15 |
| 1 Peter 3:18-22 | Romans 8:31-39 | 1 Peter 3:18-22 |
| Mark 1:9-15 | Mark 1:12-15 | Mark 1:12-15 |

### Comments on the Lessons

The Genesis 9 passage tells the story of the covenant with God in which God promised never again to destroy the earth by flood. Genesis 22:1-18 tells of Abraham taking Isaac to a place of sacrifice to offer him to God, but God provides a ram instead. It was originally a story to tell the Hebrews that God does not approve of child sacrifice. The 1 Peter passage tells of Christ's death for the unrighteous and his going to preach to the spirits in prison between his death and resurrection. In Romans 8:31-39 we have the great assurance that nothing can separate us from the love of God in Christ Jesus our Lord. There is virtual consensus on the Markan reading. Note that for (C) verses 9-11 are included which put the passage into the context of Jesus' baptism. And verses 14-15 complete Mark's introduction and give a stirring call to repentance. They also give the main theme of Mark's gospel.

### Commentary

*Genesis 9:8-17 (C)*
*Genesis 9:8-15 (RC)*

In this account of God's covenant with Noah, a covenant which included all living creatures, we find the principle of the covenant relationship for the first time. Here also appears for the first time the "sign" or "mark." The rainbow is a sign of God's promise. In the Old Testament, and to some extent in the New Testament also, we find a "sign" is some event which a person or group of God's people interpret as an indication of divine intervention. Sometimes individuals ask for a sign from God, as Gideon did. There is a concern for explaining the phenomena of the rainbow in this story also. But there is an even deeper meaning to be found in the rainbow as a symbol of God's activity in mercy now enthroned.

Compare this covenant with Noah and the later one God makes with Abraham. The one with Noah includes all living things, while the one with Abraham establishes a personal relationship between God and Abraham. We should also note that, in the preceding verses (9:1-7), the cultic taboo on eating blood is validated. Along with this emerges one of the most important symbols in the Bible, *blood* as a symbol of life.

The rainbow is a visible form of God's saying "never again." Never again will God destroy all flesh by a flood. What has changed is God's purpose. God has made a decision to be gracious to his creation and the rainbow is a sign of this decision. In the earlier chapters of Genesis (6:5—7:10), God resolves to punish the guilty. But all this has changed now. The one-to-one connection between guilt and punishment has been broken. While evil has not been eradicated and there may still be death and destruction, all human beings are now assured that these are not rooted in the anger or rejection of God. There is no longer a tit-for-tat system of retribution by God. Instead there has been a revolution in the heart of God. God's relationship to all living things is now based on unqualified grace.

The rainbow for the ancients was a symbol of a bow as a weapon of war from which thunderbolts were shot to earth. But now the bow is undrawn. The creator God has won the victory over chaos and over his tendency to punish. The rainbow is a sign or visible token that God's wrath has abated. God remembered Noah and all the creatures that were with him on the ark. (8:1) God did not and has not forgotten his people and all his creatures! This is the good news of this passage.

*Genesis 22:1-18 (L)*

This is one of the finest pieces of Hebrew prose narrative in the Old Testament. Anthropologists see in this story evidence for child sacrifice among the Hebrews early in the period of settling in Canaan. It may also be seen as a continuing protest against child sacrifice, which seems to have continued to some degree until the time of Micah, who wrote: "Shall I give my firstborn for my transgression . . .?" (Micah 6:7) For the writer of the story of Abraham this was the supreme moment of testing in Abraham's spiritual pilgrimage.

See what is at risk here. God had promised Abraham two things: land and descendants. (Genesis 12:1, 2) God gave Isaac to Abraham and Sarah in their old age when Sarah was past child-bearing. Now God puts Abraham to the test to see if he trusts God enough to sacrifice this, his only son by Sarah, his one sign of God's fulfillmment of the promise of descendants.

In this testing story we have a miracle of faith in which Abraham received back the promise, after demonstrating that he had the faith to surrender his only heir. The concept of testing may seem strange to the modern mind but it was not to the ancient world. This is not just an Old Testament concept, however. In the Lord's prayer Jesus taught the disciples to pray regularly, "lead us not into temptation." (Matthew 6:13) This is a petition that God will not put us in a testing situation where we are forced to decide or risk for our confession of faith. It reveals a fear that we will be found lacking if such a testing comes. So the prayer is that we may not be tested as Abraham and others have been pushed to the limits of their faith.

There is a second issue raised here ooncerning God. While the story begins with the testing by God, it ends with the providing by God. To believe that God, not chance, provided the ram is no less an act of faith than to believe that it was God putting Abraham to the test. God is the source of life. The test God arranges is resolved by God's graciousness.

Moriah cannot be located, although some have sought to identify it with Jerusalem. The Samaritans identified it with Shechem.

Note that in an earlier ratification of the covenant (chapter 15), God passes through the two halves of the sacrifice as the covenant is "cut." But now this reaffirmation of the covenant is a consequence of Abraham's passing through symbolic death. He and God are bound together by this shared experience. In the process a whole group of images appear which will appear again, especially in relation to Jesus Christ and his death. In this testing God provides a substitute, a ram, for the son Isaac. But at Calvary there is no ram provided and God sacrifices his only Son. Note the images: the father giving the son, the son willingly obeying the father, the symbols of sacrifice of knife, altar, wood, and the ram as a burnt offering. In this testing of Abraham we see the whole pattern of redemption prefigured.

### 1 Peter 3:18-22 (C) (RC)

The most difficult section of this epistle is 1 Peter 3:18—4:6. The core of verses 18-22 is found in verse 18: "For Christ also died for sins once for all, the righteous for the unrighteous, that he might bring us to God, being put to death in the flesh but made alive in the spirit. . . " This is a reason for what was said earlier in vrese 17: "For it is better to suffer for doing right, if that should be God's will, than for doing wrong."

The thrust of this passage is the example of Christ. An earlier passage (2:21-25) also holds up the example of Christ for Christians to emulate. The phrase "put to death in the flesh" (v. 18) puts stress on the fact that Jesus really died. "Made alive in the spirit" points to the resurrection and the fact that death could not hold him in the grave. Three things are said of Christ's death in verse 18: (1) that it is atoning "in respect of sin", (2) it is vicarious "the righteous for the unrighteous", and (3) that its aim is to restore the broken relationship between God and human beings "that he might bring us to God."

While Paul holds up the example of Christ in his passion of suffering and death, he goes beyond this in his view of the Atonement. "Once" in verse 18 sets Christ's single sacrifice apart from the repeated deaths of the sacrificial animals under the Levitical system of sacrifice.

The goal of this sacrifice is *to bring sinners to God,* which is the essential thrust of all religion in the final analysis. Peter is saying in this passage that the death of Christ enables us to get access to God, to pass from dis-grace into grace by the amazing grace of Christ Jesus.

The reference to Jesus preaching to the spirits in prison who formerly did not obey (v. 20) means that Jesus descended between his passion and resurrection to preach to certain spirits imprisoned in Hades or Sheol. (At this period Hades was no longer regarded as the dwelling of shades, but partly as a place of punishment, and partly an intermediate state.) Peter seems to be referring to the spirits of the sinners who perished in the flood. (Background for this may be in Psalm 16:10, and

Luke 16:22-23, and Isaiah 61:1) The idea of Jesus' descending into Hades and of harrowing Hell became a part of the church's theology. The point of it is that wherever people are, Christ has power to save. (See Apostles' Creed "He descended into hell")

Mention of the flood leads to a comparison with baptism. (v. 21) In the flood, water destroyed life. In baptism it saves. The power of baptism is through the resurrection of Jesus Christ. This is a typical emphasis of Peter on the central importance for salvation of the risen Christ. The risen Christ is at the right hand, the place of honor, of God, with lesser heavenly beings subject to him. (v. 22)

### Romans 8:31-39 (L)

The thrust of this passage is our confidence in God based on our experience of God's goodness in Christ. While this confidence is not new (2 Kings 6:15ff), it is greatly enhanced by what God has done and yet will do in Christ. We must read this passage against the background of being a Christian in the first century, a difficult and dangerous endeavor. In verse 32 "spare" could also be translated "begrudge" which is preferable since it brings out God's gracious generosity.

In verse 33ff we have questions which have implied answers of "Nobody, when . . ." "Who shall bring any charge against God's elect? . . . Who is to condemn? Who shall separate us from the love of Christ?" God justifies us, and Christ pleads our case.

The quote from Psalm 44:22, "For thy sake we are being killed all the day long; we are regarded as sheep to be slaughtered" was used by the Rabbis to refer to Jewish martyrs.

We are more than conquerors in all these things, says Paul, through Christ who loved us. Whether we live or die we cannot be separated from God. No supernatural beings, good or evil, can separate us from God's love. Nor can the astrological powers of the stars in their highest point (heights) or abyss (depths) separate us from God's love. Things present and things to come represent the ongoing march of human events which, apart from God, seem to be fatalistic and destructive of God-human relationships.

Notice that Paul does not deny, as modern minds tend to deny, the existence of supernatural powers. These forces which we cannot understand or control cannot destroy the one great thing that really matters in life, says Paul, namely God's love in Christ Jesus our Lord. None of these forces can separate us from the saving love of God.

### Mark 1:9-15 (C)
### Mark 1:12-15 (L) (RC)

The more inclusive reading (9-15) briefly sketches Jesus' baptism, temptation and the beginnings of Jesus' ministry in Galilee. Jesus' message is summarized in verse 15: "The time is fulfilled, and the kingdom of God is at hand; repent, and believe in the gospel." All of the Gospel of Mark is an expansion of this verse.

Jesus, the sinless One was baptized for sinners. Pictures of Jesus' baptism from early centuries show him standing in water about his knees, being baptized with water poured from a shell on his head by John the Baptizer. Or he may have immersed himself in the presence of John the Baptizer. Jesus was baptized for the forgiveness of sins of others. He was baptized for us and in his baptism we are cleansed of our sins. The words from heaven "Thou art my beloved Son; with thee I am well pleased" (v. 11)refer to God's choosing of Jesus (Isaiah 42:1), an intentional act of the will, not a feeling only. Mark regards Jesus' baptism as the moment when he received supernatural power from the Spirit which descended upon him. Jesus' baptism was an act of self-dedication as well as one of identification with the sinners he came to save.

Mark merely records the fact of Jesus' temptation. He was tempted by Satan forty days (another way of saying "a period of time") and was ministered to by the angels, God's messengers. (See Matthew 4:1-11; Luke 4:1-13.) It is significant that after Jesus' baptism when he is empowered by the Spirit and given the Father's affirmation, he is immediately driven into the wilderness where he is tempted by Satan. When one is "most spiritual" one is most vulnerable to Satan's wiles. We must remember that the temptations in the wilderness were not the final three temptations at the beginning of Jesus' ministry, but that he continually was tempted throughout his ministry. The Pharisees demanded a sign, Peter rebelled against the idea of Jesus' suffering, Jesus was tempted in the Garden but submitted to God's will, and even on the cross he was tempted. (Mark 15:29ff)

The arrest of John was the decisive moment for the beginning of Jesus' ministry in the Markan tradition. However, between the events of verse 13 and verse 14, there is room for a period of ministry by Jesus alongside that of John the Baptizer which is recorded by the Fourth Gospel.

The summary of Jesus' ministry in verses 14-15 contains the note of fulfillment, one which resounds throughout the entire New Testament. "The time is fulfilled" is a declaration of the primitive kerygma that in Jesus the prophecies and promises of the Old Testament had been fulfilled. The "right time" (kairos time) had arrived. The kingdom of God is his rule in the hearts of people. Kingship of God is rooted in two main ways in the Old Testament: (1) God is thought of as being even now the King of Israel and also of the whole world, (2) but this kingship is something yet to be realized, and so is referred to in terms of expectation and hope. Jesus could speak of the kingdom as having come near, and yet as yet to come: "Thy kingdom come" (Lord's Prayer). The future coming of the kingdom is imminent, declares Jesus. It is at hand, therefore repent and believe in the Gospel. Notice the tension between realized and future eschatology in Mark. The kingdom is present in Jesus and his ministry, but at the same time it awaits a consummation that is yet to come. Since the kingdom is at hand there is an urgency in the message to repent now and to believe in the Gospel. In contrast to John the Baptizer who proclaimed only judgment, Jesus proclaims good news.

## Theological Reflections

The graciousness of God is a theme running through these passages like a red thread. God is gracious, not only to Noah and his family, but to all living creatures in making a covenant with them, with the sign of the rainbow as a symbol to all that God remembers and will never again destroy all living things by flood. God is gracious to Abraham in sparing Isaac when putting Abraham to the test. Abraham's faith is tested by taking Isaac to offer as a sacrifice and also by the provision of a ram instead. Not chance, but God provided the ram as a gracious act. In 1 Peter we see the example of Christ who died for sins. This is God's gracious act of giving his Son for us. Paul tells the Romans that nothing can separate them from the love of God in Christ Jesus our Lord. Again God's gracious act in Christ is emphasized. Mark relates the baptism of Jesus, his temptations, and the beginning of Jesus' ministry as he proclaimed the fulfillment of time and the kingdom of God being at hand. This is good news. Those who hear are called to repent and believe in the gospel. The amazing grace of God permeates all these passages in a very distinctive fashion.

## Homiletical Moves

*Genesis 9:8-17 (C)*
*Genesis 9:8-15 (RC)*
### The Rainbow — God's Sign of the Covenant

1. God establishes his covenant with Noah and his descendants
2. God promises that never again will all flesh be destroyed by a flood
3. God sets the rainbow in the heavens as a sign of the covenant
4. The rainbow is a reminder of the covenant and that God remembers his people.
5. Trust God to be faithful in the future, as he has in the past as you live in the covenant community, the Church

*Genesis 22:1-18 (L)*
### God Will Provide

1. God tests Abraham by commanding him to offer Isaac as a sacrifice
2. Abraham obeys God and Isaac trusts Abraham
3. God provides a ram for the burnt offering
4. God promises to bless Abraham and multiply his descendants because of his faithful obedience
5. God tests us but will not allow us to be tempted beyond our endurance, therefore let us trust in God when tested

*1 Peter 3:18-22 (C) (RC)*
### Christ Died for Sins Once for All

1. Christ, the righteous, died for the unrighteous to bring us to God
2. Christ preached to those in Hades

3. Baptism which corresponds to the flood saves us through the resurrection of Jesus Christ
4. Christ has gone into heaven and is at the right hand of God
5. Trust in Christ who died for your sins and who intercedes for us at the right hand of God

*Romans 8:31-39 (L)*
## Who Shall Separate Us from the Love of Christ

1. If God is for us, who is against us?
2. Who shall bring any charge against God's elect?
3. Who shall separate us from the love of Christ?
4. We are more than conquerors through him who loved us
5. Nothing will be able to separate us from the love of God in Christ Jesus
6. Therefore, live a life of confident trust in God's love


*This Preacher's Choice*

*Mark 1:9-15 (C)*
*Mark 1:12-15 (L) (RC)*
## The Kingdom of God Is At Hand: Repent, Believe!

1. Jesus was baptized for sinners by John in the Jordan
2. The Spirit descended upon Jesus and God affirmed Jesus
3. Jesus is tempted by Satan in the wilderness
4. Jesus came preaching that the kingdom of God is at hand
5. Jesus calls people to repent and believe in the Gospel because the kingdom is imminent
6. Repent by turning from sin to God and believe the Gospel

**Hymn for Lent 1:** *Amazing Grace! How Sweet the Sound*

**Prayer**

*Gracious God, who has made a covenant with us in Jesus' death on the cross, we thank you for your gracious saving acts in history. We thank you for the promise in the rainbow that, never again, will you destroy all flesh by flood. We thank you that you were gracious to Abraham and provided a ram in the place of Isaac his son for a sacrifice. We rejoice in the assurance that no one can condemn us, for Christ died for us and was raised for our salvation. We stand firm in the assurance that nothing in this life or in the age to come will be able to separate us from your love in Christ Jesus our Lord. Grant us the courage to repent of our sins, believe in the Gospel and live henceforth in the kingdom as faithful sons and daughters. Amen*

# Lent 2

<table>
<tr><td>Common</td><td>Lutheran</td><td>Roman Catholic</td></tr>
<tr><td>Genesis 17:1-10, 15-19</td><td>Genesis 28:10-17 (18-22)</td><td>Genesis 22:1-2, 9-13, 15-18</td></tr>
<tr><td>Romans 4:16-25</td><td>Romans 5:1-11</td><td>Romans 8:31-34</td></tr>
<tr><td>Mark 8:31-38</td><td>Mark 8:31-38</td><td>Mark 9:2-10</td></tr>
</table>

## Comments on the Lessons

Since there are eight different lessons in today's lectionary readings, the discussion of each by necessity must be brief. However, the preacher is urged to do thorough commentary work on the lesson(s) selected as the basis of the sermon. The Genesis 17 reading is the account of the naming of Abraham, the making of the covenant between God and Abraham and circumcision as a sign of the covenant. The Genesis 28 reading tells of Jacob's vision of the ladder from earth to heaven at Bethel and Jacob's vow to God made there. In Genesis 22 we learn of the testing of Abraham by obeying God's command to offer Isaac as a sacrifice, the substitution of a ram, and the renewal of God's covenant with him. Romans 4 deals with Abraham's faith which was reckoned to him as righteousness, a faith which will be reckoned to believers today as righteousness. Romans 5 discusses the consequences of justification by faith. The Romans 8 passage expresses our confidence in God who has justified us through Christ's death on the cross. Mark 8 is concerned with discipleship. Mark 9:2-10 is the account of the Transfiguration of Jesus and his charge to the disciples not to tell what they had seen until after his resurrection.

## Commentary

### Genesis 17:1-10, 15-19 (C)

Here the priestly account of the covenant of circumcision is another version of the covenant with Abraham. In verse 1 "God Almighty" (El Shaddai) means "God, the One of the Mountains." This was a name for God, current in the period before Moses, and may have been brought with the patriarchs from Mesopotamia. A covenant (v. 2) was a relationship between a superior and an inferior party in which the former establiahes or "makes" the covenant. In Abraham's case the making of the covenant by God involved giving Abram a new name, Abraham, which means "the (divine) Father is exalted." It is a variant of Abram and similar to the Hebrew for "father of a multitude." (v. 5) The multitude refers to those who trace their ancestry to Abraham which included Edomites and Ishmaelites as well as Israel herself. To keep the covenant was to practice circumcision which was an external sign of membership in the covenant community. In contrast with the covenant with Noah which included all people, the covenant with Abraham was binding on Israel only, and was a covenant in the flesh. Circumcision existed before the Hebrews appeared in history, and is still an initiation rite in many savage tribes today.

Circumcision as a mark of the covenant had the same symbolic significance as the passing through the divided portions of animals by God and Abraham at sundown. (Genesis 15:7-21) Death is implicit in the ratification of the covenant so that either party breaking the covenant falls under the penalty of death.

### Genesis 28:10-17 (18-22) (L)

The story begins with Jacob leaving Beersheba and going toward Haran. The lonely traveler stops to rest when the sun goes down. The place, Bethel, which would later become famous as a place of great pilgrimages, but now is wasteland without cultic building. Jacob has two dream revelations, one of the ladder to heaven (v. 12), and the other of God's manifestation to him (v. 13ff). The dream shows what Jacob will later call the "gate of heaven." (v. 17b) This was the narrow place, according to the ancient world view, where all intercourse between earth and the upper divine world took place. (The preacher may need to remind the congregation of the "three story universe" of the ancient world.)

God's messengers go back and forth continuously fulfilling divine commands and supervising the earth. The ziggurat or temple tower was thought of by the Babylonians as the bond between heaven and earth. Now the Elohist's version of the vision concludes with verse 12. It was a great dream which made Jacob certain he had been at precisely the entrance into the heavenly world. Now begins in verse 13 the Yahwistic version which thought of the event as a theophany and solemn address to Jacob. God is thought of as the "God of the fathers." Note the twofold promise of *land* and *descendants*. (v. 13) This is a renewal of an earlier promise to his father and grandfather — a promise of tillable land and posterity.

Being an emigrant in the ancient world was dangerous, like being a "boat person" or emigrant today. God promises in verse 15 to be with Jacob and keep him wherever he goes and to bring him back to this land.

We see that in verses 16-17 this night experience was much more than an inner consolation for Jacob. God revealed himself to Jacob in a way which would affect material and spatial matters. These verses are concerned with the realistic statement of an objective fact, with the right understanding of a place. Jacob says, "Surely the Lord is in this place" (v. 16) and the result is pious shuddering: "and he was afraid, and said, "How awesome is this place!" (v. 17)

So Jacob erects a memorial column which took great strength, for such massebahs in other parts of the Orient are often seven feet high. There are other references to Jacob's great strength. (29:10; 32:25ff) But the purpose of the story is to tell how Bethel (house of God) became a cultic center and how the holiness of the place came about. But it also seeks to explain the circumstances connected with the stone at Bethel. Jacob dedicated it to God and poured oil on it. Probably in later years the participants in the cult at Bethel poured oil on the stone also. This was certainly the case with the tithe (v. 22), for Amos mentions this custom (4:4).

This cultic center at Bethel was important for the narrator(s) of the Genesis stories. This story is a "roots" story which Israelites enjoyed re-telling to explain the holiness of the cultic center at Bethel.

### *Genesis 22:1-2, 9-13, 15-18 (RC)*

In this account of the testing of Abraham we see a miracle of faith. Abraham received back the promise after showing that he had the faith to surrender his only heir, Isaac. Isaac was his one means of the fulfillment of the promise of descendants. In its oldest form, the story tells how God relaxed his claim upon the first-born and provided an animal for a substitute. (Exodus 13:2, 11-16; 22:29) God tested Abraham, put him under trial to see if he would obey in faith. This is a pedagogical test which God permits people to endure in order to push their faith to the limit, and is not new in patriarchal stories. What is new here is the appearance of testing in the very first verse of the story, as well as its destructive harshness. This testing is a part of cult life in which the ritual of the ordeal occurs. In it God seeks to bring to light guilt or innocence. The place of Moriah is unknown, although some identify it with Jerusalem.

Expositors like to compare Abraham's walk with Isaac with Elijah's last walk with Elisha. (2 Kings 2:1-6) Notice the old man's answer to the child's intelligent question: "God will provide himself the lamb for a burnt offering, my son." The answer is somewhat ambiguous, but contains a kernal of truth of which Abraham himself is not yet aware.

In verses 9-13 we are given details with frightful accuracy, like a novelist would give in creating a moment of high tension in a story. It puts the reader there as the event occurs. The angel of the Lord calls from heaven, and this is the only form in which God appears. The distinction between God and the angel is almost removed, for in everything it is God's voice that speaks to Abraham and says, "I know that you fear God." (v. 12) The "fear of God" in the Old Testament refers to obedience, not to strong emotions in the presence of God. So fear of God refers not to feelings but to obedience to the divine commands.

God provides a ram for the sacrifice and Abraham offers it up as a burnt offering. Abraham calls the name of the place, "The Lord will provide." It appears that the narrative once ended at verse 14. But God speaks a second time in a story which must have been added to the ancient cultic legend. The thrust of this second part is to link the story with the motif of promise, a motif which unites all Abraham narratives. This finale ends powerfully and celebrates the victor from Moriah. Abraham swears by himself, which does not occur any more in parallel passages.

There are many levels of meaning to this story, and, if the preacher thinks he or she has discovered them all, then another reading and reflection may reveal more meanings. It has often been compared to the crucifixion in which the Father offers the Son, but there is no ram provided for the sacrifice.

God experiences the desolation of losing his only Son. Abraham was tested in his faith, but his son was spared.

### *Romans 4:16-25 (C)*

This passage is a good compliment to the Genesis 17 and 22 reading in that it points out that the true descendants of Abraham are those who have faith in Christ, whether Jews or Gentiles. The benefits promised to Abraham are theirs, because they have faith which is reckoned to them as righteousness. Abraham was fully convinced that God was able to do what he had Promised. The essence of God's promises is that they are kept, and faith is the confidence that they are kept. The basis of salvation is thus faith on the part of human beings and sheer generosity on God's part. Abraham's faith consists in taking God at his word when he promised to make him the father of many nations. Abraham believed that God could, by his creative power, bring about the seemingly impossible.

Abraham apparently was beyond being capable of fathering a child and Sarah had been barren, but now God promises them offspring, and this is enough. Notice that verses 19-21 consist of six clauses of which the first three are constrasted with the last three. There was no weakening of Abraham's faith; he faced the fact of his and Sarah's impotence, and he never doubted God's promise. Rather, Abraham was strong in the faith, acknowledged the wonderful power of God, and was certain God could fulfill his promise.

In verse 19 "barrenness" is literally "deadness," a Hebrew usage. It was faith of this quality (v. 22) which made Abraham accepted by God.

Paul argues that what was said about Abraham is applicable to all people. (v. 24) Abraham believed that God would bring life out of deadness, and so we must believe that God has raised our Lord from the dead. Jesus died because death is the inevitable result of sin and trespasses. Christ rose again because God's purpose meant new life for a renewed humanity: "raised for our justification." (v. 25)

### *Romans 5:1-11 (L)*

Paul describes the consequences of justification in this passage, which develops further the thought of 4:25. When we rely upon God alone for justification and not on ourselves, we have peace, reconciliation, a state of harmony and wholeness with God. Although we have fallen short of the glorious destiny for which we were created by God, now we find ourselves confidently expecting it. We have peace instead of hostility with God. Because we have this peace with God and hope, Christians can keep their confident assurance although they must suffer for their faith. A sterling character is produced by such faith and courage in the face of suffering. This expectation of great things from God (v. 5) is already being realized in an experience of God's love here and now by the power of the Holy Spirit.

The underlying basis of this peace with God is the reconciling work of Christ (v. 6) who died for the ungodly. Christ in his death bore the consequences of our sin and thus reconciled us to God. Christ died at the "right time," the time of human beings' extreme need. The fact that Christ had to die to save sinners is an indication of the extreme need.

But human beings are not ready to sacrifice themselves for another person, even for the just and good. There are instances where one person risks or loses her or his life for another person. But these are rare. On the other hand, God proves his love for us by giving everything while we were worth nothing. (v. 8) Christ's sacrificial death has put us right with God, (v. 9) and this is the guarantee that we shall be saved from the final judgment.

Note that for Paul God is always the one who reconciles, and human beings are the ones reconciled. The reconciled share the life of Christ and we rejoice in God. Sharing this divine life is the true meaning of being saved.

### *Romans 8:31-34 (RC)*

In this passage Paul expresses his great confidence in God. History tells us that to be a Christian in the first century was both difficult and dangerous. But with God on the side of the Christian no one can bring a charge against God's elect or condemn the Christian.

The basis of this unshakable confidence in God is the experience of God's goodness. This confidence is not new, but was expressed in the Old Testament as well. (2 Kings 6:15ff) But God's saving actions in Christ have greatly strengthened this experience of God's love. In verse 32 "spare" can mean either "begrudge" or "spare," and the former is preferable since the emphasis here is on God's generosity. In answer to the question of "who is to condemn?" the answer comes in the account of

Christ's saving actions. (v. 34) And Christ is the one who pleads our cause. Paul concludes this section by declaring that nothing at all can separate us from the love of Christ. He lists the things which oppress people and make them wonder if God has deserted them. But in the face of all such disasters God's love in Christ remains firm.

### *Mark 8:31-38 (C) (L)*

This passage follows immediately after the Great Confession (v. 29) of Peter on behalf of the disciples. Peter confessed that Jesus was the Christ (Messiah), but Jesus charged them to tell no one about him, emphasizing the Messianic secret of Mark's theology. Then in verse 31 Jesus explains what lies ahead for him, the son of Man, in fulfilling his mission. This goes directly counter to the popular notion of Messiah who would come with force to inaugurate the rule of God on earth.

The Son of man, says Jesus, must:
1. suffer many things,
2. be rejected by the elders and the chief priests and the scribes,
3. be killed, and
4. after three days rise again. (v. 31)

But Peter reacted to this description of the role of Messiah in a very negative way. Peter rebuked Jesus. Then Jesus turned, and seeing the disciples, rebuked Peter! He said to Peter, "Get behind me, Satan! For you are not on the side of God, but of men." (v. 33)

Next Jesus outlined the self-sacrifice necessary in order to follow him:

1. let him deny himself
2. take up his cross, and
3. follow me.

Jesus goes on to give a paradox: "Whoever would save his life will lose it; and whoever loses his life for my sake and the gospel's will save it." (v. 35) Life can only be gained by losing it for Christ's sake, denying self, taking up one's cross, and following Jesus.

Jesus warns that whoever is ashamed of him now in this adulterous (perhaps a metaphor for idolatrous) generation, of him will the Son of man be ashamed when he comes at the Parousia at the End of the Age.

### *Mark 9:2-10 (RC)*

Mark gives his account of the Transfiguration of Jesus which occurred six days after the Great Confession. Jesus took Peter, James and John up a high mountain apart by themselves and there he was transfigured before them. Mark thus describes a vision of Jesus in heavenly glory as the Messiah. While the precise form of the experience is difficult to determine, the important thing is the revelation which occurred. Mark sees this event as a confirmation of the Messiahship of Jesus. "Transfigured" means having a non-earthly appearance. Elijah the prophet was expected to appear before Messiah appeared. Moses represented the Law and was traditionally the author of the first five books of the Bible. The "three booths" refer to temporary shelters. Peter proposes them as temporary dwellings in which to prolong the experience.

The voice from heaven marks the uniqueness of Jesus: "This is my beloved Son; listen to him." (v. 7) The cloud is a symbol of the divine presence in the theophanies of the Exodus (a pillar of fire by night and a cloud by day led the children of Israel through the wilderness). In the New Testament the cloud is connected with the Transfiguration, Ascension and Parousia. The cloud is the vehicle of God's presence from which he speaks.

As they came down the mountain Jesus charged them to tell no one what they had seen until the Son of man had risen from the dead. This is another instance of the Messianic secret which forms part of Mark's theology. In this instance the disciples kept the secret, but questioned among themselves what the rising from the dead meant. (v. 10)

## Theological Reflections

Genesis 17 gives the renewal of the covenant God made with Abraham, in which he is given a new name and circumcision is to be a sign of the covenant. In Genesis 28 God appears to Jacob in a dream and reminds him that God has promised land and descendants to Abraham and Isaac and now to him. Jacob erects a pillar and anoints it with oil. This is a renewal of the covenant and explanation of the origin of worship at Bethel. The theme of Genesis 22 is the testing of Abraham's faith in taking Isaac up a mountain to offer him as a sacrifice. A ram is provided by God, and God commends Abraham for his faith and renews the promise of land and descendants. In all three passages we see the central significance of the covenant made by God, the superior, with Abraham, the inferior, and renewed with his descendants. Romans 4 centers on faith as the key to righteousness, a faith like that of Abraham, the father of us all. Faith in Christ who was put to death and raised from the dead is the key to righteousness says Paul. Romans 5 spells out the consequences of justification by faith, among which are peace and hope and character. We are justified by faith in Christ's death by which we are reconciled to God. Romans 8 affirms the Christian's confidence in God who has justified us through Christ's death and resurrection. In Mark 8 Jesus outlines the role of the Son of man in fulfilling his mission on earth, and gives the conditions of discipleship: denial of self, taking up one's cross, and following Jesus. In Mark 9 we have an account of the Transfiguration which confirmed Jesus as Messiah who fulfilled the Law and the Prophets, represented on the mountain by Moses and Elijah. The covenant of the Old Testament made by God with Abraham is fulfilled in Christ's death and resurrection and God's people are saved by faith in a covenant relationship with God.

## Homiletical Moves

*Genesis 17:1-10, 15-19 (C)*
### God's Covenant with Abraham

1. God calls Abram to walk before him and be blameless
2. God gives Abram a new name, Abraham, a father of a multitude
3. God renews the promise of land and descendants
4. God gives circumcision as a sign of the covenant
5. God has given us baptism as a sign of the covenant, therefore live in covenant life with God

*Genesis 28:10-17 (18-22) (L)*
### Bethel, the House of God and Gate of Heaven!

1. Jacob dreams of a ladder from earth to heaven on which angels go up and down
2. God stood above the ladder and renews the covenant with Jacob made with Abraham and Isaac of land and descendants
3. Jacob awoke from the dream with fear and awe and said, "This is the house of God and gate of heaven"
4. Jacob rose early in the morning and set up the stone which he had put under his head, and anointed it with oil, calling the place Bethel — house of God
5. Jacob makes a deal with God to tithe if God will be with him, bring him again to his father's house in peace, and give him food and clothing.
6. God has promised to be with us by the Spirit, therefore let us live in grateful response to his covenant love

*Genesis 22:1-2, 9-13, 15-18 (RC)*
### God Tests the Faith of Abraham

1. God commands Abraham to take his only son, Isaac, up and sacrifice him
2. Abraham obeys but at the last moment God tells him not to slay his son and a ram is supplied instead
3. Abraham offers a burnt offering and calls the place "The Lord will provide"
4. God renews his covenant with Abraham, promising descendants and land, and assuring him that through him and his descendants all the nations of the earth will be blessed
5. When God tests our faith, let us trust him not to test us beyond our endurance, and put our faith in his promises

*Romans 4:16-25 (C)*
## Faith Reckoned as Righteousness

1. Abraham was justified by faith, not works
2. Abraham's faith in God was credited to him as righteousness
3. Our faith in God who raised Jesus from the dead will be reckoned to us as righteousness also
4. Therefore, accept God's justification by faith and live in faithful obedience

*Romans 5:1-11 (L)*
## The Consequences of Justification by Faith

1. We have peace with God
2. We have hope of sharing the glory of God
3. We are reconciled to God by the death of Jesus and saved by his life
4. We rejoice in God
5. Therefore, live as sinners saved by grace through faith

*Romans 8:31-34 (RC)*
## The God Who Justifies

1. Since God justifies, who can condemn?
2. God did not spare his own Son but gave him up for us all
3. God will give us all things with him
4. Christ who was raised to the right hand of God intercedes for us
5. Turn to Christ in prayer for assurance and help

*Mark 8:31-38 (C) (L)*
## The Cost of Discipleship

1. Denial of self
2. Taking up one's cross
3. Following Jesus
4. Not being ashamed of Jesus in this age
5. Will you pay the cost of Christian discipleship?

*Mark 9:2-10*
## Jesus, the Beloved Son of God

1. Jesus takes Peter, James and John up a mountain apart
2. Jesus is transfigured and his garments become white
3. Moses and Elijah appear to them
4. A voice from heaven speaks from a cloud, "This is my beloved Son; listen to him"
5. Jesus charges the disciples to tell no one until he has risen from the dead, and they question what the rising from the dead meant
6. Live in faithful obedience to the Risen Christ

**Hymn for Lent 2:**   *The God of Abraham Praise*

**Prayer**
    *Holy God who made a covenant with Abraham your servant, who tested his faith, and who renewed the covenant through the ages, we humbly bow before you to confess our sin of trusting in our good works rather than putting our faith in you. Forgive us we earnestly pray, for we trust in Christ's death on the cross for our salvation. We seek to come after him in daily living by denying self, taking up our cross and following him. Grant us a vision of the risen Christ who intercedes for us. We rejoice in the assurance that no one can condemn us for we put our trust in Christ who died in our place. Amen*

# Lent 3

| Common | Lutheran | Roman Catholic |
| --- | --- | --- |
| Exodus 20:1-17 | Exodus 20:1-17 | Exodus 20:1-17 |
| 1 Corinthians 1:22-25 | 1 Corinthians 1:22-25 | 1 Corinthians 1:22-25 |
| John 2:13-22 | John 2:13-22 | John 2:13-25 |

## Comments on the Lessons

There is consensus on the first reading which contains the Ten Commandments. There is consensus on the second reading. There is virtual consensus on the reading from John. Some omit verses 23-25 as editorial comments that are extraneous to the passage.

## Commentary

*Exodus 20:1-17*

There were two forms of law in Israel: casuistic and apodictic. Casuistic laws were characterized by a conditional style which defined specific legal cases. There was often an elaborate differentiation of subordinate circumstances. On the other hand, apodictic laws were marked by an unconditional imperative style, usually in the second person and expressed in the negative. Apodictic law was unique to Israel and provided what is called "true Israelite law" and is the kind of law found in the Ten Commandments.

The Ten Commandments or Decalogue (from Greek deka + logos, meaning ten words) are found here and in Deuteronomy 5:6b-21 and there are minor differences in the two accounts. Some religious traditions divide them differently. Judaism understanding the statement, "I am the Lord your God, who brought you out of the land of Egypt, out of the house of bondage," (v. 2) as the first commandment. Actually it is a preface which sums up the meaning of the Exodus. It therefore sets the law within the context of God's redeeming action. Judaism sees the prohibition against other gods and graven images as a single commandment. Protestants and Roman Catholics also differ in regard to verses 3-4 which Roman Catholics combine, and verse 17 which Roman Catholics divide into two commandments. Some scholars think that the original Decalogue consisted of short prohibitions and commands without any elaboration such as found in verses 4, 5, 17, etc. The explanatory comments reflect a later period in Israel's life and therefore, in their present form, cannot have been written by Moses. But without these additions they could have been written by Moses. Not all scholars agree that the Decalogue was originally a unified list of short commandments, and, even among those who do agree, not all agree that they came from Moses.

The Ten Commandments sum up the duties of human beings toward God and neighbor. The first four are concerned with God, and the last six with neighbor. The preacher will need to set the commandments in the context of Christian theology, including the views of Jesus and Paul toward the Law. Obedience to the Law must be proclaimed as response to God's saving work in Christ, rather than as a legal code by which one earns salvation.

A brief overview of the Commandments is as follows:

1. "You shall have no other gods before me." (v. 3) This is the basic demand made on Israel. Israel is here addressed in the collective second person and in what follows. The Southern "you all" is the nearest English has to this form. This is the most important commandment of all and rightly stands at the beginning. It calls for an unconditional exclusive worship of God. The reason there are to be no other gods is that the Lord is a jealous God. (v. 5)

2. "You shall not make for yourself a graven image . . ." (v. 4) This commandment forbids the making of any kind of representation of gods. The basis for this is the idea in the ancient world that an image had a firm connection with the being it portrayed, and that, with the help of an image, a man might gain power over the being represented in the image. Thus Israel is prohibited from making any image whatsoever to keep the people from attempting to gain power over God or gods.

3. "You shall not take the name of the Lord your God an vain . . ." (v. 7) Another translation is "You shall not abuse the name of Yahweh your god . . . " The word "vain" is synonymous with the word "evil" here. Behind it lies the notion that the name is a part of the being who has it, and the bearer of the name is present in some mysterious way in the name. The divine name is like the divine image. It must be protected from possible misuse. Some see the thrust of this commandment to be, "You shall not swear falsely by the name of the Lord your God." But the commandment had a wider meaning than swearing falsely, although very early, and throughout the rest of the Old Testament, the commandment was interpreted primarily in the sense of swearing falsely.

4. "Remember the sabbath day, to keep it holy." (v. 8) The origin of the word sabbath is unsettled. It probably is derived from a Hebrew word meaning "to rest, cease from work." The major thrust of the commandment falls on the verb "to hallow." This means to make holy, to set aside the sabbath for something special. The sabbath belongs to God and is tied to the act of creation. Israel is commanded to observe the sabbath in order to remember its slavery and deliverance, and so the thrust of the writer of Deuteronomy in regard to the sabbath is theological, not humanitarian. (5:12ff) The sabbath is to be observed as a day separated from the others and kept holy and apart as a period of time belonging especially to God.

5. "Honor your father and your mother . . ." (v. 12) This is a misunderstood commandment usually applied to small children or rebellious adolescents to get them to obey their parents. But the commandment applies to adults who care for aging parents and are to show honor to them! Notice that the commandment has been expanded by a promise and warning. The problem of the right of the parent grew out of a number of situations and, at the heart of the original law, was a command which protected parents from being driven out of the home or abused after they could no longer work. To honor is to prize highly, to show respect, to glory and exalt. The word has nuances of caring for and showing affection to parents. The word honor is frequently used to describe the proper response to God and is like worship.

6. "You shall not kill." (v. 13) The difficulty in understanding this commandment is in determining the precise meaning of the Hebrew verb translated "to kill." It refers to a special kind of killing. It means arbitrary killing, as over against killing in war and by the death penalty of a law court. The commandment forbids an act of violence against another person which arises from personal feelings of hatred and malice. It rejects the right of persons to take the law into their own hands because of a personal injury.

7. "You shall not commit adultery." (v. 14) The meaning is clear. The commandment seeks to maintain the sanctity of marriage and either man or woman can be the subject of adultery. Adultery was placed in a different category from fornication by Israel.

8. "You shall not steal." (v. 15) The verb lacks a specific object and can refer either to a person or object. It has a nuance of secrecy. Notice that this seems to overlap with the tenth commandment forbidding coveting.

9. "You shall not bear false witness against your neighbor." (v. 16) Another translation is "You shall not testify in the law court against your neighbor as a lying witness." The law seeks to guard the member of the covenant community of Israel against the threat of false accusation. The original commandment was not a general prohibition against lying, but is directed against lying which affects one's neighbor.

10. "You shall not covet your neighbor's house . . ." (v. 17) The form of this commandment has some features which set it apart from the other nine. For one, the verb "to covet" in the first prohibition is repeated in an independent clause, but with a different object. This led the Roman Catholic and Lutheran traditions to see verse 17b as an independent commandment. Also, the verb seems to denote a subjective emotion, while the other laws were directed against an objective action. The original command was directed against that desire which led to the acquiring of the object coveted.

*1 Corinthians 1:22-25*

The Gospel message seemed foolish because it did not meet the wants of the people. That the Jews sought signs is clear from the Gospels. (Mark 8:11-12; John 4:48) But Jesus refused to perform miracles to validate his mission, and the miracle-loving church preserved this refusal. The Greeks loved philosophy. They tried to turn the Christian faith into a logical system of doctrine. The idea of a crucified Messiah was nonsense to both Greek and Jew. The word for "stumbling-block" (v. 23) was a favorite word of Matthew for temptation to sin. In Romans 9:33 Paul connects this word with that which caused Israel to sin.

But to those who were called by God, the Gospel is both power and wisdom. The wisdom of God was considered a separate hypostasis in a considerable amount of the later Jewish writings. While it might be tempting to write Paul off as a preacher who belittled all learning, we know that this is not the case. He was a very highly educated person, although educated in a restricted way. He does not discredit such knowledge. But Paul knows that such knowledge does not bring people to know God. Knowledge of God depends on God's own act of redemption in the cross of Jesus Christ. Thus knowledge of God comes, not through human knowledge, but through the revelation of God in Jesus Christ. This foolishness of God, as Paul calls it, is wiser than men and the weakness of God is stronger than men, says Paul.

### *John 2:13-22 (C) (L)*
### *John 2:13-25 (RC)*

This account of the cleansing of the Temple follows the miracle at the wedding in Cana. The miracle at Cana suggests that Jesus' revelation fulfills and supersedes the ordinary daily ceremonies of the Jewish cultic system. Now, in the cleansing of the Temple event, the same theme is illustrated with reference to the very heart and center of Jewish sacrificial worship.

Notice that in the Synoptic Gospels this bold act of Jesus is recorded as an event in the last week of his life. There it appears as a prophetic protest against the profanation of the temple by fraudulent practices within its confines. Jesus drives out the money changers in order to make it a fit "house of prayer for all the nations" in the coming messianic age. The effect of this bold act is to solidify the opposition of the Jewish religious leaders against Jesus and to motivate them to destroy him.

In John's Gospel the incident means all this and more. John places it at the beginning of Jesus' ministry at Passover time. Although not a miracle, it is a sign of what will be fulfilled by Jesus' death and resurrection. Notice that Jesus drives out, not only the wicked money-changers, but also the innocent animals as well. In doing so Jesus points to a more drastic "purifioation" of worship in which the old cult of animal sacrifice is ended and the inauguration of a worship in "spirit and truth" is begun.

The temple was begun in 20/19 B.C. but was not finished until A.D. 64 and then was destroyed by the Romans in A.D. 70. Jesus predicted its destruction. This was used against him at his trial. (Mark 14:57-59) The original form of Jesus' prediction is probably recorded in verse 19. Jesus is the true "Lamb of God who takes away the sin of the world." (1:29) Jesus' sacrificial body is the new temple. In and through the risen Christ the disciples and believers who come after them will offer a spiritual sacrifice acceptable to God in a building not made with hands, Jesus' Body, the Church.

Animals were sold for sacrifice in the temple and Roman money was exchanged for Jewish money to pay the temple tax. In verses 15-16 Jesus expresses the energy of righteousness against the religious leaders who made religion into a business. This was not an outburst of temper, but righteous indignation in action! Jesus says "my Father's house" and so claims lordship.

In verses 23-25 we learn that faith which rests just on signs and not on Jesus to whom they point is shallow and unstable and not to be trusted. Jesus knew what was in the heart of human beings.

## Theological Reflections

The Decalogue was given to guide Israel in living as a covenant people, indicating how they were to relate to God and to neighbor. It was never meant as a code by which Israel could earn salvation, but was part of God's gracious gift at Sinai when he made a covenant with Israel. Paul writes about the stumbling block of the gospel which is the power of God and the wisdom of God in contrast to human knowledge. Jesus drives the money-changers and those selling sacrificial animals in the temple out of the temple as an act of righteous indignation. He predicts his death and resurrection which confuses the Jewish religious leaders. But after Jesus' resurrection the disciples remembered his words and could understand them.

**Homiletical Moves**

*Exodus 20:1-17*
## You Shall Have No Other Gods

1. God is a jealous God who will brook no rival
2. God demands total loyalty and the sabbath is a time to remember God
3. God calls us to love our neighbor as ourselves as the last six commandments spell this out in concrete terms

*1 Corinthians 1:22-25*
## The Power and Wisdom of God

1. Jesus demands signs and Greeks seek wisdom
2. We preach Christ crucified and risen
3. Christ is the power and wisdom of God, wiser and stronger than human beings
4. Put your trust in the crucified and risen Christ!

*This Preacher's Choice*

*John 2:13-22 (C) (L)*
*John 2:13-25 (RC)*
## The Cleansing of the Temple

1. Jesus went up to the temple and drove out those selling animals and changing money
2. Jesus refuses to allow religion to become a business
3. Jesus predicts that if they destroy the temple of his body it will be raised up in three days
4. The disciples remembered Jesus' words after the resurrection and could understand the prediction
5. God calls us to faithful worship of the risen Christ

**Hymn for Lent 3:**    *Christ is Made the Sure Foundation*

**Prayer**

*Gracious God who has given us the covenant community in which to live in relationship to you and our neighbors, forgive us when we have disobeyed your laws. Teach us to live more faithfully, remembering your saving acts in history and in our lives. Grant that we may so believe the Gospel so that it will be power and wisdom in our lives. May we not be guilty of making a business out of religion but rather live faithful lives of humble obedience. May we live in daily communion with the risen and ascended Christ by the power of the Spirit. Amen*

# Lent 4

| Common | Lutheran | Roman Catholic |
|---|---|---|
| 2 Chronicles 36:14-23 | Numbers 21:4-9 | 2 Chronicles 36:14-17, 19-23 |
| Ephesians 2:4-10 | Ephesians 2:4-10 | Ephesians 2:4-10 |
| John 3:14-21 | John 3:14-21 | John 3:14-21 |

## Comments on the Lessons

There is near consensus on the 2 Chronicles reading which summarizes what led to the exile in Babylon. The Numbers passage tells of the serpent of bronze made by Moses, which healed those bitten by fiery serpents when they looked on it. There is virtual consensus on the Ephesian reading. Note that verses 1-3 are unnecessary since their message is repeated in verses 4-10. There is near consensus on the reading from John.

## Commentary

*2 Chronicles 36:14-23 (C)*
*2 Chronicles 36:14-17, 19-23 (RC)*

Here we have described the last agonies of the doomed nation. There is no parallel to verse 14 in 2 Kings where the blame is laid primarily on the king. Note that the writer does not include the Levites and musicians in his condemnation. In verse 21 there is a reference to "her sabbaths" and according to the final Law stated idealistically every seventh year the soil was to rest uncultivated. Ten such "sabbaths" would total seventy years, or threescore (score = 20) years and ten. This implies that the legitimate worship of God was held in abeyance from the time of Jerusalem's fall in 586 B.C. until the second temple was dedicated in 516 B.C. The loyal Hebrew priests and laymen returned to Jerusalem from captivity in Babylon in 538 B.C. and from 518-516 B.C. the temple was rebuilt and dedicated.

We find that verses 22-23 occur in Ezra 1:1 3a. They probably were added to the original document. When Chronicles was put at the very last of the Hagiographa these verses were added, it seems, to the original MSS in order that the Hebrew Scriptures might conclude on a note of hope. Otherwise, the chapter would read like the tolling of a funeral bell. Chronicles was written to the Jews of the author's time as a solemn warning and also as a command to perform their duty to God, and to give hope. It seems to have been written between 350 and 300 B.C. Originally 1 and 2 Chronicles and Ezra and Nehemiah were one book. The author knew and used the books of Samuel and Kings. This book is concerned with priestly things such as worship in the Temple, the transfer of the Ark and the building of the altar. The unknown writer of the book, known only as "the Chronicler" sought to present the correct procedure for the worship of God, and secondly to show that the plan of God was to be fulfilled through the Southern Kingdom of Judah.

The passage which ends the book contains the edict of Cyrus of Persia which permitted the exiles to return home from Babylon.

*Numbers 21:4-9 (L)*

As the Israelites left Mount Hor, they turned south toward the Red Sea and Ezion-geber. The people became impatient on the way. They spoke out against Moses and God, complaining that they had brought them out of Egypt to die in the wilderness. As punishment for rebellion God sent fiery serpents among the people which bit them, and many people died. They were called fiery because the venomous serpents bit the people and set up inflammation. This caused the people to come to Moses and confess that they had sinned. They asked Moses to pray to the Lord to take the serpents from them. So Moses prayed for them. God told Moses to make a fiery serpent of bronze and to set it up on a pole. The promise was that everyone bitten, when they saw the bronze serpent, would be healed and live. This seems to imply sympathetic magic. But the editor of the material insists that the cure comes from God.

In 2 Kings 18:4 we learn that the worship of the brazen serpent was practiced at that time during the Israelite monarchy. This story is probably told as a means of strengthening the prophetic teaching, which sought to eradicate the bronze serpent and other objects of superstition, and as an effort to teach the people that it was God who cured them. This story reflects serpent magic as practiced in ancient Egypt. The worship of God would preclude the worship of the serpent.

### Ephesians 2:4-10

Verses 1-10 are an introduction to what follows in Ephesians. We noted earlier that verses 1-3 are unnecessary since they are duplicated in verses 4-5. The thrust of the passage is God's gracious saving love while we were yet dead in our sins. There is a sharp black and white contrast between the high calling of the baptized who are saved by grace and their sinful state in their unredeemed past.

Literary evidence and other clues point to a Jewish Christian author of Ephesians who is not Paul but an admirer of Paul writing in his name. This is the position of the *Workbook,* although the name Paul will be used for convenience.

The emphasis of verses 4-7 is God's saving love, and that of verses 8-10 is salvation by grace. God's judgment and God's loving compassion cannot be separated. Note that in the prologue to Ephesians God's love and mercy have been praised. (1:5-8) This theme continues here with an even greater emphasis on the graciousness of God. Even when we (includes Jewish Christians as well) were dead through our trespasses, God who is rich in mercy out of his great love has made us alive together with Christ. The emphasis throughout is on the grace, the unmerited love of God in Christ, by which we are saved. The author puts in parenthesis "by grace you have been saved" and this is developed as the chief topic in verses 8-10.

The believer's new life with Christ is in and with him. Notice that the writer uses words which have the Greek prefix "with" three times close together here: "alive . . . with Christ," "raised up . . . with Christ," and "sit with him." The turning point for believers is *baptism* when God's grace is most effectively real, and a person moves from being an unbeliever to being a member of the body of Christ, the church. The words "with" and "together with" stress that salvation is shared both with Christ and other Christians in the body of Christ. It is significant that the thought here is of a transformation already made effective.

Verse 7 refers to the coming ages. Eternity is represented in the terms by which time was conceived, not as infinity, but as a succession of ages. God's purpose of blessing was before the foundation of the world and so, in turn, it continues to all eternity in the future. "The mercy of the Lord is from everlasting to everlasting upon them that fear him." (Psalm 103:17) God's graciousness is shown toward us in Christ Jesus.

In verses 8-9 the theme of verse 5's parenthesis "by grace you have been saved" is amplified. Note that we have here a summary of Romans 1-5 which is also generalized. The thrust is on the fact that we are not saved by our own efforts, our good works or moral living or piety, but by the *free gift* of God. There is nothing we can boast of in our salvation.

One of the indications that Paul did not write this passage is the fact that the *perfect* tense is used in speaking of salvation, while Paul always thinks of salvation as a process which continues throughout life. However, the use of the perfect here is consistent with the attitude toward eschatology revealed by the writer of Ephesians. While Paul could write elsewhere that he was "in Christ" now and hopes to be "with Christ" in heaven, the writer of Ephesians feels that the Christian is both "in Christ" and "with him in the heavenly places" here and now. For this reason he is more like the author of John's Gospel than Paul's letters.

Verse 10 is a positive counterpart to verse 9 since "for good works" is the obverse to "not because of works." Good works are the result, not the cause of salvation. God has not only saved us by grace, but has prepared a particular sphere in which we may serve and has given us tasks to do. Good works are not played down as unimportant in the Christian life, but neither are they the means of salvation.

### John 3:14-21

Notice that verses 14-15 continues Jesus' conversation with Nicodemus, but verses 16-21 are a reflection of the author of John rather than a part of the conversation. The passage begins with a reference to the Old Testament incident recorded in Numbers 21:9 when the fiery bronze serpent was set up on a pole by Moses, and everyone bitten by a serpent who looked at the bronze serpent was healed. John is saying that in a similar way Jesus must be lifted up and those who look on him (believe) will have eternal life.

The verb "to lift up" (v. 14) has a double sense here as it applies to Jesus Christ. Verse 13 has just referred to the descent of Jesus from heaven in the Incarnation and now the pendulum swings upward in regard to Jesus, the Son of man, being lifted up. Lifting up refers to the lifting up of Jesus on the cross, to his being raised from the tomb, and to his ascension to heaven. Jesus' exaltation on the cross is never separated from his exaltation to heaven in the theology of John. The Hebrew word for "lift up" can mean both death and glorification. Here, in John, "being lifted up" refers to a continuous process by which Jesus returns to the Father, a process which includes death, resurrection and ascension. The word "to glorify" has an ambiguous meaning also, as it refers to Jesus' glorification through the humiliation of his death.

While some have argued for a change of speaker at verse 13 and verse 16 this proposal is being rejected by leading scholars. While the evangelist has been at work in this discourse, his work does not begin at a particular verse. The homogeneity of style and of inclusions indicate this passage is a unity.

The theme of the earlier conversation of Jesus with Nicodemus was the kingdom of God and entrance to it by being born again. John uses a synonym for the kingdom, "eternal life" which becomes the theme of the remaining verses of this chapter. The gift of eternal life begins in the love of God. A person possesses it by faith. Note that in verse 15, "in him" belongs to "may have eternal life," while in verse 16 these words are connected to the verb "believes." Thus in the first instance "the Son of man" is the source of eternal life, while in the second he is the object of faith.

God gave the gift of his only son because of his love for the world, for all sinful human beings. He was willing to even give his son to die on the cross to save them. Without such saving they were doomed to spiritual ruin and death. The purpose in sending Jesus into the world was not to judge the world but to save the world. The one who believes in Jesus is thus saved from condemnation. By believing, the person has passed from death into the true, full and lasting life.

But the person who does not believe is condemned already. The very act of rejecting the Son is judgment here and now. The person who does evil hates the light and does not come to it. But the person who does what is true comes to the light so that it may be seen that the deeds that person does are wrought in God.

Verse 16 has been called by Luther "the gospel in miniature" and is, of course, one of the best known verses of the Bible. The word for love here is in the aorist which implies a supreme act of love. It is significant that God's love is directed toward the world here, while in other places as in 1 John 4:9, for example, God's love is toward Christians. God expresses his love for the world in the Incarnation and the death of the Son. God's giving refers not only to the Incarnation but also the crucifixion, the "lifting up" mentioned in verses 14, 15.

### Theological Reflections

2 Chronicles expresses the last agonies of the doomed nation, but also contains the edict of Cyrus permitting the exiles to return home from Babylon, thus ending with a note of hope. In the Numbers passage the healing power of the serpent lifted up by Moses in the wilderness is described, foreshadowing Jesus being "lifted up" on the cross, from the grave, and into heaven. Ephesians draws a sharp black/white contrast between the condition of human beings before and after salvation by the gracious love of God. John points us to the supreme love of God that sent the only Son to die for the sins of the world, that those who believe in him might have eternal life and not perish. The gracious saving love of God toward sinful human beings permeates the readings for today. He acts to save while they were yet sinners and unable to save themselves by good works. But salvation leads believers to do good works in response to salvation.

### Homiletical Moves

*2 Chronicles 36:14-23 (C)*
*2 Chronicles 36:14-17, 19-23 (RC)*
**Devastation for Israel, But God Acts!**

1. The leading priests and people were very unfaithful to God
2. God sent messengers (the prophets) but the people despised and mocked them
3. God allows the land to be devastated and the people to be taken into exile in Babylon

4. But God stirred up the spirit of Cyrus, king of Persia who allows the people to return to build a temple in Jerusalem
5. God calls us to be faithful and to build in stone and service for God!

*Numbers 21:4-9 (L)*
## The Healing Power of the Bronze Serpent

1. The Israelites complained against Moses and God for taking them out of Egypt to die in the wilderness
2. God sent serpents whose bites cause inflammation to bite the people and many died
3. The people repent and plead with Moses to pray to God to take away the serpents
4. Moses makes a bronze fiery serpent at the command of God, which he set up on a pole and everyone who is bitten by a serpent but sees the bronze serpent shall live
5. Repent and turn to Christ lifted up on the cross for healing for your life

*Ephesians 2:4-10*
## The God Who Is Rich in Mercy

1. God who is rich in mercy loved us while we were dead throughout our trespasses
2. God made us alive with Christ and made us sit with him in the heavenly places
3. Salvation is not your own doing, not by good works, but is a gift of God
4. We are God's workmanship, created an Christ Jesus for good works, which God prepared beforehand that we should walk in them
5. Accept salvation as a gift of the gracious God and live in joyful and humble obedience

*This Preacher's Choice*

*John 3:14-21*
## God So Loved the World He Gave His Only Son!

1. As Moses lifted up the serpent in the wilderness which gave healing to those bitten by snakes, so the Son of man must be lifted up in order to give healing to those who believe in him
2. God so loved the world that He gave his only Son to die for the world
3. God sent the Son into the world, not to condemn the world, but that the world might be saved through him
4. The person who does what is true comes to the light that it may be clearly seen that his/her deeds have been wrought in God
5. Believe in Christ and do what is true in obedience to him

**Hymn for Lent 4:**   *There's a Wideness in God's Mercy*

**Prayer**
*Gracious God, who has loved us while we were still dead in our trespasses, we repent of our sins and confess our faith in the saving power of Jesus' death on the cross. As we look up to the crucified Christ we confess that our sins helped nail him to the cross. We were there when they crucifed our Lord. We rejoice that you have made us alive with Christ and raised us up with him. May we be good and faithful servants of yours, walking in the good works which you have prepared beforehand. Thank you for showing the immeasurable riches of your grace in kindness toward us in Christ Jesus. Amen*

# Lent 5

|   Common   |   Lutheran   |   Roman Catholic   |
| --- | --- | --- |
| Jeremiah 31:31-34 | Jeremiah 31:31-34 | Jeremiah 31:31-34 |
| Hebrews 5:7-10 | Hebrews 5:7-9 | Hebrews 5:7-9 |
| John 12:20-33 | John 12:20-33 | John 12:20-33 |

## Comments on the Lessons

There is consensus on the Jeremiah passage which contains the promise of the new covenant written on the heart. There is virtual consensus on the second reading and consensus on the third reading.

## Commentary

*Jeremiah 31:31-34*

Jeremiah uses the oldest expression for covenant making — cutting a covenant — which reflects the actions described in Genesis 16:7-17, where the two partners to the covenant, God and Abraham, pass between the two halves of animals which have been cut apart. The implied threat is that such would happen to the party which broke the covenant. Israel broke the covenant by her disobedience but God remained faithful. God promises in this passage of Jeremiah that he will make a new covenant with the house of Israel and the house of Judah. It will not be like the old covenant which God made with their fathers when he brought them out of Egypt, a covenant which they broke, even though God was their ''husband'' and Israel God's ''wife.'' The covenant relationship was compared to a marriage relationship by Hosea and others after him. (cf. Jeremiah 3)

The prophet affirms that God will make a new covenant in their hearts — their minds and wills. This covenant is the antithesis of the earlier covenant cut on stone or written on parchment. Terms such as ''born anew'' and ''a new creation'' were not used at this time, but this promise of a new covenant written on the minds and wills of people expresses the same idea.

Religion must be internalized and spiritualized in order to have effect. This experience could be that of every Israelite. When this happened, then no one in Israel would need to teach another about God for all would know him.

God promises to forgive their iniquity and to ''remember their sin no more.'' (v. 34) In Jesus' death on the cross we see the new covenant fulfilled which Jeremiah foretold, a covenant made in human hearts by which their sins are forgiven. When the covenant is written on the hearts of people, then they respond to God's gracious forgiveness by living in obedience to his will. God reaffirms that he will be their God and they will be his people, one of the oldest forms of the covenant and one of the simplest forms.

*Hebrews 5:7-10 (C)*
*Hebrews 5:7-9 (L) (RC)*

Here the author seeks to show that Jesus, although not a descendant of Levi is indeed a high priest, one after the order of Melchizedek. Verses 5-6 give background in which we are told that Christ did not exalt himself to be made a high priest, but was appointed such by God the Father.

During Jesus' incarnation on earth, he offered up prayers and supplications with loud cries and tears to God and he was heard for his godly fear. A high priest must be able to sympathize with others in their suffering, and here we see that Jesus suffered and so qualified himself to be a high priest. The sufferings may refer primarily to the agony in Gethsemane (Luke 22:41-44), but it could also include the times when Jesus prayed to God when his life was in great danger and he was delivered from death.

Jesus was heard in his prayers for his godly fear. Scholars have tried to explain the meaning of this closing phrase of the verse. We don't know what was in the author's mind when he wrote this. It could mean that Jesus' prayer was answered in the sense that he received strength to submit himself to the Father's will and to bear the consequences.

Jesus learned obedience through what he suffered. (v. 8) Although Jesus was God's Son he learned obedience through suffering. It was not that he learned to be obedient through suffering for disobedience as we do, for being sinners, but rather that he learned by his experience of suffering what obedience to God involved for the life of human beings on earth.

Jesus was "made perfect," which refers to being completely adequate to achieve the goal of saving human beings. It means reaching a goal or destination rather than moral perfection.

Jesus procured eternal salvation for all who obey him. Obedience to the Living Christ is an integral part of faith in Christ. Eternal salvation stands in oontrast to temporal salvation gained through the Levitical law. (9:12)

He was designated a high priest after the order of Melchizedek. This is priesthood with a difference. In Genesis 14:17-20 we learn about the mysterious priest/king Melchizedek who was greater than Abraham or his descendent Levi. He is said to be without father or mother or genealogy and has neither beginning of days nor end of life and continues a priest forever. (Hebrews 7:3) This means simply that these facts are not recorded in Scripture.

Jesus was appointed to this office of high priest by God at the resurrection. Through the cross and resurrection Jesus became the source of eternal salvation for all who accept the gospel.

### John 12:20-33

John takes a traditional incident, the Greeks coming to Jesus, and uses it as a springboard for a discourse, much as he took the conversation with Nicodemus of last week as an occasion for a discourse. The Greeks were brought to Jesus by Philip and Andrew who were from Bethsaida where Greeks and Jews intermingled. These Greeks represent the Hellenistic world, whether they were Greek-speaking Jews of the Dispersion or Gentiles. Some think they were Gentiles only, but this writer accepts the Greek speaking Jews/Gentiles position.

The Greeks asked Philip, "Sir, we wish to see Jesus," words which many ministers have lettered on a sign and placed behind the pulpit as a reminder of their task in preaching. An inclusive rendering of this would be: "Preacher, we wish to see Jesus." The task of so proclaiming the gospel that men and women may see Jesus, be encountered by the Living Christ and so transformed into new creatures, is an awesome one.

Jesus replies to the Greeks' request, "The hour has come for the Son of man to be glorified." (v. 23) The purpose of this paragraph (vv. 20-26) is to show that the world-wide Christian mission, represented by the Greeks, presupposes the death and glorification of Jesus.

Jesus develops the themes: (1) unless a grain of wheat falls into the earth and dies, it remains alone; but if it dies, it bears much fruit, and (2) I, when I am lifted up from the earth, will draw all men to myself. The Greeks cannot "see" Jesus until after he has been crucified, for only then can they experience messianic salvation.

During his earthly ministry Jesus confined his ministry almost entirely to his own people, the Jews, and his contacts with Gentiles were exceptional, and each time, there is a reluctance on Jesus' part to break the barrier. Note that it was only later that Hellenistic preachers began proclaiming the gospel to Gentiles. (Acts 11)

The mission to the Gentiles could begin only after the wall of partition between Jew and Gentile, the Jewish law, had been broken down and for this reason Jesus limited his mission to the Jews. The "grain of wheat" must die before it can bring forth its fruit (winning Gentile converts). And it is only after the Son of man is lifted up (crucified, raised from the dead and ascended to heaven), that the Gentiles can be brought into the community of faith.

Jesus prays to the Father, "Father, glorify thy name." (v. 28) A divine voice answers, "I have glorified it, and I will glorify it again" and the crowd heard it, for Jesus says it was spoken for the crowd's sake, not his. Some thought the voice from heaven was thunder, others that an angel had spoken to Jesus. The response of Jesus is that the judgment of this world has come now, and the ruler of this world will be cast out. Those who hear God's word, and those who do not, but are deaf to it, stand under judgment. This is also the time for the defeat and expulsion of Satan, the ruler of this world. Jesus, when lifted up on the cross and exalted (John has deliberately used an ambiguous word) will draw all people to himself and away from Satan.

### Theological Reflections

In the Jeremiah passage God promises a new covenant written on the hearts of people which will enable them to know God firsthand. This will mean a renewal of them and a binding them to God, as the old covenant could not do. Hebrews seeks to show us that Jesus is a high priest after the order of Melchizedek, who is able to intercede for us for he knows our sufferings, having suffered and learned obedience through it. He procured salvation for all who obey him. John's Gospel gives an account of the conclusion of Jesus' public ministry when the Greeks come seeking him, and he declares that unless a grain of wheat dies it cannot produce fruit, and that the Son of man must be lifted up from the earth and so draw all people to himself. God's gracious acts in saving human beings is a common theme in these passages. The new covenant, Jesus as high priest, and Jesus' death and resurrection and ascension reveal God's mighty acts to save sinners.

## Homiletical Moves

*Jeremiah 31:31-34*
### The New Covenant Foretold

1. God promises a new covenant in which the law will be written on the hearts of his people
2. God promises to be Israel's God, and affirms Israel as his people
3. Then everyone will know God
4. God will forgive their iniquity and remember their sin no more
5. Accept the forgiveness God offers through the new covenant in Christ

*Hebrews 5:7-10 (C)*
*Hebrews 5:7-9 (L) (RC)*
### Jesus the High Priest

1. Jesus offered up prayers and supplications with loud cries and tears
2. Although a son, Jesus learned obedience through suffering
3. Jesus achieved his goal as high priest and became the source of eternal salvation for all who obey him
4. Jesus was designated a high priest after the order of Melchizedek
5. put your trust in Christ as Savior and obey him

***This Preacher's Choice***

*John 12:20-33*
### The Attractive Power of the Crucified and Risen Christ

1. The Greeks come seeking to see Jesus
2. Jesus tells them unless a grain of wheat dies it cannot bear fruit
3. A voice from heaven declares that God has glorified Jesus' name and will glorify it again
4. Jesus tells the crowd that judgment is now come and the ruler of this world shall be cast out
5. Jesus promises that when he is lifted up from the earth (crucified, risen and ascended) he will draw all people to himself
6. Come to Christ the crucified and risen Lord!

**Hymn for Lent 5:**   *Jesus Shall Reign*

**Prayer**
*Gracious God, we thank you for the new covenant in the death and resurrection of Jesus by which our sins are forgiven and we are bound to you in love. We thank you for writing this new covenant in our minds and wills and for revealing yourself to each of us as a God of mercy. We praise you for Jesus Christ, our high priest, who learned obedience through suffering and who is the source of eternal life for all who obey him. We thank you that Jesus has broken down the barriers between Jew and Gentile and, by his death, resurrection and ascension, has drawn all people to himself. May we hear your word of salvation to us, and live in faithful obedience. Amen*

# Passion Sunday

Palm Sunday

| Common | Lutheran | Roman Catholic |
|---|---|---|
| Isaiah 50:4-9a | Isaiah 50:4-9a | Isaiah 50:4-7 |
| Philippians 2:5-11 | Philippians 2:5-11 | Philippians 2:6-11 |
| Mark 11:1-11 | Mark 11:1-10 | Matthew 26:14-27, 66 |

## Comments on the Lessons

The first reading has virtual consensus and gives the obedient response of the servant of God. There is virtual consensus on the Philippians reading which is the "Kenosis" passage describing Jesus' self-emptying in coming to earth and his passion and exaltation. Mark describes the entry of Jesus into Jerusalem on Palm Sunday. Matthew tells of Jesus' betrayal and the Last Supper.

## Commentary

*Isaiah 50:4-9a (C) (L)*
*Isaiah 50:4-7 (RC)*

This third Servant Song of Isaiah is a song of faith sung by those who have learned the meaning of Israel's tragic history through prophecy. It expresses the experience of the Israelites in exile who have ears to hear, who submit with understanding to the humiliation of the Exile and wait expectantly for God's coming act of redemption which they are confident is near at hand. Hebrew thought moved easily from the individual to the group, even as Americans refer to Uncle Sam as an individual representing the people of the whole nation. This Song seems to have been composed by an Israelite to be sung by faithful exiles as an act of trust and belief. Notice that it is intensely individual in character. It probably was used in worship in which the individual exile would embody in himself or herself the experience of Israel. By singing the song in the assembly the Israelite identifies with the "servant."

Of all the Deutero-Isaiah servant songs this is probably the easiest to understand. It has been generally accepted as an individual lament in form. But it can more accurately be called an individual psalm of confidence. The thrust of verses 7ff is a broad development of the main two motifs of the psalm: (1) the confession of confidence in God, and (2) the certainty of being answered. But verses 4-5a have nothing to do with an individual lament. Notice that the one who confesses unshakable confidence in God in verses 5b-9 is the same one who is commissioned with an office of the word. So verses 4-9 are the confession of confidence spoken by one who is mediator of the word.

Turning to verse 4 we see that it and the first clause of verse 5 is the utterance of a person whose being is governed by hearing and speaking. This person is like a disciple, meaning that, in both hearing and speaking, the person is concentrated on God and the hearing and speaking have their source in God. God opens the disciple's ears to hear. God tells the disciple what to speak. The Servant has been awakened and aroused in order to hear God's word. It is a word to the prostrate, to Israel who is not in a position to hear the word. Thus the people Israel, like the Servant, must be aroused before she can hear the word that applies to her case.

In verses 4-5b we have the call of one who in verses 5b-9 attests his faith in the office committed to him. Notice that the Servant is entirely unable to exercise any control over the reception and transmission of a word that has no establishment in which it is at home. This is the chief characteristic of the prophetic office here. A second distinctive feature of the prophetic office is that God's servant is here described as God's "disciple." The fact that God's servant is God's disciple is the most important feature in the picture of the Servant.

The Servant who is attacked and defamed because of his task develops in this song for the first time a new approach: he assents and accepts this suffering. The servant believes God himself wills his suffering and its acceptance. Notice the glaring contradiction between verse 6 and verse 7. "Shame" and "ashamed" appear. God makes the servant's face like a flint. The power of his resistance derives from his acceptance of the blows and shameful treatment which he meets. Note that it is this complete acceptance and it alone that enables him to make his face hard as flint rock.

In verses 8-9 we find the certainty that the Servant feels that God is on his side expressed in a very forceful way by means of terms taken from the legal process. We can only understand this by seeing it from his opponent's point of view. In their eyes the contest is already decided and the Servant's case is lost, since he has admitted defeat by accepting the blows and acts of shame. The Servant summons those who oppose him, however. These are the people who smite him and shame him and spit upon him. He calls them into God's law court for he is convinced that God justifies him and that no one can condemn him.

In verse 9 the Servant declares and asks, "Behold, the Lord God helps me; who will declare me guilty?" He believes that those who mock and smite him will perish. But the question of whether there is the slightest possibility of any justification or rehabilitation for the Servant according to verses 4-9 is left open. The question points forward to the final servant song.

### Philippians 2:5-11 (C) (L)
### Philippians 2:6-11 (RC)

This is the "Kenosis" passage, so called because of the Greek word for emptying. The central thrust of this passage is the example of Christ. The disciples are to live with one another after the example of Christ in and with whom they dwell. This is one of the greatest and most moving passages Paul ever wrote about Jesus. The heart of this passage is summed up in Paul's letter to the Corinthians: "For you know the grace of our Lord Jesus Christ, that though he was rich, yet for your sake he became poor." (2 Corinthians 8:9)

Earlier Paul had pleaded with the Philippians to live in unity and harmony, to put away their personal ambitions, pride, desire for privilege and prestige. Here, Paul holds up the example of Jesus whose humility and self-emptying marked his life of service to others. In order to better understand what Paul is saying here, we need to look at the meaning of the key Greek words he uses.

In verse 6 Paul says that Jesus in his very essence was in the form of God. The essence is that which cannot be changed, the very innate and unalterable characteristics of a person. Two words in Greek can mean form in English: morphe, and schema. Morphe is the essential form of something, while schema is the outward form which changes from time to time. Throughout her life a woman may change from being a baby, to a child, to a young woman, an adult woman and an older woman, but her morphe remains the same while her schema is continually changing. The key point is that the morphe doesn't change, while the schema does. In verse 6 the word which Paul uses for the Jesus being in the form of God is morphe. So Jesus is, in his essence and unalterable form, God.

Then Paul goes on in the same verse to say that Jesus did not count equality with God something to be grasped. The word for "grasped" in Greek can mean snatch, or clutch. While Jesus did not need to snatch at equality, since he was by essence equal with God, he did not clutch at equality. He did not refuse to let it go but gave it up willingly.

Jesus emptied himself, taking the form of a servant. (v. 7) The word Paul uses for form here is morphe, which we saw earlier means essence or essential form. Jesus became really human. He became like human beings, being "made in the likeness of men." (v. 7, KJV) The word for made emphasizes the full identity of Christ with the race of human beings. Hebrews says of Jesus that "in all things it behooved him to be made like unto his brethren." (Hebrews 2:17)

And being found in fashion as a man (v. 8) is a statement in which Paul uses the word for "form" which means shape, appearance, that which changes, in contrast to the essence. Here Paul is writing from the point of view of those who saw Christ as he lived on earth. The mystery of his essence, his morphe, was hidden from them. They saw him as a man like themselves, subject to human suffering and fraility.

He humbled himself (v. 8) which indicates he laid aside all the heavenly privileges that were his. He became obedient to death, even death on a cross, which took his humility to the utmost limit. The emphasis is on the word "obedient."

Note the two pictures which Paul draws side by side and contrasts them. One is of Jesus in his original glory as the Pre-existent Christ, of the same nature with God, so near to God. On the other hand is Christ as he chose to be be, emptying himself, changing the form of God for that of man, and being obedient even to death on the cross.

But then Paul holds up a third picture of Jesus for us, the exalted Christ. "Therefore God has highly exalted him and bestowed on him the name which is above every name." (v. 9) The *name* held special meaning for people in Paul's day. The person was thought to somehow be present in the name. A soldier took his oath in the name of Caesar and, in doing so, became Caesar's man. And a Christian was baptized in the name of Jesus and thus gave his loyalty to Jesus and gained his protection. Paul is saying that the new name given Christ in his exaltation with its active power came from divine authority. This transcendent name given to Christ is none other than "Lord" as Paul will say in verse 11.

Jesus was exalted at the resurrection. His exaltation will be fully acknowledged at the Parousia when Christ returns in glory. This passage is modeled on Isaiah 45:23 which describes the purpose of God as that of bringing all nations to obedience to him. The triumph described is the manifestation of messianic lordship. This is attained as a result of the Incarnation. The whole work of Jesus, his whole life and aim is not his own glory, but the glory of God the Father. The one aim of Jesus was to point people to God. As the universe gives glory to God, it thereby achieves the goal of its creation and redemption.

Scholars generally agree that we have in this passage of verses 5-11 an early hymn which Paul has incorporated in his letter. Although it may have been composed by Paul, the hymn has ideas and terms not characteristic of Paul, and it lacks other concepts which are central to Paul's theology. Therefore, this may well be a pre-Pauline hymn used here because of its pertinence to the issues with which Paul is dealing. Some would divide the hymn into six strophes of six lines each.

*Mark 11:1-11 (C)*
*Mark 11:1-10 (L)*

Here begins a new section of Mark's Gospel which depicts Jesus' ministry in Jerusalem. The passage may be divided into four parts: (1) setting (v.1); (2) procuring the colt (vv. 2-6); (3) acclamation on approaching Jerusalem (vv. 7-10); (4) conclusion (v. 11). We are so familiar, as are most church folks, with this story that we are likely to miss the peculiar point of view which Mark presents. We should make an effort not to confuse the accounts of the other Gospel writers with Mark's, but rather preserve the thrust of his text. The temptation is to interpret Mark's account with all the pomp and circumstance normally associated with Palm Sunday observances. Mark shows Jesus entering Jerusalem as a lowly one, who is a hero only to a motley crowd. But he is more of a king than they think him to be. We can see in Mark's picture of Jesus the authoritative lowliness of God revealed in Jesus Christ. The quiet dignity and hidden majesty are two marks of Jesus in this account. Lowliness is a characteristic seldom associated with God, but revealed in this account. Notice Jesus' silence in the midst of the excited, shouting crowd. It is easy enough to join in a sports cheering crowd in acclaiming a winner, but here is the case of a silent lowly figure on a colt who calls for a different kind of following.

The story of Jesus' entry into Jerusalem is a traditional one about the popularity of Jesus at this point in his ministry. Mark has theologically adapted the story to an announcement of Jesus as the Messiah, after the manner of the prophecy in Zechariah 9:9. Notice in John the disciples were not aware of any messianic significance involved in the entrance, but later they saw its true meaning as they reflected on the event. (John 12:16)

*1. Setting.* "And when they drew near to Jerusalem, to Bethphage and Bethany, at the Mount of Olives . . ." (v. 1) begins a new phase of Jesus' ministry, one toward which the passion narratives have been pointing since the first one at Caesarea Philippi. (8:27—9:1) While there are some aspects of an enthronement procession to be seen here, there is a reticence also which recalls his predictions of his passion, and a foreshadowing of the confrontation with the Temple and its authorities. The mention of the Mount of Olives is important, since, according to Zechariah 14:4, the Lord would appear there "on that day." Messianic hopes of that time were focused there. "On that day his feet shall stand on the Mount of Olives which lies before Jerusalem on the east . . ." The geographical references are peculiar, however, since Bethphage is closer to Jerusalem than Bethany, which is about a mile and a half away. It is obvious that Mark, writing at a later time, was not acquainted with these places.

*2. The colt.* (vv. 2-6) The Greek text does not specify whether it was the colt of a horse or of a donkey. The latter was more common in Palestine. The Greek word when used alone usually meant the colt of a horse. Zechariah 9:9 refers to "riding on an ass, on a colt the foal of an ass." The fact that no one had ever sat on the colt could point to the sacred use to which it was put. It is more likely an allusion to the Zechariah prophecy of the foal on which the messianic king would enter Jerusalem.

In sending for the colt, Jesus reveals his remarkable power and authority as shown by his clairvoyance, according to the text. "Lord" refers to God since Jesus is saying the colt is needed for a sacred purpose. However, as Mark communicates with his readers, he wants them to understand that Jesus is the Lord who needs the colt.

The main thrust of the colt account is that Jesus took the initiative in arranging for the acclamation which followed, and each step of the preparation was through divine foreknowledge according to a definite plan.

*3. Acclamation on approaching Jerusalem.* The central message of the passage is in verses 7-10. The spreading of garments was a coronation custom. The people shouted "Hosanna! Blessed is he who comes in the name of the Lord!" which is a quotation from Psalm 118:25-26. It is from the last of the Hallel or praise psalms sung by pilgrims approaching the Temple. It is also one of the royal psalms. The word "Hosanna" literally means "save now." As shouted by the pilgrims as Jesus passed along, it became a shout of praise. To this the people added, "Blessed is the kingdom of our father David that is coming! Hosanna in the highest!" Note that unlike in Luke and Matthew's accounts, here the people do not explicitly call Jesus "Son of David" or "King." Although this is an enthronement procession, there is a marked reticence with regard to Jesus himself. Notice that no crowds came out from the city to meet him, but only those who were with him, including the blind man, Bartimaeus (10:52) accompany Jesus into the city.

The people who follow Jesus are enthusiastic, but wrong about their expectations that Jesus will restore the fortunes of Jerusalem by force. But they are correct in regard to hoping he is the Messiah. His kingdom is radically different from the one they expect.

*4. Conclusion.* In contrast to Matthew and Luke's accounts, here Jesus does not immediately drive the money changers and merchants from the Temple. Upon entering the city he goes at once to the Temple, but only to look around and then return to Bethany for the night. In verse 11 we are directed to the Temple as the central place for what will follow in the section after this one.

### Matthew 26:14-27, 66 (RC)

We must read this against the background of the previous account in which Jesus is annointed at Bethany in preparation for his burial. (26:12). Only the woman who anointed Jesus understands what is taking place. Note the contrast between her actions and those of Judas in this passage. See how verse 13 puts special emphasis on her act of love.

In verses 14-16 Matthew records the final stage in the plot to destroy Jesus, as Judas agrees to deliver Jesus over to the chief priests for money, thirty pieces of silver. We cannot determine why Judas betrayed Jesus. Some guess that it was because he was disappointed that Jesus did not lead an uprising against Rome. But this is only speculation. Matthew doesn't make clear what Judas betrayed. It may have been simply to lead the guards to Jesus in the Garden where he spent the night outside the city walls. There the guards could take him by stealth.

The account of the Last Supper is given in verses 17-29. Our pericope ends at verse 27. Scholars generally agree that John has the historically correct chronology of the Last Supper. He considers the Friday afternoon on which Jesus was put to death to be the Day of Preparation. This meant Jesus died at the very time when the paschal lambs were being slain. The Day of Preparation began on Thursday night, and this explains the reluctance of the Jews to defile themselves by entering Pilate's hall. The first day of Unleavened Bread was the occasion for the celebration of the Passover meal. It was eaten by the family during the night.

Notice that Matthew's account says Thursday was the day when preparations were made for the feast, in contrast to John who puts this on Friday. All four gospels put Jesus' death on Friday. Thus, according to John, Jesus was crucified on the day of preparation and the Last Supper was on the preceding evening, Thursday.

It appears from Mark 14:13-16 that Jesus had friends in the city and had arranged to eat the Passover meal in the house of one of them. Matthew adds the word, "My time is at hand" as a prophecy of the crucifixion.

Jesus may have had word that one of the disciples would betray him (v. 21), or he may have gathered this from Judas' facial expression. The evangelists think of Jesus having supernatural knowledge. But verses 21-25 may not have been part of the original account of the passion.

It is doubtful that the Last Supper of Jesus was a Passover meal, since most of the characteristic elements of that meal are not recorded in the Gospel accounts: lamb, bitter herbs, etc. It may well be that the Christian understanding of the death of Jesus in the light of the Passover tradition as God's mighty act of delivering his people has, in fact, influenced the reporting of the Last Supper.

Jesus took bread, and blessed and broke it, and gave it to the disciples and said, "Take, eat; this is my body." (v. 26) Jesus took the bread as the father or host did at any Jewish meal. He used the usual words, no doubt, for blessing or thanksgiving: "Blessed art thou, O Lord our God, king of the world, who dost bring forth bread from the earth." Jesus added the word "this is my body" which suggests (1) that as the bread is broken, so will Jesus' body be broken, and (2) as they eat the bread and are nourished, so Jesus' death will not be a loss, but for their benefit.

Jesus took a cup and when he had given thanks he gave it to them, saying, "Drink of it, all of you." (v. 27) The cup represented the new covenant in the blood of Jesus which was to be poured out for them. Notice that the blood of the covenant is an allusion to Exodus 24:8. There sacrificial blood was thrown on the altar, book of the covenant and the people to confirm the people's solemn agreement to observe God's law. Here the blood is for the welfare of many people. (v. 28)

## Theological Reflections

Isaiah records the third Servant Song and in it the Servant accepts the role of transmitting God's word in spite of opposition. It is a psalm of confidence. It expresses the confession of confidence in God and the certainty of being answered by God. Paul writes the Philippians of the example of Jesus who emptied himself of heavenly power and glory and took the form of a servant and was born in the likeness of human beings. He became obedient unto death on the cross, but God has highly exalted him and given him a new name, Lord. Mark records Jesus' triumphal entry into Jerusalem as he begins the final phase of his life leading up to the trial and crucifixion. Jesus comes as a lowly, silent figure on a lowly colt, while the people with him shout words of praise. Matthew tells of the betrayal of Jesus and the Last Supper. In all these passages we see God's mighty acts to save his covenant people as God works through the servant, through the self-emptying of Jesus Christ, his triumphal entry and his death, foreshadowed in the Last Supper. Verse 66 records the verdict on Jesus, "He deserves death." But death was not the end. God raised him on the third day.

## Homiletical Moves

*Isaiah 50:4-9a (C) (L)*
*Isaiah 59:4-7 (RC)*
**Behold, the Lord Helps Me!**

1. The Lord teaches the Servant and the Servant obeyed
2. The Servant is shamed and oppressed for his work
3. But the Servant is not confounded, but sets his face like a flint
4. God helps the Servant, therefore none can declare him guilty
5. The opponents of the Servant will be destroyed
6. God calls us to be faithful in spite of persecution and he promises to help us by the Spirit

*Philippians 2:5-11 (C) (L)*
*Philippians 2:6-11 (RC)*
**Jesus Christ Is Lord!**

1. Follow the example of Jesus who, though he was in the form of God, did not count equality with God a thing to be grasped, but
2. He humbled himself and took the form of a servant, being born in the likeness of human beings
3. He became obedient to death on a cross
4. God has highly exalted him and bestowed on him the name, Lord, which is above every name
5. At the name of Jesus every knee should bow, and tongue confess that Jesus Christ is Lord
6. Confess Christ as your Lord and live in obedience to him

*This Preacher's Choice*

*Mark 11:1-11 (C) (L)*
**Hosanna! Blessed Is the One on the Colt!**

1. Jesus sends for a colt to ride into Jerusalem
2. He rode on the colt, and people spread their garments and leafy branches in the pathway

124

3. Those with Jesus shouted, "Hosanna! Blessed is he who comes in the name of the Lord!"
4. Jesus entered Jerusalem and went into the Temple and looked around
5. Live in joyful obedience to the Prince of Peace

*Matthew 26:14-27, 66 (RC)*
**The Last Supper**

1. Judas betrays Jesus
2. The disciples and Jesus share a meal together
3. Jesus identifies Judas as the betrayer
4. Jesus breaks bread and gives the cup
5. Christ invites you to share table fellowship and live in faithful obedience

**Hymn for Lent 6:**  *So Lowly Does the Savior Ride*

**Prayer**

*Holy God, who called the Servant to declare your message boldly, forgive us when we have been unfaithful messengers of yours. May we set our faces like a flint in face of opposition, knowing that you help us. Grant that we may have the mind of Christ who humbled himself, even to death on a cross. May we follow his example of obedience in faithful service. We pray that we can name him "Lord" of our lives and follow his commands to love you and our neighbor. Grant that we may not only shout "Hosanna" as Jesus comes into the city, but also stand at the cross and tomb to witness your mighty acts for our salvation. When we eat the bread of life and drink the cup of salvation, may we receive the Living Christ into our lives by faith. Amen*

# The Resurrection of Our Lord

Easter Day

| Common | Lutheran | Roman Catholic |
|---|---|---|
| Isaiah 25:6-9 | Isaiah 25:6-9 | Isaiah 25:6-9 |
| 1 Corinthians 15:1-11 | I Corinthians 15:19-28 | Colossians 3:1-4 |
| John 20:1-18 | John 20:1-18 | John 20:1-9 |

## Comments on the Lessons

There is consensus on the first reading. The epistle readings all have the same theme of the resurrection, although differing from one another. The Gospel reading is virtual consensus. Verses 8-10 are used because they include Jesus' actual appearance and the Easter proclamation, although omitted in the RC pericope.

## Commentary

*Isaiah 25:6-9*

This is part of the third major section of Isaiah which describes the judgment of the world and the salvation of Israel. It is the second of the eschatological pericopes making use of traditional mythic material. Note that the brief psalm in verse 9 speaks in the usual language found in the Psalms. The immediately preceding verses 1-5 are a psalm of thanksgiving that praise the Lord for destroying the city in defense of the poor. The oppressive rulers have been cast down. Now follows the Easter pericope.

Notice that 25:6-8 is an oracle announcing the continuation of the action of God in 24:21-23. All nations make a pilgrimage to Zion: "on this mountain." All the nations will be drawn into the salvation God brings. The image is a coronation banquet, hosted by none other than God the King. It is for "all peoples," and it should be noted that this universal celebration correlates with the universal dominion of the Lord.

The image of a feast for all nations celebrating the destruction of God's enemies and the beginning of a new era of peace and salvation is also found in northern Canaanite mythology. It is also found in later apocalyptic literature.

The picture of a great feast is often used to describe the ideal future. The familiar Isaiah 55:1-2 calls people to a victory banquet. The joy of the banquet is doubly emphasized by the reference to wine and the eating of rich meat. It is significant that the banquet is for all peoples, for God's covenant is all-inclusive. God's sovereignty is universal. "Fat things full of marrow" and "wine on the lees" refer to rich food and wine that is well matured for the heavenly banquet. Fat delicacies flavored with marrow and old wine, fermented out and standing on its lees (to be strained before the wine is served) are the menu for this world class feast for the world's citizens! Only the best is fit for the royal banquet.

It should be noted that in the Old Testament the idea of the pilgrimage of the nations of the world to Zion has the same significance as the idea of mission in the New Testament. Although the idea of salvation of the nations is a marginal idea in the Old Testament and in Judaism it nevertheless is there. Both the Old Testament and New Testament agree in looking forward to the welcoming of all nations into fellowship with God. This table fellowship brings the nations into community with God.

We shift from the picture of a banquet to the defeat of death in verses 7-8. God's presence means the lifting of the veil from the head, which seems to have been a sign of mourning in the face of death. Because death has been destroyed, the veil is removed and mourning is turned into joy. This brings an end to the time of suffering and mourning. But there is no mention of resurrection. This must wait for the New Testament and its universal hope for resurrection. The stress here is on the joy in the victory of God the King. The Lord speaks and it is done. It should be noted that both Paul and the author of the Revelation of John use this phrase or the whole verse to express the Christian hope of eternal life and the final abolition of death. (1 Corinthians 15:54; Revelation 21:4)

Finally, we come to the hymnlike response of Isaiah 25:9 which is tied to verses 6-8 by the words "on that day." This stresses that Israel's role in all this is simply to wait on God's action. Isaiah does not lay out a "Five Year Plan of Progress" or a "Mission Directive for the Decade." Nothing Israel can do will bring in the rule of God. Only faithfulness under oppression while waiting is needed. This will turn into joy.

After the conquest of the world power and the glorification of God in his people, Israel will no longer have to suffer the contradiction that has been her lot through the centuries: While being the people of the God who created the heavens and earth, who guides the course of the stars and nations, Israel has been like one nation among all the others, but worst of all, one which was subject to the Gentiles and was forced to live as pariahs in their midst.

The thrust of this pericope is in its only partly formed sense. Today we still wait for God. "Waiting for Godot" dramatizes the spirit of the age. Paul Tillich, when asked what the Church must do to receive the Spirit said, "The Church must wait!" We activists are reminded by Isaiah that waiting can be a very positive thing when we face forces beyond our ability to overcome. While we are inclined to try to bring in God's kingdom with technology and management by objectives, ultimately we must still wait on God's action. And when we wait we can "be glad and rejoice in his salvation." (v. 9)

### 1 Corinthians 15:1-11 (C)

Paul had gotten reports that some at Corinth denied the resurrection and for this reason he sets forth a restatement of the gospel he has preached all along. Paul grounds has message in Old Testament scripture whenever possible. "Christ died for our sins in accordance with the Scriptures" refers to Isaiah 53:5-12. "He was raised on the third day in accordance with the Scriptures" alludes to Psalm 16:10, "For thou dost nor give me up to Sheol, or let thy godly one see the Pit."

The fact that Paul left until last his teaching concerning the resurrection is no accident, but indicates rather that he considered it of supreme importance. The awkward style which is evident in the Greek reflects his heightened consciousness about the issue of the resurrection. He is very concerned that the readers give careful attention to it.

An early confession of faith is found in 1 Corinthians 15:5, the nucleus of which goes back to a Semitic text. Paul says that this confession was handed on to him, which very likely occurred soon after his conversion, which was not long after Jesus' death. The division between the tradition and Paul's comments probably occurs in verse 5.

As if arguing a legal case, Paul cites all the best witnesses for the fact of the resurrection. Not only did the risen Christ appear to Cephas (Peter), who was one of the first at the empty tomb and who was encountered by the risen Christ on many occasions, but the "twelve" saw him. Then to prove that this was no hallucination of a few people, Paul says the risen Christ appeared to more than five hundred brethren at one time, most of whom were still living when Paul wrote. The point he is making is that you can't fool a crowd of five hundred people with a ghost or illusion or magic trick. Some consider this a variant of the Pentecost traditon which gives the risen Christ's appearance to the disciples by the Spirit. Then he appeared to James, the Lord's brother, who of all people should be able to recognize the authentic risen Jesus. He appeared to the apostles. This was a wider company of missionaries (apostles = those sent). The "twelve" refers to the immediate band of apostles and some texts change it to eleven to reflect the defection of Judas.

Then the risen Christ appeared to Paul "as to one untimely born," which literally means an abortion or a premature birth. Paul takes this as a disparaging term. He had not had preparation for this meeting by earlier contact with the earthly Jesus. Rather, Paul as Saul had persecuted the church. Then in verse 10 Paul says his conversion was all of grace. Until this point Paul has used "grace" only three times, but now, in one sentence, he uses it three times with the deepest sense of gratitude to God in Christ. Although he worked harder than any of the other apostles in preaching the gospel, he acknowledges it was the grace of God with him in his ministry. Here is true humility. In order to avoid party strife among ministers, Paul quickly turns in verse 11 to the faith in the gospel which all of them had preached. This gospel centered on the resurrection of Jesus.

### 1 Corinthians 15:19-28 (L)

In this stirring passage Paul argues vigorously for the resurrection of the dead. He says that if, in this life, we who are in Christ only have hope, but no firm facts on which to base our faith in the resurrection, then we are of all people most to be pitied. The central thrust of the pericope is Christ's resurrection and the End. In verses 19-28 we have a counterpart to the Isaiah text. Notice many of the same motifs: the setting aside of the enemy death, God's rule over opposing forces, waiting for the future realization. But Paul, as would be expected, has drastically reinterpreted the Isaiah text in light of Christ.

Notice the two Old Testament motifs Paul introduces. First, the reference to Christ's resurrection as the "first fruits of those who have fallen asleep" (v. 20) is a direct reference to the first sheaf of the harvest, which was brought to the temple on the first day following the Passover celebration, representing the entire harvest. The harvest was given by God and is in this act consecrated to him. In the same fashion Paul sees the raising of Christ by God's power to point to the resurrection of all who belong to him.

The second Old Testament motif is that of Adam as a type of Christ. As in Adam all die, so also in Christ, the New Adam, all will be made alive, says Paul. But this is not universal salvation but the phrase "in Christ" is the key. Those who are now "in Christ" will be made alive. Those who remain in the old Adam will suffer death as a consequence of sin.

Now we come to verses 24-28, a "little apocalypse," which should be read side by side with 1 Thessalonians 5:1-11. Both stress the already fulfilled aspects, as well as the yet to be completed aspects of God's work in Christ. Paul is writing to clear up a misunderstanding of the resurrection among the Corinthians. They thought that, after baptism, they lived on the level of the Spirit and were set free from the body. This accounts for their view that there was no resurrection of dead people since they believed resurrection had already taken place. The result of this belief was rampant individualism and self-confident security. Paul counters this, arguing that the resurrection of Jesus is part of the general Gospel proclamation.

Resurrection, says Paul, is a future concept, still a hope for the Christian and not a present possession. Future events will occur in their proper order. The "parousia" is a technical term referring to the arrival of a king or his official representative. The Parousia of Jesus will also mean the end of history. Then God will be enthroned as King because all those opposing him will be overthrown. Jesus will turn over the kingdom to God the Father after every enemy including death has been destroyed. And, at the end, Jesus will be subjected to God so that "God may be everything to everyone."

This pericope warns against false complacency and calls attention to the reality of the fruit of the resurrection while we wait for its final consummation at the Parousia.


### Colossians 3:1-4 (RC)

These verses give the basis for the Christian life. Because the Christian has been raised with Christ, he or she is free to seek the things that are above. The Christian has died to enslavement to trespasses and cosmic powers. Paul urges his hearers to set their minds on things that are above as a consequence of their being raised with Christ. He points them to a radical new orientation of life regarding goals and motives, since they are now in Christ new persons. Their life is hid with Christ. This is the new heavenly life. In effect, Paul is saying that they have parted with their old life in baptism and now a new life has been born in them, but it is still hidden. Christ is not only seated at the right hand of God, but he has withdrawn into the divine nature. This concept of being hidden with Christ in God is a mystical concept which is combined with the primitive hope in the nearness of the return of Christ. The hope the Christian has in Christ will be actualized when Christ returns at the Parousia. Then those whose lives are hidden with Christ in God will appear with him in glory.


### John 20:1-18 (C) (L)
### John 20:1-9 (RC)

What happened on that first Easter? The 1 Corinthian 15:4 evidence is that the turning point came on the third day, the Sunday, after Jesus was crucified. All four gospels agree that what set in motion the following events was the visit of the women to the tomb that first Easter morning. Until recently, scholars have considered Mark 16:1-8 as the earliest account of the Easter event, but now the evidence points to this being a later account which seeks to prove the reality of the resurrection by the story of the empty tomb. John has preserved an earlier form of the same story in this pericope of 20:1ff.

According to John, Mary of Magdala went alone to the tomb at the dawn of Easter day to lament Jesus' death. But when she saw from a distance that the stone had been rolled away from the opening of the tomb, she ran back to tell Peter "and the other disciple, the one whom Jesus loved" (John), thus sounding the alarm that the body had been stolen. Grave robbing was common and laws forbidding it point to its practice. It was not likely that the governor would have released a criminal's body but fanatics could have gotten around this by stealing the body by night and burying it in one of the criminal's graves. Anti-Christian writings claim this was the case.

The empty tomb indicates resurrection, not mere immortality. Peter runs to the tomb and finds it empty according to Luke 24:12. But John's gospel tells us John got there before Peter and, stooping to look in, he saw the linen cloths lying there. John didn't go in at this point. But bold Peter who followed close behind in the race to the tomb did go in. What he found is the kind of evidence that a Sherlock Holmes delights in explaining. Peter went into the tomb which was carved out of the stone hillside with an opening about a yard high. Inside was a little room probably with several niches carved into the walls for bodies. We are told it was a new tomb so Jesus' burial was the first. When Peter entered the tomb he found "the linen cloths lying, and the napkin which had been on his head, not lying with the linen cloths but rolled up in a place by itself." (vv. 7, 8) Now John enters the tomb also and "he saw and believed." This is the goal of the account — to lead the reader to faith in the resurrection of Jesus. But Peter doesn't understand what has happened yet. Note that John's role in the story of the disciples' visit to the tomb functions in the same way as the angel interpreter in the story of the women's visit. He indicates what the empty tomb means and instantly recognizes the signficance of the arrangement of the burial clothes. Instantly he believes in the risen Jesus. John becomes a representative of all believers who accept the disciples' witness. Note that while Peter is the first to see, the beloved disciple is the first to see and *believe*. This leap of faith is the purpose of the Fourth Gospel: "these are written that you may believe that Jesus is the Christ, the Son of God . . ." (20:21) It is not enough to see the empty tomb. In fact, the empty tomb alone is not sufficient evidence for faith, for, indeed, the body could have been stolen away. But the arrangement of the grave clothes gave John an "Aha!" discovery experience of faith in which he saw and believed. The fact the clothes were not scattered on the floor or taken with the body gives the clue to what happened. The material body of Jesus was transformed into a resurrection, spiritual body. Paul describes this unique kind of body in 1 Corinthians 15:20, 44, 50. They believed, although they did not yet know the Scripture which indicated Jesus must rise from the dead.

The disciples went back to their homes, but meanwhile, back at the tomb, Mary Magdala stands weeping. She stooped, and looking into the tomb she saw two angels in white sitting where Jesus' body had lain. They asked her why she was weeping and she said because someone had taken Jesus' body and she couldn't find it. Then she turned around and saw Jesus standing, but she did not recognize him. He, too, asked why she was weeping, whom was she seeking. Mary thought he was a gardener and asked directions for finding Jesus' body so she could take it away. Then Jesus called her name, "Mary." With this she turned and answered, "Rabboni!"(teacher).

Then Jesus speaks words which have perplexed scholars through the centuries: "Do not hold me, for I have not yet ascended to the Father." (v. 17) Jesus directs Mary to return to the brethren and tell them he is ascending to "my Father and your Father, to my God and your God." Mary obeyed and went to tell the disciples, "I have seen the Lord." This is the final evidence for the Christian faith: personal encounter with the Living Christ. Mary told the disciples what Jesus had said.

Jesus did not want Mary to hold him, because she thought he had returned as he had promised at the Last Supper and that he would stay with her and the other disciples in their former relationship. But this was not his permanent presence that he had promised. Jesus is telling Mary that his permanent presence is not by way of appearance but by way of the gift of the Spirit, which can come only after he has ascended to the Father. For this reason she is told to go and prepare the disciples for that coming of Jesus when the Spirit will be given.

In both John and Mary Magdala we see models of Easter faith. John saw the empty tomb and the arrangement of the grave clothes, indicating Jesus' body had escaped without them being unwound. He saw and believed. Mary met the risen Lord at the tomb and believed for she reported to the disciples: "I have seen the Lord." The thrust of this pericope is to lead the reader to faith also.

## Theological Reflections

Victory over death is the thrust of all the pericopes for today. God has acted to overcome all his enemies, including the last enemy, death itself. God raised Jesus from the dead on the third day. The fact of the resurrection of Jesus from the dead is the base on which the Christian faith rests. Destroy this and the whole structure of the Christian religion collapses. The evidence of the empty tomb and graves clothes in place, where Jesus' body had lain, points to the transformation of his material body into a resurrection body. The encounter of persons with the risen Christ and later with the Spirit of the Living Christ confirms the fact of the resurrection. Christ's victory over death is the central thrust of the New Testament pericopes.

## Homiletical Moves

*Isaiah 25:6-9*
### God's Victory Banquet

1. God in Christ has won the victory over sin and death itself
2. We must wait patiently for the consummation of this victory
3. In the Eucharist we celebrate a victory banquet in which we rejoice and are glad in God's salvation
4. Trust in Christ's victory over sin and death and rejoice!

*1 Corinthians 15:1-11 (C)*
### Evidence for Easter!

1. Christ died for our sins in accordance with the Old Testament Scriptures
2. God raised Jesus from the grave on the third day according to the witnesses who saw him
3. By the preaching of the Gospel of the resurrection we, too, can come to faith in the risen Christ through the grace of God
4. Hear and live the good news of Christ's resurrection!

*1 Corinthians 15:19-28 (L)*
### In Christ Shall All Be Made Alive!

1. If in this life only we have hope in Christ we are hopeless
2. Christ has been raised from the dead as the first fruits of the resurrection
3. In Christ we shall all be made alive for Christ has conquered death
4. When all things have been subjected to God. God will be everything to everyone
5. Hope in Christ now, and in the life to come!

*Colossians 3:1-4 (RC)*
### A Life Hid With Christ

1. You have died with Christ therefore turn from thoughts of things that are on earth
2. You have been raised with Christ so set your minds on things above where Christ is seated at the right hand of God
3. Your life is hid with Christ in God and when Christ appears you also will appear with him in glory

*This Preacher's Choice*

*John 20:1-18 (C) (L)*
*John 20:1-9 (RC)*
### He Saw and Believed!

1. John entered the empty tomb and the evidence of the grave clothes led to faith in the resurrection of Jesus
2. Mary met the risen Lord at the tomb and believed
3. The Living Christ comes to meet us by the Spirit in worship, prayer and the events of our daily life
4. When we have seen and believed we, too, must witness to the resurrection of the Living Christ

**Hymn for Easter Day:**  *Christ the Lord is Risen Today*

**Prayer**

*O God, who has conquered death in the death and resurrection of Jesus Christ, we rejoice and are glad in your presence. Feed us with the spiritual food of your presence through prayer that we may know the joy of the feast. Help us to wait patiently for the consummation of your kingdom when Christ returns in glory. May our hearts be open to and our minds expectant of meeting the Living Christ by the power of his Spirit in the daily events of life as well as the high points of worship. Amen*

# Easter 2

| Common | Lutheran | Roman Catholic |
|---|---|---|
| Acts 4:32-35 | Acts 3:13-15, 17-26 | Acts 4:32-35 |
| 1 John 1:1—2:2 | 1 John 5:1-6 | 1 John 5:1-6 |
| John 20:19-31 | John 20:19-31 | John 20:19-31 |

## Comments on the Lessons

Notice that the community emphasis of the Acts pericope is complemented by the Fourth Gospel passage in which Jesus appears to the disciples in community and to Thomas eight days later in the community of the disciples. Acts describes some of the characteristics of this community formed by the Spirit of Christ. Also notice the complementary relationship between the concrete sense references of 1 John 1:1ff and the Thomas story of the gospel. 1 John 5:1ff relates love of God and others with obedience to God. It also proclaims the victory over the world through Jesus' death on the cross which is given to those who believe that Jesus is the Son of God. There is consensus on the John reading.

## Commentary

### Acts 4:32-35 (RC)

Acts, which was written about A.D. 77 by the Gentile physician Luke, relates how the early church was born and grew until it had spread across the Mediterranean world. Acts begins in A.D. 30 with Jesus' ascension into heaven, and 4:32-35 relates the action of the Holy Spirit in the community of believers shortly after the founding of the Church. The Living Christ has returned and is drawing his disciples together by the power of love. In each of the Cycles A, B, C, note that during the Easter season the Old Testament lessons are replaced by readings from the Book of Acts. The purpose is to give an account of the work of the Living Christ in his church.

This summary of the church's life parallels 2:42-47. Some scholars think Luke has combined two different accounts of the same thing drawn from two different sources. Our pericope has two thrusts: (1) the sharing of all things in common which was done voluntarily, and (2) the preaching of the resurrection by the apostles with great power (dynamis).

This passage and 2:42-47 have often been referred to as describing early Christian communism. However, it must be clearly noted that this is *not* based on an economic doctrine nor is it legally enforced common ownership. This sharing of goods occurred in the Jerusalem church for a while and resembled that of the Essenes. But Peter's statement in 5:4 indicates it was not a universal rule. There is no attempt to establish a new economic order. But on the other hand, the Christians in the young church took care of their needy as other passages of the New Testament reveal. But it was only in Jerusalem that this type of communal living was practiced for a period of time. It reflects the command of God set forth in Deuteronomy 15:4, "But there will be no poor among you (for the Lord will bless you in the land which the Lord your God gives you for an inheritance to possess) . . ." Evidence for the claim that common ownership was unusual is the fact that Barnabas is mentioned by name. This does not seem to be of the same kind of common ownership as that of the Essenes which was on a different basis and of a different kind. An important question is whether or not goods were shared only within the community of believers.

The mention of heart and soul reflects a similar description in Deuteronomy 6:5. The church's unity was formed by the power of the Spirit. Notice that here as in 2:42-47 the sharing of all things in common comes immediately after the outpouring of the Spirit. The disciples, in their awareness of the presence of God in their midst, are moved to rise above "me" and "my" to act on the basis of "we" and "our." Throughout the Christian church today, but especially in the Third World there is a re-emerging of this sharing of goods in common on a voluntary basis, particularly in small communities. This is happening in various societies. Whatever expression this sharing takes, there should be some expression of this principle of Christian community of goods if the church is to maintain its integrity. This spaceship earth as viewed from the moon and space craft is a small planet in the midst of a huge universe. All who live in this global village are linked together like mountain climbers connected by a common rope. With instant communication and jet travel we are neighbors with our brothers and sisters around the world. Famines and disasters, natural and people-made, are leading passengers on Spaceship Earth to share their bread and drink, as passengers on an airliner do when the stewards run out of supplies.

### Acts 3:13-15, 17-26 (L)

Luke gives the essence of Peter's sermon in the portico called Solomon's. Jesus is interpreted as fulfilling the role of the Servant of Isaiah 53. Peter declares that the people have killed the Author of life, Jesus, whom God raised from the dead. He says they acted in ignorance, as did the rulers. This is a common Lukan theme. But Jesus' suffering was in accordance with God's plan. Peter calls for repentance and conversion. However, baptism is not mentioned. He points out that his hearers are people of the covenant and that in their posterity all the families of the earth are to be blessed. The idea that the Servant is sent to Israel first is another Lukan theme. The blessing of all the families on earth is through Jesus.

### 1 John 1:1—2:2 (C)

Since we will be considering pericopes from 1 John for several future readings, as well as today, some brief background will be helpful. Written about A.D. 95, the purpose of the book is to combat the Gnostic heresy and to call the church to obedience and love. Although the author is unnamed, it was probably John the apostle, author of the Fourth Gospel. Tradition has long held this to be true. In its style, the book is not a letter but a sermon. We do not know the occasion of its writing. Notice there is no greeting, salutation or signature as a letter would ordinarily have. Chapter 1 is the testimony of the gospel and 2:1-17 is concerned with knowledge of God and resulting love.

One approach to study of this pericope would be through doing word studies of key ethical and theological words used in 1 John: love, sin, confess, confidence and testimony. For example, a study of sin in 2:1-2 might be done against the background of Camus' book *The Fall*. The novel, though a study of sin, keeps talking about God. The main character, Jean-Baptiste, could be presented against the background of John's description of sin and what God has done to overcome sin. Contemporary listeners would identify with sin described in terms of violence of self, vanity of self, and cowardice. The relevance of 1 John for contemporary living and escaping the bondage of sin can be made strikingly clear through use of contemporary novels, movies. TV movies (especially the "soaps", and drama. The minister's own study of this pericope would be given a new dimension by watching one or two TV "soap operas" one afternoon. Or seeing a movie that teenagers are going to see.

In the introduction (1:1-4), the evidence of the senses is called on to refute the gnostic heresy that Christ was not really human: heard, seen, looked upon, touched. Compare this with Thomas' encounter with the risen Christ in the Fourth Gospel. The purpose of the sermon is to lead hearers to attain fellowship with Christ and to have Christian joy.

The first main section (1:5-10) deals with right attitude toward sin. It asserts that God is light without taint of sin of any kind. Darkness is used as a symbol of habitual and intentional evil conduct. In verses 8, 9 denial of sin is cited as self-deception. But confession brings God's forgiveness. But to deny that we commit acts of sin contradicts God's declaration. (Psalm 14:1, 2, etc.)

The meaning of Christ's death and resurrection as expiation for our sins is the focus of 2:1, 2. The fact the atonement is effective for the sins of all the world reminds us of John 3:16. The ultimate goal of Christian living is that "you may not sin." (2:1) A word study of expiation in contrast to propitiation would be useful for dealing with this text.

### 1 John 5:1-6

Notice the spiral method of John in building on themes. The phrase "Jesus is Christ (Messiah)" was a primitive baptismal confession. It is by baptism into the Body that believers become children of God. With this initiation into the fellowship of believers goes responsibility to love God and neighbor. John says that through baptism we overcome the world. For John, "world" includes all the unbelieving peoples of the world who are in opposition to God and now live in sin and darkness.

An important thrust of this passage is the assertion in verse 3 that love of God involves obedience to his will. Obedience is the lost concept in the Christian religion today. But to love God is to obey

God's commandments. To be a Christian calls for responsible ethical conduct, not just feeling good about oneself or an hour of worship. Victorious faith results in eternal life. The Spirit witnesses to the water (Jesus' baptism) and to the blood (the cross). Our victory in Christ is based on the saving act of God in Christ, a real victory that triumphs over unbelief. Evidently verse 6 is a refutation of those gnostics who claimed Jesus came by water (baptism) but not by blood (crucifixion). It may also deal with a gnostic belief that Jesus was a mere man upon whom the Spirit descended at his baptism but left him before he was crucified. They compare to a person today who believes in the Incarnation but denies the Atonement.

### John 20:19-31 (C)

There are two resurrection appearances in the pericope from John: (1) to the Twelve in Jerusalem (Matthew puts it in Galilee), (2) to Thomas and the disciples, an event peculiar to John. The second appearance expresses a concern of Christians of how is it possible to believe in the risen Lord if one has not seen him? John's answer is that even to see the risen Lord, as in the case of Thomas, is no guarantee of faith. But everyone has to make the leap of faith in order to believe.

The first appearance occurs on the evening of the resurrection, the first day of the week, as the disciples are gathered behind closed doors for fear of persecution. The tradition of this appearance goes back to the account in 1 Corinthians 15:5 and is developed in Matthew, Luke and here in John 20. It is thought that the appearance in chapter 21 may be a variant of the same tradition. Notice that the frightened disciples have met behind closed doors, but Jesus appears to them and shows them the marks of his passion. His hands and side have identifying marks which are also signs of glory through suffering. The fact that Jesus appeared to them behind closed doors indicates he was no longer in a flesh and blood body but had a transformed, resurrected body, but nevertheless a *body*.

Jesus says to the disciples, ''Peace be with you. As the Father has sent me, even so I send you.'' He gives them not only the customary social greeting of ''peace'' but also peace in their hearts and consciences. He calms their fears. Then he commissions them to go out into the world.

Jesus breathed on them and said, ''Receive the Holy Spirit.'' This act of breathing on them reminds us of God's breathing into Adam a living spirit. Here at the moment of the new creation, Jesus breathes his own Holy Spirit into the disciples. The gift of the Spirit is the climax of relations between Jesus and the disciples.

Most scholars think the Spirit was given on Easter, but in a way different from that at Pentecost. It seems the gift of the Spirit on Easter was transitional and anticipates the gift on Pentecost which was complete and definitive. One is potential and the other actual, say some scholars. The Spirit's role is to take the place of Jesus after he ascended to the Father. For this reason the Spirit is sometimes called ''The Living Christ.'' The Spirit carries on Jesus' work and is his presence in the world. We may call this event the ''Johannine Pentecost.''

The church carries out Jesus' mission of forgiveness. (v. 23) But this occurs only as Jesus' life is breathed into her. Compare this to 1 John 2:1-2 regarding the forgiveness (expiation) of sins.

The second episode occurs later as Thomas, who was not with the Twelve earlier when Jesus appeared to them, is now present. They tell Thomas they have seen the Lord but he protests that, unless he physically feels the evidence of the crucifixion he will not believe. Eight days later the disciples and Jesus are in the house and again the doors are shut. John emphasizes that Jesus appeared in a supernatural fashion to the disciples, no longer limited by time and space and material barriers. Jesus stood among them and said, ''Peace be with you.'' Jesus knows Thomas wants visible proof of his being the crucified and now risen Lord.

Jesus tells Thomas ''Put your finger here, and see my hands; and put out your hand, and place it in my side; do not be faithless, but believing.'' (v. 27) Thomas' response (apparently *without* actually touching Jesus' wounds!) is the climax of the Fourth Gospel: ''My Lord and my God!'' Thomas represents all those in every age who have doubted the resurrection of Jesus but who come to faith in a leap of courage from doubt to confidence. Notice Jesus did not despise Thomas' doubt, for out of it came a great confession of faith.

Notice that John has given us in chapter 20 four slightly different episodes showing the slightly different ways in which Jesus evoked faith from the disciples. John, the Beloved Disciple, came to faith after seeing the unique arrangement of the burial cloths but without seeing the risen Jesus. Mary Magdala sees Jesus but only comes to faith after he calls her by name. The disciples see him and believe after he appears through closed doors. Thomas overcomes doubt and believes after insisting on examining the evidence himself. All four are examples of those who loved Jesus during his earthly life and who came to faith in the risen Lord. Then Jesus gives a ''stray Beatitude'': ''Blessed are those who have not seen and yet believe.'' This is aimed at the reader or hearer in whatever century who comes to faith in the risen Lord. All are equal in God's sight with those who encountered the risen Lord, on Easter or in the days that followed before his ascension.

The whole purpose of the Gospel is in verses 30-31: ''that you may believe that Jesus is the Christ (Messiah), the Son of God, and that believing you may have life in his name.'' Jesus reverses our common saying of ''seeing is believing'' to say ''No, believing is the way to seeing and knowing.'' Faith is the door to sight and knowledge in spiritual matters.

## Theological Reflections

The theological thrust of these passages is on the evidence for the risen Christ, his continuing work in the community of faith, and how one who has not seen may yet come to believe that Jesus is the Christ, the Son of God and thus have the gift of life. In 1 John we have the theology of forgiveness of sins through the expiation made possible by Christ's death and resurrection. The new life given by the risen Christ to all who believe and the victory over the world which comes to the believer is another message of 1 John.

## Homiletical Moves

*Acts 4:32-35 (C) (RC)*
### A Company of One Heart and Soul

1. The apostles preached the resurrection with great power
2. God's great grace united the believers in one heart and soul
3. As a result they had everything in common and there was no needy person among them
4. Allow God's Spirit to share your material goods with those who have need in response to God's grace

*Acts 3:13-15, 17-26*
### The Servant Sent to Bless You

1. God sent his servant to you, but you acted in ignorance to put him to death
2. Repent and turn again to God
3. God will forgive your sins and send the Living Christ to you to bless you
4. Live in joyful response to God's forgiveness

*1 John 1:1—2:2 (C)*
### What We Have Seen and Heard We Proclaim to You

1. God is light
2. We sin and walk in darkness and unrighteousness
3. If we confess our sins God will forgive us through Christ the righteous who is the expiation for our sins
4. And we will have fellowship with one another and with the Father and his son Jesus Christ
5. Therefore, repent and seek God's forgiveness so you may live in fellowship with God and with one another

*1 John 5:1-6 (L) (RC)*
### This Is the Love of God

1. Jesus Christ came by water (baptism) and blood (cross)
2. Whoever is born of God overcomes the world through faith
3. We express our love for God by keeping his commandments
4. We know we love the children of God when we love God and keep his commandments

*This Preacher's Choice*

*John 20:19-31*
## My Lord and My God!

1. Thomas the doubter who wants sensory experience of Christ is contemporary man
2. Jesus appears to the Twelve and they were glad when they saw the Lord
3. Jesus appears to Thomas who then believes without touching Jesus
4. Blessed are those who have not seen but make the leap of faith to say with Thomas: "My Lord and my God!"
5. Through believing you will have life in his name as a gift of the Spirit

In this pericope we have two appearances of the risen Christ to the disciples, one to the Twelve, and the second to Thomas who is with the disciples. Notice the flow of the passage from unbelief to faith to life in his name. The climax of the whole book is Thomas' confession in verse 28: "My Lord and my God!" The preacher may want to show how Thomas is a contemporary person seeking sensory, scientific proof of Jesus' resurrection. But he comes to faith by a leap from doubt to confession: "My Lord and my God." The confession of Jesus as Lord (ruler) is the key to obedience. It is not enough to say one believes in God. Obedience to the will of God expressed by the commandments is the evidence of love of God according to the epistle of John. The thrust of the passage is to lead people like Thomas to a living, obedient faith which offers life.

**Hymn for Easter 2:**   *Jesus Christ is Risen Today*

**Prayer**

*God of light, in whom there is no darkness at all, enlighten our minds and hearts by the gift of the Holy Spirit. Turn us from doubt to a living faith that can affirm the Living Christ as "My Lord and my God!" Grant us the peace that only he can give. Heavenly Father, as you sent your son Jesus into the world, send us by the power of the Spirit into the world to be witnesses of your love. Make us instruments of your will that through the preaching and hearing of the Word many may come to be called blessed who have not seen but have believed in the Living Christ. Amen*

# Easter 3

| Common | Lutheran | Roman Catholic |
| --- | --- | --- |
| Acts 3:12-19 | Acts 4:8-12 | Acts 3:13-15, 17-19 |
| 1 John 3:1-17 | 1 John 1:1—2:2 | 1 John 2:1-5 |
| Luke 24:35-48 | Luke 24:36-49 | Luke 24:35-48 |

## Comments on the Lessons

In the Acts pericopes, the Common and RC readings are almost the same while the Lutheran selects a different passage. In the context of the whole passage it is felt that verses 12-13 of Acts 3 will not be understood as anti-Semitic. In the Common Lectionary 1 John 5:1-6 was moved from Easter 2b to Easter 6b (in order to preserve the sequence of readings). Thus all selections from 1 John move forward one Sunday. Note that clear development of thought takes place in 1 John 3:1-7. There is virtual consensus on the third reading, but verse 48 provides a good homiletic ending.

## Commentary

*Acts 3:12-19 (C)*
*Acts 3:13-15, 17-19 (RC)*

Most scholars see the speeches in Acts as the compositions of Luke which represent his theology, rather than being the actual words which Peter and others spoke on any given occasion. They contain early christological materials very often. For example, Jesus is here called "the Holy and Righteous One," which is a descriptive title of Jesus, pointing to his earthly life as the righteous servant of God. Another very ancient title is "the Author of life." This points to Jesus as the new Moses, since the Greek word for author also means captain or leader. As Moses led the people of Israel out of bondage to the land of Canaan, now Jesus, the new Moses, leads the faithful into the Kingdom of God, the new Canaan. Jesus is also the successor of David. While the people asked for a murderer to be granted to them and freed, they killed the Author of life, whom God raised from the dead. Man's "no" of sin and rebellion is answered with God's "yes" of resurrection from the dead in Jesus Christ.

Peter calls the people to repent and turn again. This involves not only a change of mind but a turning from sin, with hatred for it, to live a new life. The promise is that those who do will have their sins blotted out, as one blots from a record book an account of criminal acts, or as one "kills" a document stored in a computer's memory. It is erased forever and can never be recalled!

Those who repent and turn and have their sins forgiven will find times of refreshing coming from the presence of the Lord. This refers to the blessings of the end time as verse 20 referring to the sending of Christ indicates.

*Acts 4:8-12 (L)*

Peter and the disciples are brought for a hearing before the council which had recently judged Jesus. They ask by what power or by what name did they heal the lame man. Peter, inspired by the Holy spirit, responded to their questioning. Notice that this reflects the idea that the Spirit comes sporadically. Peter's explanation centers on the kerygma, the death and resurrection of Jesus. While the crucifixion is the act of men, the resurrection is God's act. By the healing power of the risen Christ the lame man is standing before them, says Peter. Jesus, the rejected stone has now become the head of the corner. Essenes, as well as Christians, used the "stone" image from Old Testament passages in teaching. The quotation is from Psalm 118:22.

The assertion that "there is salvation in no one else" is a statement many modern minds find objectionable as they try to be tolerant of all religions. But the question is not one of tolerance but of truth. E. Stanley Jones, the missionary to India said the choice before us is "Christ or chaos." Those who have lived and worked on the mission field abroad often find the contrast between Christ and other religious leaders sharply defined, in contrast to religion in America or the Western world in general. But when we do a radical examination of the core of each of the world's religions, we find in Christianity the cross and resurrection, God's unique act in human history to rescue sinners from the power of evil and the grip of death. Not the moral teachings of religions, which are often similar, but *the saving acts of God in Jesus Christ* make Christianity unique. This is still a stone of stumbling and foolishness to the wise of this world.

### 1 John 3:1-7 (C)

God's love for us makes us his children, which in turn, gradually, produces resemblance to him, now and in the life to come. This is a theme also found in John's gospel: "But to all who received him, who believed in his name, he gave power to become children of God." (1:12) The power of hope and the image hope can give is pointed up in verse 3. The role of imaging in shaping personality and conduct is suggested here.

The sins mentioned in verse 6 are the habitual and constant sins. The role of Christ who was sinless himself and who came to take away sins is singled out in verse 5. Sin is described in terms of lawlessness. (v. 4)

### 1 John 1:1—2:2 (L) (See commentary on C reading in preceding Sunday's Lectionary pericopes.)
### 1 John 2:1-5 (RC)

*Obedience* is the thrust of these verses. The ultimate goal of Christian living, says Jesus, is "that you not sin." This is the thrust of Romans 6:11, "So you must consider yourselves dead to sin and alive to God in Christ Jesus."

The Advocate is one who pleads the case of another. Jesus is the person for others. He has taken our case to the Father himself. Jesus is not only our Advocate but the expiation for our sins. (v. 2; 4:10) Jesus' death wipes clean the record of our sins. Or, in computer language, his death has "killed" the document recording our sins! And not only for our sins but the sins of the whole world. (John 3:16)

The relationship between knowledge of God and obedience to God is pointed up in verse 3. Living in obedience to God's commandments makes us sure we know, have intimate communion with, God. This is not knowledge about God, or knowledge of God as an academic subject, but knowledge in the biblical sense of the most intimate personal relationship. "To know" in the Old Testament is used of sexual intercourse, as Adam knew Eve.

Keeping God's word is the way in which love for God is truly perfected. Again the integral relationship of obedience and love for God. Love of God implies and demands obedience to God.

### Luke 24:35-48 (C, RC)
### Luke 24:36-49 (L)

This resurrection story is unique in the gospels and seems to be based on tradition different from that of the Emmaus story, since the disciples are startled and frightened. If they had known he was risen his appearance would not have been so shocking.

One should read Luke 24:13-35 in order to better understand the events leading up to this appearance, and also to see the pattern there which is also repeated in verses 35-48. The pericope for today is included to refute the beliefs of docetism which asserted that Jesus only *seemed* to have a physical body. Note that Luke announces that the risen Christ has flesh and bones, by which Luke wants to avoid any idea that the Living Christ had no concrete reality. The word translated "spirit" means "ghost" and would be better translated so. Jesus is not just a disembodied ghost but can eat a piece of broiled fish, and he bears the marks of the crucifixion. While it is true that the risen Christ appeared only to those who knew and loved him during his earthly ministry, nevertheless his appearance was not a psychological inner experience of feeling him present as sometimes happens to persons in deep grief. Through the ages the church has affirmed its faith in the "resurrection of the body."

Looking at verses 13-35 and verses 35-48 simultaneously, we find this pattern:

1. the appearance of the risen Christ
2. the failure to recognize him
3. the reprimand by Jesus for their failure to recognize him
4. the sharing of food
5. the opening of the meaning of Scriptures
6. the response of joy and wonder.

Since a number of the resurrection narratives resemble one another, we should expect that details from one account would bleed into another. Notice the themes which recur in Luke's narratives which are vital to the message of the book:

1. The centrality of the Jewish Scriptures for the ministry of Jesus and the message of the church

2. The importance of eating together for Jesus' work and the mission of the church. In this pericope eating takes on an added dimension for, when Jesus eats fish and offers his hands and feet for examination, this is saying something about the resurrection. Luke is not only refuting the heresy of docetism noted earlier, but also the notion of the immortality of the spirit. At this point the material thrust of the Christian faith becomes very apparent. Jesus appeared to the disciples in a body, not as a ghost, and this also counters the idea that material things are evil or inferior. And to those who would deny that this material world has significance, Jesus says, "Look at my wounds" and "Give me something to eat." This stress on the material aspects of Jesus' resurrected body refutes those who hold to the spirituality of religion and claim it is concerned only with "souls" that can't be seen.

3. An injunction of Scripture and command to the disciples by the risen Christ. Notice the stress in verse 48 on being witnesses to Jesus' resurrection and the things related to his life.

It should be noted that this pericope is the counterpart of John 20:19-31 which we read last Sunday. The appearance takes place in the upper room in Jerusalem, the emphasis on the physical is similar and the greeting "Peace to you." (v. 36 and addition in some MSS) While the emphasis on the physical in John takes the form of the invitation to touch the risen Christ, in Luke it is found in the eating of a piece of boiled fish. Fish suggests that the original setting of this event may have been Galilee. The meal points to the association of the original resurrection with the eucharist.

But Luke's primary interest is found in the last paragraph: the instructions of the risen Christ to his disciples. This is rooted in the earliest tradition and parallels in Matthew and John should be noted. The command to mission (repentance and forgiveness of sins should be preached in his name to all nations, beginning from Jerusalem). You are witnesses to these things. And behold, I send the promise of my Father upon you . . . includes the notion of baptism also. But Luke has a unique emphasis on the Scriptures: "everything written about me in the law of Moses and the prophets and the psalms must be fulfilled." Jesus "opened their minds to understand the Scriptures . . . Thus it is written . . ." We have the same themes in the last paragraph of the Acts 3: 12-19 reading, which indicates this is a theological concern of Luke's.

Note in all the Easter narratives the restraint with which the New Testament writers used them and the realism with which the appearances are portrayed. With this Easter narrative we leave this form of witness to the resurrection to move on to other Gospel texts.

### Theological Reflections

Luke, in both the gospel and in Acts, grounds the death and resurrection of Christ in the Old Testament prophets and scriptures, which reveals a concern of Luke's to show that Jesus fulfilled prophecy. God's love in Christ is stressed in the 1 John readings. This love overcomes sin and enables the believer to live in obedience to God's will. This firmly links believing and obedience in the Christian life. The Easter narrative stresses the bodily resurrection of Jesus in opposition to various heresies, among them docetism. The Christian religion rests on the resurrection and Luke stresses the realism of this event in the lives of the disciples. The invitation to look on his hands and feet and to handle him and his request for food are very definite attempts to show the reader that the risen Christ was not a ghost but had a resurrected body. The continuity of the risen Christ with the earthly Jesus and the prophecy of Messiah come across in the pericopes. The power of the risen Christ in forgiving sins and leading believers to obedience continues this action of God in Christ in the present age.

### Homiletical Moves

*Acts 3:12-19*
## Repent and Turn to God

1. We were all there "when they crucified my Lord," acting in ignorance, denying the Holy and Righteous One, and asking for a murderer

2. But what God foretold by the prophets, that the Christ (Messiah) should suffer, he has fulfilled
3. Repent and turn again that your sins may be blotted out
4. And times of refreshing will come from the presence of the Lord when Christ returns at the end of the age.

*Acts 4:8-12*
## The Rejected Stone Has Become the Head of the Corner

1. Jesus of Nazareth was crucified by sinners
2. But God raised him from the dead
3. There is salvation in no one else, for there is no other name by which we must be saved
4. The rejected stone has become the head of the corner
5. Therefore, put your trust in the name of Jesus Christ

*1 John 3:1-7*
## We Are God's Children Now!

1. See what love the Father has given us in Jesus Christ
2. Jesus appeared to take away sins: lawlessness, rebellion, etc.
3. By faith we are adopted sons and daughters of God and thus called children of God now
4. When Jesus returns we shall be like him for we shall see him as he is

*1 John 2:1-5*
## Jesus Is the Expiation for Our Sins

1. If anyone sins we have an Advocate with the Father, Jesus Christ
2. The person who disobeys God's commandments but says "I love God" is a liar
3. Whoever keeps God's word has true love for God perfected
4. Jesus Christ the righteous is the expiation for our sins and the sins of the whole world
5. Therefore keep God's word through faithful obedience

### *This Preacher's Choice*

*Luke 2:35-49*
## You Are Witnesses of These Things

1. The risen Christ stood among them but they were startled and frightened
2. Jesus invites the disciples to handle him and asks for food which he eats
3. Jesus tells the disciples that he has fulfilled the Old Testament prophecies in the law of Moses, the prophets and the psalms
4. You are witnesses of these things
5. Proclaim repentance and forgiveness of sins to all nations

In preaching on this pericope the preacher will want to involve the congregarion in the flow of the passage from being startled and frightened by the presence of the risen Christ to faith in the bodily resurrection and accepting the mission to witness to Christ's life, work and atoning death and resurrection. The thrust is on response to God's saving acts, response in proclaiming the good news of forgiveness of sins. The power of the Holy Spirit which the disciples were told to wait for has come and empowers the church for mission today. Ways in which the hearers have experienced the power of the risen Christ in their own lives should be reviewed with the purpose of their witnessing to this to all nations.

**Hymn for Easter 3:**  *They Cast Their Nets*

**Prayer**
*O God, who has rescued us from sin by the death and resurrection of Jesus Christ, grant us power from on high to witness to what we have seen, heard and experienced of the risen Christ. Turn us from being startled and frightened to become bold witnesses. Open our minds to understand the Scriptures. Teach us how to live as obedient disciples in our time. Grant us power as you have promised that we may be faithful witnesses to the world. Amen*

# Easter 4

| Common | Lutheran | Roman Catholic |
| --- | --- | --- |
| Acts 4:8-12 | Acts 4:23-33 | Acts 4:8-12 |
| 1 John 3:18-24 | 1 John 3:1-2 | 1 John 3:1-2 |
| John 10:11-18 | John 10:11-18 | John 10:11-18 |

## Comments on the Lessons

The themes of love, faith and the caring love of the good shepherd for the sheep run through the lessons for today. They blend well with one another. The selection from Acts 4:8-12 maintains the complementary relationship between the rejection of the cornerstone (v. 11) and the image of the good shepherd in the Gospel pericope. Jesus the rejected one is crucified, thus laying down his life for the sheep. The Acts 4:23-33 passage gives an account of a giving of the Holy Spirit to the disciples and the unity and sharing which resulted. Here is ''shepherding'' of the little flock by the risen Christ by the power of the Spirit! The church is under fire but the good shepherd remains faithful: ''And with great power the apostles gave their testimony to the resurrection of the Lord Jesus, and great grace was upon them all.'' (v. 33)The epistle readings emphasize the love of the Father for the adopted children and the hope of Christ's return, and the assurance of the Spirit that the disciples abide in Christ. There is virtual consensus on the gospel reading, and a resurrection note in verses 17-18. Christ, the good shepherd, gathers the flock from all folds into one, and to this the Christian can look forward with confidence.

## Commentary

### Acts 4:8-12 (C, RC)

Jesus had assured the disciples that when under persecution they would be given the words to speak under the inspiration of the Holy Spirit: ''For what you are to say will be given to you in that hour; for it is not you who speak, but the Spirit of your Father speaking through you.'' (Matthew 10:19-20) Now Peter, ''filled with the Holy Spirit,'' defended their action in healing the lame man. He tells the rulers, elders, scribes, and particularly the Sadducees who had assembled to hear their explanation of how the lame man had been healed. Peter says it was in the name of Jesus Christ that the cripple had been made whole. Peter repeats what he had said earlier in the temple. He stresses that the Jews — or the authorities — had put Jesus to death by crucifixion but God had raised him from the dead. ''By him this man is standing before you well,'' declares Peter. Peter uses a metaphor borrowed from Psalm 68:22 in which Jesus is compared to the stone, rejected by the builders, that has become the cornerstone. Again, Peter declares that salvation cannot be gained through Judaism but only through Jesus. Here there is a play on words. Peter says, ''And there is salvation in no one else, for there is no other name under heaven given among men by which we must be saved.'' (v. 12) In verse 9 Peter says, ''If we are being examined today concerning a good deed done to a cripple, by what means this man has been healed'' and the word for ''heal'' in verse 9 is also translated ''saved'' in verse 12. There are thus two levels of understanding of Peter's message: (1) it deals with the healing or making whole of the lame man, but (2) moves on to the healing or making whole of ''whoever calls on the name of the Lord.'' (2:21) Peter is not only speaking to the Sanhedrin but also to us, the readers, for whom the lame man serves as a mirror.

Notice how Peter takes advantage of this occasion of healing the lame man and his defense of the miracle in order to proclaim to the Sadducees (who did not believe in the resurrection) and others that Jesus had been raised by God.

The absolute claim for salvation in Jesus only may strike modern ears as narrow bigotry. But, when the Christian faith is compared to other world religions, the uniqueness of its message stands forth. It proclaims salvation, wholeness, freedom from guilt, and union with God through the mediation of Jesus Christ, his death and resurrection. Not moral teachings, not religious acts, not ''fatherhood of God and brotherhood of man'' but *the death and resurrection of Jesus Christ* is the unique proclamation of the Christian faith. ''For there is no other name (nature, character) under heaven given among men by which we must be saved.'' (v. 12) No one can be argued into faith in the uniqueness of salvation through Christ, but those who have come to know the Living Christ as the Good Shepherd, who abide in Him, and who know the power of his salvation in their lives can make this claim while avoiding an arrogant, intolerant attitude.

### Acts 4:23-33 (L)

This passage follows the trial that was in the previous Sunday's lesson from Acts. Here we have the reaction of the Christian community to its first experience of oppression and threat. Note that when Peter and John are released from prison they returned to the other disciples and reported what the chief priests and elders had said to them. It appears the disciples had gathered to pray while Peter and John were in prison. The disciples reponded to the report of Peter and John with a prayer that falls into four sections: (1) verse 14b in which God is addressed as ''sovereign Lord'', the oriental title for supreme ruler which is found some twenty-five times in the Greek version of the Old Testament (Septuagint). God is described as the Creator God. Next, (2) in verses 25-26 which quotes from Psalm 2:1-2 is the second part of the prayer. Notice the phrase ''and against his anointed'' which is taken to refer to Messiah. Then (3) the text is applied to Jesus in an act of memory ( verses 27-28). Jesus' death is predestined by God, although the rulers and people put him to death. Finally, (4) there is the situation of threat (verses 29-30). The disciples pray that God will look upon the threats of the oppressors and will give to the disciples the power to speak with boldness. And they ask for more miracles to be performed ''through the name of thy holy servant Jesus.'' Suddenly an earthquake occurs which would have been interpreted as a sign and answer to their prayers.

This passage has a central thrust for the church in every age: when under persecution, PRAY! Notice that the disciples did not pray to escape persecution but that they might be bold in proclaiming the Gospel in the face of opposition. Christians are living in an increasingly hostile environment where the ethics of society set forth in TV, movies and mass media in general go *directly counter* to the Christian ethic. Christians who live under political oppression know the power of prayer to witness boldly. The church in the Western world is afflicted by the dry rot of apathy within. But only prayer can enable the church to face boldly this form of persecution.

### 1 John 3:18-24

John points up that the heart of love is not in words and speech but in deeds and truth. God judges according to our abiding in a loving relationship with others. Notice that John stresses the integral relationship between obeying God's commandments and abiding in him. He says the chief commandment is to believe in the name of Jesus Christ and to love one another. Love is caring action, not a sentimental feeling or many words. The essence of the Christian faith, according to John, is faith and love. To live as children of God requires faithful obedience to God.

### 1 John 3:1-2 (L, RC)

John points to the love of the Father expressed in the fact we are called his children. Elsewhere the Scriptures declare we are sons and daughters of God by adoption through faith. (Romans 8:17, Galatians 3:26-29, etc.) John says we have the gift of being called ''children of God; and so we are.'' (v. 1) This is the first place in this book in which the idea of Christians being God's offspring appears. In the Old Testament we find this concept of Israel as God's son, and the Davidic king is also so named. The phrase ''children of God'' claims a very special relationship for Christians and God.

There is no avoiding the fact that this claim is divisive. The world which did not know God does not know God's children. This division is caused by a commitment to God in Christ. This can be compared to the Sons of Darkness and Sons of Light theme in the Dead Sea Scrolls.

Although we are God's children now we have a future out there when we know that, when Christ appears, we shall be like him ''for we shall see him as he is.'' (v. 2) The Christian lives by hope in the Coming Christ who will transform the believer into his likeness. Life is moving toward a goal and is not a cyclic repetition of defeats and victories in the daily struggles of life. We will see Christ as he really is, the glorified Son and we shall be like him.

### John 10:11-18

The image of the shepherd and flock is a familiar one in the Old Testament. Now Jesus fulfills the Old Testament prophecies that God himself will come to shepherd his people. The false shepherds may refer to the Gnostics, and to the many "saviors" of the Hellenistic world. The "other sheep" are the Gentiles. The Old Testament references in Isaiah 40:11, Jeremiah 23:1-6 and Ezekiel 34 point to God as a shepherd. Now Jesus says boldly, "I am the good shepherd. (v. 11) This is another of the "I am's" of Scripture in which Jesus describes his role and mission in terms of a vine, door, bread, water, and now shepherd.

We have two sheep parables in John 10 and the pericope for today forms the interpretation of the second found in 10:3b-5 (the first being 10:1-3a). Notice that two applications of this second parable are given: (1) verses 11-13, and (2) verses 14-18. Each begins with "I am the good shepherd," and each makes the basic assertion that the good shepherd lays down his life for the sheep. Then each proceeds to make a different application in the life of the church. The first application is to the defense of sheep against wolves. Wolves are an image for false teachers. The second application refers first to the inner life of the church, and then speaks of the church's missionary outreach to the "other sheep," the Gentiles.

Notice that the death of the shepherd is a voluntary one, not one forced on him. Such dedication of the shepherd to the flock explains the Father's love for the Shepherd. Jesus speaks of laying down his life "that I may take it again" (v. 17) referring to his death and resurrection. Jesus fulfills the commission given him by the Father to save the sheep by laying down his life for them. He uses his power to carry out the Father's saving will. Therefore, the Father loves him and there is harmony between the two, Father and Son.

Behind the allegory of this passage there is a polemic and apologetic note which one discovers by reading this passage alongside verses 24-30. John describes in verses 14-30 a scene in the temple court where there is skeptical opposition from the synagogue to the claims of the church with its message of Christ's death and resurrection.

The shepherd is described as "good" because he lays down his life for the sheep. The purpose of the shepherd is to give life to the sheep. In this passage, the shepherd's mission extends beyond Israel to sheep which are "not of this fold," i.e. the Gentiles.

One must read this passage in its context and see that the result of this teaching about the good shepherd is that of forcing people to decide for or against him. (v. 19) Some believe in him, some reject him. Jesus' teaching in our time forces hearers to decide for or against him.

### Theological Reflections

God's caring love in Jesus Christ, the good shepherd who lays down his life for the sheep, lifts up the atoning work of Christ. God takes the initiative in Christ to make salvation possible. Salvation, not only for the Jews but for Gentiles as well. The exclusive nature of the salvation in Christ is pointed up also. There is no other name by which one can be saved. And the teachings of Jesus force one to decide for or against him. There is also future hope, hope in Christ's coming again when we shall be made like him. Thus the good shepherd cares for his flock not only now, but in the age to come. He cares for them now by the power of the Holy Spirit as Acts points up when the Spirit gave Peter the words of defense and united the church in prayer for those suffering persecution. And the Living Christ unites the disciples and leads them to share their material goods.

### Homiletical Moves

*Acts 4:8-12 (C, RC)*
### There Is Salvation in No One Else

1. By the name of the crucified and risen Christ the lame are healed
2. Jesus, the rejected "stone," has become the head of the corner
3. There is salvation in no one else
4. Therefore, accept God's offer of salvation today

*Acts 4:23-33 (L)*
### Speaking the Word of God with Boldness

1. The disciples lifted their voices together in prayer
2. When they had prayed the place was shaken
3. They were all filled with the Holy Spirit

4. They spoke the word of God with boldness
5. Great grace was upon them all and they were of one heart and soul
6. Let the Holy Spirit empower you and unite the church for witnessing

*1 John 3:18-24 (C)*
## God's Commandment: To Believe and To Love

1. Let us love, not in word or speech, but in deed and in truth
2. We should believe in the name of his Son Jesus Christ
3. We should love one another
4. All who keep his commandments abide in him and he in them

*1 John 3:1-2 (L, RC)*
## We Shall Be Like Him

1. See the Father's love for us that we are called his children
2. The world does not know us because it does not know him
3. We are God's children now, but when he appears we shall be like him for we shall see him as he is
4. Accept God's love and live as his children now

*This Preacher's Choice*

*John 10:11-18*
## The Good Shepherd Lays Down His Life for the Sheep!

1. Jesus is the good shepherd
2. The hireling shepherd flees when danger comes
3. The good shepherd knows his own and his own know him
4. The good shepherd lays down his life for the sheep of his own accord
5. There are other sheep that must be brought so there will be one flock, one shepherd
6. Come to Christ the Good Shepherd who cares for you

**Hymn for Easter 4:**   *The King of Love My Shepherd Is*

**Prayer**

*Unto you, the Good Shepherd, we turn as sheep who have gone astray, seeking your forgiveness and healing. We know your voice, for you have spoken words of eternal life. We call upon you, Christ the Good Shepherd, to guide us through the valley of the shadow of death and to provide for our daily nourishment. Heal us and make us whole persons that we may live in your love and abide with you forever. We thank you, God, that you have loved us and made us your children through adoption by faith. We pray for Christ's return when we shall be made like him. Amen*

# Easter 5

| Common | Lutheran | Roman Catholic |
| --- | --- | --- |
| Acts 8:26-40 | Acts 8:26-40 | Acts 9:26-31 |
| 1 John 4:7-12 | 1 John 3:18-24 | 1 John 3:18-24 |
| John 15:1-8 | John 15:1-8 | John 15:1-8 |

## Comments on the Lessons

The Acts 8:26-40 (C, L) pericope has a missionary thrust and deals with baptism, both very relevant to the Eastertide Season. Luke describes the conversion of the Ethiopian eunuch who was an outsider by virtue of being a Gentile and a eunuch, but who was received into the community of faith in Jesus Christ. The Acts 9:26-31 passage describes Paul's initial rejection in Jerusalem and later reception and preaching there and the growth of the church. The 1 John 4:7-12 reading contains a composite image of God's love for us his people which results in our love for each other. Compare the mutual indwelling of verse 12 and the vine and branches symbolism in the Fourth Gospel reading. The 1 John 3:18-24 reading emphasizes the nature of love involving deed and truth as well as words. The test of knowing that Christ abides in us, says John, is the Spirit. There is consensus on the third reading, the vine analogy Jesus gave the disciples.

## Commentary

*Acts 8:26-40 (C, L)*

Here Luke tells the story of Philip's mission to the Ethiopian eunuch who was the treasurer for Candace, the sovereign queen. He must have been a God-fearing Gentile. Note the role of the angel. Revelation through an angel is a common motif in Luke. Note that the heavenly messenger carries out the same function as the Spirit in verse 29. The Ethiopians were Nubians living in an area between what is now Sudan and Aswan and Khartoum in Upper Egypt.

Note that the Eunuch who is treasurer stands in sharp contrast to Simon who seeks in the preceding narrative to buy the gift of the Holy Spirit. The Eunuch has great wealth under his control, but seeks to find spiritual direction through the interpretation of Isaiah which he is reading. Simon has come down in history through the name "simony," as one who sought to use spiritual things for financial gain. The preacher can have a field day with this contrast between true faith and using faith for personal gain. The whole positive thinking and cult of success which uses religion for financial gain (TV evangelists, etc.) could be contrasted with devoted public servants who, like the eunuch, are seeking spiritual insight.

Gaza was an ancient city of the Philistines, southwest of Jerusalem on the road to Egypt. The eunuch was reading aloud as was customary in the ancient world. He was reading from Isaiah 53:7-8 which deals with the servant of the Lord. The early Christians found many prophecies of Christ in the book of Isaiah. However, the primitive church did not seem to apply this text to Jesus as did the later generations. But this is done in Philip's answer to the Ethiopian's question, a question asked down through the centuries: "Does the prophet in this passage speak of himself or of another?" Philip applies it to Jesus as he told him the good news.

Luke gives us in a brief, tightly-worded story all the necessary details. The meeting occurred at noon, in a deserted road, and the main character is the Ethiopian eunuch who had gone to Jerusalem to worship. The plot is his search for understanding of Isaiah and his conversion and baptism. Luke has packed into this brief story some of the major themes of his theology: (1) the work of the Holy Spirit in the spread of the Gospel. Here the Spirit is in the form of an angel. (2) The universal impact of the gospel as it overcomes human barriers. Not only was the Ethiopian a Gentile, but by reason of being a eunuch, he was also excluded from being a part of orthodox Israel. (Deuteronomy 23:1) The fact he was an African would exclude him from much of Western society today, including not only private clubs but churches, etc. (3) A third theme of Luke is promise/fulfillment with Jesus as the key that unlocks the meaning of the Scriptures of the Old Testament. The preaching of the Gospel

144

to the Ethiopian takes place in an area beyond Judea and Samaria and thus fulfills Jesus' command. (Acts 1:8)

The Eunuch represents the sincere searcher for spiritual guidance in whatever age. He is a God-fearer who has made a long pilgrimage in search of God, both geographically and spiritually. He was searching the Scriptures, looking in the right place for guidance, and he asked the right questions. In addition, he was eager for divine guidance for his life. He came to a decision that he wanted to follow Jesus, the Servant foretold by Isaiah, and so he asks for baptism.

Philip is a model for an evangelist. He doesn't answer questions the seeker isn't asking, or give a canned spiel to avoid having to deal with the really tough questions. He responds to the Spirit's leading. He is forthright in asking penetrating questions. And he has both knowledge and skill in interpreting the Scriptures.

The Ethiopian responded joyfully. We should note that some MSS add some or all of verse 37: "And Philip said, 'If you believe with all your heart, you may.' And he replied, 'I believe that Jesus Christ is the Son of God'." The frequent association of joy with the Spirit may imply that the Ethiopian departed with the gift of the Spirit. The idea of joy after separation and after persecution is very characteristic of Luke. Nothing more is known of the Ethiopian. Christianity was started in Ethiopia by two laymen in the fourth century, however.

Luke says that Philip was snatched away by the Spirit. Twenty years later we find him entertaining Paul and Luke. He had four daughters who prophesied as he did also. He lived in Caesarea and was head of the local church. Philip was one of many evangelists in the early church and their work, guided by the Spirit, accounts for the spread of the gospel across the ancient world like a prairie wild fire!

### Acts 9:26-31 (RC)

It is not surprising that Paul had difficulty joining the disciples in Jerusalem since he had earlier led the persecution of the church. In recent years we have heard of national figures who have had a radical change of heart from being crooks to becoming ministers, lay or ordained. When their change was first announced many questioned their sincerity, as Paul's is questioned in Jerusalem. But Barnabas took Paul to the apostles and vouched for him. The role of a friend in overcoming obstacles cannot be overestimated. So Paul was accepted and preached boldly in the name of the Lord. So boldly, in fact, that the Hellenists tried to kill Paul, and he was whisked out of the city by friends and sent off to Tarsus. There is a time to fight and a time to flee in order to fight another day.

Luke reports that the church had peace and was built up in Galilee, Judea and Samaria. It grew as members walked in the fear of God and in the comfort (strengthening) of the Holy Spirit. This is the secret to the church's growth now and in every age.

### 1 John 4:7-12 (C)

This passage sums up the epistle's central thrust: God is love. In verses 7-10 John describes God's love in sending his son as the expiation for our sins. Then verses 11-12 asserts that to love one another is the only sure way to authenticate our love for God whom we cannot see. John sums up our relations to God by saying that "God is love." Note that he does not just say that God is loving but that the very heart of God is love. Another way to put it is to say that God in Christ revealed on the cross that the heart of God is suffering love.

But we cannot turn the statement around to say that "love is God" for God is much more than love. He is justice, power, truth, etc. Just as John claims God is light, we cannot turn it around to assert that "light is God" for again God is more than light and love.

The key to our loving God and others is in verse 19 "We love, because he first loved us." We cannot love other people except as God enables us to do so in response to his love. John says "in this is love, not that we loved God but that he loved us. (v. 10) Because God has loved us in sending his son to be the expiation for our sins we ought to love one another. The expiation is a technical word for wiping clean the slate, erasing the record of past sins in this case. When we love in response to God's love then God abides in us and his love is perfected in us. (v. 12)

### 1 John 3:18-24 (L, RC)

John points to the heart of love: not just words or speech, but deeds and truth. God who knows everything judges us according to our abiding in a loving relationship to others. The relationship between obeying God's commandments and abiding in him is also stressed by John. The chief commandment, says John, is to believe in the name of Jesus Christ and love one another.

### *John 15:1-8*

The believer's true relationship to Christ is one of abiding in him. This dynamic relationship is an ongoing, continuous one of living in vital union with Christ. In John chapters 14-17 we have the message of Christ to his church. In the pericope for today and the remaining two Sundays of the Eastertide season we will be reflecting on the farewell discourses and prayers of Jesus in the Fourth Gospel.

In this allegorical parable one of the main points is that as the branch gets its life from the vine, so the disciple gets her or his life from Jesus. In other places John indicates that Jesus gets his life from the Father, but here the role of God the Father is that of tending the vine, not giving it life.

Raymond Brown and other scholars suggest that the figure of the vine and branches in verses 1-6 orginally belonged to another context. One reason for making this judgment is the fact that there is nothing futuristic about the description of the union between the branches and the vine. In verses 1-6 the disciples are already in union with Jesus, and the emphasis is on remaining in that union. Note there is no reference to an immediate departure and other themes found in the Last Supper discourses. But in verses 7-17 a different viewpoint is found. At verse 7 the imagery shifts to deal with love and obedience.

This pericope is one of the "I am" passages, along with "I am the good shepherd," "I am the door," "I am the bread of life," etc. Jesus says, "I am the true vine, and my Father is the vinedresser." (v. 1) Note that the true vine is not to be found in Israel but in Messiah, the Son of God. By the shedding of the blood of Messiah, he makes possible the existence of the true people of God, joined to him not by physical descent but by abiding in him. The use of the vine image here stands in sharp contrast to its use in the Old Testament where Israel is called the vine. This figure for Israel always led a prediction of judgment and disaster. For, in the Old Testament, the symbol of the vine is never used apart from the idea of degeneration. But Jesus takes over the image and uses it to picture the new life of God's people. Jeremiah complained that Israel had become a strange vine. In Jesus the true vine has been planted. Like all vines it will have branches that will need attention, pruning, etc. With this vivid image Jesus shows that the life of God-with-man, which should have been Israel's proper existence, has now begun in him.

The Father prunes the branches that they may bear more fruit. "He takes away" and "he prunes" are similar actions and serve the same end of bringing forth more fruit. Every branch that bears fruit is pruned (Greek = purified) that it may bear more fruit. Although we are not told what this pruning stands for, it may be temptation, responsibility, persecution, and so on. This act of pruning/purification reveals that discipleship is not a plateau, but the Christian life is one of constant demand to bear more fruit. The Christian, like the branch, is not self-secure or independent but depends upon Christ for life. Remaining in Christ is a source of power.

The branches that do not bear fruit are cast forth and thrown into the fire and burned. This appears to refer, not to Jews, but to apostate Christians.

The fruit which the disciples/branch bears is communion with God. Prayer is the means by which this intimate communion is maintained. It is also an act of glorifying the Father. Thus to bear fruit is to live the life of true discipleship and by this to glorify the Father. Fruit bearing for John is equivalent to belief for Paul, and both lead to action that demonstrates one is truly a disciple. The thought moves between God's initiative in love and the human being's loving obedience. We can best find the fruit John is referring to as a result of abiding in Christ by looking, not at Paul's listing of the fruit of the Spirit, but within the Fourth Gospel itself. For John fruit-bearing refers to preaching and witnessing to the Gospel to all nations. (12:20-27)

### Theological Reflections

Common theological themes running through the lessons for today are abiding in Christ in love, fruit-bearing through preaching, witnessing (as Philip did to the Ethiopian), and the judgment on those who do not abide and do not bear fruit. God's initiative in loving us first is stressed by the epistle, and our responsibility to respond by loving one another and abiding in Christ is a common theme. The good news of salvation in Christ, the Messiah foretold by Isaiah and other prophets, is prominent. Philip is presented as the model evangelist who guides the earnest seeker after spiritual understanding. Judgment on those who do not abide and do not bear fruit is also found.

## Homiletical Moves

*Acts 8:26-40 (C, L)*
### He Told Him the Good News of Jesus

1. The excluded Ethiopian eunuch searched for God, as a God-fearer and reader of Scripture
2. Philip, the interpreter, explains the prophecy of Isaiah as foretelling Jesus as Servant of the Lord and tells the good news of Jesus
3. The Ethiopian believes, asks for baptism, and is thereby included in the community of believers
4. The Ethiopian went on his way rejoicing, a mark of the Spirit and of faith in Jesus
5. Listen to God's Word in Scripture and rejoice in hearing it

*Acts 9:26-31 (RC)*
### The Church Was Built Up

1. Paul is at first rejected by Jerusalem disciples who did not believe his conversion
2. Barnabas, a friend, attests to his authentic conversion, and his abiding in Christ
3. Paul risked his life in boldly preaching Jesus Christ
4. As a result of the preaching and witnessing of Paul and other disciples, the church in Judea, Samaria and Galilee had peace and was built up as disciples walked in the fear of the Lord
5. Let us walk in the fear of the Lord in response to the Gospel

*1 John 4:7-12 (C)*
### Let Us Love One Another

1. Love is of God
2. He who does not love does not know God
3. God's love was made manifest among us through Jesus Christ who is the expiation for our sins
4. If God so loved us, we also ought to love one another
5. If we love one another God abides in us and his love is perfected in us
6. Therefore, let us love one another

*1 John 3:18-24 (L, RC)*
### God's Commandment: Believe in His Son and Love One Another

1. Let us love in deed and in truth
2. Believe in the Son and love one another
3. Those who keep his commandments abide in him and he in them
4. By this we know that God abides in us, by the Spirit which he has given us

*This Preacher's Choice*

*John 15:1-8*
### Abiding in Jesus

1. Jesus is the vine, the Father is the vinedresser
2. Every vine that does not bear fruit he takes away and destroys
3. Every branch that does bear fruit he prunes that it may bear more fruit
4. The person who abides in Jesus and Jesus in the person, that one bears much fruit of prayer, preaching the Gospel and witnessing
5. If you abide in Jesus and his words in you, then whatever you ask it will be done for you

The creative contribution of John to the theology of the New Testament is the *concept of loving* as the most characteristic activity of the Godhead, loving manifested at the cross. Notice the emphasis in John on abidiing in God and God in us as the key to Christian living. In an alienated society like contemporary America where walls, not bridges, mark human relationships and relationship with the transcendent, the good news of intimate communion with God through Christ the vine is cause for celebration. There is a strong gnostic taint to contemporary religion which says knowing about God is sufficient, that one's knowledge of religion and private practice of this is saving knowledge, unrelated to other people or to corporate worship of God. But John goes to the heart of it in saying that abiding in Jesus and Jesus in us is the secret to bearing the fruit of prayer, witnessing and preaching the Gospel. The preacher would do well to involve the hearers in an elementary lesson in horticulture so they can understand the meaning of vine, branches, pruning to bear more fruit, and casting away the non-productive branch to be burned.

**Hymn for Easter 5:**   *In Heavenly Love Abiding*

**Prayer**
*O God, who has sent forth your son, Jesus Christ, to be the expiation of our sins, we thank you for such great love. Open our hearts and minds to understand your revelation in Scripture and in contemporary events and worship. Turn us from our individualism which builds walls instead of bridges between us and other people. Grant us to abide in Christ and Christ in us so that we may bear much fruit. Enable us by your Spirit to live a life of prayerful communion with you each day. May we bear much fruit and so glorify you, our Father. Amen*

# Easter 6

|  Common  |  Lutheran  |  Roman Catholic  |
| --- | --- | --- |
| Acts 10:44-48 | Acts 11:19-20 | Acts 10:25-26, 34-35, 44-48 |
| 1 John 5:1-6 | 1 John 4:1-11 | 1 John 4:7-10 |
| John 16:9-17 | John 15:9-17 | John 15:9-17 |

## Comments on the Lessons

The Acts 10:44-48 reading maintains the sequence of readings from Acts, bringing out again the theme of baptism found in Acts 8:26-40 (C, L) of the previous Sunday. The immediately preceding verses 34-43 were used on Easter Day. Now we have the baptism of Cornelius, a critical turning point in the early church, along with the other Gentiles with him. The Acts 11:19-30 reading describes the growth of the church in response to persecution, building up at the church at Antioch where disciples were first called Christians, and the sending of relief to the needy in Jerusalem. In the 1 John 5:1-6 reading the relationship of love of God and keeping his commandments is central. The 1 John 4:1-11 reading stresses the initiative of God in loving us which should result in our loving one another. There is consensus on the gospel reading which gives the commission to bear fruit. Obedience to this command results in the baptizing described in Acts.

## Commentary

### Acts 10:44-48 (C)

Here is described a Second Pentecost when the Spirit comes upon the disciples, just as at Pentecost, but now the converts are Gentiles! This is a major turning point in the mission of the church. Those present knew, by the speaking in tongues, that the Spirit fell upon the believers *before baptism*. "The circumcised" with Peter were Jewish-Christians who came with him from Joppa. Notice that the fact that the Holy Spirit fell upon Cornelius and his company before baptism is another unique exception which "proves the rule." God's grace is free and not confined to any channel. However, Cornelius was baptized *after* receiving the Spirit. This shows that the early church considered baptism necessary. Baptism could not be withheld from those who had received the Spirit. Baptism involves both water and Spirit. Notice that Peter does not baptize them himself, but supervises the baptisms. They were baptized "in the name of Jesus Christ," indicating that they now belonged to Christ's people and owe allegiance to him. We should not take this as necessarily indicating the words of the baptismal ritual used, but as indicating belief in Jesus Christ as Lord or as Son of God, as some texts indicate. Peter stayed there "some days" in a legally unclean house of a Gentile, showing that he does not just visit and go away again.

### Acts 10:25-26, 34-35, 44-48 (RC)

Notice that verses 25-26 show the reverence of the devout Gentile Cornelius for Peter and Peter's disclaiming of being other than a man. Then verses 34-35 contain one of the critical announcements of Peter and all of Scripture: that God shows no partiality, "but in every nation any one who fears him and does what is right is acceptable to him." (v. 35) "No partiality" literally means "God accepts no one's face." This statement can be compared to Paul's declaration in Romans 2:11 that Jews have no special privilege. But there is no notion of salvation apart from Christianity implied in the statement that the righteous in every nation are acceptable. Rather, this message of Peter's indicates that the way is now cleared for the Gentile mission. Peter is saying that God has no favorites, not even a favorite nation but he accepts from every nation those who are devout like Cornelius.

### Acts 11:19-30 (L)

Here we have an account of the mission to the Greeks in Antioch, the largest city of the Roman Empire, boasting a population of 800,000. It was not only a prominent commercial city of the ancient world but was also noted for its blatant paganism. It is significant for several reasons that the disciples were first called Christians at Antioch. The term "Christians" was a Latin word meaning "partisans of Christ." It is thought to have been a term of reproach when first used. Antioch was a large, important city with a strong pagan influence, but this city, for Luke, represented "the world" into which the Gospel now moves. For Luke the Gospel expands geographically from Jerusalem to Samaria, to the cities of Joppa and Caesarea of Palestine and now to this great center of Greek culture, Antioch. It was in Antioch that the first offering for the poor was organized and sent to the poor who lived in Judea, with each person giving "according to his ability." There is some problem regarding identifying the "famine" foretold in verse 28. The best solution seems to be to see this as a doublet with the offering visit of 21:15. This seems preferable since Agabus appears again as a prophet in 21:10. Some think this famine occurred in A.D. 46.

Christians were scattered because of the persecution over Stephen, the first martyr, and some came to Antioch. At first, the Gospel was preached only to Jews, but then some disciples from Cyprus and Cyrene who came to Antioch preached to the Greeks also. And a great number turned to the Lord. Notice that the evangelization of the Gentiles is described unobtrusively in verse 20. It is very significant that at Antioch, where the disciples were first called Christians, the church engaged in *evangelism and social action!* This can serve as a model for the church in every age. Not preaching and teaching the good news *or* social action. But "both/and" is the thrust of the church at Antioch and has been the church's mission through the ages, when true to its original commission.

The message preached in Antioch was the "Lord Jesus" which may mean they were preaching Jesus as Lord in direct contrast to the paganism which taught the worship of the lords of the Hellenist cults. Notice that in verses 20-21 "Lord" is used three times, which tells us Luke wants the reader to hear clearly the message that Jesus is Lord of the lives of believers. In verse 22 we are told that Barnabas is sent to the church at Antioch to supervise the life of the young church there. Notice that he plays a role similar to that of Peter and John in Samaria. He is sometimes called "apostle" as in 14:14. While it may seem from this passage that Saul/Paul has dropped into obscurity, we should remember that not much time has elasped between the action of verse 9:30 and this period. And during this time Paul has been busy carrying out a mission smiliar to the one in Antioch in Syria, Cilicia and other areas.

## 1 John 5:1-6 (C)

The thrust of this pericope is that everyone who believes in the Incarnation, that Jesus of Nazareth is the Christ (Messiah), is a child of God. This has two effects: (1) it brings the believer into the Family of God, and (2) it enables the believer to conquer the evil influences of the world. Two additional implications of this are that (1) the believer should love both God and the children of God, and (2) the believer should obey the divine commandments which are not burdensome because they flow from love. There is nothing radically new here, but the convolution of thought is typical of John's style.

One should compare this reading with earlier verses: 2:13; 3:1f, 1O; 4:4. The reference in verse 6 to water and blood refers to the baptism of Jesus (water) and the cross of Jesus (blood). In verse 7 John talks about the witness of the Spirit also. The Spirit witnesses to the water and the blood. In verses 6-12 John is stressing the witness of the Spirit, water and blood in opposition to the docetic heresy that Jesus only "seemed" to appear in human flesh. The docetists had also claimed that Jesus only had the Spirit upon him from the time of his baptism to his crucifixion. But John argues that Jesus had the Spirit all along and that the Spirit testifies to this.

To John faith in the incarnate Son of God, Jesus, is victory, over the world of moral wrong. Love gives this faith to win the victory and this is the only victory that is important.

## 1 John 4:1-11 (L)
## 1 John 4:7-10 (RC)

The thrust of verses 1-6 that being children of God means distinguishing truth from error, and verses 7-11 are a unifying summary centering on God is love. Today, as perhaps never before in the history of the church, the necessity is for Christians to be critical of false religion and to take a critical approach especially to those groups and leaders who fly the flag of the Christian faith (TV evangelists, leaders of sects, popular preachers who neatly combine nationalism and religion as if the two were the same, etc.). Notice in verses 1-2 the contrast between "spirits" (the supernateral powers claimed by false prophets) and the Holy Spirit of God. The supreme test is whether or not the Spirit confesses that Jesus Christ (Messiah) has come in the flesh. This test weeds out the docetists who claimed Jesus did not really come in human flesh but only *seemed* to be a human being. In verse 5 "they" refers to the false prophets, and "we" in verse 6 refers to Christians. Those who know God listen to John and the apostles, but those who are not of God do not. To know God is to have the power to discriminate between truth and error.

The basic definition of religion is that which binds all of life together, and here John asserts that God is love. John summarizes all our relationship to God by asserting that God is love. (4:8, 16) God is not just loving but the essence of God is love. The person who loves is born of God and knows God. But the person who does not love does not know God.

Here is John's most creative contribution of the theology of the New Testament as he sets forth the nature of God as love revealed in the death and resurrection of Jesus Christ. Special attention should be given to verse 10, which declares that God's love to us is prior to our love for him. That love was revealed in his Son who was sent to be the "expiation" of our sins. The expiation refers to the wiping clean of the record of our sins by Christ's death on the cross. The motive for loving others is God's love for us, says John. (v. 11)

Victor Frankl who survived the Nazi prison camps knew of the power of love and one night while on a forced march from one unknown destination to another, he stumbled along with other prisoners, slipping on icy spots, supporting one another and dragging one another up and onward. Each man was thinking of his wife. He could see in his mind's eye his wife answering him, her smile and her frank and encouraging look. "For the first time in my life I saw the truth as it is set into song by so many poets, proclaimed as the final wisdom by so many thinkers. The truth — that love is the ultimate and the highest goal to which men can aspire. Then I grasped the meaning of the greatest seoret that human poetry and human thought and belief have to impart: the salvation of man is through love and in love." (Quoted in McGinnis, *The Friendship Factor,* page 191)

Frankl captured, or was captured by, the power of love, and this made all the difference in surviving. Others who survived prison of war experiences have indicated that they, too, came to the same conclusion: God is love and that love for one another is the answer to human survival.

### *John 15:9-17*

This continues the theme in Easter 5 from John of abiding in Christ. As the church abides in Christ through prayer and loving obedience it finds joy. The believers live in a relationship to one another of love. Jesus and the Father live in a relationship of love and Jesus has loved the disciples. Therefore the disciples are to abide in Christ's love. They abide in this love by keeping God's commandments.

The theme of verses 11-17 is that the substance of God's command is love. The disciples are to love one another because their mutual love for one another is related in a special way to the love between the persons of the Godhead. This love will be expressed in self-sacrifice. From war, prison of war and from everyday living we have accounts of heroic acts in which one person unselfishly gives his or her life for one or more companions. A mother rushes into a burning house and saves a child but is overcome by smoke herself and dies. A father jumps into a swiftly moving stream to save a son and, in doing so, is swept under by the current but the child survives. A friend in a prisoner of war camp gives food to another and in doing so starves but the friend survives. The accounts go on and on and remind us that many have lived and died by this greatest love of all, the love which leads to self-sacrifice. Jesus is the Supreme Friend who lays down his life for his friends, indeed, for the whole world. Before any of the disciples could lay down their lives for another, Christ had laid down his life for them all.

Jesus calls the disciples friends "if you do what I command you." (v. 14)

The initiative is solely Christ's in the disciples' salvation. Christ has chosen and appointed them. It is not a matter of the disciples choosing Christ, but of his choosing and appointing them that they should go and bear fruit. Notice that Jesus has called the disciples friends, not slaves. Those chosen by Christ stand within the circle of mutual love and knowledge.

The passage ends with a return of the metaphor of fruit-bearing. This time it is in connection with prayer: "that you should go and bear fruit and that your fruit should abide; so that whatever you ask the Father in my name, he may give it to you." (v. 16) Finally, the command to love ends the passage. This sets divine love apart from human love which is based on emotion alone and which may come and go as emotions wax and wane. But divine love "agape" is a love which is willed and involves the total person. Jesus commands us to love one another, to have the same care for others and their well being that he has for us. (v. 12)

## Theological Reflections

God's initiative in loving us as described in the Fourth Gospel and our responsibility to respond to that love by loving one another is a major thrust in the passages for today. The epistle and gospel readings center on God's love revealed in Jesus Christ and the need to abide in this love and to show that we love God by obeying his commandments. God's love is revealed in the readings from Acts as he gives the Spirit to Gentile as well as Jew, thus revealing that he has no favorites. This love is shown by the disciples as they obey Christ's command to love the world for which Christ died, through preaching the good news and giving to the needy in Judea. The preaching of Jesus as Lord in Acts indicates that the church called people to put off old allegiances to pagan gods, in order to give total allegiance to Jesus alone and thus to obey his command to love one another even as he has loved us.

## Homiletical Moves

*Acts 10:44-48*
### The Spirit Is Given to the Gentiles

1. The Holy Spirit fell on all who heard the word, including Gentiles
2. Those who received the Spirit were baptized with water
3. They were baptized "in the name of Jesus Christ"
4. Hear God's Word and receive the Holy Spirit anew for witnessing and service

*Acts 11:19-30*
### Antioch, Where the Disciples Were First Called Christians

1. The Gospel is preached to the Greeks in Antioch
2. Barnabas is sent to oversee the new church and he was glad when he saw the grace of God at work
3. Barnabas was a good man, full of the Holy Spirit and of faith
4. The disciples at Antioch gave according to their ability to relieve the needs of the brethren in Judea
5. Give to the needs of others in response to the Gospel

*1 John 5:1-6*
### The Victory That Overcomes the World: Our Faith

1. Faith that Jesus is the Christ makes us children of God
2. The love of God is revealed in keeping his commandments
3. Whatever is born of God overcomes the world and knows the victory of faith
4. This Jesus in whom we believe came by water (his baptism) and blood (the cross) and thereby won the victory over the evil of this world
5. Therefore believe in Jesus as the Christ (Messiah) and live in obedience to his commandment of love

*1 John 4:1-11*
### Let Us Love One Another For Love Is of God

1. Love demands that we test the spirits to see if they are of God
2. Every spirit that confesses that Jesus Christ has come in the flesh is of God
3. God has taken the initiative in first loving us and giving his Son to be the expiation for our sins
4. Since God so loved us we ought to love one another
5. If we in fact do love one another God abides in us and his love is perfected in us

*This Preacher's Choice*

*John 15:9-17*
### Abide in My Love and Love One Another

1. As the Father has loved Jesus so he has loved us
2. Abide in Christ's love
3. Greater love cannot be shown than laying down one's life for a friend
4. Christ has called us friends and laid down his life for us
5. "This I command you, to love one another" (v. 17), go and bear fruit

**Hymn for Easter 6:**   *In Christ There is No East or West*

**Prayer**

*O God, who has loved Christ and sent him as the expiation for our sins, we praise and adore you. May we be worthy to be called Christians with the disciples at Antioch and those through the ages who have suffered and died for their faith. Teach us to love one another as you have loved us. May we be willing to give ourselves in sacrifical service to those in need. We claim Christ as our Friend who calls us to abide in his love. May we know his joy and may that joy be full. Amen*

# Easter 7

| Common | Lutheran | Roman Catholic |
|---|---|---|
| Acts 1:15-17, 21-26 | Acts 1:15-26 | Acts 1:15-17, 20-26 |
| 1 John 5:9-13 | 1 John 4:13-21 | 1 John 4:11-16 |
| John 17:11b-19 | John 17:11b-19 | John 17:11-19 |

## Comments on the Lessons

There is virtual consensus on the first reading. This is the account of the replacement of Judas Iscariot with Matthias. The first epistle reading gives a strong Easter ending on eternal life. The second and third epistle readings overlap and emphasize that we love because God first loved us and we are to abide in Christ. There is virtual consensus on the Gospel reading.

## Commentary

*Acts 1:15-17, 21-26 (C)*
*Acts 1:15-26 (L)*
*Acts 1:15-17, 20-26 (RC)*

All four Gospels agree that the Eleven stayed together. But now in the events described in the pericope, the sacred number Twelve, corresponding to the Twelve tribes of Israel, is restored in anticipation of the coming age. The upper room to which the disciples went after the Ascension may have been the same room in which the Last Supper was celebrated. It has been suggested that it was located in the house of Mary, the mother of John Mark.

Here, at the beginning of the active mission of the church, the names of the eleven apostles who make up the nucleus of the church are listed. By virtue of being witnesses and chosen by Jesus they are the church's leaders. But since Judas Iscariot committed suicide this has left an empty twelveth place in the leadership. Peter makes a speech to "about a hundred and twenty" and, according to rabbinic teaching, the leaders of a community should compose a tenth of the total. So 10 X 12 = 120.

Notice that the disciples are at prayer "with one accord," a favorite phrase of Luke's. This is a prayer of expectation of the coming of the Spirit, similar to the prayer of Jesus at his baptism. Now the disciples pray for the Spirit to "baptize" the whole body of believers, who make up the church, the Body of Christ, even as the Spirit baptized Jesus while in the Jordan river.

We must note that the original function of the Twelve was quite distinct from that of the apostolate. Apostles, by definition, are those who are "sent" on mission. The Twelve had been appointed by Jesus during his ministry on earth as a sign of the eschatological community. This new Israel will be the outcome of his work. The apostles were originally missionaries and the Twelve and the apostles overlapped. Luke goes further than Mark and Matthew in making the Twelve as such apostles and almost confining the apostolate to the Twelve. Notice that the apostles serve as a bridge between the earthly Jesus who chose them and the ongoing life of the church. This is a major concern of Luke's.

The qualification for being an apostle in the full sense, in contrast to being a missionary envoy of the local church, is that an apostle needed to have been an eyewitness to the Gospel events from the beginning (John's baptism) to the Ascension. However, the primary function of an apostle is to witness to the resurrection. We may gather that there were other disciples present during the resurrection appearances.

The words "they put forward two" refers to the whole community's action and implies that popular choice was involved. We aren't told by what criteria these two were chosen. They prayed, acknowledging that the Lord knows all hearts, and asking that he show which one of the two had already been chosen to take the place of Judas in this ministry and apostleship given up by Judas. They cast lots and the lot fell on Matthias and he was enrolled with the Eleven. It is significant that we hear nothing further about Matthias, and the church does not use this method of casting lots in choosing other leaders so far as we can tell. In the casting of lots, the names of the persons are written on stones, put into a jar or other container and shaken until one falls out. Evidently to the mind of the early Christians this method gave them confidence that the ultimate choice was made by God. The Twelve are thus recognized as "whole" again and are the leaders of the church. Peter is their obvious leader.

*1 John 5:9-13 (C)*

The thrust of this pericope is that eternal life is in the Son and is to be enjoyed only by those who possess the Son. By this, John is ruling out all those who repudiate the humanity of Jesus, including the docetists.

When three witnesses agreed, their testimony was accepted as valid. Or in the case of prophets, such as John the Baptizer, who spoke for God their testimony was accepted. Here John is saying that the testimony of God is greater than that of men. God's testimony is greater because, as in human affairs, a father can speak more authoritatively about his son, or a mother about a daughter, than can anyone else. So no one knows the Son except the Father.

There is also an inward testimony. The person who places his or her faith in the Person of Jesus Christ, rather than a doctrine, is given inward testimony of Christ himself. On the other hand, the person who does not believe, who does not trust God's word, has made God a liar. This is the testimony, says John, that God gave us eternal life and that this life is in his Son. The use of "gave" indicates a reference to the earthly Jesus. The person who has the Son has life.

The progression in John's epistle :s from abiding in Christ through love to the affirmation that we are born of God, and now finally to the affirmation of eternal life. Notice that verse 13 is a more emphatic restatement of the previous verse and, in a real sense, is the conclusion to the epistle. But it is also transitional to what follows in its emphasis on the certain knowledge: "that you may know."

*1 John 4:13-21 (L)*
*1 John 4:11-16 (RC)*

This pericope's central thrust is the love for God manifested in love for neighbor. Notice that verse 11 says we should love one another and verse 21 says that he who loves God should love his brother also. This follows the reading for both the L and RC lectionaries for the previous Sunday and, in typical Johannine fashion, repeats the themes of that passage with some variation. Notice the themes of (1) the love of God, (2) the duty to love one another, (3) the mutual indwelling of God and believer, and (4) the definition of God as love expressed in terms of the saving event. But, in today's pericope, a new point is made, namely that this mutual indwelling is exhibited in the confession of Jesus as the Son of God.

Notice that to love one another is the final proof that we know God whom no one has ever seen. In verses 13-18 John makes clear that the Holy Spirit testifies that Jesus, God's Son, has revealed his Father as love. When this love is perfected or matured in us, then fear of judgment is allayed.

Verse 19 is one of the key verses of all Scripture: "We love, because he first loved us." God has taken the *prior initiative* in loving, and our love is a response to his love. Love originates in God. To fail to love is visible evidence that we have broken with the unseen God and is a violation of his commandment.

*John 17:11b-19 (C) (L)*
*John 17:11-19 (RC)*

This reading continues the High Priestly Prayer which begins with verse 1. It is also called the Prayer of Consecration, because in it Jesus consecrates himself for his redemptive death. He offers himself to the Father as an obedient sacrifice. He prays that the Father will keep the disciples in his name and that they may be one, even as the Son and Father are one. Since the disciples have received Christ's revelation, they no longer belong to this world but still have to live in it.

There is a sense in which the Prayer of Consecration represents the Johannine equivalent of the words of institution through which Christ consecrates himself as the messianic sacrifice. Jesus offers the benefit of his sacrifice for the disciples so that they may partake in advance.

Notice that in verse 11 Jesus prays "I am coming to thee" which, in John's understanding, refers to the whole atoning work of Jesus' death, resurrection and ascension. While especially meaningful when read on Maundy Thursday, this passage is appropriate during Eastertide. We must understand that, as a result of Jesus' departure to the Father, the mission of the apostles is begun. For this reason the prayer is fitting for today, the Sunday before Pentecost, since it looks forward to Pentecost and yet beyond it to the mission of the church.

In order better to interpret today's pericope, we should look at an outline of the whole prayer. There are four centers of concern: (1) Jesus offers himself for his Father's purposes (vv. 1-5);

(2) he is concerned for the destiny of his disciples after his ascension (vv. 6-19); (3) the mission to all future believers until the end of time (vv. 20-23); and (4) the expectation of the final consummation of the age yet to come. (vv. 24-26)

Jesus prays "and these things I speak in the world, that they may have my joy fulfilled in themselves." (v. 13) The gift of Christ is joy through an abiding relationship with him. He prays that the disciples may be kept from the evil one, reminding us of the phrase in the Lord's Prayer "But deliver us from evil (the Evil One)."

## Theological Reflections

The work of the Holy Spirit is central to the pericopes for today. The Spirit guides the disciples in selecting a replacement for Judas. They pray for the promised gift of the Spirit to empower them for mission. They are united in one place in prayer. The Spirit makes real in the believers the love God has shown in Jesus Christ's death and resurrection. In the gospel Jesus prays to the Father to keep the disciples in his name and unite them into one fellowship, even as he and the Father are one. By implication the Spirit is the agent through which the Father will carry out this prayer of Jesus. He prays that the Father will protect them from the evil one, again a work of the Spirit. And he prays that the Father will sanctify them in the truth, another work of the Spirit.

## Homiletical Moves

*Acts 1:15-17, 21-26 (C)*
*Acts 1:15-26 (L)*
*Acts 1:15-17, 20-26 (RC)*
### Choosing A Twelfth Apostle

1. The disciples with one accord devoted themselves to prayer
2. The disciples select two men who had been with them from Jesus' baptism to his ascension as candidates
3. They cast lots for the one to be enrolled as the twelfth as a way of leaving the final decision to God
4. Matthias is enrolled as a witness to the resurrection with the eleven apostles
5. Respond to God's call in faithful obedience

*1 John 5:9-13 (C)*
### Eternal Life in the Son

1. The person who believes in the Son of God has the testimony within
2. The person who does not believe in God has made him a liar, because he/she has not believed the testimony that God has borne of his Son
3. God gives us eternal life by Jesus' atoning life and death
4. The person who has the Son has life. Therefore choose Jesus

*1 John 4:13-21 (L)*
*1 John 4:11-16 (RC)*
### We Love Because God First Loved Us!

1. God has sent his Son as the Savior of the world
2. Whoever confesses that Jesus is the Son of God has God abiding within and abides in God
3. Perfect love casts out fear
4. God's commandment is that the one who loves God should love one's brother/sister also

*This Preacher's Choice*

*John 17:11b-19 (C) (L)*
*John 17:11-19 (RC)*
### Jesus' Concern for the Disciples After His Ascension

1. He prays that the disciples may be one
2. He prays that the Father will keep the disciples from the evil one
3. He prays for the sanctifying of the disciples in the truth
4. He consecrates himself for the disciples
5. Jesus sends the disciples into the world as the Father sent him into the world
6. Jesus calls and sends you into the world on mission

**Hymn for Easter 7:** *All Hail the Power of Jesus' Name*

**Prayer**

*Holy Father, who sent your Son into the world to save us from the evil one, we thank you for your great love. Thank you for calling us to abide in you and for the giving of yourself to abide in us. We pray that we may so possess your Son that we may have eternal life. Send us forth into the world by the power of the Spirit that we may be faithful witnesses to the resurrection. May we love you whom we do not see and love our brothers and sisters whom we do see. Amen*

# The Day of Pentecost

| Common | Lutheran | Roman Catholic |
| --- | --- | --- |
| Ezekiel 37:1-14 | Ezekiel 37:1-14 | Acts 2:1-11 |
| Acts 2:1-21 | Acts 2:1-21 | 1 Corinthians 12:3-7, 12-13 |
| John 15:26-27; 16:4b-15 | John 7:37-39a | John 20:19-23 |

## Comments on the Lessons

The Ezekiel reading is an alternative reading for those churches which do not observe the Pentecost vigil and is drawn from that occasion. The Acts passage is used as the second reading by (C) (L) and includes the Joel citation. The RC lectionary has the 1 Corinthians reading. Each of the third readings describe either the promise of the Holy Spirit, the Comforter, or the gift of the Spirit by the risen Christ. It should be noted that the readings for Pentecost are *repeated* each year. Regarding the Day of Pentecost itself, this is not the commemoration of a single historical event, but John places the giving of the Spirit on Easter evening. The important point to remember is that the giving of the Spirit is the work of the risen Christ. There were successive *outpourings* of the Spirit as Acts records.

## Commentary

### Ezekiel 37:1-14 (C) (L)

Ezekiel has a vision of a valley or plain of dry bones. The bones are the exiles who have no more hope of raising the kingdom of Israel to life than of putting flesh on these bones and calling them to life. This plain may be the same as that where the glory of God appeared to the prophet. In the vision it is a vast battlefield strewn with the bones of men who have been dead a long time. God leads the prophet about over the field to see that there are very many, very dry bones in it. The point of "very dry" is that the life had long since gone out of them.

God asks the prophet in verse 3 if these bones can live, to which the prophet has no answer. To bring them to life again would seem utterly impossible. In this rather surrealist setting of the dream, God commands the prophet to speak to the bones and to call them to life: "Say to them, 'O dry bones, hear the word of the Lord.' " (v. 4)

One of the keys to understanding this passage is to note the constant word-play on the Hebrew word "ruah" which means spirit, breath, wind. The phrase "four winds" may refer to God's omnipresence. We must be careful not to project this vision onto the Christian doctrine of resurrection. The date of the vision seems to be fairly close to the fall of Jerusalem, time during which the prophet's work of administering consolation had not yet been able to take effect.

Notice that what happens in 37:1ff stands in complete contrast to all that has gone before. The valley-plain in which judgment was suffered now becomes the place where God triumphs over death. But there is no hope here of human resuscitation. Rather, God calls the prophet to speak the authoritative prophetic word by which the bones are to be once again transformed into living persons. But will the prophet obey, or shrink back from lack of faith?

The prophet obeys God's call and the bones arrange themselves together, and they are connected by sinew to each other and are given flesh clothed with skin. Here is a parallel to how the first man was made. But the forms do not yet have life. God must, as with Adam, breathe in the breath of life before they can really live again.

The prophet is commanded to summon the spirit of life from each of the four winds to come in its full power to fill the lifeless bodies. Notice the underlying idea here of a spirit of life. This is a very old Israelite conception. The prophet seems to think of the spirit as being a sort of invisible fluid which pervades all the world and which gives life as God commands it to do so. This is based on an ancient Hebrew idea that says the mystery of natural life is comprised in spirit, and the created world is assured of being kept alive by the ever-renewed pouring out of this breath of life from God. But when God withholds this spirit, then death and corruption take over. This is very closely related

158

to the breath of life in Genesis 2:7. But with Adam, the breath which God gives distinguishes him in a peculiar fashion from all other created beings. In verse 10 we see the way in which the concentration of spirit inundates the field where the dead lie. This is a major offensive against death and all its power which results in victory for life. The dead stand up on their feet and become an exceedingly great number.

In verse 11 God equates the bones with the house of Israel. Notice carefully that it is not the dead Israelites who are to be resurrected to take part in salvation. But the house of Israel itself is to experience liberation from the power of death which now dominates it. Now we see that this vision of the prophet has come as a mighty answer from God to the despairing laments of the exiles. Since they had regarded Jerusalem as the ultimate guarantee of their survival as a nation the fall of Jerusalem made them feel as if they had been given up to death itself. They felt their bones were dried up, "very dry," deprived of the last remnants of life. Ezekiel uses the image of actual dead bones to represent the present condition of his people, and, as a result, the people's lamentation can be followed by the victory of divine salvation.

Note how in verse 12 the original form of the dry bones symbol retreats into the background and words of promise follow. The revival of the nation Israel resembles that of a corpse raised out of a grave. Again, the imagery is vivid: the land of exile has become a grave, where death dwells. Those who suffered in prisoner of war camps have expressed much of the same feeling. Babylon is the great graveyard of the nations.

But now the people return to their home country. (v. 12) This is the land of life. The opening of the grave is like the breaking through of the prison door of Babylon. The bringing out of those from their graves symbolizes the exodus of the people from Babylon. In this miracle God says: "And I will put my Spirit within you, and you shall live, and I will place you in your own land; then you shall know that I, the Lord, have spoken, and I have done it, says the Lord." (v. 14)

*Acts 2:1-11 (RC) (See commentary below)*
*Acts 2:1-21 (C) (L)*

There is no agreement in the New Testament about a single outpouring of the Holy Spirit. The Fourth Gospel places the gift of the Spirit on Easter Sunday evening, while Acts puts it on Pentecost, with other outpourings in the early church recorded in Acts. It may be that the gift of the Spirit was originally associated with each of the resurrection appearances. In this case, the Pentecost story would correspond to the appearance to the five hundred. (1 Corinthians 15:6)

The feast of Weeks gained the name Pentecost because it was observed fifty days after Passover. At first an agricultural festival, by Luke's time it had become a commemoration of the giving of the Law. Luke historicizes the giving of the Spirit to this one occasion. "All" would naturally refer to the one hundred and twenty disciples, but it is not clear whether this group or the twelve are meant.

The miracle of the giving of the Spirit is accompanied by the sound as of a mighty wind and the appearances of tongues like fire which rest on each person present. "Wind" is another translation of the Greek word for "Spirit." Now the prophecy of John the Baptizer has been fulfilled: "He will baptize you with the Holy Spirit and with fire." The fact that the disciples were "all together in one place" is significant. Earlier we are told that "with one accord (they) devoted themselves to prayer." (1:14) The disciples were united when the Spirit came. They were praying for the gift of the risen Christ which he had promised and he came as the Holy Spirit.

Further evidence that the Holy Spirit has been given is found in the speaking in tongues. This may originally have been an outburst of emotional babbling, since those around thought they were filled with new wine. Luke interprets this as a miracle by which each one heard them speaking in their own tongue. The event may have included both unintelligible utterances and speaking in foreign tongues. It is symbolic of the whole theme of Acts, which is the Spirit-inspired proclamation to the whole world. The Gospel heard at Pentecost is universal and is heard by representatives of all nations. The rabbis thought that, at the giving of the Law, all nations were offered an opportunity to accept it. And according to Philo, the giving of the Law was accompanied by signs of fire and Spirit. Thus the parallel of the giving of the Law and giving of the Spirit on Pentecost is complete!

Peter explains why the ecstatic speech by saying they are not drunk, since it is only 9 A.M. Instead, the words of Joel the prophet are being fulfilled. The Spirit is being poured out on all flesh. Luke uses the Greek translation of the Old Testament to quote from Joel, which indicates Luke composed Peter's message in its present form. Peter would have used an Aramaic version of Joel. Notice that various apocalyptic signs of blood and fire, and vapor of smoke are indicated to symbolize the importance of this event which has occurred in history. The hearing of various foreign tongues and understanding them is meant as a reversal of the Tower of Babel event in which a common language is divided into many.

### *1 Corinthians 12:3-7, 12-13 (RC)*

Paul says here that the real test of whether or not the Spirit has come from God is does it contribute to the common good. In verses 4, 5 we have a suggestion of the Trinity: Spirit, Lord, God. There were Christians in Corinth who claimed to speak under the inspiration of the Spirit, but those who possessed such spiritual gifts were producing divisions in the church. They were provoking rivalries and disorders. Ecstasy is not enough to prove that one is speaking under the power of the Holy Spirit.

In verses 12-13 Paul speaks of the body and its members as a figure of the church, the body of Christ. There are parallels to Paul's figure of the body and its members in Greek and Jewish literature. But Paul's application is unique. The body is a perfect unity. It is made up of many parts, each interdependent, and the function of each, however humble, is needed for the proper functioning of the body as a whole. Notice that Paul starts with the one body and explains why it must have more than one member. For a good illustration of the interdependence of Mount Everest climbers see page 134 of *Across China* by Peter Jenkins (NYC; William Morrow/Sweet Springs Press, 1986).

### *John 15:26-27; 16:4b-15 (C)*

Jesus gives the promise of the Counselor whom he will send from the Father. This is the Spirit of truth who proceeds from the Father and will bear witness to Jesus. Jesus tells the disciples that they are his witnesses because they have been with him from the beginning.

Jesus goes on to tell the disciples that there were things he could not tell them while he was still with them, but now that he is going to the Father he will send the Counselor to them. If he does not go, the Counselor cannot come. But when he comes, he will convince the world concerning sin, righteousness and judgment. The Counselor can convince the world that sin is unbelief, that Jesus is the Christ, that the cross reveals God's righteousness, and that this brings judgment by triumphing over evil. He then points out that when the Spirit of truth comes, he will guide them into all truth. He will glorify the risen Christ and declare to the disciples the things that are to come. The sorrow of the disciples over Jesus' departure is transformed by the truth that his death and resurrection make possible the Spirit's work. The guidance of the Spirit into the full truth about the historic Jesus will glorify (reveal) the essential nature of him.

### *John 7:37-39a (L)*

In this very brief pericope Jesus invites those who thirst to come to him and drink. John takes this as a symbol of the giving of the Spirit to those who were to receive him later. The Spirit had not yet been given at this point because Jesus was not yet glorified. Now Jesus promises the Spirit as rivers of living water. His opponents see this as a promise to carry the gospel beyond Judea and the people of God to even the Gentiles. They refuse to see Jesus as a fulfillment of God's purpose for his people Israel. They cannot accept his coming as a fulfillment of God's purpose for Israel. Their pride and exclusiveness blind them to God's plan.

### *John 20:19-23 (RC)*

Here is the Fourth Gospel's account of the giving of the Spirit on the evening of Easter. The doors to the room were closed for fear of the Jews. But nevertheless, Jesus came and stood among them and said, "Peace be with you." We can presume the room was in Jerusalem where the frightened disciples are hiding. Jesus shows them the marks of his passion to identify himself. He gives the disciples true peace, the inner security and fearlessness which will enable them to carry out their mission. He commands them to take up his work, even as the Father sent him into the world. He breathes on them, reminding us of God's breathing the breath of life into Adam. John wants us to see this as the work of Jesus in making a New Creation. He said to the disciples, "Receive the Holy Spirit" and told them that if they forgive sins of any, they are forgiven, but if they retain sins, they are retained. It is by the gift of the Spirit alone that the disciples can declare the forgiveness of sins. The church embodies Christ's mission of forgiveness only as his life is breathed into her. Here is a New

Creation which comes into being through the work of the second Adam. While verse 23 may refer to baptism in which sins are forgiven when administered, or retained if not administered, the whole ministry of Jesus was one of remitting and retaining sins. It is this ministry which is carried forward through the church's mission. The twofold effect of the Spirit is not arbitrary but has divine significance.

## Theological Reflections

The gift and work of the Spirit in renewing God's People is the central thrust of the lessons for today. Ezekiel sees a vision in which God breathes life again into Israel, although she has become like a valley of dry bones. At the end of Jesus' earthly ministry, he promises the disciples that the Counselor will come to enable them to carry out their mission. On pentecost the Spirit is given to the assembled disciples which enables them to understand one another, although speaking different languages. John places the giving of the Spirit on Easter evening when Jesus appears to the disciples behind closed doors. The Spirit comes and gives them power to forgive sins and thus to carry out the church's mission as the Body of Christ.

## Homiletical Moves

*This Preacher's Choice*

*Ezekiel 37:1-14 (C) (L)*
### Come Home and You Shall Live!

1. The valley of dry bones as an image of life apart from God
2. God acts to cause breath to enter the reconstructed bodies
3. God brings his People home into the land of Israel
4. God's People live as a gift from God
5. Accept God's gift of life through Christ

*Acts 2:1-21 (C, L, RC)*
### The Power of Pentecost

1. The disciples were all together in one place praying
2. The promised Spirit came upon them and they were all filled with the Spirit and spoke in tongues
3. They understood one another while speaking foreign languages
4. The Spirit came upon all flesh in fulfillment of Joel's prophecy
5. Open your life to receive God's Spirit in greater measure

*1 Corinthians 12:3-7, 12-13*
### The Spirit Given for the Common Good

1. There is one God who gives the Spirit with a variety of gifts
2. The Spirit is given for the common good
3. By one Spirit we were all baptized into one Body, the Church
4. Pray for God's Spirit to empower your life for the common good

*John 15:26-27; 16:4b-15 (C)*
### When the Spirit of Truth Comes

1. Jesus promises the Spirit of truth
2. The Spirit bears witness to Jesus
3. The Spirit will guide you into all truth, convincing the world of (1) sin, (2) righteousness, and (3) judgment

*John 7:37-39a (L)*
### Rivers of Living Waters

1. If anyone thirsts let her/him come to Jesus and drink
2. Out of Jesus' heart flows rivers of living water, the Spirit
3. On Pentecost Jesus' promise is fulfilled
4. Come to Jesus, the Fountain of Living Water and receive life by the Spirit

*John 20:19-23 (RC)*
# Receive the Holy Spirit

1. Jesus appeared to the disciples behind closed doors on Easter evening
2. He showed them the marks of his passion
3. He commissions the disciples even as the Father sent him
4. Jesus gives the disciples the Holy Spirit to enable them to forgive sins in carrying out the church's mission
5. Open your life to receive God's Spirit to empower you for mission

**Hymn for Pentecost:**   *Holy Spirit, Truth Divine*

**Prayer**

*Holy God, breathe on us the Spirit of the Living Christ. We who have become like dry bones from our sins repent and turn to you, the source of Life. We thank you for Jesus who came and promised the gift of the Counselor, even the Spirit of truth. Grant to us a greater measure of your Spirit that we may become more faithful in our mission to the world. Enable us to live as one body, united by one Spirit, with a variety of gifts used for the common good. Amen*

# An Overview of the Sundays After Pentecost

This is the non-festival half of the Christian Year. It has been called a variety of names: "Ordinary time," "Season after Pentecost," "Kingdomtide," etc. Each Sunday stands on its own and the preacher has some freedom in selection of which passages to choose from for the sermon each Sunday. Some preachers follow a nine year cycle, preaching on the Gospel on one cycle, the Epistles another cycle, and the Old Testament lesson on the third cycle of using A, B, C years of the Common Lectionary.

Preaching during this period may follow a semi-continuous cycle using either Old Testament, Epistle or Gospel lessons for a given year as the basis for the sermon. In addition, the other readings can create greater interest and knowledge of the Bible's teaching as the minister or reader gives an introduction of the reading of a given Sunday with a brief recapping of the story or book of the Bible to this point. These readings can be a kind of "mini-series" of stories from the Bible, such as the life of David in cycle B.

While Sundays are called "the Sunday after Pentecost" the lectionary readings are determined by the days within which a Sunday falls on the calendar. For example, the readings for one Sunday will be designated for "the Sunday between July 10 and 16, regardless of the date of Pentecost.

Or the minister may choose to "go off the lectionary" for the sermon Scripture during the time, choosing rather to preach through a part or whole of a book of the Bible, deal with doctrines such as the Apostles' Creed, or social issues of special concern to the congregation.

While the basic color is green for this season, other colors may be used, such as white on Trinity Sunday and Christ the King, red on the days of saints who were martyrs, and red symbolizing the fire of the Holy Spirit during evangelistic services, or ordinations and consecrations, etc. Combinations of colors and colors other than the basic green — red, purple and white — may be used during this half of the year and are being used more often.

Since this half of the church year is less structured, churches may be more creative in celebrating each Sunday. Green, a symbol of life in nature and growth of grass, trees, etc., can also symbolize the growth of Christians and congregations in Christ-likeness.

Special occasions such as July 4 in the USA, Labor Day, Thanksgiving and other special occasions give the preacher a number of possibilities for preaching "occasional" sermons. When this is done, Scripture appropriate for the sermon is selected and the prescribed readings from the lectionary may also be used if desired. When Holy Communion is celebrated during this half of the year the preacher will want to select appropriate Scripture for the occasion, if none of the three lectionary readings for the day are fitting.

From what has been written in these essays on the seasons of the Christian Year, it should be obvious that the Christian Year is not a sequential following of the life of Jesus from cradle (and before) to grave and beyond. Rather the Christian Year is a *theological ordering of the church's living commemoration*. The reforms that have taken place in the Christian Year in recent years since Vatican II have been a return to earlier practices, not innovations. What may seem new to congregations and preachers is, in the main, the restoration of the oldest of Christian practices.

# The Holy Trinity

| Common | Lutheran | Roman Catholic |
|---|---|---|
| Isaiah 6:1-8 | Deuteronomy 6:4-9 | Deuteronomy 4:32-34, 39-40 |
| Romans 8:12-17 | Romans 8:14-17 | Romans 8:14-17 |
| John 3:1-17 | John 3:1-17 | Matthew 28:16-20 |

## Comments on the Lessons

The readings for Trinity Sunday all point to the nature of the Godhead. The Trinity is implied or reflected in them as we reflect on God who reveals himself and who enables the believer to respond to his revelation. The Isaiah passage is an account of the call of Isaiah and his response, "Here am I, send me." The Deuteronomy readings are concerned with knowing God. The Romans passages have virtual consensus. The John reading is the familiar encounter of Nicodemus and Jesus. The Matthew account of the "Great Commission" contains a trinitarian formula which likely was added later by a redactor to reflect the church's faith about God. Baptism in Palestine was always in the name of Jesus alone (See Acts and Paul's letters). The triple formula of Father, Son and Holy Spirit only arose toward the end of the first century and then outside Palestine. But, even so, baptism was always trinitarian by implication, since it was initiation into the New Age ordained by God acting in Jesus the Messiah by the Spirit. The doctrine of the Trinity is, of course, implied rather than explicit in Scripture.

## Commentary

*Isaiah 6:1-8 (C)*

We know little about Isaiah the prophet. Chapters 1-39 tell us most of what we know of his life. We know that he was called to his prophetic role in the year of Uzziah's death (c. 742 BC) and was probably born two decades earlier. His boyhood coincided with the ministry of Amos. He was married and had at least two sons. He had easy access to the king and appears to have been from a good family. if not a member of the court itself. His career extended over half a century. The passage for today is the account of his call, and is one of the best known passages of all of the book of Isaiah.

Isaiah 6 is the beginning of what is called the testimony of Isaiah which continues as far as chapter 9:7. The prophet gives an account of his activity in the period of the war with Syria and Ephraim. Isaiah 6:1-8 may be outlined as follows: verses 1-4, The vision of Isaiah; verses 5-7, The preparation for service, and verse 8, Calling and sending.

While other prophets such as Jeremiah have recorded their call to service (Jeremiah 1), none are as dramatic or majestic as the call of Isaiah. The setting is the temple, probably on some special festival occasion when Yahweh's kingship was cultically affirmed. With this his choice of Zion and David were celebrated. Isaiah in the temple heard the massed choirs, and gazing toward the doors to Yahweh's throne, saw a vision of Yahweh the king. The throne was the ark of the covenant. The seraphim were possibly griffin-like creatures which may be compared with the cherubim who were also associated with the glory of God. In verse 3 "holy, holy, holy" is used for emphasis. Isaiah was filled with terror at what he saw for, as a sinful man of a sinful people, he had gazed on God face-to-face — something no person could do and live. (Exodus 33:20) But he had lived!

In verses 5-7 we have Isaiah's preparation for service. In the darkness he cries out, "Woe is me! For I am lost . . . for my eyes have seen the King, the Lord of hosts!" He could not join in the songs of praise. Nor did his people have a right to do so. The description of God as king came into use as early as the period of the judges, when God was worshiped at Shiloh as enthroned upon the cherubim.

Then one of the seraphim flew to Isaiah, not to kill him, but to purify him with a burning coal taken from the altar. Touching Isaiah's lips with the coal, he symbolically purifies his whole life, purging him of sin. Now he could stand before God without fear. Because the coal comes from the consecrated altar it possesses in itself an atoning and purifying force. The seraphim says, "Behold, this has touched your lips; your guilt is taken away, and your sin forgiven.'' (v. 7) The Hebrew words for sin and for guilt are virtually the same in basic meaning. Their basic thrust is departure from the norm which is demanded. But Isaiah is now cleansed of sin and guilt and can hear the voice of God and answer it appropriately. Only when one has recognized his or her sin and has been set free from it can that person do the will of God.

Verses 8-11 record the calling and sending of Isaiah on his mission for God. As Isaiah stood on the outskirts of the heavenly company, he heard God's voice asking, ''Whom shall I send, and who will go for us?'' Now having been cleansed of his sin, Isaiah can answer rightly, ''Here am I! Send me.'' Then God gives him his commission: to speak again and again a word which will be heard but never understood.

The movement of this passage is from vision of God to vision of self to vision of service. This is particularly appropriate for Trinity Sunday, when the thrust of the message should be not merely standing in awe at the mystery of God and the impossibility of understanding the complexity of the trinity as a doctrine, but rather coming to a face-to-face meeting with the living God, which results in obedience to his will. Knowledge of God, not about God is the goal.

### Deuteronomy 6:4-9 (L)

In Jewish tradition these verses are known as the Shema, so named because of the first word in the Hebrew ''shema'' which means ''hear.'' Here is the great commandment, as Jesus called it. (Mark 12:29-30) It is essentially a restatement of the first commandment, but in positive form. In contrast to pagan religions, Israel has only one God who is sovereign and unique. For this reason she can have but one loyalty: total allegiance to this one God.

The believer is to love this one God with ''all your heart'' which includes the whole mind and will, ''all your soul'' which is the vital self, the whole person, and ''with all your might'' meaning completely. Might expresses the idea of loving God with all one's devotion. This love for God is to be taught to the children, and taught diligently, throughout the day. The words are to be bound on their hands and as frontlets between their eyes, and are to be written on the doorposts of the house and on the gates. This is an emphatic way of saying that love for God is to permeate all of life. There are to be reminders all around to love God, to love him with head and hands in going out and coming in and in all the activities of life.

This, too, is a fitting passage for Trinity Sunday for it focuses our thoughts on the love of God, which is to permeate and transform all of life and is to be passed on to future generations.

### Deuteronomy 4:32-34, 39-40 (RC)

Here is a portrayal of God as the merciful, faithful, remembering God who revealed himself at Horeb and earlier had rescued Israel from bondage in Egypt. It is the Lord's mighty deeds in history by which he chose and formed Israel as his people which have demonstrated his sole deity. There is no other God beside him.

So Israel must know that there is no other God in heaven above or in earth beneath. (v. 39) Because there is only one God and this God has formed and cared for Israel, she is to keep his statues and commandments. Here is God's action and human response to that action. In these verses we find an expression of Israel's art: her theocentric faith. Israel revels in God and this theocentric art underlies many parts of the Old Testament.

Again, a very fitting passage for Trinity Sunday since it focuses on God and his mighty acts in history which call for obedient living from his people Israel. With this obedient living comes a promise: ''that it may go well with you and with your children after you, and that you may prolong your days in the land which the Lord your God gives you for ever.'' (v. 40)

### Romans 8:12-17 (C)
### Romans 8:14-17 (L, RC)

Paul declares that the first obligation of Christians is to embrace the spiritual way of life and to forsake the way of the flesh which leads to death. The Spirit can enable Christians to put to death the deeds of the body and in doing so grants life. The theme of this passage is ''the Spirit and sonship'' and the fact that the Spirit prompts the prayer ''Abba! Father!'' proves our sonship. (v. 16)

Spirit-led and Father-adopted in verse 14 refer to the same persons. They spend their lives in the service of God their Father, not as slaves in fear, but as sons of a loving Father. ''Sonship'' literally means adoption here. The Spirit of God makes us sons and daughters, not slaves. We are reminded of the prodigal son, who in returning home, was planning to ask to be as a hired servant but his father restored him to sonship.

Abba is the Aramaic word meaning "father." This is the word which Jesus used in his own prayers and corresponds to our family word "daddy." For Paul the hall-mark of the Christian religion was to call God "Father" and to call Jesus "Lord." The Spirit works in the lives of believers to enable them to make both these affirmations.

In verse 17 it would be better to translate "provided we suffer" as "if, as is the case, we suffer." The life of the Christian is one of taking up the cross of suffering in following Christ. The sufferings are not hypothetical but actual: "I consider that the sufferings of this present time . . ." (v. 18) Paul assures the Romans that those who suffer will also be glorified with Christ, an inheritance as sure as the sufferings endured. (v. 17)

## John 3:1-17 (C, L)

This pericope contains the working of the three persons of the trinity: the Father God who sent his Son and the work of the Spirit by whose power a person is born anew. The best way to understand the nature of the Godhead is not in philosophical discussion of the three persons and their interaction, dependence and interdependence, pre-existence, etc. but rather in the Biblical revelation of the three persons of the Godhead and their action in salvation history.

This pericope which contains what is undoubtedly the best known verse of the Bible, John 3:16, describes the saving action of God the Father, Son, and Holy Spirit. God is described as going forth out of himself (from his deity) in revelation (he gave his only Son), and redemptive activity (so must the Son of man be lifted up), and creating in human hearts a believing response to this action of revelation and redemption, as the Spirit apparently did in the life of Nicodemus.

Nicodemus was a man of the Pharisees, the most devout Jews, and a member of the Sanhedrin, "a ruler of the Jews." Jesus tells him that a person enters the Kingdom of God, not by moral achievement but by the transforming power of the Spirit of God. Entrance comes through a rebirth by water (baptism) and the Spirit. Jesus tells him that the Son of man descended from heaven, referring to his Incarnation. He would be lifted up even as the serpent in the wilderness was lifted up by Moses. Those with Moses who had been bitten by serpents were cured when they looked at the brazen serpent. Even so those who believe in the Son of man lifted up on the cross will be saved. Both the Incarnation and the Crucifixion demonstrate the love of God which is their cause and motive.

One appropriates this gift of salvation by faith: whoever believes in him should not perish but have eternal life. Jesus did not come to judge but to save the world. The person who believes in him, who accepts him as Savior and Lord, is not condemned.

## Matthew 28:16-20 (RC)

This account of the Great Commission contains the trinitarian formula "Father, Son and Holy Spirit" and so is particularly appropriate for Trinity Sunday. Jesus commissions the disciples and sends them forth to make disciples of all nations, baptizing them, and teaching them to observe all that he has commanded them. And he assures them that he will be with them until the close of the age. For he will come back soon as the Comforter, the Counselor, the Holy Spirit. Jesus' charge to them, with "all authority in heaven and earth" having been granted him, indicates he has been glorified and is now the enthroned Messiah, the King.

Baptism in Palestine was in "the name of Jesus" as we learn from Acts and Paul's letters. But a redactor expressing the faith and practice of the church toward the end of the first century outside Palestine, has included the trinitarian formula in Jesus' commission. Most commentators doubt that the formula was original at this point in Matthew's gospel. For one thing, nowhere else does the New Testament know of such a formula. But it does express the faith of the early church and the action of God the Father, Son and Holy Spirit in salvation history. God the Father sends forth the Son into the world to die for the sins of the world, and after he is raised from the dead the Spirit is given to believers to make effectual in their lives the grace given by God.

### Theological Reflections

Trinity Sunday is a thrilling occasion each year as we seek new ways not only to know about God, but more importantly *to know him face-to-face* as Isaiah did in the temple. While there will always be awe in our hearts as we stand before the mystery of the Godhead, one God in three persons, nevertheless we are led by the Spirit who leads us into all truth to seek to understand the nature and working of God more clearly. We seek understanding through God's revelation in Scripture. The passages today, like spotlights from different angles, seek to reveal more of the hidden mystery of God. God takes the initiative in coming to us, as he did to Isaiah. He sent forth his Son, as John tells us, to save the world. And he has given the Spirit to apply in our hearts the grace he offers. A simple, uneducated believer can know God as fully or more so than the most scholarly theologian, for knowledge of God is a gift of God received through faith, not knowledge learned with the mind alone.

## Homiletical Moves

*This Preacher's Choice*

*Isaiah 6:1-8 (C)*
## Responding to a Vision of God

1. Seeing God in worship
2. Seeing self in relation to God
3. God's good gift of pardon
4. Hearing God's call to service
5. Redeemed to respond in obedience

*Deuteronomy 6:4-9 (L)*
## The Lord Our God Is One!

1. There is but one God
2. You shall love the Lord your God with all your: (1) heart, (2) soul, and (3) might
3. This command to love God shall be taught to your children and shall be made a daily reminder of God for your mind and hand in all your going out and coming in

*Deuteronomy 4:32-34, 39-40 (RC)*
## You Shall Keep God's Statutes

1. God acted in history to call a people and constitute Israel a nation
2. God delivered Israel out of Egypt
3. There is no other God in heaven or on earth
4. Therefore, you shall keep his statutes that it may go well with you and your descendents

*Romans 8:12-17*
## Abba! Father! — The Cry of Faith!

1. We are led by the Spirit of God and therefore children of God
2. The Spirit bears witness with our spirit that we are children of God and heirs of God
3. We cry "Abba! Father!" as God's faithful children who suffer now that we may also be glorified with Christ
4. Place your trust in God and live as children of God

*John 3:1-17 (C, L)*
## For God So Loved He Gave

1. God the Father sent the Son into the world
2. God the Son was lifted up on the cross for the healing of the nations
3. God the Spirit enables those who believe to be born again and enter the Kingdom of God
4. In response to God's love give him your life on the altar of joyful service

*Matthew 28:16-20 (RC)*
## Jesus Sends the Disciples Forth

1. By his authority as the enthroned Messiah Jesus commissions the disciples
2. He sends them forth to (1) make disciples, (2) baptize in the name of the Father, Son and Holy Spirit, and (3) to teach all that he commanded them
3. He promises to be with them to the close of the age
4. Jesus calls you to service in the world and promises to be with you by the Spirit

**Hymn for Trinity Sunday:**  *All Creatures of Our God and King*

**Prayer**

*Unto you, Father, Son and Holy Spirit, we lift our hearts in humble prayer. In your temple we confess that we are people of unclean lips dwelling in the midst of a people of unclean lips. Touch our mouths with the burning coal of your Spirit that we may be pardoned. Open our ears to hear your call to go forth on mission so that we may answer. "Here am I! Send me." Reassure us that, as we go, the Presence of the Living Christ will go with and remain with us until the close of the age. Amen*

# Proper 4
May 29—June 4

# Pentecost 2

# Ordinary Time 9

| **Common** | **Lutheran** | **Roman Catholic** |
|---|---|---|
| 1 Samuel 16:1-13 | Deuteronomy 5:12-15 | Deuteronomy 5:12-15 |
| 2 Corinthians 4:5-12 | 2 Corinthians 4:5-12 | 2 Corinthians 4:6-11 |
| Mark 2:23—3:6 | Mark 2:23-28 | Mark 2:23—3:6 |

## Comments on the Lessons

The reading from Samuel begins Year B's semi-continuous treatment of the narrative of David beginning with his anointing in today's lesson and continuing to his death. The pericope for today reveals that David was chosen for the role of king by God, rather than his rising up through the ranks. The Deuteronomy reading deals with Sabbath observance and is a perfect background reading for the Gospel lesson for today dealing with Jesus and the Sabbath. There is virtual consensus on the epistle reading. Notice that the immediate mention of Christ in verse 5 picks up the link between David in the Samuel reading and Christ in the Gospel reading. There is virtual consensus on the Gospel reading. The long form includes the healing on the Sabbath and picks up on the death/life note in the epistle reading in terms of Jesus' healing.

## Commentary

### 1 Samuel 16:1-13 (C)

While the present form of this story is probably late, it provides the inevitable sequel to the story in the preceding chapter. The breach between Samuel the prophet and Saul the king led quite naturally to the choice of a candidate to replace Saul. Since God had rejected Saul, it followed that God would provide his successor. So Samuel goes to the house of Jesse, the Bethlehemite to seek a king from among his sons. Notice that this account of the anointing of David has the same position in the traditions about the rise of David that the episode of the asses has in the Saul history. Both share the unique secret anointing commanded by God. Both Saul and David were young men at the time of their anointing, known only as the son of their father.

God orders Samuel to anoint a new king so that the kingdom will not fall with the "rejected" king. The anointing is a sign of a call from the Lord to take up the office of king. David, like Saul before him, is elected entirely by divine grace.

Samuel must go through Gibeah where Saul is on his journey from Ramah to Bethlehem. He feels under Saul's constant surveillance, and so Samuel is ordered to offer sacrifice in Bethlehem as a means of avoiding arousing Saul's mistrust. The anointing is not to be regarded as a public affair. Samuel carries out the consecration of the male members of Jesse's family through the offering of sacrifice. The real purpose of Samuel's visit thus remains hidden from the elders of the town and even from Jesse's sons.

Eliab, the oldest son of Jesse, is an imposing young man but he is turned down, as are the other brothers present. The youngest, David, was keeping the sheep and was sent for. He was ruddy and had beautiful eyes and was handsome. Some have thought "ruddy" indicated he was redheaded, but the reference is to his complexion. Not only was David's complexion fair but, as later developments show, his whole attitude displays something fair and winning. But the selection of David is based not on his appearance and Samuel's judgment but on God's command given to Samuel. The Lord commanded Samuel to arise and anoint David in the midst of his brothers. But some commentators deduce from the earlier precautions Samuel took that this action was performed in secret. In this case "in the midst" would be translated "from the midst."

With his anointing David is chosen as the instrument of God, and, as with the anointing of Saul and the prophets, the Spirit of God descends on him. At the baptism of Jesus, which corresponds to the anointing, the Spirit of God descends on him.

Now Samuel can leave Bethlehem. Here, in a very short account, is the keynote to the whole history of David. He has not risen up through the ranks by his own prowess and courage, but rather is the long foreseen, pre-elected, forethoughtfully anointed king. David is now the man with whom God is present by the Spirit. Thus the rise of David has its theological foundation in the anointing at Bethlehem. David is a charismatic person. Kingship for Israel is thus a religious as well as a political office. It should be noted that possession by the Spirit was not just a mark of God's favor but was limited almost exclusively to kings and prophets.

### Deuteronomy 5:12-15 (L, RC)

This commandment regarding keeping the Sabbath is the only one that shows a difference between the Exodus version and the one here. "Observe the Sabbath day" is used instead of "remember." Jewish tradition sees a purpose in this distinction, suggesting that "remember" refers to positive acts like sanctification through candles and wine and Sabbath joy, while "observe" refers to abstinence from any form of labor. "Keep it holy" refers to setting it apart from the other days. Note also that "As the Lord your God has commanded you" is not found in the Exodus version. Some hold that "observe" means "keep in mind" and that one should keep the Sabbath in mind all week long.

The Sabbath is the day that belongs to God in a special way. Notice that nothing is said about it in a cultic fashion. The command "you shall labor" in verse 9 was interpreted by the Rabbis to be a positive commmand. By labor human beings would emulate God's creative process in both work and rest. The command not to do any work was spelled out in detail, with thirty-nine main types of prohibited labor. Even cattle were to rest and not to be used as a substitute for human labor.

The Sabbath has been called Israel's most original contribution to world law. It reveals a marriage of social and cultic legislation. It enjoins rest from labor in a cultic framework. Observing the Sabbath was the Israelites' way of recognizing God's dominion over time and over himself. Keeping the Sabbath was acceptance of the sovereignty of God. The Jews have a saying that "more than Israel has guarded the Shabbat, the Shabbat has guarded Israel." The Sabbath was observed from dusk on Friday to sundown on Saturday and is marked by family observance, synagogue attendance, and total rest. Its mood combines both a serene and joyous one. It is a time for remembering God's goodness and acknowledging his sovereignty. It provides for intellectual growth, gives social balm and shuts out the day's cares.

While rules for keeping Sabbath were marked out in great detail, its purpose was not to make it a day of painful restrictions. Several rules, such as the duties of circumcision or of saving life were considered to have precedence over Sabbath laws.

Early Christians observed the biblical Sabbath, but as the influence of Ebionite Christians waned, the observance was shifted to Sunday, the first day of the week and called "the Lord's Day" in memory of Christ's resurrection. The fourth commandment was declared abrogated along with the biblical law of circumcision. However Sunday was made the official day of Christian worship in A.D. 321. But at first it did not carry the demand for rest attached to the biblical and post-biblical Sabbath. Only much later in medieval Catholicism and in British-American Puritanism do we find the emphasis on Sabbath rest. With the Puritans the restrictions of the Sabbath were not balanced by the innate joy of the Jewish Sabbath. Instead, it tended toward a pleasureless day enforced by "blue laws." Rather than thinking in terms of what cannot be done of the Sabbath, it would be more appropriate to think of what should be done in terms of worship, rest and service. The Jews regulated the distance a person could travel outside the city on the Sabbath to about one-half mile. But instead of thinking of how far we can go in distance we should think of how far we can go in service, in re-creation of our souls, bodies and minds, and in worship of God.

### 2 Corinthians 4:5-12 (C, L)
### 2 Corinthians 4:6-11 (RC)

Paul begins this pericope by stating that his purpose in preaching was not to promote self but to preach Jesus Christ as Lord, with himself as a servant of his hearers. Then he links the God of creation with the God revealed in the Incarnation of Jesus Christ. The God who spoke at creation to command light to shine out of darkness (Genesis 1:3) is the same God who has shone in our hearts to give us the light of the knowledge of God in the face of Christ. Paul evidently thought of it as a visible brightness for he saw the face of Christ on the Damascus road. But it was more than external light and consisted of a spiritual presence and power.

We have this treasure in earthen vessels, says Paul, to show that the transcendent power belongs to God and not to us. Earthen vessels is a reference to the weakness of the body (Genesis 2:7) and stands for all human limitations. Paul sees a divine purpose involved in preaching, since the transcendent power has enabled him to overcome great obstacles in spite of being an earthen vessel. The revelation of God's life and power come through a life like Paul's of unselfish service and suffering for others. During his life, Paul felt he was always being given up to death for Jesus' sake, so that the life of Jesus might be manifested through his mortal flesh. Thus Paul finds meaning and purpose in suffering endured for the gospel's sake. While death is at work in Christ's ministers, the result is life for Corinthians and other Christians. One person suffers for another. The supreme example is in Christ's death on the cross. But the follower takes up the cross and suffers with Christ for the sake of others. Paul felt that he always carried in the body the death of Jesus, so that the life of Jesus might be manifested in his body. His sufferings were a kind of death because of his union with Christ. He was continually laying down his life for the sake of the gospel, so that others might hear and have life. Paul, rather than bitterly complaining about his many hardships and sufferings, offered them up to the purpose of God. He consecrated his hardships to God's plan of salvation gladly.


*Mark 2:23—3:6 (C, RC)*
*Mark 2:23-28 (L)*


In the longer pericope we have two Sabbath violation stories. They show one of the ways in which the religion of Jesus and Jewish legalism differ. While it is officially a Sabbath violation in both instances, the unlawfulness in the grain field is not clear. There are historical inaccuracies which point to a Gentile background for Mark. The grain field story contains the strongest anti-Sabbath statement by Jesus in all the gospels, one which is omitted in both the parallel versions.

These stories were probably preserved because of the interest of the early Christians in Sabbath observance. Reaping, grinding, and sifting are among the thirty-nine kinds of work forbidden on the Sabbath in the Mishnah. Notice how Jesus replies to the criticism of the Pharisees with a characteristic counter-question. He appeals to the example of David. But the high priest was not Abiathar but his father Ahimelech. However, in association with David, Abiathar was much better known.

The action is not clear in the Greek MSS. Matthew makes the offense plucking and eating, while Luke makes it a kind of crude threshing. The Pharisees permitted "plucking and eating" when one was in need. It may be that Mark is caricaturing the legalism of the the Pharisees. Notice that, although it is only the disciples who break the law, it is Jesus who is accused by the Pharisees. Jesus' answer consists of three sayings. (1) The first is much like a rabbinic argument. With a counter-question Jesus asks about what David did when he and those with him entered the house of God and ate the bread of the Presence. Here is an instance of the priority of human need over law. The drift of the argument is that, since Scripture did not condemn David for his action, this reveals that the rigidity with which the Pharisees interpreted the law was not consistent with Scripture, and therefore was not a proper understanding of the Law. (2) Next Jesus quotes "The Sabbath was made for man, not man for the Sabbath." This grounds Sabbath law in the welfare of humanity. This remarkable statement seems to have been understood in early Gentile Christianity as the reason for abandoning the Sabbath entirely. The changeover from Sabbath observance to Sunday worship was accomplished by the early second century. (3) And Jesus says, "So the Son of man is lord even of the Sabbath." This appears to justify Jesus for his actions on the basis that he was privileged to do things on the Sabbath others were not allowed to do. This asserts that the Sabbath remains God's day. Since it was designed for the welfare of humanity the proper use of it is determined by the Son of man.

Turning next to the healing on the Sabbath, according to the Rabbis, the sick or injured were to be treated on the Sabbath day only if life was actually in danger. The withered hand obviously did not endanger the man's life. Therefore, to heal it on the Sabbath was in the Pharisee's view an infringement of the Sabbath and punishable. Jesus looked at them with anger, thus revealing his righteous indignation and his emotional involvement with the cause. Jesus is angry because they are blind to real moral values.

Notice that in this miracle Jesus does not touch the sufferer or use material means in healing. Rather, he commands the man to stretch out his hand. When he did so, his hand was restored.

The Pharisees went out and consulted with the Herodians how they might destroy Jesus. Instead of amazement as onlookers of Jesus' miracles have shown elsewhere, the Pharisees have only cold hostility. This is the first explicit reference in Mark to Jesus' death. It is the climax and conclusion of this first controversy division. Notice that it foreshadows the climax of the whole Gospel in the passion narratives.

## Theological Reflections

God's selection and anointing of the young man David as king foreshadows the anointing of Jesus at his baptism who follows in the Davidic line of rulers. The passages dealing with the Sabbath emphasize that God's sovereignty is revealed in the Sabbath for he is Lord of time, and human actions and healings should reflect God's ruling of human life. Not human interpretation but God's revelation in law should determine human actions. The end of the Gospel stories point to the death of Jesus which is one of the themes of Paul's message to the Corinthians in our epistle reading. The centrality of the death and resurrection of Jesus for Paul and the Gospel is clear from this passage.

## Homiletical Moves

*1 Samuel 16:1-13 (C)*
### Anoint Him for This Is He!

1. Human beings look on the outward appearances but God looks on the heart
2. David is chosen by the grace of God
3. Samuel anoints David with oil and the Spirit of the Lord came mightily upon David from that day forward
4. Since we are chosen by the grace of God let us respond in faithful service to God and others

*Deuteronomy 5:12-15 (L, RC)*
### Observe the Sabbath Day and Keep It Holy

1. Six days you shall labor
2. The seventh day is a Sabbath to the Lord your God and in it you shall not do any work
3. You shall remember that you were a servant in Egypt and God delivered you with a mighty hand
4. Therefore, in response to God's redemptive acts keep the Sabbath day holy
5. The Sabbath was made for humans, therefore keep it in grateful response to God in joyful worship, rest and service

*2 Corinthians 4:5-12 (C, L)*
*2 Corinthians 4:6-11 (RC)*
### We Preach Jesus Christ As Lord!

1. God who said let light shine out of darkness has given us the light of the knowledge of God in Christ
2. We have this treasure in earthen vessels
3. We are afflicted in every way but not crushed
4. We are always being given up to death for Jesus' sake so that the life of Jesus may be manifested in our mortal flesh
5. Live by the light of our knowledge of God in Christ

*This Preacher's Choice*

*Mark 2:23—3:6*
### The Son of Man Is Lord of the Sabbath

1. The disciples and Jesus break the rules of the Pharisees governing the Sabbath
2. Jesus cites the example of David and those with him who ate the bread of the Presence but Scripture did not condemn them
3. Jesus declares the Sabbath was made for humans, not humans for the Sabbath
4. Jesus declares that the Son of man is lord even of the Sabbath
5. In Christ we are set free from the legalism of the Sabbath to live in freedom and joy, celebrating Christ's resurrection on the first day of the week

**Hymn for Pentecost 2:** *God Himself is With Us*

**Prayer**

*Holy God, who has created us for yourself and commanded us to keep a day for rest, worship and service, give us wisdom to use time to glorify you. As we bear witness to the death and resurrection of Jesus Christ by following him in suffering, may we never give in to the legalism that puts law before human need. May we, like Paul of old, be willing to give ourselves up to death for Jesus so that the life of Jesus may be manifested in our mortal flesh. Help us to observe the Sabbath, remembering the day of rest during the other six days, and giving thanks for work and rest. Enable us to use the Sabbath rest to draw closer to you, to remember that we were made for you and not for work alone, and to know that you are Lord of the Sabbath. Amen*

# Corpus Christi

## Roman Catholic

**Exodus 24:3-8**
**Hebrews 9:11-15**
**Mark 14:12-16, 22-26**

## Comments on the Lessons

The lessons were selected for the feast commemorating the institution and gift of the Holy Eucharist. In the Western Church it is observed on the Thursday or Sunday after Trinity Sunday, although the natural day for the celebration would be Maundy Thursday, the day on which the Eucharist was instituted. The institution of the feast was largely due to the influence of Juliana (d. 1258) who took action in response to a vision. Keeping of the feast was commanded by Urban IV in 1264 and observance became universal in the Fourteenth Century. The services of the day were drawn up by Saint Thomas Aquinas. While there are no variations from the above texts, the Hebrews reading could more appropriately continue to verse 21 (which would then include verse 20, which cites Exodus 24:8).

## Commentary

*Exodus 24:3-8*

Here we have a description of the ceremony of covenant ratification. This first version of the covenant ceremony emphasizes the people's participation. ''The words'' in verse 3 refer to the Decalogue. The ordinances are the laws of the Covenant Code. This refers to laws formulated, often in the third person, to deal with various cases. These stand in contrast to the Decalogue, a set of unconditional laws. The ordinances reflect the agricultural way of life in Canaan and resemble other laws of the ancient Near East.

The twelve pillars of verse 4 symbolize the twelve tribes of Israel and emphasize the participation of all the people. They offered burnt offerings and sacrificed peace offerings of oxen to the Lord.

In verses 6-8 the ritual of taking half the blood and putting it in basins, and taking the other half and throwing it against the altar, dramatizes the uniting of the two parties in the covenant: God and his people. God's presence is represented by the altar. The book of the covenant contained the covenant laws, and so is identified with the laws and ordinances of verse 3. The blood of the covenant in verse 8 reflects the view that blood was life and so was efficacious in making covenant between God and human beings.

This passage is central to the understanding of Christian redemption and its symbolism in the Eucharist. Mark 14:24 speaks of ''my [Jesus'] blood of the covenant.'' The covenant blood of Christ is contrasted with the blood which Moses threw upon the people and against the altar. The second reading from the New Testament relating to this Exodus passage is Hebrews 9:15-21, particularly verse 20. It even cites Exodus 24:8.

The biblical understanding of covenant made it necessary for a covenant to be ratified in blood. The blood was believed to have a finality about it that makes it and the covenant itself irrevocable. The sacrifice expresses the offerer's total commitment to be faithful to the terms of the covenant lest a similar fate, death, befall the one who breaks covenant.

But before the covenant can become complete, the people have to become participants in it. This occurs in the Sinai covenant when Moses sprinkles half the blood on the people, and the other half on the altar representing God. In Jesus' crucifixion the sacrificial death is completed from God's side when the son gives his life (blood) in surrender to God. On the human side the covenant is complete when the believer receives the cup of salvation in communion. The cup conveys a participation in the new covenant by faith.

*Hebrews 9:11-15*

''But when Christ appeared'' in verse 11 contrasts Christ with all earthly priests. In this passsage are described the characteristics of the sacrifice of Christ. Christ's sacrifice through the offering of his blood is incomparably superior to the sacrifices of the blood of goats and bulls and the ashes of a heifer. The blood was recognized as the seat and the mysterious essence of life itself. The book of Hebrews is the main New Testament source for the imagery of blood.

In verses 13-14 the writer employs the familiar "how much more" type of argument. The blood of Christ, who through the eternal Spirit offered himself without blemish to God, is set over against the Old Testament sacrifices of goats, bulls and ashes of heifers. The sacrifice of Christ was as tangible and real as blood, as central and decisive as life represented by blood. But it was not an offering on the level of animal existence. It was transmuted into an eternal redemption precisely because it was made through the eternal Spirit. God through his eternal Spirit entered by his Son to rob death of its sting and victory. For this reason Christ is the mediator of a new covenant by which those called may receive the promised eternal inheritance. This is possible because a death has occurred (Christ's on the cross) which redeems them from the transgressions under the first covenant. Christ's death redeemed the Old Testament saints also and inaugurated the new covenant in his blood.

Christ surpasses the qualifications for priesthood and is both priest and sacrificial victim offered for the sins of the world. Christ the Son of God is priest because he fulfills all the requirements — and even surpasses them. He fulfills them in the following ways:

1. By his human experience in which he has sympathy with human temptations and suffering
2. By being called of God to this ministry
3. By his adequate offering
4. By bearing this offering through the curtain into the Holy of Holies
5. Because his priesthood is established by God's oath
6. Because he is without sin
7. Because he remains a priest forever
8. Because he is a priest in the heavenly sanctuary where he continues permanently
9. Because his sacrifice is once for all
10. Because his sacrifice cleanses the conscience.

Christ's sacrifice ends the sacrificial system of the past. At the same time he assures those who trust him an unhindered access to God. Such is the chief function of a priest.

In verse 20 there is a direct quote from Exodus 24:8: "This is the blood of the covenant which God commanded you." Hebrews develops the concept of Christ as fulfilling and far surpassing the sacrificial system of the Old Testament, described in Exodus and elsewhere, as Christ fulfills the role of the High Priest.

### Mark 14:12-16, 22-26

In this passage we have Mark's account of the Last Supper, concluding with verse 26 and the singing of a hymn before going out to the Mount of Olives. When we examine Mark's account apart from the Gospel parallels and Paul we find that the supper Jesus and the disciples ate together was:

1. An anticipation of their reunion in the kingdom, or even of the "messianic banquet" although the evidence for this concept is late.

2. A sacrament. Every Jewish meal was sacred, particularly those of religious groups. This meal bound Jesus to his disciples and they to him in a bond of loyalty. Sharing a meal in the ancient world was a rite of sharing life and incorporated persons into a group.

3. It was a sacrifice in which the disciples were to participate — not only by eating and drinking with Jesus but also by dying with him. The blood of Jesus, symbolized by the cup, was the blood of the covenant poured out for many.

There are a number of indications that this was *not* the Passover (unless by a kind of anticipation). Reasons are as follows:

1. Bread, not matzoth was used.
2. There is no mention of the lamb which was the main dish at the Passover meal.

3. There is no mention of the bitter herbs, or of the attire of the participants as prescribed in Exodus 12.

4. If this had been a Passover meal, beginning after 6:00 p.m. on Thursday, therefore making it the start of Friday by the Jewish calendar), this would mean Jesus would have been tried and executed on the Passover, which would have been impossible.

The above differences from a Passover celebration have led many scholars to view this as simply the last supper Jesus ate with his disciples which Mark has rewritten as an account of a Passover meal. The original account of the meal seems to have been a narrative explaining the origin of the Lord's Supper as observed in Gentile churches. Notice that Paul in 1 Corinthians 11:23-25 does not refer to Passover but to "the night when he was betrayed."   Since the common meal was close to that of the Passover, there is some kind of identification of the supper with the paschal meal. However, Jesus' death was the event which later interpreted both the new supper and the Passover feast for Christians. And this is true for Mark. The Passover was a memorial of God's mighty acts in delivering his people, as well as an actual act of worship. These factors influenced the early church and led to its repetition. The Eucharist thus became the Christian Passover. But in Mark there is none of this emphasis since his story is more primitive.

Jesus "blessed" *not* the bread *but God*. He said the blessing of God, or thanksgiving. This was in keeping with Jewish custom. God blesses living things, giving them the grace of life. God blesses Noah, Abraham and others. In return human beings respond to God by blessing him, that is to say, in thanksgiving.

In Mark's Christian community the Eucharist was celebrated at the end of a common meal. Notice that in Paul's earlier account of the Lord's supper in 1 Corinthians the bread *precedes* the meal and the cup *follows it*. There were seven actions involved:

1. Taking the bread
2. Blessing God (as noted above)
3. Breaking of the bread loaf so that the congregation might share the one loaf in communion
4. The administration, not consecration. In Jewish thought the consecration was effected by thanksgiving
5. Taking the cup
6. Giving thanks over the cup
7. Administration

In Mark's account there are three especially key words: (1) the bread word, (2) the cup word, and (3) the eschatological saying: "Truly, I say to you, I shall not drink again of the fruit of the vine until that day when I drink it new in the kingdom of God." (v. 25)

In verse 23 the giving thanks is both parallel and equivalent to the blessing. Both are directed to God. Notice that in the meal Jesus takes the initiative: He took . . . blessed . . . broke it . . . gave it to them . . . and said . . . and he took a cup . . . when he had given thanks he gave it to them . . . and he said to them . . . For Mark and the early church the supper had a sacramental significance. There is no way it can be interpreted as a borrowing from some mystery religion.

The blood of the (new) covenant of verse 24 refers to the Sinai covenant of Exodus 24:8 and the ratification by blood. While the word "new" covenant is not found in the best texts for Matthew and Mark, it is found in Paul's writings and in the longer reading of Luke 22:20. The reference to the new covenant is probably derived from Jeremiah 31:31-34. However, this is a later development than we find in Mark's words of institution.

In verse 25 the words "I shall not drink again of the fruit of the vine" implies that Jesus had already drunk with the disciples the paschal cup. There are a number of variants on this, such as: "I will never again," "I will not hereafter," "From now on I will not." The Jews had a formula used in the Passover which ended with "this year as slaves, in the year to come as freemen." The reference to drinking anew in the kingdom of God in verse 25 points forward to the time of freedom in the New Age, new as the first creation.

We are not told what the hymn was which the disciples and Jesus sang together before going out to the Mount of Olives. It may have been the final part of the Hallel (Psalms 115—118), which was sung at the conclusion of the Passover meal.

## Theological Reflections

All three Scripture passages focus on the theme of the covenant God made with his people, first at Sinai and then a new covenant in Christ's blood shed on the cross. The Last Supper, in which Jesus instituted the Eucharist, is the focus of the Gospel which describes Jesus' initiative in the sacramental meal. Hebrews shows the relationship of the far superior new covenant in the blood of Christ to the old covenant of the Old Testament. The blood of Christ redeems those who are called of God and grants them an eternal inheritance. The theme of Corpus Christi is thus the institution of the Lord's Supper as the new covenant in the blood of Christ.

## Homiletical Moves

*Exodus 24:3-8*
### God's Covenant and the People's Promise to Obey

1. Moses came and told the people the words of the Lord, the Decalogue, and the ordinances, and after a sacrifice sprinkled blood on the altar and on the people, ratifying the covenant of God with his people
2. The people promise to obey the words of the Lord
3. God in Christ has made a new covenant with his people through his blood shed on the cross
4. God calls us to obedience, loving God and our neighbor as ourself

*Hebrews 9:11-15*
### Christ the High Priest and Sacrificial Offering

1. Christ appeared as the high priest of the good things that have come and entered the Holy Place, once for all, taking his own blood and thus securing an eternal redemption
2. The sacrifice of Christ the high priest purifies our consciences from dead works so that we may serve the living God
3. Christ is the mediator of a new covenant so that those who are called may receive the promised eternal inheritance
4. Let us trust in Christ who forgives our sins and follow him in our daily living

*This Preacher's Choice*

*Mark 14:12-16, 22-26*

1. Jesus shared a last supper with his disciples before his arrest and crucifixion
2. During the meal Jesus took bread, blessed God, broke the bread, gave it to them and said, "Take, this is my body"
3. Jesus took a cup and when he had given thanks he gave it to them and said to them, "This is my blood of the covenant, which is poured out for many." He told them he would not drink again of the vine until the day he would drink it new in the kingdom of God
4. Jesus invites us to eat the bread and drink the cup, so that we may receive salvation and be nurtured in the faith
5. Let us put our trust in the Living Christ and live in obedience to him in covenant love

**Hymn for Corpus Christi:** *Gift of Finest Wheat*

**Prayer**

*Gracious God, who has called us into covenant living with you through the death of Christ on the cross, we ask you to purify our consciences from dead works, that we may serve you, the living God. May we so live in covenant love and obedience to you that we may receive the promised eternal inheritance. Grant that we may be nourished in our faith by the bread and cup of the new covenant in Christ's blood. Amen*

# Proper 5

June 5-11

# Pentecost 3

# Ordinary Time 10

| Common | Lutheran | Roman Catholic |
|---|---|---|
| 1 Samuel 16:14-23 | Genesis 3:9-15 | Genesis 3:9-15 |
| 2 Corinthians 4:13—5:1 | 2 Corinthians 4:13-18 | 2 Corinthians 4:13—5:1 |
| Mark 3:20-35 | Mark 3:20-35 | Mark 3:20-35 |

## Comments on the Lessons

In the first reading from 1 Samuel we learn how David was called into Saul's service to refresh Saul when the evil spirit came upon him. The Genesis reading as the account of God confronting Adam and Eve in the Garden, after they have eaten the fruit from the forbidden tree, and God curses the serpent who tempted them. The epistle reading has virtual consensus and the third reading has consensus.

## Commentary

### 1 Samuel 16:14-23 (C)

This is an account of how David gains a position in Saul's court. It is also an account of the beginning of Saul's suffering from mental illness which was attributed to an evil spirit. Saul has been rejected by God and, in losing the influence of the Spirit of God, he is tormented by an evil spirit.

In both the Old and New Testaments the stories of the people chosen by God are told generally as a history of the Spirit of God being with them. The narrators make a point that it is not just a human history. In Saul's case, when he is anointed the Spirit of God is with him. But when he is rejected by God the Spirit departs. Note that, although he is still king for a number of years yet, he is king without the divine legitimation.

Note that the evil spirit which visits Saul from time to time is said to come "from God," which expresses how, in the Hebrew way of thinking, in the final analysis all things are caused by the one God. This avoids dualism, but at the same time raises the question of how can God be the ultimate source of an evil spirit. The Old Testament speaks of Satan only three times, and then only in later passages. In Saul's case the evil spirit describes theologicelly what we today would describe psychopathetically or psychologically.

Saul is still held in great esteem by his court, and his servants prescribed an ancient remedy for a distraught person: music. The Greek physicians knew and prescribed not only music but drama and other forms of the arts for afflicted persons. In modern times the soothing and healing effect of music is being rediscovered and used in therapy. The instrument named as the lyre, smaller than the harp.

David is recommended by one of Saul's young men as a skillful player of the lyre and also as a very attractive person, "a man of valor, a man of war, prudent in speech, and a man of good presence; and the Lord is with him." (v. 18) Saul was on the lookout for good soldiers and so recruited David. Saul is able to have David brought from Judah, which indicates Saul's power extends beyond his own tribe. The writer of the narratave does not tell us whether or not Saul knows that David had shortly beforehand been anointed. The impression is that Saul does not know. Nor do Jesse and David seem to be afraid that Saul's request to come to the court is connected with this anointing. The presents which Jesse sends with David are gifts representing homage to the king.

David comes to the court and quickly wins the heart of Saul, as he later will win the heart of Jonathan, Saul's son, and then the heart of Saul's daughter. Note that David is not only the musician to Saul but also becomes his armor-bearer. But his chief task is to use his music to help the king when he is possessed.

This story is really the continuation of the account of David's anointing. The Lord not only allows David to be anointed but arranges for David to be taken to Saul's court while Saul is still king. David, all unknowing and unexpectant, is allowed to make the first steps towards becoming king which will be fulfilled later according to God's will.

### Genesis 3:9-15 (L, RC)

The story of Adam and Eve is a part of the first eleven chapters of Genesis, which are generally accepted as myth rather than history. A myth is not a story which is untrue but rather is a story which conveys truth of a kind which cannot be expressed in historical categories. While Adam and Eve are referred to by name this does not imply that these are historical figures.

God's call to Adam "Where are you?" is one of the most profound questions God can speak to a person. "Where are you in relationship to God? Where are you in terms of sin and disobedience? Where are you in relationship to Christ?" Note that Adam answers not with a "Here am I" of Isaiah, but rather in terms of how he came to disobey God. Adam's guilt had led him to attempt to hide from God. God is described anthropomorphically as strolling in the garden.

The essential knowledge for man and the knowledge which set Israel apart from all other nations was the knowledge of God. But obedience was the condition for life. But Adam and Eve disobeyed God and so became subject to pain and suffering and death itself.

The serpent was a familiar character in ancient myths. He was said to have magic knowledge, promises of life and fertility and was the fitting symbol of guile which would lure men and women away from God. Here the serpent offers Adam and Eve vital knowledge.

The curse of the serpent explains why the serpent crawls on its belly rather than walking on feet and why human beings are instinctively hostile to it. The serpent becomes the age-long enemy of God and man. The serpent has come to symbolize evil. The author of this passage is describing in symbols drawn from ancient myths truths which cannot be described effectively any other way. Here he tells how human beings marred what God had made.

### 2 Corinthians 4:13—5:1

Paul begins with a reference to the courage and faithfulness of the writer of Psalm 116:10, who spoke out in the midst of all his troubles a word of faith. In typical rabbinic style Paul quotes only the first few words of the passage, leaving it to the reader to supply the rest from memory, much as one today might quote the first words of a poem or song and leave it to the hearer to supply the rest. Paul says that it is faith that sustains his preaching, as indeed, it sustains each preacher of integrity. Paul expresses faith in a coming salvation in which he will be joined with the Corinthian readers as members of the body of Christ. It is the same God who raised Jesus from the dead who will raise believers at the last day.

Both Greek and Jewish readers would understand Paul's language as he appeals to the underlying faith of both his converts and himself. God will place them all in his presence. Paul felt he would die before the parousia as he speaks of his outer nature wasting away. But he also felt his inner nature was being renewed every day. He also writes about the seen and the unseen, a way of thinking which would have appealed especially to Greek minds. (Plato in *The Republic* developed this seen versus unseen, real versus shadow concept.) Paul says that if the life of Jesus is made effective in the Apostle's body here and now, then a spiritual life is being developed in it that will soon triumph. There is a momentary affliction now that is preparing us for an eternal glory, says Paul.

It is Paul's thought of God's grace abounding for many that leads Paul to be confident of victory in the face of destructive forces. "So that as grace extends to more and more people . . ." (v. 15) The decisive turning point from death to life is baptism which the resurrection of the body begins.

Since 5:1 begins with "for," we know it is introducing an idea based on what has just been said but going on to develop it. Paul uses the image of a tent to describe our present bodies. And if this tent is destroyed we have a building from God, a "house not made with hands" which is eternal. This building Paul speaks of is the "spiritual body." Note carefully that Paul is not speaking of the immortality of the soul here but of the spiritual body of the resurrection. It is conceived first as a heavenly house and then a heavenly garment "so that putting it on we may not be found naked." (v. 2) The spiritual body is eternal for it is prepared by God.

### Mark 3:20-35

Both Matthew and Luke omit verses 19b-21, but they are necessary for the best understanding of the verses which follow since they provide the reason for Jesus' refusal to go with his family. Matthew and Luke emphasize the harmony of Jesus with his family and, for this reason, carefully eliminate the suggestion that Jesus was at odds with his family. The infancy narratives of Matthew and Luke stress Jesus' good relationship with his family.

In this passage we have a series of stories and brief sayings which point up the conflict of Jesus with the authorities and what they charged against Jesus. People were saying that Jesus was mad. His family and friends believed and acted on this rumor. They were concerned for his safety and welfare. To say that he was ''beside himself'' meant that his spirit was outside his body, that it was being directed by a demon or foreign spirit.

Mark is well-known for his ''sandwich'' passages, a passage in which one event is inserted into another. Here is one such ''sandwich'' and the two events are the coming of Jesus' family/friends to take him home, and the Beelzebul controversy with the scribes.

Turning first to the Beelzebul dispute we discover this outline: (1) the scribes accuse Jesus of being possessed by the devil, (2) the scribes accuse Jesus of casting out demons by the prince of demons, and (3) Jesus answers the second charge by saying that a house divided against itself cannot stand. (4) He answers the first charge by saying that he is the stronger one who is binding the strong one (Beelzebul). Jesus says that no one can enter a strong man's house and plunder his goods unless the first binds him and then he may plunder his house. (v. 27) Here Jesus refers to the overthrow of Satan when the kingdom of God finally comes.

Notice that added on to this is a very difficult saying about the blasphemy against the Holy Spirit. Many have come up with fantastic ideas of what this refers to, including suicide. It has to do with Jesus' exorcisms and his Christological claim. To blaspheme against the Holy Spirit is to fail to recognize the Holy Spirit, calling it a demon instead. The heart of this saying is found in Matthew 12:31, and in a different setting in Luke 12:10. Only Mark has the saying in verse 30 which is the most satisfactory interpretation. To blaspheme against the Holy Spirit by confusing the Holy Spirit with unclean spirits is to cut oneself off from the very power which can forgive: the Holy Spirit.

Next we come to the outside of the sandwich. (verses 20-21, 31-35) Jesus' family appears only twice in Mark's gospel, here and in 6:1-6. In both instances, the family members appear as outsiders rather then supportive members of his group. Jesus makes the point that true kinship and relationship of brother or sister is a spiritual, not a physical one. To do the will of God is to become a part of an eschatological family by responding to Jesus' eschatological message in obedient following of him. Jesus does not mean to exclude his family from following him, but they must become disciples on the same basis as anyone else.

### Theological Reflections

In both the 1 Samuel and Mark passages we find the contest between good and evil portrayed. Saul, who had been anointed with God's Spirit, had become possessed by an evil Spirit from time to time. In Jesus' case his enemies accuse him of being possessed by Beelzebul and of casting out demons by the prince of demons. The answer Jesus gives is that a house divided against itself cannot stand indicating that he claims the Holy Spirit has given him power to cast out demons. The Genesis passage describes in story form the appearance of evil in the world. In Paul's epistle to the Corinthians we have a contrast between this present seen world which is being destroyed and the eternal unseen world which is coming and indeed has appeared in the resurrection body of Jesus. God's victory over the power of evil is the basic theme found in all the passages for today.

### Homiletical Moves

*1 Samuel 16:14-23 (C)*
### David Comes to Saul's Court

1. Saul is tormented by an evil spirit
2. David is brought to Saul's court to play the lyre to refresh Saul's spirit
3. David finds favor in Saul's sight for he is a man of good presence and the Lord is with him
4. God calls you to serve in the court of the King of Kings and his Spirit will be with you.

*Genesis 3:9-15 (L, RC)*
### Where Are You?

1. God called to Adam ''Where are you?''
2. God confronts Adam and Eve with their disobedience

3. God curses the serpent who has tempted them
4. God punishes Adam and Eve for their disobedience
5. God has sent Jesus Christ as the Second Adam to forgive us for our disobedience, therefore trust in him.

*2 Corinthians 4:13—5:1*
## Looking to the Things That Are Unseen

1. Our outer nature is wasting away
2. Our inner nature is being renewed every day by God
3. He who raised the Lord Jesus will raise us also with Jesus
4. If our earthly "tent" is destroyed we have a building from God, eternal in the heavens
5. Trust in God's promises for life with him beyond the grave

*This Preachers Choice*

*Mark 3:20-35*
## Jesus' True Family

1. The scribes accuse Jesus of demon possession
2. Jesus says that a house divided against itself cannot stand
3. Jesus warns that anyone who blasphemes against the Holy Spirit by confusing the Holy Spirit and the evil spirit never has forgiveness
4. Jesus declares that whoever does the will of God is his true family
5. Therefore, trust in Christ and obey his commandments and thus live as his brothers/sisters in faith

**Hymn for Proper 5:**  *Jesus, Thou Joy of Loving Hearts*

**Prayer**

*O God of love and truth, we praise and adore you. We come into your presence remembering that we are sinners saved by grace. Lead us not into temptation but deliver us from evil. Help us to look to the things that are unseen, and not to the things that are seen which are being destroyed. We know that this present body is but a tent and that our true and eternal home is built by you in heaven. May we do your will and so be included as true members of the family you have created through Jesus Christ. Amen*

# Proper 6  Pentecost 4  Ordinary Time 11

June 12-18

| Common | Lutheran | Roman Catholic |
| --- | --- | --- |
| 2 Samuel 1:1, 17-27 | Ezekiel 17:22-24 | Ezekiel 17:22-24 |
| 2 Corinthians 5:6-10, 14-17 | 2 Corinthians 5:1-10 | 2 Corinthians 5:6-10 |
| Mark 4:26-34 | Mark 4:26-34 | Mark 4:26-34 |

## Comments on the Lessons

The first reading describes David's devotion to his king and to Jonathan his friend. In it we have one of the authentic psalms of David which is a lament and prayer for deliverance from enemies. David expresses confidence that this deliverance will happen. The Ezekiel reading contains the messianic allegory of the cedar. Its imagary is based in part on the cosmic tree of 31:1-9. There is virtual consensus on the epistle reading. There is consensus on the final reading.

## Commentary

*2 Samuel 1:1, 17-27 (C)*

This may be seen as David's elegy over Saul and his son Jonathan. We know that David played on the lyre and his name is traditionally connected with the composition of psalms. This is great lyric poety, but note the absence of any specifically religious reference. The fact that it lacks any religious feeling is the best possible proof of its genuineness. If it had been composed by another writer but attributed to David, the writer could hardly have resisted the temptation to copy the psalmody so closely associated with David elsewhere. If we had no other poetry from David this would be sufficient to establish him as one of the great lyric poets of all time.

Unfortunately for us the text is very corrupt. The translations into English have tried to disguise the corruption of the text without remedying them. *The Book of Jashar* was an anthology of the early poems of Israel, composed sometime after the dedication of Solomon's temple. The RSV translators have repeated ''he said'' at the end of the verse in order to introduce the poem. But the Hebrew text contains ''the Bow'' which is put as a footnote in the RSV since it does not make sense in the present oorrupted text. The best solution to this puzzle of missing text is suggested by G. B. Caird who says the first line of the poem is missing. All that is left of the first line are the words which cause the translator problems. The most likely reconstruction, says Caird is:

*Weep, O Judah,*
*Be grieved, O Israel,*
*On thy heights are the slain!*
*How have the mighty fallen!*

While the mountain areas had always been the stronghold of Israel they now are her grave.

The lament begins with verse 19 describing how the flower of Israel, the young men, have fallen in war. The ravenous sword is a common image in the Old Testament. The bow was Jonathan's weapon as the spear was Saul's. It is significant that in verse 23 the bonds of Saul and Jonathan, father and son, were not divided in life or death, in spite of the close relatioship between David and Jonathan. The lament has special meaning as David thinks of his friendship with Jonathan. (v. 26) In this lament David has sung not only in memory of Saul and Jonathan but also thinks of himself and his relationship to them.

Later in 4:10 David describes the message brought to him as ''good news,'' which is what the messenger thought and was, in fact, the case. Saul's fall and Jonathan's death leave the way open for David, and so began a new leaf in the history of God's people. While only sorrow is expressed here in the lament, sorrow which seems uninterested in the consequences for David himself, we must remember that at the beginning of the history of David it was said that the Lord is "with" David. Reading the account from this vantage point in history we cannot but be amazed by the miraculous way in which David's career was guided by the hand of God.

### Ezekiel 17:22-24 (L, RC)

The mountain referred to here is Mount Zion in Jerusalem. In contrast to the work of earthly rulers is this news in Ezekiel that God himself is planting a cedar shoot. This reveals his power to guide the course of history. Jesus may have had this parable in mind when he told the parable of the mustard seed (Mark 4:30-32 in Gospel for today). The striking thing about this story is that God's way of working so closely resembles that of Babylon, for he, too, works with what is small and unimportant. But his purpose is very different. The great eagle of the opening parable (v. 3) wanted to keep the vine turned toward itself, meaning that Babylon wanted to keep Judah weak so that it might not ever again become dangerous. God wills that this tiny twig would one day grow so large that it would provide shelter for birds from all over the world.

The cedar becomes a miraculous tree full of life-giving fruit. It is a refuge for all, for even the birds dwell in its branches. This implies that the ruler appointed by God gains world-wide significance. Everything is centered upon the religious recognition of the world-God and subjection to his righteous will. The parable is messianic only in the sense that it is concerned with what God will do for his people in the future. The young twig probably refers to Judah rather than to an individual king who is to arise one day. Judah will prosper when she has learned what God's will for her is.

In verse 24 we find one of the major themes of the Bible: man's judgment and God's. It may be compared to the Magnificat in which the high and mighty will be brought low, and the lowly raised up. Also compare it to the song of Hannah. (1 Samuel 2:1-10) God's judgment reverses human values and judgments! All the nations will know the wonder of God's work, how he brings low the powerful and exalts the humble, how he dries up the green tree, but gives life to the dry tree.

### 2 Corinthians 5:6-10, 14-17 (C)
### 2 Corinthians 5:1-10 (L)
### 2 Corinthians 5:6-10 (RC)

Paul writes to the Corinthians to express his longing to be at home with the Lord. Now he is at home in the body and away from the Lord, for he walks by faith, not by sight. But whether at home or away he says his aim is to please the Lord. Paul knows that, while he is in the present body, he is away from the Lord, although elsewhere he could write of being "in Christ". He is saying that in this life we have to live by faith without seeing Christ. But when he dies he can abide with Christ. Paul can face the dissolution of this earthly body because God will replace it with a resurrection body. And that will be a great gain.

He goes on to say that everyone must appear before Christ at the judgment to receive reward or punishment according to what one has done in the body. The belief in a last judgment is an integral part of the Christian faith. While we are justified by faith the Scriptures makes it plain that faith must result in works of love if genuine. We are responsible persons and will receive a reward for our good works, even if they are the fruit of the Spirit.

In verses 14-17 Paul reveals that the primary reason he cannot live for himself is because of his keen apprehension of the love of Christ which controls him. This love was made known in Jesus' death for all. The Greek verb translated "we are convinced" refers to a conviction formed in the past. It may be that this conviction came to Paul on the road to Damascus when he met the risen Christ and acknowledged he was the Messiah whose death brought life for all and who was raised from the dead.

The meaning of "therefore all have died" is not clear and interpreters are divided on its meaning. It could mean that, since Christ died, the death which sinners deserve to die, he died in their place. Or it could refer to the death, the crucifixion of self, one undergoes in giving a faith response to the cross and in dying to self in baptism. The point that Paul is making in this section is that the outcome of Christ's death and resurrection is that Christians are constrained to live no longer for themselves but for Christ.

Paul says that he no longer regards anyone from a human point of view. Literally Paul is saying "according to the flesh." Before his conversion Paul opposed the Church, Christ and persecuted Christians. He thought of Christ as being just another man. But, now that he is converted, he is convinced that a new creation has begun. As a member of this new creation he takes a fresh, new viewpoint of life. Christ, the new Adam, has begun a new creation. The Spirit re-creates persons and makes them new persons.

*Mark 4:26-34*

In this pericope we have two parables: the Seed growing secretly (found only in Mark) and the Grain of Mustard Seed. They both give insight into the nature of the kingdom of God. Jesus may have had the tree from Ezekiel in mind when he told the Grain of Mustard Seed parable for they resemble one another. As we look at these two parables we should remember that each contains one main point, which is its basic message. The thrust of the parable of the Seed growing secretly is that the growth of the kingdom of God in the world is beyond our understanding or control. Yet we may recognize its progress and play a part in it. The kingdom is already at work in Jesus' ministry, although hidden at that point. But in due time it will be manifested and consummated.

When Jesus told this parable it may have been a polemic against the Zealot policy of armed rebellion against Rome. It speaks to our time against any efforts to force the kingdom of God to come by use of human power or force. Management by objective of the church locally or nationally cannot bring in the kingdom, effective though it may be in organizing people to work toward goals. The main point of the parable is that the kingdom is a divine act and not a human accomplishment. It teaches us to be patient with the apparent delay in the coming of the kingdom.

The parable of the Mustard Seed is a contrast between the small, insignificant beginnings of the kingdom and the final tremendous kingdom that is its destiny. Mark has grouped these three ''seed'' parables together, apparently because they teach related truths about the kingdom.

It is crucial in understand both parables to see that they *do not* speak of the evolutionary growth of the kingdom or of the Church. In the Mustard Seed parable birds of the air can make nests in the shade, as birds can do in the cedar tree of Ezekiel 17.

In verses 33-34 Mark tells us of Jesus' usual practice. However verse 33 conflicts with verses 11ff. It may be that verse 34 was added to this section by Mark to carry out his theory of Jesus' teaching, or may mean that Jesus gave further teaching to the disciples.

## Theological Reflections

The miraculous power of God in effecting his will in the world is a central theme of the pericopes for today. The miracle of God's working in the career of David and the mystery of God's providence is found in the 2 Samuel reading. God creates a great tree from a little twig, says Ezekiel, and Jesus tells a similar parable of the Mustard Seed which grows to a large shrub. The miracle of the new creation by the power of God in Christ's death and resurrection is a theme of Paul in the 2 Corinthians passage. These pericopes point us to God as the one who is at work in human life and history to effect his purposes.

## Homiletical Moves

*2 Samuel 1:1, 17-27 (C)*
### How Are the Mighty Fallen!

1. Saul and Jonathan are slain in midst of battle
2. David laments the death of both his king and friend
3. God works in a mysterious way to open the way for David to be king
4. Follow the sometimes mysterious leading of God's providential hand leading you into the future

*Ezekiel 17:22-24 (L, RC)*
### God's Noble Cedar

1. God plants a cedar sprig (the Davidic dynasty) on a high and lofty mountain — Zion
2. The twig becomes a noble cedar which bears fruit and shelters beasts and birds
3. God brings low the high tree, and makes high the low tree, dries up the green tree, and makes the dry to flourish
4. God works in mysterious ways in our lives to renew us and guide us in his paths so trust in him always

184

*2 Corinthians 5:6-10, 14-17(C)*
## The Love of God Controls Us

1. While we are in this body we walk by faith and are away from the Lord
2. We are of good courage and make it our aim to please the Lord
3. We must all appear before the judgment seat of Christ to receive good or evil for what we have done in this body
4. The love of Christ controls us because he died for us
5. If anyone is in Christ he is a new creation
6. Therefore, entrust your life to Christ today

*This Preacher's Choice*


*Mark 4:26-34*
## The Seed and the Kingdom of God

1. God makes the seed grow secretly without the planter knowing how it does
2. God makes even the smallest seed grow into the greatest of all shrubs by his miraculous power
3. The kingdom of God is God's act rather than a human accomplishment and its culmination will be tremendous
4. Entrust your life to Christ and enter God's kingdom

**Hymn for Pentecost 4:**   *God of Grace and God of Glory*

**Prayer**

*God of miracles, thanks for the miracle by which you are bringing in your kingdom on earth. Thank you for the life, death and resurrection by which we are made a new creation. Help us to see all people from a new perspective as a result. Give us a deeper faith in your miraculous working to bring about your kingdom and help us to become more obedient to your will. Amen*

# Proper 7  Pentecost 5  Ordinary Time 12

June 19-25

| Common | Lutheran | Roman Catholic |
| --- | --- | --- |
| 2 Samuel 5:1-12 | Job 38:1-11 | Job 38:1, 8-11 |
| 2 Corinthians 5:18—6:2 | 2 Corinthians 5:14-21 | 2 Corinthians 5:14-17 |
| Mark 4:35-41 | Mark 4:35-41 | Mark 4:35-41 |

## Comments on the Lessons

In the first reading, David becomes king of both Judah and Israel and establishes Jerusalem as the capital city. In the Job reading, God speaks to Job out of the whirlwind to remind Job of his power in creating the world and ordering it. The whirlwind was a frequent setting for a theophany. The 2 Corinthians reading appears on Ash Wednesday also. Here they are used to highlight the "favorable time" signified by Jesus' stilling of the waves in the Markan reading. There is virtual consensus on the Mark passage.

## Commentary

*2 Samuel 5:1-12 (C)*

This section is of very great importance for the promise to David is fulfilled as he becomes, not only king over all the people, but also king in Jerusalem. What comes later is only confirmation and assurance of this very great event. Although there are four sub-sections in this passage it is well to take it as a whole, since the two most important factors — the king of Judah and Israel and his capitol are linked together.

In verses 1-2 we have what appears to be the work of an editor in the spirit of the Late Source of 1 Samuel, since in the Early Source David was not a general in Saul's army, nor was he promised the kingship of Israel. The transfer of the kingship over Israel to David follows as a direct consequence of the murder of Ishbaal. David is the only possible candidate and his reign is supported by three reasons: (1) his connection with Saul's family by blood, (2) his historical right as leader of the troops by which David exercised the office of ruler in practice, and (3) by the promise of the Lord.

The enthronement and anointing of David seems to have taken place in two stages: (1) the first was done by the active and responsible men of the tribes and is a preliminary action, and (2) by the "elders" who form a higher authority and are an official body. David concludes a covenant with them, and not they with him, indicating that David takes pledges of their loyalty. They offer their homage and recognize him as king.

The anointing takes place at the sanctuary of Hebron which is indicated by the phrase "before the Lord." By this David becomes king in the full sense. The role of the sanctuary or holy place in the enthronement of kings and queens continued in Europe: French royalty at Rheims, and English at Westminster Abbey, etc.

Note the similarities and differences between Saul and David as they are enthroned. In the case of David it is not a united state that is achieved but a personal union.

In verses 4-5 Jerusalem is mentioned, but it was captured only after David was enthroned. Note the statistics regarding David's reign: seven and a half years in Hebron and thirty-three years in Jerusalem.

Note that the capture of Jerusalem is achieved not by the host of Israel but by "David's men." The city was regarded as a foreign city in Israel — Judah and this, in fact, was the case, since it was a fortress city off the main north-south routes. The reference to the blind and lame is puzzling. It could be translated: "You will not come in except after you get rid of the blind and the lame." This would be a better lead into David's command to attack the blind and lame. The meaning of this is that the inhabitants of Jerusalem thought it so impregnable that it could easily be held by the blind and lame against attack.

The reference to the way to capture Jerusalem in verse 8 of "let him get up the water shaft to attack" raises some problems in translation and interpretation. In later times there were two water shafts: siloam tunnel and Warren's shaft, but there is no evidence that these or a similar shaft existed in David's time. The verb translated "go up" normally means "touch, reach or strike" and not "go up." The LXX has "dagger" instead of water shaft. If we follow this approach the verse is better translated: "let him stab the lame and blind, who are hated by David's soul, with his dagger."

The Millo refers to rampart or earthworks, a part of the fortifications from which David could begin building his own city. Hiram of Tyre sent messengers, workmen and materials to David to build the city. The Israelites were semi-nomads and apparently were glad to get technical help in the building of the city. David perceived that the Lord had established him king over Israel and that he had exalted his kingdom. Kingship in Israel differed from that in pagan nations, in that the king ruled under the kingship of God and was responsible to God for his actions (cf. Nathan condemns David in God's name for his adultery), while pagan kings had absolute power of life and death over their subjects and answered to no one.

## Job 38:1-11 (L)
## Job 38:1, 8-11 (RC)

For a detailed examination of the overall message of Job see the commentary for Ordinary Time 5 for Job 7:1-7. In the past many commentators considered 38:1—42:6 to be editorial additions but more recent scholarship affirms their linguistic and literary homogeneity with the main part of the poem in Job.

The answer which God gives to Job's question regarding why calamity and suffering fall on the innocent is in the form of questions which point Job to the wonder of God's creation. Verses 4-7 celebrate the creations of the earth, with a praise from the morning stars, and verses 8-11 celebrate the birth of the sea. The whole scene of creativity is posed to Job as two questions: Who are you? and Where were you?

The depths of reality have been disclosed through Job's experience as having the character of deep darkness. God's design is a "design of darkness to appall." Job in verse 2 has described God's creative purpose as a design of darkness, but, in doing so, he has obscured God's creative intent. Job doesn't know what he is talking about! The divine strategy in 38:2 is revealed by the fact that God calls into question Job's words, as Job himself had called into question his wife earlier, "You speak as one of the foolish women would speak." God calls on Job to assess the propriety of his words as over against the character of his experience of God as a whole.

Job must come to terms with the brute fact of the place of the sea in creation and human affairs. (vv. 8-11) The sea, even as primal chaos, is limited to, yet given a place in the scheme of things, says God.

Throughout the discussion Job has asked why misfortune happened to him, and now God offers Job the right to challenge the divine rule. The point is that the sovereign of the universe is not subject to human ideas about what constitutes justice and God's acts are inscrutable.

## 2 Corinthians 5:18—6:2 (C)
## 2 Corinthians 5:14-21 (L)
## 2 Corinthians 5:14-17 (RC)

This passage (5:14—6:2) which includes the readings of all three lectionaries (C, L, RC) will be dealt with as a whole. In verse 14 Paul writes "for the love of Christ" which means Christ's love for us. "All have died" (v. 14) refers to the death of the Christian who no longer lives for self, but for Christ, and does not refer to physical death. The phrase "though we once regarded Christ from a human point of view" has several possible interpretations. The best is this: Paul no longer thought of Christ simply as another human being who was shamefully crucified. Instead, he now knows Christ as the risen Lord he met on the road to Damascus. This Lord is head of a new creation into which the believer is incorporated. The phrase "be reconciled" means "accept God's forgiveness in Christ and be united to him." Note that in verse 21 Paul does not say "made him a sinner," which would put Jesus on the same level as all human beings, but rather says "he made him to be sin" indicating that Jesus was sinless but bore the burden of our sin. He did this so that we might be acquitted of sin. And in 6:1-2 Paul urges the Corinthians to respond faithfully to God's grace in Christ. There is an urgency about this, however. They are to respond before Christ returns at the End.

The primary reason Paul cannot live for self (me-ism of our age) is that he has experienced the love of Christ revealed in his death for all. Note that "we are convinced" refers to a conviction Paul formed in the past. Paul's life was controlled by a compelling influence: the self-giving love of Christ. Paul is convinced from that first experience of Christ in his life that, if Jesus as Messiah brought divine forgiveness to those he called to follow him, then the benefits of his death are for all persons.

Because of this re-direction of his life (v. 16-17), Paul is now unable to judge anyone from a human point of view although he did so before his conversion. He had seen the cross as a shameful thing and Jesus' death on it as a curse. But now those who are in Christ no longer think or live according to the flesh but according to the Spirit.

In 5:8—6:2, notice that in this new creation, as in the first creation, all things are the work of God. In Christ, God was reconciling the world to himself. He was overcoming his rebellious creation. God took the initiative in sending Christ. Paul sees this saving act against the background of the sin of human beings. There is a great urgency to this reconciliation in light of the coming again of Christ at the End.

Paul shares with other New Testament writers the view that Jesus knew no sin. He did not sin by his own decision or action. Yet in a real sense Christ took upon himself the sin of the world. (John 1:29-34) This understanding of Jesus' role in salvation as the "sin-bearer" is at the root of all "substitutionary" theories of the atonement. Beginning at his baptism Jesus identified with sinners and was baptized for sinners, though sinless himself. The ultimate identification was on the cross where he shared our fate and dealt effectively with our predicament. Paul does not attempt to give a rational explanation of this, however. Rather, he is so conscious of the imminent End that he stresses the urgency of accepting immediately God's grace.

## Mark 4:35-41

Miracles are the work of divine compassion on the one hand and are signs of the new age that is already breaking in on the other. We in this scientific age seek to explain and understand natural phenomena. But this was not the case in the ancient world. Miracles were an accepted part of life. While miracles are a problem for us today, they were regarded as proofs of the divinity of Jesus. But the ultimate miracle of the Bible is the Incarnation and, once we accept this miracle by faith, we can accept the miracles the Incarnate Son of God performed. The central thrust of this miracle is that Jesus trusted in God and his trust was not in vain. Mark seems to imply also that the One who could calm the storm was present still with his own amid the storms and stresses, and especially the persecutions, of life.

Someone has said that the ultimate question posed for Christian theology is: Is it proper to pray for meteriological change? The answer given by this miracle is a resounding "yes." For Jesus who lived a life of prayer simply spoke to the storm as he earlier had spoken to the demon (1:25) and says "be still." In the calm which follows, the disciples ask the question which the story is meant to raise in the mind of the reader: "Who then is this, that even wind and sea obey him?" (v. 41)

There must be a place for God's intervention in the creation which he created and continues to create, unless we take a Deist view in which God has wound up creation as one winds up a clock and is simply letting it run down. But this is not the God revealed in Christ in the Scriptures who interacts with his creatures and with creation. To answer the question of whether it is proper to pray for meteriological change with a "no" is to refuse to affirm the God of Scripture who repents, who delivers his people with mighty acts in nature, such as the crossing of the Red Sea, etc. When we read history and learn that the outcome of critical battles in the past were apparently determined by weather conditions beyond the control of human beings, the act of Jesus in stilling the storm is more believable. The Heisenberg principle, named for the German physicist who developed it, has given modern science an entirely new approach to the possibility of the unexpected occurring in natural phenomena. The deterministic view of reality has been replaced by one in which miracles can and do occur!

Notice how graphic the miracle story is and the attention to detail which Mark shows here. He even mentions the cushion. This miracle and the three that follow are different in style from those already related by Mark. All four stories tell of happenings which took place on one side or the other of the lake which was subject to sudden storms. This author visited the lake on which the storm occurred and was told by the guide that sudden storms still occur as they did in biblical times.

Notice the calm serenity of Jesus and the contrast with the terror of the disciples. One thing we may learn from this miracle is the example of absolute faith and confidence shown by Jesus which reveals his trust in God. While this is one point of the miracle it is not the whole story. The miracle points us beyond our storms and stresses of life to the One who controls nature and raises in our minds the question: "Who then is this?" This is the question the gospels and all Scripture seek to answer in the words of John's gospel: "But these are written that you may believe that Jesus is the Christ, the Son of God, and that believing you may have life in his name." (20:31)

## Theological Reflections

God's initiative in saving human beings is a thrust of the passages for today. Job questioned God but God pointed him to his work in creation, which was beyond Job's understanding, as a way of saying he was at work in human lives. God worked in raising up David as the great king and placing him on the throne in Jerusalem. Paul emphasizes the new creation which God has begun in Christ Jesus. God was, in Christ, reconciling the world to himself, declares Paul. In the miracle of the stilling of the storm we see God's power working through Christ to control nature itself for the sake of his creatures. God takes the initiative to still the storms and stresses of life. Through the eyes of faith we can see God at work. Through prayer we can seek God's intervention in nature for the sake of his people.

## Homiletical Moves

*2 Samuel 5:1-2 (C)*
### The Lord Establishes David As King

1. The people acknowledge David as king at Hebron
2. David makes a covenant with the elders of the people before the Lord
3. David is anointed king
4. David conquered Jerusalem and became greater and greater because God was with him
5. Christ has promised to be where two or three are gathered in his name to empower them, so accept his gracious promise

*Job 38:1-11*
### The God of the Whirlwind

1. To Job's question regarding God's justice God points to his creation
2. God asks Job where he was at the foundation of the earth
3. God asks Job who controls the seas
4. Job is pointed to the majesty and power of God in creating and controlling creation as Job seeks understanding of his working
5. Trust in the God of the whirlwind to bring you through adversity and suffering

*2 Corinthians 5:18—6:2 (C)*
*2 Corinthians 5:14-21 (L)*
*2 Corinthians 5:14-17(RC)*
### Behold the New Has Come!

1. Christ died for all and was raised
2. If anyone is in Christ he/she is a new creation
3. God in Christ reconciled us to himself
4. God has given us the ministry of reconciliation
5. Accept the grace of God for now is the day of salvation

*This Preacher's Choice*

*Mark 4:35-41*
### Who Then Is This?

1. A great storm arose and the boat was filling with water
2. Jesus rebukes the wind and says to the sea "Be still"
3. The disciples were filled with awe and said, "Who then is this, that even wind and sea obey him?"

4. The answer of faith is that this is the Christ, the Son of God
5. Believe in Christ who is Lord of nature and all of life

**Hymn for Pentecost 5:**   *We Sing the Mighty Power of God*

**Prayer**

*Lord of nature and Lord of history, we bow before you in humble trust. You have created the heavens and the earth, the seas and all that in them is. Too often in our stresses and suffering we have questioned your wisdom and your justice. Yet your ways are beyond our understanding. The mystery of the Incarnation fills us with awe. Thank you for reconciling us to yourself through Christ and for giving us the ministry of reconciliation. Help us to trust you as Jesus did amidst the storms of life. Amen*

# Proper 8
June 26 — July 2

# Pentecost 6

# Ordinary Time 13

| Common | Lutheran | Roman Catholic |
|---|---|---|
| 2 Samuel 6:1-15 | Lamentations 3:22-33 | Wisdom 1:13-15; 2:23-24 |
| 2 Corinthians 8:7-15 | 2 Corinthians 8:1-9, 13-14 | 2 Corinthians 8:7, 9, 13-15 |
| Mark 5:21-43 | Mark 5:21-24a, 35-43 | Mark 5:21-43 |

## Comments on the Lessons

In the first reading we have an account of David bringing the ark of the covenant to Jerusalem which helped consolidate his rule. It likened the religious symbol of the tribal federation with his monarchy. The Lamentation reading focuses on steadfast love, a love based on the covenant of God with his people. The Wisdom reading assures the reader that God made human beings imperishable, made in his image of his own nature. The thrust of the letter to the Corinthians is the offering for the church at Jerusalem. Mark gives two accounts of healing by Jesus, another "sandwich" for which he is famous: Jairus' daughter, and the woman with a flow of blood. There is virtual consensus on both the Corinthian and Markan readings.

## Commentary

*2 Samuel 6:1-15 (C)*

David wanted to make Jerusalem a religious as well as a political and military center and therefore it was fitting for him to bring the ark there. The ark was the sacred object of the northern tribes. Now in Jerusalem it becomes the symbol of the national God, Yahweh. In verse 2 there is some confusion regarding the name where the ark had rested. Baalejudah is either an error or another name for Kiriath-jearim where the ark had been left. Regarding the term "Lord of Hosts," it was originally "Lord of armies" or "God of battles" which referred to God's leading his people in war. The reference to "who sits enthroned on the cherubim" reflects the practice in Phoenicia where the king was sometimes represented as sitting on a throne supported by the cherubim. The writer here suggests that the Lord God of Israel is similarly enthroned. An alternate interpretation is that God dwells in the cherubim.

Some scholars think that verse 5, which refers to a full orchestra making merry before the Lord, is an embellishment from a later period since it seems more appropriate to the time of the temple.

Uzzah apparently was trying to steady the ark when the oxen pulling the new cart carrying it stumbled. Uzzah died when he took hold of the ark. People in the ancient world attributed disaster to the work of the gods. Even in these early times the ark was considered "hot" religiously and therefore very dangerous.

The question arises of why Eleazar is not mentioned here. Some think that Uzzah could be a short form of the name Eleazar.

Uzzah's sudden death arouses David's anger. But was it not fear rather than anger? Perhaps both were aroused and so David is unwilling to go farther. So David took the ark aside to the house of Obededom the Gittite for three months while things cooled off. The Lord blessed Obededom and all his houshold, which was told David. So with this assurance that God was no longer angry, David went and brought the ark from Obededom's house to Jerusalem with rejoicing. Each time the ark was moved six paces David sacrificed an ox and a fatling.

The description of David dancing before the Lord is one of the best known aspects of David's religious life. He wore a linen ephod which was probably the same kind of garment Samuel wore as a boy. The ephod was a priestly garment. But all were not impressed by David's cavorting and dancing as he brought the ark into the city. Meanwhile, back at the palace Michal, David's wife, looked out the window and saw David leaping and dancing before the Lord and despised him. (v. 17) Evidently Michal, as Saul's daughter, is concerned for what she thinks is proper for a king to do. She despised David for his dancing because it did not seem appropriate for the royal dignity. But what a fitting way to bring the ark into Jerusalem. The earliest form of religion was dance. When two primitive people met they danced to express who they were and what they believed. Religious dance has come to take on a new meaning and place in contemporary worship. (See *The Dance of Life* by Havelock Ellis.)

## *Lamentations 3:22-33 (L)*

One of the great words of the Old Testament is "hesed" translated "steadfast love." This refers to God's love for his people. It includes both the love which was at the heart of the covenant relationship of God with his people and also reflects God's determination to maintain the covenant. The writer affirms that God's steadfast love never ends but is new every morning. Israel's faith in God's steadfast love is rooted and grounded in God's great saving act of bringing Israel out of bondage in Egypt.

In each of the three verses 25-27 the first word is "good" in the Hebrew. This reflects a description of the commendable style of life — one of waiting for God and seeking him, waiting quietly for God, and bearing the yoke of his youth.

In verse 29 "His mouth in the dust" refers to self-abasement.

In verse 33 the writer affirms that God does not "willingly" afflict or grieve the sons of men. "Willingly" literally means "from the heart." The Hebrew thought of the heart as the center especially of the will.

## *Wisdom 1:13-15; 2:23-24 (RC)*

In this reading from the Apocrapha the writer declares that death is not God's doing, and he takes no pleasure in the death of the living. God's creation and all that conforms to God's will is made for life and an undying life. (1:13-15)

In 2:23-24 the conclusion is drawn that since humans were made in God's image, according to the Genesis account of creation, they are by nature immortal. Death is the work of the devil: "It was the devil's envy that brought death into the world." (v. 24) Notice that here, for the first time in Jewish thought, Satan is identified with the serpent of the Garden of Eden.

The declaration that God made man imperishable, since he was made in God's image, goes counter to the doctrine of death and resurrection in the New Testament which says humans die as a result of sin, but through faith in Christ they are raised to a new life. This is not something inherent in the human nature but is an act of God's saving power. It is possible to find strains in the New Testament which seem to teach immortality of the soul, while there is the affirmation of the resurrection of the body. The two concepts cannot be reconciled but both approaches to life beyond the grave must be considered by the Christian who reflects on the future life.

## *2 Corinthians 8:7-15 (C)*
## *2 Corinthians 8:1-9, 13-14 (L)*
## *2 Corinthians 8:7, 9, 13-15 (RC)*

In this passage (vv. 1-15) Paul holds up the example of the churches in the area of Macedonia as a model for the Corinthians. Paul was a master psychologist and strategist in working with individuals and churches. Here he plays on friendly rivalry between the Corinthians and Macedonians to promote the offering for the church in Jerusalem. The churches of Macedonia, in spite of their poverty and difficulties, poured out generously and joyfully their gifts of money to relieve the poor in the Jerusalem church. The secret to their giving was their commitment of their lives to God first, after which they gave generously to God's people. The entire chapter 8 is concerned with Paul's collection for the church in Jerusalem.

In Galatians 2 we learn that Paul had begun to raise money for this need several years earlier at the apostolic conference. He had carried out his side of the agreement. In 1 Corinthians 16:1-4 Paul tells how the collection could be organized.

During the interim a great crisis had developed in Paul's relationship with the Corinthians. This was the result of false prophets who appeared in Corinth. In the church fight which followed, the collection had been forgotten. Paul had taken a sudden and disastrous visit to Corinth, wrote a severe letter (some think this is 2 Corinthians 10-13), Titus visited Corinth and other events occurred in the dispute and reconciliation. Now that the crisis is over Paul returns to the earlier program of raising a collection for the Jerusalem church.

Notice that Paul pulls out all the stops in his hard-driving fund-raising drive. He gets their attention and uses all the motivations he can devise to bring the collection to completion. The greatest motivation for Christian giving is in verse 9: "For you know the grace of our Lord Jesus Christ, that though he was rich, yet for your sake he became poor, so that by his poverty you might become rich." Gratitude to God for the riches Christ has brought through his self-emptying in the incarnation. Compare this passage with Philippians 2:6-11, the "Kenosis passage" in which Paul appeals to the self-emptying of Christ as an example of humility.

Notice that Paul makes it clear that he is neither commanding them to give (v. 8) nor telling them how much they are to give. Rather he calls on them to respond to the grace of our Lord Jesus Christ revealed in his self-emptying. In verse 9 it does not appear that Paul is appealing to the humility of the earthly Jesus of Nazareth, but rather to the voluntary abasement of the pre-existent Christ who, in becoming a man, brought the riches of heaven to the poor. This divine love motivates the Christian to give. According to Paul, the proof of genuine love lies in the Christian's readiness to give, not in the amount of the gift. What is all important is the intention to give what one desires without reservations. Paul points to the example of God's gift of manna to the Children of Israel in the wilderness who had just enough, not too much and not too little.

Notice that Paul's ethical teaching is rooted in doctrine. Giving is a theological matter, based on God's action in Jesus Christ. Stewardship which is based on the giver's need to give in response to God's great Gift, rather than on the object of the giving alone, is more effective. There is a "push" and "pull" in such authentic giving: the push of God's love which motivates us to give, and the "pull" of the need toward which we give.

Paul says he is not seeking to make the Corinthians poor and the Jerusalem Christians rich, but rather to provide a "give and take," to make things equal. And the mother church in Jerusalem would gain spiritual wealth by which the Corinthian church would be repaid. Paul makes it clear that selfishness is not the best policy, that me-ism, looking out for Number One, charity beginning at home, etc. is not the Christian principle of living or giving. Charity must begin at home, someone has said, but not end there but go on to the ends of the earth!

*Mark 5:21-43 (C, RC)*
*Mark 5:21-24a, 35-43 (L)*

Here is another example of a "sandwich" story which is charactertistic of Mark. There are two miracle stories, one contained within the other. The story of the raising of Jairus' daughter (vv. 21-43) is interrupted by another miracle, the woman with a flow of blood (24b-34). Matthew tells the same story of the raising of Jairus' daughter but places it earlier and tells it more briefly. Luke tells a parallel story also. However, both Matthew and Luke abandon the seaside setting which Mark has. Luke also eliminates the disparaging reference to doctors in verse 26 since he was a physician himself. While the synagogue had only one ruler, Mark may be referring to a class of synagogue rulers in verse 22.

In verse 23 it is difficult to tell whether Mark intended this to be an account of a healing at the point of death, as this verse suggests, or the bringing back to life of one who has died as verse 35 suggests. In the ancient world "sleep" was used of death. The point of the story is to demonstrate Jesus' power over life and death. The raising from the dead was modeled after the raisings by Elijah and Elisha. They proclaim Jesus as the eschatological prophet. The background of this story is Palestinian.

The healing of the woman with a flow of blood is a remarkable example of Jesus' healing power. She was led to Jesus by faith, and her faith is specifically mentioned at the end of the story as the reason she was cured. But the actual curing was by the power of Jesus. The woman's faith was that which allowed the power of Jesus to be effective.

This story seems to be more Hellenistic. The woman thought of Jesus as a kind of divine man, as revealed by her touching his garment. Luke adds that Jesus knew that power had gone out of him as she touched him. But notice how Mark seems to try to change this notion by transforming the woman's superstitious acts into an expression of faith. Mark makes the whole story into a personal encounter with the Savior.

Notice that, at the end of this "sandwich," Jesus strictly charges them not to tell about the raising of Jairus' daughter. This is the messianic secret theme. It makes sense theologically, but it is doubtful such a command was ever obeyed if given. What Mark is saying to the reader is that the real meaning of the miracle is not revealed here, but will only be known at the resurrection when the veil of secrecy over Jesus will be lifted. Only then will Jesus be seen as the victor over death. The raising of the little girl was not Jesus' victory over death, since she had to die again sometime. But it is a prefiguration or parable of Jesus' resurrection by which he overcame death once for all. Notice that the healing of the woman is a symbol of Jesus' death which cleanses from sin.

## Theological Reflections

Death occurs in a number of the passages today. As David brings the ark of the covenant to Jerusalem, Uzzah died when he touched it when the oxen stumbled. Lamentations says that though the Lord causes grief he will have compassion according to the abundance of his steadfast love. Wisdom assures us that God does not take pleasure in the death of the living. Wisdom affirms that, since humans are made in God's image, they are by nature immortal and death is the work of the devil. Death is not a theme in Paul's letter to the Corinthians, but rather he urges them to complete the offering they had begun earlier for the poor in Jerusalem. In Mark's gospel Jesus raises a little girl from the dead and heals a woman with a flow of blood. God's power over death is a theme which is demonstrated in Jesus' resurrection. The raising of Jairus' daughter prefigures the resurrection.

## Homiletical Moves

*2 Samuel 6:1-15 (C)*
### David Dances Before the Lord with All His Might!

1. David brings the ark toward Jerusalem but temporarily halts for three months when Uzzah is struck dead when he touches the ark
2. David makes a sacrifice every six paces as they bring the ark to the city
3. In his great joy David dances before the Lord and the house of Israel celebrates with shouting and the sound of the horn
4. Michal despised David when she saw him leaping and dancing
5. Respond to God's presence in your life with joy as you follow the "lead" of the Lord of the Dance, Christ

*Lamentations 3:22-33 (L)*
### The Steadfast Love of the Lord Never Ceases

1. The Lord is good to those who wait for him, who wait quietly and who bear the yoke in their youth
2. The steadfast love of God never ceases
3. Therefore, hope in him

*Wisdom 1:13-15; 2:23-24 (RC)*
### Death Is Not God's Doing!

1. Do not court death by the error of your ways
2. Death was not God's doing, but the work of the devil
3. God made man imperishable in his own image
4. In Christ God has given us victory over death, so commit your life to Christ

*2 Corinthians 8:7-15 (C)*
*2 Corinthians 8:1-9, 13-14 (L)*
*2 Corinthians 8:7, 9, 13-15 (RC)*
### Excel in the Gracious Work of Giving

1. You know the grace of God in our Lord Jesus Christ who, though rich, became poor
2. Complete now the project you began a year ago to aid the church in Jerusalem, Paul tells the Corinthians
3. Your abundance at the present time can supply their want, and their spiritual abundance can supply your want, thus creating equality
4. Since you excel in everything, excel in this gracious work of giving also, after the example of Christ who gave his all

*This Preacher's Choice*

*Mark 5:21-43*
## Little Girl, I Say To You Arise!

1. Jairus' daughter was at the point of death but he believed Jesus could make her well
2. The little girl died, but Jesus assured Jairus not to fear but to believe
3. Jesus told her, "Little girl, I say to you, Arise"
4. She immediately got up
5. Jesus told them to give her food
6. Jesus commanded them not to tell others about this miracle
7. Put your trust in Christ and he will heal your brokenness

**Hymn for Pentecost 6:**  *Father, Whose Will is Life and Good*

**Prayer**

*God of life who does not will that any should die, we praise you for creating us and giving us life. Grant us faith to live with joy and hope, dancing out our faith in a life lived in harmony with you. Forgive us when we have doubted your steadfast love or failed to wait quietly for you. Grant us faith like that of the woman with a flow of blood to boldly approach Jesus and touch the hem of his garment that we might be healed. Thank you for his death and resurrection by which death itself has been conquered and we have the assurance of life eternal. Amen*

# Proper 9  Pentecost 7  Ordinary Time 14

July 3-9

| Common | Lutheran | Roman Catholic |
|---|---|---|
| 2 Samuel 7:1-17 | Ezekiel 2:1-5 | Ezekiel 2:2-5 |
| 2 Corinthians 12:1-10 | 2 Corinthians 12:7-10 | 2 Corinthians 12:7-10 |
| Mark 6:1-6 | Mark 6:1-6 | Mark 6:1-6 |

## Comments on the Lessons

The first reading tells of David's plans to build a house for God, but Nathan the prophet tells him God will build a "house," a dynasty for him instead! This reveals the divine origin of the Davidic dynasty. The Ezekiel reading describes God calling Ezekiel, the son of man, to be a prophet in spite of the rebelliousness of the people to whom he speaks. There is virtual consensus on the epistle reading. In (C) it begins with verse 1 in order to pick up on the revelations mentioned in verse 7. There is consensus on the third reading.

## Commentary

*2 Samuel 7:1-7 (C)*

Chapter seven is the only serious interruption of the Early Source in all of 2 Samuel. It is a late theological commentary inserted into an early historical source. It is placed here to try to explain why David was not chosen to build the temple. To some extent it is based on Psalm 89. While the historical Nathan does not appear in the Early Source, Nathan the prophet is used here as a mouthpiece of the author. Note that verses 4-17 are often called "The Prophecy of Nathan" and verses 18-29 is called the "Prayer of David." Notice that in verse 6 the author ignores the temple at Shiloh.

The key to understanding this passage is the play on the various meanings of the word "house." (1) In verses 1-2 it means "palace", (2) in verses 5, 6, 7, 13 it means "temple", (3) in verses 11, 16, 19, 25, 27, 29 it means "dynasty" and in verse 18 it means "family status." From the historical point of view the dynasty of David was not everlasting for it fell in 587 (586) B.C., most probably after the author wrote this chapter. The writer may have been thinking of a literal restoration of the kingdom of David while at the same time anticipating in some vague way the Kingdom of God which, of course, is the only eternal kingdom.

Notice that the king who wants to build a house for the Lord is told by the prophet Nathan that the Lord will "build" him a " house" instead. The real point of this passage is that the Lord will make a house for David, not a house of cedar, but a dynasty. This is explained in further detail in the verses which follow this passage.

It is interesting that after David proposes building a house for the Lord, Nathan's immediate response is "Go, do all that is in your heart; for the Lord is with you" (v. 3), but then Nathan receives another word from the Lord that very night telling David not to build a house for him. The reason being that the Lord has not dwelt in a house, but in a tent, since the day the Lord brought the Israelites out of Egypt.

*Ezekiel 2:1-5 (L)*
*Ezekiel 2:2-5 (RC)*

Ezekiel was overawed by the likeness of the glory of the Lord and when he saw it he fell down on his face. (1:28) But God spoke to him and told him to stand upon his feet and he would speak to him. When God commands he also empowers. The Spirit entered into the prophet and set him on his feet. Again, he heard God speak to him to send him on his mission. God will sustain Ezekiel throughout his whole ministry by his Spirit. His message is to be the word of Yahweh but the content of the message is not given.

Notice that Ezekiel is addressed by the title "son of man" meaning "man" or "mortal man." This expresses the prophet's sense of remoteness and finitude in the presence of the divine glory. This title occurs eighty-seven times in the book but rarely elsewhere. The phrase "Thus says the Lord God" may reflect the form of the oracles sent to the kings of the ancient Near East. Ezekiel is to make known to his rebellious people the royal message of God. Although the words of his hearers may be harsh he is not to fear them but to be bold, for the people will know that there has been a prophet among them.

### 2 Corinthians 12:1-10 (C)
### 2 Corinthians 12:7-10 (L, RC)

Paul's statement in 11:30 introduces the theme of 12:1-10: "If I must boast, I will boast of the things that show my weakness." Paul protests that there is nothing to be gained from boasting but, at the same time, Paul feels compelled by his accusers to tell of the experiences of ecstasy which had been given him. He singles out one extraordinary vision and audition of the third or highest heaven. He recalls that it was fourteen years earlier that the vision occurred. The experience burned itself into Paul's memory. Since it is pinned down at fourteen years earlier, we cannot equate it with Paul's Damascus road conversion when the Risen Christ met him and struck him blind. While boasting for Paul is out of place, he is forced to recall one in which he, "a man in Christ," had a heavenly vision. He was snatched up to the third heaven, which according to Jewish belief was the highest heaven of all. Paul heard things that cannot be told, which a person may not utter.

But Paul does not want to offer incommunicable experiences, no matter how important they are to his inner life, as evidence of his divine commission. Paul says that he will boast only of his weakness. (11:30) However, if he wished to he could boast of much else without being a fool.

This passage is from Paul's severe letter written at the height of his controversy with the Corinthians over the false prophets who were undermining his influence at Corinth. (2 Corinthians 10-13) This passage is from an earlier time in Paul's relationship to the Corinthians than that of the previous lectionary readings of recent weeks. The false prophets had boasted of their ecstasies, visions, miracles, etc. But Paul says that, whenever he is tempted to boast of his own spiritual visions, he is humbled by the "thorn in the flesh" which keeps him from being too elated by the abundance of revelations. This thorn was given him by Satan to harass him, and to keep him from being too elated.

Paul says that he prayed to the Lord three times about the thorn, asking that it might be taken away. This reminds us of Jesus' three prayers in Gethsemane that the cup of the cross might pass from him. But Paul, like Christ, did not get the answer he sought but rather had to recognize that God wills otherwise.

The nature of Paul's "thorn in the flesh" has been the subject of countless discussions and articles through the centuries. The thorn or stake as it can be translated continually tortured Paul. While Paul says it came from God, the agent by which it came was Satan. The thorn was a messenger of Satan. Its purpose was to teach Paul humility and to keep him reminded of the need of it. The buffeting by the thorn is in the present tense, implying that it was a continual process. Many commentators think the thorn was a physical ailment of some kind: epilepsy, offensive eye trouble, malarial fever, etc. Some wags have said the thorn in the flesh was his wife, but this must be dismissed as a joke and nothing more. The problem in trying to diagnose Paul's ailment is that the patient has been dead nineteen hundred years!

Karl Bonhoeffer, the father of Dietrich who was executed in World War II in a Nazi prison camp, was a medical authority who thought Paul's thorn in the flesh might have been chronic depression. This illness is often accompanied by periods of excessive activity. He described Paul's illness as "hyperrhythmic temperament." Notice that Paul doesn't complain about his illness but uses it in a positive fashion. For Paul it points up the grace of God in his life. The thorn continually reminded Paul of suffering, a real part of an authentic Christian life. It was a daily drain on his body and nerves but God sustained him with his grace. And so Paul could write: "I am content with weaknesses, insults, hardships, persecutions, and calamities; for when I am weak, then I am strong." (v. 10)

### Mark 6:1-6

This event may be titled "The Rejection at Nazareth." Luke places this story at the beginning of Jesus' ministry. It has been suggested that Mark puts it at this point in Jesus' ministry as the first sign of his waning public interest. In the next section, the disciples are warned to expect similar indifference and antagonism: "And if any place will not receive you and they refuse to hear you, when you leave, shake off the dust that is on your feet for a testimony against them." (v. 11)

Here, in his own hometown where everyone knew Jesus, he could not make an impression. As Thomas Wolfe the novelist has reminded us so well in his novel, *You Can't Go Home Again*. Jesus was evidently quoting from a popular saying of that time when he commented, "A prophet is not without honor, except in his own country, and among his own kin, and in his own house." (v. 4) The townsfolk looked on Jesus, not as a prophet, but as just another hometown boy. When this writer visited Nazareth in 1953, he commented to the guide that he had heard so much about Nazareth and wanted to visit there for a long time, to which the guide replied, "Why, what is so special about Nazareth?" Even though he could point out holy places for tourists he shared the view of Jesus' townsfolk in not giving him honor!

The fact that Jesus was called "son of Mary" may indicate that Jesus' father had died. It was not customary for Hebrews to call a man by the name of his mother. Note that instead of "carpenter" Matthew calls him "son of a carpenter."

The mention of the brothers and sisters of Jesus has created much discussion and even controversy. There are three main views of who they are: (1) they were full brothers and sisters, or (2) they were sons and daughters of Joseph by a former wife, or (3) they were cousins of Jesus. Jerome holds to the third position. There are strong and conclusive objections to the third explanation, but either of the first two may be the case. If Jesus was younger than his brothers and sisters, we may more readily understand their attitude toward him, the kid brother.

Mark is unique in the bold way in which he points out that Jesus was unable to do any mighty work in Nazareth. He was not able to do any mighty work there, but laid his hands on a few sick people and healed them. Jesus required faith on the part of those who sought healing for themselves or for others. However, there are occasional apparent exceptions to this, as in John 5:13.

Jesus marveled because of their unbelief. This amazement is significant for it shows how natural trust in God seemed to Jesus. Mark tells us that this rejection in Nazareth did not defeat Jesus, but rather "he went about among the villages teaching."(v. 6) This example of persistence in the face of opposition speaks to lay and clergy as they run into opposition in bearing witness to Jesus Christ.

## Theological Reflections

David offers to build a house for God, but instead God builds a "house," a dynasty for David. David was not allowed to show his strength and wealth by building for God, but rather God built for him a lasting house. Ezekiel is called to be God's messenger to rebellious people who will not hear him, reminding us of Jesus' experience in Nazareth where the hometown folks reject him. Paul ran into rejection at Corinth because of the phony prophets who came to Corinth boasting of their visions, dreams, etc. But he overcame this rejection by boasting, not of his strength, but of his weakness. Someone has commented that we help others more by sharing our weaknesses, our failures, our sufferings with them than by boasting of our successes, our strength, our making it big through possibility thinking, etc.

## Homiletical Moves

*2 Samuel 7:1-17 (C)*
### God Builds a "House" for David

1. David proposes building a house for God who dwells in a tent while the king lives in a house made of cedar
2. But God rejects David's offer since he lived in a tent since the escape from Egypt
3. God promises to build a "house," a dynasty for David
4. God promises not to take his steadfast love from David as he took it from Saul
5. David's kingdom and throne is to be established for ever, pointing to the kingdom of God which is everlasting
6. Believe in Christ and enter the kingdom of God, for God's steadfast love endures forever

*Ezekiel 2:1-5*
### Ezekiel Is Sent to the Rebellious People

1. The prophet is commanded to stand on his feet

2. God speaks to the prophet and sends him to the people of Israel, a nation of rebels
3. He is commanded to say "Thus says the Lord"
4. Whether they hear or refuse to hear they will know that there has been a prophet among them
5. God calls us to be faithful witnesses in spite of the response we may receive, so obey his call to service

### *This Preacher's Choice*

*2 Corinthians 12:1-10*
## Boasting of Weakness

1. Paul was caught up in a vision into the third heaven
2. Paul is given a thorn in the flesh by Satan to buffet him and keep him from being too elated
3. God tells Paul, "My grace is sufficient for you, for my Power is made perfect in weakness"
4. Paul confesses that "when I am weak, then I am strong"
5. Entrust your life to Christ whose grace is sufficient for your every circumstance of life

*Mark 6:1-6*
## You Can't Go Home Again!

1. Jesus went to Nazareth his own city and taught in the synagogue on the Sabbath
2. His townsfolk are astonished and took offense at him
3. Jesus quotes, "A prophet is not without honor except in his own country, etc.
4. Jesus in his own deep faith marveled at their unbelief
5. Jesus was not defeated by rejection but "went about among the villages teaching"
6. God calls us to be faithful witnesses to the Gospel in spite of opposition

**Hymn for Pentecost 7:**  *Amazing Grace! How Sweet the Sound*

**Prayer**

*God of grace who has loved us in spite of our rebelliousness and who sent Jesus to save us from our sins, have mercy on us. Forgive us for boasting of our own strength, instead of relying upon your grace which is sufficient for our every need. Forgive us for boasting of our spiritual superiority and of playing spiritual one-upmanship with our brothers and sisters. Teach us humility even though it may be through a thorn as Paul was taught. Let us not be defeated by opposition as we witness to the good news of Jesus Christ. But send us to those who will hear and obey your Word. Amen*

# Proper 10        Pentecost 8        Ordinary Time 15

July 10-16

| Common | Lutheran | Roman Catholic |
|---|---|---|
| 2 Samuel 7:18-29 | Amos 7:10-15 | Amos 7:12-15 |
| Ephesians 1:1-10 | Ephesians 1:3-14 | Ephesians 1:3-14 |
| Mark 6:7-13 | Mark 6:7-13 | Mark 6:7-13 |

## Comments on the Lessons

The first Old Testament reading is David's prayer in reponse to God's promise to build him a "house." The Amos reading contrasts the professional prophet Amaziah with Amos the herdsman and dresser of sycamore trees who heard God's call to prophesy to Israel. There is virtual consensus on the Ephesians reading. Note that verses 1, 2 give the context of the passage and therefore are necessary. There is consensus on the last reading.

## Commentary

*2 Samuel 7:18-29 (C)*

As noted in the previous Sunday's reading from 2 Samuel the key to understanding this chapter is the play on the various meanings of the word "house." It can mean palace, temple, dynasty or family status. While the dynasty of David was not everlasting but fell in 586 B.C. which was some time before our author wrote, he may have been thinking of a literal restoration of the kingdom of David, but also at the same time anticipating the Kingdom of God which, of course, is the only everlasting kingdom and "house."

In this passage David offers a prayer of gratitude to God for the promise and the initial acts of grace shown to the nation in the Exodus and Settlement. (v. 23) Note in verse 23 the reference to "making himself a name" which is achieved by God through the events of the Exodus. This concept of the "great name" plays an important role in subsequent writers of Isaiah, Jeremiah, and Ezekiel. The referenoe to "a nation and its gods" in the same verse includes both the Canaanites and Philistines who occupied the land before Israel.

This prayer was apparently made in the tent of the ark where David sits or lies down on the ground. (v. 18) The thrust of the prayer is David's thankful acceptance of God's promise to establish his house. Notice that David, like Nathan earlier, begins with a remembrance of the divine guidance which David has already received. Next comes the promise "for a great while to come." (v. 19) It appears David is thankful that God has allowed him to look into the hidden secrets of the future. This as an act of God's grace. David recalls the long established relationship between the Lord and Israel and the mighty acts of God in Israel's history. While some commentators have seen this as an insertion this need not be the case, since personal prayers are enlarged to take in the people and community in some of the Psalms, such as Psalm 22, 130, etc. Just as God has chosen Israel to be the people of God forever, so now God promises that the house of David will be forever. The house of David and the people of Israel are bound together forever by the promise of Nathan.

The prayer concludes with the request that the Lord will make what he has promised a reality — that the house of David will be forever. The spotlight is on David, and the contrast between him and Saul makes David stand out even more brilliantly. But in spite of this focus on David, the central thrust of the whole era of David is not on the man David but on the grace of God. For David is king by the grace of God. It is not because of, but in spite of David and his greatness and sins, that God's will is worked out in history. "Amazing grace" permeates the life and work of David.

*Amos 7:10-15 (L)*
*Amos 7:12-15 (RC)*

In this passage we learn that Amos, a lay prophet, is expelled from Bethel where Amaziah is the priest of the royal sanctuary. Amaziah is the professional who expells Amos from northern Israel because he thinks Amos is preaching conspiracy. (v. 11) It was at Bethel that Amos narrated his third vision in which he foresees destruction of both the sanctuaries and the royal house.

It may be that Amaziah fears that Amos has magical powers by which he will bring to pass his prophecy of destruction in verse 11. For this reason the land is not able to bear the words of Amos and so he must be expelled from Israel. Amaziah says that Amos may "eat bread," earn his living in Judah, but not in Israel. In 3:13-16 Amos has predicted inescapable disaster for Israel. The nation as a whole will perish. The mighty and swift will not be able to save even themselves, but rather they run away.

This reading goes with the reading from Mark regarding the mission of the Twelve. Here Amos is sent by God to speak God's word to the people in Israel, even as later the Twelve are sent to God's people in Galilee.

Notice that we have here two conceptions of religion: Amaziah represents civil religion, the religion which supports nationalism and makes a deity of nation rather than God. This religion is still rampant today as it promotes patriotism and loyalty to the status quo. Bethel was a kind of national cathedral, and Amaziah saw himself as a kind of court chaplain whose role it was to speak smooth things.

Amos, by contrast, was an outsider. He was a common workman who was called by God to speak God's word. We don't get the basic message of Amos here, but we do learn that his calling is to deliver the word of God and not to follow the professional line of the court chaplains who are uncritical of king and nation. God calls Amos to denounce the government for its injustices and ungodly policies which oppress the common folk.

*Ephesians 1:1-10 (C)*
*Ephesians 1:3-14 (L) (RC)*

The first two verses give the context for what follows and should be included in this section. Note that the greeting is like that in Colossians 1:2. Many New Testament scholars believe that the author of Ephesians was *not* Paul but an admirer of Paul in the Pauline school of thought who wrote in his name. The author's literary style is quite different from that of Paul, as a study of Ephesians and letters known to be from Paul reveals. The position taken in the *Workbook* is that Ephesians was *not* written by Paul but by an admirer writing in his name. In the *Workbook* the author will be referred to as Paul for convenience, or as "the author of Ephesians." Evidence points to the author being a Jewish Christian who wrote to Christendom at large.

After the conventional greeting of verses 1, 2, the letter goes into a hymn of blessing which reads like a baptismal hymn. "In the heavenly places" is a phrase found only in this letter and refers to the unseen spiritual world. Notice the stress on the high calling of God's adoptive sons on the remission of sins, and on the seal of the Spirit. These call the believer to realize in this life the qualities of the life to come.

We may read verses 4-10 in summary as "God chose us . . . and destined us to be his sons in accord with his eternal purpose in Christ . . . to unite heaven and earth in him." Paul is writing to counter gnostic claims to supply heavenly riches through esoteric knowledge of heavenly beings considered superior to Christ. He is also answering the question of why the church as a divine fellowship has appeared only recently. In verse 9 Paul says that the church from the beginning was in the mind of God and appeared in the fullness of time. Christ is head of all angelic powers. All things find their fulfillment in Christ. He is their uniting power. Christ has been called the great linchpin in the chain of being.

The ancient world sought the source of harmony in the world. In a world of diversity and freedom, thinkers sought to find the source of harmony. In Christ we find the source of harmony. In him is the power of God which providentially guides the universe.

In verses 12, 13 Paul contrasts "we who first hoped in Christ" with "you also, who have heard the word of truth . . ." The literal reading is "in *the* Christ" which puts its emphasis on its primary sense of "the Messiah." This refers to the Messianic hope in Israel now fulfilled in Jesus, the Christ (Messiah). However, Gentile readers were not prepared by generations of hope for the coming of the Messiah. But through hearing the gospel, they have come to faith in Jesus as the Messiah and by the Holy Spirit have been sealed for God's possession. The Holy Spirit is the guarantee of our inheritance, a down-payment until we receive the full possession of it. The "earnest" is more than a guarantee, but is a partial payment, a down-payment, which binds the bargain and obliges both buyer and seller to complete the deal. So the Holy Spirit is the first installment of the great treasure that God will give in the future.

The passage ends with a repetition of praise: "to the praise of his glory." (v. 14) God's glory is revealed with increasing clearness as his purpose of grace unfolds with greater and greater revelations of his blessings, as a stone in a pond creates ever widening circles of waves. So the renewal of the song of praise increases in ever increasing fashion.

*Mark 6:7-13*

Here we have the commissioning and instruction of the Twelve. This action is prepared for in 3:14, 15, "And he appointed twelve, to be with him, and to be sent out to preach and have authority to cast out demons . . ." Some question the historicity of this section. A circle of twelve leaders is very seldom found in Jewish fellowships. It appears that Jesus called the twelve as a special inner group of his followers. But Jesus did not intend to form an exclusive group but looked on the twelve as a symbol of his claim upon Israel.

The fact that Jesus sent the twelve out two by two symbolizes the fact that service for Jesus is always service to the church and involves teamwork. Notice the emphasis on authority. He gave them authority over unclean spirits. Preaching is not entertainment or theoretical instruction but is exhortation by the authority and power of God. Preaching with such authority confronts every hostile power with God's truth.

The twelve are sent out in poverty, without provisions, without money in their pockets or additional protective clothing. They are to live in dependence upon God and God's people, trusting like the "birds" and the "wild flowers" in God's providential care. But at the same time they are not ascetics. They are to make use of whatever they need without hesitation. They are not to burden themselves with extra clothing, etc., but, like long distance backpackers going for months at a time, they are to strip off all but the bare essentials.

We must remember that in every Jewish city a social welfare worker provided food and clothing for wanderers as the twelve would be on this mission. While rabbis were undecided about how long a stranger might stay as a guest, the early church said that anyone who stays more than two days is a false prophet. Jesus warns the twelve that they are not to move to more pleasant quarters in the same town. (v. 10)

The act of shaking off the dust from their feet if rejected by a town reflects the action of Jews who, when they returned from a Gentile region to the Holy Land, shook off the dust as a way of leaving everything unclean behind them. It might also be a sign for those who were not ready to repent to indicate to them the seriousness of their rejection of the Gospel, which might move them to repent. Or it might be a sign against them on the Day of Judgment. It is an indication that the place is to be regarded as heathen. It is not an actual curse. Its purpose is to motivate people to think and to repent. The content of the call to repentance preached by the twelve is found in 1:4 ". . . preaching a baptism of repentance for the forgiveness of sins" and in 1:14f ". . . preaching the gospel of God, and saying 'the time is fulfilled, and the kingdom of God is at hand; repent, and believe in the Gospel.' " The disciples' work of healing is also mentioned: ". . . and anointed with oil many that were sick and healed them." (v. 13) While oil was often used as a salve, it is used here as something objective which may be interpreted as the sign reinforcing the message which announces the healing.

How important is authenticity in preaching is a thrust of this passage. The medium is the message, but not the whole message. The poverty and unpretentiousness of the messengers, their courage in preaching an unpopular message which might mean their rejection are all part of the message. All point to God who is more important, of course, than anything else.

## Theological Reflections

God promises David a dynasty, a house, and David responds with a prayer in which David reflects on God's saving actions in Israel's life. Here is God and a person in dialogue, God promising and the person responding. Responding in trust and obedience. The grace of God is prominent in this passage. In the Amos reading we see the contrast between two kinds of religion: civil religion which supports the state and is used by the state, and the Word of God which calls a lay person to preach a warning to king and people. This foreshadows the sending out of the Twelve by Jesus to preach a message of repentance in light of the coming Kingdom of God. The Ephesians reading is a hymn of blessing with its emphasis on what God has done in calling people to be his sons and daughters by adoption, on the remission of sins, and on the sealing of the Spirit. The believer is called to realize in this life the qualities of the life to come. Mark records the sending out of the Twelve to preach and the instructions of how they are to go and their response to being rejected. They are to go as God's messengers and to heal as well as cast out demons and to preach repentance in light of God's coming Kingdom. This Kingdom is the fulfillment of the "house" God promised to David, an everlasting dynasty

## Homiletical Moves

*2 Samuel 7:18-29 (C)*
### Bless the House of Thy Servant!

1. David praises the greatness of God in his prayer
2. God has redeemed Israel and brought her into the Promised Land
3. David prays that God will confirm his promise to establish his house forever
4. David prays that God will bless his house that it may continue forever with God's blessing
5. Come by faith into God's kingdom and you will be blessed forever

*Amos 7:10-15 (L)*
*Amos 7:12-15 (RC)*
### Civil Religion Versus Authentic Religion

1. Amaziah accuses Amos of conspiracy against king Jeroboam
2. Amaziah commands Amos to leave Israel and to live in Judah and prophesy there
3. Amos defends his prophetic role as a lay person called of God from working as a herdsman and dresser of sycamore trees
4. Amos obeyed God's call to prophesy judgment of God against Jeroboam and Israel
5. God calls us to be faithful to him and to reject nationalism and other false religions, therefore, obey his call

*This Preacher's Choice*

*Ephesians 1:1-10 (C)*
*Ephesians 1:3-14 (L, RC)*
### Chosen by God to Be Holy and Blameless

1. God has destined us in love to be his sons and daughters through Jesus Christ, according to the purpose of his will
2. In Christ we have redemption through his blood, the forgiveness of our sins
3. He has made known to us in all wisdom and insight the mystery of his will to unite all things in Christ, things in heaven and on earth
4. We have been destined and appointed to live for the praise of his glory
5. We have been sealed by the promised Holy Spirit, which is the guarantee of our inheritance, therefore live in response to God

*Mark 6:7-13*
### So the Twelve Went Out As Commanded

1. Jesus sends out the Twelve, two by two, to preach and heal
2. They are to go in poverty with only the bare essentials for this urgent mission
3. If rejected by a place, they are to leave it
4. The Twelve went out and preached repentance, cast out demons and healed the sick
5. Heed God's call to join other Christians in mission to a broken world relying on his power

**Hymn for Pentecost 8:**  *O Master, Let Me Walk With Thee*

**Prayer**

*O God who called prophets of old to proclaim your Word, may we hear and obey your call in our time. Like Amos, may we be charged with a message. Or we may be sent with another believer like the disciples Jesus sent out to preach and heal. May we respond with trust and obedience when we hear your call to serve. O God, remind us that we are your sons and daughters by faith and that you called us to be your people from the foundation of the world. Grant to us a greater measure of the Holy Spirit to seal us for service and to empower us for our mission in the world. Amen*

## Proper 11     Pentecost 9     Ordinary Time 16

July 17-23

| Common | Lutheran | Roman Catholic |
|---|---|---|
| 2 Samuel 11:1-15 | Jeremiah 23:1-6 | Jeremiah 23:1-6 |
| Ephesians 2:11-22 | Ephesians 2:13-22 | Ephesians 2:13-18 |
| Mark 6:30-34 | Mark 6:30-34 | Mark 6:30-34 |

### Comments on the Lessons

The Samuel reading is the account of David's sin with Bathsheba and against Uriah her husband. The Jeremiah passage is a "woe" against false shepherds and a promise of a righteous Branch of David who will reign as king and deal wisely. From this side of the cross we see this fulfilled in Jesus Christ. There is virtual consensus on the Ephesian reading. The longer version of the readings is preferred, since it preserves the contrast between the precovenant situation with the reality for believing Gentiles after Christ. There is consensus on the Mark reading. It is a short gospel reading chosen because of the long previous readings. Note the reference in verse 34 to the shepherd since next Sunday's John reading of the miracle of feeding reflects a similar concern. The Jeremiah passage with its reference to false shepherds foreshadows the Markan reference to the great throng who were like sheep without a shepherd.

### Commentary

*2 Samuel 11:1-15 (C)*

The story of David and Bathsheba is one which arouses both dismay and astonishment. It is a story which paints David, "warts and all," and shows that the ancient writers had no concern to whitewash even kings and national heroes. The story produces dismay over the fact that a chosen king like David could sink so low into sin. Readers are astonished that the Bible would record such a damaging story. The writer of Chronicles omits it. The sordid account points up the fact that God's cause is advanced, not through perfect people, but by God himself in spite of the sinfulness of his best people.

The setting is in the spring of the year when kings go forth to war. David is at war with the Ammonites. Joab, the general in David's army, is beseiging Rahab while David remains in Jerusalem. David not only satisfies his lust for Bathsheba and commits adultery in doing so but also arranges for the death of her husband in a battle. Notice the amazing realism of the account which reflects first hand knowledge of what happened. The consequences of this sinful act is so much a part of the account which follows that the cause must be clearly described. Psalm 51 is thought by some to be David's personal prayer of repentance for this particular sin.

David sends Joab and his servants into battle. The servants are David's outstanding men from the royal bodyguard. "All Israel" refers to the army in general. The name Bathsheba means "daughter of oath" and "Uriah" is a pure Hebrew word meaning "Yahweh is my light." Hittite may refer to the derivation of his family. Uriah the Hittite is listed in 23:39 as one of David's heroes, and he was probably a member of one of David's foreign troops.

Note that Bathsheba's simple message "I am with child" forced David to take action. While kings of pagan nations were accountable to no one but themselves for their actions, Israel's kings were accountable to God, as we shall learn from Nathan's accusation of David. David tries to conceal his sin of adultery with Bathsheba by giving Uriah leave to visit his wife so that it will appear the child is his. David tells him "Go down to your house and wash your feet." (v. 8) This may mean simply "Make yourself comfortable." The Hebrew word for feet may also allude to the male genitals. David sends food to put Uriah an a good frame of mind. It may well be that Uriah got wind of the affair from court gossip. Uriah may have seen in the king's generosity confirmation of his suspicions from court gossip.

Uriah refuses to sleep with his wife Bathsheba while his fellow soldiers are on the field of battle away from their wives. Even David's ploy in getting Uriah drunk doesn't work. Uriah feels a loyalty to the holy war and his religious obligations and so abstains from intercourse with his wife during this visit. This is Uriah's weapon and revenge against King David and Bathsheba, his wife, but he loses his life as a result.

David writes the ''Uriah letter'' to Joab, commanding him to place Uriah in the forefront of battle and then to withdraw and leave him exposed so he may be killed. As it worked out in fact, Uriah is placed where there were valiant men but the soldiers around him were not withdrawn as David planned. Instead, the men of the city came out and fought with Joab and Uriah was killed in the battle. David wanted it to appear that Uriah was killed in normal battle action and not by strategy against one of his heroes. Note that the different stages of David's sin are described with great truthfulness, much like the stages of Cain's sin.

### Jeremiah 23:1-6 (L) (RC)

Israel's rulers are referred to here as shepherds. This is a messianic oracle in which the coming of the righteous Branch is foretold, one we see fulfilled in the life and work of Jesus Christ.

Jeremiah reproaches the rulers of Israel for scattering Judah, the flock. The rulers have been like wolves devouring the flock but now God will judge them. But in verse 4 there is a comforting assurance that God will set shepherds over his flock who will care for them. This foreshadows the coming of Jesus the ''Good Shepherd'' who lays down his life for his sheep.

Jeremiah foretells the coming of a righteous Branch of David who will reign as king and will deal wisely and execute justice and righteousness in the land. (v. 5) This king will not be a weakling like Zedekiah whose name means ''the Lord is righteous'' but a new king, a real king who is a righteous Branch. Here is a play on the word ''righteous'' which forms the first part of Zedekiah's name. When this king comes, Judah will be saved and Israel will dwell securely. This will be a deliverance even more glorious than that from Egypt. ''The Lord is our righteousness'' will be the king's name.

### Ephesians 2:11-22 (C)
### Ephesians 2:13-22 (L)
### Ephesians 2:13-18 (RC)

As indicated in earlier commentary on Ephesians, literary evidence and other clues indicate that a Jewish Christian other than Paul is the author of Ephesians, although the author is in the Pauline school of thought and claims the name Paul. The author will be referred to as Paul for convenience.

God's unlimited grace has reached down so far that it extends even to the Gentiles, says Paul. They are made inheritors of God's promises to his people. In verse 11 Paul says that the distinction between Jew and Gentile is removed in Christ and now are obsolete. The hinge on which this passage ''turns'' is verse 13 which begins *But now in Christ Jesus you who once were far off have been brought near . . .*'' Now the reconciling work of Christ is available for Gentiles who once were far off from God and his people. They have been brought near in the blood of Christ, the new covenant in his blood. Christ is our peace. He has made both Jew and Gentile one, and has broken down the dividing wall of hostility between the two. Christ has reconciled both Jew and Gentile to God in one body, the Church.

The unity of Christians in one body, the church, is based on their participation in the one Spirit. (v. 18) This is no human creation of unity of those who think alike, look alike, feel alike, but rather is a divine gift by the power of the Spirit. One of the tests of whether a spirit is God's Spirit or a demonic spirit is whether or not it creates unity and breaks down dividing walls. Too often those claiming to ''have the Spirit'' have been divisive with their claims of spiritual elitism.

In verse 19 the reference to strangers echoes the reference in verse 12. Those who once were strangers to God's covenants of promise, who had no hope and were without God are no longer strangers and sojourners but are fellow citizens with the saints and members of the household of God. (v. 19) It is this incorporation of Gentiles into the church which makes it something altogether new on the stage of human history. Gentiles are now part of the one new man, Christ Jesus. The unity which is achieved is derived entirely from Christ who is our peace.

Paul uses two metaphors and fuses the metaphor of a body with that of a building. As a consequence, the building is said to grow. This building is God's temple and the foundation is the prophets and apostles. Christ is the cornerstone. Christ is the uniting factor who joins the building into a unity.

Paul says that the individual Christian is built into this temple as a dwelling place of God in the Spirit. The whole structure is joined together and grows into a holy temple in the Lord, says Paul. Thus the body of Christ is thought of in dynamic rather than static terms. The church is the body of Christ and grows because Christ is a living being who empowers the church to grow by the Spirit.

### Mark 6:30-34

Jesus calls the apostles to come away from the crowds to rest after the mission. This withdrawal in Matthew is linked to the news of John's death. The apostles are called such only here and in 3:14. The word "apostle" means one who is sent. It is used to translate the Hebrew term denoting an authorized agent or representative. The term here does not seem to be an official title but rather means simply "the missionaries." The significance of the Twelve lies in the fact that they are commissioned by Jesus. They are dependent on him and accountable to him who has commissioned them. The apostles have carried out their temporary commission and now have come back to Jesus and to his "school" to learn even more. In addition to their need for rest after their mission, the apostles also need to escape the pressure of the crowds. But the people recognize them and their trip by boat to a lonely place and so run ahead by foot from all the towns and get there first! Anyone who has tried to escape the pressures of daily demands of the pastorate or other demanding vocations, only to have the phone ring at the vacation cottage, can understand something of the apostles' frustration. The disciples needed solitude and rest from all the commotion "for many were coming and going, and they had no leisure even to eat." (v. 31)

Although Jesus has withdrawn to avoid the crowds he had compassion on them and went out to teach them, for they were like sheep without a shepherd. The shepherdless flock of people reminds us of the description of the people of Ezekiel's time: "So they were scattered, because there was no shepherd; and they became food for all the wild beasts. My sheep were scattered, they wandered over all the mountains and on every high hill; my sheep were scattered over all the face of the earth, with none to search or seek for them." (Ezekiel 34:5-) Jesus' compassion is inspired by their lack of leadership. Later in 8:2 Jesus has compassion because of their hunger.

We are not told the place to which Jesus and the apostles retreated for rest but somewhere on the northeast shore of the Sea of Galilee is very probable. The next event in Jesus' ministry is the feeding of the multitude following this period of teaching.

## Theological Reflections

The account of David's sin with Bathsheba and the arranged murder of her husband Uriah ranks as one of the most dastardly deeds in the Bible. The fact that the biblical writers record it indicates that they know God's grace which can forgive even this evil. And God is able to use David in spite of his sin. Jeremiah speaks "woes" against the false shepherds who destroy and scatter the sheep, but then gives the promise of a righteous Branch who will reign as king and execute righteousness and justice. This coming One stands in contrast to the human David who does injustice and is unrighteous. God will raise up for David this righteous Branch, says Jeremiah. The letter to the Ephesians stresses the loving work of God in Christ who has united Gentile and Jew and brought them together in the one body through the cross. God's power working through the Spirit to unite both Jew and Gentile to him in peace is set forth. Here again God's grace is the focus of the passage. Mark tells of the return of the apostles from their missionary journey and their retreat with Jesus, which is frustrated by the crowds who are anxious to hear Jesus. The compassion of Jesus is central in this passage. For he sees the crowd as sheep without a shepherd, reminding us of the Jeremiah passage and reading from Ezekiel 34:5-6 which describes the people as wandering without a shepherd.

## Homiletical Moves

### 2 Samuel 11:1-15 (C)
### Love in the Afternoon

1. David lusts after Bathsheba, wife of Uriah
2. David took her and lay with her and she conceived a child
3. David seeks to cover up his sin by sending Uriah home but he refuses to go
4. David arranges for Uriah's death in battle
5. Later Nathan the prophet confronts David with his sin, he repents, and is forgiven, and God continues to use David rather than reject him
6. Repent of your sin and turn to God that he may use you in his service

*Jeremiah 23:1-6 (L) (RC)*
## The Promised Righteous Branch of David

1. The shepherds (rulers) have scattered God's sheep, Israel
2. God will judge the false shepherds
3. God will gather the remnant of his flock and bring them back to the fold
4. God will raise up a righteous Branch who will reign as king
5. The new just king will be called "The Lord is our righteousness"
6. Put your trust in the Righteous Branch Jesus Christ

*This Preacher's Choice*

*Ephesians 2:11-22 (C)*
*Ephesians 2:13-22 (L)*
*Ephesians 2:13-18 (RC)*
## No Longer Strangers But Fellow Citizens with the Saints

1. You Gentiles were once separated from Christ and strangers to the covenants of promise
2. But now in Christ Jesus you have been brought near
3. Christ is our peace who has made us both one
4. We both have access to God in one Spirit
5. You are fellow citizens with tha saints and are growing into a holy temple in the Lord, therefore live as citizens of God's kingdom

*Mark 6:30-34*
## Jesus Had Compassion on Them

1. The apostles returned to Jesus and told all they had done
2. Jesus calls them apart to rest and they go by boat
3. The crowd runs ahead and meets them as they go ashore
4. Jesus has compassion on the crowd for they are like sheep without a shepherd
5. Jesus begins to teach them many things
6. Come to Jesus the Good Shepherd and follow him

**Hymn for Pentecost 9:**   *In Christ There is No East or West*

**Prayer**

*Almighty God who has created us for yourself, we thank you that you have redeemed us from the power of sin through Christ's death on the cross. When we commit sins we know that you continue to love us and shepherd us back to your fold. Forgive us when we have strayed from you. Forgive us when we have not been faithful shepherds of the flock entrusted to us, either as lay or clergy leaders. Grant to us a greater measure of your grace by the power of the Spirit. May we continue in the household of faith. Amen*

## Proper 12
July 24-30

## Pentecost 10

## Ordinary Time 17

| Common | Lutheran | Roman Catholic |
|---|---|---|
| 2 Samuel 12:1-4 | Exodus 24:3-11 | 2Kings 4:42-44 |
| Ephesians 3:14-21 | Ephesians 4:1-7, 11-16 | Ephesians 4:1-6 |
| John 6:1-15 | John 6:1-15 | John 6:1-15 |

### Comments on the Lessons

The Samuel reading is an account of Nathan the prophet's confrontation of David through a parable of his murder of Uriah and adultery with his wife, Bathsheba. In the Exodus passage we have the ceremony of the covenant ratification between God and Israel as blood is thrown upon the altar and on the people. The 2 Kings pericope is the miracle in which Elisha multiplied the barley loaves and ears of grain to feed a hundred men. A parallel to this miracle is found in the Feeding of the Multitude miracle in the Gospel for today. The Ephesians 3:14-21 reading contains the famous doxology and is included here because it does not appear elsewhere in the lectionary. In the (C) lectionary, Ephesians 4:1-6 is moved to the following Sunday. There is near consensus on the Gospel reading from John of the Feeding of the Multitude.

### Commentary

*2 Samuel 12:1-14*

Nathan the prophet rebukes David for both murder and adultery with the use of a parable. Note that the parable of the ewe lamb is narrated without an introduction. Nathan shows great courage in confronting David with his sins, for it was within the power of a king to execute or exile those who displeased him. What David had done was wrong for king or peasant to do, according to the moral principles of that time. We learn that later Nathan became an active supporter of Bathsheba. (1 Kings 1:5-14)

The point of the parable is that a great injustice has been done. David is so enraged by it that he pronounces the verdict on himself: "The man who has done this deserves to die; and he shall restore the lamb fourfold . . ." (v. 6) Nathan increases the effect of the parable by making the lamb which the poor man had to struggle to buy for himself the darling of the whole family. But the way in which the rich man acts is thus made to appear not only parsimonious but also crude and arrogant. David's response reveals his sense of justice, justice which does not escape him when the real point of Nathan's parable breaks in on his consciousness. He doesn't blame Nathan for confronting him with his sins. Instead, the opposite occurs. From this point on, until David's death, Nathan is his trusted adviser as well as prophet of God. It appears that the prophet played the same role to David that confessors did in later courts. While some have criticized David for demanding four-fold restitution in addition to the death penalty, this is understandable in light of David's concern that the poor man as well as the rich should have justice done.

Nathan's piercing words, "You are the man" go right for the jugular! It has been called one of the "most apt" sayings in the Bible. See how it takes up the verdict spoken by David without having to spell it out: it is a sentence of death. We must note this in order to understand what follows. This sentence is annulled, but only on David's acknowledgment of his sin. But until then it stands.

Nathan reminds David in words of "Thus says the Lord, the God of Israel" that God had given him his master's house and "your master's wives." This makes David's crimes even more heinous. The sin which David is accused of first is murder, murder of Uriah, and then taking his wife for himself. These sins are mentioned twice and are described as despising the word of the Lord. The punishment for the sins is that "the sword shall never depart from your house, because you have despised me." (v. 10)

The second threat does mention David's adultery, but avoids mentioning the murder. It announces a fitting punishment. Notice the relationship between guilt and punishment regarding the commandment against adultery found in Job 31:9-12. Nathan tells David that the child of this adulterous relationship shall die, although God has put away his sin. The child will die because David has utterly scorned the Lord.

### Exodus 24:3-11 (L)

God's revelation of himself on Mt. Sinai concludes with the solemn making of a covenant between God and Israel which is described in 24:1-11. After even an initial reading, it is readily seen that there are two different literary strata here. In verses 1f and 9-11 the covenant is made on the mountain, but these two sections are separated by verses 3-8 which are a different telling of the story. In verses 3-8 the events take place at the foot of the mountain.

The first version of the covenant ceremony stresses the people's participation, while the second says the people did not take part but were represented by the seventy elders or chief priests. In this story Moses who is the covenant mediator is accompanied by the priestly family. The leaders did not see God directly but saw only the lower part of his heavenly throne-room. They did not dare to raise their eyes to God himself. They saw what was under God's feet, the heavens. Sapphire is a sky-blue, semi-precious stone. It is pictured as "like the very heaven for clearness." (v. 10) So the summit of the mountain was in heaven and here in heaven the God of Israel makes himself known.

The sealing of the covenant with blood was an ancient rite, reflecting the view that blood was efficacious in establishing community between God and his people. Compare this with the cutting of the covenant in Genesis 15:17. The book of the covenant seems to have contained the covenant laws and ordinances. Moses built an altar at the foot of the mountain and twelve pillars, representing the twelve tribes. He sent young men who offered burnt offerings and sacrificed peace offerings of oxen to the Lord, after which Moses took half the blood and threw it against the altar, which represented God's presence. The other half he threw over the people, the second part of the covenant. This ritual dramatized the uniting of the two parties in the covenant. Notice that Moses does not sprinkle the blood on the twelve altars but on the people. This forms a valid conclusion to the covenant. To emphasize this Moses uses the declarative perfect tense in verse 8b. In verse 11 we read that the chief men of the people of Israel beheld God and ate and drank. This refers to a covenant meal, which just as a common meal can form a seal among human beings, so this covenant meal joined God and his people in covenant. Of course, both parties do not share in the meal, but God lets the representatives of Israel hold a meal in his presence on the mountain. The content of the covenant is now binding!

### 2 Kings 4:42-44 (RC)

This is a little known story from the collection of stories about Elisha. It has become very important in recent New Testament scholarship since it offers a literary prototype of the miraculous feeding of the multitudes in the Gospels. It was chosen for the (RC) lectionary as a parallel to the account in John's Gospel for today of the feeding of the multitude.

The pattern of the "feeding stories" is very similar:

1. Food is brought to the man of God
2. The quantity of food is indicated
3. Someone objects that the quantity of food is not adequate
4. But the man of God takes charge of the situation, ignores the objections and commands those about him to distribute the food
5. As a result the crowd not only has a sufficient amount to eat but there is some left over

Looking at the pericope from 2 Kings we find this outline holds:

1. A man came bringing twenty loaves of barley and fresh ears of grain in his sack (v. 42)
2. The quantity of food is indicated (20 loaves, ears in sack)
3. Someone objects that the food is insufficient (v. 43)
4. But the man of God takes charge: "So he (Elisha) repeated, "Give them to the men, that they may eat"
5. There is food left over: "And they ate, and had some left, according to the word of the Lord" (v. 44)

Parallels to this are found in the New Testament in Matthew 14:13-21; 15:32-38 and John 9:1-15.

*Ephesians 3:14-21 (C)*

In verses 14, 15 there is a play on words in Father and family: Greek, "pater," "patria." God himself is the source of all fatherhood. God is also the source of all motherhood, since God created both man and woman and united them in marriage to live in families. The main point here is that the Church as God's family is a society that in its ultimate sense must be conterminous with humanity because creation is the ground of redemption. While there are various interpretations of this term "every family," the RSV meaning is more likely right for it means that "every family, no matter where, is a family because it is derived from God's Paternity." It may also refer to gnostic theories of the propagation of heavenly powers, and be written as a refutation of them.

Note that verse 18 refers to the "breadth . . . and depth" of Christ's love. Then comes the marvelous doxology in verse 20f, which celebrates God's boundless generosity and his glory both in the church and in Jesus Christ. God can do far more for us than we can ask or think.

*Ephesians 4:1-7, 11-16 (L)*
*Ephesians 4:1-6 (RC)*

In these verses and those that follow to the end of the book we have ethical implications of the doctrines found in chapters 1-3. In verses 1-6 there is an appeal to maintain the unity of the faith. Note in verses 4-6 the seven elements of unity: (1) one body, (2) one Spirit, (3) one hope, (4) one Lord, (5) one faith (6) one baptism, (7) one God and Father of us all.

In verses 7-16 the author sets forth Christian unity and diversity of spiritual gifts. The gifts were that some should be: (1) apostles (those sent) (2) prophets (those who speak for God) (3) some evangelists (who preach and teach the gospel) (4) some pastors (shepherds of the flock), (5) teachers. Their purpose is to equip the saints for the work of ministry, for building up the body of Christ. The goal is to enable all to attain to the unity of the faith and of the knowledge of the Son of God, to mature development as persons, to the fullness of Christ. The apostolic ministry is a gift of the ascended, triumphant Christ who empowers persons and the church and his Spirit. He gives them their authority.

The development of the saints toward maturity is to prevent their being tossed about by various doctrines, by the cunning of men and their craftiness in deceitful wiles. The method is by "speaking the truth in love." (v. 15) The verb used here in verse 15 means both speaking and doing. Christ is the head of the church who enables each part of the church to work properly and to work together for bodily growth and upbuilds it in love.

The thrust of this passage is that all Christians are to be equipped for the work of active spiritual service so that the unity of the Body may be maintained and expressed. Unity is both a gift and a task which requires work. "There is one body" (v. 4) is an indicative. Paul can urge his hearers to express this unity in practice because unity is a gift and is already present in the Church. He can say in effect, "Become what you already are!"

*John 6:1-15*

The feeding of the five thousand is the only miracle recorded by all four gospels. There is strong historical evidence for it and all four gospel writers accept it as miraculous. Since this event in chapter 6 occurs immediately after ministry in Jerusalem in chapter 5, which seems an odd arrangement some scholars would place chapter 6 after chapter 4 and *before* chapter 5. If this is done it does make the itinerary seem more logical; however there is reason to think that from a theological perspective chapter 6 is in the right order.

As noted in the analysis of Elisha's miraculous feeding in 2 Kings there is a pattern in these feeding stories. When we examine Jesus' feeding of the five thousand we find the events fit this pattern nicely:

1. Food is brought to the man of God: "There is a lad here who has five barley loaves and two fish." (v. 9)

2. The quantity of food is indicated: five loaves, two fish. (v. 9)

3. Someone objects that the quantity of food is not adequate: "But what are they among so many?" (v. 9)

4. But the man of God takes charge of the situation, ignores the objections and commands those with him to distribute the food: "Jesus said, 'Make the people sit down''. . . Jesus then took the loaves, and when he had given thanks, he distributed them to those who were seated; so also the fish, as much as they wanted." (v. 11)

5. The result is that the crowd not only has enough to eat but there is some left over: "He told his disciples, 'Gather up the fragments left over, that nothing may be lost.' So they gathered them up and filled twelve baskets with fragments from the five barley loaves, left by those who had eaten." (vv. 12, 13)

Jesus asked Philip who was from that area, "How are we to buy bread so that these people may eat?" in order to test Philip. The feast of the Passover is mentioned, and, according to John, this is the second Passover in Jesus' ministry. This is not, of course, the Passover at the end of Jesus' earthly ministry. Barley loaves were food of the poor. The fish were pickled fish eaten with bread.

In all the Gospels, the feeding is a pivotal point in their narrative of Jesus' ministry. Although we are not told what happened, it is apparent that the feeding event represented a crisis in Jesus' ministry. Mark's Gospel tells us that, after Jesus fed the multitude, he sent the disciples off in a boat while he dismissed the crowd. In John's account we see why this was done: it was to get the disciples away from the dangerous nationalistic-messianic enthusiasm of the crowd: "Perceiving then that they were about to come and take him by force to make him king, Jesus withdrew again to the mountain by himself." (v. 15)

There are motifs in the feeding of the multitude also found in the Eucharist, and in the messianic banquet expected at the End when Messiah returns. Note the key words: Jesus *took, gave thanks, distributed,* the people were *filled.* The word "filled" is used elsewhere in describing the messianic banquet. Most of these acts were natural acts at a Jewish meal. After the feeding the crowd tried to take Jesus by force to make him king, a political Messiah opposing Rome. But he would not accept this. Note that this was one of the ways Satan had tempted him in the wilderness at the beginning of his ministry. The onlookers took this action because of the miracle, but Jesus cannot submit to being made a king by men. But note that the thought of Messiahship is in the background of the verses which follow. (vv. 22-59)

## Theological Reflections

God's gracious acts on behalf of human beings is a major thrust in the passages for today. David is confronted by Nathan with his sins, but God does not reject David when he repents of them, but forgives him and continues to use him. The Exodus Passage tells of the covenant ceremony by which God and Israel pledge themselves to each other through sacrifices, the sprinkling of blood and a ceremonial meal. The blood which seals the covenant foreshadows Jesus' death on the cross where the New Covenant is made in his blood. The story of Elisha feeding the hungry is another gracious act of God through his prophet. There was not only enough, but some left over. God's grace is full and overflowing! The first Ephesians passage (3:14-21) is a prayer that the readers may be strengthened by God's Spirit, that they may know the love of God in Christ which surpasses knowledge. The doxology contains the assurance that God is at work within us and is able to do more abundantly than all that we ask or think. Again, the overflowing graciousness of God. The second Ephesians passage is concerned with the gift of unity in the church and the gifts of various kinds of functions in the church. Again, the emphasis lies in the gracious gifts of God for individuals and the church. John records the feeding of the five thousand in which Jesus' miracle is clear evidence to the crowd that he is Messiah. But they have the wrong concept of Messiah, a Messiah who is a nationalistic king, not a suffering-servant. But God's graciousness in feeding the multitude so that they not only had their fill but twelve baskets of fragments are left over is a central thrust.

## Homiletical Moves

*2 Samuel 12:1-14 (C)*
## You Are the Man!

1. Nathan confronts David with the parable of the ewe
2. David's rage over the injustice done the poor man

3. Nathan confronts David, "You are the man"
4. Punishment is meted out for David's crimes
5. But God puts away David's sin and he is forgiven
6. Confess your sin, turn to God and he will forgive you

*Exodus 24:3-11 (L)*
**God's Covenant with Israel at Sinai**

1. Moses tells the people the words and ordinances given by God
2. The people respond with a vow of obedience
3. The covenant is sealed with the sprinking of blood on the altar and the people, and a covenant meal
4. God has made a new covenant in Christ's death
5. Put your trust in Christ and live in obedience to him

*2 Kings 4:42-44 (RC)*
**Elisha Feeds the Hungry**

1. Elisha commands that barley loaves and ears of grain be given the hungry
2. His servant objects that there is not enough to go around
3. By a miracle all are fed and there is some left over
4. The gracious God of Elisha will be gracious to you also

*Ephesians 3:14-21 (C)*
**That You May Know the Surpassing Love of Christ**

1. Paul prays that his readers may be strengthened within by the Spirit
2. He prays they may know the fullness of Christ's love
3. Paul offers a doxology that God who is at work in them is able to do far more abundantly than all they ask or think
4. Trust God to do more than you can ask or think as you venture into the future strengthened by the Spirit

*Ephesians 4:1-7, 11-16 (L)*
*Ephesians 4:1-6(RC)*
**One Body and One Spirit and One Lord**

1. Paul's prayer that his readers may live a life worthy of their calling in all lowliness, meekness, etc.
2. There is *one body and one Spirit,* therefore live out this unity
3. There are gifts to enable us to build up the body of Christ
4. We are to speak the truth in love and to grow up in every way into Christ

*This Preacher's Choice*

*John 6:1-15*
**The Feeding of the Five Thousand**

1. The multitude which had followed Jesus was hungry
2. A lad offers his five barley loaves and two fish to Jesus
3. Jesus gave thanks for the food and distributed it to the multitude
4. They ate their fill and there was food left over
5. The crowd thought Jesus was the Messiah/national king
6. Jesus withdraws from the crowd to the mountain alone
7. Offer what you have to Jesus and he will bless it and use it to bless others

**Hymn for Pentecost 10:**   *Guide Me, O Thou Great Jehovah*

**Prayer**
*Gracious God who has made a covenant with us in the blood of Jesus Christ, we confess that we are sinners before you. We have sinned against our neighbor and against you. We repent and turn in trust that you are a covenant-keeping God. Thank you for your gracious supplying of our physical needs, and for the abundance of your grace in Jesus Christ. Thank you for the gift of the unity of the church. May we live out that unity, using our particular gifts for your glory. Grant that we may grow up in every way into Christ, the head of the Church. Amen*

# Proper 13        Pentecost 11        Ordinary Time 18

July 31 — August 6

| Common | Lutheran | Roman Catholic |
|---|---|---|
| 2 Samuel 12:15b-24<br>Ephesians 4:1-6<br>John 6:24-35 | Exodus 16:2-15<br>Ephesians 4:17-24<br>John 6:24-35 | Exodus 16:2-4, 12-15<br>Ephesians 4:17, 20-24<br>John 6:24-35 |

## Comments on the Lessons

The first reading describes the death of the first child of David and Bathsheba, David's repentance, and the birth of Solomon. The Exodus passage tells the story of the murmurings of the children of Israel in the Wilderness and God's provision of manna and quails for food. This foreshadows the Gospel story in which Jesus says he is the bread from heaven, relecting God's gift of manna from heaven. Note that Ephesians 4:1-6 was dealt with in the previous Sunday's readings (RC) and so will not be commented on again today. In the Ephesians 4:17-24 passage Paul tells the Ephesians that they must put off their old nature as one puts off old, worn-out clothes, and put on the new nature created after the likeness of God. There is consensus on the Gospel reading in which Jesus declares himself to be the bread from heaven.

## Commentary

*2 Samuel 12:15b-24 (C)*

The child born to Bathsheba becomes ill, as expected from Nathan's prophecy. (v. 14) Note that Bathsheba is not mentioned. David takes a variety of measures in order to move the Lord to change his mind and allow the child to live: he offers special prayers, enters a special fast which seems to last the whole period of the child's illness, puts on sackcloth, and lies upon the ground at night. David also refrained from bathing and anointing himself as further means of self-abasement. The elders of his house, his trusted officials, try to persuade him to get off the ground and to eat food with them but he refused.

Then on the seventh day the child died. This is the hinge or turning point in the story. What is naturally expected at this point is that David would go into deep mourning, curse God for the death, and possibly wreck havoc on all around him in his guilt and grief. The servants naturally are afraid to tell David the child has died since he had grieved so bitterly while the child was still living, and they feared he might harm himself on learning of the child's death. It seems they feared he might commit suicide out of guilt.

But David himself finds out the child has died, and when the servants confirmed this was true, he arose from the earth, washed and anointed himself and changed his clothes. Then he went into the house of the Lord to worship, and then to his own house where he ate. Hardly normal behavior for someone in grief. The court is amazed. It is as if he had worked through his grief over the child as a penitent and, now that Nathan's prophecy has come true, he is released from grief to live normally again.

The death of the child is confirmation that nothing more will happen to David. This may be one reason for his sense of relief. Nathan had earlier pronounced him absolved of his sins. Now, by the death of the child, David's sins seem to be expiated. In a time when child sacrifice by pagans was common practice, the death of the child seems to have been accepted as a sacrifice.

When asked about his behavior, David explains by saying that while the child was yet alive he fasted and wept in hope that the Lord would repent and let the child live. But now that he is dead there was no reason to fast. "Can I bring him back again? I shall go to him, but he will not return to me," explains David. (v. 23) This verse reflects the concept of Sheol, the underground cavity where all the dead go and from which there was no return.

Then David comforted Bathsheba, his wife, and lay with her and she bore a son which he named

Solomon. And the Lord loved Solomon. The name Solomon is connected to the word for peace and conveys the thought that God loved him. The fact that the child continued to live in contrast to the first one is further evidence of the love of God. The grace of God is revealed once again and shines over Solomon and over David also. This confirms what was said by Nathan earlier.

*Exodus 16:2-15 (L)*
*Exodus 16:2-4, 12-15 (RC)*

It is significant that the chapter and section begins with an itinerary which puts these stories which follow in a precise geographical and chonological order. Note that time is measured in terms of lapsed time since departing from Egypt. However, we are unable to trace th route with any certainty.

The major theme of the wilderness wanderings is the murmuring of the children of Israel. Although the complaint against Moses and Aaron for bringing them out of Egypt is very stereotyped, the content of the grumbling in various stories relates to a particular need within the story. Here the need is the lack of food. So like kids at summer camp or college students eating institutional food they grumble about the lack of food they enjoyed in the "fleshpots of Egypt." Note that the author begins the account with the murmuring. The eating of meat was a rare event for the common peasant in that time and place.

The murmuring about lack of food also introduces the theme of the exodus from Egypt. Moses is even accused of causing the death of Israel by leading them out into the wilderness. (v. 3. This complaint against the deliverance from Egypt strikes at the heart of Israel's relationship to God. The complaint of the people is not just a causal grumbling, but is more basic. It is *unbelief* which has called into question God's election of Israel as his people!

Then God tells Moses he will rain bread from heaven and the people can go out and gather a day's portion every day (cf. "daily bread" in Lord's Prayer). God tests the people to prove whether or not they walk in his law. (vv. 4, 5) While the story begins with the people finding fault, and trying to put Moses to the test, here God tests Israel instead! God gives the gift of bread on his own initiative, and his gift carries its own conditions. Later God speaks to Israel's complaint in confirming Moses' statement.

Then Moses and Aaron deal with the murmuring itself. (vv. 6-8) Note that murmuring is referred to seven times in the next eight verses. Now Moses and Aaron throw the charge back at the people: "For what are we, that you murmur against us?" The people are fighting against God and reveal their unbelief in doing so. They express their anger and frustration against Moses and Aaron, but the real object of their unbelief is God.

Then the glory of God appears in a cloud. (v. 10) Note that in the wilderness stories there is a cycle: the people complain, people dispute, but finally God himself appears to them and brings the immediate matter to a halt with a decisive judgment.

In verse 11 God addresses Moses in the climax of the section: "I have heard the murmurings of the people of Israel; say to them 'At twilight you shall eat flesh, and in the morning you shall be filled with bread; then you shall know that I am the Lord your God.' " In the evening quails came up and covered the camp. And in the morning when the dew was gone there was a fine, flake-like thing, fine as hoar-frost on the ground. When the people asked what it was, Moses told them "It is the bread which the Lord has given you to eat." (v. 15) God meets the people's request not to pacify their grumblings, but in order to teach Israel who *He is* through this gracious act of feeding Israel. Earlier (v. 4) it seems God had not heard the people's complaint. But now Moses' point is illustrated by the fact that the God who had been accused is also the same God who will make himself known by supplying Israel's need.

We are told that quails fly low in their migration in great numbers from Africa in the spring and some fly over the Sinai Peninsula. The manna, according to scholars, is the well-known honeydew excretion of so many plant lice and scale insects. The rapid evaporation in the dry air of the desert changes this into sticky solids, which later turn a whitish, yellowish or brownish color. While this may be a rational explanation for what happened, the theological understanding of the events by Israel came from her faith in God.

*Ephesians 4:1-6 (C) (See previous Sunday's reading for RC.)*
*Ephesians 4:17-24 (L)*
*Ephesians 4:17, 20-24 (RC)*

Paul moves from a theological statement about the church in the previous verses to an account of Christian conduct contrasted with the pagan decadence of the culture. Paul sees the Christian moral life as response of the Christian to the love of God in Christ. The two ways of life are pictured as two garments. The old garment of the old nature is to be put off, since it belongs to the former way of life and is corrupt through deceitful lusts. This old way of life is described in terms of being darkened in understanding, alienated from the life of God because of ignorance due to their hardness of heart, callousness being given up to licentiousness, greedy to practice every kind of uncleanness, and corrupt through deceitful lusts. A British debating team won a debate with an American team some years ago on the proposition that "America has passed from barbarism to decadence without passing through civilization." The Gentiles had not learned Christ and so were still in a decadent state of immorality.

But those who have learned Christ and have been taught in him as the truth is in Jesus are to be renewed in the spirit of their minds, putting on the new nature, created after the likeness of God in true righteousness and holiness.

Often one needs the perspective of travel, especially to another country, to see the contrast between the Christian and non-Christian way of life. In some parts of the world cannabalism is still practiced. Children are maimed at birth to make them better at begging, or a son's eye is put out to prevent his being drafted into the army as an adult. But the daily newspaper and TV news reveals the decadence of American life in which child abuse is common, and abuse of spouses and the elderly is surfacing more often.

It was said of early Christians by their pagan neighbors, "How these Christians love one another!" Love continues to be the characteristic mark of the Christian way of living. Love is the distinctive mark of the new garment the Christian wears. The new nature is created after the likeness of God.

### *John 6:24-35*

The pericope for today is part of a longer discourse on "Bread from Heaven." (vv. 22-59) The thrust of this discourse is summed up in verse 27: "Do not labor for the food which perishes, but for the food which endures to eternal life, which the Son of man will give to you; for on him has God the Father set his seal." The whole discourse is introduced by verses 22-27 which prepare the reader for it both topographically and in terms of theme. There are four parts to the longer discourse as follows:

1. Preparation for discourse and summary (vv. 22-27)
2. Jesus claims to be the bread of life (vv. 28-40)
3. An objection develops (vv. 41-51)
4. Through Jesus' sacrifice of himself people may feed on him, i.e. enter into a relation with him like that of his with his heavenly Father (vv. 52 59)

In this discourse on the bread from heaven, Jesus brings out the meaning of what was dramatized in verses 1-15 in the feeding of the multitude, namely his power to give people the bread of life. We should note that there is no parallel to this discourse in the Synoptic gospels, but we should keep in mind as we read this the account of the words and actions at the Last Supper, recorded in the Synoptics which do not have parallels in John. There are very definite allusions to the Eucharist in this passage in which Jesus emphasizes that in his death for all he gives eternal life.

The crowd had followed Jesus clamoring for more bread. While they were aware that a miracle had been performed in the feeding of the multitude, the crowd did not understand the significance of what they had seen. Jesus confronts them with the fact they are seeking him because of the food they ate and not because they saw signs pointing to Jesus as food for the soul. Son of man was Jesus' usual term for himself which had an eschatological thrust. (1:51) The "seal" (v. 27) probably refers to the affirmation of Jesus at his baptism by the words from heaven. The seal authenticated Jesus.

John contrasts the question of the people about doing "the works of God" with the answer of Jesus "This is the work of God, that you believe in him whom he has sent." (v. 29) The works are the religious works they hoped would be pleasing to God. But the *work* Jesus points to is obedient trust, or believing. God sent Jesus who reveals God and is the one in whom they are to believe.

It is important to recall that the Jews expected Messiah to reproduce the miracle of the giving of manna from heaven. The crowd reminds Jesus of the manna their fathers ate in the wilderness and asks for a sign that they may see and believe him. They wanted to see a proof, but faith is beyond the kind of proof they sought.

Jesus replies that it was not Moses that gave bread from heaven but God gave it. And it was not bread from heaven that Moses gave them, but only bread which perishes. Here two points have been pressed into one sentence. (v. 32) Jesus tells them that God gives them the true bread from heaven, bread which gives life to the world. Note that in verse 33 the people understand Jesus to say "that which comes down" rather than "he that comes down" which is Jesus' meaning. So he corrects them in the first of the great "I am" sayings: "I am the bread of life; he who comes to me shall not hunger, and he who believes in me shall never thirst." (v. 35) The mention of thirst points to the eucharistic cup. But here John is not referring to the eucharist as such but the "coming" is a once for all coming in faith.

In verses 35-50 we have what has been called the "Great Bread of Life Discourse." When Jesus says "I am the bread of life" he means the bread that gives life, eternal life now and in the age to come. The fundamental reaction to Jesus' description of himself as the bread of life is unbelief. So the reader is confronted by Jesus as the bread of life with a decision: to believe or to reject this bread from heaven. Jesus' claim to be the bread of life is a claim to be the revealer of the truth, the divine teacher who has come into the world to nourish and give life to the world. Compare this metaphor with other metaphors Jesus uses such as "life" and "water," which refer to the same reality of Jesus as the source of eternal life. Jesus gives this bread, water, and life through his death and resurrection.

## Theological Reflections

Samuel tells of David's penitent seeking to change God's judgment on the child born to Bathsheba. When David's fasting, praying, etc., are futile and the child dies, then David is relieved of fear of further punishment and takes up a normal life again. The themes of judgment for sin with the innocent child being a sacrifice and God's assurance that David's sins are forgiven and he himself will not die are prominent in this passage. Exodus tells of the murmurings of the people of Israel against Moses and Aaron (but really against God) for bringing them out into the wilderness to starve. The people do not believe God's promises but rebel and want to return to the fleshpots of Egypt. But God hears their murmurings and gives them quail for flesh and manna for bread. These are gracious acts of God in sustaining Israel and demonstrating that he is their God. Ephesians 4:1 6 is concerned with the unity of the church which is a gift from God, and the living out of this unity in a Godly life. Ephesians 4:17-24 contrasts the pagan way of life with the Christian way of life, using the metaphor of a garment for each. Paul says to put off the old nature which is corrupted by sin and put on the new nature which is created after the likeness of God. In John's Gospel Jesus declares that he is the bread of life in the first of a series of "great I am's" in the Bible. The crowd that was fed on the plain misunderstood the nature of the sign and in this discourse Jesus points to himself as the true bread from heaven which comes down and gives life. The graciousness of God in giving the true bread to satisfy the souls of believers is the theme of this pericope.

## Homiletical Moves

*2 Samuel 12:15b-24 (C)*
### David's Penitence and God's Graciousness

1. Bathsheba's child became sick
2. David prayed and fasted for the child
3. The child died and David ends his fast
4. David comforts Bathsheba his wife, and they later have Solomon
5. The Lord loved Solomon
6. Trust the gracious God who forgives and blesses in spite of our sin

*Exodus 16:2-15 (L)*
*Exodus 16:2-4, 12-15 (RC)*
### You Shall Know That I Am the Lord Your God

1. The people murmur against Moses and Aaron (and God)
2. God hears their murmuring and promises quails and manna
3. God feeds Israel so that Israel will know he is God who is faithful
4. When the people ask what the manna is, Moses explains it is bread which the Lord has given them to eat
5. Trust in the faithfulness of God who cares for you

*Ephesians 4:17-24 (L)*
*Ephesians 4:17, 20-24 (RC)*
## Put On the New Nature!

1. Put off the old nature which belongs to your former manner of life
2. Put on the new nature created after the likeness of God in true righteousness and holiness
3. For you have learned Christ and were taught in him as the truth is in Jesus.

*This Preacher's Choice*

*John 6:24-34*
## I Am the Bread of Life, Says Jesus

1. Do not labor for the food which perishes but for the food which endures to eternal life
2. Jesus says he is the true bread of God from heaven which gives life
3. The people ask, "Lord, give us this bread always"
4. Jesus replies, "I am the bread of life"
5. Feed on Christ, the Bread of life, and you will truly live

**Hymn for Pentecost 11:**   *Break Thou the Bread of Life*

**Prayer**

*Gracious God who has sustained your people through the ages with the bread of life, grant that we may do the work you require of believing in Christ. Grant that we may put off our old nature which is corrupted by sin and put on the new nature created after your likeness. Grant that we may trust your leading in all of life, through the wilderness and deserts of life as well as in the valleys of plenty. May we always feed on the true Bread of Life who sustains our souls, even Christ Jesus who came down from heaven that we might have life and have it abundantly! Amen*

# Proper 14     Pentecost 12     Ordinary Time 19

August 7-13

| Common | Lutheran | Roman Catholic |
|---|---|---|
| 2 Samuel 18:1, 5, 9-15 (C) | 1 Kings 19:4-8 | 1 Kings 19:4-8 |
| Ephesians 4:25—5:2 | Ephesians 4:30—5:2 | Ephesians 4:30—5:2 |
| John 6:35, 41-51 | John 6:41-51 | John 6:41-51 |

## Comments on the Lessons

The reading from 2 Samuel is part of the Succession Narrative which sketches the story about attempts by David's sons to seize the throne. Here we have the account of the killing of Absalom, David's son, despite specific orders from David to deal leniently with him. The 1 Kings passage is the account of Elijah's fleeing from the wrath of Jezebel into the wilderness where he sat and later slept under a broom tree. An angel provided food and drink for him, and he went to Horeb where God earlier gave the Law to Moses. There is virtual consensus on the Ephesians reading, with the earlier (vv. 25-30) verses making an interesting parallel with 2 Samuel dealing with anger and gentleness. There is virtual consensus on the reading from John. Note that verse 35 is necessary in order to provide the context for the response of those present (v. 41) about Jesus's statement that he is the "bread of life."

## Commentary

*2 Samuel 18:1, 5, 9-15 (C)*

Although Absalom, David's son, had rebelled against his father and raised an army in an attempt to overthrow David, the father's love prevailed as David instructed his commanders, Joab and Abishai and Ittai to deal gently with Absalom for his sake. The two armies fought in a thick forest east of the Jordan, the forest of Ephraim. There were high trees and deep undergrowth and rocks, not simply the usual forest. The forest itself caused many casualties: "and the forest devoured more people that day than the sword." (v. 8) Absalom himself falls victim to the forest and is caught by the head in the branches of a great oak tree as he was riding his mule through the forest. There is a popular idea based on 14:26 that Absalom was caught by his hair. The text here implies that his whole head was caught, perhaps in a forked branch, and he could not extricate himself.

Joab disobeys David's command to deal gently with Absalom. Joab never withheld a death blow to an enemy when he felt that it would be to his or David's advantage. Joab knows better than David, who is governed here by fatherly love for a son, that further pardon of Absalom will only further jeopardize the kingdom and his own life. Note that the soldier who first saw Absalom remembered David's command to deal gently with him and so merely reported seeing Absalom hanging in an oak. If the soldier had killed Absalom he knew he would be left alone by Joab in the decisive hearing before David. He knew nothing was hidden from the king.

Joab breaks off the conversation and takes three darts which he thrusts into the heart of Absalom hanging from the tree. The expression "in the heart" does not mean a part of the body but rather "in the middle" as it means here and in connection with the oak. In verse 15 we learn that Absalom is killed by ten of Joab's armor-bearers who struck and killed him. Joab's thrusting of the three darts seems to be more a symbolic action which clears the way for the killing of the king's son. This may explain why Joab uses darts instead of spears. We are not told where Joab wounded Absalom, but the flow of blood marked him as a doomed man. The slaying of Absalom by ten soldiers indicates the execution was by the troops as a whole, and not by an individual. Compare this story with that of Achan. (Joshua 7:25)

*1 Kings 19:4-8 (L) (RC)*

Elijah flees from the wrath of Jezebel after his triumph over the prophets of Baal at Mount Carmel.

Initially, Elijah goes to Beer-sheba which was practically the southern limit of the settlement of the Hebrews (from Dan to Beer-sheba).

By God's miraculous help Elijah the prophet arrives at Horeb, where according to the tradition of Israel, God revealed the Law, and which was called Sinai in the southern or Judah tradition. The distance Elijah traveled is forty days and nights which is a round number indicating a great distance. The traditional site of Mount Horeb is some two hundred miles to the south of Beer-sheba and some scholars think it probably is not intended here. Horeb was probably a place of pilgrimage from an early time.

The broom tree has a delicate white flower with a maroon center and is usually found along the beds of wadis. As Elijah sat under the tree he asked God that he might die. "He requested his life to die" is a literal translation. The Hebrew thought of the life-breath as a gift directly from God and therefore it belonged to God, although a person might wish to die. For this reason, among Hebrews, a person was not free to commit suicide, a rare occurrence among Hebrews of that time. The angel is a messenger from God.

The angel touched Elijah and told him to arise and eat. He looked and saw at his head a cake baked on hot stones and a jar of water. So he ate and drank and lay down again. A second time the angel aroused the prophet, touched him and urged him to eat, and he ate. The cake he ate was a round flat cake of bread, baked on hot stones in the ashes. Or, in the desert, charcoal of dried camel dung is often used instead of hot pebbles. When this writer was touring modern Israel in 1953, he met Arab nomads at a well near Beer-sheba and rode one of their camels. They lived in tents and carried on life much as in Elijah's day.

The sustenance Elijah received reminded him of the experience at Zarephath (17:8-16) and renewed his courage and will to carry on. He believed God was still sustaining him, although he had come near despair. Elijah may have made the pilgrimage to Horeb, not only to escape Jezebel, but to renew his faith in God there. God had appeared to Moses there and given him the Law and it was believed this was God's special dwelling place.

*Ephesians 4:25—5:2 (C)*
*Ephesians 4:30—5:2 (L) (RC)*

This passage is part of a section (4:17—5:20) in which Paul urges the Ephesians to renounce pagan ways. In verse 22 he urges them to put off their pagan ways like old, worn-out clothes and in verse 24 he tells them to put on the new nature created after the likeness of God. Now in this passage he continues the contrasts of pagan and Christian conduct. Paul relates the moral demand of the gospel to the response of the believer to the love of God in Christ.

Paul urges truthful speaking with neighbors in the community since we are members of one another. Community life is based on honest and truthful dealing with one another. Falsehood and dishonesty destroy community. Paul goes on to urge his readers to "be angry but do not sin." We are to "own our feeling" of anger, but not to allow it to fester and become resentment, a toxic emotion. He says "do not let the sun go down on your anger, and give no opportunity for the devil." (v. 26, 27) Anger flashes up like black gunpowder burning in a pan, but resentment is anger which smolders like a pile of old rags which burn without a flame but just as surely destroy, and may at any moment burst into flame by spontaneous combustion. Resentment is one of, if not the most, destructive of all human emotions. Resentment lies behind much of the emotional and physical illness of our time. Resentment is anger which is nursed and kept smoldering by an unforgiving spirit. It can create emotional stress which leads to disease and even death in severe cases. But anger is to be "owned" and not repressed. To feel one's anger does not mean one should act out of anger to strike out against others or harm oneself. Far too often we have thought of anger as evil, as somehow unnatural and to be denied. But anger is a normal emotion which moves us to act when we see injustice being done, when a child is abused, a class of people are discriminated against, or the poor and weak are denied their rights as human beings.

Paul urges the thief to no longer steal but rather to do honest work with his hands so he may give to those in need. The giving of the honest worker is not merely in restitution to those from whom he or she has stolen in the past, but giving in liberality to those in need. In a world in which technology is making it possible to produce more goods with fewer people, and much less manual labor, the question of what society owes those unable to find honest work is a pressing one. This writer was in a small group discussion at Taizé, the community for Christian renewal and reconciliation in France, in which industrialists from northern Italy were raising just this issue. It is an issue which the writer and the DuPont Company community in which he lives are struggling with also. How to provide jobs for the unskilled who can and want to work with their hands in a highly technological and mechanized "high tech" society is a problem which won't go away and with which the Church and society in general must devise creative answers. More and bigger prisons for thieves who steal is only a stop-gap solution. Prisons become colleges for crime in which older, more experienced criminals teach the younger and less experienced how to succeed in criminal activity in and out of prison.

Paul urges the Ephesians "let no evil talk come out of your mouths, but only such as is good for edifying, as fits the occasion, that it may impart grace to those who hear." (v. 29) We live in a society in North America in which gutter language has been accepted in movies and novels and on the street. Cable television and satellite dishes have enabled TV watchers to tune into programs which are moral sewage. While no one would think of paying a stiff monthly fee to the local sewage department to pipe raw sewage into one's living room, yet the even more destructive evil talk and acts are being piped in twenty-four hours a day. A minister of a very conservative denomination told this writer that, while his denomination was on record opposing their members attending movies, nothing has been said about watching X-rated movies at home on TV or VCR's. While technology races ahead, the human moral response remains eons behind. Paul faces just this issue in this text of verse 29.

It has been said that "no matter how much of a a sewer your life may be, kindly refrain from opening it to public view." While cursing and filthy language was associated with the lower class or the sophisticated upper class in years gone by, now the evil talk which Paul condemns is socially acceptable in many communities.

Instead of evil talk Paul urges talk which is good for edifying, for building up, and which fits the occasion. Such conversation imparts grace to those who hear. There are those who know what to say and how to say it. Genuine love for one's neighbor is the underlying motivation for speaking the right words which build up, rather than tear down. The word "edify" is from the Latin and refers to building a house. It means to instruct or improve in moral and religious knowledge. We enjoy being around those who affirm us and the values and goals we share.

Paul tells the Ephesians not to grieve the Holy Spirit. The Spirit is given by God as our guide and director in living. Just as when we act contrary to our parents when we are young and thus grieve them, so to act contrary to the Holy Spirit is to grieve the Spirit. Evil words and deeds hurt the very heart of God. They crucify Christ anew.

Then Paul lists things which must be put out of the Christian's life: bitterness, wrath, anger, clamor, slander, and all malice. Bitterness is long-standing resentment. It is the unforgiving spirit. It is the spirit which buries the hatchet but marks the spot! Paul says put away wrath or outbreaks of passion, along with anger. While in verse 26 Paul has just said "be angry but do not sin" in this verse (31) he says to control anger. Wrath is an outbreak of passion which blazes up like a paper set on fire, and just as quickly dies out. But the anger he refers to is that which has become habitual and unmanageable. Both the burst of temper and the long-lived anger are forbidden to the Christian way of living. Note it is not "feeling anger" that is forbidden, but the bursts of temper. No one likes to be around someone who is like a box of fireworks accidentally set on fire, who is shooting off at the mouth and calling attention to his or her hurt feelings.

Loud talking and insulting language is also forbidden in Christian living. While there are some-ethnic groups which ordinarily speak loudly to convey normal feelings, Paul is urging self-control in Christian conversation. The person who speaks loudly to get his or her way does so out of a sense of powerlessness. The person with real self-confidence and power usually speaks softly.

Then Paul urges the reader to "be kind to one another, tenderhearted, forgiving one another, as God in Christ forgave you." This is good guidance for all human relationships, but particularly within marriage and family living. Someone has observed that we ordinarily treat strangers on the street with much more common courtesy than we treat our spouses or family. Paul is urging that we forgive one another even as God in Christ has forgiven us.

Then in 5:1 he says we are to imitate God as beloved children. Here is an image from family life in which a child imitates a parent. So we are to imitate God our heavenly parent. Then he urges us to walk in love. Life is often compared to a walk, a way, a pilgrimage in the Bible. We are to walk in love, to follow the path of love all through life, remembering how Christ loved us and gave himself up for us as a sacrifice. The ultimate motive for Christian living is not common decency or middle class morality but the sacrificial love of Christ. Middle class morality has fallen on hard times and has been almost destroyed. But Christian morality is another style of living and is motivated by divine love, not human desires to be accepted or to appear socially approved.

*John 6:35, 41-51 (C)*
*John 6:41-51 (L) (RC)*

Verse 35 provides the context for the response of those present in verse 41 regarding Jesus' claim to be the bread of life. Since the theme of bread of life was dealt with at length in the previous Sunday's lesson from John, it will be given briefer treatment here. The discourse on bread from heaven (vv. 22-59) advances in this passage (41-51) by means of an objection. The Jews murmured at Jesus and his claim to be the bread which came down from heaven and said, "Is not this Jesus the son of Joseph, whose father and mother we know? How does he now say, 'I have come down from heaven?'' His claim to have come down from heaven is absurd according to those who knew this "home town boy from Nazareth." Those who are drawn to and taught by God (Isaiah 54:13) come to Jesus. (v. 44) However, this does not mean that people have an immediate knowledge of God in virtue of which they are able to pass judgment on the claims of Jesus. Only Jesus has such knowledge. The drawing by God is not coercive or mechanical. If his opponents had heard and learned God's voice in their scriptures, then they would have recognized its accents in Jesus who alone has direct communion with aod the Father. By their actions in responding to Jesus, people show whether God has knowledge of them and wills to give them to his Son.

Notice that in verses 47-51 some points already made are reemphasized and two new ones are added: (1) Jesus is now the living bread *come* down from heaven. In verse 33 there was an allusion to the Incarnation, but here it becomes explicit. (2) In verse 51b Jesus says that that the bread which he gives is his flesh which is given for the life of the world. This points to the fact that only in his death will Jesus' self-giving be complete. This is necessary if people are to have life. It is also likely a pointer to the Eucharist. The declaration by Jesus that "the living bread . . . is my flesh" means that the One who became flesh, i.e. assumed complete human nature, offered himself to God in death and by doing so released his life for the life of the world.

### Theological Reflections

Controlling of anger and dealing gently are two themes in the reading from 2 Samuel and Ephesians. God deals gently with Elijah who is escaping the anger of Jezebel by fleeing into the wilderness and going to Horeb. God by an angel supplies the prophet with bread and water. God acts graciously in sending Jesus as the bread of life to give eternal life, in contrast to the manna from heaven which God gave in Moses' time which the people ate and later died. Ephesians contrasts two life styles: the pagan and the Christian. Paul urges the reader to put off the evil ways of pagan living and to put on the new life of gentleness, love, tenderheartedness, and forgiveness. The key to such new living is walking in love in response to God's love in Christ.

### Homiletical Moves

*2 Samuel 18:1, 5, 9-15 (C)*
## Deal gently with the Young Man Absalom

1. David's fatherly love overrides his concern for the kingdom as he asks his commanders to spare his rebellious son Absalom's, life
2. Absalom is caught by a tree, stabbed by Joab and killed by ten soldiers
3. By contrast, Jesus was obedient to his heavenly Father and gave his life for the world that the rebellious human race might be saved from ultimate death from which they alone cannot extricate themselves
4. Put your trust in Christ who died to save you from the death you could not otherwise escape

*1 Kings 19:4-8 (L) (RC)*
## God Strengthens His Prophet Elijah

1. Elijah flees the wrath of Jezebel
2. Elijah despairs of life itself and asks God to take his life
3. Instead, God ministers to him by an angel who gives bread and water
3. Elijah is strengthened by the divine provisions for his pilgrimage to Horeb
4. Trust in God's providential care of your life in your pilgrimage through life

*This Preacher's Choice*

*Ephesians 4:25—5:2 (C)*
*Ephesians 4:30—5:2 (L) (RC)*
## Be Imitatiors of God

1. Do not grieve for the Holy Spirit, but put away those things of your former pagan life: (1) falsehood, (2) stealing, (3) evil talk, (4) bitterness, (5) wrath, (6) anger, (7) clamor, (8) slander, (9) all malice
2. Be imitators of God as beloved children
3. You were sealed by the Spirit for the day of redemption, so walk in love by (1) speaking the truth, (2) being angry but not sinning, (3) doing honest work, (4) giving to those in need, (5) speaking only such as is good for edifying and fits the occasion, (6) being kind and (7) tenderhearted to one another (8) forgiving one another as God in Christ forgave you
4. Live this new life of love in response to Christ who loved us and gave himself as an offering and sacrifice to God

*John 6:35, 41-51 (C)*
*John 6:41-51 (L) (RC)*
## Jesus, the Bread Which Gives Eternal Life

1. Jesus declares, "I am the bread of life" which came down from heaven
2. The Jews object that he is merely the man whose father and mother they knew
3. Jesus declares that anyone who believes has eternal life
4. Jesus promises that if anyone eats of the bread from heaven, his flesh, that person will live forever, pointing to the Eucharist in which by faith we feed on the Living Christ
5. Feed on Christ, the Bread from heaven, who gives eternal life

**Hymn for Pentecost 12:**   *Bread of the World*

**Prayer**

*Gracious God, who has dealt gently with us while we were yet sinners and who gave your Son to die in our place, we bow in gratitude for your great love. You have fed us when we were in the wilderness of our sin, despairing even of life itself. You have given us a radically new life by the power of the Spirit. Give us power by your Spirit to walk in the way of love and to be imitators of you, our heavenly Father. May we walk in love even as Christ loved us and gave himself as a sacrifice for us. Amen*

# Proper 15     Pentecost 13     Ordinary Time 20

August 14-20

| Common | Lutheran | Roman Catholic |
| --- | --- | --- |
| 2 Samuel 18:24-33<br>Ephesians 5:15-20<br>John 6:51-58 | Proverbs 9:1-6<br>Ephesians 5:15-20<br>John 6:51-58 | Proverbs 9:1-6<br>Ephesians 5:15-20<br>John 6:51-58 |

## Comments on the Lessons

In the 2 Samuel reading David receives the news of his son, Absalom's death and mourns over the young man, in spite of his rebellion against him. The passage describes the problem of succession and why Solomon succeeded David. The reading from Proverbs is a poetic allegory in which Wisdom, the gracious hostess, invites the unwise to her feast. Wisdom's house is the world and the "pillars" are the pillars of heaven. There is consensus on the Ephesian reading and virtual consensus on the John passage. Note that verse 51 is included to provide the remark of Jesus which gave rise to the dispute that follows.

## Commentary

*2 Samuel 18:24-33 (C)*

David sits between the outer and inner gates on the city wall. The city wall must have been several feet thick with one gate at its outer side and another at the inner side. Above this was a room and a staircase went up to the roof. The roof would be level with the rest of the wall. The watchman on the roof saw a man running alone. David is in a place where he can keep in touch with the watchman who is posted at the place where the gate joins the battlements. A man running would be either a messenger or a fugitive. A fugitive would have others about him pursuing him, or such a group could have been interpreted as a rout. Soon a second man appears in the distance.

Soon the first man is identified as Ahimaaz. David seems confident that he is bringing good news, which may be based on wishful thinking, but partly on the idea Joab had expressed earlier that a friend would not be in a hurry to bring bad news. When Ahimaaz arrives he uses only one Hebrew word to say "It is well" — shalom. Today in Israel "shalom" is used as a greeting and parting word on the streets of cities. It cannot be translated precisely into English but means health, wholeness, welfare, prosperity, or peace. It was a conventional greeting. Note that David picks up the word at the beginning of his question, "Is it well (shalom) with the young man Absalom?" (v. 29) Ahimaaz was too excited to remain behind but when he faced King David he lacked the courage to tell the whole story. It was not uncommon in the ancient world to punish or put to death the bearer of bad news to the king.

Ahimaaz may not have meant by "shalom" any more than a respectful form of address. Even if he had only seen a great tumult the truth is that Joab had mentioned Absalom's death in Ahimaaz's presence. Thus he must have known more than he claimed to know. David suspected there was more news so he told Ahimaaz to turn aside and stand still.

Then the Cushite (Ethiopian slave) came to David and told the true story. But even his story was an aroundabout way of saying that Absalom had been killed: "May the enemies of my lord the king, and all who rise up against you for evil, be like that young man." (v. 32) Note that while Ahimaaz brings news of victory in battle, David is only interested in what has happened to Absalom his son. In his personal grief he forgets about his military victory and public duties. When the Cushite gives David the news, David was deeply moved. He went up to the room over the gate and wept and, as he went, he cried out words that express one of the most distressing scenes in all literature: "O my son, Absalom, my son, my son Absalom! Would I had died instead of you. O Absalom, my son, my son!" (v. 33) Note the repetition of "my son" as David cries out in deep grief.

A parallel can be drawn between David's sorrow over the death of his son Absalom and God's sorrow over human sin which takes saving action through the death of Christ. The Psalmist wrote, "As a father pities his children, so the Lord pities those who fear him." (103:13) In Christ's death God the father did what David longed to do, He died for his rebellious children so that they might live!

### Proverbs 9:1-6 (L) (RC)

The writer of this passage contrasts Lady Wisdom and Dame Folly (see also vv. 13-18). There are two influences in the world and two ways of living. In this poetic allegory Wisdom invites the unwise to her feast. Those who come and eat of her bread and drink of the wine she has mixed, allegories for the truth Wisdom imparts, will walk in the way of insight. The seven pillars are the pillars of heaven.

This concept of Wisdom's heavenly banquet is part of the background of Jesus' discourse about bread of life in John's gospel for today. However, it is not as appropriate for today's reading (John 6:51-58) as for the previous reading (Ordinary Time 18) in which Jesus says "and he who believes in me shall never thirst." (6:35) Wisdom's wine relates better to this than to the reading for today.

Note that in today's reading we have the close of the prologue on Wisdom. Both Wisdom and Folly invited the simple and those without sense to come into their houses to a banquet. They are free to choose to accept or reject the invitation. Today's reading gives Wisdom's invitation and rewards for drinking her "wine" of wisdom. But in verses 3-18 Folly invites those passing by to come in to dine, but the reward is death and Sheol.

### Ephesians 5:15-20

This is the concluding passage of the section whose theme is an appeal to renounce pagan ways. (4:17—5:20) This passage might be called "prudent living." Verse 15 has a parallel in Colossians 4:5, and verses 19-20 has a parallel in Colossians 3:16. In Colossians 4:5 the admonition to use time and opportunities wisely is applied specifically to relations with non-Christians, while in Ephesians 5:16 it applies generally upon the whole of the moral life. "Making the most of time" literally means "buying up" the time. "Because the days are evil" refers to the conditions which often are in direct opposition to Christian witnessing. The lines between Christian and pagan are being drawn more clearly in North America and the world in general today as in Paul's time of writing. Because much of American life seems to have passed from barbarism to decadence without pass!ng through civilization is no reason for the Christian to give up. Rather, it is an even greater motive to seek to maintain the Christian ideal in daily living.

The admonition to "understand what the will of the Lord is" is an equivalent to the more common expression of "the will of God." The use of "Lord" instead of "God" reveals how Christians had become used to thinking about Jesus Christ, the Lord, as God.

The instruction not to get drunk with wine which is debauchery is cited from Proverbs 23:31 (LXX, Codex A). While the warning is meant literally, there is an overtone of reference to the use of wine in the cult of Dionysus and possibly other mystery religions. Also wine-induced frenzies were characteristic of some pagan worship. It is interesting to note that the Greek word for debauchery is a negative formation from a root word closely related to the word for salvation. Thus debauchery is the opposition of salvation, the ruin of life in dissolute living of whatever kind. With the growing number of alcoholics in North America, especially among young people, this admonition has very contemporary application.

Instead of being drunk with wine Christians are admonished to be filled with the Spirit. But the contrast here is not between the two states of being overcome by wine or the Spirit, but between the degrading effects of overindulgence in alcohol and its degrading effect versus the progressive fulfillment of the spiritual life on the other hand.

The spiritual life is fulfilled in a life of thanksgiving and joyful fellowship marked by singing. The Christian religion is a singing faith and in some pagan cultures Christian hymn tunes and words have been adapted for use in pagan worship but without success. For the Christian sings of Christ whose distinctive life and death and resurrection gives joy in word and song. Note that this section of verses 19-20 is modeled on Colossians 3:16-17. But here "addressing one another" suggests the joyful fellowship is over a broader area than that indicated by the Colossian passage. Christian singing is done "to the Lord" in Ephesians while it is "singing to God" in Colossians. Again, this reflects the high Christology which was reflected in Christians thinking about Jesus Christ as about God. They felt his presence with them in their joyful gatherings. The practice of singing Psalms goes back to the beginning of the Christian church, along with singing hymns and spiritual songs which denote words and music written by human beings rather than the more directly inspired words of the Psalms. Martin Luther, the Reformer, said that the person who sings prays twice, meaning that one prays in the words of the hymn but also in the music offered to God with joy and thanksgiving.

Ephesians urges the reader to live ''always and for everything giving thanks in the name of our Lord Jesus Christ to God the Father.'' (v. 20) All of the Christian life should be lived in an atmosphere of worship, of offering up one's life to God in gratitude, and all worship should be filled with thanksgiving. This rules out the whining kind of religion that uses religion to achieve one's own desires. Or that calls on God as a Cosmic Bellhop to get the good things of life or fix life's tragedies.

The Christian life is a singing life, a life of gratitude to God, a life of seeking to understand what the will of the Lord is and living that will, a life of making the best use of the opportunities that come our way.

### John 6:51-58

(Note the difference in numbering of the verses in the Latin Vulgate from that of the Greek in verse 51ff which is reflected in Catholic and Protestant translations. The RSV used here reflects the Greek text.)

This discourse continues Jesus' debate with the Jews who misunderstand him to mean cannibalism when he calls himself the bread of life that his followers must eat. The whole discourse is summed up in verse 57: ''As the living Father sent me, and I live because of the Father, so he who eats me will live because of me.'' This discourse is a duplicate of the preceding one, but in this one the Bread of life is now the Eucharist.

The Eucharistic theme, which was secondary in the preceding passage, is not the exclusive one here. Instead of being told that eternal life is the result of believing in Jesus as in the former passage, that Jesus dominates this passage as the agent and source of salvation. And note the new vocabulary which runs through verses 51-58: ''eat,'' ''feed,'' ''drink,'' ''flesh,'' and ''blood.''

There are two main indications that the Eucharist is referred to in this passage: (1) the stress on eating (feeding on) Jesus' flesh and drinking his blood, and (2) the formula found in verse 51: ''the bread which I shall give for the life of the world is my flesh.'' Since John does not report the Lord's words over the bread and cup at the Last Supper, it is possible to consider verse 51 to be the Johannine form of the institution of the Lord's Supper. Note that it resembles the institution found in Luke: ''This is my body which is given for you.'' John speaks of ''flesh'' while Luke speaks of ''body.'' Since there is no Hebrew or Aramaic (language Jesus spoke) word for ''body'' as we know the term, many biblical scholars think that what Jesus actually said at the Last Supper was the Aramaic equivalent of ''This is my flesh.'' A number of the Church Fathers use ''flesh'' in referring to the Eucharist. Thus it may well be that in this regard John is the *closest of the Gospels to the original eucharistic language* of Jesus! From earliest times scholars noticed that John 6:51 resembles a eucharistic formula.

The two forms of the Bread of Life Discourse (35-50; 51-58) represent a juxtaposition of the two ways in which Jesus is present to believers: (1) in the preached word, and (2) in the sacrament of the Eucharist. These two themes date back to the very beginning of Christianity and are reflected in the Eastern Liturgy, Roman Mass and Protestant liturgies that evolved from the Mass.

Jesus' use of ''flesh'' has a certain crudeness and reality which recalls the Incarnation. It may have been used intentionally to refute docetism which held that Jesus only appeared to be in human form. When Jesus says that ''the bread which I shall give for the life of the world is my flesh'' (v. 51), he is describing his voluntary death (cp. 1 Corinthians 13:3), so John may here be hinting at the connection between the Eucharist and the death of Jesus.

The Hebrew phrase ''flesh and blood'' means the whole person and during the Reformation verses 53-55 were the center of the debate over whether it was necessary to receive both bread and wine in the Eucharist.

The term ''feeds'' in secular Greek was originally used of animals feeding but later applied to human beings as well. It had a crude connotation and meant ''gnaw, munch, etc.'' and here emphasizes the realism of the flesh and blood in the eucharist.

The thrust of this discourse is that the One who became flesh (in the Incarnation assumed complete human nature) offered himself to God in death and, in doing so, released his life for the life of the world. The separation of flesh from blood (v. 53) emphasizes the reality of Jesus' death. To eat and drink (v. 54) is to believe as indicated in verse 47 but also to appropriate, assimilate and to abide in Christ. Since Christ is bread from heaven the person who eats him will live for ever. (v. 58)

While, in the earlier part of the chapter (v. 32), we learn that the Father gives the heavenly bread in the sense that the Son comes from the Father, now in this passage, when the bread is identified with the flesh of Jesus, he must give it himself. Jesus gives up his life on the cross voluntarily and it is this voluntary death which makes the eucharistic participation in his flesh possible. Recall that in 1:29 Jesus is called the Passover Lamb who takes away the world's sin. In this present discourse set in the context of Passover, we hear that Jesus gives his flesh for the life of the world.

To have eternal life is to be in close communion with Jesus. The Christian remains in Jesus and Jesus remains in the Christian. Communion with Jesus is actually a participation in the intimate communion that exists beween Father and Son. While verse 57 just mentions the communion between Father and Son it is assumed the reader will understand. Jesus gives human beings a share in God's own life.

While the other three Gospels record the institution of the Eucharist, it is significant that John's Gospel explains what the Eucharist does for the Christian. The words of the Eucharist reflect the covenant theme in "blood of the covenant," and here in John the *mutual indwelling of God (and his Son Jesus) and the Christian* reflect the covenant theme also. To be united with Christ is to live forever. Eternal life means both duration and quality of life. To feed on Jesus, the bread from heaven, is to enter a relationship with Jesus like that of God the Father with God the Son and thus to have life.

## Theological Reflections

The mourning of David for his son Absalom is the theme of the 2 Samuel passage. In his deep grief he forgets his military victory and public duties and cries out, "Would I had died instead of you" which points to the cross and God's love for his rebellious children. The Father gives the Son to die in their place. Proverbs describes Wisdom as a hostess who makes wise the simple in contrast to Folly who destroys them. The theme of Ephesians also deals with wise versus foolish living and urges the reader to make the most of the time and to understand what the will of the Lord is. Ephesians tells the reader to be filled with the Spirit, to rejoice in Christian fellowship and to live a life of gratitude to God. In the passage from John, Jesus describes himself as the bread of life from heaven which gives life to all who feed on him. This is John's version of the Eucharist in which he relates Jesus' death to the Eucharist and the communion of God and human beings.

## Homiletical Moves

*2 Samuel 18:24-33 (C)*
### O My Son Absalom!— The Cry of a Grief-Stricken Father

1. Ahimaaz brings the message that all is well from the battlefield, although there had been a tumult
2. The Cushite (Ethiopian) brings news of Absalom's death in the tree
3. David wept and was deeply moved and said, "Would I had died instead of you, O Absalom, my son, my son!"
4. God gave his son on the cross to die for us the rebellious children that we might have life and dwell with the Father forever
5. Come to God in faith and you will dwell with him forever

*Proverbs 9:1-6 (L) (RC)*
### Walk in the Way of Insight

1. Wisdom has built her house in this world with seven pillars of heaven
2. Wisdom invites the simple to eat of her bread and drink of her wine
3. Wisdom calls her guests to live in simpleness, to live and to walk in the way of insight
4. Therefore, follow the way of Wisdom

*Ephesians 5:15-20*
### Always and for Everything Giving Thanks!

1. The days are evil
2. Walk, not as unwise, but as wise persons making the most of the time
3. Be filled with the Spirit and understand what the will of the Lord is

4. Live in joyful fellowship with one another singing and making melody to the Lord
5. Always and for everything give thanks to God the Father

*This Preacher's Choice*

*John 6:51-58*
# Jesus, the Bread from Heaven, Who Gives Eternal Life

1. The Father sent Jesus the Son from heaven as the living bread
2. The person who eats Jesus' flesh and drinks his blood has eternal life and abides in Jesus and Jesus in that person
3. The bread from heaven is not like the manna which the Israelites ate and died
4. The bread which Jesus gives for the life of the world is his flesh which he gave on the cross
5. Feed upon Christ that you may have eternal life

**Hymn for Pentecost 13:**   *Now Thank We All Our God*

**Prayer**

*O God who nourishes us as a mother nourishes her baby or a father feeds his child, so feed us with the bread from heaven that we might have eternal life. May we turn from our rebellious ways and seek to understand your will and walk in your ways, making the most of the time. Grant that we may live the Christian life with joy, always giving thanks to you our God and making melody to the Lord. May we be filled with the Spirit. Grant that we may feed upon Jesus, the Bread from Heaven, and so abide in him and he in us. May we be given this bread and so live forever. Amen*

# Proper 16     Pentecost 14     Ordinary Time 21

August 21-27

| Common | Lutheran | Roman Catholic |
| --- | --- | --- |
| 2 Samuel 23:1-7 | Joshua 24:1-2a | Joshua 24:1-2, 15-18 |
| Ephesians 5:21-33 | Ephesians 5:21-31 | Ephesians 5:21-32 |
| John 6:55-69 | John 6:60-69 | John 6:60-69 |

## Comments on the Lessons

The 2 Samuel reading contains the last words of David in which he compares God's care for his people with the sun and the rain that make the grass grow. The Joshua passage is a record of the covenant at Shechem in which the generation which had conquered Palestine now makes a covenant with God similar to the one made earlier at Sinai. There is virtual consensus on the Ephesian reading. It is a self-contained theological piece. There is virtual consensus on the passage from John. Note that it overlaps in (C) with the previous Sunday by beginning with verse 55 in order to pick up the reason for the disciples' difficulty.

## Commentary

### 2 Samuel 23:1-7 (C)

Here we have a brief hymn of praise to God for his favor to David with whom God has made an everlasting covenant. David stands in sharp contrast to godless scoundrels who come to no good. Note that these last words of David follow immediately after the royal psalm of chapter 22, just as the blessing of Moses follows the song of Moses. The royal psalm and the last words of David have been put together here on purpose.

The basic structure of David's life and house is presented clearly, along with the theological program for the future of the dynasty of David. The context of the poem is very well chosen. Even as a "last will" of a dying person has always been respected, so these words carry special meaning. Note that they are not express words of blessing as in the case of Isaac, Jacob and Moses. The poem runs into six strophes, each of four lines, and the individual lines are in three-stress metre. The last strophe has four short verses of two stresses each, making for an effective conclusion. The high quality of the poetry found here is significant. It is outstanding in every way. There is a growing opinion among scholars that regards David as the author from verse 3b onwards. This is a strongly defended position.

Note that two strophes make up the introduction, which follows a stylistic form found in other passages. (Numbers 24, Proverbs 30:1ff) There is a kind of presentation at the beginning as David gives himself his full names. It is a self-characterization. He calls himself "the sweet psalmist of Israel." David is not only anointed but has skill in making poetry. He bears the divine spirit and mediates the divine word. In Israel the king is a sacral figure. So David can be said to be in a unique way "filled with God" which refers not to ecstasy but rather to the Word, as in the case of prophets who speak God's Word.

The message of the poem (vv. 3b-5) contain two similes: (1) the rising sun, and (2) the effect of the rain. They cannot be joined into one. The first simile gives the saying of God and describes the righteous ruler. Both righteousness toward people and the fear of God make up this person. The ruler is compared to the rays of the rising sun. (v. 4) The "sun of righteousness" in which the sun is associated with righteousness is well known in the East.

In the second simile the ruler is compared to rain that makes grass to sprout from the earth. A better parallel is "to sparkle." This simile was also current in the East, for after a long summer drought the rain would make the grass sparkle. The point of both these similes is that the covenant God made with the house of David is life-giving and produces blessings like the rains.

From the fourth strophe on, the singer, rather than God, speaks and the words are like a confession. God has been faithful to his covenant and has made the king share in salvation.

Then in verses 6-7 the godless people are compared to thorns that are thrown away. They cannot be taken in hand, and the person who takes them does so armed with iron and the shaft of a spear. In the end they are consummed by fire. This is a dramatic description of a king and his enemies. At the end of David's life all the thorns that had goaded David are withered and burnt.

Here in these few lofty lines of poetry we are shown the essential makeup of David's life and character. While chapter 22 does this in a psalm, chapter 23:1-7 is prophetic. Both passages point to God who is with David and his house.

*Joshua 24:1-2a, 14-18 (L)*
*Joshua 24:1-2, 15-18 (RC)*

In this well known passage of Scripture, Joshua invites the people to choose the Lord which he and his house have chosen. The people join with Joshua saying, "Therefore we also will serve the Lord, for he is our God." The generation of Israelites who had conquered Palestine makes a covenant with God similar to the one made at Sinai.

It was customary for people of that time, upon entering a new country, that the people placed themselves under the jurisdiction of the gods of the new country. They gave up the gods of their former country. The group whose leader was Joshua had already made their decision — to claim the Lord as their God. In addition to Joshua's group, there were those sympathetic to Israel. A decision for the Lord will make a united community of two groups who were ethnically related already but divided by differences. But a decision in favor of the local religion would bring about a breach between the two groups.

Notice that Joshua's invitation to join him and his house in claiming the Lord has no escape clause and no room for compromise. The decision is clean cut: either join with Joshua and his houseshold or, if they decide differently, then the relations are terminated.

From this passage we learn a historical fact of great importance. There was a group around Joshua who already had made a choice for the Lord, while there was another, second group, in the process of making a decision. This division between Israel (the north) and Judah (the south) continued to recur throughout the pre-exilic history of Israel.

In verse 16-18 we have the reply of the people to Joshua's challenge to join him in claiming the Lord as God. They make an unequivocal decision for the Lord based, on his mighty acts on their behalf in the past. The people realize it is not a matter of throwing out an old god and choosing a new one, but rather a decision of a fundamental choice. This God they choose has no place of his own, for all the world, every place in it, is his. This almost fanatical zeal for the Lord carried on through the generations. And so it was no accident that the only Jews to return to Palestine after the edict of Cyrus (539 BC) were those who were determined in their theology and unwilling to compromise with other gods. For this reason the Samaritans were expelled from the community for they had compromised and were called "apostates of the Jewish nation." And foreigners were also expelled who had become part of the nation, since foreign wives who worshiped pagan gods could decide the religious training of their children and thus lead them into paganism.

The people all joined in choosing to serve the Lord for he had rescued them from Egypt, brought them safely to Canaan, and aided them in the conquest of the land. In response to God's mighty acts, the people unite in declaring "therefore we also will serve the Lord, for he is our God." (v. 18)

*Ephesians 5:21-33 (C)*
*Ephesians 5:21-31 (L)*
*Ephesians 5:21-32 (RC)*

This section is part of a larger part of Ephesians dealing with the Christian household. (5:21—6:9) In this part the relationships of husbands and wives (21-31) is dealt with, followed by children and parents (6:1-4) and masters and slaves (6:5-9). The key to all these relationships is mutual subjections as summed up in Philippians 2:3: "Do nothing from selfishness or conceit, but in humility count others better than yourselves." There are a number of parallels to this passage in other early Christian literature, especially in Colossians 3:18—4:6.

We may read 5:21 as an introduction to the whole larger part dealing with the Christian household: "Be subject to one another out of reverence for Christ." In each relationship, husband/wife, parent/child, master/slave, the emphasis is on loyal obedience. But clearly this is not servile capitulation. but rather reciprocal responsibility. While the concern for husband/wife relationships is briefly dealt with in Colossians 3:18-19, they are greatly expanded here because of the author's pressing concern to define the nature of the church. He finds a parallel in the institution of marriage to Christ and the church.

This passage contains two basic convictions about marriage: (1) the unity of husband and wife in marriage, "and the two shall become one flesh"; and (2) the husband is regarded as the head of the body, "for the husband is the head of the wife as Christ is the head of the church."

This passage creates problems for many people when taken out of the context of the culture in which it was written and out of the New Testament view of equality of male and female in Christ. The feminist movement has sought to correct the injustice in society toward women. The companionship model of marriage described by David Mace and others is a corrective for the extremes of seeing either husband or wife as dominant and the other submissive in marriage. In a companionship marriage, leadership roles are shared and changed in various tasks and stages of marriage.

This passage is primarily important because of what it reveals about Paul's view of the church. Note the head-body metaphor. Christ is both head and savior of the church. He had a self-sacrificing love for the church. There is stress on the church's duty of unconditional obedience to Christ. A new understanding of lordship is revealed in that Christ's lordship is closely related to his love for the church, shown in his death. The church is the "bride" of Christ who is presented washed and in proper attire. The washing of water is baptism. The "word" may be the baptismal formula. By water and the word Christians are called to serve God, both individually and in the corporate body.

The mystery referred to (v. 32) is Christ's spiritual union with our humanity. This is of particular importance in understanding the nature of human marriage. Notice that in the command to love one's wife and to respect one's husband polygamy is prohibited.

*John 6:55-69 (C)*
*John 6:60-69 (L) (RC)*

We should note that verses 60-71 describe the close of Jesus' ministry in Galilee, a ministry that ends in almost total failure. Only the confession of Peter (v. 68ff) prevents it being a complete failure. He confesses faith in Jesus as the "Holy One of God" on behalf of the Twelve.

The (C) reading begins with verse 55 in order to pick up the reason for the disciples' difficulty, although this overlaps with the reading of the previous Sunday. The core of the difficulty is Jesus' declaration: "He who eats my flesh and drinks my blood abides in me, and I in him." (v. 56) This is clearly a reference to the Eucharist, but since the Lord's Supper had not yet been instituted, many scholars think verses 52-56 are a later editorial insertion. John is speaking on a number of different levels here. This anticipates chapter 13 and the Last Supper and footwashing scene. While hard for the disciples to understand, the Christian today sees them as pointing to an institution of the Lord's Supper of "This is my body; this is my blood."

The meaning of "hard saying" for the disciples is that it is offensive or difficult, not that it is obscure. In verse 62-63 Jesus speaks of the ascension of the Son of man by which he will be taken away as regards the flesh. This indicates that Jesus has been speaking of spiritual things and not of the actual eating of his flesh: "It is the spirit that gives life, the flesh is of no avail; the words that I have spoken to you are spirit and life." (v. 63) The key to understanding this "hard saying" and unlocking the difficult and offensive door is *faith*. And faith is God's gift, not a human achievement: "But there are some of you that do not believe . . . And he said, 'This is why I told you that no one can come to me unless it is granted him by the Father'." (vv. 64-65) When one receives the gift of faith from God one is enabled to know God in Christ. But to refuse this gift is to become a partner with the devil. Note the division between people based on faith/unbelief.

While the words about eating his flesh and drinking his blood created a crisis of belief for the disciples and were an offense to the Jews the disciples are confronted with a decision: to believe that Jesus is speaking of final things and is speaking of spiritual matters, or not to believe and to remain on the literal level.

It is Peter who makes the leap of faith and speaks for all but Judas, when he says that they have come to know that Jesus is "the Holy One of God." Notice that, from this moment on, only the Twelve and a few others continue to follow Jesus. This is the first mention of Judas the betrayer. From this point on the shadow of the cross falls more fully over the life and ministry of Jesus. And even greater tests of the disciples' faith will come as the cross is approached.

## Theological Reflections

The 2 Samuel passage is a hymn of praise to God for his favor toward David with whom God made an everlasting covenant. They reveal the essential nature of David's life and character. The Joshua reading describes the leading of Joshua of not only those with him, but of all the people to decide for the Lord as their God. *Decision* is the thrust of this passage. In Ephesians the mutual relationship in Christian marriage is compared to that between Christ and the church, his bride. There is a mystery about this relationship. But it is characterized by self-sacrificing love, reciprocal responsibility and mutual caring. John relates the end of Jesus' ministry in Galilee, when he confronts the disciples with the necessity of making a leap of faith from the literal meaning of "eat my flesh, drink my blood" to understand and believe that he is the Holy One of God. Decision is a central theme in these passages as individuals and groups decide for or against God.

## Homiletical Moves

*2 Samuel 23:1-7 (C)*
### The Sweet Psalmist of Israel, David

1. David was the anointed of God, the sweet psalmist of Israel
2. A just ruler who rules in the fear of God is like the sun shining
3. A just ruler is like the rain that makes grass to sprout
4. God has made an everlasting covenant with David and his house
5. But godless people are like thorns that are thrown away and consumed with fire
6. Therefore, live in covenant obedience with God

*Joshua 24:1-2a, 14-18 (L)*
*Joshua 24:1-2, 15-18 (RC)*
### Choose This Day Whom You Will Serve!

1. Joshua calls on the people to fear the Lord and put away the gods their ancestors served before
2. Joshua confronts the people with the decision: choose this day whom you will serve
3. The people remember God's mighty acts in bringing them out of Egypt, preserving them in the wilderness, and driving out the people who occupied Palestine before them
4. The people reply, "Therefore we also will serve the Lord, for he is our God"
5. Choose you, this day, whom you will serve: God or idols

*Ephesians 5:21-33 (C)*
*Ephesians 5:21-31 (L)*
*Ephesians 5:21-32 (RC)*
### Love and Respect in Christian Marriage

1. Be subject to one another out of reverence for Christ
2. Husbands should love their wives as Christ loved the church and gave himself up for her, and are the head of their wives as Christ is the head of the church
3. Husbands should love their wives as they love their own bodies
4. A man and a woman leave their parents in order to be joined in marriage as one flesh
5. Husbands and wives should have mutual love and respect for each other in Christian marriage, sharing leadership in companionship marriage

*John 6:55-69 (C)*
*John 6:60-69 (L) (RC)*
### You Are the Holy One of God!

1. The disciples complain about the hard saying of Jesus regarding eating his flesh and drinking his blood
2. Jesus says that the spirit gives life but the flesh is of no avail
3. Many disciples drew back and no longer followed Jesus

4. Peter, speaking for the Twelve, says, "We have believed, and have come to know, that you are the Holy One of God"
5. Commit your life to Jesus, the Holy One of God, and live in joyful obedience to him

**Hymn for Pentecost 14:**   *The Church's One Foundation*

**Prayer**

*Almighty God who has delivered us from the bondage of sin, who has sustained us by your Spirit and fed us on the Bread from Heaven, we now confess that you are our God whom we will serve. We put away all false idols of greed, pride, and power. When we remember what you have done for us in the covenant relationship you have formed with us, we are humbled and confess with Peter and the Twelve that Jesus has the words of eternal life. There is no one else to whom we can go. For we have believed and have come to know that he is the Holy One of God. Amen*

# Proper 17    Pentecost 15    Ordinary Time 22

August 28 — September 3

| Common | Lutheran | Roman Catholic |
|---|---|---|
| 1 Kings 2:1-4, 10-12 (C) | Deuteronomy 4:1-2, 6-8 | Deuteronomy 4:1-2, 6-8 |
| Ephesians 6:10-20 | Ephesians 6:10-20 | James 1:17-18, 21-22, 27 |
| Mark 7:1-8, 14-15, 21-23 | Mark 7:1-8, 14-15, 21-23 | Mark 7:1-8, 14-15, 21-23 |

## Comments on the Lessons

The first reading contains David's charge to Solomon, the record of David's death, and Solomon's ascension to the throne of David. The Deuteronomy reading teaches that obedience to God's law is the condition for life in Canaan and is a witness to the wisdom which the Lord gives his people. The Ephesians reading concludes the readings from this letter. The James passage deals with true religion and the need to be doers of the word and not hearers only. There is consensus on the Markan reading.

## Commentary

### *1 Kings 2:1-4, 10-12 (C)*

In verses 1-4 we have the first example in the book of the editorial work of the first Deuteronomist. Solomon is warned that he must follow the "law of Moses." The alternative is national ruin. David gave Solomon practical advice for securing dynastic stability. The dying charge of David is made up of two distinct sections: (1) the first giving sound advice in the orthodox seventh-century style, and (2) the second giving practical counsel after the fashion of an earlier age which was more brutal in dealings. The two sections are very different in style and temper. In verses 2-4 we have David's charge to piety. It appears that the Deuteronomist inserted many phrases to act as a preface to his whole history of the kings in an attempt to suggest that David was a model Deuteronomic king. David thus becomes the measure by which other kings are judged, and they are judged by how they obey the commands of David.

Briefly, the model king must worship God faithfully in Jerusalem, must reject all immoral cults and have nothing at all to do with any foreign gods. He must care for the poor and oppressed so that God's justice may reign in the land. As long as the kings do this, there will always be an heir of David's throne to rule in Jerusalem. In verse 4 a better translation of "all their soul" is "with all their self." Neither the Old Testament nor New Testaments use "soul" to refer to an immortal part of a person's nature.

In verses 10-12 we have a chronological insertion by the editor to mark the close of David's reign. It is an obituary notice, indicating how long he reigned over Israel, etc., and the fact that he was buried in the city of David and was succeeded by his son Solomon whose kingdom was firmly established.

### *Deuteronomy 4:1-2, 6-8 (L) (RC)*

The words "And now" (v. 1) introduce the second part of the sermon. They begin a section which shows how Israel must work out her salvation in the future with fear and trembling. The preacher has turned in this section from:

1. the past to the present
2. the illustrations to the tasks
3. from the story to the moral

There is a unity to chapter 4 and it belongs to chapters 1-3 in theme. Together, chapters 1-4 provide the introduction to the whole Deuteronomic history. Notice that "the statutes and the ordinances" is frequently used by the Deuteronomic writer to refer to the divinely revealed law. "Teach" here means "what I am about to teach." Israel is commanded to keep the statutes and ordinances and to do them. The ground for Israel's obedience to the law is the uniqueness of Israel among all the nations of the world. Israel is unique in three ways: (1) She possesses a divinely revealed law, (2) her law is more righteous than any other law, and (3) she enjoys the nearness of God which is expressed in the hearing of prayer. (v. 7)

The first and greatest step in a person's religious pilgrimage is to learn to know God, to affirm that God is, and what God is. The second step is to know with certainty what his will is. It was here that Israel found her pride and joy. So great was Israel's love for the law that she has been called "the people of the book."

### Ephesians 6:10-20 (C) (L)

"Be strong in the Lord" or simply "Strength in the Lord" are appropriate titles for this section. This passage is the only significant remnant of Jewish apocalyptic within the theological structure of Ephesians. The language of divine warfare is drawn from Isaiah 59:17ff:

*He put on righteousness as a breastplate, and a helmet of salvation upon his head; he put on garments of vengeance for clothing, and wrapped himself in fury as a mantle. (v. 17)*

A similar description of preparation for divine warfare is found in Wisdom 5:17-20:

*For armour he will take his jealous love, he will arm creation to punish his enemies; he will put on justice as a breastplate, and for helmet wear his undissembling judgments; he will take up invincible holiness for shield, he will forge a biting sword of his stern wrath . . .*

The coming final battle at Armageddon in Revelation may be compared with these passages. The conflict between good and bad angelic powers is the one piece of apocalyptic which can easily be fitted into a Hellenised or "gnostic" doctrine of redemption.

As Paul concludes this exhortation to the Ephesians, it is appropriate that he conclude with words regarding spiritual strength. He urges them to put on the whole armor of God which God supplies and to maintain their vigil of prayer both in their own fight against evil and for the apostolic ministry. Paul thinks of the great struggle which lies in the future. It has been said that life was much more terrifying for the ancients than for us today. They believed the world was filled with evil spirits which were determined to work harm to human beings. So for Paul and his contemporaries the whole world was a battleground. But, in light of the possibility of a nuclear holocaust and the destruction of all living things by that or other means, the future for contemporary persons without God is terrifying. Only faith in God and the conviction that, through Christ's death on the cross, the victory has been finally won over the forces of evil can give the Christian hope and confidence.

Paul was chained by the wrist to a Roman soldier in prison. As Paul (or the Pauline school writer interpreting Paul's experience) looks up at the soldier beside him night and day, the image of the Christian's armor comes to him. So Paul looks at each piece of the Roman soldier's armor and translates it into Christian terms. "Flesh and blood" in verse 12 refers to mere mortal beings. The principalities and hosts of wickedness are the organized forces of evil spirit beings. In verses 13-17 Paul cites the armor which the Christian wears. Notice that the sword is the one offensive weapon mentioned here and refers to the word of God which God speaks through his servants. Continuous prayer is an aid in standing. (vv. 18-20)

The Christian is to put on God's armor because the battle is serious, one not against human beings but against supernatural evil powers. The image of a holy war is found in other ancient religions. Note the pieces of armor:

1. The belt of truth — the soldier's belt girded in his tunic and his sword was suspended from it. It gave him freedom and movement. Even so truth as a belt gives the Christian freedom to move quickly in any situation. The Christian is not bound by the lies he or she has told, but is set free by knowing the truth.

2. The breastplate of righteousness — a righteous life, one made righteous through faith in Christ and lived in right relationship with God in Christ, is impregnable.

3. The sandals indicated one is ready to move. For a Christian the sandals of the Gospel of peace means the Christian is eager to preach the Gospel to those who have never heard it.

4. The shield of faith. Paul uses a word meaning, not the small round shield, but the great oblong shield which the heavily armed soldier wore. The shield of protecting faith defends the soldier against all "the flaming darts of the evil one." Faith is complete and perfect trust in Christ. It is a personal relationship with Christ which protects in all circumstances.

5. "Take" the helmet of salvation. The word "take" means literally "accept." Salvation means not only forgiveness for past sins but is strength to deal with evil in the future.

6. The sword of the spirit which is the Word of God. God's Word is both a weapon of defense and a weapon for attacking the enemy. God's Word in Scripture, in preaching, in Christ, and in the Sacraments equips us for the battle.

7. Finally, the greatest weapon of all is *prayer*. "Pray at all times in the spirit," says Paul. He says three things about prayer here: (1) it must be constant. Too often we pray only in foxholes or on deathbeds. Paul says prayer must be a constant on-going activity of the Christian. (2) Prayer must be intense. It demands concentration. And (3) prayer must be unselfish, prayer not for one's own wants and needs only, but for all the people of God. Paul says to pray for "all the saints." And Paul asks them to pray for him. He asks them to pray, not for his comfort, but that he may be able to witness boldly to the gospel for which he is "an ambassador in chains." He asks that he may be able to declare the gospel boldly as he ought to speak. This suggests that the preacher should ask for the prayers of the congregation she or he serves, for no preacher can be successful without prayer.

*James 1:17-18, 21-22, 27*

The central thrust of this passage is religion that is pure and undefiled. In contrast to the spirituality which is concerned only with devotional exercises and inward piety, the definition of pure religion here is one of visiting orphans and widows in their affliction, and keeping oneself unstained from the world. "Be doers of the word, and not hearers only" (v. 22) carries out this same theme.

James declares that every good endowment and perfect gift comes down from above, from the Father of lights. The Father of lights is the creator of heavenly bodies. In verse 18 James says that God makes us his children through the knowledge of his truth. We are to be a kind of first fruits of his creatures. The first fruits of a harvest were holy and often offered to God.

James urges his readers to "put away" all evil as if it were soiled and old clothing. "The implanted word" is the gospel which has been received and is now growing. It is not enough to merely listen to God's word. True religion is characterized by *obedience* to God. Pure and undefiled religion is one which is characterized by benevolence to those in need and by avoiding the evils of this world. God is Father and elsewhere symbolized as Mother. Such a God receives the worship of God towards his or her needy children.

*Mark 7:1-8, 14-15, 21-23*

In this passage we see the contrasts between the common people who were moved by basic needs, and Jesus' compassion for human suffering set apart from the religious leaders who were concerned with details of ritual. Jesus' controversy with the Pharisees, in this section which is a composite, deals with three issues. The three issues are directed to three different groups:

1. Verses 1-8 deal with the problem of unwashed hands
2. Verses 9-13 treat the Corban vow, and
3. Verses 14-23 deal with the problem of kosher food

Note that while the first two problems are directed to the Pharisees the third is expressed first to the people and then to the disciples. Verse 16 is omitted since most ancient MSS does not have it.

The general unity of the section reflects the early church's problem of loyalty to Jewish customs. The solution is simply freedom from them, which is attributed to Jesus himself. However, Paul deals with the same problem as if it were a new one and seems unaware of the fact that Jesus had already solved it in principle.

In verses 1-8 Mark by his description of Jewish customs seems to imply that his intended readers are Gentiles who need this kind of explanation. It also implies that Mark is probably outside this circle which has firsthand knowledge of the customs discussed, since Mark's explanation is somewhat inaccurate. For example, Mark for whatever reason attributes to "all the Jews" the custom which was one of strict Pharisees only.

A theme word of this whole section is a Greek word meaning "ritually unclean." In classical Greek it means "common" as opposed to "private." The meaning of it as used here would not have been understood by Gentile readers and for this reason Mark explains it in verse 3ff.

Notice how in this section and those before it the conflict between Jesus and the authorities is building up. It is unlikely that verses 1-5 describe an actual investigation of Jesus (the first was in 3:22) since the Jews who did not observe this custom of ritually washing hands were numerous.

The violence of verses 6-7 seems out of proportion to the matter and seems to express the later hostility between church and synagogue as seen from the Christian point of view.

In vv. 14-23 the question of ritually unclean food is described from the viewpoint of the Gentile church for it makes it appear as if the problem is clearly solved.

The key verse is verse 15, and the rest is explanation:

*There is nothing outside a man which by going into him can defile him; but the things which come out of a man are what defile him.*

In verses 21-23 there are various things pointed out which come out of a person. The Greek word in verse 21 for fornication means any kind of sexual vice. Envy here means literally "an evil eye" and may refer either to a common superstition or to a jealous or grudging disposition. Slander is literally "blasphemy," which was a word used of untrue accusations used against either God or persons. The thrust of this section is that what comes out of a person is what makes the person unclean, not what he or she eats, etc.

## Theological Reflections

Instructions for leading the Godly life is a common theme in the readings for this Sunday. David gives instructions to his son Solomon on piety and on securing the dynasty. Solomon is to worship God in Jerusalem, to reject all immoral cults and to have nothing to do with any foreign gods. And he must care for the poor and oppressed (a theme in James also). Deuteronomy describes how Israel must work out her salvation in the future with fear and trembling, following the statutes and ordinances of God. Israel is compelled to do this for she stands in a unique relationship to God possessing the divinely revealed law, a law more righteous than other laws, and she enjoys the nearness of God expressed in prayer. Ephesians gives the reader instructions for preparing for the battle with the evil powers by putting on the armor which God gives. Prayer is the greatest weapon of all, a theme in the Deuteronomy passage also. James describes religion that is pure and undefiled as religion which does acts of charity and which keeps unstained from the evils of the world. James emphasizes the necessity of *doing* rather than merely hearing God's Word. In Mark, Jesus instructs his followers in living the Godly life, pointing out that it is not what goes in a person but what comes *out* that is critical.

## Homiletical Moves

*1 Kings 2:1-4, 10-12 (C)*
### Keep the Charge of the Lord Your God

1. David charges Solomon to be strong and to walk in God's ways, keeping his commandments
2. David reminds Solomon that God has promised to bless him if he is faithful and obedient
3. David died, and Solomon became king and firmly established the kingdom
4. In response to God's love, be strong and walk in God's ways, keeping his commandments

*Deuteronomy 4:1-2, 6-8 (L) (RC)*
### Obey God's Law That You May Live

1. Give heed to and do the statutes and ordinances God gives you, God says to Israel

2. If you Israel are obedient you will live and go in and take possession of the land
3. Obedience to God's law will reveal to other nations that you, Israel, are unique, have a unique law, and are near to God who hears when you pray
4. Come to the God of Israel, obey him, and be assured that God hears you when you pray

*This Preacher's Choice*

*Ephesians 6:10-20 (C) (L)*
## Be Strong in the Lord!

1. Put on the whole armor of God in order to stand against the wiles af the devil
2. We are not battling flesh and blood but principalities, powers and the world rulers of this present darkness, against the spiritual hosts of wickedness in the heavenly places
3. Accept the whole armor of God:
   a. the belt of truth
   b. the breastplate of righteousness
   c. the sandals of the Gospel of peace
   d. the shield of faith
   e. the helmet of salvation
   f. the sword of the Spirit, the Word of God
4. Pray at all times in the Spirit

*James 1:17-18, 21-22, 27 (RC)*
## Be Doers of the Word and Not Hearers Only

1. Every good and perfect gift comes from God
2. God brought us forth as a kind of first fruits of his creatures
3. Put away all evil and receive with meekness the implanted word
4. Be doers of the word
5. Religion that is pure and undefiled is to (1) visit orphans and widows, and (2) to keep oneself unstained from the world

*M... 7:1-8, 14-15, 21-23*
## What Defiles a Person: Garbage Out, Not Garbage In!

1. There is nothing outside a person which by going into the person can defile him or her
2. But the things which come out of a person defile:
   a. evil thoughts
   b. fornication
   c. theft
   d. murder
   e. adultery
   f. coveting
   g. wickedness
   h. deceit
   i. licentiousness
   j. envy
   k. slander
   l. pride
   m. foolishness
3. Hold to the commandments of God, not the traditions of human beings

**Hymn for Pentecost 15:** *God of Our Fathers*

**Prayer**
*Holy God, who has called us to worship you and to abstain from false gods, we confess our sins. We have left your commandments to follow human traditions. We have failed to visit and care for the orphan, widow, and the oppressed near and far. We have failed to accept the armor you offer to enable us to stand firm against the evil forces around us. Forgive us as we claim Christ's death and resurrection for our salvation. Grant that we may put on the whole armor you offer and stand firm against evil. Grant that we may live in freedom from the rules and regulations that humans have devised and rather may follow your commandments. May we be doers of the word and not hearers only. Grant that we may follow your law and thus live in daily communion with you and our God. Amen*

# Proper 18    Pentecost 16    Ordinary Time 23

September 4-10

| Common | Lutheran | Roman Catholic |
|---|---|---|
| Proverbs 2:1-8 | Isaiah 35:4-7a | Isaiah 35:4-7 |
| James 1:17-27 | James 1:17-22 (23-25) 26-27 | James 2:1-5 |
| Mark 7:31-37 | Mark 7:31-37 | Mark 7:31-37 |

## Comments on the Lessons

The Proverbs text is concerned with the fruits of seeking the wisdom that the Lord gives. For those using the (C) lectionary note that Isaiah 35 appears on Advent 3 (A). James 1:17-27 was dealt with in the previous Sunday. James 2:1-5 (RC) concerns servility to the rich and oppression of the poor. There is consensus on the third reading.

## Commentary

*Proverbs 2:1-8 (C)*

The entire second chapter deals with the fruits of the search for wisdom. Pursuing wisdom brings both understanding and morality. Those who possess wisdom have an inner safeguard against bad companions and sexual immorality. The structure of the chapter is: verses 1-4, introduction, with a conclusion in five parts: verses 5-8, verses 9-11, verses 12-15, verses 16-19, and verses 20-22.

The introduction points out that the search for wisdom demands a receptive and expectant attitude. One must be attentive with senses (ear) and reason (heart) and must be actively searching for wisdom. The search for wisdom demands total commitment which sacrifices everything else. Only those who are pure in heart can find wisdom. In verse 1 the "commandments" are a synonyn for wisdom and the means to it. But they cannot be equated here with the laws of Israel's covenant.

The greatest gift of all is "the knowledge of God." (v. 5) The Lord is the source of wisdom and he gives knowledge and understanding. In this text it is impossible to determine if God is synonymous with wisdom in its fullest sense. The metaphors used in this passage show the influence of the rest of the Old Testament. God is affirmed as the giver of wisdom, the protector of those who walk in integrity, the one who preserves the way of his saints. (vv. 7-8)

*Isaiah 35:4-7 (L) (RC)*

This passage along with the preceding chapter describes Zion restored. The combined chapters probably originally belonged to chapters 40-66. The transformation of nature is a prominent feature as is the highway along which God leads his people home to Zion. Just as God's judgment has burned and ruined, so now his redemption makes the desert blossom. God's people see his glory. In order to understand this pericope it must be seen in the context of the verses which precede and follow it.

The despondent (vv.3, 4) should take heart for God is coming to rescue his own. Those who have been blind will see, the deaf will hear, the lame be healed and the dumb will sing for joy. God's broken people will be whole again. This picture of the coming new age came to be associated with the work of the expected Messiah. The reading from Mark 7:31-37 for today tells of Jesus' healing a man who was deaf and had an impediment in his speech, which was a sign that Messiah had arrived in Jesus Christ.

Deutero-Isaiah has more than one prophecy of joy and of the transformation of the desert into a forest. This was an image associated with the first exodus and journey through the desert from Egypt to Canaan. But the coming exodus would be surpassed by the second journey from Babylon to Jerusalem. The desert will now be covered with trees and flowers. (vv. 1-2)

The Jews who had doubted God's power and who were fainthearted will see what is promised to all peoples (40:5), the revelation of "our God." Note that the exclamation "Behold your God!"

s a quotation from 40:9. The phrase "vengeance comes" brings to mind 43:8a. In this way the prophecy against Edom is linked with the prophecy of salvation.

Beginning with verse 5 the instruction to the messengers and the promise of salvation is concluded, and now the author is once again speaking to the reader. In verse 6 there is something new and original. We cannot be sure how the author intended verses 5, 6 to be interpreted. Was he thinking only of bodily healing or also of liberation from prison? And could it be a prison of spiritual blindness? There is rejoicing at both the beginning and the ending of this first train of thought. (vv. 1-6) It can be assumed that it is joy in God, although this is not explicit.

In verses 6b-10 our attention is turned again to the desert with the assurance that it will be full of water and no longer hold the terrors for travelers it held in the past. The writer assures the people that there will not be lions or jackals or other dangerous beasts along the highway to Zion. Along this highway (v. 8) God has prepared will travel the redeemed of God. They have been set free by his coming and his revenge upon the nations. Instead of fear and weakness there will now be joy and gladness. For sorrow and sighing shall flee away. (v. 10)

### James 2:1-5 (RC)

The thrust of this passage is that God shows no partiality, therefore the Christian must not show partiality but treat all persons equally. In verse 2 the word translated "assembly" means literally "synagogue," which was where the early church had its roots. For parallel passages dealing with God's special concern for the poor in this world see Luke 6:20, and 1 Corinthians 1:26-29. The 1 Corinthian passage says:

*For consider your call, brethren, not many of you were wise according to worldly standards, not many were powerful, not many were of noble birth; but God chose what is foolish in the world to shame the wise, God chose what is weak in the world to shame the strong, God chose what is low and despised in the world, even things that are not, to bring to nothing things that are, so that no human being might boast in the presence of God.*

There is no place for class distinctions in the church, since Christ himself humbled himself and took the form of a servant. (Philippians 2:5ff) To show partiality is to reveal that a person is divided in mind, like the judges who give unjust and corrupt decisions. God has chosen the rich in faith, not the rich in material goods, to be the heirs of his kingdom. The rich, on the other hand, were often the oppressors of the poor who dragged their debtors into court. (v. 6) They filed vexatious lawsuits and blaspheme the "name." (v. 7) Those rich who are referred to here were not necessarily Jews or Christians or even doers of such injustice, but they were members of the same class.

In a global village in which the gap between the "haves" and "have nots" is growing at an increasing pace this passage has particular relevance. Down through the ages the church often has been captive of the rich and powerful, and all too often on the side of the "haves" against the "have nots." Special seats for the land owners were provided in Scottish churches in the balcony, while the common folk sat down below. In slavery days in America, Blacks were relegated to the slave gallery in the balcony. When churches were supported by pew rents, the rich obviously were able to rent the better seats and leave the poor to less desirable seating or to stand. The church often sides with the rich owners against the poor workers, and management against labor. The church today must examine itself to discern where it is continuing to discriminate against the poor and show partiality toward the rich.

### Mark 7:31-37

The route which Jesus took described here is circuitous, since Jesus went northward from Tyre to Sidon and then south-eastward past Caesarea Philippi and through Philip's territory to reach a place on the eastern shore of the Sea of Galilee in the territory of the Decapolis. Some think Jesus was still avoiding the territory of Antipas.

The miracle described by Mark is peculiar to Mark. Matthew knew of it but omitted it, some think because it seemed magical. There are parallels to the miracle of healing the deaf-mute man in Jewish and pagan sources.

The man brought to Jesus was deaf and had an impediment in his speech. The Greek word used to describe him means "blunt" or "dull" and thus can mean both deaf and dumb, and can also be used with regard to sight or intelligence. Here it means deaf. Some think he stuttered. They asked Jesus to lay hands on him, a common way of healing. Notice that Jesus took the man aside from the multitude to be in private. Jesus put his fingers into his ears. He spat and touched his tongue. Saliva was believed to have curative powers in the ancient world. Then Jesus looked up to heaven, sighed, and spoke to the man. Looking to heaven and sighing were, like laying on of hands and using saliva, common gestures used in healing. The sighing of Jesus indicates the strong emotion of Jesus as he wages war against the power of Satan which caused the impairments, and so he seeks divine aid in urgent prayer. Jesus then said to the man "Ephphatha" that is "Be opened." And at once the man's ears were opened and his tongue was released and he heard and spoke. The word Jesus spoke could also mean "be released" as well as "be opened." Jesus' command to the man shatters the fetters by which he had been bound by Satan. The man who had been shut up by deafness and impairment of speech is now being released by the power of God working through Jesus. Note that verse 35 implies that the man had an impairment of speech, perhaps stuttering, rather than being unable to speak at all.

Next Jesus charged the people to tell no one of the miracle, but the more he charged them the more they told it! Jesus was up against a kind of "Murphy's Law" in which the more he tried to prevent the Messianic secret from being told the more those around him told it!

The people were amazed exceedingly. They commented to one another, "He has done all things well; he even makes the deaf hear and the dumb speak." (v. 37) This healing forms a pair with Mark 8:22-26. We see that 7:31-37 concludes the complex containing the Feeding of the Five Thousand, and that 8:22-26 concludes that containing the Feeding of Four Thousand. One thing which both miracles have in common is the fact that in both the cure was accomplished with difficulty and not instantaneously. Both concern miracles which figure in Isaiah 35:5f which is the Old Testament reading today for (L) (RC). Mark seems to have regarded these miracles as a pair.

Mark seems to imply more than just the healing of one man who was deaf and dumb by this miracle. Mark is saying that true faith and all true confession of Christ is a miracle. Note that the ears were healed first, and then the tongue, which is a reminder that it is only as the Church *hears* the Word of God that it has a message to speak! The miracle has eschatological significance. It leads up to the christological confession of Peter in 8:29 and then corrected in 8:33.

We are not told whether or not the man who was healed followed Jesus or not. But the fact is that Jesus met his needs and in doing so revealed his own glory, and this is absolutely clear.

### Theological Reflections

The reading from Proverbs deals with the search for Wisdom and the fruits of such a search. It brings both understanding and morality, and the greatest gift of all, the knowledge of God. The Isaiah passage describes Zion restored. The healings mentioned foreshadow the healing by Jesus in Mark of the man who was deaf and dumb. These indicate God's power overcoming Satan and point forward to the eschaton when evil will be completely destroyed. The passage from James 2:1-5 tells us that God does not show partiality toward people and therefore neither should we favor the rich or put down the poor. Rather God has chosen the poor in the world to be rich in faith and heirs of the kingdom. Mark's miracle story has overtones beyond the healing of man who was deaf and dumb, in that it points to the Church's need to hear God's Word and then speak that message to the world. It has an eschatological thrust as it points to the coming age when Satan will be defeated.

### Homiletical Moves

*Proverbs 2:1-8 (C)*
### The Fruits of Seeking Wisdom

1. If you seek wisdom and understanding with all your might, then you will understand the fear of the Lord and find the knowledge of God
2. For the Lord gives wisdom, knowledge and understanding
3. The Lord is a shield to those who walk in integrity, guarding the paths of justice and preserving the way of his saints
4. Therefore, seek wisdom from God and he will give you wisdom and guard your ways

*Isaiah 35:4-7 (L) RC)*
### God Will Come and Save You

1. Say to those who are fearful, "Be strong, fear not!"

2. Behold your God, he will come and save you
3. The blind, deaf, lame and dumb will be healed and sing for joy
4. God will make the waters break forth in the wilderness, and streams in the desert
5. Trust in God who has come and saved you in Christ, therefore sing for joy

*James 2-1-5*
## God Shows No Partiality

1. Do not show servility to the rich or put down the poor
2. Do not make distinctions among yourselves and become judges with evil thoughts
3. God has chosen the poor in the world to be rich in faith and heirs of the kingdom promised to those who love him

*This Preacher's Choice*

*Mark 7:31-37*
## Jesus Even Makes the Deaf Hear and the Dumb Speak!

1. A man is brought to Jesus who is deaf and has an impediment of speech
2. Jesus takes him aside from the crowd to heal him
3. Jesus put his fingers in his ears, spat and touched his tongue, looked up to heaven, sighed and said to the man "Be opened"
4. The man's ears were opened and his tongue was released
5. The people were astonished exceedingly and said, "he even makes the deaf hear and the dumb speak"
6. Believe in Christ who can make you whole

**Hymn for Pentecost 16:**   *O For a Thousand Tongues to Sing*

**Prayer**

*O God, we seek for wisdom, knowledge and understanding with all our might. We seek to know you more fully. In this time of seeking we ask that you reveal yourself to us that we may have true wisdom. When you come to us we shall say with the people of God of old, "Behold your God!"*

*O God of healing, heal our deaf ears that we may hear you speak to us. Release our bound tongues that we may sing and speak your praises. We sing, "O for a thousand tongues to sing" and ask that you enable each of us to use the tongue we have to speak your message of love to the world.*

*Forgive us when we have shown partiality toward the rich and have put down the poor. Help us to see all people as you see them and to know that the ground is level at the foot of the cross. May we be among those who love you, who are rich not in worldly goods but in spiritual faith and who are heirs of your kingdom. Amen*

# Proper 19

September 11-17

# Pentecost 17

# Ordinary Time 24

| **Common** | **Lutheran** | **Roman Catholic** |
|---|---|---|
| Proverbs 22:1-2, 8-9 | Isaiah 50:4-10 | Isaiah 50:4-9 |
| James 2:1-5, 8-10, 14-18 | James 2:1-5, 8-10, 14-18 | James 2:14-18 |
| Mark 8:27-38 | Mark 8:27-35 | Mark 8:27-35 |

## Comments on the Lessons

The reading from Proverbs lifts up the value of a good name and the virtue of sharing with others. In (C) the Isaiah reading appears at Lent 6, but in (L) and (RC) here. Isaiah 50:4-11 is the third Servant Song. The Servant brings God's comfort to his fellow Israelites but he is treated despicably. James 2:1-5 was dealt with in the previous Sunday's reading (RC). But verses 8-10 and 14-18 are additional. There is virtual consensus on the Markan reading, but (C) elects to extend the reading through verse 38, since the Proverbs reading is short.

## Commentary

*Proverbs 22:1-2, 8-9 (C)*

Proverbs 10:1—22:16 is attributed to Solomon. Any proverb written by Solomon would have been composed by 931 B.C. The book came into its present form about 350 B.C. Classified as Wisdom literature, the book deals in practical matters of living. They were transmitted from parent to child, scholar to scholar, friend to friend and, over the years, were gradually refined and sharpened and compiled into the present collection.

Solomon stresses the greater value of a good name, reflecting ethical behavior, over against riches. And he says that favor or goodwill is better than silver or gold. In the money economy of capitalist America, with the emphasis on the ''bottom line'' rather than moral decisions and ethical behavior, these words of Solomon are particularly relevant. Youth must be trained in value judgments and taught that ethical behavior is far more valuable than dollars, in spite of the message of mass media to the contrary.

Solomon warns that the person who sows injustice will reap calamity. We are seeing this on an international scale, as the injustices against Third World Nations results in calamity not only for them but for the world village. The world economy links the peoples and nations of the world together like mountain climbers tied together on the same rope. If one falls, all may be pulled down too.

But the person who is generous toward the poor and who is bountiful will be blessed. The God of the Bible takes up the cause of the poor over against the rich who oppress them. The person who is bountiful toward the poor will be blessed by God. This verse reminds us of the Beatitudes of Jesus in which he describes what the blessed life of the Kingdom is like.

Notice that verse 1 is not a polemic against wealth but rather seeks to develop a framework of values within which material wealth can make its contribution to a full life. Otherwise wealth may be a snare and delusion. Thus reputation is to be preferred over great wealth, and engaging personal qualities are to be valued more highly than silver or gold.

In verse 8 we have a typical expression of the doctrine of theodicy — the person who sows iniquity will reap evil.

A person with a keen social conscience and concern for the poor is commended in verse 9, as this concern reveals itself in practical expression. The paradox in this verse is the fact that, because the benevolent person does not live to himself or herself and is not a prisoner of selfish desires and ambitions, that person achieves the highest degree of self-fulfillment. True blessedness is not to be found in going all out for self, with no concern for neighbor and the neighbor's well-being. The blessed person is the one who sees the brother or sister as one for whom he or she is responsible and who does acts of mercy for them. Such a person sees the world as a global village and shares bread with the person in need.

*Isaiah 50:4-10 (L)*
*Isaiah 50:4-9 (RC)*

This third Servant Song of Isaiah is a song of faith sung by those who have learned the meaning of Israel's tragic history through prophecy. It expresses the experience of the Israelites in exile who have ears to hear, who submit with understanding to the humiliation of the Exile and wait expectantly for God's coming act of redemption, which they are confident is near at hand. The Hebrew thought moved easily from the individual to the group, even as Americans refer to Uncle Sam as an individual representing the people of the whole nation. This Song seems to have been composed by an Israelite to be sung by faithful exiles as an act of trust and belief. Notice that it is intensely individual in character. It probably was used in worship in which the individual exile would embody in himself or herself the experience of Israel. By singing the song in the assembly the Israelite identifies with the "servant."

Of all the Deutero-Isaiah servant songs this is probably the easiest to understand. It has been generally accepted as an individual lament in form. But it can more accurately be called an individual psalm of confidence. The thrust of verse 7ff is a broad development of the main two motifs of the psalm: (1) the confession of confidence in God, and (2) the certainty of being answered. But verses 4-5a have nothing to do with an individual lament. Notice that the one who confesses unshakable confidence in God in verses 5b-9 is the same one who is commissioned with an office of the word. So verses 4-9 are the confession of confidence spoken by one who is mediator of the word.

Turning to verse 4 we see that it and the first clause of verse 5 is the utterance of a person whose being is governed by hearing and speaking. This person is like a disciple, meaning that in both hearing and speaking the person is concentrated on God and the hearing and speaking have their source in God. God opens the disciple's ears to hear. God tells the disciple what to speak. The Servant has been awakened and aroused in order to hear God's word. It is a word to the prostrate, to Israel who is not in a position to hear the word. Thus the people Israel, like the Servant, must be aroused before she can hear the word that applies to her case.

In verses 4-5b we have the call of one who in verses 5b-9 attests his faith in the office committed to him. Notice that the Servant is entirely unable to exercise any control over the reception and transmission of a word that has no establishment in which it is at home. This is the chief characteristic of the prophetic office here. A second distinctive feature of the prophetic office is that God's servant is here described as God's "disciple." The fact that God's servant is God's disciple is the most important feature in the picture of the servant here.

The Servant who is attacked and defamed because of his task develops in this song for the first time a new approach: he *assents* and *accepts* this suffering. The Servant believes God himself wills his suffering and its acceptance. Notice the glaring contradiction between verse 6 and verse 7. "Shame" and "ashamed" appear. God makes the servant's face like a flint. The power of his resistance derives from his acceptance of the blows and shameful treatment which he meets. Note that it is this complete acceptance and it alone that enables him to make his face hard as flint rock.

In verses 8-9 we find the certainty that the Servant feels that God is on his side expressed in a very forceful way by means of terms taken from the legal process. We can only understand this by seeing it from his opponent's point of view. In their eyes the contest is already decided and the Servant's case is lost, since he has admitted defeat by accepting the blows and acts of shame. The Servant summons those who oppose him, however. These are the people who smite him and shame him and spit upon him. He calls them into God's law court for he is convinced that God justifies him and that no one can condemn him.

In verse 9 the Servant declares and asks, "Behold, the Lord God helps me; who will declare me guilty?" He believes that those who mock and smite him will perish. But the question of whether there is the slightest possibility of any justification or rehabilitation for the Servant according to verses 4-9 is left open. The question points forward to the final servant song.

*James 2:1-5, 8-10, 14-18 (C) (L)*
*James 2:14-18 (RC)*

These verses will be considered together. Note that verses 1-5 were discussed in the previous Sunday's readings for (RC) and so will not be dealt with again here.

The thrust of these passages is living the Christian faith in practical matters such as respect due the poor and deeds of mercy to those in need. God shows no partiality and neither should the disciple. In verses 1-13 there is the theme of sin of deference toward the rich. There is not a sustained argument, but rather a loosely connected group of reproaches, which were written down apparently as they came to the mind of the author. The Christian faith has as its object our Lord Jesus Christ who ascended to heaven and reigns in heavenly glory.

After a digression in verses 5-7 the author returns in verses 8-9 to the theme of verses 2-4. In verse 8 an objector offers an excuse for favoring the rich by quoting the commandment to love your neighbor as yourself. But the answer given to this excuse is that such behavior would be praiseworthy if it were true, but they do not show the same attention to the poor that they show the rich. And, in so favoring the rich, they are not loving the poor neighbor as oneself, and thus are breaking the commandment. Thus they are transgressors of the law and rebellious against God.

The theme of faith versus works is taken up in verses 14-18 with the concrete example of expressing genuine faith by doing works of mercy to those in need. James has misunderstood the Apostle Paul in pitting faith over against works, since for Paul faith was no intellectual acceptance of monotheism which demons could share with believers. Rather, for Paul faith was self-surrender of the whole person to God, a surrender which cannot be "dead" or without moral actions in daily living.

The polemic here is not against genuine Pauline theology, but rather against a distortion of what Paul taught, and even Paul rejected such a distortion.

We find in verses 14-17 a little parable which has its application in verse 17: "So faith by itself, if it has no works, is dead." "Be warmed" (v. 16) is by proper warm clothing. The arguments in verses 18-19 disregard verses 15-17 altogether. The opening word of verse 18 "But" looks back to verse 14 and is a contrast to the "faith-not-works" false doctrine the author is refuting. We must take verse 18 as a unit. He says works can be shown and the works reveal true faith which underlie them. The writer assumes that both he and his readers are Christians. Thus he is not thinking of the possible value of good works performed by unbelievers.

*Mark 8:27-38 (C)*
*Mark 8:27-35 (L) (RC)*

This section stands at the opening of a new division of the Gospel. In the first division we heard a series of deeds and incidents in the life of Jesus which raise the question: "Who then is this, that even wind and sea obey him?" (4:41) The question may be expanded to, "Who is this that can do such amazing things?" Jesus by his ministry had raised the question so clearly that even ordinary people who were not disciples asked the question and answered it by saying that he must be some very great figure. But the real answer to the question posed by Jesus is "You are the Christ (Messiah)" which Peter answered for the disciples. These words express the Christian understanding of Jesus.

While we might expect such an answer to be met with an enthusiastic response by Jesus this is not the case here, although he does in Matthew's account. (19:17) But according to Mark, Jesus' reaction to the confession is ambiguous. He charges them to tell no one about him. Here is the Messianic secret of Mark's theology. But this is a tacit acceptance of their description of who he is. But notice how carefully Jesus avoids calling himself Messiah. There was some sense in which Jesus did not want to be known as Messiah. The word for charged (v. 30) has in Greek the normal meaning of "rebuke" which suggests that there is a hint of censure in Jesus' reply to Peter, and perhaps even displeasure.

The reason Jesus rejected the title of Messiah becomes clear when we understand that the general agreement at that time about Messiah was that he would accomplish his work by the possession of and exercise of brute force in one form or another. This concept of Messiah was one who would achieve his victory without suffering and defeat.

For this reason Jesus outlines the kind of Messiah he has come to earth to be, referring to himself by the usual term "Son of man." The Son of man must:

1. suffer many things, and
2. be rejected by the elders and the chief priests and the scribes, and
3. be killed, and
4. after three days rise again. (v. 31)

Clearly such a route to fulfilling his mission on earth was shocking to Peter and the disciples. Peter took Jesus and began to rebuke him. But Jesus replied, "Get behind me, Satan! For you are not on the side of God, but of men." (v. 33)

This encounter and the Great Confession lead up to the radical teaching about discipleship in 8:34—9:1. Jesus says that anyone who would come after him, must deny himself, and take up his cross and follow him. The Romans forced a condemned criminal to carry part of the cross to the place of execution, hence the metaphor. The present formulation of words of the saying may be the work of the early Church as it looked back on Jesus' crucifixion. Jesus then states a paradox: whoever would save his life will lose it; and whoever loses his life for my sake and the gospel's will save it. (v. 35) Then Jesus asks what gain is it to have the whole world but lose one's own soul. And he warns that whoever is ashamed of him and his words in this adulterous (perhaps a metaphor for idolatrous) generation of him will the Son of man be ashamed in the Parousia when the Son of man returns in glory at the End of the Age.

## Theological Reflections

Both Proverbs and James give practical advice for living a Godly life. In Proverbs Solomon seeks to develop a framework of values in which material wealth can make its contribution to a full life. He stresses the importance of a good reputation and engaging personal qualities over against wealth. James stresses showing no partiality toward the rich but treating all people the same. And James deals with the faith versus works issue by showing that good works reveal true faith which motivates them. Isaiah gives a third Servant Song in which the servant accepts suffering as part of his role in hearing and speaking God's message to weary Israel. He expresses confidence in God who vindicates him before his enemies. In Mark's gospel Peter confesses the disciples' faith that Jesus is the Christ. Jesus corrects their misunderstanding of who Messiah is and what he must undergo in fulfilling his mission. Then he spells out the radical demands of Christian discipleship which call for denying self, taking up one's cross and following Jesus. The paradox of finding one's life by losing it is described. And Jesus warns that those who are ashamed of him now he will be ashamed of when he returns in his glory.

## Homiletical Moves

*Proverbs 22:1-2, 8-9*
### Reputation Versus Riches

1. A good name is preferable to great riches
2. Engaging personal qualities are valued more than silver and gold
3. The bountiful person who shares bread with the poor is blessed
4. Therefore, live a godly life, sharing with the poor

*Isaiah 50:4-10*
### Confidence in the Lord

1. God wakens the ear of the prophet/Servant to hear his word
2. The Servant submits to shame and abuse without rebelling
3. Because the Servant accepts suffering his face is set like a flint
4. The Lord helps the Servant who is God's disciple, so who will declare him guilty?
5. The Servant knows he will not be put to shame for God is near
6. Trust in Christ, God's Suffering Servant, who accepted suffering and death for us that we might be forgiven of sin

*James 2:1-5, 8-10, 14-18 (C) (L)*
*James 2:14-18 (RC)*
### Works That Prove Faith Is Real

1. Show no partiality as you hold the faith
2. Give to the poor who lack food and clothing as an expression of faith
3. Works in the Christian faith are an expression of genuine faith
4. Therefore, express your faith by doing good works in response to God's love in Christ

*This Preacher's Choice*

*Mark 8:27-38 (C)*
*Mark 8:27-35 (L) (RC)*
### You Are the Christ!

1. Peter confesses for the disciples that Jesus is the Christ (Messiah)
2. Jesus charges them to tell no one about him being Messiah

3. Jesus describes what he must undergo in fulfilling his mission: suffering, death, and resurrection
4. Jesus outlines discipleship as (1) denying self, (2) taking up cross, and (3) following him
5. Whoever is ashamed of the Son of man now, the Son of man will be ashamed of when he returns in his glory at the End of the Age
6. Therefore, witness boldly for Christ now by denying self, taking up your cross and following him

**Hymn For Pentecost 17:**  *In the Cross of Christ I Glory*

**Prayer**

*Almighty God whose love enfolds us like a mother holding a baby in her bosom, we thank you for all your tender mercies. Grant that we may always so live that our reputation will reflect that we are your disciples, and that we put goodwill and reputation above silver and gold. May we express our faith in good works of mercy toward those in need. Forgive us when we have shown partiality toward the rich and oppressed the poor. Grant that we, with Peter and the disciples, may always give a good confession of Jesus as the Messiah who was crucified for our sins and raised for our salvation. May we daily die to sin, take up our cross, and follow him who loved us and gave himself up for us. Amen*

# Proper 20     Pentecost 18     Ordinary Time 25

September 18-24

| Common | Lutheran | Roman Catholic |
| --- | --- | --- |
| Job 28:20-28 | Jeremiah 11:18-20 | Wisdom 2:12, 17-20 |
| James 3:13-18 | James 3:16—4:6 | James 3:16—4:3 |
| Mark 9:30-37 | Mark 9:30-37 | Mark 9:30-37 |

## Comments on the Lessons

Job 28:20-28 gives the central statement of Wisdom. The Jeremiah passage is Jeremiah's first personal lament and contains an account of a plot against his life. Wisdom 2 uses language which suggested to the early church the circumstances of Jesus' crucifixion. The James 3:13-18 (C) reading omits verses from the next chapter since they introduce a new subject. The theme is wisdom from above. James 4:1-6 deals with the source of war in the passions. There is consensus on the Markan reading which deals with Jesus' foretelling his passion, and with true greatness.

## Commentary

### Job 28:20-28 (C)

Scholars are generally agreed that Job 28 does not properly belong to the discourses of Job. It is not written in his style or connected with the Joban context. The theme is wisdom and verses 1-13 say that man digs in the ground but cannot find wisdom, and the deep and the sea do not know wisdom (vv. 14-22), and that only God understands the way to wisdom. (vv. 23-28)

This passage has been called one of the most impressive bits of literature in all of the Old Testament. This poem about wisdom and where to find her speaks to the modern person who seeks wisdom in intellectual pursuits and scientific knowledge. Wisdom is hidden from those who seek her in the physical world (v. 21) and even from the deities of the underworld. (v. 22) Religious techniques and science and technology cannot supply answers to the search for wisdom.

God alone knows the way to wisdom, says the poet. (v. 23) Wisdom is the supreme possession of God. But the poet does not say that God created wisdom. Rather he insists that God at the moment of his creative activity took note of Wisdom. (vv. 23-28) The hymn originally ended at verse 27 say some commentators. Up to this point, the kind of wisdom dealt with is a metaphysical type which is forever beyond human beings. But in verse 28 the practical wisdom referred to is a way of life fully accessible to humans, which is summed up in (1) the fear of the Lord, and (2) to depart from evil.

The question of the whole book of Job is, "How can a person truly fear God the Creator and truly depart from evil?" This remains unanswered. Human beings are unable to discover wisdom precisely because its price — the perfect fulfillment of the law — is beyond the reach of human beings.

### Jeremiah 11:18-20 (L)

This first of Jeremiah's personal laments tells of an assassination plot against him. This is the first of six personal laments of Jeremiah. He learns that he is the unwitting object (gentle lamb) of a plot against his life, and so prays to God who knows all to protect him. (v. 20) This lament wrestles with the problem of theodicy, the justice of God. Jeremiah affirms such justice (12:1) but then mentions evidence that makes this idea problematic, such as why the wicked prosper, the wicked who made a plot on his life. The central thrust in this first lament (11:18—12:6) is Jeremiah's impression that evil thrives on earth precisely because God is negligent or capricious.

### Wisdom 2:12, 17-20 (RC)

These verses use language that suggested to the early church the circumstances of Jesus' crucifixion: "Let us lie in wait for the virtuous man," "if the virtuous man is God's son, God will take his part," "let us test him with cruelty and torture," "let us condemn him to a shameful death." The preacher who develops this passage for a sermon will find parallels in the accounts of Jesus' trial and crucifixion. These verses from Wisdom add meaning to the crucifixion accounts and may be called up in a sermon on the crucifixion. But with the crucifixion must also be proclaimed the good news of the resurrection of Jesus on the third day and the meaning of both crucifixion and resurrection for Christian living today. Thus this text, like all texts before the cross and resurrection, must be interpreted in light of God's mighty acts of salvation in Jesus Christ.

*James 3:13-18 (C)*
*James 3:16—4:6 (L)*
*James 3:16—4:3 (RC)*

The James readings overlap and will be dealt with in two sections: 3:13-18, and 4:1-6.

*James 3:13-18*

The thrust of this passage is true wisdom which is not a human achievement but is from God and reveals itself in a good life. The earlier part of this chapter (vv. 1-12) points out the two besetting sins of the teacher and rebukes them, namely intemperate speech, and arrogance. True wisdom is revealed in works, in daily actions and not in philosophical speculation. But where there is bitterness and rivalry the boastful pretence to wisdom is a sham. Such wisdom, says James, is not from God in heaven above, but is earthly, unspiritual, devilish. (v. 15)

One of the marks of true wisdom is gentleness to the opinions and even the faults of others. Meekness gives a wrong sense in modern English, but in Elizabethan English "meek" and "gentle" were used as synonymns.

In sharp contrast to the disorder produced by false, human wisdom is the divine wisdom from above. The author describes the results of true wisdom in eight terms. This listing of items is a procedure from Hellenistic teachers of rhetoric and ethics who made their pupils memorize lists of virtues or vices to be used in moral instruction. Such instruction had as its goal good conduct and the avoidance of evil. Such lists are not found in the Old Testament, but were adapted for Jewish use in Hellenistic Judaism. In the Greek this list is arranged partly by alliteration: five of the terms begin with epsilon, and three with alpha, two letters of the Greek alphabet. Notice that this is not a general list of moral virtues but is a list of terms relevant to the theme of wisdom. True wisdom is:

*1. Pure.* It is unmixed with evil. This is the basic quality underlying the other items that follow.

*2. Peaceable.* It doesn't cause disorder, in contrast to false wisdom which does. (v. 16)

*3. Gentle.* It respects the feelings of others.

*4. Open to reason.* It is not locked into a position like the person who said, "I know what I believe, don't confuse me with facts!"

*5. Full of mercy.* Mercy toward those who are in the wrong, which seeks to win them back to the truth.

*6. Producing good fruits.* True wisdom produces good fruits in daily living.

7. Without uncertainty. This is single-minded, aiming for the truth.

*8. Without insincerity, or hypocrisy.* This is similar to the former item, but the emphasis is on the moral rather than intellectual aspect of wisdom.

In verse 18 we have the climax to this passage, which says that the purpose of life is to find righteousness. Righteousness not only in one's self but also in one's relationship to others, thus helping them to find righteousness also. Those who make peace will sow in peace and reap the harvest of righteousness.

*James 4:1-6*

Here are listed wrongful desires, in contrast to the virtues of true wisdom just mentioned. Note here that war is set in direct contrast to peace of 3:18. In the previous section the special harm done by false wisdom is described, but here James points out the far greater harm done by wrongful desires in general.

This section lacks unity. The opening verses 1:-2b do not seem appropriate for Christian readers. Wars and fightings are not just quarrels and disputes within the community of faith, but refers to literal wars waged which result in killings. The prophets saw the covenant as a marriage between God and Israel and verse 4 condemns the unfaithful as covenant breakers who have made friends with the world and thus enmity with God. The writer sees the passions of desire, a Stoic cardinal vice, and passions (lusts) as the basis for wars, fightings and killings.

The origin of the quote in verse 5 is not known. There is no such text in the Old Testament or other Jewish writing that has survived. In verse 6 the main thought seems to be that God who yearns for every human being gives more grace or special help to those fitted to receive it by their humility. He quotes Psalm 3:34. See also 1 Peter 5:5. The main thrust of verses 5 and 6 is to point out the deadly evil of unlawful pleasures and desires and to help the reader to overcome them.

## Mark 9:30-37

As in the previous James reading we have two separate sections here: verses 30-32 deal with the foretelling of Jesus' Passion for the second time, and verses 33-37 deal with true greatness.

*Section verses 30-32*

This second prediction of Jesus' passion is shorter than the first (8:31-33) and has no reference to suffering or rejection specifically. It is not only the briefest but may be the oldest, and in one sense is the most sweeping of the three. (See Mark 10:33-34) Here Mark quotes Jesus saying, "The Son of man will be delivered into the hands of men, and they will kill him . . ." (v. 31) This indicates that Jesus must suffer at the hands of representatives of the whole human race! All human beings are implicated in the death of the One who died for all human beings. Thus, to the questions of the spiritual, "Were you there when they crucified my Lord?" we all must answer, "Yes, I was there. My sins helped nail him to the cross." Jesus wants privacy with the disciples in order to give them further instructions. Notice that Jesus refers to "delivering into" for the first time. Some see this as a reference to the treachery of Judas. But it more likely refers to the "delivering up" of the counsel of God (Acts 2:23 and Romans 8:32). The disciples fail to understand because they are still thinking in terms of the coventional Messiah who will take over by force to bring in the rule of God.

Notice that the response of the disciples was that they did not understand Jesus and were afraid to ask him. But Luke 9:45 excuses them, and Matthew 17:23 omits any mention of the misunderstanding.

*Section verses 33-37*

True greatness is the thrust of this passage. Note in verse 37 that "in my name" means "because of who I am by my very nature." In this passage the action builds by two stages to the climactic saying of the section. The mention of Capernaum brings the disciples and Jesus back home "in the house." We should be alert to special instructions Jesus will give the disciples.

In the first stage verses 33-34 Jesus asks for an explanation of what they had been discussing on the way. But the disciples were silent. The word for "discuss" here means private remarks or asides not intended to be overheard. The disciples are struck dumb, for they recognize the sharp difference between Jesus' denial of self (8:31-34) and their desire for self-promotion as they argue about who will be the greatest. The disciples have more than a mere intellectual misunderstanding about life in the Kingdom of God. They have followed him only outwardly and have missed the essence of his message. So Jesus challenges them at a key point — the real meaning of true greatness.

In the second stage of verses 35-37 we have the climactic saying of "If any one would be first, he must be last of all and servant of all." (v. 35) See how this second stage is introduced by a three-fold formula: (1) he sat down, which indicates formal teaching, (2) and called the twelve, which focuses the teaching on the leaders of the disciples, and (3) "he said to them," which introduces the climatic saying of ''If any one . . .''

The saying about the first and the last is a reversal of the world's values and a signficant advance over the instruction in the first passion prediction of 8:34—9:1. The measure of greatness by lowly service is a characteristic of Jesus who said he came '' not to be served but to serve, and to give his life as a ransom for many.'' (Matthew 20:28) Even as service was characteristic of Jesus, so it runs counter to the world and its values.

Jesus reinforces his teaching on true greatness by an acted parable in which he took a child, put him or her in the midst of them (the Greek leaves uncertain the age and sex of the child), and taking the child in his arms, or putting his arms around the child, he spoke to the twelve. Children were held in low esteem in the Greco-Roman world, so Jesus' gesture is even more striking. We should note that the word used here for ''child'' in the Greek is the same used of the suffering servant in the Greek version of Isaiah 53:2 ''We heralded him as a child.'' Those who read this story as it circulated in the early church would see Jesus identifying himself as the lowliest, least and servant of all as he embraced the child.

While we might expect Jesus to exhort the twelve to be like children, which is what Matthew 18:3 records, Mark shifts the argument at verse 37 from being lowly like a child to urging the twelve to receive a child in the name of Jesus. We should note that Mark uses ''receive,'' ''child,'' and ''in my name'' as catchwords to attach the following series of loosely connected sayings to the second passion prediction of 9:30-32. This linking passage gives a blessing to all who work with and care for children. However, ''child'' applies to anyone who has need of help and is applied especially to new disciples, as the verses which follow make clear.

## Theological Reflections

Wisdom is praised in Job as a virtue which only God can give for only he knows the place it is found. Wisdom is found in the fear of God and departing from evil. James contrasts wisdom from earth with wisdom from heaven and shows that God's gift of wisdom leads to a life of righteousness and peace. The second section of the James reading focuses on passions and desire as the underlying cause of wars and killing. There is a kind of wisdom in the saying that God oppposes the proud, but gives grace to the humble. (4:6) The Jeremiah reading is his first personal lament and tells of the plot against Jeremiah's life. He prays to God for protection and he commits his cause to God. Mark gives the account of the second prediction of his passion which Jesus gives the disciples. They misunderstand what he is saying for their concept of Messiah is radically different from his and does not include suffering, death and resurrection. Then Jesus imparts wisdom to them as he describes true greatness in terms of being the servant of all. Then he acts out a parable with a child and blesses all who work with and care for ''children,'' not only children as young people, but anyone who has need of help and especially new disciples who are ''children in the faith.'' This, too, is divine wisdom about the nature of life in the Kingdom.

## Homiletical Moves

*Job 28:20-28 (C)*
### Whence Comes Wisdom?

1. Wisdom is hidden from the eyes of all living, and even cannot be found in the deities of the underworld
2. Only God knows the way to wisdom
3. Wisdom consists of the fear of the Lord and departing from evil
4. Choose wisdom and live in fear of the Lord always

*Jeremiah 11:18-20 (L)*
### Like a Lamb Led to the Slaughter

1. Jeremiah's enemies conspire against his life
2. He felt like a gentle lamb led to the slaughter
3. Jeremiah prays for God's vengeance on his enemies as he commits his cause to God
4. Commit your life to God as you offer yourself on the altar of service knowing he will care for you

*Wisdom 2:12, 17-20 (RC)*
## The Testing of a Virtuous Person

1. The virtuous man annoys the wicked and oppresses the way of life of the wicked
2. The wicked set out to test the righteous man with cruelty and torture, and even condemn him to a shameful death
3. They taunt the righteous man saying that God will look after him
4. We see this Scripture fulfilled in the passion of Jesus Christ
5. The crucified Jesus was ''looked after'' by God the Father who raised him from the dead the third day
6. Trust in Christ to care for you now and in the life to come for he has overcome sin and death itself

*James 3:13-18 (C)*
*James 3:16—4:6 (L)*
*James 3:16—4:3 (RC)*
## True Wisdom from Above

1. True wisdom is expressed by works in a good life
2. Earthly wisdom is destructive of human life and consists of jealousy, selfish ambition which lead to disorder and every vile practice, and is expressed in lusts and desires
3. Wisdom from above is pure, peaceable, gentle, open to reason, full of mercy and good fruits, without uncertainty or insincerity.
4. God opposes the proud but gives grace to the humble
5. Therefore, humble yourself before God and seek wisdom from above

*This Preacher's Choice*

*Mark 9:30-37*
## True Greatness in the Kingdom

1. Jesus predicts his passion and resurrection but the disciples do not understand him
2. Jesus teaches the twelve that true greatness consists of being the ''last of all and servant of all''
3. Jesus acts out a parable with a child, pointing out that the person who receives one such child in his name receives him
4. Whoever receives Jesus receives God the Father who sent him also
5. Receive Christ into your life and live as his servant giving yourself as the servant of all

**Hymn for Pentecost 18:**   *We Love Your Kingdom, Lord*

**Prayer**

*O God of wisdom, grant us a greater measure of wisdom and understanding. May we learn that wisdom consists in fearing you and departing from evil. May we learn to trust you more and ourselves and material things less. Grant us wisdom from above that we may lead peaceable lives with a harvest of righteousness. Help us to turn from passions and desires which lead to fightings, wars and killing. May we be your friends in covenant relationship and turn from being friends of this world. Grant us the grace of humility that we may walk with you in faithful obedience. O God, teach us that true greatness consists in being the last of all and servant of all. Enable us to receive the weak and lowly of this world in Jesus' name and in so doing to receive Jesus and you who sent him, even God the Father. Amen*

# Proper 21

September 25 — October 1

# Pentecost 19

# Ordinary Time 26

| Common | Lutheran | Roman Catholic |
| --- | --- | --- |
| Job 42:1-6 | Numbers 11:4-6, 10-16, 24-29 | Numbers 11:25-29 |
| James 4:13-17; 5:7-11 | James 4:7-12 (13—5:6) | James 5:1-6 |
| Mark 9:38-50 | Mark 9:38-50 | Mark 9:38-43, 45, 47-48 |

## Comments on the Lessons

In the first reading Job answers the Lord after reflecting on what the Lord has done. Numbers gives an account of the murmuring of the Israelites in the wilderness and the Lord's power to support them in the wilderness. The readings from James contrast godliness and worldliness, and give encouragement for living a Christian life. There is virtual consensus on the Markan reading.

## Commentary

### Job 42:1-6

In this passage we have Job's confessional response to God. It is a response to God's second speech and reveals Job's knowledge of the purposefulness of God. (v. 2) However, the replies of Job are unimpressive. A reading of the book of Job reveals Job's longing throughout the dialogue to confront God. Now when the movement brings Job to it, he can only speak a few unimportant platitudes. Note his complete surrender and humiliation. While courage and fortitude are virtues of the highest kind, the submissive Job is not marked by them. Rather, he has a craven attitude according to the replies he makes to God. Some scholars think that the replies of Job are not by the author of the Dialogue.

A brief outline of the passage is: (1) Beginning of Job's confessional response (v. 2ab), (2) God's first address quoted and Job's response (v. 3ab), (3) God's second address quoted (v. 4ab), (4) Job's concluding words begin (v. 5), and (5) Job's concluding words (v. 6).

In verse 3a we find a quote from 38:2. Job recognizes his finitude. There is an echo of the divine questioning in verse 4 (40:7) which prepares for the confession that follows in verse 5.

Verse 5 "I had heard of thee by the hearing of the ear, but now my eye sees thee" is one of the best known verses of Job and of Scripture. In it we find the contrast between belief through tradition (hearing of the ear) and a living faith through prophetic vision and confrontation with God (my eye sees thee). Although God has not justified Job he has come to him in person and revealed himself as a God who cares for a lonely man. Although Job is not vindicated he has gained far more than the recognition of his innocence. Job has been accepted by the Creator God who is ever-present. This encounter face to face with God makes vindication superfluous.

Most commentators see in verse 5 the supreme teaching of the entire book. All through the book Job has expressed almost as pedantic an academic knowledge of God as that of his so-called friends. His knowledge of a personal God had been affected by the unjust suffering and disasters that befell him. He desperately searched for a formula which at the same time preserves the justice of God and his own righteousness. His knowledge was that of the hearing of the ear as he went down blind hallways to blank walls. This was wisdom from that of the wisdom schools. While such traditional theology might satisfy a person's needs when health and affluence are the order of the day, it could not sustain a person struck by destitution, pain, rejection and isolation from God himself.

If we would make a comparison, Third World Christians are the Jobs of the world today. We might include Christians behind the Iron curtain also, since they suffer for their faith. We Christians in the Western World have much to learn from our Christian brothers and sisters who go on believing in the face of political and economic oppression and personal suffering because of lack of medical care, food, housing and other basics of life. They are the Jobs who see God face to face and in this personal relationship are sustained in spite of their destitution and hardships.

In verse 6 the word translated "despise" is a difficult Hebrew word which is intransitive and has the thrust of "to flow" or "to melt." The meaning here is "I flow into nothingness," or "I sink into the abyss of nothingness."

Job repents in dust and ashes. Job is no longer egocentric. His desire at this point is no longer for righteousness — this is annihilated. Therefore he is able to truly repent. He repents, not from moral guilt, but from a reckless display of distrust of God. Job now trusts God and says in effect, "Thy will be done." This trust is a result of his personal communion with God and is the motivation for his repentance. Job's repentance means total dedication.

## *Numbers 11:4-6, 10-16, 24-29 (L)*
## *Numbers 11:25-29 (RC)*

In this pericope we have two stories: the full story of the complaints against manna which begins with verse 4 and continues to the end of the chapter, and the inserted story of the seventy elders (vv.11-12, 14-17, 24b-30). The story of the manna has marks of being a composite. Note the difference between the threat in verse 20 and the actual punishment in verse 33.

The difficulty began with the rabble among the Israelites who had a strong craving for the rich foods they had in Egypt in contrast to the manna they now subsist on in the wilderness. This rabble is mentioned in Exodus 12:38, "A mixed multitude also went up with them, and very many cattle, both flocks and herds." There were other Hebrews or rootless people with Israel. Exodus 1:15 refers to the Hebrew midwives. Hebrew was an older and broader and more inclusive term than Israelite. Hebrew was used when foreigners spoke about or to Abraham's people. The "rougher element" led the others in complaining against Moses and God, reminding us of another incident recorded in Exodus 16:3: ". . . and said to them, Would that we had died by the hand of the Lord an the land of Egypt, when we sat by the fleshpots and ate bread to the full; for you have brought us out into this wilderness to kill this whole assembly with hunger." Here they complain, "O that we had meat to eat! We remember the fish we ate in Egypt for nothing, the cucumbers, the melons, the leeks, the onions, and the garlic; but now our strength ("throat" is better) is dried up, and there is nothing at all but this manna to look at." (vv. 4-6) They craved the seasoned dishes of Egypt.

The story in verses 4-34 seeks to explain the place name at the end, verse 34: "Therefore the name of that place was called Kibroth-hatta-avah, because there they buried the people who had the craving." Nothing is known of the place now. The original meaning of the name could have been "the graves at the boundary." But for the present writer and the tradition he recorded the meaning is "the graves of desire or craving." However, this is somewhat forced. It appears to have been a place of a divine judgment (graves) inflicted on Israel for its sinful craving. This happened after the Exodus and during the period of wandering. The people craved food, and although God provided manna for them in the wilderness and guided them, the people craved something more, and better. So the people murmured.

The manna they ate was a resinous gum from the manna-tamarisk plant of the Sinai peninsula. Eating it left the throat dry, a better translation of verse 6 that "now our strength is dried up."

Moses is enraged by the people's desire for more and better food but turns his anger, not toward the people as might be expected, but to God. And verse 10 tells us the anger of the Lord blazed hotly.

Then in verses 12-13 we have one of the rare occurrences in which the connection between Israel and God is expressed by the idea of motherhood. This indirectly attributes the concept of femininity to God (see Isaiah 49:15; 66:13). In verse 12b notice that the image shifts slightly when Moses complains that he is supposed to be the nurse charged by the mother with the care of the child.

In verses 14-17 we have a new section with a new thought, namely, that Moses alone cannot bear the burden of leading the people. He says to God he would rather be killed than live in such wretchedness. The people seem a burden to be borne. So Moses' burden is lightened by investing seventy elders with power in order to assist him. This story presupposes the tradition about the tent of meeting. Moses is regarded as a charismatic leader who has the divine spirit. The number seventy should be taken simply as a large number. The selection from among the elders is made by Moses himself.

In verses 18-24a the basic narrative is resumed about food. God tells Moses that he will see whether his word will come true to him or not. (v. 23) The story emphasizes the miraculous power of God to support a large population in the wilderness.

Moses gathered the seventy men and placed them round about the tent and God came down and spoke to him (Moses) and took some of the spirit of Moses and and put it upon the seventy elders. And when the spirit rested upon them they prophesied. While the King James Version says "they prophesied, and did not cease,'' the RSV is a correct translation of the Hebrew which means ''they did so no more.'' Prophetic frenzy was at times a common characteristic of Semitic religions. Great importance was attached to it. Notice that the spirit is not confined to certain officers or people. This fact is emphasized in the story of Eldad and Medad who did not go outside the camp to the tent, but stayed in the camp and prophesied there. It is assumed the tent of meeting was outside the camp. The prophetic ecstasy probably shows Canaanite influence.

Joshua asked Moses to forbid Eldad and Medad from being a part of the seventy, but Moses asked him if he was jealous for his sake. But Moses wished that all God's people were prophets and that God would put his spirit upon them. Here we have an early conviction of the Old Testament that the Spirit ''bloweth where it listeth.''

### James 4:13-17; 5:7-11 (C)
### James 4:7-12 (13—5:6) (L)

Since these two pericopes have some overlapping they will be treated together, and James 5:1-6 (RC) will follow in a separate section.

This section is concerned with wrong desires and how to resist them. The author urges submission to God since God is stronger than the devil. The Testaments of the Twelve Patriarchs contains similar sayings to verse 7 which indicate that, if a person turns to God, then Satan or evil will flee away.

The promise of verse 8 ''Draw near to God and he will draw near to you'' is well known and is borne out in Christian experience. People draw near to God by repenting of sin, by rejecting the evil desires and pleasures in which they have indulged, and by rejecting the double mind which tries to serve both God and the world at the same time. (1:8)

Cleansing the hands originally referred to ceremonial purity but here is used symbolically of not doing evil. Purifying the heart suggests the proper inward attitude toward God, a pure heart which enables one to see God. All the laughter and joy must be turned into mourning and sorrow for sins. This is not suggesting sackcloth and ashes, etc., however. The way to proper relationship with God is through *humbling oneself* before God. Then God will exalt the person who does so.

Speak no evil is the thrust of verses 11-12. This section is complete in and of itself, although it deals with evil speaking which is a result of evil desires and pride. The evil speaking against another person reflects the teaching of Leviticus 19:16-18 against slandering another. When a person slanders another, that person speaks evil against the law which forbids such, as well as speaking evil against the neighbor. In doing so the person sets him or herself up as judge in the place of God.

In verses 13-17 the writer rebukes those who plan their future with complacency, forgetting that God is the author and giver of life and that they live at his mercy. Human life is as evanescent as mist, vapor or smoke. The Lord refers to God, not Christ, in this section.

The author says that whoever knows what is right to do but fails to do it, for him it is sin. (v. 17) This verse doesn't relate to what went before or what follows. The author must have thought it a saying worth repeating and so inserted it here. But we should not stress the verse too much which could give the impression that righteousness consists in knowing and doing, or that only the person who knows can sin. Sin is a Christian and Jewish concept, not a Greek one.

### James 5:1-6 (RC)

This passage is a very sharp criticism of the rich who are held up as examples of the folly of accumulating riches. The last days (v. 3) have already begun, and in the light of the end time all earthly values lose their meaning. In verses 2-3 the verbs are in the perfect, indicating that judgment has already taken place on riches.

Next comes judgment on those who defraud workers of their pay, which was a grave crime in Judaism. (Leviticus 19:13) The cries of those who are injustly treated are heard by the Lord of hosts, or Almighty (Judge).

We find in verses 5-6 that the idea of the rich preparing their doom by their own acts is continued. They have fattened their hearts, like cattle are fattened before the slaughter. The selfishness of the rich has resulted in murder. (v. 6) The term ''righteous man'' used here does not refer to a particular individual, but is a generic term. It means any righteous person who has suffered.

The application of this passage to society today is obvious. Western countries are rich at the expense of the poor in Third World countries. The latter, working at minimum, subsistence wages, provide much of the labor to make the things enjoyed by the rich. Management and labor relations, the oppression of women in the work force who are paid much less for the same work, the suffering of children of single parents who go to bed hungry every night and who lack medical care, and other aspects of contemporary life are spoken to by this passage of James.

The final clause "he does not resist you" points up the utter helplessness of the poor, and thus heightens the guilt of the oppressors.

*Mark 9:38-50 (C) (L)*
*Mark 9:38-43, 45, 47-48 (RC)*

This last portion of chapter 9 contains proverbs for disciples and expanded instruction on discipleship. In verse 38 we have the brief setting in which the disciples report seeing a man casting out demons in Jesus' name and they forbade him. The rest of the chapter is made up of originally independent sayings now linked together by catchwords such as "in my name," "for," "little ones," etc. They are also linked in a general way by subject matter. This section is the result of a complex redaction history. As we have it now, the text consists of two clusters of sayings, plus a concluding trio. An outline goes like this: (1) the unauthorized exorcist, verses 38-41; (2) warnings against causes of sin, verses 42-48; and (3) the conclusion, verses 49-50.

A summary of this section is as follows: Disciples are like flavorless salt if their lives are not characterized by (1) lowly service, (2) by openness to Christians different from them, (3) by care of those who are "little ones" or young in the faith, nor by (4) rigorous self-discipline. The disciples are urged to be salty in the sense in which Jesus was salty (v. 1, 35-37) in that he suffered and died in obedience to God. The disciples will be at peace with one another (v. 50c) since they are harder on themselves than on others, and they will welcome and help others in the common journey of discipleship.

The story in verses 38-40 is linked to the previous section and to verse 41 by the phrase "in my name." It is significant that this is the only place in Mark where John is named alone. Some scholars have questioned the historicity of this story since exorcisms were unlikely in the lifetime of Jesus. The point at issue in the story is whether or not to welcome a prophet who calls on the name of Jesus to cast out demons but does not belong to the apostolic group. The problem is that the man was not a follower of the Twelve, the established leadership of the church. Jesus states categorically: "Do not forbid him."

Then follow two "for-sayings" which urge the disciples to be gracious and generous in dealing with others who call on Jesus' name. In verse 41 a third "for" saying begins with a solemn "Truly" and gives a promise of reward for anyone who does even a simple act such as giving a drink of water in the name of Christ. There were traveling missionaries and needy persons to whom the disciples had opportunity to show kindness in Christ's name. This giving and receiving of hospitality was to be given to all who follow Jesus and not to just an in-group.

Next begin warnings against causes of sin which begins with "these little ones" being cited. The little ones correspond to the "one such child" of verse 37 and refers not only to the young but also, or even primarily to the new believers in Jesus.

There are three parallel sayings about hand, foot and eye which are linked together by verse 42. In Jewish thought there was the notion that an individual part might commit a sin. Some clever persons might even try to excuse themselves by pointing to their eye, foot or hand as the responsible party to relieve themselves of punishment for sin. Notice that one is not required to observe these statements literally. (Matthew 19:11f) They point up the fact that God is even more important than the most important parts of our bodies. There is no merit in cutting off a hand, plucking out an eye or cutting off a foot, although some persons have done this in an effort to rid themselves of sin and guilt. The thrust of this section is to free oneself from what might hinder fellowship with God.

Hell mentioned here is Gehenna in Greek and refers to the valley south of Jerusalem where in the past offerings had been presented to idols, and since the prophets threatened it with the judgment of God, it came to be associated with the place where the damned would be punished. We should not read into "hell" here later ideas of eternal punishment, nor should the sternness of Jesus' sayings be taken lightly.

In modern versions verses 44 and 46 are rightly omitted since they are textual variants not found in the early manuscripts. "Where the worm does not die, and the fire is not quenched" is from Isaiah 66:24, and this vivid description of punishment held a fascination for ancient copyists who repeated it for the sake of emphasis.

The sayings on salt form the conclusion. There are three sayings which are grouped editorially, but are unrelated to each other in meaning. "For every one will be salted with fire" (v. 49) is not found in any other Gospel. It seems to teach the acceptance of suffering as a normal experience. "Fire" links it to verses 43-48, and "salt" to the two sayings in verse 50. A textual variant is "and every sacrifice will be salted with salt." Evidently some early copyist noted that Leviticus 2:13 "With all your offerings you shall offer salt" contained a command and so inserted it here. Salt was used in ritual sacrifices and would be known to Mark's readers. Salt and fire both suggest purification.

The hardships that disciples undergo are compared to the fire of a sacrificial offering that purifies or to salt which stings and smarts but has a preserving effect. On his way to Jerusalem, Jesus is the supreme example of the sacrificial offering which has been "salted with fire." Jesus sets the example for every disciple in that his death shows the costly obedience of discipleship.

The section concludes with an exhortation to "be at peace with one another." If one fulfills the exhortations of the preceding verses, then one can live at peace with one another.

## Theological Reflections

Job finds the answer to unjust suffering in a face-to-face encounter with God. He moves from an academic knowledge of God to an existential knowledge which satisfies his search for self-justification. Numbers gives an account of the murmurings of the Israelites in the wilderness and God's miraculous power to support them. The selection of seventy elders to assist Moses reveals a theology of administration in which authority and power are delegated and shared with others. James is concerned with wrong desires and how to overcome them by drawing near to God. There is also a sharp criticism of the rich who oppress the poor and cause their death. It points up the folly of accumulating riches. The Markan passage contains a collection of proverbs now linked by catchwords and themes which deal with discipleship. Jesus urges generosity and graciousness, self-discipline, and acceptance of hardship and sacrifice as disciples. And Jesus exhorts disciples to be at peace with one another.

## Homiletical Moves

*This Preacher's Choice*

*Job 42:1-6 (C)*
### But Now My Eye Sees Thee — Job's Answer to Suffering

1. Job had searched for an answer to undeserved suffering
2. Job had an academic knowledge about God, having heard of God by the ear
3. God reveals himself to God in a first-hand encounter
4. Job responds by repenting of his distrust of God and his egocentricity melts away into nothingness
5. Repent of your distrust of God, open your life to him, and in God's Presence you will find an answer to undeserved suffering

*Numbers 11:4-6, 10-16, 24-29 (L)*
*Numbers 11:25-29 (RC)*
### God Answers Moses' Plea for Assistance

1. The rabble led the people to murmur against God and Moses because of the lack of the foods they enjoyed in Egypt
2. Moses complained to God about the burden of the people God has laid on him
3. God commands Moses to select seventy men of the elders to help him
4. God puts some of the spirit that was on Moses on the seventy
5. Two men who remained in the camp, also registered, received the spirit and prophesied also
6. Trust in God and humbly obey his call to service in the world, relying on the Spirit

*James 4:13-17, 5:7-11 (C)*
*James 4:7-12 (13—5:6) (L)*
*James 5:1-6 (RC)*
### What Is Your Life?

1. Cleanse your hands and hearts, humble yourselves, and repent of your love of riches
2. Draw near to God and he will draw near to you

3. Put your trust in the God of the future who is eternal
4. Examine your life and do what is right in response to God's saving act in Jesus Christ
5. Humble yourselves before God and he will exalt you

*Mark 9:38-50 (C) (L)*
*Mark 9:38-43, 45, 47-48 (RC)*
## Be at Peace with One Another

1. Be gracious towards those who differ but serve Jesus
2. Give hospitality in the name of Christ to all
3. Examine and discipline yourself
4. Endure hardships and suffering as a disciple, having salt in yourselves, after the example of Jesus who was sacrificed on the cross
5. Be at peace with one another

**Hymn for Pentecost 19:**   *Where Cross the Crowded Ways of Life*

**Prayer**

*O God who has been gracious to us, feeding us on the bread of life and the wine of salvation, forgive us when we have grumbled and murmured in self-pity. We rejoice in your gracious saving us from our sins. Let us draw near to you so that you may draw near to us and we may see you face-to-face. We confess that an academic knowledge about you does not satisfy our longing for an answer to our undeserved suffering. But we know that in your presence our egocentricity melts away and we find your presence is sufficient for our every need. Enable us to cut off that which hinders our fellowship with you, whether it be riches, security, or pleasures. Enable us to live at peace with one another. Amen*

## Proper 22
October 2-8

## Pentecost 20

## Ordinary Time 27

| Common | Lutheran | Roman Catholic |
|---|---|---|
| Genesis 2:18-24<br>Hebrews 1:1-4, 2:9-11<br>Mark 10:2-16 | Genesis 2:18-24<br>Hebrews 2:9-11 (12-18)<br>Mark 10:2-16 | Genesis 2:18-24<br>Hebrews 2:9-11<br>Mark 10:2-16 |

### Comments on the Lessons

There is consensus on the first reading which tells of the creation of woman and the institution of marriage. Today begins a semi-continuous reading of the book of Hebrews. There is virtual consensus. The first four verses provide an introduction to the book. The theme of the book (vv. 1-2a) is the finality and perfection of God's revelation in the Son, in contrast to other revelations. What follows is the beginning of the argument centering on Christ who was once lower and is now exalted. There is total consensus on the Markan reading.

### Commentary

*Genesis 2:18-24*

In this second creation story we read that the man was created and put in the garden of Eden to till it. God said that it is not good for the man to be alone. Man is social by nature, created in the image of the Triune God (1:26), who by nature is social, one God in three persons.

The Priestly writer in the first account of creation (1:1—2:4) presents male and female as created together in one act. Their name was called Adam. But the Yahwist in the second account pictures the man as created at first alone. Next comes one of the profoundest images of the entire Old Testament in which God builds woman out of man's essential stuff. Someone has commented that woman was made, not from man's head to be over him, or from man's foot to be under him, but from his rib to be equal and a companion to him. The deep relationship between man and woman is pictured by the creating of woman from the man's rib.

God creates the animals but none are suitable for the man as a helper. God does not intend to be man's "helper," none of the creatures are suitable, so there must be a new creature. This calls for a fresh creative act of God. The creation of woman is stunning and unpredicted. The two creatures of surprise, the man and the woman, now belong together. They are one in covenant in one flesh. The garden exists as the context for the human community in which the man and woman are the first members.

It is interesting that God himself, as the father of the bride, leads the woman to present her to the man. (v. 22) The man has an "Aha" experience in which he instantly recognizes that the new creature, woman, is one belonging completely to him (and by implication, he to her) and he gives her the name, Woman. The naming here, as with the other creatures earlier, is an expression of a previous inward interpretive appropriation. From man, "ish" is made woman, "ishshah."

In verses 24-25 we have a conclusion summary of the narrator like a short epilogue. It is not a continuation of the first man's speech, but is an explanation of the extremely powerful attraction of the male and female human being for each other. This strong attraction does not come to rest until it again becomes one flesh in the child. The man and woman were originally one flesh and thus by destiny belong together. The thrust of this conclusion is to explain something already in existence — the attraction of the sexes.

The statement about the man forsaking father and mother and cleaving to his wife does not fully correspond to the patriarchal family customs of Israel, since the woman breaks from her family more than the man does. However, it could preserve something from an earlier matriarchal culture. Still, the point of the passage is not legal customs but natural drives.

It appears that verse 24 is a conclusion and chapter 3 begins something new in theme and material.

See how verse 25 serves a coupling function which points both backward and forward. The man and woman were naked but not ashamed. Shame is the correlative of sin and guilt. (3:7) They had not yet sinned and thus had no reason to fear that the body would show sin in them.

The Hebrew words for "one flesh" imply one personality. This is the ideal of companionship marriage in which two persons unite in love and form a third personality, their marriage. So the mathematics of marriage is both 1 + 1 = 1 (the two become one flesh) and 1 + 1 = 3 (the man and woman retain their identities while still forming a third, their marriage).

One way of interpreting verses 24-25 is as follows:
1. A man leaves his father and mother — severance
2. He cleaves to his wife — permanence
3. They become one flesh — union in companionship marriage
4. They were both naked and were not ashamed — intimacy

## *Hebrews 1:1-4, 2:9-11 (C)*
## *Hebrews 2:9-11 (12-18) (L)*
## *Hebrews 2:9-11 (RC)*

The prologue (vv. 1-4) declares the author's theme, the superiority of Christianity to Judaism. Note the sharp contrast between "of old" and "in these last days he has spoken to us by a son." Yet God is the same God who spoke then in the old days who has spoken now. God's Son is the exact counterpart of the Father. (v. 3) The Son not only had part in creation (John 1:1-3), but continues to sustain the universe. (v. 3) After completing his priestly work of purification for sins, the Son was enthroned in royal splendor. Christ is prophet in that God spoke forth in him, and is also priest, the mediator, and king, the ruler.

In these verses the progressive character of Biblical revelation is described. God spoke of old to our fathers by the prophets, but this was piecemeal and partial. But in the later stage God has spoken by the Son which is fulfillment. "In these last days" (v. 2) is an Old Testament phrase indicating the time of fulfillment.

"When he had sat down at the right hand of the Majesty on high" stresses the finality of his work. The right hand was the place of honor. Christ is enthroned at God's right hand which echoes the words spoken to the Davidic king. (Psalm 110:1) Here the enthronement is seen as evidence of the perfect and unrepeatable nature of Christ's sacrifice on behalf of the people. It is evidence of the finality of Christianity. Sitting in the presence of God was a royal prerogative of Davidic kings.

The Son was as much superior to angels as the name he has obtained is more excellent than theirs. (v. 4) He is superior to the angels both by the title "Son" and by his exaltation to the throne of God. "Superior" is used thirteen times in Hebrews of Christ and his new order as it is contrasted with what went before.

In chapter 2:9-11 we find that the exaltation of Jesus is the consequence of his humiliation described in 12:2: ". . . Looking to Jesus the pioneer and perfecter of our faith, who for the joy that was set before him endured the cross, despising the shame, and is seated at the right hand of the throne of God."

There are two difficulties in verse 9, one in regard to the relation of the phrase "crowned with glory and honor" to the rest of the sentence, and the other arises from the phrase "by the grace of God." In regard to the first, unless the text has been disturbed, and it does not appear to be from MS evidence, then it is best to take these words as a parenthesis reminding the reader that the humiliation had a glorious outcome. This would not interrupt the flow of thought. The second problem "by the grace of God" could at one time have been "apart from God" since in Greek the words for grace and apart are similar in spelling. The original meaning would be that Jesus tasted death for everyone except God. But the words "the graoe of God" fits well with the opening words of verse 10 and probably are the original. Note that "to taste death" does not mean to sample death lightly as we might taste a gourmet dish, but rather means to *experience* death.

"But we see Jesus" is a great turning point in contrast to all that has happened in the past. Jesus is the answer God gives to our every human failure, and is our hope when we despair. When the pessimist reads the headlines of the daily paper or watches the evening TV news he/she views it as if there were a period, when the story ends. But the Christians puts a comma, for "we see Jesus" who is the Lord of the nations, the Prince of Peace, the Hope of God to human beings.

In verse 10 we find that high destiny of human beings which is described in Psalm 8 is to be gained through the work of Christ. "It was fitting" means that it was in accord with God's gracious nature. The idea of "to make perfect" is characteristic of Hebrews and means to make complete or bring to maturity. There is no thought of moral process leading to moral perfection, but rather of a completely adequate qualification for leading people to full and complete salvation. It was fitting that God should achieve the goal of salvation for all human beings by the means of Christ's Incarnation.

The word translated "pioneer" in Greek can also mean author and leader. Jesus is the pioneer, not in the sense of the lone hero breaking trail to salvation, but rather as the victorious leader of salvation.

### Mark 10:2-16

This section is concerned with marriage and children. In verses 2-12 Mark records the test the Pharisees put to Jesus when they asked him if it was lawful for a man to divorce his wife. And verses 13-16 deal with the blessing of children and the rebuke of the disciples to the parents which made Jesus indignant.

In chapter 10 Jesus and the disciples move from Galilee to Jerusalem. The setting for Jesus' teaching is given in verse 1 but is omitted because it is not essential for the understanding of the section.

The section on marriage and divorce (vv. 2-12) gives a Gentile-Christian adaptation of Jesus' original teaching reflecting the Markan community. Proof of this is in verses 11-12 which describes a Greco-Roman world which was the world of the Gentile-Christian church rather than a Palestinian Jewish community. For in Jesus' community adultery was not a crime against the wife but against the other wife's husband. In Matthew 19:9 we find a more accurate statement of Jesus' teaching which omits the phrase "against her." He says, "And I say to you: whoever divorces his wife except for unchastity, and marries another, commits adultery." While the wife did not have the right to divorce her husband in Jesus' environment she did in the Roman society's customs. Notice that Matthew omits this verse entirely and Luke cuts out the whole account.

The issue of marriage and divorce in Jesus' day, as in ours, was not a mere academic question discussed by the Rabbis but was very much an existential issue. There were two positions in Jesus' time on divorce: (1) Rabbi Hillel and his followers practiced a very lenient interpretation of Deuteronomy 24:1 which permitted a man to divorce his wife for minor matters, such as burning his dinner or if he found someone he liked better; (2) Rabbi Shammai and his school of thought allowed divorce only on grounds of adultery. Matthew 19:9 adapts Jesus' statement to the views of the stricter school of thought. Apparently Mark was not familiar with the Jewish discussion and so gives a view of divorce that is stricter than Shammai's, one which is also found in 1 Corinthians 7:10-11: "To the married I give charge, not I but the Lord, that the wife should not separate from her husband (but if she does, let her remain single or else be reconciled to her husband) — and that the husband should not divorce his wife."

The law of Deuteronomy 24:1ff was a concession to the hardness of the hearts of people. Jesus cites Genesis 1:27 and 2:24 as revealing the real purpose of God regarding marriage from the time of creation. From this Jesus draws the inference: "What God has joined together, let no person put asunder." The key issue here is the ideal of marriage set forth by Jesus. We probably should not treat his teaching legalistically, however.

The provision of Deuteronomy was one of mercy and justice, since it helped women by requiring divorce rather than mere abandonment. It is likely Jesus saw it as an excuse for irresponsible conduct and so adopted a stricter view of divorce. Jesus puts both sexes on the same level, in contrast to the Jewish law which allowed divorce only by men. Verse 12 seems to reflect conditions in the Gentile world.

In the ancient world the thing which united a man and woman in marriage was not love or the marriage ritual but the sexual act. The uniting of a man and woman was regarded as an act of God, an act so mysterious that one cannot explain it in human terms. The question remains, "How does God unite two persons so they become one flesh (personality) in a companionship marriage. The sex act alone is obviously too simple a solution.

In verses 10-12 we see that the disciples need Jesus to give them a private explanation, which is characteristic of Mark's Gospel but omitted by Matthew.

Jesus and children brought to him are the topic of verses 13-16. It was customary to bring children to a great person, such as Jesus, on the child's birthday. There is a poignant beauty about this passage since Jesus was on his way to the cross and he knew it, yet he found time for children! There is a simple beauty and vivid realism about the account.

The children are brought to Jesus so that he might touch them. But the disciples rebuked them (the parents). The parents wanted Jesus to touch the children and give them his blessing. Apart from the Gospels, there is no sympathy toward children in other Christian literature or in secular literature of that period.

The disciples fail to understand the relation of children to the kingdom and seem to try to save Jesus from embarrassing attentions. But Jesus is indignant toward the disciples. The disciples are put in a poor light by their actions. Now Jesus gives one of the best known sayings of the Bible: "Let the children come to me, do not hinder them; for to such belongs the kingdom of God. Truly, I say to you, whoever does not receive the kingdom of God like a child shall not enter it." (vv. 14, 15)

There were qualities about a child which Jesus liked and valued: humility, obedience, trust and short memory which doesn't bear grudges. To receive the kingdom of God as a child is to depend in trustful simplicity on the grace which God offers.

## Theological Reflections

The Genesis account of marriage ties in with the Markan passage dealing with the ideal of marriage in which man and woman become one flesh. The theological thrust here is one of permanency, fidelity and intimacy in marriage. Jesus blesses the children brought to him as a sign of his love for children. Jesus expresses his love for a group ordinarily not held in high regard in society and thus expresses his unique kind of love. The Hebrews passage introduced the book with its theme of the superiority of Christianity to Judaism. The revelation of God in Jesus Christ who is the exact counterpart of God is an expression of the Incarnation.

## Homiletical Moves

*Genesis 2:18-24*
### God's Ideal for Marriage

1. A man and woman leave their parents to be joined in marriage — severance
2. They cleave to each other — permanence
3. They become one flesh (personality) — union
4. They were naked but not ashamed — intimacy
5. God commands them to be fruitful and multiply (1:28) — procreation
6. Partners are to be subject to one another in marriage out of reverence for Christ (Ephesians 5:21) — companionship
7. Follow God's principles for living in marriage

*Hebrews 1:1-4, 2:9-11 (C)*
*Hebrews 2:9-11 (12-18) (L)*
*Hebrews 2:9-11 (RC)*
### But We See Jesus!

1. God spoke in the former days in many and various ways by the prophets
2. But in these last days he has spoken to us by a Son who reflects the glory of God and bears the very stamp of his nature
3. The Son has made purification of our sins by his death as the pioneer of our salvation through suffering
4. God has raised him from the dead and he sits at the right hand of God on high
5. He sanctifies those who believe in him and calls them brethren (and sisters)
6. Believe in Christ that he may be sanctifying you

*Mark 10:2-16*
### No Longer Two, But One Flesh

1. From the beginning of creation the ideal of marriage is for a man and woman to be so joined in marriage that they become one flesh
2. But because of the hardness of human hearts Moses allowed for written divorce
3. Divorce divides what God intended to be permanent, but by the grace of God, broken relationships can be forgiven and a new relationship formed
4. Jesus blesses children as a sign of his love for them and for family life

**Hymn for Pentecost 20:**  *For the Beauty of the Earth*

**Prayer**

*O God who has created marriage good, and who calls some men and women to this vocation, we thank you for love which enables marriage to endure. We thank you for forgiveness for the hurts we cause one another in marriage. We thank you for the joys of marriage and family life, for children which you give as a gift. Thank you for the love and example of Jesus who blessed the children who were brought to him. Enable us to receive the kingdom like a child in simple trust and humility. Grant us wisdom, courage and love to create more loving and caring relationships. Amen*

# Proper 23    Pentecost 21    Ordinary Time 28

October 9-15

| Common | Lutheran | Roman Catholic |
|---|---|---|
| **Genesis 3:8-19** | **Amos 5:6-7, 10-15** | **Wisdom 7:7-11** |
| **Hebrews 4:1-3, 9-13** | **Hebrews 3:1-6** | **Hebrews 4:12-13** |
| **Mark 10:17-30** | **Mark 10:17-27 (28-30)** | **Mark 10:17-30** |

## Comments on the Lessons

The Genesis passage fits well with the passage from Hebrews 4:1-3, 9-13 and is in sequence with the previous Sunday's reading from Genesis 2. The Amos reading is a call to seek the Lord and to forsake evil, with the promise of life for all who do so. God knows the evil of humans. The Wisdom passage praises Wisdom who is portrayed as an attractive woman.

The first and third readings from Hebrews is concerned with both the entering Sabbath rest, which points back to God's rest after creating all things, and forward to the coming eternal rest with God. They also contain a description of the word of God and its ability to discern the secrets of the heart, even its intentions. The second reading points to the faithfulness of Jesus. There is virtual consensus on the Markan reading which deals with the man who asked Jesus what he needed to do to inherit eternal life.

## Commentary

*Genesis 3:8-19 (C)*

The reading picks up after the account of the disobedience of Adam and Eve in eating the forbidden fruit. Their eyes were opened and they knew they were naked. God is portrayed in human terms as walking in the garden in the cool of the day. The anxiety of the man and woman lead them to make a guilty attempt to hide from God. The Psalmist must have had this scene in mind when he wrote, "Whither shall I go from thy Spirit? Or whither shall I flee from thy presence? . . . (Psalm 139:7-12) Adam and Eve found that there is no hiding place down here, as the hymn line puts it.

When God called to the man, "Where are you?" (v. 9), he put one of the most penetrating questions ever asked. It is not a matter of geographical location but of theological location. Not a matter of where in the garden he is hiding, but where he stands over against God. The man condemns himself when he says "I was afraid, because I was naked; and I hid myself." (v. 10) Knowing good and evil, and recognizing that he had disobeyed God drove Adam to hide in an attempt to avoid an encounter with God. This myth tells the story of how human beings behave in light of their guilt and shame in a vivid fashion. The man blames the woman for giving him the fruit of the tree, and even accuses God of being responsible as he says, "The woman whom thou gavest me to be with me, she gave me the fruit of the tree, and I ate." Then the woman accuses the serpent of beguiling her. There is an attempt to pass the buck and put the responsibility for disobedience on someone else rather than to accept it oneself. The genius of the narrator is that he explains each person's seeking to avoid responsibility for obeying or disobeying God.

The scene in the garden is a trial with the Gardener as the questioner. Adam's answer, "I was afraid" is the same given by Abraham, Isaac and all who cannot trust the goodness of God and obey him. Notice how the speech of Adam and Eve indicts them as they say "I heard . . ." "I was afraid . . ." "I had . . ." "I ate . . ." etc. They have turned from centering on the Gardener, his call to them, his permission and prohibition to center on self, on "I." Life is turned back on self.

In verses 14-18 we find the explanation of a number of mysteries: (1) why the serpent crawls rather than walks, (2) why humans are instinctively hostile to serpents, (3) why women have pain in childbirth, (4) why a woman has sexual desire for her husband, (5) her subordinate position in ancient society, (6) why man must struggle to eke out a living from the soil, and (7) why humans have a lifelong fear of death.

Notice that work is not essentially evil (2:15), but after the Fall it is under the curse along
all creation. It has become toil as a result of man's broken relationship with God. But notice
the curse is on the ground and not on man.

It is significant that the mortal nature of human beings was implicit in the circumstances of
origin (2:7) out of earth. But now because of their disobedience, God makes death the inevitable
that haunts human beings throughout life.

### Amos 5:6-7, 10-15 (L)

In verse 6 Amos calls the people to seek the Lord and live, lest God break out like a fire i
house of Joseph with none to quench it for Bethel. God's judgment will be a miraculous fire,
no rain magic of the cult at Bethel can put it out.

In verse 7 Amos speaks to those who turn justice to wormwood and cast down righteousne
the earth. Wormwood was a very bitter tasting plant. "Wormwood" here may be the source o
name for the character in C. S. Lewis' delightful "Screwtape Letters," in which Wormwood
assistant devil. It may be that the call in verse 6 is addressed to those who turn justice to wormw
but the Hebrew is not in the second person. Some translators emend it to read, "Woe to those
turn . . ." and transpose it to form the beginning of verse 10.

Amos does not define justice or righteousness but only speaks of its perversion or absence. A
seems to use these terms in the sense of the law court and of the rights of citizens in Israel. Altho
Amos does not use the term "covenant," the righteousness to which he refers is based on the cove
between God and Israel. It may well be that the reason Amos doesn't define righteousness is bec
it was such a well-known duty at the center of Israel's life.

Amos takes to task those who exploit the poor in verses 10-13. They even hate those who rep
them for exploiting the poor and they abhor those who speak the truth. The gate was the civic ce
where the elders and judges held court. In verse 11 there is a shift to the second person and this
indicate the beginning of a separate oracle. In verse 11 Amos cites those who take exactions, or e
tions in the grain market and in verse 12 those who take a bribe. Amos warns that those who so
vert justice will never enjoy their security and riches even though their houses are made of st

While some commentators take verse 13 as a reader's marginal comment copied into the text
meaning is probably that, in the coming "evil time" of God's coming judgment, those who
manipulated God and their neighbors will find they have not been successful (better word than
dent). Their shock will turn them silent.

In verses 14-15 Amos issues a third call to seek and live. In this final plea for right seeking a
good, Amos by implication defines what it means to seek God. This, like a musical theme, is repe
from verse 4b and 6a. To seek good is to respond in obedience to God. Amos exhorts the pe
to seek good and not evil in order to live. Good and evil include a whole range of moral and spiri
possibilities. But here Amos speaks in very specific and concrete terms: to do good is to estab
justice in the gate, i.e. in the law court held at the gate. But this must be more than outward acti
it must involve inner motivation as well. Israel must not only do good acts and refrain from d
evil acts, she must hate evil and love good. It is only by such inner commitment to good and
that, in the coming judgment, a remnant will be left by God's grace. In verse 3 Amos has expre
the hope that there will be some survivors in the coming holocaust. However, remnant of Jos
may mean all Israel which was seen as small and unimpressive.

So Amos denies the false illusions of those who say that Israel's present prosperity is evide
of God's presence with them (v. 14cd): "and so the Lord, the God of hosts, will be with you
you have said."

### Wisdom 7:7-11 (RC)

In verses 1-6 Solomon describes his birth and declares that his wisdom was not due to any unu
native gifts. He says that all kings enter life the same way and leave it the same way.

In the verses of our reading, Solomon expresses his respect for Wisdom. He gained Wisdom thro
prayer. (v. 7) Solomon tells how he put the highest value on wisdom, far above royal power and p
tige, riches, gold and silver, and even more than health or beauty. He says he prefers her to the l
since Wisdom's radiance never sleeps.

When Solomon found Wisdom then all good things came to him, including riches not to be n
bered. But he put Wisdom first in his search. In the following verses (vv. 22-30) he continues to pr

Wisdom and refers to Wisdom as a person, comparing her to a woman. He refers to Wisdom as the "mother" of the things in which he delighted. In verses 14 Solomon says that those who acquire Wisdom win God's friendship.

*Hebrews 4:1-3, 9-13 (C)*
*Hebrews 4:12-13 (RC)*

The "rest" referred to is the real Sabbath rest which is eternal. It corresponds to the well-founded city and the heavenly country of 11:10, 16. The writer urges readers to strive to reach this rest and not to miss their goal as the Israelites failed to reach Canaan. They failed to reach Canaan because they did not accept the good news with faith. (v. 2) There is in verse 2 a primitive corruption in the text, but the conjecture "because it did not meet with faith in the hearers" is plain enough and expresses the thrust of the thought. Another conjecture says "they were not united in faith with the hearers."

God's true rest is given to people of faith. (v. 3) The rest refers to the Sabbath rest of God after creation. (Genesis 2:2) This is the unending Sabbath rest of God which people may forfeit by failing to believe.

In verses 9-13 the theme of Sabbath rest continues as the author reaffirms the Sabbath rest for the people of God. God's people will enter this rest when their labor on earth is ended, even as God ceased his work and rested when creation was finished. The author emphasizes that God is not to be trifled with and that the Sabbath rest can be missed by disobedience.

God's Word is compared to a two-edged sword. In the Old Testament God's Word is seen as his messenger or agent, as it is here. It is living and active. God's Word is the supreme judge and discerns the thoughts and intentions of the heart. Like a security X-ray machine at an airport which "sees" within suitcases and bags, God's Word "sees" the hearts of all. No creature is hidden from him, "but all are open and laid bare to the eyes of him with whom we have to do." (v. 13) The words "laid bare" in Greek mean literally "with neck bent back" ready for the death stroke. The thrust of this passage is expressed in the familiar prayer, "O Thou unto whom all hearts are open, all desires known, and from whom no secrets are hid."

*Hebrews 3:1-6 (L)*

The focus of this passage is on Jesus who is greater than Moses. Jesus is the apostle and high priest who was faithful to him, who appointed him. Moses was also faithful, but Jesus has been counted worthy of as much more glory than Moses as the builder of a house has more honor than the house. Moses was but the chief servant in the house, but Christ was faithful and set over God's house as a son. One of the reasons for stressing the superiority of Christ over Moses is to show the superiority of Christianity over Judaism, but also because in some Jewish/Christian circles Jesus was seen as a second Moses. But here Jesus is presented as more than a second Moses.

"We are his house if we hold fast our confidence and pride in our hope." (v. 6) Some MSS add "firm to the end." The emphasis here is on the holding fast to our hope and was written at a time when the first expectant enthusiasm was growing dim.

We should carefully note that whether under Moses or under Christ there is but *one continuous* household of God by faith (11:40), "Since God had foreseen something better for us, that apart from us they should not be made perfect."

*Mark 10:17-30 (C) (RC)*
*Mark 10:17-27 (28-30) (L)*

Note that Mark is not making poverty a special virtue in this account of Jesus and a man, Everyperson, as we may think of him or her. The story does not specify who the person is on purpose, so that each of us can identify with the person who came to Jesus. The point of all this discussion is found in verses 25-27:

*"It is easier for a camel to go through the eye of a needle than for a rich man to enter the kingdom of God." And they were exceedingly astonished, and said to him, "Then who can be saved?" Jesus looked at them and said, "With men it is impossible, but not with God; for all things are possible with God."*

This is said in another way in Romans 3:23f: "Since all have sinned and fall short of the gl
of God, they are justified by his grace as a gift, through the redemption which is in Christ Jes
whom God put forward as an expiation by his blood, to be received by faith." The thrust of b
passages is that salvation is a *free gift* of God and cannot be earned or deserved. Salvation is a mira
since with God all things are possible!

To get the full thrust of the passage we must avoid attempts to water down the difficulty of ve
25. Later rabbis spoke maxims concerning an elephant who goes through the eye of a needle. A
by altering one Greek letter the verse can be made to read "rope" instead of camel. A ninth cent
A.D. commentary note said that a small gate to the city of Jerusalem was called the Needle's
and that a camel could pass through it, but only with great difficulty by bowing down. But such
tempts to get around the hard saying here add to the problem rather than solving it. The preac
must be careful *not* to be taken in by such simple solutions which often appear in older commentar

The story deals with a man who wants to accomplish something more than what an ordinary p
son does. He wants to inherit or receive what God has promised. In Israel it was common to sp
of inheriting God's promises, since the future inheritance depended on God's gracious promise alo
This ruled out any merit just as it would in inheriting family wealth. The man who asks the quest
is not seeking a life of possibility thinking, or positive thinking, or a well-adjusted life as self-h
books promise. He is concerned to gain "eternal life" which is the final existence in the prese
of God on the other side of death itself. Thus the conversation is about ultimate issues: eternal l

He calls Jesus "Good Teacher" which was not customary for either Jew or Greek to do. Je
refused to accept this name. This has been a problem for exegetes through the ages. It may be t
Jesus is simply saying that it is not fitting to exchange compliments when discussing a matter wh
concerns God. Here Jesus acts in the place of God. The man's idea of goodness is of a goodn
that is man's achievement. Jesus points to the Father alone who is good, who is the only source a
norm of goodness. "The Son can do nothing of his own accord, but only what he sees the Fat
doing . . ." (John 5:19) seems to explain Jesus' reply to the man.

The man declares that he has kept all the commandments, which is not an assertion of pride, si
Mark says Jesus loved him. Jesus searchingly looks at the man. He loved him as God loved h
and the miracle of divine grace was ready for him to receive. The statement that all things are poss
with God indicates that anyone can be saved and that discipleship comes only as the act of God.
can only receive salvation as a free gift and continue to hold it as we live in obedience to Chr

The man went away sorrowful for he had great wealth. We are not told whether or not he la
repented, sold his goods as Jesus commanded and became a disciple. It serves in a sense as a para
which is open-ended as it poses the searching question to each reader: "Are possessions standing
the place of God in my life and preventing my receiving eternal life?"

With verse 28 we begin the third section of the passage, the first two being: (1) verses 17-22;
verses 23-27. While each of these parts could exist independently, it is probable that (1) and (2) w
historically connected. The first part seems incomplete without part 2. But part 3 could be ea
detached from parts 1 and 2. While Mark thinks of verses 17-31 as a unit, he does not link ver
27 and 28 with a conjunction of any sort. This may indicate he did not take over all three parts
a unit. Note also that verse 31 is what is called a "floating logion." It is omitted by Luke's acco
of this event, and occurs elsewhere in the Gospels. It seems likely that part 3 existed independer
originally, but that Mark has attached it to 1 and 2 because of their similar theme. It serves h
to provide a contrast to the man who valued wealth above eternal life, since the disciples did in f
give up all for Christ's sake and the Gospel's. Notice that the warning in verses 17-27 is matchec
this part by the promise in verse 29f.

It seems verse 28 was inserted for transition to the promise in verse 29. While Peter first menti
the forsaking of all things and then discipleship, the proper order would be discipleship and then
result which is forsaking all things. In 1 Corinthians 9:5 we note that at a later time Peter actua
took his wife on his missionary journeys, and it is interesting that "wife" is omitted from the
of verse 29.

In Luke's Gospel (18:29) "for the sale of the Kingdom of God" is used, instead of "for my s
and for the Gospel." Luke's version is probably nearer to the original wording. The promise of Je
in verse 30 is remarkable since it covers every aspect of earthly life.

Jesus calls persons to find the gift of life in the giving of self. Discipleship, according to Jes
does not lead to poverty and deprivation but to wholeness, to the experience of genuine living.
find such joyful life in the fellowship of the church. But discipleship also included persecutions. T
part of the fulfillment of Jesus' promise is different from the complete fulfillment which comes o

in the age to come. Then life will be free of temptation and persecution.

Jesus is saying that life can be experienced in real fullness here and now, and Christianity is not "pie in the sky by and by when you die" as the detractors of the faith have put it. But what happens to us here and now is only a taste, a token of what salvation consists of in the fulfillment in the age to come.

Note that verse 31, the floating logion, is omitted from the readings, but serves to accentuate the strangeness of the divine law which Jesus states in earlier verses.

## Theological Reflections

The Genesis passage deals with the disobedience of Adam and Eve and their shame. It explains a number of mysterious things about life in terms of the affect of sin on relationships. The Amos reading calls people to turn from evil and to seek the Lord in order to live. Hate evil and love good, do justice in the law court and in the daily affairs of life, exhorts Amos. The promise is that it may be that the Lord will be gracious to the remnant of Joseph. The Hebrews 3 passage is concerned with Jesus as the superior son of the household of God in comparison to Moses the servant. Readers are promised that they are in God's house if they hold fast to their confidence and pride in their hope. The readings from Hebrews 4 center on the promise of "eternal rest" for the Christian who receives God's gift by faith. God's Word is compared to a two-edged sword which pierces to the inner parts of the person is a dramatic way of saying God knows what is in the heart of each person. In Mark we see that Jesus knew what was in the heart of the man who came seeking eternal life and so prescribed the only remedy that could give him eternal life: putting God first over his love for possessions. Jesus lifts up salvation as a miracle of God, a free gift, and not something that can be earned or deserved. And he promises a full life here and now to those who forsake all to follow him, but also persecutions here and now. All things are possible with God is the central thrust of Jesus' teaching here.

## Homiletical Moves

*Genesis 3:8-9 (C)*
### Where Are You?

1. God seeks Adam and Eve who are hiding in the Garden
2. Adam admits his shame over being naked
3. God confronts Adam and Eve with their disobedience
4. God curses the serpent, relationships between the serpent and humans, childbearing, the ground, etc. and death hangs over human life
5. The good news in Jesus Christ is that sin and death have been conquered by his death on the cross, for Christ is the New Man and in him creation is being redeemed
6. Commit your life to God in Christ and thus find where you are in relationship to God: at one through faith in Christ

*Amos 5:6-7, 10-15 (L)*
### Seek the Lord and Live!

1. Seek the Lord and live lest he break out like fire to judge you
2. Stop oppressing the poor and instead establish justice in the law court
3. Turn from evil and seek good that the Lord of hosts will be with you as you claim he is
4. God comes by the power of the Spirit to all who seek him to give them a new life in Christ
5. Life in the Spirit is one of doing justice and taking up the cause of the poor and oppressed
6. Therefore, seek the Lord and live in the Spirit

*Wisdom 7:7-11 (RC)*
### The Rewards of Loving Wisdom

1. Solomon prays for wisdom and it is given him
2. Wisdom is esteemed more highly than anything else by Solomon
3. When Wisdom was given him he was also given all good things beyond numbering
4. Wisdom is a gift of God given to those who seek after it with all their might
5. Therefore, seek after Wisdom with all your might

*Hebrews 3:1-6 (L)*

## We Belong to the House of God

1. Jesus was far more worthy than Moses, even as a builder (God) is more worthy than the house (his people)
2. Christ was faithful over God's house as a son
3. We are God's house if we hold fast our confidence and pride in our hope
4. The body is the temple of God's Spirit who has created us and who sustains us
5. Enter by faith the household of God and let God's Spirit dwell in your body

*Hebrews 4:1-3, 9-13 (C)*
*Hebrews 4:12-13 (RC)*

## The Living and Active Word of God

1. God has promised eternal rest to those who believe
2. Let us strive to enter that rest and not lose it by disobedience
3. The Word of God is living and active and pierces to the innermost parts of human life
4. God knows the thoughts and intentions of the heart, but nevertheless saves us by the grace of Christ in spite of our sins
5. By God's grace we can enter the eternal rest after death if we accept God's gift of salvation by faith here and now
6. Therefore, accept God's grace and the promise of eternal rest after death

*This Preacher's Choice*

*Mark 10:17-30 (C) (RC)*
*Mark 10:17-27 (28-30) (L)*

## The High Cost of Living!

1. A man, Everyperson, came to Jesus seeking eternal life
2. Jesus reminds him of the commandments of Moses and the man says he has kept them
3. Jesus loved him and told him to sell his goods, give them to the poor and come follow him
4. Jesus points out to the disciples that salvation is only by the miracle of God's grace, not by good works
5. Jesus promises a full life here and now, with persecutions, as well as eternal life in the age to come to those who follow him
6. Accept God's miracle of salvation and live by grace

**Hymn for Pentecost 21:**   *O God, Our Help in Ages Past*

**Prayer**

*Gracious God who has loved us while we were yet sinners, and who has promised us eternal rest if we continue in the faith, look down with mercy upon us. Forgive our disobedience which has ruptured our relationship with you, with our neighbor and with creation itself. We thank you for Jesus the New Adam who died that the sin of the old Adam might be destroyed. May we have the courage to divest ourselves of all that keeps us from putting you first in our lives, whether it be wealth, power or prestige. Grant that we may forsake all to follow Jesus in the way of discipleship and so receive the gift of life now and eternal rest beyond the grave. We praise you for the miracle of salvation for we know that with you all things are possible. Amen*

# Proper 24

October 16-22

# Pentecost 22

# Ordinary Time 29

| Common | Lutheran | Roman Catholic |
|---|---|---|
| Isaiah 53:7-12 | Isaiah 53:10-12 | Isaiah 53:10-11 |
| Hebrews 4:14-16 | Hebrews 4:9-16 | Hebrews 4:14-16 |
| Mark 10:35-45 | Mark 10:35-45 | Mark 10:35-45 |

## Comments on the Lessons

There is virtual consensus on the Isaiah reading which is part of the fourth Servant Song which declares God's judgment on sin and his mercy on his people. The Hebrews reading has virtual consensus. The (C) and (RC) readings pick up where last Sunday's left off, while the (L) reading overlaps some. This concludes the chapter. There is consensus on the Markan reading.

## Commentary

*Isaiah 53:7-12 (C)*
*Isaiah 53:10-12 (L)*
*Isaiah 53:10-11 (RC)*

The readings today are part of the fourth Servant Song. (52:13—53:12) There are differing views among scholars regarding who the Servant was in these Songs. Some hold that he was an individual, others the nation Israel and still others that he was both. The position of this writer is that he was both individual and nation, much as "Uncle Sam" represents both an individual (mythical) and the nation of the United States of America. The Hebrew mind does not seem to have difficulty with blending the notion of individual and corporate people in one image.

In these verses, in contrast to Jeremiah or Job, the Servant suffers silently. Notice that he is unjustly condemned, executed, and buried in a grave with the wicked. The Servant's suffering manifests God's judgment on sin and his mercy upon sinful human beings.

In verse 7 the report which was interrupted by the confession in verses 4ff now continues. There is a parallel in this chapter with the Apostles' Creed in that verse 2 corresponds to "was born" since it tells of the Servant's origin, and now verses 7ff corresponds to "suffered . . . was dead . . . and buried." Here the prophet thinks of the Servant as an individual. But the individual's suffering is an image of Israel's in which Israel as a kingdom comes to an end, and her exile is a "death" of the Servant. The text does not make it clear whether the Servant died of a disgraceful disease or by violence, or by normal condemnation and execution.

The difference between the portrayal of the Servant's suffering in verses 3-6 and in verses 7ff is significant for understanding chapter 53. We find in these two passages the two strands of suffering as in the psalms of lamentation. Note in Psalm 22 where the suffering is an illness and also persecution and hostility. Isaiah 53 thus shows the Servant as a typical sufferer in that he suffers in the two basic ways as given by the tradition. For this reason we need not take either the one (illness) or the other (conviction and violence) as a literal, true to life description.

The Servant's death is appropriate for his suffering and comes quickly. Suffering and death for the Servant have both been in view from the beginning, and both form a unity. Notice that it was a violent death which was not due to the Servant's guilt, and death came to him because of the sins of those who now report it.

Shame was part of the Servant's death we learn from verse 9 since he was buried with the wicked. This points to an individual who actually died and was buried, but from the narrator's perspective the event is in the past. But there was no indication at the time of his death of its great significance.

In verses 10-11a we learn that God has been on the Servant's side all along. After the Servant's death God intervened on his behalf by reviving or by healing him. Some scholars see this as the Servant's resurrection from the dead. But this is not clearly said. Note that verses 10b and 11a give the consequences of God's act of restoring his Servant. He is to have a long life and see his offspring. "See his offspring" is literally "see his seed." Recall the theological importance of seed for Abraham recognized by Isaiah elsewhere. This means that the promise made to Abraham will now be fulfilled.

We have in verse 11 a textual crux which is not easy to solve. One translation which seems the best is "After his travail he shall see light, he shall be satisfied with his knowledge" and light means "happiness, salvation." The Servant is righteous and will make many to be accounted righteous. God justifies the Servant who was previously condemned to shame.

In verse 12 the prophet announces the national vindication of Israel as represented by the Servant, and the tribute of the nations. Atonement at the depth at which the Servant makes it depends on the righteousness of the Servant. While this passage is not understood in Judaism, Christians on this side of the cross and resurrection see it fulfilled in the vicarious suffering of the sinless Son of God, Jesus Christ.

The "yet" is verse 12c presupposes that something has been left unsaid, namely, "Yes, he let himself be counted with the transgressors but actually he was no transgressor at all, but . . ." Two brief statements sum up the Servant's work: (1) "he bore the sin of many," and (2/)"and made intercession for the transgressors." With his life the Servant through his suffering and death took the place of sinners and underwent their punishment in their place.


## Hebrews 4:14-16 (C) (RC)
## Hebrews 4:9 16 (L)


Note that verses 9-13 were dealt with in last Sunday's lectionary and will not be repeated here for (L). These verses (14-16) form a transition from what has gone before to what follows. However, these verses are not a full statement of the theme to be developed. While there is no careful and complete thematic sentence, nevertheless the author makes a very practical application of his thinking to the needs of Christian readers. This transitional passage (vv. 14-16) closes with a warm personal conclusion. This is an example of the purpose of the whole book: to urge readers to hold fast to their Christian confession, not in the sense of a creed, but of their Christian convictions.

In this passage the theme of Jesus as our great high priest is resumed (see 2:17-18). There are two qualifications for a priest and Jesus has both: (1) divine appointment (5:4) and (2) the ability to sympathize with our weaknesses. (v. 15) The author sees Jesus' high priestly office as an incentive for Christians to persist in their convictions. This is due to the fact Jesus as our great high priest endured all the trials a person can undergo and yet remained steadfast throughout. And he has passed "through the heavens" to the very throne of God.

Although Jesus is the Son of God, this did not prevent his sympathizing with human beings in their weaknesses. The fact that he was tempted in every respect as we are, yet remained sinless, reveals that he underwent even greater trials than ordinary humans. It was not necessary for Jesus to sin himself in order to experience our trials. In fact, the fact that he remained sinless indicates that he knew the strength of the temptation in a way that only the sinless can since he knew temptation *in its full intensity*. Ordinary human beings fall into sin before the last strain, but not so with the Son of God. He was not only tempted by Satan in the wilderness immediately after his baptism at the beginning of his public ministry, but tempted throughout his life, particularly in the Garden as he prayed that the cup of suffering and death might pass from him. Yet he submitted to the will of God and resisted the temptation to take another course of action. Only the person who has won through victoriously can best help others who are tempted. (v. 16)

Now Jesus is on the throne of grace where he gives mercy and grace to all who come in time of need. Therefore we can come near to the throne of grace in our time of need because we know that the Ascended Christ understands us, and is indeed one of us. He has taken our humanity into the Godhead.

The author of Hebrews is the first to ascribe to Jesus full human experience and at the same time full divinity without compromising either. The thrust of this final verse 16 is to run through all the discussions which follow in Hebrews.

Although the phrase "let us hold fast our confession" (v. 14) does not come at the end of this section, it is the conclusion of the thought. We have a high priest who knows our trials and temptations and who can strengthen us to withstand them. Therefore we can perservere in our Christian convictions.

*Mark 10:35-45*

In this passage James and John seek honor. Matthew has their mother asking for the seats of honor for her sons (Matthew 20:20-28) but neglects to correct verses 22, 23, and 24 in which Jesus speaks directly to James and John and not to their mother who made the request! Matthew evidently is offended by this very uncomplimentary description of the disciples and so puts the request in the mouth of their mother.

The request of James and John reveals the fact that they have not understood the nature of Jesus' Kingdom and his coming suffering and death. The seats on the right and left hand were places of honor, especially the seat on the right. Although Jesus has told them three times of his coming passion they still have not comprehended its meaning but are jockeying for personal power and special dignity.

Jesus' saying about the cup is also found in John 18:11. The saying about baptism is in Luke 12:50. As far as we know James and John were not martyrs. Jesus' saying to them has all the marks of an authentic saying of Jesus, since it is not likely the church would have worded it this way.

The cup and baptism are symbolic of Jesus' messianic sufferings. "Father, if thou art willing, remove this cup from me; nevertheless not my will, but thine, be done." (Luke 22:42) "I have a baptism to be baptized with; and how I am constrained until it is accomplished!" (Luke 12:50) The cup of suffering is an Old Testament metaphor: Isaiah 51:17, 22, Psalm 75:8, etc.

When James and John tell Jesus they are able to drink his cup and be baptized with his baptism Jesus replies by saying that it is not his decision to determine who sits on the right and left in glory. This indicates that Mark and the community out of which he wrote accepted the limitations of Jesus power.

The other disciples were indignant over the request of James and John. (v. 41) This then leads to a discussion of true greatness in the Kingdom, ending with the "ransom" saying. (v. 45) Jesus makes the point clear that discipleship is not a privilege but is *service*. Jesus' greatest service is that he finally gave his life as a ransom for many. But the ransom phrase goes contrary to the thinking of Luke and Matthew. While the idea of Jesus' death as a ransom is not developed in Mark's gospel, it is undoubtedly related to 1 Corinthians 6:19-20; 7:23, and Galatians 1:4; 2:20. Through this idea of ranson Gentile Christians expressed their conviction that Christ's death is God's action to rescue people who were powerless in the grip of sin. This may be a development of Jesus' own attitude as it was shaped by Isaiah 53. The "ransom" saying is one of the most important in the gospels and can be interpreted by Isaiah 53:11f (see earlier commentary for today on Isaiah 53). Greatness in the Kingdom is measured by service. In verse 45 "for many" is a typical Jewish phrase and may mean "for the sake of all." "Many" indicates the vast multitude in contrast to the individual. There was a widespread idea in Judaism that all innocent suffering was borne due to one's own sin, as well as due to the sins of others. But this concept could not express the uniqueness of the sufferings of Jesus.

As a result of Jesus' suffering and death there can be no hierarchy in the church. (v. 42) Discipleship does not allow one to claim any special reward. Thus Jesus rejects the claim that suffering is meritorious. The fact that a Christian suffers in following Jesus, in taking up one's cross, does not qualify one to a reward in the Kingdom nor to make any special demand as James and John did. But God will not forget even a cup of water given in the name of Christ. (9:41)

## Theological Reflections

Isaiah portrays the Servant of God who is righteous and who suffers for the unrighteous. He does not protest his unjust suffering. The Servant dies as he makes himself an offering for sin. The Lord does not forget him but he shall see his offspring, which points to his being revived. While Judaism cannot understand the significance of this Suffering Servant, Christians see it fulfilled in Jesus' vicarious suffering for the sins of the world. Hebrews deal with the theme of Jesus as the great high priest who knows the temptations of human beings but remains sinless himself. He is able to sympathize with us in all our weaknesses. The Ascended Christ is at the throne of grace to which Christians may approach with confidence, since we know he will forgive and grant mercy. For this reason Christians are urged to hold fast their confession. Mark relates the ambition of James and John who misunderstand the nature of the Kingdom and Jesus' coming suffering and death. Jesus points out that service to others is the way to greatness in the Kingdom. Jesus says that the Son of man came not to be served but to serve and give his life as a ransom for many. Ransom was a Gentile Christian concept explaining the power of Christ to set people free from the bondage of sin. We can best interpret ransom in light of Isaiah 53:11f which describes the Servant who is righteous but bears the iniquities of others. True greatness in the Kingdom is measured by service and Jesus has set the example by giving his life on the cross.

## Homiletical Moves

*Isaiah 53:7-12 (C)*
*Isaiah 53:10-12 (L)*
*Isaiah 53:10-11 (RC)*

### Jesus the Righteous Servant Who Bears Iniquities

1. The Servant was afflicted but opened not his mouth and so was Jesus
2. The Servant dies and is buried with the wicked; Jesus was crucified and buried in a borrowed tomb
3. The Servant, though righteous, bore the sin of many and made intercession for the transgressors, and so did Jesus
4. The Lord revives the Servant so that he sees his offspring; Jesus was raised from the dead
5. The Ascended Christ is alive and grants forgiveness and strength to all who trust in him
6. Put your faith in Christ who is alive and grants forgiveness and strength to those who trust in him

*This Preacher's Choice*

*Hebrews 4:14-16 (C) (RC)*
*Hebrews 4:9-16 (L)*

### Our Great High Priest Jesus Christ

1. Jesus can sympathize with us an our weakness, for he has been tempted in every respect as we are, but is sinless
2. Let us draw near to the throne of grace that we may receive mercy and find grace to help in time of need
3. Therefore let us hold fast our Christian faith as we face trials and temptations on the journey of life

*Mark 10:35-45*

### Discipleship: Not a Privilege But Service

1. The world creates classes with some ruling over others
2. James and John thought discipleship should bring a heavenly reward
3. Jesus declares the radical New Order in which the first place goes to the slave of all who serves God and others
4. Jesus set the example of service by giving his life as a ransom for many in his death on the cross
5. Therefore follow his example of self-giving in response to his love

**Hymn for Pentecost 22:**   *O Master, Let Me Walk With Thee*

**Prayer**

*Gracious God who gave your Son to ransom us from bondage to sin, we gladly offer our lives upon the altar of service in response. We thank you for Jesus the servant who though sinless bore the sins of many, and made intercession for us the transgressors. We come boldly to the throne of grace in prayer because we know we have a great high priest in Jesus Christ who has been tempted in every respect as we are tempted and yet remained sinless. Enable us to hold fast to our Christian faith when we are tried by temptations. May we join "The Order of the Towel" of those who follow Jesus' example of washing the disciples' feet and who look for ways to serve, rather than expecting to be served. Forgive us when we have sought places of prestige and have forgotten that the ground is level at the foot of the cross, where we all stand as sinners saved by grace. Amen*

# Proper 25      Pentecost 23      Ordinary Time 30
October 23-29

| Common | Lutheran | Roman Catholic |
|---|---|---|
| Jeremiah 31:7-9 | Jeremiah 31:7-9 | Jeremiah 31:7-9 |
| Hebrews 5:1-6 | Hebrews 5:1-10 | Hebrews 5:1-6 |
| Mark 10:46-52 | Mark 10:46-52 | Mark 10:46-52 |

## Comments on the Lessons

There is consensus on the first reading which is part of a message of consolation that gives assurance of the restoration of Israel. There is near consensus on the Hebrews reading. Note that verses 7-9 appear on Lent 5 (B) and so is omitted from (C) and (RC). There is consensus on the Markan reading.

## Commentary

*Jeremiah 31:7-9*

This is part of a longer passage (vv. 7-14) dealing with Homecoming. God will bring back the dispersed Israelites and assemble them in their homeland. There are parallels in Isaiah 35:5-10. This providing for Israel reminds us of Psalm 23:2-3 in which God cares for the poet and leads him in the paths of rightness, the right paths.

Jeremiah speaks of "Israel . . . Ephraim" (v. 7, 9) which indicates that as Ephraim is restored so is all of Israel, including Judah.

The prophet portrays the scattered Israelites coming back amid universal joy: "Sing aloud with gladness for Jacob, and raise shouts for the chief of the nations." (v. 7) He pictures the worn men, women and children shouting glad "hosannas" as they return home. They come from all parts of the earth, and among them are the blind, the lame, and the woman with child and "her who is in travail." Their tears mingle with shouts of joy as God gently leads them like a shepherd: "I will make them walk by brooks of water, in a straight path in which they shall not stumble" which parallels Psalm 23:2-3 in thought. God cares for Israel like a father, and for Ephraim as for a first born. (v. 9)

In verse 7 it has been suggested that the Hebrew should be emended that reads "for the chief of the nations" so that it reads "on the top of the mountains."

It would seem more appropriate to place "for I am a father to Israel, and Ephraim is my first-born" after verse 20 than in its present place. This would make verse 20 and verse 9c read:

*Is Ephraim my dear son?*
*Is he my darling child?*
*For as often as I speak against him,*

*I do remember him still.*
*Therefore my heart yearns for him;*
*I will surely have mercy on him (v. 20)*

*for I am a father to Israel,*
*and Ephraim is my first born. (v. 9c)*

In dealing with this passage we should note the close similarity to the ideas and phrases of Second Isaiah who is also concerned with the return from the Diaspora and note also the presence of ideas foreign to Jeremiah. This indicates that this passage is later than Jeremiah and from a writer who lived in the early post-exilic age. Perhaps only verse 9c dealt with above can be considered from Jeremiah himself. And verse 14 seems very foreign to the prophet's thought and not likely to be authentic Jeremiah.

274



*Hebrews 5:1-6 (C) (RC)*
*Hebrews 5:1-10 (L)*

This continues the theme of Jesus as our high priest which began with last Sunday's pericope. Since we have a high priest who is adequate for our human needs we should draw near to the throne of grace with confidence. The author of Hebrews is aware that Jesus did not qualify as a priest on the earthly level, but is concerned to show that Jesus qualifies for the heavenly priesthood.

Hebrews describes Jesus as high priest in terms of the requirements for a high priest in the order of Aaron and the priests who came after him. They were: (1) appointed to represent people before God, particularly in the presenting of gifts and sin-offerings, (2) they were required to be sympathetic toward human weaknesses since they too were human, (3) since they were sinners they had to present sin-offerings for themselves as well as others, (4) they had to be duly appointed in accordance with the divine ordinance.

The high priest can "deal gently" was a term from Greek philosophy which contrasted with the Stoic notion of a developed lack of feeling. It refers to a golden mean between indifference and sickly sentimentality. There is a gentle strength which cares for others in the priest's manner.

Notice how Hebrews moves from the "confidence" the Christian should have in Jesus as priest (4:16) to the qualifications of priesthood as required in the earthly official (vv. 1-4), as noted above. Then he moves to the fulfillment of these requirements (vv. 5-10) and to the bitter experience of Jesus as a human being especially as it has significance for us.

We should note that in the Old Testament there was no atoning for deliberate and defiant sins, but only for unwitting sins committed by the "ignorant and wayward." (v. 2)

In verse 6 there is reference to "the order of Melchizedek" which means according to the rank which Melchizedek held. (Psalm 110:4; and Hebrews 7:1-10) Melchizedek was a mysterious priest-king who was greater than either Abraham or his descendent, Levi. Neither his birth nor death are recorded in Scripture.

It is interesting that there is no documentation of verse 7 or the verses that follow it. It seems that an account of Jesus' Passion, either written or oral, underlies these verses. However, a comparison with the Synoptic Gospels reveals that this description does not exactly tally with them. However, the Gethsemane events are the closest parallel to this section. When the author wrote, there may have been a still fluid account of the Passion before it was set down in the Gospels as we have them. Note carefully that it is only here that the author deals in detail with the life of Jesus and that, in doing so, he deals only with the his Passion! This supports the modern thesis that the passion narrative was the first connected form which tradition took.

In describing Jesus' Passion as offering up "prayers and supplications, with loud cries and tears, to him who was able to save him from death, and he was heard for his godly fear" (v. 7), it appears the author has no problem in going all out in equating Jesus' agony with the greatest depths of human despair.

The phrase "and he was heard for his godly fear" (v. 7) is a puzzle for scholars, and we are unable to know what was in the author's mind when he wrote these words.

In verse 8 the thought seems to be that Jesus could learn the real, inner meaning of obedience only through suffering.

We find in verses 9-10 a reference to Jesus being made "perfect" which seems to mean completely adequate but also to have a connotation of moral perfection. Jesus is qualified to be a high priest, not only because he fulfilled tha requirements of a priest in a formal way, but also because he dealt with human weakness and sins in a radical way. He faced them from inside humanity itself. Jesus was a priest, but a different kind of priest, for he was after the order of Melchizedek. In the following verses he expounds on this difference.


*Mark 10:46-52*

This passage is a transition between the section on discipleship (chapters 8-10) and the section on Jesus' confrontation with the religious authorities in Jerusalem (chapters 11-13). It is the last healing story in Mark's Gospel, and although not as spectacular as some, it is climactic in that its outcome lifts up the goal of this Gospel: to motivate readers to also follow Jesus "on the way." Notice how Mark transforms the story into a picture of discipleship by the addition of the last few words. It emphasizes the importance of the Passion story which comes immediately afterwards.

While some scholars regard this healing event as legendary, it appears to be a narrative based on the reminiscence of an eye-witness. This is due to the vivid details it contains and the fact that it is an account which goes back and forth. The fact that it is located in Jericho indicated that the original teller of the event remembered the connection with Jericho.

It hardly seems accidental that the story was placed where it is, since it contributes to the progress of the Gospel in such a marked fashion. It is told from a special angle which suggests that the story had been told for a long time in the church as instruction for particular aspects of Christian discipleship, as Mark uses it also.

The mention of Jericho is a signal to the reader that Jesus and the disciples are now only fifteen miles from their goal of Jerusalem. Thus a new phase of the story opens in what follows. The Blind Bartemaeus' healing serves a two-fold role: to conclude the present section, and to make a smooth transition to the next. The character of the story corresponds to this.

Note that this is the first public and unrebuked recognition of Jesus as Messiah! The Messianic secret is out! No longer is Jesus recognized as Messiah only by the demons and disciples, but the blind beggar also greets him as "Son of David." Jesus endures this messianic title by healing the man rather than rebuking him. This prepares the way for the people in the crowds, in the Palm Sunday account which follows, to shout "Hosanna! . . . Blessed is the kingdom of our father David that is coming! Hosanna in the highest!" (11:9, 10)

It can hardly be accidental that the section of Mark (8:27—10:45) which is so concerned with Jesus' efforts to open the eyes of his disciples to the fact and meaning of his Messiahship is completed by a story of Jesus opening a blind men's eyes, even as it was introduced in 8:22ff by the miracle of restoring sight to another blind man. We must see these healings of blind men in sharp contrast with the disciples who, though they see, are yet spiritually blind to the meaning of the Kingdom. It serves as a repudiation of the attitude of Jesus' followers who in verse 48 rebuked Blind Bartimaeus and told him to be silent. It also serves as an object lesson on the meaning of service which Jesus had been unsucessfully trying to teach in 8:27—10:45.

One of the most striking aspects of this healing miracle is the great amount of interest that centers on the blind man, rather than on Jesus. Of course, the healing reveals the compassion and power of Jesus and thus shows his messianic role (cf. Isaiah 42:18 "Hear, you deaf; and look, you blind, that you may see!") This focus on the blind man suggests that, when the story was told in the early church, the blind man was held up as a model and encouragement for others, either believers or potential believers. Bartimaeus is aware of his blindness and consequent helplessness, but when Jesus comes near he realizes that his only hope has come. Therefore he calls on Jesus for help. (Recall that in the previous section we are shown that we are all blind until Jesus opens our eyes, although the disciples in sharp contrast to Bartimaeus, remain unaware of their condition.) Notice the persistence of Bartimaeus whose faith persists despite all discouragement until Jesus, through the disciples, calls to him. That call and Bartimaeus' immediate reponse to it means that he is saved from his helpless plight. As a result he must begin to follow Jesus at once, to follow in the way of Christian discipleship. Soon we will see that this discipleship of Christians leads to danger and suffering at Jerusalem. But it is significant that "faith," "save," "follow," "way" are all used in their full religious meaning as they relate to "The Way," an early title for the Christian religion.

The fact that Jericho is mentioned twice in verse 46 probably means that the story was associated with Jesus' departure from Jericho when the story reached Mark. Mark had to introduce it with a formula to get Jesus into the town so he could heal the blind man as he was departing. Some scholars think the story referred originally to a nameless blind man who later came to be identified with Bartimaeus of Jericho, who was well known in the early Church as a person who had followed Jesus on the way. Some MSS have "the blind begger" which supports this thesis even more.

Bartimaeus calls Jesus "Son of David," and in the Greek it reads "Son of David, Jesus" which is simply a messianic title. Although it doesn't refer to Jesus' family descent, it was valued in the early church as a useful and vital title for Jesus when properly understood.

In verse 50 we have an interesting detail which shows the eagerness and quickness with which the blind man answered Jesus, as he sets an example for others: "And throwing off his mantle he sprang up and came to Jesus." A beggar in the Orient would already have his cloak off and spread on the ground to receive alms. Some scribes have attempted to deal with this by altering the text to read "put on his cloak."

In verse 52 Jesus says to the man, "Go your way; your faith has made you well." The Greek word translated "made you well" can mean both healing and "salvation."

Similarly "on the way" in Greek can mean both "along the road" and "in the way" (of discipleship)."

The central thrust of this healing story is the invitation, implied, to all readers who, like Bartimaeus, are both outsiders and blind to come to Jesus and so to see, and seeing to follow Jesus. Thus the story of blind Bartimaeus is not simply a story with a moral for Christians. Rather it is a *witness* to Jesus Christ and a *call* to follow him. Notice that the Old Testament lesson from Jeremiah 31:7-9 is an oracle of salvation and restoration in which the blind and lame from all over the earth are brought home. It may be that the framers of the lectionery saw in Bartimaeus a particular example of the fulfillment of that promise in Jeremiah, as Jesus goes up to Jerusalem to seal in his death and resurrection the new covenant which Jeremiah announced in 31:31-34. All may now enter that new covenent, both the house of Judah and Israel and all who know their blindness and want to see, and seeing, are willing to follow Jesus on the way. Thus this passage contains both miracle and call to discipleship. The story of Bartimaeus witnesses to the power of Jesus to restore (both make well and save) those who know they are blind. This blind man serves as a model of faith for all "blind people," both seeing and non-seeing!

## Theological Reflections

Jeremiah tells of a God initiated Homecoming in which he will assemble the dispersed from over the world, the blind and lame, and woman with child, and a great company. They will return with shouts of joy and God will lead them by brooks of water in a straight path, for He is the father to Israel and Ephraim is his first-born. Hebrews describes the role of high priest and points out how Christ fulfilled the heavenly high priest role, suffering for others and learning obedience through what he suffered. He was made perfect and became the source of eternel salvation to all who obey him, for he was designated a high priest by God himself. The account of the healing of Blind Bartimaeus is both a healing miracle and a call story. A blind man comes seeking healing, but he represents all those who are spiritually blind. He is an "outsider" and not part of the disciples. He calls Jesus "Son of David" or Messiah, and Jesus affirms this title by healing the man. Jesus tells him to go his way, his faith has made him well. Mark tells us that he not only received his sight but followed Jesus on the way. So this is a teaching story to lead those who hear it to seek spiritual sight from Jesus and then to come follow him. The initiative of God in the healing and salvation of human beings is a common thread through all three of these passages.

## Homiletical Moves

*Jeremiah 31:7-9*
### God's Homecoming for His People

1. The Lord commands the dispersed Jews to sing and shout for joy because he will bring them home to their homeland
2. He will gather the blind, lame, woman with child, etc. from the farthest parts of the earth
3. They will return with joy mixed with weeping as God leads them by brooks of water in a straight path
4. God brings us home to live with him who created us and to whom we belong through the death and resurrection of Jesus Christ
5. Hear and obey Christ's invitation to come to him

*Hebrews 5:1-6 (C) RC)*
*Hebrews 5:1-10 (L)*
### Christ Our High Priest

1. Christ has been appointed a heavenly high priest by God
2. Through his passion and resurrection Jesus suffered for us and became the source of eternal salvation
3. Therefore believe in Jesus Christ and obey him that you may draw near to the throne of grace
4. Through Christ our high priest we have forgiveness of our sins and eternal salvation beginning here and now and continuing after the grave

*This Preacher's Choice*

*Mark 10:46-52*
### The Healing and Calling of Blind Bartimaeus

1. Bartimaeus a blind beggar cries out to Jesus to have mercy on him
2. The disciples, insiders, rebuked him

3. But Jesus tells the disciples to call Bartimaeus, an ''outsider'' which they do
4. Jesus answers his cry by healing him through his faith
5. Bartimaeus responds to Jesus' healing by following Jesus on the way, thus setting an example for all who are blind spiritually
6. Believe in Christ and follow him on the way of life

**Hymn for Pentecost 23:**   *Hail to the Lord's Anointed*

**Prayer**

*Almighty God who has taken the initiative in our salvation, we praise you for appointing Christ as our high priest. We thank you that he learned obedience through suffering and has become the source of eternal salvation for all who obey. Through Christ we can come home again to you, our Heavenly Father, and find rest and peace for our souls. For you have made us for yourself and outside of you we can find no rest or peace. We confess the blindness of our spiritual sight and cry out for mercy. Heal us and set our feet on the paths of righteousness to follow the Living Christ all our days. May we hear his call to us, spring up in joy and come to Jesus. Grant us the faith that will enable us to find healing and wholeness of life. Amen*

# Proper 26    Pentecost 24    Ordinary Time 31

October 30 — November 5

| Common | Lutheran | Roman Catholic |
|---|---|---|
| Deuteronomy 6:1-9 | Deuteronomy 6:1-9 | Deuteronomy 6:2-6 |
| Hebrews 7:23-28 | Hebrews 7:23-28 | Hebrews 7:23-28 |
| Mark 12:28b-34 | Mark 12:28-34 (35-37) | Mark 12:28-34 |

## Comments on the Lessons

There is virtual consensus on the first reading which gives the purpose of the law and sets forth the law of love of God. Note that verse 1 is needed for meaning and verses 7-9 for a proper completion. There is consensus on the Hebrews reading. There is consensus on the Marken reading.

## Commentary

*Deuteronomy 6:1-9 (C) (L)*
*Deuteronomy 6:2-6 (RC)*

The pericope is the beginning of a longer explanation of the meaning of the first commandment. (vv. 1-25) In this chapter Moses deals with *the commandment* and in a later passage Moses explains the statutes and ordinances (chapter 12ff).

In verses 1-3 we have a transition in which Moses turns from the revelation in the past to the duty in the future before them. The God-centered life which began at Horeb is to continue in Canaan. In 5:31 the Lord speaks to Moses saying: "But you, stand here by me, and I will tell you all the commandment and the statutes and the ordinances which you shall teach them, that they may do them in the land which I give them to possess."

"Now this is the commandment . . ." (v. 1) introduces a new section which differs from similar titles in 5:1 and 12:1, in that it uses the word "commandment" which is translated "commandments" by error in the KJV. A better rendering of the word is "charge" which is suggested by George Adam Smith. Moses gives the charge to Israel which was earlier given to him at Horeb. The purpose of the charge is to ensure that the present and all the following generations may learn to reverence (or fear) God. Such reverence of God will reveal itself in obedience. The purpose of obedience to God's commandments and statutes is "that your days may be prolonged." (v. 2) This is a similar promise to that in verse 3 "that it may go well with you." This promise of divine blessings, fruitfulness and welfare (5:33; 6:18-19) is a characteristic of Deuteronomy.

The milk and honey promised would be an ideal of a nomadic rather than an agrarian society. In Exodus 3:8 Canaan is called a "land flowing with milk and honey," which made it a paradise in the eyes of the semi-nomadic Israelites.

The Great Commandment is set forth in 6:4-19. Here Israel's faith and duty are described. In Jewish tradition verses 4-9 are known as the "Shema" from the first word in the Hebrew (shema) which means "hear." Notice that this Great Commandment (Mark 12:29-30) is basically a restatement of the first commandment of the Ten Commandments but in a positive form. It declares that there are not many gods but only One Lord. This Lord is sovereign and unique. There are several possible translations for the Hebrew of verse 4 which the RSV gives as footnotes. In addition to "The Lord our God is one Lord" it could read:

1. the Lord our God, the Lord is one
2. the Lord is our God, the Lord is one
3. the Lord is our God, the Lord alone.

These four Hebrew words which can be translated in any one of the four ways above can emphasize the unity of the Lord, or may declare the uniqueness of the Lord. From the context, we cannot really tell whether it is the unity in God or the uniqueness of God over against other gods which is stressed here. It seems the first emphasis, on the unity of God, is more likely. The commandment is almost the same as the first commandment, but restated in light of Israel's encounter with the Canaanite deities. The thrust of the commandment is that the object of Israel's exclusive attention, affection and devotion in worship is not several gods but One God. Israel's attention is undivided and is confined to the One God called Yahweh (translated "Lord" by both the KJV and RSV). The thought expressed is not that there are no other divine beings that exist but that the Lord alone is sovereign Lord and there is no other Lord, power or authority who rules the destinies of the earth.

In verse 5 Israel is commanded to love this Lord completely. By using the word love the writer of Deuteronomy seeks to avoid a legalism of obedience required by duty or necessity. The Hebrew is to love God because God first loved him or her and expressed this love especially in the Exodus experience.

The word "love" is derived from family life and except for its use in the Ten Commandments (Exodus 20:6) and Song of Deborah (Judges 5:31), love was not used in relation to God before Hosea. God is love and can transform even the inability to love into the capacity to love. John puts it, "We love, because he first loved us." (1 John 4:19) God is lovable. Such love contains awe and reverence, for the love for God inevitably takes on a part of the character of the person who is loved.

"With all your heart, and with all your soul, and with all your might" (v. 5) is a favorite phrase of Deuteronomy. Heart in the Hebrew thought is the seat of the mind and will, along with a whole range of psychical emotions. Soul is not the Greek soul imprisoned in the fleshly body, but was the source of vitality which dies when the body dies. These two words mean that a person is to love God with his or her total being. This notion is reinforced by the third phrase, "with all your might." This has the thrust of "all your force or strength." It means completely to love God. The New Testament adds "with all your mind" (Mark 12:30) to the above three (see commentary on Mark for today).

The stress laid on this commandment is evident from the verses 6-9. The words are to be "upon your heart." (Jeremiah 31:33) The words are to be taught diligently to children, talked constantly all day long, and bound upon the hands, forehead and doorposts. This is another way of saying that the commandment to love God is to be the central and controlling interest in the Hebrew's life.

The commandment to bind the commandment on the hand and frontlets between eyes, and to place it on the doorposts, was later carried out literally by Jews who wrote Deuteronomy 6:4-9, 11:13-21 and Exodus 13:1-10, 11-16. These verses were written on small scrolls and attached to their forehead, left arm or to the doorposts of their houses. There is always the danger of taking something literally which was meant figuratively. The point of this section (vv. 4-9) is to make love for God the controlling force in one's life. The literal placing them on the arm, forehead and doorposts could easily become a substitute for the daily obedience of the commandment. At the same time human beings need aids for devotion, and when such phylacteries serve as reminders to love God they serve their function. The commandment to love God is to be a perpetual reminder to the Hebrew of his or her relationship to God.

### Hebrews 7:23-28

This is a continuation of the comparison of the priesthood of Melchizedek and the Levites. (7:1-28) The Levitical priests were impermanent, for death ended their term of office. But Jesus holds his priesthood permanently since he continues forever. Jesus was appointed with a divine oath (vv. 20, 21, 28) as foretold by the Psalmist "The Lord has sworn and will not change his mind, 'You are a priest for ever after the order of Melchizedek'." (Psalm 110:4) While the earthly priest took office without an oath, our priest, Jesus Christ, has taken an oath and therefore has behind his ministry the divine guarantee. Hebrews declares that "the word of the oath, which came later than the law, appoints a Son who has been made perfect for ever." (v. 28)

The permanence of Christ's priesthood which is guaranteed by the divine oath ensures a covenant superior to others. The central thrust of this whole passage is the permanence of the ministry of Jesus as high priest. Because Jesus' priesthood is permanent he is able "for all time to save those who draw near to God through him, since he always lives to make intercession for them." (v. 25) While the function of earthly priests was to bear people up to God in intercession there is now in Christ a high priest who does not need angels and especially Michael as intercessors for human beings. Nor does he need to offer sacrifices for his own sins and then for others. Notice how the author blends together rather loosely his description of the annual sacrifice of the high priest on atonement-day to which he referred earlier in 5:3 and the daily sacrifices of the priests. The daily offering of the priests was a cereal offering and not a sin offering.

The author describes how radically different Jesus as high priest is from earthly priests in verse 26: "For it was fitting that we should have such a high priest, holy, blameless, unstained, separated from sinners, exalted above the heavens." Jesus offered a sacrifice once for all, the sacrifice of his life on the cross which made a perfect atonement. Those who draw near to God through Jesus the high priest can always count on him because he always lives to make intercession for them. (v. 25) He is a living high priest who continually intercedes on our behalf. Thus the personal character of the high priest, Jesus, makes the chief difference in his priesthood. It appears that in verse 26 we have a part of an early Christian hymn in praise of Christ.

The passage concludes with an affirmation that Jesus is the kind of high priest that suits our case, since he has no sins of his own to expiate like the earlier priests appointed by the law. Jesus who has received his priestly appointment by the oath of God is the "Son who has been made perfect for ever." (v. 28) This priesthood after the order of Melchizedek satisfies the human hunger for God. He is the perfect high priest forever.

*Mark 12:28b-34 (C)*
*Mark 12:28-34 (35-37) (L)*
*Mark 12:28-34 (RC)*

This passage is concerned with The Great Commandment, which we have dealt with in the Deuteronomy passage for today. It comes after three insincere questions. The basic thrust of this paragraph is a clear presentation of a central doctrine of early Gentile Christianity. It makes the point that righteousness is not a matter of obedience to a complex code of laws and customs, but rather obedience to the law of *love*.

It is significant that in the parallels to this event (Matthew 22:35; Luke 10:25) the attitude of the lawyer is hostile, but there is no sign of this in Mark. Rather, Jesus commends the scribe (v. 34) for his answer: "You are not far from the kingdom of God."

Notice that the words of Deuteronomy 6:4 which are both preface to, and part of, the first commandment define the quality of the complete love which God requires. These are among the most treasured verses of Judaism, known as the "Shema" from the first word in Hebrew which means "hear." The question of which was the greatest commandment was one that was often discussed by the Jewish scholars, but there was no real doubt as to the greater commandment.

The distinctive aspect of Jesus' reply is that he added to Deuteronomy 6:4 the quote from Leviticus 19:18: ". . . You shall love your neighbor as yourself . . ." This second quotation could hardly be offensive to anyone. It expresses a Christian concern. The comment "There is no other commandment greater than these" appears to be the affirmation of early Gentile Christianity. Matthew and Luke both omit it, however. Matthew 22:40 changes the account to make all the other laws grow out of these two. And Luke has completely rewritten the story (10:25-28) and has the scribe say what Jesus says in Mark.

There is no evidence for the combining of these two commandments of love for God and love for neighbor before the time of Jesus. Love to God finds its only complete fulfillment in love to one's neighbor, and in turn love to one's neighbor must be grounded in love of God.

In Luke's account the lawyer sought a further explanation and Jesus gave him the parable of the Good Samaritan.

Jesus told the scribe that he was "not far from the kingdom of God" (v. 34), meaning that he recognizes the sovereignty of God and has the right spiritual outlook as described in the Sermon on the Mount. Jesus speaks to the scribe as Lord and not merely a Teacher.

## Theological Reflections

The Deuteronomy and Mark readings focus on the great commandmant, to love God with all one's being. In Mark Jesus adds to this the commandment to love one's neighbor as one's self. Love for God and for neighbor is our response to God's prior love. We love God because he first loved us in Jesus Christ. We love our neighbor because God in Christ has shown us his love. Hebrews stresses the permanence of Christ as our high priest who is able to save those who draw near to God through him. God's love for us in Christ in making Christ our permanent high priest is the central thought of this passage. God's love for us which motivates our love for God and neighbor is the message of the passages for today.

**Homiletical Moves**

*Deuteronomy 6:1-9 (C) (L)*
*Deuteronomy 6:2-6 (RC)*
## You Shall Love the Lord Your God

1. You shall love the Lord your God with all your heart, soul and might
2. You shall love God because he first loved you by delivering you from the power of sin and death by Christ's death
3. You shall love the Lord your God all the time, in all circumstances of life, and provide reminders to love God
4. You shall teach your children to love God
5. If you obey the commandment to love God and keep his statutes and ordinances, then your days will be prolonged, it will go well with you, you will multiply greatly in a land flowing with milk and honey

*Hebrews 7:23-28*
## Christ Is Our Permanent High Priest

1. Christ, in contrast to earlier priests who died, is a priest forever because he lives forever
2. He has made a sacrifice once for all on the cross for our sins
3. Christ is a high priest who is holy, blameless, unstained, separated from sinners and exalted above the heavens
4. Christ is able to save those who draw near to God through him, since he always lives to make intercession for them
5. Draw near to God through faith in Christ our high priest

*This Preacher's Choice*

*Mark 12:28b-34 (C)*
*Mark 12:28-34 (35-37) (L)*
*Mark 12:28-34 (RC)*
## You Shall Love God and Neighbor!

1. A scribe asks Jesus which is the greatest commandment
2. Jesus replies that you shall love God with all your being, and a second commandment is to love your neighbor as yourself
3. The scribe agrees with Jesus and comments that this commandment is much more than all whole burnt offerings and sacrifices
4. Jesus tells the scribe that he is not far from the kingdom of God, since he recognized the sovereignty of God and has the right spiritual outlook
5. Love for God finds its only complete fulfillment in love for one's neighbor, and love for one's neighbor must be grounded in love for God
6. Therefore, love God and neighbor in response to God's love

**Hymn for Pentecost 24:**  *Spirit of God, Descend Upon My Heart*

**Prayer**

*O God of love who loved us while we were yet sinners, teach us to love you. Descend upon our hearts and make us love you as we ought to love. We thank you for Christ, our permanent high priest, who made a complete sacrifice once for all on the cross for our sins. Thank you that he is able to save all those who draw near to you through him since he always lives. O God of everlasting love, teach us to love our neighbor as ourself. May we see that love for you finds its only complete fulfillment in love for our neighbor, and may we discover that our love for our neighbor must be grounded in love for you. Amen*

# Reformation Sunday

Lutheran Only

## Lutheran

Jeremiah 31:31-34
Romans 3:19-28
John 8:31-36

## Comments on the Lessons

The Jeremiah reading is a prophecy of a new covenant which God will make with Israel and Judah, not like the old covenant, but a covenant written on the hearts of people, assuring them of forgiveness of sins and in that time everyone will know the Lord. The central thrust of the Romans reading is justification by faith through Christ Jesus apart from the law, the basic principle of the Reformation. Jesus declares in the reading from John that the truth will make one free and says that if the Son makes you free you will be free indeed. All three passages deal with the *grace of God* in the new covenant in Jesus Christ which justifies and sets us free.

## Commentary

### Jeremiah 31:31-34

This passage has the only occurrence in the Hebrew Bible where "covenant" is qualified by "new." This new covenant is coming in the future and the Hebrew indicates this with a formula translated: "Look, days are coming," (v. 27, 38 also) The new covenant will replace the old one broken by the community. (v. 32) Here is a reversal motif, what once existed and is broken is now replaced with a new covenant. The breaking of the old covenant had reversed the relationsip of God with the people by making him disgusted with them. But with the giving of the new covenant the people of Israel will become God's people and He their God once more: "And I will be their God, and they shall be my people." (v. 33)

The new covenant projects the Law interiorly in the minds of the people, and this may constitute the "new" of the covenant, since Biblical theology sees one covenant made by God with Abram and renewed through the centuries and fulfilled in Jesus Christ's death as the new covenant. This is a continuation of the relationship of God and his people based on grace from the time of Adam and Eve's Fall.

Under this new covenant there will be a cessation of the human teaching of God because each person will know God already. Every person, from the least to the greatest, in the nation will know God. This new status will reverse that described in Jeremiah 5:1-5 and 8:7 where the people do not know the way of the Lord (5:4) and "my people know not the ordinance of the Lord (8:7).

Another result of the new covenant will be the divine forgiveness of the nation's sin. (v. 34) Thus the prophet sees that, although the nation's fathers had brought the people into dire straits, there is hope through the promised new covenant. The situation of the past will be reversed through the making of this *unbreakable* covenant. Although only the past and future generations are mentioned here, the present generation is referred to in 2:9: "Therefore I still contend with you, says the Lord, and with your children's children I will contend." It is this present generation which is being given the promise of the new covenant.

In foreseeing this new covenant the prophet ignores the problems of the past and foretells a relationship between God and the nation Israel which avoids the defects of the old covenant, since it will internalize the teachings of God. But this is a pious hope and may be described as utopian rather than a program of social organization. That this is utopian is revealed by the prediction that individuals in the nation will not need to teach each other about the knowledge of God or justice, because each person will know it already and the nation's sin will be forgiven. The Old Testament scholar John Bright has ventured to ask in this regard, "And what about the future beyond this new covenant? Will the people no longer sin after this new covenant?" The answer to this is that an answer lies beyond Jeremiah's field of vision. This promised new covenant is God's gracious act of salvation for his people.

If the people truly know God within as promised here then they will be sinless, which is utopia and a victory of hope over experience. Such a time has yet to come, of course, even though the covenant made in Jesus' death on the cross is called the new covenant in his blood. It points yet forward to the coming Messianic Age at the End.

Some scholars have called this passage one of the most profound and moving passages of the Bible. This is given from a Christian perspective which reads into this Old Testament text the new covenant of the New Testament. This complicates the treatment of the section, however.

Some question whether or not Jeremiah spoke this prophecy, or if one of his disciples is the author. The reader is referred to the commentaries for detailed discussion of this issue.

"Covenant" is used as a metaphor to describe a state in which the faith community will automatically keep the Law for it will be written on their hearts. This future covenant is not an obligation between two parties with national and moral requirements which must be kept. Rather it is a metaphor of an arrangement of an imaginary community in the future. Such a utopian society does not and cannot exist, but these images serve to transform the disintegrating society of Jeremiah's time described in chapters 4-21. The promise is that God will restore the nation and create the kind of society which past generations failed to create.

### *Romans 3:19-28*

In verses 19-20 we are told that the law speaks to those who are under the law and that the whole world is accountable to God. For no human being will be justified in God's sight by doing works of the law, for it is through the law that knowledge of sin comes. In other words, the law succeeds only as it makes people aware of their sinful condition. And this was God's purpose in giving the law: (7:7, and Galatians 3,19-29). The law of Moses revealed God's will so that people might recognize their transgressions. The law, according to Paul, serves like a custodian of a child to train the child. These two verses set the stage for what follows in verses 21-28 which is the central thrust of the Reformation movement of Martin Luther which continues in Protestant churches today: the righteousness of God through faith in Jesus Christ for all who believe.

The true righteousness of God is described in verses 21-26, a righteousness revealed in Jesus Christ which rests not on obedience to the law, but rather on God's gracious act of redemption in Christ Jesus. Note that verses 22b-23 are really a parenthetical explanation of "all" in verse 22a: "for all who believe." (v. 22) "For there is no distinction; since all have sinned and fall short of the glory of God, they are justified by his grace as a gift, through the redemption which is in Christ Jesus." (vv. 22b-23)

"Fall short of the glory of God" reflects the creation of all humanity in the image of God and the fact that the divine image has now been distorted by sin, and the glory of God which should show in the way one lives is lacking. But this image of God was expected to be restored in the coming age.

"The law and the prophets"(v. 21) refers to the Hebrew Scriptures. Paul says that all who believe are justified by his grace as a gift. "Justified" is a verbal form from the same root as "righteousness." The thrust of the word is not so much "made righteous" in the moral sense of being perfect, but rather "pronounced righteous." Thus it means "acquitted." The prisoner is set free to leave the courtroom rather than go to prison. Human beings appear before God as guilty, but by the mercy of God they are pronounced acquitted and treated as if innocent. This is the "amazing grace" which touched the life of John Newton, the slave trader, and transformed him. He sang and wrote the hymn about this amazing grace.

"Redemption" (v. 24) refers to a ransoming or buying back, as in the case of a prisoner or war or a slave. The word means emancipation or deliverance. As used in this verse, it means that those who are slaves of sin are freed from the power of sin through God's act in Christ. While ransom of a slave implies a price paid, there seems to be no thought of a price paid here. If the question is raised, the price is Christ's blood (v. 25), which is his life.

God put Christ Jesus forward as an "expiation" by his blood. (v. 25) Expiation refers to wiping away the sin which marred human life. Expiation is by the blood of Jesus Christ which shows the seriousness with which God takes sin, and it reveals the depths of his love. God shows his forebearance in passing over former sins. Expiation may also refer to the "mercy seat" where reconcilation was effected. Calvary is the mercy seat for Christians!

The difference between God's justification of sinners and their attempt to justify themselves by works of the law is summed up in *grace*. The way of obedience to the law is based on what a human being tries to do to please God. But the way of grace is based on what God *has done* for us in Christ Jesus. Thus the right relationship with God (one meaning of righteousness) is based on God's grace and our acceptance of that through faith in Jesus Christ, not on our own striving to be good.

Boasting is excluded, says Paul, on the principle not of works but of faith. (v. 27) If we were righteous because of good works, there would be room for boasting. But since salvation is by faith pride is excluded. We are justified by faith apart from works of law. The word for "boasting" in Greek is a favorite word of Paul's and it was an aspect of zeal characteristic of Judaism. We see what he means by boasting in the story of his life in Galatians 1:13-14; Philippians 3:3-6 and 2 Corinthians 11:16—12:10. The person who is saved by grace claims no moral progress of his or her own achievement. The Christian could never title an autobiography, *Goodness and How I Achieved It*. Rather, the Christian's life is summed up in "Amazing Grace."

### John 8:31-36

Jesus is now speaking to the Jews who believed in him. He raises the question of freedom.

The truth which is the key to freedom here is not truth in the sense of knowledge in general, but rather saving truth: "Jesus said to him, 'I am the way, and the truth, and the life; no one comes to the Father, but by me'." (14:6) The "truth" meant is the revelation of Jesus. In verse 36 it is the Son who sets free. The preacher should caution against the use of the phrase "the truth will set you free" in political oratory appealing for national or personal liberty. Such use is a distortion of a purely religious meaning of both truth and freedom in this passage. Deliverance from sin by truth is not a concept found in the Old Testament.

In verse 31 there is a subtle difference in the Johannine use of the verb "believe" in Greek. In verse 30 John said that "many believed in him" but in verse 31 the more correct translation is "the Jews who had believed him," rather than the RSV "the Jews who had believed in him." In verse 30 John uses the verb with a preposition to mean "believed *in* him" but in verse 31 there is no preposition used with the verb, hence the meaning "believed him." The meaning of "believed *in* him" is that they gave credence, plus intelligent understanding and reliance, upon Jesus who is believed. But in verse 31 "believed him" means no more than that they gave credence to what has been stated.

In this passage Jesus is speaking to those who have simply given credence to his words as he says, "If you continue in my word, you are truly my disciples." (v. 31) Jesus is thus defining belief as more than intellectual knowledge about or giving credence to words. Rather belief is placing personal reliance upon another person and continually staying with that person by continuing in her/his word.

In this passage John brings together Hebrew and Greek thought regarding freedom and truth. For the Jew law was truth. The study of the law made people free. But in the Hellenistic thought world the Stoics said that a person could obtain freedom by regulating one's life in accordance with the Logos. Truth for the Jew brought freedom from worldly care. Truth for the Stoic delivered the person from ignorance, error and final loss of being. For John's Gospel here and elsewhere, freedom means deliverance from sin.

The Jews responded to Jesus' statement that the truth will make you free by claiming they had never been in bondage to anyone. While this was not true in a literal sense, for they had been in bondage in Egypt and in Exile, they must be claiming that they have never lost their spiritual autonomy. But in making this claim they are showing a profound ignorance of their own spiritual situation. Jesus is not speaking of physical bondage, of course, but of slavery to sin: "every one who commits sin is a slave to sin." (v. 34) Jesus begins this verse with "truly, truly, I say to you," which indicates the key importance of what he is now saying.

It was more of a Greek than Hebrew notion to think of sin as bondage. The Hebrew thought of sin as breaking the law. But for Jesus, sin is a manifestation of a condition of slavery. Here Jesus attacks the Jews' confidence in their being descendants of Abraham. The word for "descendant" in Greek is a collective singular, and while the Jews may have been thinking of themselves as descendants of Abraham, John seems to be using it in the sense that Jesus is the real descendant of Abraham! If to sin is to become a slave and, since the Jews were sinners for having rejected Christ, then it follows that they are slaves and are not free sons of Abraham. The Jews were proud of the fact they were descendants of Abraham through the free-born son, Isaac, and not Ishmael the slave-born. Thus the slaves, the Jewish sinners, must be considered outside. But Jesus the Son is the true descendant of Abraham and inherits the Father's property and so can free his father's slaves. Note that it was through Jesus' death and resurrection that he entered upon his inheritance from the Father and thus could free Jews, giving them real liberty, freedom from sin.

In verse 35 freedom, sonship and sinlessness of Jesus underlie the thought of the verse.

Paul writes in Galatians 5:1, "For freedom Christ has set us free; stand fast therefore, and do not submit again to a yoke of slavery." This seems to be the same thought Paul had in mind in verse 36 which could be translated better: "So if the Son makes you free, you will be *really* free." Only the Son has power to set a person free from the slavery of sin. "So" or "consequently" at the beginning of the verse 36 gives this thrust of meaning.

Notice that verse 35 seems to be a parenthetical insertion. The slave mentioned here is not the slave of sin in verse 34. The contrast is not between slave and free, but in gradation between slave and son. Verse 35 seems to be a short parable since definite articles appear before the main nouns *slave* and *son* as they do in parables. Slave and son are stock characters in the parables of the Synoptic Gospels. For John the slave has no permanent place in the household.

### Theological Reflections

Freedom from slavery to sin is the theological thrust of all three passages for this Reformation Sunday lectionary. Jeremiah foretells a new covenant which will be written on the hearts of all the house of Israel and Judah in a coming utopia. Then all persons will know God, and God will forgive their iniquity and no longer remember their sin. God will be their God and they shall be his people. Sin is slavery and to be free from sin is true freedom. In Romans 3 Paul declares that all have sinned but that those who believe in Jesus Christ are justified by his grace as a gift. God has passed over former sins. Again, freedom is the result of being free from the slavery of sin. In John's Gospel Jesus declares that "You will know the truth, and the truth will make you free." Sin makes us slaves but Jesus the Son makes us really free.

### Homiletical Moves

*Jeremiah 31:31-34*
## The New Covenant upon Their Hearts

1. The days are coming says the Lord when he will make a new covenant written on the hearts of his people
2. In that utopian society everyone will know the Lord and no one will need to teach the neighbor about the Lord
3. God will forgive the iniquities of his people and remember their sin no more
4. In Jesus Christ God has made a new covenant and forgiven our sins
5. The Christ who came is coming again when he shall reign forever and everyone will know the Lord
6. Trust in the new covenant in Christ's blood, and watch expectantly for his return

*This Preacher's Choice*

*Romans 3:19-28*
## We Are Justified by His Grace as a Gift

1. No one will be justified in God's sight by works of the law
2. The righteousness of God through faith in Jesus Christ has been manifested
3. Those who believe in Christ are justified by God's grace as a gift
4. We are justified through the redemption in Christ Jesus whom God put forward as an expiation by his blood for our sins
5. Since we are justified by faith we have no room to boast of works, so live in freedom giving God the glory
6. Accept the gift of justification by faith and live in obedience to Christ

*John 8:31-36*
## The Truth Will Make You Free!

1. Everyone who commits sin is a slave to sin
2. If you continue in the word of Jesus you are truly his disciple
3. Then you will know the truth, and
4. The truth will make you free

5. If the Son, Jesus Christ, makes you free you will be really free!
6. Become a follower of Christ and live in true freedom

**Hymn for Reformation Sunday:**   *Take Thou Our Minds, Dear Lord*   or
*A Mighty Fortress is Our God*

**Prayer**

*O God who is our mighty fortress against the powers of evil, we who were the slaves of sin claim Christ and his righteousness for our salvation. Give us the mind of Christ. Teach us to know the truth that sets us free. Help us to turn from boasting in our own good works to trust in you alone. Write your new covenant in Christ upon our hearts. We claim the redemption which is in Christ as the expiation of our sins. We rejoice that we are accepted by you as justified through Christ's death and resurrection. Enable us to live as free people through bondage to Christ and Christ alone. Amen*

# All Saints' Day/All Saints' Sunday

| Common | Lutheran |
|---|---|
| **Revelation 21:1-6a** | **Isaiah 26:1-4, 8-9, 12-13, 19-21** |
| **Colossians 1:9-14** | **Revelation 21:9-11, 22-27 (22:1-5)** |
| **John 11:32-44** | **Matthew 5:1-12** |

## Comments on the Lessons

The lessons have been selected for their relevance for the celebration of All Saints' Day which marks a transition in the non-festival half of the liturgical year. The first part of the post-Pentecost season has an emphasis on grace, and the last part focuses on the "last things" of eschatology. For Protestants all Christians are saints. (1 Corinthians 1:2) Christians are saints, not because of moral purity, but because of being made objectively holy (set apart for God) by baptism. Thus All Saints' Day is a commemoration of all the faithful departed when we give thanks for their lives. Revelation 21:1-6a is a vision of the holy city, new Jerusalem, in which God will dwell with his people and wipe away every tear from their eyes and death shall be no more. Revelation 21:9-11, 22-27 (22:1-5) is a vision of the holy city Jerusalem which had no temple, for its temple is the Lord God Almighty. There people will see God's face and his name shall be on their foreheads. The Isaiah 26 passages foretell the time when people who are as though dead shall rise. It gives the assurance of perfect peace to those who think on God and trust in him who is an everlasting rock. Colossians 1 is Paul's prayer for the Colossians in which he gives thanks for sharing in the inheritance of the saints in light. John 11:32-44 is the account of Jesus raising his friend Lazarus from the dead, a foreshadowing of the raising of the dead in the Day of the Lord. Matthew 5:1-12 contains the Beatitudes in which Jesus describes the life that is blessed by God. "Blessed are the pure in heart, for they shall see God" (v. 8) is especially fitting for All Saints' Day as we recall those who have died and now are in the presence of God.

## Commentary

*Revelation 21:1-6a (C)*

John sees a vision of the new Jerusalem predicted by the prophet Isaiah. (65:17) In this new city all creation will be renewed and will be set free from imperfections. All creation will be transformed by the glory of God. Paul, writing to the Romans, foretold this coming new creation: "For the creation waits with eager longing for the revealing of the sons of God; for the creation was subjected to futility, not of its own will but by the will of him who subjected it in hope; because the creation itself will be set free from its bondage to death and obtain the glorious liberty of the children of God." (Romans 8:19-21)

The sea will be no more, says John, in this new creation. The sea was a symbol of chaos with its turbulence and unrest. Jews had an awe and dread of the sea because of its mysteries and dangers. New Jerusalem is a symbol for the church. It will be the eternal dwelling place of the community of faith. The new Jerusalem is prepared as a bride adorned for her husband. A bride is a symbol of all that is beautiful and lovely.

In this new city God will dwell with his people and death and sorrow will be no more. All former things will have passed away.

In verse 5 the speaker is God who says, "Behold I make all things new." God calls himself "Alpha and Omega," the first and last letters of the Greek alphabet, indicating that he is the beginning and end of all things.

*Isaiah 26:1-4, 8-9, 12-13, 19-21 (L)*

Isaiah 26:1-6 is a processional psalm of victory sung on entering Jerusalem which was called the strong city. There is a call for the city's gates to be opened that the righteous nation may enter in.

The prophet gives one of the great assurances of Scripture: "Thou dost keep him in perfect peace, whose mind is stayed on thee, because he trusts in thee." (v. 3)

In verses 8-9 we have part of an apocalyptic psalm. God's chastisements are designed to benefit those judged by God. In verses 12-13 confidence is expressed in God who will ordain peace for his people. Although other lords have ruled over them, the faithful Israelite will give worship to God alone.

The last section (19-21) speaks of Israelites who though as dead will be raised up by God. God's light will illumine the gloom of despair. In verses 20-27 we have the fourth eschatological section which follows logically the preceding petition. The theme again is judgment. The people should await God's victory, for he is coming out of his place to punish those guilty of iniquity.

### Colossians 1:9-14 (C)

It was usual to begin a letter with a thanksgiving and prayer following the salutation and so Paul does this here. There is thanksgiving in 1:3-8. In verses 9-14 we have a prayer consisting of a petition (9-11) and a second thanksgiving. (12-14)

The petition consists of a prayer that (1) they understand what God's will is, (2) they live in a manner befitting Christ their Lord, and (3) they be strengthened with his power for joyful endurance and patience. The knowledge which Paul prays for is insight into truth which is granted by the working of God to those who are open to spiritual wisdom and understanding. (v. 9) This wisdom results in Christian conduct in the daily affairs of life and is sustained by divine strength. Such a life bears fruit "in active goodness of every kind" (New English Bible). The gospel bears fruit and grows when those who have been grasped by its power bear fruit in their transformed lives. J. B. Philipps translates this: "We also pray that your outward lives, which men see, may bring credit to your master's name, and that you may bring joy to his heart by bearing genuine Christian fruit, and that your knowledge of God may grow yet deeper." (v. 10)

A thanksgiving follows in verses 12-14. The petitions move without a break into a thanksgiving. God is called Father three times in Colossians, and each time it is in connection with the thanks due God for salvation. "Giving thanks to the Father who has qualified us to share in the inheritance of the saints in light. (v. 12)

In verses 13-14 believers are reminded of their baptism. Baptism marked the transferral from darkness to light and delivered us to the kingdom of his beloved Son. In the Son we have redemption and the forgiveness of sins. Our ground for hope is God's own act of deliverance in which he forgives our sins through Christ's death.

### Revelation 21:9-11, 22-27, (22:1-5) (L)

In these verses we have a picture of the heavenly Jerusalem. Many of the images here are drawn from Ezekiel to describe the new Jerusalem. The city, of course, is symbolical. So are its measurements. All of them are multiples of twelve. The new Jerusalem exists in its perfection in heaven and is now ready to descend on the new earth. Notice the seer's guide, one of the seven angels, and it may be the same angel that has been his interpreter since 17:1. The vision has been foretold in verse 2: "And I saw the holy city, new Jerusalem, coming down out of heaven from God . . ."

The new Jerusalem has the glory of God and God's presence makes itself known in a revelation of light: "having the glory of God, its radiance like a most rare jewel, like a jasper, clear as crystal." (v. 11)

In verses 22-27 we move to a more detailed description of the new Jerusalem. In 3:12 and 7:15 John anticipated a temple in the new heavenly city. But now he says it will have no temple for the presence of the Lord God will make any other sanctuary unnecessary. Nor is there a need for sun or moon to shine upon it, for the glory of God is its light, and its lamp is the Lamb (Jesus Christ).

The nations of the earth will pay homage to God and will enter by gates that are always open. (v. 25) But only those whose names are written in the Lamb's book of life will share in this new age. (v. 27) The Book of Life was the register of God which contained the names of the redeemed. The Old Testament has many references to such a book of names of the elect, and the image was drawn from royal records of citizens.

In 22:1-5 the seer is shown the river of the water of life flowing from the throne of God and of the Lamb, and, on either side of the river, the tree of life with its twelve kinds of fruit, one for each month. And the leaves were for the healing of the nations. "The tree" is used here generically of many trees on either side of the river. This is related to the river that flowed out of the Garden of

Eden and to the tree of life. But Ezekiel is the immediate source of these images. The twelve fruits may be John's interpretation of Ezekiel's fresh fruit every month and means twelve fruits in succession, rather than at one time.

There is but one throne there: of God and of the Lamb.

Nothing and no person is allowed in the city that would desecrate it. Those there will see God's face, which is the crowning joy of heaven. They will experience God's immediate presence without any temple or other intermediary. God will be their light and his servants shall worship him. The saints will reign forever with God and Christ, and this marks the climax of the visions. And this concludes the visions.

### John 11:32-44 (C)

This very moving account of the raising of Lazarus from the dead reveals the humanity of Jesus and his power over death. "Jesus wept" (v. 35) shows that Jesus felt the loss of his friend and so he grieved. This impressed the crowd. (v. 36) That Jesus was "moved" (v. 33) may indicate his indignation over the power of death which had taken Lazarus from them. It is like Jesus' agony in Gethsemene. (12:27) "Laid" in verse 34 means buried. The fact Lazarus was dead four days indicates he was truly dead, for the Jews believed that the spirit of a person lingered near by the body for three days and then left.

In verse 40 the "glory of God" refers to God acting to reveal his nature as lifegiver. We learn that Jesus lifted up his eyes and thanked the Father that he had heard him. Jesus wants the people to know that he is not a magician but that God has sent him.

Jesus calls Lazarus to come forth from the grave and he comes out. He was bound with grave clothes, and Jesus told them to unbind him and let him go. Hoskyns has called this a "miracle within a miracle." Lazarus comes out of the tomb with hands and feet bound with bandages and his face wrapped in a cloth. How could he come out so wrapped except by supernatural power inspired by the Word? The wrapping of hands and feet suggests embalming but does not prove it. Here is fulfillment of the prophecy of 5:25 that the "hour is coming and now is, when the dead will hear the voice of the Son of God, and those who hear will live."

The real miracle here is not that Jesus restored a man to physical existence (who later died as all humans must die), but Lazarus dead in the tomb hears the voice of the Son of God and lives! The story of Lazarus has been called the "crux interpretationis" of the whole gospel of John, since it compels the reader to decide whether or not he or she will accept John's view of miracle that miracle is always in essence the gift of eternal life. Eternal life here is knowing the one whom God has sent and obeying him. The other choice is to take this from the point of view of the Jews as a performance of magic or miracle in that sense.

Thus the miracle within a miracle is that Lazarus obeys Jesus' command to come out while he is still *a dead man!* But when he is still dead he heard tha voice of the Son of God and so lives eternal life. The real miracle is the life that is given by Jesus Christ to those who believe in him, not the restoration of Lazarus to his family.

### Matthew 5:1-12 (L)

Jesus went up on the mountain, reminding us of Moses going up Mount Sinai to receive the Ten Commandments. He also went up on a mountain when he was transfigured, and when he gave his parting commandment. (28:16) Jesus sat down to teach, the usual posture. His disciples came to him. "He opened him mouth" points to the speaking of solemn truth.

In the Sermon on the Mount (or Plain, as Luke calls it) Jesus gives the disciples the New Law which is designed for the community which will inherit the Kingdom. Matthew has a great interest in the moral life of the Christian community, and this discourse of Jesus deals with the righteousness which exceeds that of the scribes and Pharisees. Notice that the Sermon on the Mount is a whole new teaching tradition, and not just a new lawbook. In these teachings Jesus describes the blessedness or happiness of those who live in accordance with God's will. The Greek word for "blessed" as used in pagan literature denotes the highest stage of happiness and well-being, the kind which the gods enjoy. Here the word stands for the Hebrew term which means "how happy." (Psalm 1:1; 32:1, 112:1) The Beatitudes describes those who are happy in God's sight.

Some say there are seven Beatitudes, and seven is a holy number. Others see eight or ten (in which case they are a new Decalogue). This is a revolutionary teaching, whatever the number.

"Blessed are the poor in spirit, for theirs is the kingdom of heaven." (v. 3) Some think this is the root Beatitude from which the others grow. It summarizes all of them and gives the central thrust of them all. The "poor" not only denotes their poverty, but points to them as the despised, oppressed and pious poor. But they are not only poor in body but are afflicted in spirit. Matthew adds "in spirit" and this indicates those who feel their spiritual need. The poor in spirit put their trust in God rather than self.

"Blessed are those who mourn, for they shall be comforted." (v. 4) These are the people who mourn for their own sins and those of Israel. They also mourn because of the evil of the world which oppresses their spirits. They shall be comforted, strengthened by God.

"Blessed are the meek, for they shall inherit the earth." (v. 5) The meek are the humble minded rather than the gentle. Moses was "very meek, above all men" and so the English word "meek" does not mean weakness. This verse is almost a direct quote from Psalm 37:11.

"Blessed are those who hunger and thirst for righteousness, for they shall be satisfied." (v. 6) This refers to the people who depend on God's power and not their own to achieve righteousness. One can only hunger and thirst for this righteousness. Those who seek God's righteousness will have their hunger satisfied.

"Blessed are the merciful, for they shall obtain mercy." (v. 7) The merciful are those who show lovingkindness toward the unfortunate, as the Good Samaritan did to the man who fell among thieves and was left for dead. Those who show mercy to others will receive mercy. God deals with the merciful as they deal with their neighbors. Because they are loving to others they need not fear the day of judgment for God will be merciful to them.

"Blessed are the pure in heart, for they shall see God." (v. 8) Heart for the Hebrew included the mind as well as the emotions and so referred to the whole personality. The pure need not be thought of as morally perfect, and there is no reference to sexual purity. Another translation could be "those who are right with God." The pure in heart will see God does not mean "see God" in the metaphorical way of worshiping in God's house or even in a mystical sense. It points to the End time when God will allow them to see him face-to-face. (Revelation 22:40) Those who have a singleness of mind, who try to do God's will, will be permitted to come face-to-face with God in the End when the kingdom is fulfilled.

"Blessed are the peacemakers, for they shall be called sons of God." (v. 9) Peace, "shalom" in the Hebrew, means more than a mere absence of conflict or war and points to a sense of social well-being in the fullest sense of the term. It is a positive condition, not a mere absence of strife. While "sons of God" sometimes refers to angels or divine beings in the Old Testament, it usually means the Hebrews who are created by God and are persons (men and women) cared for by him. Further in the Sermon Jesus says: "But I say to you, Love your enemies and pray for those who persecute you, so that you may be sons of your Father who is in heaven; for he makes his sun rise on the evil and on the good, and sends rain on the just and on the unjust." (5:44-45) The peacemakers are those who love their enemies, one of the unique aspects of Jesus' teaching, since no Old Testament passage commands love of enemies, only love of neighbor. To love one's enemies is to follow the example of God who loves those who reject and hate him. To love one's enemies and be a peacemaker is to be truly a son or daughter in the fullest sense.

"Blessed are those who are persecuted for righteousness sake, for theirs is the kingdom of heaven. Blessed are you when men revile you and persecute you and utter all kinds of evil against you falsely on my account. Rejoice and be glad, for your reward is great in heaven, for so men persecuted the prophets who were before you." (vv. 10-12) "For righteousness sake" seems to be earlier and perhaps the original saying, rather than Luke's "on account of the Son of man." (Luke 6:22) "Falsely" may have been added by a scribe since several MSS omit it, and Luke omits it. The reward is not confined to heaven, although it will be enjoyed in heaven. But reward in heaven is not based on heavenly bookkeeping. Reward in heaven is seeing God face-to-face and this is identical for all, and reward is out of proportion to service rendered. In the final analysis, reward in heaven is a gift of God, not something earned. The Old Testament records some of the persecutions of the prophets such as Amos and Jeremiah.

## Theological Reflections

The readings for All Saints' were selected for their relevance to the remembrance of those who have died in the faith and to the hope we have in Christ. There is the vision of the new Jerusalem coming down out of heaven. In this city the saints will see God face-to-face and there will be no need of sun or moon for the glory of God is its light. "Light" is a frequent symbol for the heavenly presence. The raising of Lazarus indicates the power of Jesus over death as a dead man hears the voice of the Son of man and responds. The Beatitudes describe the New Law designed for the community of faith which lives in the Kingdom of God. The readings have hope as a common theme, since they point to the fulfillment of God's purpose.

## Homiletical Moves

*Revelation 21:1-6a (C)*
### The New Jerusalem

1. The first heaven and earth, along with the sea, are passed away in John's vision of the future
2. In this new city God will be with his people and thcy with him
3. Death, sorrow, pain and the former things will have passed away since God rules completely
4. God, the beginning and end, will make all things new
5. In Jesus Christ God is working to renew people and all creation
6. Commit your life to God in Christ who is making all things new

*Isaiah 26:1-4, 8-9, 12-13, 19-21 (L)*
### The Lord Will Ordain Peace for His People

1. God is an everlasting rock in whom we can put our trust
2. God will keep the person in perfect peace whose mind is stayed on him
3. God will punish the wicked for their iniquity
4. God has sent Christ as the Prince of peace to bring wholeness of life to persons and society
5. Therefore, earnestly seek God in daily living and trust in him always

*Colossians 1:9-14 (C)*
### Lead a Life Worthy of the Lord

1. May you be filled with the knowledge of God's will in all spiritual wisdom and understanding
2. May you be strengthened with all power according to his glorious might
3. In Christ God has delivered us from the darkness of sin and transferred us to the kingdom of his Son
4. Therefore, may you lead a life worthy of the Lord, fully pleasing to him, bearing fruit in every good work and growing in the knowledge of God

*Revelation 21:9-11, 11-17 (22:1-5) (L)*
### The City Without a Temple

1. The new Jerusalem will not have a temple since its temple is the Lord God the Almighty and the Lamb (Jesus Christ)
2. Its gates shall never be shut and kings of the earth shall bring their glory into it
3. Only those whose names are written in the Lamb's book of life shall enter the city
4. The saints will reign with God forever and ever in the new Jerusalem
5. Believe in Christ that your name may be written in the Lamb's book of life and you will live in communion with God

*John 11:32-44 (C)*
### The Dead Man Came Out

1. Jesus was so distressed when he learned of Lazarus's death that he wept and was deeply moved in spirit and troubled
2. Jesus prays to the Father thanking him that he has heard him
3. Jesus shouts for Lazarus to come out of the tomb
4. Lazarus hears the command of Jesus while still a dead man and comes out
5. The Living Christ gives eternal life to those who hear his voice and obey, therefore listen for his call and obey it

*Matthew 5:1-2*
## True Happiness in the Kingdom

1. Blessed are the poor in spirit, for to them belongs the kingdom of heaven
2. Blessed are those who seek God's righteousness for they will be filled
3. Blessed are those who mourn, those who are meek, those who are merciful, those who are peacemakers, for they shall be rewarded in an appropriate fashion
4. Blessed are the pure in heart, for they shall be given the ultimate reward of seeing God face-to-face
5. Trust in Christ and know the blessedness of living in obedience to him in the kingdom

**Hymn for All Saints' Day:**  *For All the Saints, Who From Their Labors Rest*

**Prayer**

*Gracious God who has promised to be our God in the future as in the past, we claim your promises and put our trust in you, our Rock. Grant us a vision of the new Jerusalem where there will be no more death, no mourning, pain or tears. Give us strength and courage to lead a life worthy of you, pleasing in your sight, which bears the fruit of righteousness. We thank you that you have transferred us from the dominion of darkness to the kingdom of Christ in whom we have redemption, the forgiveness of sins. We thank you for the assurance that you will keep that person in perfect peace whose mind is stayed on you. We thank you for all our departed brothers and sisters who died in the Lord and we commend them to your keeping, looking forward with eager anticipation to the Day when Christ will come in power and glory to reign for ever and ever. Amen*

# Proper 27

November 6-12

# Pentecost 25

# Ordinary Time 32

| Common | Lutheran | Roman Catholic |
|---|---|---|
| 1 Kings 17:8-16 | 1 Kings 17:8-16 | 1 Kings 17:10-16 |
| Hebrews 9:24-28 | Hebrews 9:24-28 | Hebrews 9:24-28 |
| Mark 12:38-55 | Mark 12:41-44 | Mark 12:38-44 |

### Comments on the Lessons

The 1 Kings passage is an account of Elijah being fed by the widow whose supplies then never run out. The reading should begin with verse 8 as in (C) (L). There is consensus on the Hebrews reading and near consensus on the Markan reading. The Markan passage is the story of the widow giving her two small coins in the Temple treasury and Jesus' commendation of her gift. Both 1 Kings and Mark tell of widows whose faith enables them to give at risk to themselves.

### Commentary

*1 Kings 17:8-16 (C) (L)*
*1 Kings 17:10-16 (RC)*

To understand the pericope for today we should note the following background information: The name "Elijah" means Yahweh is God and the name may identify the prophet as a member of a group seeking to put Baal worship aside as chapter 18 indicates. 1 Kings 17:1 tells of a drought which is an important development for the stories thet follow, including the widow and Elijah episode for today. It also poses the question which chapter 17 develops, namely, "Is Elijah's word a believable word from God?" In verses 2-6 the prophet obeys the command and the promise of God is fulfilled. Thus the way of faith is one of obedience and dependence. It shows the protecting care of God for his prophet and his support of the prophet's message. But in the background there is the reality that the drought is taking effect. Zarephath was located on the coast, some seven or eight miles south of Sidon, and was in territory beyond the control of Ahab.

The story for today, verses 8-16, follows a similar pattern to that which has gone before, but, another stage of the story. The basic elements are the same, God commands and promises. Elijah obeys and witnesses the fulfillment of the promise. The internal development of the story, however, is more complicated. It is the widow who is the obvious one to fulfill God's promise. But she appears to be unlikely to be able to do that which tests Elijah's faith. Then Elijah puts the widow's faith to the test in a similar way with command and promise. She obeys in faith, and all involved are rewarded. Thus Elijah has become a mediator of God's Word as well as its recipient.

The position of widows and orphans without a breadwinner was precarious in the ancient world. Levirate marriage in which a brother of the deceased husband took the widow under his protection was designed, not primarily to relieve the widow, but to provide an heir to the name and property of the deceased brother. A childless widow was the responsibility of the famiy. But a widow who was a mother also, as in the case of this widow, had no such provision other than charity. A good government might provide for them. With this historical background to the widow's plight we see that Elijah's dependence on her was even more poignant.

The unfailing supply of meal and oil was a familiar motif in the ancient Near-Eastern king-ideology. The king was the dispenser of the water of life in some folk stories. This may point to the saga nature of the Elijah story.

The miracle stories of the Elisha and Elijah cycles dealing with the multiplication of food foreshadow the miraculous feedings in the Gospels.

The widow is seen to be of the same character as the widow in the Markan story in that both gave away all that they possessed. They are supreme examples of persons who throw themselves upon the Providence of God in faith.

*Hebrews 9:24-28*

The finality of Christ's redemption is the thrust of this passage. The author says that Christ has penetrated into the very presence of God on our behalf. (v. 24) Christ's work as high priest in heaven is permanent, in contrast to earthly high priests. His sacrifice does not need to be repeated since it is completely effective and has come "at the end of the age." (v. 26) The author shows the meaning of this by using a human analogy. "And just as it is appointed for men to die once, and after that comes judgment." (v. 27) "So Christ, having been offered once to bear the sins of many, will appear a second time." (v. 28) Human beings die *once* but Christ has been offered *once* for our sins.

Here in verse 28 is one explicit reference to the Second Coming" of Christ in the New Testament. Nowhere else is the parousia or presence called a "second" coming. Notice how the author has combined two ideas here: (1) the dominant idea of Christ as the priest who introduces us to the heavenly sanctuary, and (2) the primitive eschatology which moves in terms of a time sequence. While such a combination would have seemed out of character for a Hellenist, it reveals that the author is a primitive Christian and not a thoroughly consistent philosopher.

The thrust of the author here is to arouse his readers to a sense of urgency and crisis in view of Christ's imminent second coming. Time is short! Christ *will return,* there is no doubt about it. Therefore Christians must be prepared for the second coming of Christ. He says that the judgment is coming after the individual's death. (v. 27) This would suggest that for each person judgment follows immediately after his or her death. This is consistent with the author's thought elsewhere.

Christ's first coming marks the end of the old age and heralds the beginning of the age to come. Even as the Israelites on the Day of Atonement eagerly awaited the reappearance of the high priest after he had entered the holy of holies, so Christians await Christ's parousia, his second coming, knowing that he will not have to repeat his sacrifice but will fulfill for his people the final and eternal benefits of his sacrifice.

## *Mark 12:38-44 (C) (RC)*
## *Mark 12:41-44 (L)*

These two brief stories come at the end of Jesus' public ministry. The story of the widow giving her last two coins to the Temple treasury stands as an example of a person who lets go of every security and casts herself on the mercy of God. The widow's giving is a quiet, matter-of-fact act which does not call attention to itself. She stands as a Christ-figure, one who gives her all. This story sums up what has gone before in the Gospel and makes a fine transition to the story of how Jesus "gave everything" for human beings.

This teaching is directed by Mark at the church. The clue to this is in the phrase "he called his disciples to him, and said to them." Mark holds up the widow as an example for all disciples, while the scribes stand as a warning to the crowd in general and particularly for the leaders of the church.

Mark, in a masterful way, contrasts the hypocrisy of the scribes with the genuine piety of the widow. This is a powerful section of Scripture when we see the two stories in contrast with one another.

These two stories are part of a three section passage beginning with verse 35, "And as Jesus taught in the temple, he said . . ." and the other two sections begin with verse 38 "And in his teaching he said . . .", and verse 41 "And he sat down opposite the treasury . . ." Note that Matthew in 22:41—23:36 separates these units, while Luke, like Mark, holds them together. Mark and Luke use the initiative of Jesus, and the unifying theme of religious posturing versus costly discipleship to unite the three units.

The clue to understanding verses 38-40 is in the words translated as the warning by phrases such as "beware of," "watch out for," and "be on guard against the scribes." Notice how the scribes are pictured by Mark as (1) loving religious show and honors (long robes, salutations, best seats, places of honor at feasts), (2) their greed is exposed and made even more repugnant by the fact they attempt to hide it behind their false piety, and (3) they are "wolves in sheep's clothing" who will "receive the greater condemnation." (v. 40) God at the last judgment will judge these false religious leaders who are hypocrites with a special severity.

While Jesus does not attack Judaism or Jewish religious practices as such he does attack egotism and avarice which parade in religious vestments and make a show of their false piety. This judgment is directed against such practices as they began to appear in the early church to whom Mark wrote. We in the church must give special attention to these words of warning of Jesus.

In stark contrast to the hypocrites who "devour widows' houses" stands the poor widow who put her whole living into the treasury of the Temple. She put in two copper coins which make a penny. The coins were the smallest unit of money of that time. The woman might have kept one for herself, but the point is that *she gave them both!* She gave all she had!

Jesus sat opposite the treasury and watched the multitudes putting their money into the treasury. He was "people watching" with a purpose. The gifts of the rich were probably guided by the law of the tithe, one tenth of one's income. There was a long tradition on how the tithe was to be figured. But the poor widow gave, not a tithe, but all she had, and gave out of her poverty. She put in her whole living and Jesus says that her gift was more than all the combined gifts of the rich who gave out of their abundance.

Some scholars think that this beautiful story is best explained as being originally a Jewish parable, which Jesus took over in his teaching and which was later transformed into an incident in his life. There are parallels to the story in Jewish writings. In one a woman gave her offering of a handful of flour to the priest who scorned it. But in a vision that night he received a rebuke, "Don't despise her because, in her gift, she has offered her life." Some think that a common theme, of the sacrificial gift of a poor widow, has been clothed in the form of a conversation between Jesus and his disciples. Or it may be possible that the story developed from an illustration Jesus gave the disciples. Jesus was not able to see how much she gave since the coins went into trumpet-shaped receptacles in the Temple, nor had he a way to know this was all the living the widow had.

John Calvin comments on this story by saying that in two ways this teaching is useful to us: (1) the poor, who appear not to have the power of doing good, are encouraged by Jesus not to hesitate to express their love cheerfully out of their meager means, since if they consecrate themselves with their gift which may appear worthless, nevertheless it will not be less valuable than the gift of the treasures of Croesus; (2) it stands as a reminder to those who have great wealth that it is not enough to give more than the poor give, because the gift of a rich man out of his abundance is less than the gift of a poor person who in giving little gives all he or she has.

This passage of verses 41-44 is called a pronouncement story and its connection with the Temple may be the reason it was placed here in the Gospel. It may well belong here historically. Some scholars think that Jesus, without thinking of his supernatural powers, would have been able to sense the situation from the woman's manner and could tell how much she gave and the fact it was all her living. The incident is in harmony with Jesus' teaching elsewhere. (Mark 9:41; Luke 12:15)

### Theological Reflections

The faith of the two widows, one who shared the last of her food with Elijah, and the other who gave her last two coins to the Temple treasury, reveals the quality of faith required of disciples. They gave their all and cast themselves on the mercy of God. Hebrews speaks of the finality of Christ's redemption in which he gave his all for the sins of the world. His sacrifice does not need to be repeated. Christ is coming again, therefore we should live with the kind of lives of faith-ful obedience to the will of God exemplified by the two widows. In light of Christ's coming again we should be on guard against the sins of hypocrisy and greed which parade under a cloak of false piety. For Christ is coming again to judge all people, and the poor who give their all in simple trust in God give far more than the gifts of all who give out of their abundance, and their faithful obedience will be rewarded.

### Homiletical Moves

*1 Kings 17:8-16 (C) (L)*
*1 Kings 17:1-16 (RC)*
## The Faithful Obedience of a Poor Widow

1. There was a famine in the land when Elijah went to a widow's home in Zarephath
2. Elijah asked the widow for water and bread
3. The widow replied she had only a handful of meal and a little oil and she was going to prepare a little cake for her son and herself and then die for that was all their food
4. Elijah asks her to make a little cake for him first and assures her that the Lord says the meal will not be spent or the oil fail until rains come
5. The widow acted in faith and God fulfilled his promise to the widow
6. Trust God's providential care of your life

*Hebrews 9:24-28*
# Our Permanent High Priest in Heaven

1. Christ has appeared in the presence of God on our behalf
2. Christ has put away sin by the sacrifice of himself
3. Christ will come again at the end of the age to save those who are eagerly waiting for him
4. Believe in Christ and watch expectantly for his return

*This Preacher's Choice*

*Mark 12:38-44 (C) (RC)*
*Mark 12:41-44 (L)*
# The Widow Who Outgave Them All

1. Jesus warned the disciples to avoid the hypocrisy of the scribes who are greedy and who devour widow's houses
2. Jesus commends the poor widow who gave two copper coins to the Temple treasury
3. Jesus declared that the widow's gift was greater than all the other gifts combined since out of her poverty she put in everything she had, her whole living
4. Jesus gave his all for us that we might live for him
5. Cast yourself on God's providential care and give sacrificially in response to Christ's sacrifice of his all

**Hymn for Pentecost 25:**   *When I Survey the Wondrous Cross*

**Prayer**

*Gracious God who has given us Christ as our permanent high priest who offered himself up for us all, we confess our sins. We have paraded about with false piety and trusted in our long prayers and show of religious practices. Forgive us as we repent and turn to you in faith that Christ died for us, once for all. May we so die to the sin of greed that we may give as the poor widows gave, and cast ourselves on your mercy. May we turn from our search for security in the things of this world to live in greater trust of you and your provision for our daily needs. Give us the courage and faith to risk our all for the Kingdom. Amen*

# Proper 28      Pentecost 26      Ordinary Time 33

November 13-19

| Common | Lutheran | Roman Catholic |
|---|---|---|
| Daniel 7:9-14 | Daniel 12:1-3 | Daniel 12:1-3 |
| Hebrews 10:11-18 | Hebrews 10:11-18 | Hebrews 10:11-14, 18 |
| Mark 13:24-32 | Mark 13:1-13 | Mark 13:24-32 |

## Comments on the Lessons

The Daniel 7:9-14 reading gives the vision of the kingdom of the Son of man. Commentary on verses 9-10 is found in Pentecost 27, and commentary on verses 11-14 in today's commentary which follows. Daniel 12:1-3 passage is concerned with the resurrection and is one of the finest in the Old Testament on the topic. The Hebrews reading picks up from the previous Sunday passage and centers on Christ as the permanent high priest who has made a single perfect sacrifice for all time and now sits at the right hand of God. The Mark 13:24-32 (except for verse 32, which will be discussed in brief) reading is dealt with in the Pentecost 27 commentary. Mark 13:1-13 is concerned with the destruction of Jerusalem and the end of the age. Both Markan passages are part of the "Little Apocalypse" as Mark 13 is called.

## Commentary

### Daniel 7:11-14 (C)

Commentary on Daniel 7:9-10 is found in Pentecost 27. "Great words" (v. 11) refers to blasphemies which are greater than any human being has any right to speak, no matter how exalted the person may be. The beasts referred to in verses 11, 12 are somewhat vague but the best theory is that they represent the Babylonian, Median, Persian, and Greek-Macedonian empires. The speaking of such blasphemies as the horn spoke is evidence of the great iniquities and the final judgment which is near. In his vision Daniel continues to look and sees the final judgment on the four beasts. The blasphemies of the little horn (v. 11) include the destruction of the entire empire whose guilt comes to its fullness in him.

We are not told how the beast is slain, but its body is burned with fire while the other three beasts are killed with the sword. The body of each of the four beasts stands for the structure and organization of an empire. The body of the beast burned refers to the Greek Empire which was completely abolished. This empire had sorely oppressed the Jews and so, as fire destroys a body, there would be nothing left of the Greek Empire.

Notice that the other three beasts were not destroyed but had their dominion taken away. These were Oriental empires which had been somewhat friendly to the Jews and so were not to be annihilated as the Greek Empire was. Their life was to be extended for a "season and a time" in order that they might be incorporated in the coming kingdom of God in which their separate identities would finally cease.

Now in verse 13 the vision changes, changes in a dramatic way as often happens in dreams, and Daniel sees the arrangements being made to have the judgment followed by the eternal kingdom. The old order has been judged and now the new begins. The "one like a son of man" symbolizes the new era that begins. Notice the contrast of the human form with the beasts. The son of man comes from heaven. Heaven is a place of orderliness, purity and peace, in contrast to the sea which is a place of chaos, turbulence and evil. Here the writer is not so interested in who this figure is as in what he accomplishes.

Although verses 13, 14 are metrical and would appear to be a quote from some source, they are apparently the writer's composition. Care is used in arranging the scene in this vision. The figure comes with the clouds of heaven and when he arrives he is presented before the Ancient of Days in formal court procedure. After this the Ancient of Days gives him the kingdom: "and to him was given dominion and glory and kingdom, that all peoples, nations, and languages should serve him; his dominion is an everlasting dominion which shall not pass away." (v. 14)

This "one like a son of man" represents a king and a kingdom. Further on in verse 22 it is the saints who are to possess the kingdom. So this figure symbolizes the kingdom of the saints of God. Even as the beasts represented not peoples but kingdoms, so here the son of man represents not individual saints but the kingdom of saints. The king who inaugurates that kingdom is the messianic king. Here we find the connection between the son of man and the messianic king. In Daniel we find that the king and kingdom interchange, and so this figure may represent both the saints as a body, and the Saint of saints as an individual, much as Uncle Sam for citizens of the USA can represent both citizens as a body and as an individual.

We are not told who presented the son of man to the Ancient of Days, but it was in order for the new king to be "proclaimed" according to ancient ceremonial usages. In verse 14 "dominion and glory and kingdom" make this verse sound like official protocol from a royal document. The peoples, nations, and languages whom Nebuchadnezzar and Darius considered to be under their command come now to place themselves under God's rule. If the son of man is a messianic figure, then this prophesies a great conversion of the Gentiles in the last days. In the religions of Zoroastrian, Samaritan, Mandaean, and Muslim their image of End Time calls for the conversion of all peoples as a result of the coming of Messiah.

### Daniel 12:1-3 (L) (RC)

These verses are part of the larger section (12:1-13) concerned with the final consummation. Chapter 12 passes from temporal to eternal things, with chapter 11 having dealt with human history already past or about to be realized. Notice that 12:1-3 are metrical verses.

The death of Antiochus Epiphanes marks the beginning of the final consummation. In view of the imminent end Michael, the patron saint of the Jews, arises. The great tribulation becomes very great at this point in the final spasms of the dying world and the "birth pangs" of the Messiah. It ends with the general resurrection and the great separation of the blessed from the damned. The vision ends in verse 4 with the sealing of the book.

"At that time" (v. 1) refers to the time of the overthrow of Antiochus. The author is going to write about the final consummation which comes at the end of time and he regards the last days as beginning immediately after the death of Antiochus. The end will usher in the rule of the saints and therefore it is appropriate that Michael, the patron angel of the Jewish people, would be active in preparation for it.

"Has charge of" refers to protecting. "Your people" means the Jewish people as a whole nation.

"There shall be a time of trouble." (v. 1) means the great tribulation. There is found in all descriptions of the great tribulation the great war in which Gentile nations gather for a final assault on Jerusalem and its inhabitants. To refer to it as "a time of trouble, such as never has been" (v. 1) is characteristic of other descriptions of the last times.

"Your people shall be delivered" (v. 1) is a smaller group than the earlier "your people" which Michael guards, for it is not the whole Jewish people but only the true Israel who have their names written in the book. These are those who remained faithful keepers of the law throughout the persecutions. The people to be delivered are the saints (7:18, 27) who will inherit the coming kingdom.

In the Persian Empire a register of citizens was kept, and in the Old Testament the practice of keeping a register of the members of the theocratic community is noted. (Exodus 32:32ff; Psalm 69:28, etc.) Those who have been faithful and thus proved that they are saints of God have been recorded as members of the new kingdom and are delivered from the great tribulation. Note that the "book" (v. 1) is not necessarily the same as the "books" of 7:10. The latter seems to refer to a register of good and evil deeds.

In verse 2 we have for the first time in the Old Testament a clear mention of a resurrection of the wicked as well as of the righteous. But even here it is not a general resurrection, but it is only the "many" who will rise. However, some scholars think that the "many" should not be forced in meaning and that the writer is referring to a general resurrection.

The idea that death is a sleep in the dust of the earth where the dead rest until the resurrection was a common notion. Sleep is a biblical image for death. Since humans were created from the dust, and to dust they return, it is not surprising that dust would be the dwelling of the dead. "Dust of the earth" is a peculiar expression, used along with "soil of dust" and "land of dust," etc. While some scholars take this to refer only to the grave, others see it as a description of Sheol, the abode of the dead in Old Testament theology.

Next, after the resurrection, comes the great division of the good and evil people, made vivid for us in the parable of the sheep and goats. (Matthew 25:31-46) The right and left sides are the places of division. (v. 33) Here in Daniel the actual judgment is not mentioned but is assumed. Those who rise face their deeds recorded in the book, and the deeds are the basis on which they will be separated.

If we think of general resurrection here, then the division is of the righteous from the wicked, those who will enter the kingdom and those who will be sent to shame and everlasting contempt. But some scholars who insist that "many" refers to another gathering than the general resurrection say that this is the division of the martyrs from the arch-sinners, or whatever group they see referred to in this passage.

"Everlasting life" is mentioned only here in the Old Testament. But it is a common expression in apocalyptic literature from which it came into rabbinical writings.

"Everlasting" points to life without ending since the kingdom promised to the saints is unending. "Shame," mentioned with "contempt," does not refer to the actual punishment but rather suggests it. The way the sentence is worded the meaning could be either that they are annihilated, or that they went to an eternal punishment.

Those who inherit the kingdom "are wise" and "shall shine like the brightness of the firmament" and will "turn many to righteousness, like the stars for ever and ever." (v. 3) The wise are the leaders among the faithful. (11:33-35) In the kingdom they will be singled out for their shining like the brightness of the firmament. We cannot be certain what is meant by their shining "like the brightness of the firmament." This may have come from astral theology of the time.

A second group is made up of those who "turn many to righteousness, like the stars for ever and ever. (v. 3) They turn many to righteousness by their precept and example, and not in any legal sense. They also shine brightly like the stars. This may be just a repetition of the earlier "shine" so that only one group is mentioned. But the LXX sees this verse as referring to two classes. The first has deep insight and so are teachers of the people. The second group, according to the LXX, are those who receive the teaching and hold it with tenacity.

It is clear that there is no hint of universal salvation here. Judgment will extend beyond death. Some have damaged their souls by disobedience and continue to reject God. There is everlasting life. There is shame and contempt, now and beyond the grave.

A final observation is that verse 2 is one of the more highly developed insights of the Old Testament into life after death.

## Hebrews 10:11-18 (C) (L)
## Hebrews 10:11-14, 18 (RC)

With verse 11 we have the beginning of the final section of formal argument which begins with verse 11 and continues through verse 18. This passage does not add anything new but emphasizes two points made earlier: (1) Christ's death was a sacrifice made as a single offering perfecting for all time those who are sanctified (v. 14), and (2) it also achieves the promised goal of the new covenant by which sins are forgiven.

This continues the theme of last Sunday's pericope from Hebrews, Jesus as the great high priest. This passage stands in a larger unit (9:1—10:18), whose focus is on the characteristics of the sacrifice of Christ. In verses 1-12 we see that Christ is both priest and king. A priest stands, but a king sits. The priests in the order of Aaron always stood in performing their duties, both in daily services and on special occasions. They stood, for their work was never done. However, Psalm 110 pictures the Messiah as a seated priest: "The Lord says to my lord: 'Sit at my right hand, till I make your enemies your footstool.'" (v. 1) In verses 16-17, the new covenant is described which assures full and final remission of sins (see Jeremiah 31:33-34).

Christ as the enthroned high priest means that his sacrificial work is finished and his self-oblation has been completed, once for all, in contrast to the Levitical sacrifices which were never finished.

The sacrifice of Christ has assured his people of a right relation with God in a permanent way. The complete removal of sin was promised in Jeremiah's prophecy of the new covenant. (31:34)

Notice the contrast between the earthly priests who stand and repeat their sacrifices daily on the one hand, with Christ who sits in triumph at the right hand of God, having made the single sacrifice on the cross for sins. While the priestly sacrifices were a constant reminder of sin, Jesus' perfect offering of himself resulted in God speaking through the Holy Spirit to say, "I will remember their sins and their misdeeds no more." (v. 17)

In verse 18 the negative form, "Where there is forgiveness of these, there is no longer any offering for sin" prepares the way for what follows. While forgiveness should give confidence (vv. 19-25), the fact is that there is no longer any offering for sin, which carries a terrible warning. (vv. 26-31)

## Mark 13:24-32 (C) (RC)

We will deal only with verse 32 here since verses 24-31 are dealt with in Pentecost 27. The meaning of verse 32 is difficult to understand and has created a lot of discussion in the past. In the context in which Mark uses it, the verse means that although the parousia is imminent its precise date is not known. "That day" seems to have been a Christian technical term for the Day of Judgment. This suggests that this was originally an independent saying about the Day of Judgment. In this case the profession of ignorance would be more absolute and reflects an attitude alien to apocalyptic speculation, which emphasized an orderly succsssion of events leading up to the End.

Some of the best scholars hold opposing views about the authenticity of these words. Some say no Christian would have invented such a self-limiting saying to attribute to Jesus. Others doubt if Jesus ever referred to himself absolutely as the Son for there is no parallel in Mark, and only one possible one elsewhere, Matthew 11:27/Luke 10:22. This would indicate the language is that of the early Church.

The early Church could have ascribed these words to Jesus as an attempt to deal with the delay of the End by showing that even he did not know exactly when the End would arrive. If the words are authentic, and this writer accepts them as such, then it is one of the glorious marks of the Incarnation that Christ accepted those limitations of knowlege which characterize a true humanity.

## Mark 13:1-13 (L)

Some scholars think that verses 10, 11b and 13 disturb the poetic structure of the remaining verses and regard them as additions to the original source for this chapter. The original would then have consisted of three four-line strophes. Notice that each of the additions contains an assurance designed to help those beset by the troubles described in the preceding strophe: "And the gospel must first be preached to all nations" (v. 10), etc. This passage deals with both the foretelling of the destruction of Jerusalem and the End time events. In verses 1-2 Jesus foretells the destruction of Jerusalem. The Temple which was begun by Herod the Great was still unfinished and was destroyed in A.D. 70.

Jesus predicts the destruction of the Temple in response to the admiring remark of one of the disciples. He says that not one stone will be left standing on another, so complete will be the destruction. Prophets such as Micah (3:12) and Jeremiah (26:6, 18) also foretold the destruction. The prediction of the destruction also appears in all four gospels, and it figures in Jesus' trial and crucifixion, and underlies the story of Stephen.

The rest of the chapter is more difficult to understand. This is the longest discourse attributed to Jesus and scholars generally agree that it is a composite. Mark seems to have combined several groups of sayings, some of which contained apocalyptic elements.

In verses 3-4 the scene changes from the Temple to the Mount of Olives, where Peter, James, John and Andrew asked him when the destruction of the Temple would take place. They asked him this privately.

The important thrust of the passage is the injunction against alarm in verse 7: "And when you hear of wars and rumors of wars, do not be alarmed; this must take place, but the end is not yet." Jesus says this is but the beginning. (v. 8)

Jesus foretells various disastrous events which lie within the scope of God and therefore should not greatly alarm the disciples. But they must not be mistaken for the "birth-pangs," the great sufferings which will immediately precede the end of the world.

In verse 6 Jesus warns that some of the false prophets will claim to be the returning glorified Jesus and will lead many astray. This actually happened in Palestine as false Messiahs gathered large numbers of followers on the promise of working miracles.

The best commentary on verse 7 is 2 Thessalonians, in particular chapter 2 which shows there were Christians who had been persuaded by events that the End of the world had arrived. So 2 Thessalonians tries to persuade people that the End is not yet and uses similar language to that of Mark 13.

In verse 8 "the sufferings" is literally "the travail pangs." It was commonly believed by the rabbis and was contained in Old Testament passages that the messianic age would come to birth only through a period of woes, as a baby is born through birth pangs.

Then in verses 9-13 Jesus gives a series of warnings to Christians. They will need to keep a firm watch on themselves (v. 9a), but if they do their reward will be great. (v.13b) In verse 11b they are given forewarning, guidance and promise of divine help. Most commentators think that as the passage is now found it reflects to some extent the experience of the early Church, especially the ministry of Paul, and the circumstances of Nero's persecution of the church. Mark's readers would have been helped by this passage.

The catchword "deliver" links verse 9 and verse 11. Mark has used distinctively Markan verse in verse 10 "And the gospel must first be preached to all nations."

In verse 13 it appears Jesus' words have been transposed into another key, although he may well have foretold the unpopularity facing his followers. For in this verse we seem to be in a period when the Christian faith is universally known in the Roman Empire and Christians are hated on account of Jesus' "name."

"To the end" (v. 13) translates Greek which has no article, and thus may simply mean "finally" or "without breaking down." Those who keep the faith to the end will gain salvation without passing through death seems to be the meaning.

## Theological Reflections

The Daniel 12:1-3 passage and Mark 13 passages refer to the End events when all will be judged by God. They predict a time of trouble and tribulation before the judgment takes place. Daniel describes a general resurrection of the dead, some to be judged and given everlasting life, others to be given shame and everlasting contempt. Jesus assures his hearers that those who endure to the End will be saved, those who rely on God in their times of persecution and suffering. Hebrews portrays Christ as the permanent high priest who sits at the right hand of God, having made a single sacrifice on the cross for the sins of all. The assurance of forgiveness of sins and the covenant promise of God is made by the Holy Spirit.

## Homiletical Moves

*Daniel 7:11-14 (C)*
### The Coming Rule of the Son of Man

1. The four kingdoms will be judged by God
2. The Son of man will be given dominion, glory and kingdom over all
3. We see this prophecy fulfilled in Jesus who called himself the "Son of man" and who is Lord of the nations forever

*Daniel 12:1-3 (L) (RC)*
### The Dead Shall Be Raised!

1. There shall be a time of trouble before the Judgment
2. Those whose names are found written in the book shall be delivered
3. Those who are raised from the sleep of death will be raised to everlasting life, or to shame and everlasting contempt
4. Jesus Christ will be our judge and we will be judged on our faithful obedience to him
5. Place your trust in Christ who gives eternal life now and beyond the grave

*Hebrews 10:11-18 (C) (L)*
*Hebrews 10:11-14, 18 (RC)*
### Christ Our Priest/King Who Forgives Sins

1. Christ sits at the right hand of God as priest/king
2. Christ by a single sacrifice on the cross has perfected for all time those who are sanctified
3. The Holy Spirit assures us that God will put his laws on our hearts and minds and not remember our sins
4. Christ has fulfilled the covenant God made with his people and graciously forgives sin
5. Believe in Christ and accept forgiveness of your sins

*This Preacher's Choice*

*Mark 13:1-13 (L)*
# The One Who Endures Will Be Saved!

1. Jesus foretells the destruction of Jerusalem
2. Jesus tells the disciples not to be alarmed over wars and rumors of wars which must take place before the End
3. The coming wars, earthquakes, etc. are the birth-pangs of the End
4. The Gospel must first be preached to all nations before the end comes
5. When you are persecuted, hated for the name of Jesus, etc., the Holy Spirit will give you the words to say and encourage you
6. Those who endure faithful to God to the End will be saved, therefore persevere in your faith in God

**Hymn for Pentecost 26:**  *O Worship the King*

**Prayer**

*Gracious God who has forgiven us by Christ's single sacrifice on the cross, enable us to face persecution, trials and troubles and endure faithful to the End. Give us wisdom to avoid false prophets who claim to be Messiah. Grant us courage to proclaim the good news of Jesus Christ to all nations. We ask for the power of the Holy Spirit to give us strength and wisdom when we are persecuted. Grant that we may so live in daily communion with Christ, our great high priest, that we may know the forgiveness of our sins, and may your covenant be written on our hearts and minds. Amen*

# Pentecost 27

Lutheran Only

---

**Lutheran**

Daniel 7:9-10
Hebrews 13:20-21
Mark 13:24-31

---

## Comments on the Lessons

Presbyterian and Lutheran lectionaries omit unneeded readings at the end of the liturgical year when Easter is late, while other denominations and the new Consultation on Common Texts proposes the omission at the beginning of the post-Pentecost period. In the CCT schedule Proper 29, the last Sunday after Pentecost, is "Christ the King" Sunday, the Sunday before the first Sunday in Advent. There is consensus on all three readings for today.

## Commentary

*Daniel 7:9-10*

In this passage we have a vision of the Son of man as he is presented before the "Ancient of Days." This is not a coming of the Son of man to earth but rather his being brought before the Presence of God. This is analogous to the Ascension instead of the Second Coming. When Jesus' face at the Transfiguration shines like the sun and his garments are white as light, we recognize that Jesus is being glorified like the Son of man. While nothing is said in Daniel about the shining face or the white garments of the Son of man, we find in Revelation 1 similar features are combined with the image of the Ascended Christ as the Son of man in Daniel.

The earlier part of Daniel's vision is of the sea and what comes out of it, but now he lifts his gaze to the celestial sphere. In contrast to the chaos and beasts of the sea, Daniel in his vision now sees the orderliness of the judgment scene and the calm dignity of the heavenly beings which appear in human form. Notice that verse 11 gives the reason for shifting his gaze, namely the loud-mouthed utterances of the little horn. As Daniel looked at the little horn he realized that this could only be the final depravity which comes just before the End. Therefore he looks up and sees the preparation for the grand judicial inquest was at hand.

The picture here of the grand judgment or assize figures prominently in later eschatology and many of the forensic elements mentioned here become standard images for the eschatology. For example, (1) the judgment is set, (2) the Judge comes down to occupy the seat of judgment, (3) the members of the divine court take their respective places around the Judge, (4) the record books are brought out and opened, (5) judgment is given according to works, and (6) the judgment is executed.

While the writer is undoubtedly influenced by the secular images of judgment in surrounding cultures, the main source of his material is from the Old Testament. (Joel 3, 2ff; Psalms 50, 72; 1 Kings 22:19) Again and again, the fact that the deeds of human beings are the substance of judgment is repeated. The record books are mentioned in Isaiah 65:6; Malachi 3:16, etc.

The "Ancient of Days" has parallels in the Ugaritic texts in which El is called "king, father of years." The image of God sitting as a man on a throne was familiar to Jewish audiences. (Job 36:26, etc.) The title means that the judge had been living a long time, not that he was decrepit. The whiteness of his hair is not from age but refers to the purity and resplendent brightness of things associated with the realm of light. It may be that he stands as the ancient of days in contrast to the new gods.

"Took his seat" points to the action of his taking the judge's place on the judgment seat, rather than delegating the task.

His raiment was white as snow, dazzling in brightness, is an image commonly associated with celestial beings.

The throne was a movable one, for the judgment seat was also a chariot on wheels. It was a fiery throne. Fire is commonly associated with the appearance of God. The sun-gods of pagan religions all had their blazing chariots.

Since the Hebrew believed fire always accompanied a theophany or revelation of God, the stream of fire (v. 10) confirms that this was God himself present at the judgment. In one sense the fiery river marks the boundary of the throne area so that no one can draw near to the throne without passing through the river of fire. As the righteous pass through it, they are purified of their remaining dross, but the wicked are consumed by the fiery river.

The reference to the "thousand thousands" who served the judge is to the celestial attendants who execute the duties associated with the judgment. The number before the throne is beyond count.

"The court sat in judgment" (v. 10) is the translation of the literal "the judgment sat," and from this we get "the rendering court" which refers to those to whom the judgment has been committed. In Egyptian and Iranian religions there was an image of a heavenly court. We find figures assembled for judgment at Babylon and Ugarit.

"The books were opened" (v. 10) is a parallel to the Babylonian texts in which tablets of good deeds and tablets of sins are mentioned. If human kings kept records of the good and evil deeds of their subjects, it was reasonable that the heavenly Judge should do so also. It followed that these records should be produced and examined at the grand judicial inquest. It may be, as some suggest, that the deeds of the four empires in particular are brought out for examination.

### Hebrews 13:20-21

This is the benediction which is followed by a postscript. (vv. 22-25) These two verses of the benediction are structured like a collect in the third person. The structure of the benediction is as follows:

1. The invocation: "the God of peace"
2. An adjective clause: "who brought again . . . covenant"
3. The main petition: "Equip you with everything good"
4. A secondary petition: "Working in you . . ."
5. A prayer for the merits of Christ: "through Jesus Christ"
6. An ascription of glory to Christ: "to whom be glory for ever and ever"
7. The "Amen"

Notice that in verse 20 the reference to the resurrection "who brought again from the dead our Lord Jesus" is the only reference to the resurrection of Christ in the whole epistle. The argument of Hebrews makes it more appropriate to emphasize his direct passage from the cross to the throne of glory in the heavenly sanctuary.

We have an echo of Isaiah 63:11 "Where is he who brought up out of the sea the shepherds of his flock?" in the phrase "the great shepherd of the sheep." (v. 20) And in the phrase "the blood of the eternal covenant" (v. 20), there is an echo of Zechariah 9:11: "As for you also, because of the blood of my covenant with you, I will set your captives free from the waterless pit."

### Mark 13:24-31

In this "Little Apocalyse," as the whole chapter 13 is called, we have a foretelling of the End. We find in it the themes of divine necessity and scriptural fulfillment. These, along with the prophetic self-consciousness of Mark point to Mark 13 as the basis of the witness of the Markan community. One of Mark's purposes was to correct the mistaken notions of false prophets within the early church. For Mark the world is passing and the coming of the Kingdom will climax with the return of the Son of man on clouds of glory. (13:24-27) Mark's community of which he wrote expected this to happen any day. (13:28-36) When the Son of man does come this present world will be declared obsolete as he gathers his elect and moves with them into the "age to come." (10:30) Mark puts the climax of Jesus' teaching here in chapter 13, where his final christology is seen in the apocalyptic Son of man. We cannot avoid the overall apocalyptic flavor of Mark's theology.

While the prevailing expectation of Jesus' day was that the Jewish Messiah would come in the form of a charismatic warrior like David to free the Jewish people from their Gentile oppressors, namely the Romans, Jesus' life and ministry was the opposite of this notion. He died at the hands of the government a Davidic type warrior was expected to overthrow. So how could this Jesus be the Messiah? According to Mark he was a Son of man Messiah whose work would climax, not in the political events of a holy war in which he would win the decisive victory, but in an apocalyptic drama when he would return from heaven on clouds of glory at the end of the age. (13:24-27)

It is significant that this passage from Mark starts at exactly the same place as the selection from Daniel for today, namely at the point where the apocalypse moves from future historical events vaguely conceived to a series of cosmic events. These cosmic events are expanded with images gathered from other parts of the Old Testament, such as the failure of the sun, moon and stars. (cp. Isaiah 13:10, 34:4, etc.) This is picture language which we should not force into a literal interpretation. Then comes the last judgment. But Mark differs from Daniel in the role assigned to the Son of man. (Daniel 7) In Daniel the Son of man appears as a symbol and personification of the people of God, while in Mark's Gospel he is an individual figure who carries out the eschatological judgment. Jesus declared that the Son of man would judge people according to their acceptance of his own eschatological message. After the resurrection Jesus was manifested as himself, the heavenly Son of man, who ratified his own word and work. In the early Church we find that it expanded the apocalyptic imagery to express its faith that the Son of man would come again as Jesus.

Notice the warning which runs like a red thread through the whole chapter. Jesus' speech to the four disciples begins with "Take heed" (v. 5) and the final parable begins with a "Take heed, watch." (vv. 33, 35, 37) In between, the Christian community is warned to be on guard by a number of expressions. It is significant that the specific words of warning come almost exclusively in redaction material. (vv. 5, 9a, 23, 33, 35, 37) with the exception of verse 21f. This underscores the fact that Mark was addressing the speech to specific dangers which threatened the Christian community and needed attention. The second point to be noted about the warnings is that they are not all aimed at the same danger.

The four disciples asked Jesus when would the destruction of the Temple take place and what will be the sign when all these things are to be accomplished. Jesus replies to them in three parts. Our pericope for today includes the second part of Jesus' answer (vv. 24-27) and some of the third part (vv. 28-37). Some scholars have suggested that originally verses 32-37 were the entire answer of Jesus to the question of the disciples about the end, with the other material added by Mark.

The make-up of Mark 13 is a combination of authentic eschatological sayings and parables of Jesus fused with traditional apocalyptic material. This appears especially in the sayings about the Son of man. Through this combining of these two elements, he creates an impression very different from that of Jesus' own proclamation that announced the inbreaking of the kingdom and the quick vindication of his message. Mark's message evidently spoke meaningfully to the church community of which he was a part, a church beset by temptations of a divine-man Christology and by persecution.

In verses 24-27 we have the signs of the eventual parousia of the Son of man. The tribulation on earth of earlier verses 14-22 is replaced now with cosmic portents: the forces that held the stars in their places will be shaken. Then they will see the Son of man coming in clouds with great power and glory (v. 26), which is a picture of the Daniel Son of man. (7:13-14) Jesus is now exalted to glory at the right hand of God.

Compare the image of "his angels" in verse 27 with the picture of the Son of man coming in glory with the holy angels of 8:38. He sends out the angels to gather his elect from the ends of the earth to the ends of heaven, which continues a theme from verse 20, "'but for the sake of the elect, whom he chose, he shortened the days."

The final third part of Jesus' speech (vv. 28-37) is concerned with the date of the Parousia. This is the climax of the apocalyptic discourse which contains practical exhortations and final counsel written entirely from the Christian perspective. Some suspect that verse 31 belongs to an earlier Jewish or Christian Jewish source, but there are parallels in Matthew 5:18 and Luke 16:17 which suggests that a detached saying of Jesus has been used in the apocalypse. In this section the discourse returns to the question of verse 4 regarding the end and the signs of the end.

The parable of the fig tree (vv. 28-29) is brief and simple, like many other parables in the Gospels, and compares the approach of "the end" to the signs of coming summer, particularly the leafing of the fig tree. When the signs of the promise appear then we may know that he is near "at the very gates." This fulfillment will take place before this present generation has passed away. "My words" (v. 31) are Jesus' whole teaching, his whole revelation of God. Jesus' words are presented as eternal, a position which they share in Luke and Matthew with "the law and the prophets." Matthew and Luke are more conservative than Mark who presents a more radical Markan Christianity.

### Theological Reflections

Both Daniel and Mark deal in apocalyptic material and to interpret it correctly we should avoid the trap of a literal imminent expectation of the end. The material is mythological in character. It is crucial to see the meaning of the imminent expectation which is a mode of expressing certainty of conviction. Despite the troubles and tribulation as pictured by Daniel and Mark and the troubles of the church at present, we can be sure that Jesus' promise that there will come vindication and God's saving purpose is the thrust of these two passages. Hebrews pictures Jesus as the great shepherd of the sheep and uses the image of the covenent in his blood to describe his saving work. The author prays that the God of peace will equip the hearer with everything good for the purpose of doing God's will. It ends with an ascription of glory and "Amen."

## Homiletical Moves

*Daniel 7:9-10*
### The Judgment by the Ancient of Days

1. God is seated on the throne of judgment as the ancient of days surrounded by his court
2. The books are opened with the good and evil deeds of people
3. The Christian will be judged, not on good works, but on faith in Christ Jesus
4. Therefore, believe in Christ and live in obedience to him

*Hebrews 13:20-21*
### The Great Shepherd of the Sheep

1. The God of peace raised Jesus the great shepherd from the dead
2. The blood of the eternal covenant made in Jesus' death on the cross equips us with his grace to do God's will
3. May God work in us what is pleasing in his sight through Jesus Christ
4. Therefore, live in obedience to the Living Christ, doing God's will

*This Preacher's Choice*

*Mark 13:24-31*
### The Son of Man Will Come in Great Power and Glory

1. The sun, moon, and stars will be changed and the powers in the heavens will be shaken before the Son of man comes
2. The Son of man will send out the angels to gather his elect from the ends of the earth
3. Although heaven and earth will pass away, Jesus' words will not pass away
4. Take heed and watch for Christ's return in power and glory at the end of the age whose time is known only by God the Father

**Hymn for Pentecost 27:**   *Ancient of Days*

**Prayer**

*O God, Creator of the heavens and the earth, before whom we must stand on the day of judgment, we confess our trust in Christ who died for us. Help us to take heed and watch for his return. May we be found faithfully doing your will, O God, when Christ returns in great power and glory. We claim Jesus as our great shepherd who was raised from the dead and by whose blood of the eternal covenant we are saved. Amen*

# Christ the King

| Common | Lutheran | Roman Catholic |
|---|---|---|
| Jeremiah 23:1-6 | Daniel 7:13-14 | Daniel 7:13-14 |
| Revelation 1:4b-8 | Revelation 4b-8 | Revelation 1:5-8 |
| John 18:33-37 | John 18:33-37 | John 18:33-37 |

## Comments on the Lessons

The Jeremiah passage was selected by (C) in order to use the semi-continuous Davidic material and is particularly appropriate to the theme of "king." It brings the Davidic strain of Year B to a conclusion. It was dealt with in Proper 11 B and so will not be commented on again here. Daniel 7:13-14 was commented on in Proper 28 B and will not be repeated here. There is virtual consensus on the Revelation reading. There is near consensus on the reading from John. Note that verse 33 provides the identity of the speaker.

## Commentary

*Revelation 1:4b-8 (C) (L)*
*Revelation 1:5-8 (RC)*

The pericope is the salutation and ascription (vv. 4-8) of The Revelation to John. Notice the number seven which is considered sacred and is the symbol of wholeness or perfection, a concept which determines much of the structure of Revelation. The letter is written to seven representative churches in the Roman province of Asia (western Asia Minor). Verse 4b begins "grace to you and peace" and grace is substituted for the usual secular term "greetings." Peace has overtones of the Hebrew word for "salvation."

The message is from God "who is and who was and who is to come" and from "the seven spirits" which just possibly may refer to the Holy Spirit symbolized here as sevenfold, and from "Jesus Christ the faithful witness" (martyr). The reference to God the Father as "he who is and who was and who is to come" probably refers to Exodus 3:14 where God says he is I AM WHO I AM. This came to be understood by many Jews to be "I am he who is and who will be" (LXX). The Jerusalem Targum expanded this to "I am he who is, and who was, and I am who will be." Notice that John gives the name a "twist" by replacing the future tense in "who will be" with the phrase "who is to come" and, in doing so, says that God not only transcends the ages but it is of his nature that he "comes" from the future and works out his plan for his creation. When we think of God's coming in the future we naturally think of Christ's parousia: God intervening in history in Christ. Jesus is called the faithful witness and the word for witness can also mean "martyr" and in its present reference to Jesus Christ it should probably be translated "martyr" in regard to his death on the cross. This is the first instance in literature of the term "witness" (martus) being synonymous with the specialized meaning "martyr." A martyr is a witness who seals his or her testimony with his or her blood. The early Christians remembered that Jesus was the faithful One who made the good confession before Pilate and the Jewish authorities. His faithful witness was an inspiration to them as they stood trial for the sake of his name.

It has been suggested that the seven spirits may refer to Babylonian or Persian symbols of the deity, but may more likely refer to the archangels of Judaism. But it seems unreasonable that the writer would place these here between the first and third persons of the Trinity, and so the Holy Spirit is the more likely reference.

The reference to Jesus as "first-born" may not be chronological but rather procedural, and the whole phrase "the first-born of the dead, and the ruler of kings on earth" ( v. 5) means "Lord of the dead and king of the living."

The Greek tenses of "to him who loves us and has freed us from our sins" are significant. The present tense "loves us" is followed by the aorist "has freed us" and the author means that God's love is continuous, (present tense), but that the act of atonement was a once for all action (aorist tense).

It is clear that verses 5b-8 refer to Jesus Christ. Notice that verse 7 draws on the imagery of Daniel 7:13 (one of readings for today), but it reinterprets the passage to apply to Christ and his imminent second coming. (See 1:12-13a)

In verse 7 the words "Even so. Amen." mean "yes, yes;" "Amen" is also a proper name for Christ.

Beginning with verse 8 God is the speaker and calls himself the "Alpha and the Omega," the first and last letters of the Greek alphabet. It means the same as "the first and the last, the beginning and the end" (v. 22:13) which refers to Jesus. The thrust of this is the English equivalent of saying God is from "A to Z, " implying that he is also all the things in between the first and the last.

### John 18:33-37

The Jews charge Jesus with political treason, for Pilate asks Jesus if he is the "King of the Jews." Jesus replies, "My kingship is not of this world; if my kingship were of this world, my servants would fight, that I might not be handed over to the Jews; but my kingship is not from the world." (v. 36) This is the central thrust of this passage. From this side of the cross we see that Jesus reigns from the Tree as King. Jesus' kingdom, like the disciple, is *in* the world but not *of* it.

In verse 33 it is not clear whether Jesus is already inside the praetorium or not. In all the Gospel accounts, Pilate's first words to Jesus are "Are you the King of the Jews?" When Pilate speaks of "the Jews" he refers to the Jewish nation, and is using the term in John's sense of the hostile Jewish authorities. It may be that "The King of the Jews" was a specific title used first by the Hasmonean priest/kings who were the last really independent rulers of Judea before Roman power appeared in Palestine. Josephus uses the title to refer to Herod the Great, and it may have been the term for the expected liberator of the Jews.

It may be that the "you" in Pilate's question to Jesus is emphatic meaning "Are *you,* such an unlikely, lowly man, are *you* the King of the Jews?" To say it this way would express Pilate's incredulity. "The King of Israel" was also used of Jesus on other occasions.

In the Synoptic Gospels Jesus answers Pilate "You say so," but here in John's account he replies, "Do you say this of your own accord, or did others say it to you about me?" If Pilate had said this on his own he would have been giving an unconscious prophecy, much like that of Caiaphas earlier in Jesus' ministry: "But one of them, Caiaphas, who was high priest that year, said to them, 'You know nothing at all; you do not understand that it is expedient for you that one man should die for the people, and that the whole nation should not perish.'" (John 11:49, 50)

Pilate replies to Jesus' question, "Am I a Jew?" which is not an undertone of Roman contempt for the Jews as some think, but is Pilate's way of saying he has no real knowledge of Jesus other than what the Jewish authorities have reported to him.

The "nation and chief priests" (v. 35) is the only indication of the participation of a larger group than the Sanhedrin authorities. Luke refers to "the chief priests, and the rulers, and the people." (23:13)

Notice that Jesus does not answer Pilate's last question, "What have you done?"(v. 35) Rather he answers the question of verse 33 "Are you the King of the Jews?" but his answer is in terms of a *kingdom* rather than a kingly title, which is significant. Jesus says that his kingdom is not of this world. In Johannine thought the ultimate goal of the disciples is to be withdrawn from the world: "In my Father's house are many rooms; if it were not so, would I have told you that I go to prepare a place for you? And when I go and prepare a place for you, I will come again and will take you to myself, that where I am you may be also." (14:2, 3)

Notice in verse 36 that Jesus' reply "If my kingship were of this world, my servants would fight, that I might not be handed over to the Jews; but my kingship is not from the world" has the first and second lines in a type of staircase parallelism where the second line takes up an expression from the first.

The reference to "subjects" is only in a contrary-to-fact statement of Jesus in which he says that, if he did have a kingdom of this world, he would have subjects. But he does not think of his disciples as subjects in the sense of their being his servants. Elsewhere he does not call them servants but friends. (John 15:15)

Recall that earlier Peter took his sword and cut off a man's ear. Jesus ordered him to put away his sword, thus affirming that his kingdom was not of this world.

"Being handed over to the Jews": Jesus has been handed over to the Romans, but he ignores the importance of the Romans for the real enemies are "the Jews."

Pilate says "So you are a king?" (v. 37) but does not repeat "the King of the Jews?," and the reason may be that he has come to see that this title is not accepted by Jesus who speaks of "the

Jews" as his enemies. The repetition of the question was in keeping with Roman court procedure in which, if the defendant made no real attempt to defend himself, the direct question was put to him three times before his case was allowed to go by default.

In Jesus' reply, "You say that I am a king" Jesus is saying in effect, "It is you who say it, not I," and so Jesus does not deny that he is a king, but it is not a title that he would choose to describe his role.

Jesus says, "For this I was born, and for this I have come into the world, to bear witness to the truth." (v. 37) This is a parallelism, and both being born and coming into the world refer to the same thing. Here John makes it clear that Jesus' birth was the coming into the world of divine truth.

Jesus tells Pilate that he came into the world to "bear witness to the truth." (v. 37) The revelation of truth has the effect of judgment on the world. "Every one who is of the truth hears my voice," says Jesus. "Hears" as constructed in the Greek here means to listen with understanding and acceptance. Compare this to sheep hearing the voice of the shepherd. Jesus has come into the world to bear witness to the truth, to reveal God whose kingdom is the truth faintly foreshadowed by every earthly kingdom. Only those who are directed by the truth can recognize it, and so Pilate need not stay for an answer to his question, "What is truth?" (v. 38)

Everyone who belongs to the truth listens to Jesus. But does Pilate belong to the truth? From this point in the trial on, we see that the trial is no longer whether Jesus is innocent or guilty. Pilate proclaims that Jesus is *not* guilty. (v. 38b) The thrust of the trial now is whether or not Pilate will respond to the truth. And so Pilate asks "What is truth?" and by this John means to show that Pilate is turning away from the truth. Pilate does not accept the charges of "the Jews" nor will he listen to the voice of Jesus. Thus he does not recognize or accept the truth.

Finally, John is the only gospel writer who takes the trouble to answer the charge "the King of the Jews" and to explain that Jesus' kingship was not political. John puts words into Pilate's mouth that he could not have spoken as they stand now, and makes Jesus say things that Pilate could not have understood. But if we accept this dialogue as the Church's apologia to the Empire in the 70s and 80s, we must accept that there is a vague resemblance of a historical fact here. Pilate did look into the claim of the Jews that Jesus was a pretentious revolutionary, and one evidence against this claim was the fact Jesus' followers made no armed resistance when he was arrested. John here gives us a splendid theological exposition of Jesus' kingship.

## Theological Reflections

The Jeremiah passage describes the righteous Branch of David who shall reign as king who will be called "The Lord is our righteousness." Jeremiah speaks woes to the shepherds who scatter the sheep, and foretells the remnant of Israel who will be brought back to the fold and the shepherds who will care for them. Daniel has a vision of one like a son of man who comes to the Ancient of Days to whom is given dominion, glory and kingdom and whose kingdom is an everlasting one which shall not pass away. Revelation 1:4b-8 gives an introductory salutation to the whole book and describes Jesus as the "first-born of the dead," and the ruler of kings on earth. It pictures his coming again with the clouds at the Parousia. God who is the Alpha and the Omega, the beginning and the end of all things speaks of his being now and in the past and his coming again. The John 18:33-37 passage focuses on the kingship of Jesus, which is not of this world but of the heavenly world. Jesus turns Pilate's question about whether he is the "King of the Jews" into an answer about his kingship by which he has come into the world to bear witness to the truth. The common theme running through all these passages like a red thread is the role of Jesus as king. It is appropriate that the final Sunday of the church year focuses on Christ the King who is, and was, and is yet to come.

## Homiletical Moves

*Revelation 1:4b-8 (C) (L)*
*Revelation 1:5-8 (RC)*
### The Coming King Who Is the Faithful Witness

1. Jesus is the first-born of the dead, and ruler of kings on earth
2. Jesus loves us and has freed us from our sins by his blood as the faithful witness (martyr)
3. Jesus has made us a kingdom of priests to his God
4. The Ascended Christ is coming again with the clouds at the Parousia

5. The Lord God is the Alpha and the Omega who is, and was and who is to come
6. Commit your life to Christ, the faithful witness, who is coming again at the End of time

*This Preacher's Choice*

*John 18:33-37*
## The King Who Rules from a Tree!

1. Jesus declares that his kingship is not of this world or else his servants would have fought for him.
2. Jesus affirms that he was born for kingship and has come into the world to bear witness to the truth
3. Jesus Christ the King won the victory over sin and death by his death on the cross and resurrection from the grave
4. The Ascended Christ rules the hearts of men and women by his love revealed in his death for them, ruling from the Tree on which he died
5. Trust in Christ who rules by the power of love

**Hymn for Proper 29:**   *The King of Love My Shepherd Is*

**Prayer**

*Almighty God, the Ancient of Days, we come before you with praise and thanksgiving. We thank you for Christ our King who reigns from the Tree where he died for us. We thank you for raising him from the dead for our salvation, thus conquering sin and death. We look forward with eager expectation to the coming again of our King who will reign forever in a kingdom that is everlasting. He is our King of Love whose love never fails. Now we dedicate ourselves to him as members of his Kingdom who are called to faithful obedience and joyful service. Enable us to be faithful until he is coming again at the End. Amen*